SHAKESPEARE STUDIES

An Annual Gathering of Research, Criticism, and Reviews

VII

Edited by J. Leeds Barroll

UNIVERSITY OF SOUTH CAROLINA PRESS

Columbia, South Carolina

FIRST IMPRESSION, 1974

All editorial correspondence concerning *Shakespeare Studies* and the South Carolina Shakespeare Monographs should be addressed to: The Editorial Office, The Center for Shakespeare Studies, University of South Carolina, Columbia SC 29208. Orders—and correspondence pertaining thereto—for past, present, and future volumes of both series should be addressed to: Order Department, University of South Carolina Press, Columbia SC 29208.

ISBN 0-87249-656-2
Library of Congress Card Catalog Number 66-4496
Library of Congress classification PR2885.S64

Manufactured in the United States of America

Contents

Contributors

J. Leeds Barroll
Professor of English, the University of South Carolina

Dennis Bartholomeusz
Senior Lecturer in English, Monash University

Herbert Berry
Professor of English, the University of Saskatchewan

Carol J. Carlisle
Professor of English, the University of South Carolina

Nan Cooke Carpenter
Professor of Comparative Literature, the University of Georgia

Thomas Clayton
Professor of English, the University of Minnesota

John Scott Colley
Assistant Professor of English, Vanderbilt University

Ann Jennalie Cook
Assistant Professor of English, the University of South Carolina

Norman Council
Assistant Professor of English, the University of California, Santa Barbara

Alan C. Dessen
Professor of English, the University of North Carolina

Bettie Anne Doebler
Associate Professor, Center for the Humanities, Arizona State University

Bertrand Evans
Professor of English, Emeritus, the University of California, Berkeley

René E. Fortin
Professor of English, Providence College

John Freehafer
Professor of English, Temple University

James A. Freeman
Assistant Professor of English, the University of Massachusetts, Amherst

George L. Geckle
Associate Professor of English, the University of South Carolina

John B. Harcourt
  Professor of English, Ithaca College
Jeffrey Helterman
  Assistant Professor of English, the University of South Carolina
S. K. Heninger, Jr.
  Professor of English, the University of British Columbia
Richard Henze
  Associate Professor of English, Colorado State University
T. H. Howard-Hill
  Associate Professor of English, the University of South Carolina
Robert G. Hunter
  Kenan Professor of English, Vanderbilt University
A. L. Kistner
  Associate Professor of English, the University of Colorado
M. K. Kistner
  Boulder, Colorado
Richard C. Kohler
  Associate Professor of English, California State University, San Diego
Kenneth Muir
  King Alfred Professor of English Literature, Liverpool University
M. Kay Nellis
  Instructor in English, State University College of Arts and Sciences, Geneseo, New York
Kurt Olsson
  Assistant Professor of English, the University of Virginia
D'Orsay W. Pearson
  Assistant Professor of English, the University of Akron
Jarold Ramsey
  Associate Professor of English, the University of Rochester
Julian C. Rice
  Assistant Professor of English, Florida Atlantic University
Philip Rollinson
  Assistant Professor of English, the University of South Carolina
Peter Saccio
  Associate Professor of English, Dartmouth College
Thomas E. Scheye
  Associate Professor of English, Loyola College, Baltimore
John Shaw
  Professor of English, Hiram College

A. P. Stabler
   Professor of French, Washington State University

Marvin L. Vawter
   Assistant Professor of English, the University of Illinois, Urbana

Albert Wertheim
   Associate Professor of English, Indiana University

Michael West
   Associate Professor of English, the University of Pittsburgh

Robert F. Willson
   Associate Professor of English, the University of Missouri, Kansas City

Preface

This present volume of *Shakespeare Studies* represents the beginning of what we hope will be a long and happy association with the University of South Carolina Press, which will also early next year initiate a series of South Carolina Shakespeare Monographs as a continuation of the annual monographs formerly published in "Shakespeare Studies Monograph Series." Because such various vicissitudes as labor strikes and trucking accidents delayed a former volume to such an extent that Volume VI of *Shakespeare Studies* appeared oddly in arrears with the rubric 1970 on its title page in the spring of 1972, the Editor has decided to avoid confusion by allowing the intervening years to slip into a merciful oblivion as years of record. Readers will please note that while Volume VI did indeed bear the date 1970 on its title page, the present volume, Volume VII, appears for the year 1974 and is so dated. *Deo volente*, Volume VIII will thus be dated 1975, and Volume IX, 1976, and so forth 'till the last syllable of recorded volumes.

Volume VII for the first time contains an index and, in response to many requests from interested readers, this volume also indexes *Shakespeare Studies*, Volumes I–VI. This latter composite index is subdivided so as to isolate references to authors and their works prior to the year 1640, an arbitrary date which does, however, correspond with the upper limits of the Pollard and Redgrave *Short-Title Catalogue*.

Authors submitting manuscripts should observe that the deadline for Volume IX is July 1974. Contributors need not include abstracts of their papers, but they are urged to take care to have their manuscripts conform to the following specifications to avoid the inevitable delays occasioned by return for requisite alterations. Articles and reviews may be of any length deemed appropriate by the authors, consistent with economy of expression. Pages should be typed double-spaced (including extracts), leaving an inch or so of margin on either side. Double-spaced footnotes should follow the end of the article or review: do not place them at the foot of the individual page. Thus they should be numbered consecutively. For other mechanical details, authors should consult *The MLA Style Sheet* (2nd ed.), which is the style manual for *Shakespeare Studies*.

Articles and reviews should be submitted to: The Editorial Office, The Center for Shakespeare Studies, University of South Carolina, Columbia, South Carolina 29208.

THE EDITOR
Columbia, South Carolina
September 1973

SHAKESPEARE
STUDIES

The Senecan Background of Despair in
The Spanish Tragedy and *Titus Andronicus*

A. L. AND M. K. KISTNER

The influence of Seneca on early Elizabethan tragedy has been precisely demonstrated for some time now, and it is usually agreed that Seneca's contributions to the Elizabethans were in the areas of content and external form.[1] Formal borrowings from the Latin master were the employment of the chorus as a commentator on the action; the use of functional characters such as the messenger or the ghost; the inclusion of stock characters: the nurse, the servant, and the tyrant; stichomythia as a means of conducting argument; retention of the unities; and the division of the tragedy into five acts. The material adapted by the English writers from their Latin predecessor was characterized by its sensationalism or violence, its rhetorical passages filled with extravagant diction, and its expression of philosophic ideas or individual lines of philosophy in aphorism. English dramatists also adopted the long, reflective passages by hero, villain, victim, or bystander on commonplace themes such as fortune's fickleness, war's cruelty, youth's rashness, and poverty's advantages; the revenge motif; the inclusion of presentiments of coming destruction; the use of description to evoke a mood or place a setting; and the narration of violent action which occurs offstage.

But in addition to Seneca's content and external form, there exists an internal form, a governing pattern, which underlies many of his plays and which was adopted by many Elizabethan dramatists. Briefly stated, the pattern includes a character, usually the protagonist, who discovers that whatever means most to him, his absolute, is irrevocably taken from him. The character then falls into despair, which produces one or more reactions: (a) madness, (b) desire for suicide, (c) desire for revenge, or (d) any combination of these responses.

It has commonly been assumed that one of these reactions, revenge, which dominates many Elizabethan tragedies, was of native and contemporary continental origin and that only the sensational trappings of revenge were borrowed from Seneca. According to this theory, revenge tragedy began with Kyd, and Senecan revenge expired with *Gorboduc* and its immediate offspring.[2] To seek vengeance, however, is but one of the compulsions that a despairing Elizabethan protagonist may experience when he realizes that his absolute has been taken from him. Revenge is not the only reaction to despair, but it is the one most inducive to dramatic conflict and action; it is the protagonist's desperate action considered and attempted during a time when the man feels that he can bear no more. J. M. R. Margeson has recently attempted to describe the "overpowering passion for revenge," "the driving passion that

1

moves Elizabethan tragic characters toward their fatal destiny." This passion, he concludes, is of utmost importance in Elizabethan tragedy, is the basis for the emotional pattern of the plays, and is the focus of the dramatic stress of the tragedies.[3] This passion, we believe, is the protagonist's despair, which did not originate with Kyd, but descended in a direct line, through *Gorboduc* and its followers, from Seneca. Revenge is definitely a part of the domestic and imported backgrounds of Elizabethan tragedy, and perhaps one can generalize that the Senecan pattern was adopted by the English because of their inherent interest in and feelings for the subject of revenge, but nonetheless the form which they adopted for expressing these thoughts and feelings is Senecan.

Seneca's pattern of despair and its reactions, simple as it seems, is open to great variation. The playwright can alter the nature of the absolute, the emphasis placed on its importance, the manner in which the absolute is taken from the character, the means by which the discovery of his loss is made known to the character, and the time in the play at which the discovery is made. In addition, the writer can select from or combine the common responses—desire for revenge, suicide, or madness—with which the character reacts to despair. Further, he can modify the structure by assigning the responses, or some of them, to more than one character.

The plays, by various hands, published as *Seneca: His Tenne Tragedies* in 1581 reveal the pattern and a few of its many possible variations.[4] The first play in the collection, *Hercules Furens*, shows two characters—Hercules and his father, Amphitryon—who despair and then desire suicide. They exemplify the simple use of despair and one of its reactions (desire for suicide) as a source of a play's conflict, emotion, and motivation. Thyestes, in the play of the same name, likewise despairs and calls for death when he learns that his children have been killed. Being refused the means of suicide, however, he begs the gods for revenge. Moreover, in *Thyestes*, Seneca has emphasized a portion of the pattern, establishment of the character's absolute prior to its removal, which is left undeveloped in *Hercules*: Thyestes' love for his children is stressed before he learns of their deaths (I.71–72, 89). This slight but dramatically important variation of the pattern was widely imitated by Elizabethan dramatists.

Seneca often modifies the pattern by either dwelling on or skimping the development of one or more of its parts. In *Agamemnon*, *Troas*, and *Thebais*, for instance, he stresses the characters' desire for death (I.107; II.124–25, 129, 136–37, 139). In *Medea*, he emphasizes despair accompanied by frenzy or madness and by desire for revenge rather than for death (II.55–56, 60, 65, 72, 75, 84, 95–96).

Seneca develops despair, madness, and vengeance in only one character in *Medea*; however, he increases the complexity of plot and action in other plays, as he did in *Hercules*, by augmenting the number of people who lose absolutes. The pattern is arranged for two characters in *Hippolytus*—Phaedra and Theseus. Plunged into despair over Hippolytus's death, Phaedra desires death as a relief from her despair *and* as vengeance for his death; over his corpse, she stabs herself (I.179–80). Theseus despairs and prays to the gods for death when he learns that he has been tricked into destroying his innocent son (I.181–83). *Oedipus* is another play whose complexity of plot and action is partially owing to Seneca's doubling of the number of individuals who despair; Oedipus despairs and begs the people of the plague-torn city to slay him, and Jocasta, nearly mad from grief and despair, stabs herself (I.221–22, 227–29).

The unknown author whose *Hercules Oetaeus* appears in the venerable position as the last in Newton's book of translations attributes despair and its reactions to several characters in the play: Iole despairs and yearns for a rather unusual form of self-destruction, metamorphosis by the gods (II.199–201); despairing Deianira plans to kill Hercules in revenge for his infidelity (II.203, 205); then after his death she despairs anew, desires to commit suicide, and goes mad (II.223–24, 226–28); finally, Hercules' mother somewhat conventionally despairs over the death of her son (II.251–54).

In his tragedies, then, Seneca establishes a pattern of motivation and action, one which he repeats with variations in play after play. With certain additions and developments of content and formal devices, it was borrowed by early Elizabethan playwrights and incorporated into their own tragedies. In Thomas Norton and Thomas Sackville's *Gorboduc* (1561), the Senecan pattern begins in the opening scene, which establishes that Queen Videna loves her elder son, Ferrex, above all else and prizes him as her "chiefest ioye" (I.i.22–29).[5] Although her absolute has thus been established, the queen does not reappear until Act IV, and in the interim, the king, Gorboduc, learns of the impending war between his two sons, Ferrex and Porrex; fearing the loss of his sons, Gorboduc sinks into despair. Lest there be doubt as to Gorboduc's state of mind, a counselor admonishes, "Yelde not, O king, so much to weake dispeire!" (III.i.104); however, the messenger's report that Porrex has slain Ferrex causes Gorboduc to despair further. He first demands revenge on his remaining son and then asks for his own death at the hands of the gods (III.i.163–67). The news of Ferrex's death also plunges Videna into despair. She considers suicide but soon thinks of revenge. Addressing Porrex in her mind, she ends her eighty-line soliloquy of despair:

> Doest thou not know that Ferrex mother liues,
> That loued him more dearly than herselfe?
> And doth she liue, and is not venged on thee?
>
> *(IV.i.79–81)*

The final round of hopelessness in the play is Gorboduc's. He learns that Videna has slain Porrex, despairs, and begs for death (IV.ii.191–94). Sackville and Norton base the nonpolitical portion of their play on despair and two of its reactions—desire for suicide and desire for revenge.[6] This pattern which we have seen in the plays of Seneca and in *Gorboduc* is also apparent in the widely imitated *Spanish Tragedy* and a popular early tragedy of Shakespeare, *Titus Andronicus.*

In *The Spanish Tragedy*, Thomas Kyd follows Seneca in the accepted areas of content and external form and also in the Senecan pattern. The former may be seen in the employment of Don Andrea and Revenge as a chorus, in the prologuing ghost seeking revenge, in the messenger's speech to report offstage action (see the general's account of the battle between Spain and Portugal[7]), and in Bel-Imperia's presentiments of misfortune (II.iv.6–7, 14–15). Other possible borrowings are the long reflective passages by major characters, violent and sensational action, and liberal sprinklings of philosophic aphorisms, usually in the speeches of Hieronimo. It is, however, the close following and working out of the Senecan pattern which shows how greatly Kyd is indebted to the Latin playwright. In order to employ the pattern, Kyd establishes an absolute: the first three speeches Kyd gives to Hieronimo in Act I reflect the delight the knight marshal takes in his son.[8] Furthermore, as late as the second to the last scene of the play Hieronimo, showing his son's body, is still explaining to us and his courtly audience how much Horatio meant to him:

> See here my show, look on this spectacle!
> Here lay my hope, and here my hope hath end;
> Here lay my heart, and here my heart was slain;
> Here lay my treasure, here my treasure was lost;
> Here lay my bliss, and here my bliss bereft:
> All fled, fail'd, died, yea, all decay'd with this.
> From forth these wounds came breath that gave me life;
> They murd'red me that made these fatal marks.
>
> *(IV.iv.89–97)*

The absolute established, the next step in the pattern is the protagonist's discovery that he has lost it. Hieronimo's first speech after discovering Horatio's body ends by emphasizing his misery over the loss. "Ay me most wretched, that have lost my joy / In leesing my Horatio, my sweet boy!" (II.v. 32–33). Only a few lines after this first note of despair, Hieronimo reflects that "To know the author were some ease of grief / For in revenge my heart would find relief" (II.v.40–41). From this time on, his thoughts alternate from general expressions of despair and madness to desires for revenge or suicide. And at times, so frequently do these expressions appear that it seems as if Kyd is pressing a set of buttons whereby he rings the various changes on the Senecan pattern.[9] During one speech in which Hieronimo contemplates suicide, he carries the traditional medieval symbols of despair, the rope and the dagger. He has come on stage prepared to kill himself but is prevented by the reflection:

> Soft and fair, not so:
> For if I hang or kill myself, let's know
> Who will revenge Horatio's murder then?
> No, no! fie, no! pardon me, I'll none of that.
>
> *(III.xii.16–19)*

Like Atreus in *Thyestes* and Videna in *Gorboduc*, he turns from thoughts of suicide to desire for revenge.

In addition to thoughts of revenge and suicide, Hieronimo displays the third possible reaction to despair—madness. Three instances of his loss of self-control are his directions to the two "Portingales" seeking Lorenzo (III.xi), his fury during the long-sought audience with the king (III.xii), and his destruction of the citizens' bonds (III.xiii). Madness which accompanies despair, however, must be distinguished from the fixed and consistent loss of mental powers which we commonly consider madness. Hieronimo's insanity is similar to, and probably derives from, the Senecan frenzy; it is an expression of the despairing state of mind, brought on by overpowering emotion, grief too great to bear without outlets (revenge, suicide, or madness itself); and it alternates with more normal, logical periods, although the logic of the saner interludes is primarily motivated by despair.

For additional complexity, the pattern of despair and its responses is imposed upon another figure in Kyd's tragedy, Isabella. She, too, despairs upon the discovery of Horatio's body (II.v.38–45) and laments, "And ile close vp the glasses of his sight, / For once these eyes were onely my delight" (II.v.50–51). In her next appearance, she is depicted as mad and calling for revenge (III. viii); and in her third and final scene, she insanely attempts to revenge herself upon the site of Horatio's murder. Her lines "For sorrow and dispaire hath cited me / To heare Horatio plead with Rhadamant" (IV.ii.27–28); her frustration over Hieronimo's laxness in revenge and the king's neglect of justice; and the complaint that she has bestirred herself to no end—these all reveal why Isabella commits suicide. Alone she is not capable of gaining revenge by attacking Lorenzo and Balthazar, and once she feels that all avenues of avengement are closed, her despair brings her to self-slaughter.

The motivations and actions of Hieronimo and Isabella, their despair and reactions to it, are close imitations of the motivations and actions of Senecan characters. The action of the plot is based upon the Senecan pattern we have seen in *His Tenne Tragedies*—the character's loss of his absolute, his despair, and his various responses to it.

Seneca's direct influence in *Titus Andronicus* is, perhaps, most clearly notable in a few individual scenes. *Troas* supplies the incident of the sacrifice at the tomb of the Andronici, and *Thyestes* the banquet of slain sons. Other influences, such as the legends of Virginius and Coriolanus, Ovid's *Metamorphoses* and Virgil's *Aeneid*, appear frequently in the text itself, but the non-Senecan background, ample as it is, does not provide the structure Shakespeare is realizing in the actions of his hero. Seneca's pattern does: Titus's absolutes are his remaining children, and by the middle of Act III, scene ii, Lavinia has been ravished and mutilated, Quintus and Martius falsely accused of murder and put to death, and Lucius banished for attempting to save his brothers. Titus's despair resulting from these losses is readily apparent; for his sentenced sons, he laments:

> For these, tribunes, in the dust I write
> My heart's deep languor and my soul's sad tears:
> Let my tears stanch the earth's dry appetite;
> My sons' sweet blood will make it shame and blush.
> . . . . .
> O reverend tribunes! O gentle, aged men!
> Unbind my sons, reverse the doom of death;
> And let me say, that never wept before,
> My tears are now prevailing orators.
>
> (III.i.12–15, 23–26)[10]

For Lavinia he cries:

> It was my deer; and he that wounded her
> Hath hurt me more than had he kill'd me dead:
> For now I stand as one upon a rock
> Environ'd with a wilderness of sea,
> . . . . .
> This way to death my wretched sons are gone;
> Here stands my other son, a banish'd man,
> And here my brother, weeping at my woes:
> But that which gives my soul the greatest spurn,

Is dear Lavinia, dearer than my soul.
Had I but seen thy picture in this plight,
It would have madded me: what shall I do
Now I behold thy lively body so?

(III.i.91–94, 98–105)

He has one further expression of despair (III.i.217–30) before the messenger
returns from court with the heads of his sons and the hand Titus sacrificed to
buy their lives. When Marcus expects him to give way to further grief, Titus
laughs and declares his desire for vengeance (III.i.267–79). From this time
forth, Titus's thoughts are on revenge.[11]

As we have seen, one of the ways in which Seneca occasionally varies his
pattern is to eliminate or to neglect one or more of the reactions which despair
invokes. Just as Norton and Sackville omitted madness in *Gorboduc*, Shakespeare, in *Titus Andronicus*, does not include references to suicide in Titus's
speeches, nor do any of the Andronici seem to have it in mind. Shakespeare
does, however, pay some attention to Titus's madness, in addition to the desire for revenge. If, when, and how mad Titus is, and to what degree Shakespeare is capable, at this time, of delineating his lunacy are difficult questions,
but the intention of portraying Titus mad is clear. Concentration on the madness begins in Act IV, scene ii, and continues up to the last scene of the play.
One method employed to depict Titus's lunacy is exposition by other characters: Aaron refers to Titus's verses to Demetrius and Chiron as "some mad
message from his [Young Lucius's] mad grandfather" (IV.i..3); Marcus, watching Titus bearing arrows with letters to the gods attached to them, remarks, "O
Publius, is not this a heavy case, / To see thy noble uncle thus distract?"
(IV.iii.25–26). At the court, Saturninus complains of the arrows Titus shot and
partially ascribes the cause to madness resulting from misery:

And what an if
His sorrows have so overwhelm'd his wits,
Shall we be thus afflicted in his wreaks,
His fits, his frenzy, and his bitterness?

(IV.iv.9–12)

Finally, Tamora confidently declares to her sons that Titus is insane:

This closing with him fits his lunacy:
Whate'er I forge to feed his brain-sick humours,
Do you uphold and maintain in your speeches,

> For now he firmly takes me for Revenge;
> And, being credulous in this mad thought,
> I'll make him send for Lucius his son[.]
>
> (V.ii.70–75)

Actual examples of Titus's lunacy, however, are confined to his actions in Act IV, scene iii, in which he instructs his kinsmen to search for justice in the sea and then in the underworld. When Publius humors his speeches, Titus claims that he will dive into the burning lake and pull justice out of Acheron by the heels. The lines are reminiscent of Hieronimo's frenzied ripping of the court floor to bring Horatio back from the underworld and fiends from hell to gain justice. Titus then decides there is no justice on earth or in hell and proceeds to shoot his arrows to the gods.[12]

To conclude, the hero's motivations and actions in *Titus Andronicus* are governed by the Senecan pattern, just as they are in *The Spanish Tragedy* and *His Tenne Tragedies*. Titus's despair, desire for revenge, and madness are the despair, desire for revenge, and madness of Hieronimo and Medea. In these plays and in many Elizabethan tragedies which follow them, the Senecan pattern provides the motivation and subsequent course of action for the tragic hero, regardless of the wide variety in characterizations of the many protagonists.

Notes:

1. John W. Cunliffe, *The Influence of Seneca on Elizabethan Tragedy* (New York, 1907), p. 14 ff.
2. Fredson Bowers, *Elizabethan Revenge Tragedy 1587–1642* (Princeton, 1966), pp. 63, 65; Percy Simpson, "The Theme of Revenge in Elizabethan Tragedy," *Studies in Elizabethan Drama* (Oxford, 1955), p. 149; and A. P. Rossiter, *English Drama from Early Times to the Elizabethans* (London, 1966), pp. 142, 162, 169, 174.
3. *The Origins of English Tragedy* (Oxford, 1967), pp. 134, 169, 185.
4. Thomas Newton, ed., *Seneca: His Tenne Tragedies* (London, 1927). All references to the plays of Seneca are to this text. It is now recognized that some of the plays included in this text are spurious Senecan plays, but since the Elizabethans evidently did not know they were, they are included in the discussion. Almost all of the translations in this edition had, of course, appeared earlier, chiefly between 1559 and 1567.
5. *Chief Pre-Shakespearean Drama*, ed. Joseph Quincy Adams (Cambridge, Mass., 1924). All references to *Gorboduc* are to this text.
6. In addition to *Gorboduc*, see *Appius and Virginia, Damon and Pithias, Promos and Cassandra, Soliman and Perseda, The Misfortunes of Arthur, Locrine*, and

Tancred and Gismunda, among others, as examples of pre-Shakespearean efforts governed by the playwrights' exploitations of the Senecan pattern.

7. Thomas Kyd, *The Spanish Tragedy,* ed. Phillip Edwards, The Revels Plays (London, 1959), I.ii.22–84. All references to the play are to this text.

8. The additions by the unknown hand reinforce this declaration of the absolute. See the third addition, between III.xi.1 and 2, ll. 28–34.

9. For example, Hieronimo's despair, III.ii.1–4; III.vii.1–14; III.xiii.162–69. For his desire for revenge, II.v.51–56; III.vii.67–73; IV.iii.27–30. For his thoughts of suicide, III.xii.6–16. One might add that the writer of the additions does the same, alternating expressions of despair, madness, desire for revenge, and desire for suicide in the additions in II.v; III.xi; and between III.xii and III.xiii.

10. *The Complete Works of Shakespeare,* ed. Hardin Craig (New York, 1962), pp. 369–93. All references cited are to this text.

11. For examples, see III.ii.1–3, 69–77.

12. It is Marcus's idea, not Titus's, to loose the arrows into the court; Titus has no practical plan for them.

Two Gentlemen of Milan

Thomas E. Scheye

Mark Van Doren put *The Two Gentlemen of Verona* in its place when he said it is "a slight comedy and it minces uncertainly to an implausible conclusion, but it is Shakespeare's own and it sets his course."[1] The most recent editor of the play has said much the same thing, admitting that "No one is likely to claim that *The Two Gentlemen of Verona* is a masterpiece, or anything like it," but admonishing that "students of Shakespeare have to keep this comedy in mind. Not only does it anticipate in all sorts of ways the 'romantic' plays that followed, it also gives us a clue to the interpretation of Shakespeare's writing as a whole."[2] Almost everyone agrees about *The Two Gentlemen*: it is a poor thing but Shakespeare's own, and rich in intimations of things to come.

It is Shakespeare's first story of true love, whose course never did run smooth until the happy ending. It is also the play where Shakespeare maps out his comic territory. In Northrop Frye's familiar formula, "the action of the comedy begins in a world represented as a normal world, moves into the green world, goes into a metamorphosis there in which the comic resolution is achieved, and returns to the normal world."[3] The forest which provides the scene for the resolution of *Two Gentlemen* is Shakespeare's earliest venture into the green world: it is the place where Valentine is reunited with Silvia and Proteus reconciled to Julia, as a reconstructed society, which even includes the outlaws, forms up around the young couples. But before it moves into the forest, this comedy of Verona stops for nearly three acts in another setting, the city of Milan,[4] where all the preparations for a quick and easy denouement are laid. Milan is no green world; Valentine falls in love there and is almost ready to elope with Silvia, but his plans are foiled. He is slandered and betrayed by his best friend, and condemned and banished by the duke; then he can describe being in Milan as "living torment" (III.i.170).[5]

The action in Milan is clearly played for comedy, but the fact remains that the second world of the play is not idyllic; it is an unpleasant and even somewhat dangerous place for the protagonist. Of course, there is usually a place like this in Shakespeare's romantic comedies; in the phase when the fortunes of the hero run down, the cross-wooing threatens to get out of control, and games of disguise and mistaken identity take unexpected, unhappy turns. This phase can be more conveniently isolated for examination in *The Two Gentlemen of Verona* because of the changes of scene; and perhaps by attention to what happens to the two gentlemen in Milan we can approach a paradigm to describe what happens in the green world.

The paradigm I want to propose has to do with the search for identity since that would seem to be Valentine's motive for coming to Milan in the first place. In the opening scene he has told Proteus that he is making a journey "To see the wonders of the world abroad" (I.i.6), possibly because he has considered, as Proteus's father has, "how he cannot be a perfect man, / Not being tried and tutor'd in the world" (I.iii.20–21). The journey is part of his education, a way of making himself a perfect or complete man, or of growing up; Proteus says it is a search after "honor" (I.i.63). In *Two Gentlemen* Valentine comes to Milan in search of "honor" or experience so that he can realize himself to the fullest. But as soon as he arrives, he forgets about honor and education and the rest; he sets eyes on Silvia and falls in love. Now love will be seen as learning: in love in Milan Valentine will learn about himself.

At first, though, love makes Valentine lose his old self. In Verona he was someone who scorned Proteus's love as "shapeless idleness" and "folly bought with wit" (I.i.8, 34); in Milan he is love's abject servant, the fool who goes ungartered. And the effect of this radical change in Valentine, "from the mocker to the votary of love,"[6] is apparent even to Speed: "when I look on you, I can hardly think you my master." Valentine has lost himself in love so that now he is the mirror image of Proteus instead of his opposite. Speed says,

> . . . you have learned, like Sir Proteus, to wreathe your arms like a malcontent, to relish a love-song like a robin-red-breast, to walk alone like one that had the pestilence, to sigh like a schoolboy that had lost his A B C. . . .

And he concludes, "You are metamorphosed with a mistress" (II.i.17–30), recalling to us Proteus's apostrophe, "Thou, Julia, thou hast metamorphosed me" (I.i.66). By love's metamorphosis Valentine has lost his identity until he no longer even looks like himself; he looks like Proteus instead.

Valentine's resemblance to his best friend is not too surprising since it was traditional during the Renaissance to describe friendship in terms of identity, or one soul in two bodies.[7] This resemblance is especially acute in Milan where Valentine executes his protean about-face and turns lover like his friend, and both men for a time are in love with the same woman. When the duke of Milan asks Valentine about Proteus, he says,

> I know him as myself, for from our infancy
> We have conversed and spent our hours together;
> And though myself have been an idle truant,
> Omitting the sweet benefit of time
> To clothe mine age with angel-like perfection,
> Yet hath Sir Proteus—for that's his name—
> Made use and fair advantage of his days;
>
> .　.　.　.　.
>
> He is complete in feature and in mind
> With all good grace to grace a gentleman.
>
> (II.iv.59–71)

Valentine claims to know Proteus as he knows himself (Julia, disguised as the page, will tell Silvia she knows Julia "Almost as well as I do know myself" [IV.iv.141]); for the two friends have grown up in identical circumstances, enjoying "equality of status and congeniality of minds."[8] Valentine has been temporarily separated from his friend so that experience can do the work of time and bring his character closer to angel-like perfection. And Proteus is the image of that perfection, "complete in feature and in mind" as Valentine would like to be, his ideal and his model.

Their friendship is strained when Proteus too falls in love with Silvia, the competition in love causing the conflict in Milan. Such competition belongs to the conventions of the literature of friendship which Shakespeare reflects in *The Two Gentlemen of Verona*, with the most apposite source, apparently, being the story of Titus and Gisippus as told by Sir Thomas Elyot in *The Governor*. Although this story could be found in a number of places, some of the details Shakespeare uses are unique to Elyot's version, notably Gisippus's handing over his true love to his true friend.[9] Gisippus says, "Here I renounce to you clerely all my title and interest that I nowe haue or mought haue in that faire mayden,"[10] and his accents may remind us of Valentine's "all that was mine in Silvia I give thee" (V.iv.83). While this feature of Elyot's version has often been remarked upon, another detail, apparently also unique to Elyot, has received less attention: the description of the two friends as identical in appearance:

Gisippus . . . was equall to . . . Titus in yeres, but also in stature, proporcion of body, fauour, and colour of visage, countenance and speche. The two children were so like, that without moche difficultie it coulde nat be discerned of their propre parentes, whiche was Titus from Gysippus, or

Gysippus from Titus. These two yonge gentilmen, as they semed to be one in fourme and personage, so, shortely after acquaintaunce, the same nature wrought in their hartes suche a mutuall affection, that their willes and appetites daily more and more so confederated them selfes, that it semed none other, whan their names were declared, but that they hadde onely chaunged their places, issuinge (as I mought saye) out of the one body, and entringe in to the other.

(II.134)

The fact that Titus and Gisippus resemble each other not only in appearance but also in will or appetite provokes the conflict in the story. Given their "similitude" it is only natural that the two of them should fall in love with the same woman. Titus upbraids his friend for introducing the lady Sophronia to him:

For where as god of nature, lyke as he hath given to us similitude in all the partes of our body, so had he conioyned our willes, studies, and appetites to gether in one

. . . . .

Why wolde ye haue me see that, whiche you youre selfe coulde nat beholde without rauisshinge of mynde and carnall appetite? Alas, why forgate ye that our myndes and appetites were euer one? And that also what so ye lyked was euer to me in lyke degree pleasaunt?

(II.138–39)

And Gisippus agrees: "I knowledge my foly, wherwith ye haue with good right imbrayded me, that, in showing to you her whom I loued, I remembred nat the commune astate of our nature, ne the agreablenesse, or (as I mought saye) the unitie of our two appetites" (II.140). Resemblance or identity in this sense is at the root of the problem for Titus and Gisippus. It is also the solution for their problem since, when Gisippus allows Titus to take his place on the wedding night, the bed-trick can be managed because no one, not even the bride presumably, can tell the two men apart.

When he comes to borrow from this version of Titus and Gisippus for *The Two Gentlemen of Verona*, Shakespeare carries over the competition in love along with the notion of spiritual kinship and similitude of appetite. On the other hand, he does not include any suggestion of physical identity between the two friends, possibly because he had just written, or was about to write, a play about a pair of actual twins in *The Comedy of Errors*. Even so, twinship might provide a model for the relationship between Valentine and Proteus as it does for the two Antipholi. And perhaps from this perspective *The Comedy of Errors* can also help to explain the paradigm for *Two Gentlemen.*

The Comedy of Errors is set on the day when Antipholus of Syracuse arrives in Ephesus in search of his twin brother and the rest of his family; he has made the voyage because he believes that without relations his identity will be incomplete.[11] And though he tells a friendly merchant he meets there that he will spend the day in Ephesus sight-seeing ("I will go lose myself, / And wander up and down to view the city"), he later elaborates the figure of losing himself:

> I to the world am like a drop of water
> That in the ocean seeks another drop,
> Who, falling there to find his fellow forth,
> Unseen, inquisitive, confounds himself.
> So I, to find a mother and a brother,
> In quest of them, unhappy, lose myself.
>
> (I.ii.30–31, 35–40)

Antipholus loses himself in Ephesus hoping that, like the drop of water, he can make sense not as a single body, but in the world's body. He loses himself in order to find himself through his twin. At first, though, the fact that Antipholus of Syracuse looks exactly like his brother and is called by his name only heightens his sense of self-loss; since he is continually taken for someone else by the citizens of Ephesus, he is almost convinced that he is "Known unto these, and to myself disguised" (II.ii.213). Until they are re-united, the twins will seem to share a single identity in Ephesus, that of the native brother, since the existence of another Antipholus is unknown. And in a continual interchange of roles one brother gains identity as the other loses it. Even when the twins stand together on stage they are so alike that the duke of Ephesus concludes,

> One of these men is genius to the other;
> And so of these, which is the natural man,
> And which the spirit?
>
> (V.i.333–35)

At the denouement the native Antipholus can be seen to have acted, un-wittingly, as genius to his brother, who gains not only his family but also his individual identity once the confusion is sorted out.

On the day of errors, then, Antipholus of Syracuse has lost himself and found himself through the mirror image which is provided by his twin brother. And something like this happens to Valentine in *The Two Gentlemen of Verona*. The process begins when Valentine comes to Milan and falls under Silvia's spell; he is "metamorphosed with a mistress" and he begins to lose his old identity. At first Valentine's appearance changes so that he no longer resembles his former self. Then Love deprives him of his senses, making him blind, as Speed remarks (he is talking about Silvia):

> *Speed.*   If you love her, you cannot see her.
> *Valentine.* Why?
> *Speed.*   Because Love is blind. O, that you had mine eyes, or your own
>   eyes had the lights they were wont to have when you chid at
>   Sir Proteus for going ungartered!
> *Valentine.* What should I see then?
> *Speed.*   Your own present folly . . .
>
>   *(II.i.64–70)*

In love-blindness Valentine cannot see himself or see how much he looks like Proteus. And love has not only blinded Valentine; it has also struck him dumb. As he cannot know himself yet, he cannot express himself either. Though he is eloquent to Proteus in praise of his beloved, Valentine cannot tell Silvia of his devotion directly. And so he has resorted to letters, to which she has not replied. Letters are normally an unsuccessful means of communication, as Act I has shown with the letter Proteus has written to Julia. He has sent it to her by Valentine's servant, Speed, but when Speed returns he brings no answer and tells Proteus,

> Sir, I could perceive nothing at all from her: no, not so much as a ducat for delivering your letter. And being so hard to me that brought your mind, I fear she'll prove as hard to you in telling your mind.
>
>   *(I.i.130–33)*

The resemblance between the letters is more obvious after Speed interprets them. (Is this a reason for having Valentine's servant deliver Proteus's letter?)[12] When Silvia bids Valentine write a letter to a "secret, nameless friend" (II.i.96)—Valentine himself at this point—and then tells him to keep it, Speed asks, "do you not perceive the jest?" (II.i.141). Valentine does not perceive it, and yet the jest is so transparent that the foolish servant has caught it immediately:

O jest unseen, inscrutable, invisible,
As a nose on a man's face, or a weathercock on a steeple!
My master sues to her, and she hath taught her suitor,
He being her pupil, to become her tutor.
O excellent device—was there ever heard a better?
That my master, being scribe, to himself should write the letter!

(II.i.125–30)

Silvia's device is as plain as the nose on your face, Speed says. Valentine can see it only as well as he can see himself, as he will only understand his love after he understands himself.

The letter Silvia returns to Valentine is meant to teach a lesson: that he must love himself, and know himself, before he can love another. But for that lesson Proteus, the mirror image, will be a better teacher. When he arrives in Milan and falls in love with Silvia at first sight, Proteus understands immediately that the selfless devotion of friendship must give way before self-interest in love:

Methinks my zeal to Valentine is cold,
And that I love him not as I was wont.
O, but I love his lady too too much,
And that's the reason I love him so little.

(II.iv.199–203)

Proteus hesitates for a moment—his soliloquy is broken into two parts by an intervening comic scene between Launce and Speed—but when he resolves to move against his friend he knows that Valentine must lose himself if he (Proteus) is going to find himself:

I cannot leave to love, and yet I do:
But there I leave to love where I should love.
Julia I lose and Valentine I lose.
If I keep them, I needs must lose myself;
If I lose them, thus find I by their loss:
For Valentine, myself;

(II.vi.17–22)

Proteus imagines that he will gain his selfhood at the price of Valentine's self-loss, and the situation may recall that of the Antipholus twins in *The Comedy of Errors* sharing a single identity between them: when one of the brothers had identity, the other was selfless. Antipholus of Syracuse had taken over his twin's identity without meaning to, but Proteus consciously wishes to usurp Valentine's identity, to displace him in Silvia's affections and to replace him at the court of Milan. So he discloses Valentine's planned elopement, and Valentine is banished; banishment confirms Valentine's loss of identity. When he pronounces sentence the duke not only exiles Valentine but damns him for aspiring beyond himself to Silvia, calling him "base intruder" and "overweening slave" (III.i.158). The duke is denying Valentine his status, his position at Milan and his state as a nobleman, two essential props to his identity at this point. When he threatens Valentine, "as thou lov'st thy life, make speed from hence," Valentine says he is as good as dead already, in a state of nonexistence:

> To die is to be banished from myself.
> And Silvia is myself; banished from her
> Is self from self, a deadly banishment.
>
> .   .   .   .   .
>
> She is my essence, and I leave to be,
> If I be not by her fair influence
> Fostered, illumined, cherished, kept alive.
>
> (III.i.171–73, 182–84)

Death is nothing more than absolute selflessness; and since his fulfillment depends on Silvia—his "essence," or self-image—without her Valentine is so lacking in selfhood that he says he is no longer Valentine.

His situation is tragic in its implication, and the parallel with Romeo has often been pointed out.[13] Now as if to distance us from a potentially tragic reaction, Proteus and Launce are brought on for comic relief. Launce makes a significant malapropism about exile: "Sir, there is a proclamation that you are vanished" (III.i.216). Then Valentine and Proteus have their cross-talk on the subject:

> *Proteus.*   Valentine?
> *Valentine.* No.
> *Proteus.*   Who then? His spirit?
> *Valentine.* Neither.
> *Proteus.*   What then?
> *Valentine.* Nothing.
>
> (III.i.193–98)

Valentine is not above making jokes about his situation, and he goes on to make a pun on his name; *Valentine* no longer stands for the man himself, since he does not exist. Now the name means only a love token, a valentine with a lowercase v:[14]

> Valentine. Is Silvia dead?
> Proteus.   No, Valentine.
> Valentine. No Valentine indeed, for sacred Silvia.
>   Hath she forsworn me?
> Proteus.   No, Valentine.
> Valentine. No Valentine, if Silvia have forsworn me.
>   (III.i.209–14)

The point has been made then, at considerable length, both seriously and humorously, that Valentine without Silvia is dead or nonexistent, utterly without identity. If his fate were tragic, like Romeo's, the play might end here, or go on to show the death of the hero. But Valentine has only come two-thirds of the way along the comic curve. He has lost himself now that Proteus has displaced him in Milan; but he will find himself. He has been told by the duke to "Bestow thy fawning smiles on equal mates" (III.i.158), and, though the duke was talking about other women, Valentine will find his equal mates when he moves into the green world of the forest.

Valentine is accosted by the outlaws as he is going "to Verona" (IV.i.17). He is headed home, but he will find a new home with the outlaws as he had hoped to do with Silvia in Milan; in the forest it is the outlaws who offer a mirror image of his condition. Valentine has been banished for trying to elope with the duke's daughter, though he tells the outlaws that his offense was murder.[15] The second of the outlaws too has been exiled as a murderer, while the third one says,

> Myself was from Verona banished,
> For practicing to steal away a lady,
> An heir, and near allied unto the Duke.
>   (IV.i.47–49)

This duplication—in which one outlaw has committed Valentine's pretended crime and another his actual crime—is strange,[16] and yet it enforces the parallel between Valentine and the outlaws who are already allied as fellow exiles. One of them refers to Valentine as "a man of such perfection / As we do in our quality much want—" (IV.i.57–58), recalling Valentine's praise of Proteus to the duke. The outlaws offer Valentine to be their king, and instead of robbing him of what little he has been left after banishment, they lead him to their

treasure which they put "at thy dispose" (IV.i.76). In the forest the process
of self-loss will be reversed and the scene laid for Valentine to find himself.

In this green world Valentine regains all the friends he has lost in Milan, and
though he has one more moment of selflessness when he hands Silvia over to
Proteus,[17] he gains by this too. Valentine's proof of friendship, along with the
sudden discovery of Julia, brings pressure on inconstant Proteus to execute a
second about-face—mercurial changes come as easily to Proteus as to his
namesake—which puts him back where he started:

> O heaven, were man
> But constant, he were perfect! That one error
> Fills him with faults, makes him run through all the sins;
> Inconstancy falls off ere it begins.
> What is in Silvia's face, but I may spy
> More fresh in Julia's with a constant eye?
>
> *(V.iv.111–16)*

So Valentine and Proteus are reconciled while Valentine is reunited with his
"essence," Silvia, and Proteus with Julia; the symmetry of the scene further
enforces the parallel between the two gentlemen. In this moment Proteus has
come to some kind of self-realization in part through the efforts of Valentine;
in the same moment Valentine is reunited with his sworn brother and his
beloved. Proteus and Silvia are the two people who have provided the mirror
images in which Valentine might see himself, and the scene in which they are
reconciled also demonstrates their effect on Valentine. When his rival Thurio
makes a claim on Silvia, Valentine shows how much he has recovered his
identity, since for the first time he stands up for himself:

> Thurio, give back, or else embrace thy death.
> Come not within the measure of my wrath.
> Do not name Silvia thine; if once again,
> Verona shall not hold thee. Here she stands;
> Take but possession of her with a touch—
> I dare thee but to breathe upon my love.
>
> *(V.iv.127–32)*

The duke applauds this show of spirit and self-interest, pardons Valentine,
and approves the marriage:

> Know then, I here forget all former griefs,
> Cancel all grudge, repeal thee home again,

Plead a new state in thy unrivalled merit,
To which I thus subscribe: Sir Valentine,
Thou art a gentleman, and well derived;
Take thou thy Silvia, for thou hast deserved her.

(V.iv.143–48)

The duke had once confirmed Valentine's loss of identity by exiling him and condemning him as "base" and "overweening." Now he confirms Valentine's true identity by subscribing to his "new state," inviting him "home" to Milan, and attesting to his nobility as "Sir Valentine." The search for identity will come to an end when Sir Valentine returns to his new home and marries Silvia.

And so Milan will be the state where Valentine loses himself to find himself. The conceit is fairly familiar in Shakespeare, with the most famous statement of it coming in *The Tempest* and Gonzalo's description of the action:

in one voyage
Did Claribel her husband find at Tunis,
And Ferdinand her brother found a wife
Where he himself was lost; Prospero his dukedom
In a poor isle; and all of us ourselves
When no man was his own.

(V.i.208–13)

Gonzalo describes the effect of the voyage toward the green world with more vision and eloquence than anyone in *Two Gentlemen* can muster. But the earlier play can show more clearly how things are managed.

The Two Gentlemen of Verona is such a thin play that one can almost see through it, and the process of self-discovery is almost external to the character of the hero. Valentine has identity thrust upon him rather than achieving it for himself. There is no evidence that the mirror images Valentine confronts act like the glass Hamlet sets up before his mother, "Where you may see the inmost part of you" (III.iv.20). It is his status—what other people think of him rather than what he thinks of himself—which is seen to change. But this very lack of interest and definition in the character of Valentine leads away from theories of personality to a consideration of the scene in which the action is played out, and the second world, of this play at least, emerges as a house of mirrors, in Spenser's phrase "a world of glass." Before he sets about the creation of full-blooded characters the playwright must construct a place for them to live. And for Shakespeare's comic world *The Two Gentlemen of Verona* may be a slightly smudged blueprint.

Notes:

1. *Shakespeare* (1939; rpt. Garden City, N.Y., 1953), pp. 40–41.
2. Clifford Leech, ed., *The Two Gentlemen of Verona,* The Arden Shakespeare (London, 1969), pp. lxxi, lxxv.
3. "The Argument of Comedy," in *EIE,* 1948, ed. D. W. Robertson (New York, 1949), p. 68.
4. There is some confusion in the text about the name of the city. In the opening scene Valentine is clearly setting out for "Milan" (I.i.57, 61, 71); and after his banishment he tells the outlaws that he is coming "From Milan" (IV.i.19). But Speed has welcomed Launce to "Padua" (II.v.1), while Silvia's father, when he is trying to trick Valentine, says that he himself is in love with "a lady in Verona here" (III.i.81). Still, it is not quite true that "The topography of this text is as confused as everything else about it" (Sir Arthur Quiller-Couch and J. Dover Wilson, eds., *The Two Gentlemen of Verona,* 1969, p. 92). The references to the city as Milan outnumber the others and Valentine at least is consistent in calling it Milan. See Arden edition, pp. xv–xviii.
5. Quotations are from *The Complete Pelican Shakespeare,* General Editor, Alfred Harbage (Baltimore, 1968).
6. H. B. Charlton, *Shakespearian Comedy* (1938; rpt. London, 1966), p. 35.
7. Laurens J. Mills has traced the history of this commonplace in *One Soul in Bodies Twain: Friendship in Tudor Literature and Stuart Drama* (Bloomington, Ind., 1937). Examples from the period of Shakespeare are collected in chapters 4 and 5.
8. Ralph Sargent, "Sir Thomas Elyot and the Integrity of *The Two Gentlemen of Verona,*" *PMLA,* 65 (1950), 1169.
9. Sargent, p. 1178n. Clifford Leech finds Shakespeare closer to Boccaccio's version of Titus and Gisippus than to Elyot's. But he believes it "more than probable that Shakespeare knew *The Governor,* and the story of Titus and Gisippus is likely enough to have been in his mind when he told his own friendship story of Valentine and Proteus" (Arden edition, p. xxxviii).
10. Sir Thomas Elyot, *The Boke Named The Gouernour,* ed. H. H. S. Croft (London, 1883), II, 141–42. Subsequent citations are to Croft's edition.
11. See Harold Brooks, "Themes and Structure in *The Comedy of Errors,*" in *Early Shakespeare,* ed. John Russell Brown and Bernard Harris (New York, 1966), p. 58; Gwyn Williams, "*The Comedy of Errors* Rescued from Tragedy," *RES,* 5 (1964), 70.
12. For another guess about this, see Harold Brooks, "Two Clowns in a Comedy (to say nothing of the Dog): Speed, Launce (and Crab) in *The Two Gentlemen of Verona,*" *E&S,* 16 (1963), 93–94.
13. See *Rom.,* III.iii. 12–70.
14. The pun on the name has been pointed out by Dover Wilson, who prints *Valentine* in lines 209 and 214 with a lowercase *v* in the New Cambridge edition.
15. M. C. Bradbrook explains, in *Shakespeare and Elizabethan Poetry* (1951; rpt. London, 1964), that by lying to the outlaws about the real reason he has left Milan, Valentine "conceals his love according to the best courtly code" (pp. 133–34). She cites as an analogue Drayton's *Endimion and Phoebe,* where the shep-

herd "vows secrecie, the crown of a true lover" (p. 237). The code itself is a medieval inheritance, typified by Andreas Capellanus's admonition, "The man who wants to keep his love affair for a long time untroubled should above all things be careful not to let it be known to any outsider, but should keep it hidden from everybody" (*The Art of Courtly Love*, trans. John Jay Parry [1941; rpt. New York, 1969], p. 251).

16. In his notes to this scene Clifford Leech comments about the duplication that "The dramatist was doubtless saving the trouble of further invention." But in the introduction he suggests that "fighting and eloping, being . . . multiplied, seem to become minor and ordinary happenings, and Valentine's love-predicament all the less involving for us" (Arden edition, p. lxv).

17. See Bradbrook, p. 151; Sargent, p. 1178.

The Pattern of
Love's Labour's Lost

S. K. HENINGER, JR.

Love's Labour's Lost ends in a most curious way. The action has led predictably to the matching of the four young gentlemen of Navarre with the four young ladies of France. In the last moments of the play, however, the decision about marriage is postponed for a year, and the question of whether the mating ever takes place may be raised.[1] The action is suspended rather than terminated. It is as though the young lovers of *A Midsummer Night's Dream* returned to Athens from the woods and decided to date for a year before making up their minds about marriage; or as though Romeo and Juliet did not die in the tomb, but the Montagues and Capulets said, "Well, we'll think about it." Contrary to any other comedy of Shakespeare, the ultimate relationship of the lovers in this play is not consummated in the eye of the beholder. Love's labor is lost.

In the final lines of the play having to do with plot—that is, before preparation for the closing song—Berowne and the king comment upon the unexpected turn of events and specifically note the incompleteness of the action:

> *Ber.* Our wooing doth not end like an old play:
> Jack hath not Jill. These ladies' courtesy
> Might well have made our sport a comedy.
> *King.* Come, sir, it wants a twelvemonth an' a day,
> And then 'twill end.
> *Ber.* That's too long for a play.
>
> *(V.ii.862–66)*[2]

It is rare in Shakespearean drama for characters to stand outside the play and comment upon it. But this is what happens here. Berowne complains that the action has not gone according to expectation, that the lovers are not united at the end according to the convention of comedy. The king replies that the issue will be resolved within the usual span of time required by impossible feats in fairy tales, a year and a day. Berowne rightly rejoins that a conclusion postponed until then lies outside the bounds of the play, and hence is improper. The terminus of the action has been projected beyond the limits of this artwork,[3] thereby leaving the plot deficient. And this colloquy between Berowne and the king stops there. The play then closes quickly with a song "in

25

praise of the Owl and the Cuckoo" performed by the secondary characters
divided into two groups representing spring and winter.

This ending of *Love's Labour's Lost* raises two sets of problems that the
critic must face. One set has to do with the thematic statement of the play, the
other with its esthetics. Ultimately, of course, questions about theme and
questions about technique merge in our summary understanding of the play
—in fact, the closing song is the adequate clue to solving both the thematic and
the esthetic problems. The song is Shakespeare's way of telling us what the
play means and how we should go about appreciating its artistry. Since criticism is necessarily discursive, however, we must deal with these two sets of
problems seriatim, and we shall proceed most expeditiously by looking first
at the problems of esthetics.

The primary esthetic question can be stated briefly. Since Shakespeare does
not finalize the relationship between the lovers in this thwarted comedy, since
the main action is inconclusive, how does he give a sense of completeness to the
play? How does he manage a *terminus ad quem* for his artifact? The answer
is obvious: by means of the final song. This duet between cuckoo and owl is not
an incidental excrescence, but rather an integral part of *Love's Labour's Lost*—
indeed, the artistic and thematic conclusion of the play.

The question of *how* the song completes the play's action is more complex.
The central characters of *Love's Labour's Lost* come to a point where two
eventualities are possible, one leading to marriage of the four couples, the
other leading to failure and separation of the lovers. If the play continued,
Shakespeare would have had to make a choice between these two possibilities:
he would have had to decide between ending his play like a conventional comedy or producing something that we may call a comitragedy, a potentially
happy action that ends sadly. By stopping the action where he did, however,
Shakespeare left either possibility a viable alternative; we can make our own
choice, depending upon whether we wish to view the action *sub specie
comœdiæ* or *tragœdiæ*. Or perhaps, by stopping the action where he did, by
excluding neither possibility, Shakespeare left both options open. The ending
is intentionally ambiguous so that both options have validity. The situation is
both/and, rather than either/or. A well-rounded, full-bodied view of life is
thereby achieved, neither comic nor tragic, but somehow embracing both.

My argument, quite simply, is that Shakespeare stops the action at that
point where a choice between an optimistic or a pessimistic ending must be
made. He ducks this limiting choice (for thematic reasons to be considered
more fully) and emblematizes the intentional ambiguity by means of the
closing song. The characters are halted in their narrative; they reach the end

of their existence in a recognizably physical world, in the three-dimensional kingdom of Navarre postulated as the setting for *Love's Labour's Lost*. The mode of poetic statement shifts at this point from action transpiring within a time-space continuum to a different order of poetry, to lyric. Time and space are suspended. The characters are atomized into a different order of being. The song abstracts the lovers, expands them into a universal statement about love and life and time—the concepts that serve as counters in philosophy. Poetry here transmutes toward philosophy, as Sidney defined the two disciplines in his *Apology for Poetry*.

In dealing with the set of thematic problems in the play, the best procedure is to examine the song as a poem existing independent of the play. It can be analyzed as an autonomous lyric, self-contained and self-sufficient. Of course, it is related to the dramatic action of the play, and my focal intent is to demonstrate this interrelationship. But first we should look at the song by itself, *sui generis*, and then we can see how the play embodies the poetic statement of the song in dramatic terms.

The song is introduced as a "dialogue that the two learned men [that is, Holofernes and Nathaniel] have compiled in praise of the Owl and the Cuckoo." This attribution places it in the venerated tradition of the academic debate, wherein two erudite disputants argue the relative merits of two opposites, such as day and night,[4] almost always inconclusively. Perhaps more pertinent here is the literary tradition of the *débat*,[5] inherited from France and enormously popular in England since the thirteenth century. Most immediately to mind comes *The Owl and the Nightingale* (ca. 1250), an extensive dialogue between two birds, one representing austere attitudes toward love, and the other a more natural and indulgent point of view. A germane analogue is the large number of dialogues between body and soul which bridge the gap between secular and religious poetry. Perhaps the literary dialogue most cogent for *Love's Labour's Lost* is an English *débat* between an old man and a self-confident youth entitled *The debate and stryfe betwene somer and wynter* (London, 1530?).[6] In *Love's Labour's Lost* the two parts of the song are similarly differentiated by identification with contrasting seasons of the year. When the secondary characters come on stage to sing the song, Don Armado acts as master of ceremonies and efficiently organizes them into two groups:

> *Arm.* This side is Hiems, Winter; this Ver, the Spring—the one maintained by the Owl, th'other by the Cuckoo. Ver, begin.
>
> (*V.ii.878–80*)

The song then immediately follows, with two stanzas sung by the cuckoo-group representing spring followed by two answering stanzas sung by the owl-group representing winter.

The stanzas of the song devoted to spring are replete with the appropriate accoutrements of the season. There are flowers in abundance: English daisies, violets, cuckoo-buds, and lady-smocks—each adding its own bright color to the painted meadows of the fourth line. There are birds other than the two disputants: larks, turtles, rooks, and daws—each adding to or partaking of the merry pleasures of spring. There are human figures: shepherds, ploughmen, maidens—each participating happily in a suitable occupation. Over all shines the sun, showing off the colors of the brave flowers, requiring the larks to summon ploughmen to their day's labor, and bleaching the smocks of the maidens.

The stanzas of the song devoted to winter are likewise replete with the appropriate accoutrements of that season. There is abundant evidence of cold: icicles and snow, numb fingers and red noses, frozen milk, foul roads, blustery winds, disconsolate birds. And these scenes take place in darkness, after the milking, when a fire is built in the hall, supper is cooked, and a warming bowl of ale is prepared for the long evening. There is sharp contrast to the scenes offered in the spring-stanzas.

Another contrast between the halves of the duet is less obvious but nonetheless operative. The spring-stanzas present an idealized landscape in the pastoral mode, where "shepherds pipe on oaten straws." The items in this landscape are generalized: the human figures belong to categories (shepherds, ploughmen, maidens), and the flowers, though brightly colored in the sunshine, are deprived of much distinction by the formulaic use of a single inverted epithet ("daisies pied and violets blue") or by use of common names ("cuckoo-buds" and "lady-smocks"). The birds also are quite ordinary and undistinguished: the larks are merry and the turtledoves make love. The ambience, except for the grating cry of the cuckoo, is purely pastoral, simplified of complexity, refined from ugliness, ethereal. In contrast is the harsh concreteness of the winter-stanzas. Rather than types of humans, there are specific individuals: Dick, Tom, Joan, Marian. Rather than the pastoral vision of shepherds playing on pipes, there are unusual and starkly realistic vignettes, such as Dick blowing upon his fingers to warm them and Tom bringing logs into the house. Rather than the well-worn image of turtledoves in love, there is the distinctly conceived image of birds brooding immobile in the snow. Rather than the prettiness of maidens bleaching summer smocks, there is the graphic ugliness of Marian's raw, red nose. Vivid scenes projected in single lines follow in rapid succession: "Icicles hang by the wall," "Milk comes frozen home in pail," "Coughing drowns the parson's saw," "Roasted crabs hiss in the bowl." Little in the winter-stanzas is conventional; all is sharp, concrete, circumstantial. Instead of prettiness and optimism, there is harshness and a strong sense of human vulnerability.

The contrast between the two halves of the song, then, is distinctly drawn. The cuckoo tends to giddiness; the owl declares his worldly wisdom. The scene in spring is idealized; the scene in winter is grimly realistic. The dialogue of Ver and Hiems is like a *débat* between youth and age, between young love and old experience. The song presents diametrically opposed views of the human condition.

But the relationship between spring and winter is not simply one of contrast. Both inhere in a larger system. Both are integral parts of a larger whole, of the annual cycle of the seasons. So not only is there opposition between spring and winter, but a mutual dependence; each exists only in relation to the other. The two halves of the song, then, partake of the same continuum. In fact, the juxtaposition of spring and winter implies the seasonal cycle in its entirety, a truncated calendar. To be simplistic, the song concluding *Love's Labour's Lost* is a poetic ideogram for the year reduced to an elementary scheme of two seasonal extremes. Moreover, since the song, like the seasonal cycle, can be repeated, it becomes a poetic ideogram for time. Spenser had used a calendar of months for the same poetic purpose.[7] The pattern thereby delineated is a circle, composed of disparate parts, but all harmoniously integrated into a unit which is continuously repeated—what Spenser in the Mutability Cantos described as "the ever-whirling wheele of *Change*" (FQ, VII.vi.1.1–2) which nevertheless generates order.

The interrelationship of the seasons to form the basic unit of time and the application of this pattern to human affairs was a Renaissance commonplace—indeed, an unquestioned premise. It appeared in many modes. Perhaps the mode most helpful in our discussion is the emblem tradition, since it provides a visual as well as a verbal image. As expected, Alciati, the grand master of emblem-books, offers a brilliant example well-suited to our purpose. His Emblem 100 is entitled "On the Four Seasons of the Year," and beneath a woodcut of a tree with birds and rocks and plants, there is the following quatrain:

> The cold sparrow reports to the winged creatures that winter has come.
> The twittering swallow returns again to us. The cuckoo proclaims that he
> is ready for summer. In autumn birds flock to the fig-trees.[8]

Claude Mignault, a noted French academician, edited Alciati's emblems and prepared an extensive commentary for each—Mignault's, in fact, became by far the best known version of the *Emblemata*. His commentary on this emblem is long, but well worth quoting in full because it demonstrates the rich tradition at work here:

> This is seen to refer to the changes of the seasons within the annual cycle, especially to those things which are naturally seasonal, occurring at their own, not at some unpredictable time, and whose power lies in being used at the proper time. Ovid has rightly said:
>
> *Medicine is effective according to the times; tonics when timely given are helpful, but untimely given are noxious* [De remedio amoris, 131–32].
>
> About this cyclical mutability of time various authors have playfully said various things which it would not be out of place to include here, especially those which seem to me to have a strong affinity with this quatrain of Alciati. Gladly I cite Horace, *Odes*, II.9, and Ovid, *Ad Pisonem*, IV.vii:
>
> *Winter goes, and in spring animal coats dry out. Spring flees before summer; then summer gives way to fruitful autumn, which in turn yields to clouds and stormy seas.*[9]
>
> The same idea appears early in the *De remedio amoris*:
>
> *Autumn gives fruit, summer is beautiful with the standing crops, spring offers flowers, winter is mitigated by fire* [187–88].
>
> And in the fourth book of the *Tristia*:
>
> *Sooner will you number the flowers in spring, the ears of grain in summer, the fruits in autumn, and the snowflakes in the wintry season* [IV.i.57–58].
>
> Barthélemy Aneau in his *Picta poesis* applied this idea to the perpetual and eternal mutability of men:
>
> *Spring, summer, autumn, winter—these are the four seasons as the years roll by in a cycle. Likewise man in his lifetime has four ages: he is first a child, then a youth, next an adult, and finally an old man—so that the cycle of human life, like the undying world, reveals to us that men are undying.*
>
> See also Erasmus' *Adagia*, "Spring follows winter," and Giovanni Pierio Valeriano's *Hieroglyphica* in several places. Seneca says the same thing in the letter to his pupil, Lucilius: Nothing comes to an end, but everything is connected in a circle; they flee before and they follow after. Night presses upon day, and day upon night. Summer gives way to autumn, and

autumn is pushed out by winter, which is ended by spring. All things pass by as they roll around.[10]

When we look in Aneau's *Picta poesis*, we readily find the hexastich that Mignault quotes.[11] Aneau's emblem is entitled "The Undying Nature of Man" (*Aeterna hominum natura*) and visualized by the accompanying woodcut, which I have called an ideogram of time. The tradition that Mignault and Aneau recapitulate is the optimistic view of mutability: man by going through his four ages performs the cyclical pattern of the seasons and thereby participates in eternity. There was, of course, also the pessimistic view of this process: though nature repeated the pattern endlessly, for each man the cycle ended in death.

In Shakespeare's song, the pattern of annual cycle constructed of seasons is supplemented and reinforced by the presence of the daily cycle constructed of day and night. The cuckoo's stanzas take place in sunshine, but "nightly sings the staring owl." Again there is contrast, between day and night, as in Milton's companion poems, *L'Allegro* and *Il Penseroso*. But day and night also subsist within a single continuum; as Mignault quotes Seneca, "Night presses upon day, and day upon night." They combine to form a whole, a two-phase system making up the *diurnal* unit of time. This pattern of day and night contributes to the comprehensiveness of the song as a poetic ideogram for time.

A sense of moving time dominates the song. The first word in every stanza is "when," and the structure of each stanza depends upon a grammatical scheme wherein an adverbial clause introduced by "when" is followed by a main clause whose chronological sequence is emphasized by the adverb "then." The repetition of this "when . . . then . . ." structure in each stanza generates a sense of passing time. Moreover, every verb in the song is in the present tense, suggesting on the one hand co-temporaneity, but also mutability. It is a world of *now*, but also a world of action, and therefore of change, of impermanence. Only the fact of circular movement, rather than linear movement —the fact that spring becomes winter, which then returns to spring—permits the song to be an ideogram of eternity.

In actual fact, the contrast between the spring-stanzas of the song and the winter-stanzas is not absolute, but elements of one half inhere in the other, thereby binding the two together more closely and suggesting a fusion within the whole. For example, in the winter-stanzas Tom's logs hold the promise of some warmth and the hissing crab apples are certain tokens of conviviality. Even Joan, whose presence permeates the winter-stanzas, stirs a tempting pot; and if, as likely, "greasy" is an epithet with sexual connotations,[12] she will offer other pleasures later in the evening. The owl, indeed, quite out of season, sings "a merry note." Coordinately, the placid scene of the spring-stanzas is shaken by the cry of the cuckoo, mocking married men, evoking the unpleasant and discordant response of fear.[13] When the cuckoo sings, his very note—"cuckoo"—brings to mind "cuckold," warning that love is transient. Like all things vernal, it is subject to mutability, to time. This is the reply that Raleigh's nymph makes to Marlowe's passionate shepherd when she rejects his invitation to a life of pastoral bliss. As experience shows, cuckoldry, the result of inconstancy in both marriage partners, is a common aftermath to young love in the spring. In both halves of the song, then, in the spring-stanzas as well as the winter-stanzas, there is a refrain which insistently intrudes upon the distinctive world view fabricated in the verse lines of each stanza.[14] The cuckoo issues a fearful warning to the heedless Arcadians of the spring-stanzas, while the owl's merry note adds to the mounting joviality in the winter-stanzas as Tom's logs burn in the fireplace and Joan engagingly entices us with her concoction.

Closer examination reveals that the song further fuses its two halves by providing quite definite transitions between them. The last line of the spring-stanzas before the refrain is the most distinct and unusual line in this half of the song: "And maidens bleach their summer smocks." This image picks up the "lady-smocks" in the second line of the song, expanding the flower from its static existence as a mere item in nature to an animated scene of human activity. The flower is personalized, so that it assumes human meaning. The same process of humanizing a flower is the controlling image of Herrick's "To Daffodils":

> 1. Fair daffodils, we weep to see
>   You haste away so soon:
>
>   .   .   .   .   .
>
> 2. We have short time to stay, as you,
>   We have as short a spring. . . .

In Herrick's poem, the daffodil becomes an icon for all nature, including man, and its departure is a confirmation of mutability.[15] In Shakespeare's song, the development of the lady-smocks as an icon for nature is less insistent but unmistakable, I believe, for an Elizabethan; and when they later become identified with maidens preparing themselves for summer pleasures, even we should view the scene with the same wistful melancholy that we lavish upon the rosebuds which the maidens soon will gather, but which similarly are doomed to die. The point to make is that when lady-smocks become maidens bleaching summer smocks, we are moved in the direction of a world view of cold, of darkness, of death. Spring has become summer; the seasons have progressed one stage nearer to winter:

> For never-resting time leads summer on
> To hideous winter, and confounds him there;
> Sap check'd with frost and lusty leaves quite gone,
> Beauty o'ersnow'd, and bareness everywhere.
>
> *("Sonnet 5," 5–8)*

Conversely, the last line of the winter-stanzas before the refrain depicts the only scene of unmitigated pleasure in that half of the song: "When roasted crabs hiss in the bowl." This line of epicurean sensualism leads back to the delights of spring, thereby completing the circle. A continuity between winter and spring, paralleling the transition between spring and winter, is explicitly provided.

The song is so compressed a statement, and so comprehensive in its meaning, that it requires careful and extensive explication. Moreover, much of its meaning is conveyed through its form, a mode of poetic expression which is particularly difficult to deal with verbally. But to conclude this analysis of the song, the duet between the cuckoo and the owl constructs the basic unit of time, expressed as both the diurnal cycle of day-night and the annual cycle of the seasons. First comes spring, then winter. But the cycle continues into a new year; so it becomes an abstract of eternity, the integer of infinity, the microcosmic icon of human experience. By this conclusion, *Love's Labour's Lost* expounds a well-known Renaissance dictum: *contraria coincidunt in natura uniali*. The opposites of day and night, of spring and winter, of youth and age, of Arcadia and reality—all pairs of extremes are reconciled in unified nature. When seen in this largest possible frame, the song presents the totality of human life, bringing together the two extremes of optimism and despair. This reconciliation of opposites is the condition necessary for stability, for order despite mutability. In the cosmos it is demonstrated by universal harmony, the cosmic love that human society should reflect.[16]

Despite the fact that few critics have treated *Love's Labour's Lost* with any degree of seriousness, and even fewer have ascribed seriousness to it,[17] there is no doubt that the plot of the play develops the same thoughtful theme that the closing song expounds. Like the song, the dramatic action searchingly examines opposing attitudes toward human experience in the context of time and strives to reach a synthetic conclusion.

The opening speech of the play, in fact, introduces overtly all the large concepts that the song comprehends in its icon of the human condition. Fame, life, death, grace, time, honor, eternity—the loftiest terms of philosophical debate are strewn before us in great profusion:

> Let fame, that all hunt after in their lives,
> Live regist'red upon our brazen tombs,
> And then grace us in the disgrace of death;
> When, spite of cormorant devouring Time,
> Th'endeavour of this present breath may buy
> That honour which shall bate his scythe's keen edge,
> And make us heirs of all eternity.
>
> > *(I.i.1–7)*

The youthful king of Navarre seeks to elude Time's scythe by achieving fame, a universal desire in the Renaissance as the king notes. Enthusiastic but inexperienced, he wishes by his present efforts to transcend the world bound by time, to escape mortality—in his words, to become the heir of all eternity. Underlying this speech is the dilemma which provided impetus for the best Renaissance thought: how to relate the temporal and the eternal, the physical and the spiritual, the particular and the abstract, man and the godhead? The most common solution in human terms was the concept of fame. Through honorable deeds in this life, a man could establish a reputation which insured a continuing afterlife. This fame is equivalent to grace in the Christian scheme, as the king intimates, because it bestows blessed immortality.

Poetry when properly contrived could award this sort of fame, a theme that Shakespeare stressed in his sonnets. The way to fame as the king sees it, though, lies through study, and therefore he exhorts his companions to eschew worldly pleasures and retire with him behind the walls of an academy reminiscent of Plato's:

> Therefore, brave conquerors—for so you are
> That war against your own affections
> And the huge army of the world's desires—
> Our late edict shall strongly stand in force:
> Navarre shall be the wonder of the world;
> Our court shall be a little Academe,
> Still and contemplative in living art.
>
> > *(I.i.8–14)*

As though this were the opening of a *débat*, this speech of the king serves as a postulate which the play will test. Given the human urge for grace-bestow-

ing fame, it draws the traditional dichotomy between the active and the contemplative life, a dichotomy at least as old as Aristotelian ethics. The lines of
argument are so familiar that the king's speech elicits a knowing smile of
indulgence for his idealism and a pitying frown at his naïveté. Even the language suggests the familiarity of this debate; the king uses clichés so reverend
that their Latin tags are commonplace: *tempus edax, falx temporis, vita contemplativa, ars vivendi*.[18] The outright *contemptus mundi* expressed by the king
implies a series of rhetorical questions: Is the contemplative life possible, or
even desirable? Can fame be won by withdrawal to a little academe? Can time
be thwarted in this fashion? Can eternity be gained by academic study of the
"living art" divorced from society? Although the context of this opening scene
militates against a serious exploration of these questions, they nonetheless
have been raised and continue to hover in the air above Navarre.

In any case, the edict of the king confronts his comrades with a choice
between the world and the academy. Longaville is aware of the need to choose
and rejects the flesh for the soul: "The mind shall banquet, though the body
pine" (I.i.25). The incipient dichotomy is further emphasized by Longaville's
rhetoric, by a couplet in which antithesis is twice employed:

> *Fat* paunches have *lean* pates; and dainty bits
> *Make rich* the ribs, but *bankrupt* quite the wits.
>
> *(I.i.26–27; italics mine)*

Dumain is also aware of the crucial decision and expresses his choice in comparable terms using the opposition of life to death:

> My loving lord, Dumain is mortified.[19]
> The grosser manner of these world's delights
> He throws upon the gross world's baser slaves;
> To love, to wealth, to pomp, I pine and die,
> With all these living in philosophy.
>
> *(I.i.28–32)*

To his *contemptus mundi*, Dumain like Longaville adds rhetoric to emphasize
the dichotomy. In an oxymoronic antithesis, revealing paradoxical self-con-
tradiction, Dumain swears to be dead to love, wealth, and pomp, the values
of this world, in order to live in philosophy.

When it comes his turn, however, Berowne does not so readily comply. He
drags his feet along the path which leads to cloistered virtue. Berowne recog-

nizes the sterility of the king's proposal as well as its difficulty, and in the debate he takes a firm stand against the *vita contemplativa*:

> O, these are barren tasks, too hard to keep,
> Not to see ladies, study, fast, not sleep!
>
> *(I.i.47–48)*

When the king is insistent that Berowne not only study with the group but also desist from the world's desires—that is, when the king presses him for a clear-cut choice between the academy and the world—Berowne counters by challenging the validity of the king's assumption that fame can be achieved through study. He parries with a question:

> *Ber.* What is the end of study, let me know.
> *King.* Why, that to know which else we should not know.
> *Ber.* Things hid and barr'd, you mean, from common sense?[20]
> *King.* Ay, that is study's god-like recompense.
>
> *(I.i.55–58)*

This exchange reinforces the king's noble aims, but at the same time it pushes him to the edge of folly and even impiety. For it raises an issue that obsessed the Renaissance: what are the acceptable limits of human knowledge? From study, the king seeks "to know [that] which else we should not know," repeating in his own experience the sin of Adam and Eve in eating of the fruit of the tree of knowledge, the act that required the institution of divine grace. Berowne manipulates the king into admitting his expectation of a "god-like recompense," thereby revealing yet another pitfall of the contemplative life. Though trying to avoid the world's desires, the king is susceptible to the fourth temptation.

Berowne is fully aware of the Faustian implications—"To know the thing I am forbid to know" (I.i.60). But the play has no intention of plumbing such murky depths, so Berowne quickly deflects the conversation to a series of jests about dining and mistresses. By this maneuver Berowne demonstrates that study can lead to delights of this world with arguments to justify the enjoyment of them, but it cannot achieve the high-flown aims of the king. Fame acquired through study while ignoring the world is as empty of content as Falstaff's word "honor"; so Berowne concludes his nimble display of wit: "Too much to know is to know nought but fame" (I.i.92). Berowne realizes that the ideal must incorporate the real, that the spirit must be meddled with the flesh, that eternity must subsume the present. He has a broad view of human experience which the king lacks, but which is the rightful "end of study." Berowne has at least a glimmer of life's totality expounded at the end of the play by the song between the cuckoo and the owl.

Not surprisingly the dialogue at this point falls into terms reminiscent of the concluding song. When caught up in a round of rhetoric, Berowne answers his peers with this cryptic comment: "Spring is near, when green geese are a-breeding" (I.i.97). Green geese, of course, belong to the same genus as the cuckoo and the other birds that strut in spring's song. The epithet "green" associates them with new growth and also implies immaturity and foolishness. When applied to the king, Longaville, and Dumain, as Berowne certainly intends, the phrase categorizes the young men with the other idyllic inhabitants of the spring stanzas. The time when they breed—that is, when they flourish, when their ideas dominate—is correspondent to spring, "fit in his place and time" (I.i.98). Dumain resents the comment and denies the validity of Berowne's argument; it is "in reason, nothing." But Berowne replies that it does have validity in poetry—"Something then in rhyme" (I.i.99)—perhaps alluding to the closing song of the play. The king joins in by charging Berowne with intentional malice and labels him an agent of wintry destruction: "Berowne is like an envious sneaping frost / That bites the first-born infants of the spring" (I.i.100–101)—a statement that achieves its full meaning only when read in the context of the final song. But this attempt to relegate Berowne to the winter-stanzas fails. Instead Berowne presents himself as a moderate who sees life whole:

> At Christmas I no more desire a rose
> Than wish a snow in May's new-fangled shows;
> But like of each thing that in season grows.
>
> (*I.i.105–7*)

Berowne realizes that Christmas and May both make their appropriate contribution to the year's variety; each like spring is "fit in his place and time." Berowne could happily cite Alciati's emblem "On the Four Seasons of the Year" and could approvingly quote Mignault's comment that the power of things lies in their being used at the proper time.

This first hundred or so lines of dialogue provide the dialectic which invigorates the remainder of the play. Two opposing attitudes are argued in familiar terms of the contemplative versus the active life. A synthesis is at least hinted at by Berowne, who "like[s] of each thing that in season grows," an idea that receives full development in the final song. In his desire to escape mortality, the king has glibly posited the pursuit of fame as the goal of life;

but Berowne more wisely knows that only by attunement to the natural harmonies of the physical world can we, paradoxically, transcend that world. The present provides a pattern for eternity.

The plot can now proceed, and it proves to be the simplest plot in all Shakespeare because the issue has been clearly delineated and the outcome is obvious. The king's plan for academic isolation is immediately threatened when the princess of France arrives with her ladies, and the proposal is soon abandoned. The attractions of a little academe pall to nothingness in the presence of these beauties. The action therefore moves rapidly toward its foregone conclusion, toward a denouement which finds the lovers paired off in a way suitable for comedy.

The proposition that learning and love are mutually exclusive, set up as a straw man in the first scene, is laid aside while the ladies complete their conquest. But it comes to the fore again at the end of Act IV, when each gentleman in turn reveals his overriding passion for a particular mistress. Despite their choice of eternity in principle in Act I, the world has proved to be their choice in practice. Consequently, they are all forsworn, as Berowne wryly reminds the love-smitten lords (IV.iii.279). Faced with self-incrimination, the king turns to Berowne to resolve the contretemps: "Good Berowne, now prove / Our loving lawful" (IV.iii.281–82). Longaville pleads, "Some authority how to proceed" (IV.iii.283), and Dumain joins in, "Some salve for perjury" (IV. iii.285). Berowne obliges with a long speech of seventy-five lines, wherein he wittily uses his learning to explain and justify their loving. As though in the Academy indeed, he adopts the Platonic definition of love, with the steps leading to universal love so carefully laid out by Renaissance commentators: first, physical attraction to a particular woman, which is enlarged to love of women in general, then further expanded to love of all mankind, and finally universalized by successive expansions to participation in cosmic love, which is universal harmony. By all rights, then, in their quest for ultimate knowledge the young lovers should have started at the bottom of the Platonic ladder, by studying the faces of their ladies. By seeking knowledge from books alone and by disregarding their bodies, they have acted contrary to human nature. In these terms Berowne admonishes his three companions:

> Consider what you first did swear unto:
> To fast, to study, and to see no woman—
> Flat treason 'gainst the kingly state of youth.
> .   .   .   .   .
> For when would you, my lord, or you, or you,
> Have found the ground of study's excellence

Without the beauty of a woman's face?
From women's eyes this doctrine I derive:
They are the ground, the books, the academes,
From whence doth spring the true Promethean fire.
(*IV.iii.287–300*)

Prometheus stole fire from heaven and brought it to earth for mortals, thereby permitting them to become civilized and participate in godlike experience.[21] The sparkles in a lady's eyes are consequently likened to Promethean fire, because they similarly by love engendered, permit man to rise to higher experience, transcending the physical. Berowne continues his discourse:

But love, first learned in a lady's eyes,
Lives not alone immured in the brain,
But with the motion of all elements
Courses as swift as thought in every power,
And gives to every power a double power,
Above their functions and their offices.

. . . . .

And when Love speaks, the voice of all the gods
Make heaven drowsy with the harmony.
(*IV.iii.323–41*)

Comprehension of this heavenly harmony is the ultimate knowledge that the young men seek through study, their "god-like recompense." Participation in this heavenly harmony is also the ultimate aim of love. Therefore, since ascent to that blessed state must begin with love of a particular woman, Berowne concludes that he and his companions have properly begun by studying the sensuous allurements of their ladies:

From women's eyes this doctrine I derive.
They sparkle still the right Promethean fire;
They are the books, the arts, the academes,
That show, contain, and nourish, all the world,
Else none at all in aught proves excellent.
(*IV.iii.346–50*)

By rhetoric and logic—and poetry—Berowne proves that love and learning are complementary pursuits, both necessary to the full life, neither separable from the other.

Along the path of action that leads to this synthesis of learning and love, the two concepts have been given dramatic definition by the secondary characters. There are only the most rudimentary subplots in *Love's Labour's Lost*; rather, the subsidiary characters are arranged in two groups who serve to define the concepts of love and of learning as they should be properly understood. One group centers around Jacquenetta, the wench loved by both Costard and Don Armado, and includes Moth. The other group is composed of Holofernes, Nathaniel, and Dull. The actions of neither group can be called convincingly a subplot; Shakespeare merely brings one or the other on stage when he wishes to use the group as commentary on the main action involving the noblemen and the ladies.

When the play opens, the young lords are already committed to learning, so they must be instructed in the meaning of love. Hence the arrival of the young ladies. But as commentary on this central action, Shakespeare offers the wooing of Jacquenetta by Don Armado and by Costard. Very early, in the first scene of the play (I.i.160–77), he introduces the two extremes of love. The fantastical Spaniard is an affected melancholy lover, like Romeo at the beginning of his play, exaggerated to caricature. In absolute contrast, the rustic Costard is an animal-like lover, direct and sensual. True love, of course, as the play assumes from these negative examples, lies somewhere between these two extremes, while partaking of the best qualities of both. True love is a reconciliation of these opposites.

The play defines the concept of learning in a similar fashion, by introducing a formal opposition between two characters, Holofernes and Dull. By the conclusion of Act III, the young noblemen have learned their lesson in love—if anything, too eagerly. Then at this point Holofernes arrives on the scene—significantly, not until well into Act IV, because not until this point is love clearly ascendent, as indicated by Berowne's final speech in Act III: "And I, forsooth, in love!" (III.i.175 ff.). With love dominant, however, learning can come center stage. Indeed, the young men have proved so foolish in love that they are now in sore need of discipline. To this end, the extremes of learning are represented in the two characters, Holofernes and Dull. Holofernes is a ridiculous and parasitic pedant, with his long-winded latinate speeches, which are ultimately meaningless. Dull is a dim-witted citizen, reduced to silence except for a few monosyllables. Again, the desirable mean, learning in its proper perspective, lies somewhere between Holofernes and Dull.

In the definition of love through the contrast of Don Armado and Costard, Shakespeare provides an additional complication, a further refinement, in Moth, Don Armado's page. Moth draws out the folly of the excessive lover, as we see in the long witty dialogue between the two when Don Armado first appears in the second scene of Act I. Symmetrically, in the definition of true learning through the contrast of Holofernes and Dull, Shakespeare provides Nathaniel the curate to draw out the folly of the excessively learned man. When Holofernes first appears in the second scene of Act IV, there is a long witty dialogue between him and Nathaniel. In both cases, the patterns are made carefully analogous; only in this way, in fact, can the presence of Holofernes and Nathaniel in the play be explained, since they are in no way involved in the main plot. Furthermore, it is worth noting that the excessive practitioner of each (of love and of learning) is revealed to be deficient in the other: Don Armado abuses learning in his pursuit of love, so that his professions of love are schoolboyishly rhetorical; and Holofernes is shamelessly lacking in human feeling in his pursuit of learning. The character patterns which reveal the true nature of love and of learning are finely articulated and subtly played off against one another. The interaction between these two sets of characters— Don Armado, Costard, and Moth on the one hand, and Holofernes, Dull, and Nathaniel on the other—culminates in the nonsensical interlude presenting the Nine Worthies, a fiasco which exposes their complete misunderstanding of human achievement and their inability to comprehend meaning in human life, even the most heroic. They are utter failures in both love and learning, the two major components of a full life which this play postulates.

By the end of Act IV, then, both love and learning have been adequately defined by the dramatic action as well as in the sophistry of Berowne, and the two are shown to be not mutually exclusive, but complementary. With this "authority how to proceed," the young lords can rush toward consummation of the romance without reservation, so in the spirit of confident wooers they troop off to join battle with the opposite sex. In the name of Saint Cupid they resolve not only "to woo these girls of France," but to "win them too" (IV.iii. 367–68). As part of their stratagem, they propose some entertainment, "for revels, dances, masks, and merry hours, / Forerun fair Love" (375–76). Clearly the expectation is aroused that the young lords will succeed in their suit to the ladies. All is about to end well.

As Act V proceeds, it bears out this expectation. In celebration of the impending marriages, Don Armado and Holofernes plan "some delightful ostentation" (V.i.98), much as the rude mechanics in *Midsummer Night's Dream* plan a performance of Pyramus and Thisbe for the nuptials at the Athenian court. There is a prolonged scene in which each of the ladies gloatingly displays a gift and a letter from her lover, a scene which ends with the princess's shrewd observation: "None are so surely caught, when they are catch'd, / As wit turn'd fool" (V.ii.69–70). "Navarre and his book-men," as the princess earlier called them (II.i.226), are now without a doubt made fools by love. When the lords as a caper mask themselves like Muscovites and appear to titillate the ladies—when "Love doth approach disguis'd" (V.ii.83)—the princess and her companions respond in kind. Continuing the martial metaphor that concluded Act IV, they eagerly meet their suitors in the name of Saint Denis, the patron saint of France, against Saint Cupid. The scene of youthful, zestful fun-making is developed at great length, and victory in this courtly tilt between the sexes tends first to one side and then the other. But there is no doubt that all contend for the same consequence, for the mutually satisfactory mating of the men and the women. A resolution of this sort is taken for granted. Following the lead of the characters, the audience also loses itself in the sportive love play—so much so that when Don Armado and Holofernes offer their presentation of the Nine Worthies, mirth has degenerated to the most light-headed frivolity, and pageant has been reduced to broken farce.

It is for this very reason that the entrance of Marcade is so dramatically effective. When he arrives to announce that the king of France is dead, not only is the news a reversal in the plot, but also the grimness of Marcade's sudden communication contrasts starkly with the heedless joy exhibited by the lovers. In this last scene of the play the young gentry have been through a conventional exercise in comedy, the mix-up of assumed and mistaken identity, and now are suitably paired off in appropriate couples. No obstacle to the happy consummation of the mating game is visible. Then Marcade— quite extraneous to any action we have witnessed, even contrary to the expectations aroused in us—arrives with his disastrous news.

As the princess puts it, something "interrupts our merriment" (V.ii.705). Marcade's intrusion is complete because it introduces death, a human absolute. The presence of death abruptly halts the merrymaking. A favorite Renaissance phrase rings in our ears, "Et in Arcadia ego." We then realize with overwhelming soberness that the entire action of the play has taken place in the king of Navarre's park, in Arcadia; and the total context of the pastoral convention is brought to bear on what we have witnessed.[22] Arcadia is an ideal, a fabrication of the literary imagination to embody concepts and values outside of time, without relation to physical reality. The sort of synthesis between learning and love that Berowne has contrived is purely Platonic, academic, ideal, romantic. As Berowne now confesses to the ladies, "For your fair sakes have we neglected time" (V.ii.743). In order for the four young men and four young women to live in the perfect bliss of this synthesis, time must have a stop. That is the message of *Romeo and Juliet*. And so time is stopped here. Each lady interrupts the suit of her gentleman. The pairs of lovers, on the verge of satisfaction, are suddenly frozen in their efforts to perfect a relationship—like the pastoral lovers on Keats's Grecian urn, and for the same reason. The lovers will continue to love, but in expectation, not in consummation. Art fixes the lovers at that crucial point in the action where they must proceed toward the fairy-tale ending of living happily ever after, heedless of time, or they will follow the natural course of passion past climax through the doldrums of indifference to eventual senility.

Unlike Keats, however, Shakespeare went beyond "cold Pastoral." He was not satisfied merely to confirm the ideals of Truth and Beauty, but wished to bring his poetic statement down to the level of unaccommodated man. Willing to deal in realities, Shakespeare provided a denouement which "doth not end like an old play" (V.ii.862). The king, as he feels his vitality attenuating in the static chill of Arcadia, pleads desperately with the ladies, "Now, at the latest minute of the hour, / Grant us your loves" (V.ii.775–76). But the princess refuses "to make a world-without-end bargain" so quickly (776–77), and she demands that the king submit his love to the test of reality. He must retreat for one year to the deprivation of "some forlorn and naked hermitage" (783), in contrast to the elegant but vain academy he had proposed at the beginning of the play. The king has blithely assumed that life is constant spring, but this assumption is dangerously false as shown by the broken oath of the gentlemen and the death of the princess's father. To round out his vision so that it includes wintry hardship, therefore, the princess prescribes a stint of austerity and a trial of his love through severest tribulation:

> If this austere insociable life
> Change not your offer made in heat of blood,
> If frosts and fasts, hard lodging and thin weeds,
> Nip not the gaudy blossoms of your love,
> But that it bear this trial, and last love,[23]
> Then, at the expiration of the year,
> Come, challenge me.
>
> (V.ii.787–93)

The terms of this charge recall the colloquy in the first scene of the play when the king accused Berowne of destroying his pleasures "like an envious sneaping frost / That bites the first-born infants of the spring" (I.i.100–101), when Berowne tried unsuccessfully to educate the king to "like of each thing that in season grows" (I.i.107). But now the king realizes that a vision of life which excludes hardship, neglects time, forgets winter, is not viable, but rather deadly; and therefore, he swears, if he fails the princess's test, "The sudden hand of death close up mine eye!" (V.ii.803). An earnest of the king's growth in understanding has been shown in his sensitive response to the princess's grief, especially his speech on "the extreme parts of time" (V.ii.728 ff.).

In a parallel action, Rosaline sets a comparable trial for Berowne. Rosaline demands that he—"the merry mad-cap lord," earlier in the play (II.i.214)—employ his wit to some more serious purpose than mockery and sophistry. He must, in fact, seek service in a hospital, "visit the speechless sick . . . / To enforce the pained impotent to smile" (V.ii.839–42). To be acceptable, Berowne's love must embrace charity as well as sex. The other two ladies impose similar demands on their respective lords, and all decree the same period for this penitential service:

> There stay until the twelve celestial signs
> Have brought about the annual reckoning.
>
> (V.ii.785–86)

If the love of the gentlemen survives the grimness of one year's confrontation with "the weariness, the fever, and the fret," to use a Keatsian phrase, then the ladies will marry them. They will have removed faults from their personalities and broadened their experience. They will have reconciled opposites, reconciled the comic and the tragic views of life. They will have triumphed over time by subjugating death to vitality.

But given human limitations, this is an unreasonable expectation, as Berowne, the realist among the four gentlemen, well knows. When Rosaline imposes upon him the task of bringing joy to the dying, he remonstrates:

> To move wild laughter in the throat of death?
> It cannot be; it is impossible.
>
> (V.ii.843–44)

And the scene closes with Berowne's insistence on the incongruity of the ladies' demand:

> A twelvemonth? Well, befall what will befall,
> I'll jest a twelvemonth in a hospital.
>
> (V.ii.858–59)

Berowne's skepticism is justified. But it is not certified by the action presented within the bounds of the play. We are not shown the incongruity of jesting in a hospital. Rather, standing outside the action, Berowne then makes his observation that the play has not ended like a conventional comedy, and the song between the cuckoo and the owl follows.

Just as the song is composed of spring-stanzas and winter-stanzas, so the play has described a vernal world of growing love which is contradicted by the arrival of Marcade. Until that point, the princess tells the gentlemen, "[We] met your loves / In their own fashion, like a merriment" (V.ii.771–72). But Marcade, like a death's-head, transforms the park of Navarre from a world of timeless youth and mirth to a world of mortality and human anguish. In the words of Berowne, "The scene begins to cloud" (V.ii.710), a richly metaphorical phrase heralding the storms that destroy Arcadia, the darkness that precedes night, the cold that foreruns winter. At this point the play changes abruptly from comic to tragic themes. But the last scene of the play harks back to the opening scene and brings it round full circle. Not only is the broken oath of the lords made prominent, but the "forlorn and naked hermitage" to which the princess assigns the king must be compared with the "little Academe" which he originally proposed. And Rosaline's charge to Berowne, "Enforce the pained impotent to smile," provides the answer to Berowne's question, "What is the end of study?" Not to gain fame, the play says—a vain pursuit, in the sense of being both empty and selfish—but rather to alleviate human suffering. This understanding—of death as well as of life—is the only way to mitigate the doom of mortality, to transcend time.[24] This triumph over death is the summum bonum of life. This is the "god-like recompense" that study can bestow.

This poetic theme is epitomized by the final song, made explicit through lyric rather than dramatic poetry. A dramatic conclusion to the play would have necessitated a choice between a happy and a sad ending, thereby limiting the comprehensiveness of the poetic statement. To avoid such limitation, Shakespeare resorted to a nondramatic conclusion, to poetry of a different order, to lyric song, where the counters are less substantial than characters in a three-dimensional setting. Through attitudes—consonant with spring and then with winter—Shakespeare presents the extremes of human experience and their reconciliation in a basic unit of time. Looked at in another way, this compressed calendar of spring and winter represents "the annual reckoning" marked by "the twelve celestial signs," the smallest possible compass within which all that the young men need to know can be synthesized. Only through a twelvemonth penitential service encompassing these extremes can they adequately realize the full potential of their love.

To summarize our solution to the esthetic and thematic problems raised by the play's ending, we may say that the poetic statement of the plot is epitomized by the song, and the song fulfills this artistic function by its form as much as by its content. The song, in a real and immediate sense, provides the pattern for the play. To use Sidney's term, the song may be considered the "fore-conceit" of the play, the *idea* (in the Platonic sense) which a poem embodies.[25] In fashioning that fore-conceit, writes Sidney, lies "the skill of the artificer." In the concluding song Shakespeare makes fully visible his fore-conceit for *Love's Labour's Lost*.

The contrarieties of spring and winter so prominent in the song and the contrarieties of youthful love and death so obviously opposed in the dramatic action are reinforced by a number of other contrarieties presented through a variety of means. Several critics have noted the formality of the play,[26] its constant attention to form. Much of this formality is conveyed through the character groupings, such as four young gentlemen and four young ladies with the two groups quickly paired off in couples. For those inclined to think in alchemical terms, the mating of four lords and four ladies might suggest the alchemical hermaphrodite, the self-sufficient unit composed of both male and female. For other character groupings that juxtapose opposites we may look to the contrast of Costard and Don Armado and of Dull and Holofernes, useful in defining the concepts of love and learning, respectively.[27] The pattern of contrasting opposites is kept operative throughout the play, in fact, by means of rhetoric, by repeated use of the figure *antithesis*. The opening speeches of both Longaville and Dumain depend upon *antithesis*,[28] and there is an unusually large number of other examples in *Love's Labour's Lost*, expressed frequently in terms of light/dark,[29] day/night,[30] young/old,[31] life/death.[32]

Some patterns which contribute to the formality of the play do not emphasize the opposition of contrarieties, but rather the continuity of the structure. By exhausting the possibilities, they suggest a plenum, a continuous whole. For example, there are formal patterns in the arrangement of speeches, such as this exchange among the four gentlemen:

> *King.* How well he's read, to reason against reading!
> *Dum.* Proceeded well, to stop all good proceeding!
> *Long.* He weeds the corn, and still lets grow the weeding.
> *Ber.* The spring is near, when green geese are a-breeding.
>
> (I.i.94–97)

There is a similar tetralogue distributed among the four ladies:

> *Ros.* But will you hear? The King is my love sworn.
> *Prin.* And quick Berowne hath plighted faith to me.

> *Kath.* And Longaville was for my service born.
> *Mar.* Dumain is mine, as sure as bark on tree.
>
> *(V.ii.282–85)*

This pattern of four items, the total number of possibilities, subsumed in a whole is sometimes given more expansive development in the arrangement of a scene. For example, in the final scene of Act IV each gentleman comes on stage in turn, reads the sonnet he has composed to his lady (thereby revealing the love he has sworn to forego for study), and then hides in order to overhear the next of his colleagues, who repeats the procedure, until all four noblemen are on stage. The sense of continuity in the play is given further support in a most effective though subtle way through the extensive use of formal patterns in the metrics. Berowne knows that love as cosmic harmony should be expressed in measured verse: "I do love, and it hath taught me to rhyme" (IV. iii.13–14). It is a fact that *Love's Labour's Lost* has a higher proportion of rhyming couplets than any other Shakespearean play, and there are also numerous quatrains and six-line stanzas[33] embedded in the verse, as well as several sonnets[34] and songs. Each of these formal patterns—in the character groupings, in the rhetoric, in speech assignments, in scene arrangements, in the metrics—is developed independently, of course, being a different order of discourse than the others. But all of them interact with one another, support and affirm one another, and coalesce to give the play a pervasive and dominant sense of formality, of pattern.

This critique of *Love's Labour's Lost* is intentionally schematic. It emphasizes the formal structure, concerning itself with esthetic and thematic problems to the detriment of the mirth and vitality of the play. The play's dramatic quality, especially the interplay of human personalities, is thereby considerably diminished. I have, admittedly, ravaged Navarre's park, perhaps rendering it desolate. Moreover, I do not even touch upon the verbal wit of the play[35] or the possibility of topical allusions,[36] concerns which have dominated earlier criticism of *Love's Labour's Lost*. But I have tried to reveal the unusual and highly successful artistry of the play. Its structure and its poetic theme depend upon the integration of drama and song, two disparate orders of poetic endeavor. More compellingly—and here life may return to Navarre—I have tried to penetrate the play's surface glitter with an eye for its serious implications. I have looked at the dark side of its comedy, at the serious comment on the human condition which animates Shakespeare's best efforts in the comic genre.

Notes:

1. Some critics have speculated, not idly, that the gentlemen will fail in their suit to the ladies. See, for example, G. Wilson Knight, *The Shakespearian Tempest*, 3rd ed. (London, 1953), pp. 80–82; and E. M. W. Tillyard, *Shakespeare's Early Comedies* (London, 1965), pp. 150, 176–79.

2. Line references are to Peter Alexander, ed., *William Shakespeare: The Complete Works* (New York, 1952).

3. Anne Righter also makes this observation, though she uses it for another purpose: to illustrate the presence of the play metaphor in *Love's Labour's Lost* (*Shakespeare and the Idea of the Play* [London, 1962], pp. 111–12).

4. Cf. Milton's prolusion, *Utrum Dies an Nox praestantior sit?* In *Love's Labour's Lost*, of course, the academic context is adduced playfully, since the pedantry of Holofernes and Nathaniel is patent.

5. See F. J. E. Raby, *A History of Secular Latin Poetry in the Middle Ages*, 2 vols. (Oxford, 1934), II.282–308.

6. Reproduced in facsimile by E. W. Ashbee, *Occasional Facsimile Reprints*, XII (London, 1869); also reprinted in W. C. Hazlitt, *Remains of the Early Popular Poetry of England*, 4 vols. (London, 1864–66), III.29–39. I am not suggesting that Shakespeare knew this particular debate between summer and winter, but only that the literary dialogue was a continuing tradition that would have been familiar to his audience.

7. See my article, "The Implications of Form for *The Shepheardes Calender*," *SRen*, 9 (1962), 309–21.

8. There are, of course, numerous editions of Alciati's emblems. I have used the following: *Emblemata*, ed. Claude Mignault (Christopher Plantin; Antwerp, 1577).

> *Advenisse hyemem frigilla renunciat ales:*
> *Ad nos novo garrula hirundo redit.*
> *Indicat æstatem sese expectare cucullus:*
> *Autumno est tantùm cernere ficedulas.*

> (*p. 344*)

Mignault in his commentary offers this textual annotation:

> *frigilla.*] a bird so called from *frigus* [coldness], as some would say; cf. Aristotle, *De historia animalium*, VIII.iii.
> *frigilla.*] avis à frigore dicta, ut quibusdam placet; de qua Aristot. lib.8. cap.3.De hist. animal.

Exercising the license which Mignault suggests, I have translated *frigilla* as "cold sparrow." I could have translated it as "owl," but resisted the temptation. There is no question that the cuckoo (*cucullus*) appears in Alciati's verse. Unfortunately, Mignault offered no note for *ficedulas*.

9. I cannot identify this passage.

10. Hoc referendum videtur ad quasque temporum & annorum vicissitudines, vel

ad ea quæ suo non alio tempore solent esse tempestiva, quorumque magna vis
est, si suo tempori usum accommodemus. Rectè Ovidius:

> *Temporibus medicina valet, data tempore prosunt:*
> *Et data non apto tempore vina nocent.*

In hanc temporis quasi cyclicam μεταβολὴν varii varia luserunt, quæ huc non
piguerit ascribere, eaque potissimùm, quæ maiorem cum hoc Alciati tetrasticho
affinitatem habere mihi videntur. Lubens enim prætermitto Horatianum Odam
9.lib.2. & septimam quarti. Ovid. ad Pisonem:

> *Cessat hyems, madidos & siccat vere capillos:*
> *Ver fugit æstates, æstatum terga lacessit*
> *Pomifer autumnus, nebulis cessurus & undis.*

Idem primo De remedio amoris:

> *Poma dat autumnus, formosa est messibus æstas,*
> *Ver præbet flores, igne levatur hyems.*

Et Tristium quarto:

> *Vere prius flores, æstu numerabis aristas,*
> *Poma per autumnum, frigoribusque nives.*

Barthol. Anulus in Poësi picta, ad hominum perpetuam & æternam μεταβολὴν
traduxit:

> *Ver, æstas, autumnus, hyems, hæ quatuor annis*
>   *Sunt tempestates orbe volubilibus.*
> *Quatuor ætates homo sic habet integer ævi,*
>   *Qui puer, hinc iuvenis, mox vir, & inde senex:*
> *Aeterno ut similis mundo revolutio vitæ*
>   *Nos itidem æternos arguat esse homines.*

Vide Proverb. in Chiliad. Ver hyemem sequitur; & varios locos Hieroglyph.
Pierii. Idipsum ait Seneca, Epistola quadam ad Lucilium discipulum: Nullius rei
finis est, sed in orbem nexa sunt omnia, fugiunt atque sequuntur. Diem nox
premit, dies in noctem: æstas in autumnum desinit: autumno hyems instat, quæ
vere compescitur: omnia transeunt ut revertantur.

11. Aneau, *Picta poesis. Ut pictura poesis sit* (Lyons, 1552), p. 26. The tradition
which Aneau enunciates can be traced at least as far back as Pythagoras:

> He [Pythagoras] divides man's life into four quarters thus: "Twenty
> years a boy, twenty years a youth, twenty years a young man, twenty years
> an old man; and these four periods correspond to the four seasons, the boy
> to spring, the youth to summer, the young man to autumn, and the old

man to winter" (Diogenes Laertius, *Lives of Eminent Philosophers* [VIII. 10], trans. R. D. Hicks [London, 1925], p. 329).

Cf. Diodorus Siculus, *The Library of History*, X.ix.5; and Ovid, *Metamorphoses*, XV. 199–213. Frances Yates has expressed an opinion that *Love's Labour's Lost* may contain allusions to "a Neo-Pythagorean harmony of the universe," a central interest of French academies which provided the model for Navarre's "little Academe" (*The French Academies of the Sixteenth Century* [London, 1947], pp. 264–65). The measured dance accompanying the song at the end would convey the notion of an ordered cosmos.

12.   Cf. "You talk greasily; your lips grow foul" (IV.i.130).
13.   Alciati also has an emblem on cuckoos, which with Mignault's commentary serves as a perfect gloss on the cuckoo's cry in Shakespeare's song:

Emblem 60

What is the reason that rustics, country-folk, are usually called "cuckoos"? In early spring when the mocking-bird sings, he who has not pruned his vines is rightly said to be lazy. Like that bird, the countryman produces eggs in someone else's nest while his wife commits adultery in his own bed.

Alciati speaks more clearly about this emblem for us in his book entitled *Parergon iuris libri tres priores* [*libri septem posteriores*; Lyons, 1554], VII.v: "They call him a 'cuckoo' who is negligent in marriage and drives his wife to lechers. They have coined a word, *cucubitare* [to lie down on the job], like *cuculitare* [to play the cuckoo]. I have read that in ancient times among farmers those who were negligent, foolish, and slow were said with a degree of scorn to be 'cuckoos,' because they didn't have their vineyard in order before the cuckoo had begun to sing." . . . And so Alciati says that the name "cuckoo" has been abusively given to those whose wives are unchaste; although more rightly they ought to be called "cuckoos" who commit adultery with other men's wives in the accustomed manner of birds, who frequently place their own eggs in someone else's nest. You can find this in the Erasmian adage, "Cuckoos." Also see Pliny, *Natural History*, XVIII.26, and Valeriano, *Hieroglyphica*, XXV.

Emblem LX

Ruricolas agreste genus plerique cucullos
    Cur vocitent, quænam prodita caussa fuit?
Vere novo cantat Coccyx, quo tempore vites
    Qui non absoluit, iure vocatur iners.
Fert ova in nidos alienos, qualiter ille
    Cui thalamum prodit uxor adulterio.

Id nobis luculenter enarravit Alciatus ipsemet lib.7. Parerg. iuris, cap.5. his verbis: Cuculum vocant, qui matrimonii sui incuriosus sit, quíque uxorem suam mœchis permittat. Cucubitare verbum confinxerunt, quasi cuculitare. Ego Cuculos peculiari convicio agricolas dictos apud veteres legi, qui negligentes, socordes, tardíque essent, quòd non priùs putatas vites haberent, quàm cuculus canere cœpisset. . . . Ait itaque Cuculi nomen abusivè in eos esse traductum, quorum impudicæ sunt uxores; cùm ii contrà cuculi potius vocari debeant, qui alienas uxores adulterant, habita scilicet ratione naturæ avis; quæ sua in nidis alienis ova ponere soleat. Idem reperies Adagio Erasmico, Cuculi. Vide Plin.18.c.26. & Pierium lib.25. Hieroglyph. (Alciati, *Emblemata*, ed. Mignault [Antwerp, 1577], pp. 240–41.)

14. Bertrand H. Bronson comments urbanely, though very briefly, on the "obvious contrast that sets song against song [i.e., 'spring' against 'winter']" and the "further conflict of elements within each separate song" (*MLN*, 63 [1948], 35–38).

15. Herrick's intention, a commonplace, is succinctly stated in his shorter poem, "Divination by a Daffodil":

> When a daffodil I see,
> Hanging down his head towards me;
> Guess I may, what I must be:
> First, I shall decline my head;
> Secondly, I shall be dead;
> Lastly, safely buried.

Sir Walter Raleigh gave beautiful expression to the sentiment in a list of comparisons between the parts of the microcosm and the macrocosm: "The beauty of our youth [may be resembled] to the flowers of the Spring, which, either in a very short time, or with the Sunnes heat drie up, & wither away, or the fierce puffes of wind blow them from the stalks"; and he continued: "Our leafe once fallen, springeth no more, neither doth the Sunne or the Summer adorne us againe, with the garments of new leaves and flowers" (*Historie of the World* [London, 1614], pp. 30–31).

16. Another ideogram of this concept of universal harmony in ordered nature, expressed in aural terms, is the symphony of the Muses under the direction of Apollo. In this context, the last line of the play, which has proved troublesome to annotators, becomes intelligible. Don Armado, as stage manager of the closing song-and-dance, says: "The words of Mercury are harsh after the songs of Apollo." It was common for the actor in Don Armado's position to recite an epilogue begging approval of the audience; Puck in *Midsummer Night's Dream* and Rosalind in *As You Like It* are obvious cases in point. Since Mercury is the god of commerce, this appended appeal to the customers could well be called "the words of Mercury." The harmonious view propounded by the concluding song would place the dialogue of spring and winter among "the songs of Apollo," however, after which a crass commercial pitch seems harsh; and therefore Don Armado, quite uncharacteristically, desists from delivering an epilogue.

17. Notable exceptions are Bobbyann Roesen, "Love's Labour's Lost," *SQ*, 4 (1953),

411–26; Cyrus Hoy, "*Love's Labour's Lost* and the Nature of Comedy," *SQ*, 13 (1962), 31–40; J. D. Wilson, *Shakespeare's Happy Comedies* (London, 1962), p. 73; E. M. W. Tillyard, *Shakespeare's Early Comedies*, pp. 173–81; Peter Phialas, *Shakespeare's Romantic Comedies* (Chapel Hill, 1966), esp. pp. 80–101; and Catherine M. McLay, "The Dialogues of Spring and Winter: A Key to the Unity of *Love's Labour's Lost*," *SQ*, 18 (1967), 119–27.

18. See J. S. Reid, "Shakespeare's 'Living Art'," *PQ*, 1 (1922), 226–27.

19. This word should be read literally, "made dead"; cf. *NED*, "mortified," sense 1.

20. I.e., ordinary perception; cf. *NED*, "common sense," sense 2c.

21. The tradition surrounding Prometheus was unusually rich. Most mythographers recorded the story of his making a human figure and his stealing fire from heaven to animate it. For this impingement upon the godhead, Zeus chained him to the rock and assigned an eagle to gnaw incessantly at his vitals. But this impious act is subordinated here to his equally important function of supplying fire to mortals and encouraging the consequent arts that fire makes possible. Charles Estienne called him "vir prudentissimus, qui astronomiam primus Assyriis indicavit" (*Dictionarium historicum, geographicum, poeticum* [Oxford, 1671], p. 670). For Thomas Cooper, "he was studious, and a greate Astronomer" (*Thesaurus linguae romanae & britannicae*, 2 vols. [London, 1584], II. "Prometheus").

22. Richard Cody has recently discussed *Love's Labour's Lost* as an expression of Renaissance pastoralism (*The Landscape of the Mind* [Oxford, 1969], pp. 105–26). I came to my interpretation of the play before reading Mr. Cody, however, and in any case share but few thoughts with him.

23. I.e., last as love; cf. *NED*, "last," sense 3.

24. G. Wilson Knight makes this point with considerable poignancy: "The poet's mood will not shirk the tragic realities which condition all human joy" (*Shakespearian Tempest*, p. 83).

25. Sidney uses the terms "*Idea* or fore-conceit" in a passage deriving the etymology of *poet* from the Greek word ποιεῖν and explaining why the poet is called a "maker" (*An Apology for Poetry*, ed. Geoffrey Shepherd [London, 1965], pp. 99–101). The fore-conceit bears the same relation to the extended literary fiction as the idea in the godhead bears to the created universe. Each is an intellectual form which by the will of the creator (be he god or poet) is given sense-perceptible extension in the physical world of becoming. These *ideas*, of course, are "the forms of things unknown" which the poet's "imagination bodies forth" (*Midsummer Night's Dream*, V.i.14–15). The locus classicus for this theory of creation is Plato's *Timaeus*, 27d–29e.

26. See, for example, C. L. Barber, *Shakespeare's Festive Comedy* (Princeton, 1959), p. 89; and Wilson, *Shakespeare's Happy Comedies*, pp. 69–71.

27. See pp. 40–41, above.

28. See p. 35, above.

29. Cf. I.i.78–79, 236–37; IV.iii.265; V.ii.19–25, 622.

30. Cf. I.i.45; IV.iii.23–25, 229.

31. Cf. I.ii.8–10; III.i.170; IV.iii.213; V.i.54.

32. Cf. I.i.1–3, 31–32; V.ii.668–70, 708.

33. The *Venus and Adonis* stanza, rhyming *a b a b c c*.

34. E.g., I.i.80–93, 160–73. Some sonnets, as in *Romeo and Juliet,* are distributed as dialogue between two speakers, e.g., V.ii.343–56.

35. But see M. C. Bradbrook, *Shakespeare and Elizabethan Poetry* (London, 1951), pp. 212–19; Barber, *Shakespeare's Festive Comedy,* pp. 95–113; E. W. Talbert, *Elizabethan Drama and Shakespeare's Early Plays* (Chapel Hill, 1963), pp. 33–39, 237–51; William Matthews, "Language in *Love's Labour's Lost,*" *E & S,* 17 (1964), 1–11; James L. Calderwood, "*Love's Labour's Lost:* A Wantoning with Words," *SEL,* 5 (1965), 317–32; Tillyard, *Shakespeare's Early Comedies,* pp. 152–64; and A. C. Hamilton, *The Early Shakespeare* (San Marino, Calif., 1967), pp. 128–42.

36. But see Rupert Taylor, *The Date of Love's Labour's Lost* (New York, 1932); Eva Turner Clark, *The Satirical Comedy Love's Labour's Lost* (New York, 1933); Frances A. Yates, *A Study of Love's Labour's Lost* (Cambridge, 1936); M. C. Bradbrook, *The School of Night* (Cambridge, 1936); Richard David, ed., *Love's Labour's Lost,* 4th ed. (London, 1951), pp. xxxvii–l; W. Schrickx, *Shakespeare's Early Contemporaries* (Antwerp, 1956); Robert Gittings, *Shakespeare's Rival* (London, 1960); J. Dover Wilson, ed., *Love's Labour's Lost,* 2nd ed. (Cambridge, 1962), pp. xi–xx, xxxiv–liii; A. L. Rowse, *William Shakespeare: A Biography* New York, 1963), esp., pp. 211–20; and Phialas, *Shakespeare's Romantic Comedies,* pp. 75–80.

The Function of the Songs at the End of
Love's Labour's Lost

ROBERT G. HUNTER

Mr. Peter Seng, in his excellent book on Shakespeare's songs, sums up his view of the dramatic function of "the dialogue that two learned men have compiled in praise of the owl and the cuckoo" as follows:

> To press a dramatic function on songs which could be easily omitted—and probably often were—is to weave a rope of sand. . . . Shakespeare was merely giving his audience what would please it; these songs have pleased many and pleased them long.[1]

Like most critics of Shakespeare, I feel a compulsion to press at least one function on every moment of Shakespearean art. I recognize that the impulse is irrational and I try to resist it, but I find a statement like Mr. Seng's an unbearable temptation and I lapse, particularly since I am among the many whom Shakespeare's songs have merely pleased. In fact, I find I can take two distinct sorts of pleasure in them. When I experience them as separate lyrics —as anthology pieces—I find them very pretty. As pretty as, perhaps even prettier than, for example, George Peele's similar seasonal lyric "Whenas the rye reach to the chin." When I return Peele's song to its dramatic context in *The Old Wives' Tale*, I still find it very pretty. When, however, I put the owl and the cuckoo back where they belong, at the end of *Love's Labour's Lost*, and particularly if I am experiencing the play in the theater, I find the moment moving, right, and meaningful, and I cannot believe that this would be the case if there were not some significant connection between this conclusion and the comedy that has gone before it. Inspired by the rather dubious authority of my theatrical experience, therefore, I will try to refute Mr. Seng and those who agree with him. I will take my stand with—but definitely to one side of—such recent commentators on the play as Catherine McLay[2] and Gates Agnew.[3] Unlike them I cannot quite make out a series of detailed correspondences between the imagery of the songs and the specific dramatic concerns of the play. I see the connections as more broadly thematic, and I take my cue from C. L. Barber who, in *Shakespeare's Festive Comedy*, identifies the songs as "an expression of the going on power of life."[4] I do agree with Miss McLay, however, that these lyrics can serve as a key to the unity of *Love's Labour's Lost*.

The unity of any good play is the product of conflict, and the conclusion of traditional comedy usually consists of an attempt to resolve conflict. The conflict which our songs presumably try to resolve is described in appropriately military metaphor in the opening speech of the play. Navarre is speaking to and about his three companions and himself:

> Therefore, brave conquerors—for so you are,
> That war against your own affections
> And the huge army of the world's desires. . . .
>
> (I.i.8–10)[5]

Navarre, Berowne, Longaville and Dumaine begin the play resolved to do battle against the world, the flesh, and the devil. But the world is their world and the flesh is their flesh and the devil is in it. The battle is inevitably a psychomachy, and the young men will necessarily become battlefields as well as combatants. To gain advantage in the struggle, they have decided to enter into a kind of secular monasticism. They will scorn delights and live laborious days, and their reason is the Miltonic one:

> Let fame, that all hunt after in their lives,
> Live register'd upon our brazen tombs,
> And then grace us in the disgrace of death. . . .
>
> (I.i.1–3)

Fame is the spur, and the last infirmity of noble minds spurs the young men into one of the basic conflicts of Shakespearean and Renaissance comedy, a conflict which I would like to label—borrowing my phrase from the title of a picture painted by Brueghel in 1559—the battle between Lent and Carnival.

In Shakespeare this is the "battle" between Malvolio and Sir Toby, between Hotspur and Falstaff, between Angelo and his own affections and the huge army of Viennese desires. In Ben Jonson, Adam Overdo, Humphrey Waspe, and Zeal-of-the-Land Busy fight this good fight against the enormities of Bartholomew Fair. In Rabelais, the battle—if a little one-sided—is constant, although it is allegorically most clear in Book IV where Pantagruel and his companions find themselves caught between the surrealistic figure of Quaresmeprenant and his enemies, *les andouilles farouches* ("the savage sausages"), who are fanatical followers of the winged pig, Mardigras.

Such literary conflicts are, obviously, basic ones between two embodied views of life. Lent sees life as material from which something must be made or achieved—fame, honor, art, power, salvation, success. Carnival sees life as material to be consumed; as Sir Andrew Aguecheek has noticed, it consists of eating and drinking. And sleeping and waking and making love and so on.

Native to each of these embodied views of life is an appropriate view of time. For the followers of Lent, time is rectilinear; it moves expeditiously between two points—birth and death for the individual, creation and apocalypse for the race. It takes survey of all the world and must have a stop. For Carnival, time is circular, as round as Falstaff's belly; day follows night, the seasons return. We thirst and drink and thirst and drink, fill our bellies and empty them and fill them again. The larger battle contains a smaller battle between two apprehensions of time: Hotspur time versus Falstaff time, Malvolio time versus Sir Toby time, Protestant ethic time versus hippie time, superego time versus id time.

The view of time which obtains at the beginning of *Love's Labour's Lost* is uncompromisingly Lenten. Fame, according to Navarre, will grace the young men when they are dead:

> When, spite of cormorant devouring Time
> Th' endeavour of this present breath may buy
> That honour which shall bate his scythe's keen edge,
> And make us heirs of all eternity.
>
> *(I.i.4–7)*

"Cormorant devouring Time" is a monster who must be fed, according to the Lenten view of things, if honor is to be kept bright. The young men propose to feed him their pleasures, sacrificing to him love, leisure, food, and sleep:

> O, these are barren tasks, too hard to keep,
> Not to see ladies, study, fast, not sleep.
>
> *(I.i.47–48)*

Berowne is right. Such resolutions are preposterous, especially when they are made in a comedy:

> The sea will ebb and flow, heaven show his face;
> Young blood doth not obey an old decree:
> We cannot cross the cause why we were born. ....
>
> *(IV.iii.213–15)*

The main action of the play is concerned with bringing the young men to a knowledge of this basic truth. The task is not a difficult one. Four pretty, bawdy, witty girls arrive, and by Act IV, scene iii, the brave conquerors who war against their own affections find themselves enlisting under quite another banner:

> Have at you then, affection's men-at-arms:
> Consider what you first did swear unto,
> To fast, to study, and to see no woman;
> Flat treason 'gainst the kingly state of youth.

(IV.iii.287–90)

The followers of Lent have become "affection's men-at-arms," loyal soldiers in the army of Carnival. They assume their new roles with enthusiasm. "Saint Cupid, then! and, soldiers to the field," becomes Navarre's war cry. To which Berowne adds:

> Advance your standards, and upon them, lords!
> Pell-mell, down with them! but be first advis'd,
> In conflict that you get the sun of them.

(IV.iii.363–66)

A new use has been found for the military metaphor with which the play opens, and I would maintain that there are thematic as well as the usual reasons for the bawdy here. At the beginning of the play the young men are determined to fight time by conquering their desires. By Act IV they have decided to turn their former adversaries into weapons. But ultimately they are fighting the same good fight, for the merry war between men and women is one more skirmish in the larger battle against time. At first the young lords are determined to defeat time by achieving immortality through fame and honor, a process whose purpose is, according to Navarre, "To make us heirs of all eternity." I take this rather cryptic statement to mean both that all generations to come will inherit the memory of the young men's honor and also that they (the young men) will come to inherit a kind of eternity through fame. The phrase Shakespeare uses to express the thought is, to say the least, a suggestive one. If we dwell briefly on it, it occurs to us that there is another way "to make us heirs"—one provided by nature—and a very pleasant way, too. Down with the ladies, then, pell-mell, and get sons of them.

Although they are far from putting it in such terms, the young men are here proposing to embrace a different method for conquering time. Faced with linear, Lenten, "cormorant devouring Time," the individual can only perish, but the race, through procreation, can survive. In switching allegiance from Lent to Carnival, the young men have decided, so to speak, to heed the message of the procreative sonnets rather than those in which Shakespeare promises youth immortality through art.

This decision releases a burst of Saturnalian energy. The next time we see the young men they come on disguised as Russians, dancing the trepak, I suppose, and making perfect asses of themselves, behaving that is to say, with the decorum that young men in the throes of love and carnival normally have. Their disastrous masquerade is followed by an even sillier one—the show of the Nine Worthies. In form and function this is nearly identical to the tragical mirth of Pyramus and Thisbe at the end of *A Midsummer Night's Dream*, though it is far less funny. But just as "Pyramus and Thisbe" mocks and parodies the tragedy which threatened Hermia and Lysander at the beginning of their play, so this insubstantial pageant asserts the claims of comedy by giving a good drubbing to the serious pretensions which inspired the anticomic monasticism of the young men in Act I, scene i. Here on show are the bravest conquerors of them all—Pompey, Alexander, Hercules, Judas Maccabeus, and Hector—but if the show of the Worthies is an example of that eternity promised by the immortal poet, then we must entertain serious doubts about the value of fame and honor as antidotes to time, and we begin to suspect that of all vanities a desire for eternal fame is the vainest.

The mockery with which the young men greet the playlet is excessive and, to me at least, annoying—not because it is rude, but because it is less funny than the festivity it interrupts. For me, the result is to dampen to a very small degree the enthusiasm for Carnival, which up to this point I had shared with Navarre and his followers. I am predisposed, as a result, to listen sympathetically to Armado's defense of himself as Hector:

> The sweet war-man is dead and rotten; sweet chucks, beat not the bones of
> the buried; when he breathed, he was a man.
>
> (*V.ii.651–53*)

Armado is reasserting, mildly and perhaps ridiculously, the claims of what I have been calling Lent and is universalizing and humanizing those claims in his reassertion of them. The memory of Hector, the man Armado stands for, deserves respect, not because he was a hero, but because he was a man, transfixed like the rest of us by linear time and ending up buried bones. And so will we, Carnival or no Carnival. But these pretensions to Lenten high seriousness are destroyed at once by irrefutable evidence of Armado's own Carnival propensities. Jaquenetta is pregnant. "The child brags in her belly." The sweet war-man may be dead and rotten, but the race will survive and Carnival will continue.

The discomfiture of Armado exaggerates and parodies that of Navarre, Berowne, and the rest. They too have aspired to the role of worthies, been mocked for their pains, and finally been forced to acknowledge the common

humanity of their sexual desires. This process has been presented in the play
as a very good thing, completely in keeping with the Saturnalian spirit of one of
Shakespeare's festive comedies. Armado has functioned as a caricature of the
young men throughout the play, and in mocking him they are mocking themselves, which might explain the intensity of the mockery. In any case, the
degradation of Hector/Armado, the pregnancy of Jaquenetta, and the wild
good spirits of the young men mark the height of Carnival's triumph.

It is a short-lived triumph. Marcade's interruption of festivity with news of
death makes a brilliant and much commented upon change of tone. Here, in
my terms, is the genuine reassertion of the Lenten claims abortively made
before by Armado. The death of a "real" king and father forces upon us, as the
death of a legendary Hector could not, a knowledge of the inadequacy of a
purely Carnival view of life. The power of "cormorant devouring Time" is made
shockingly vivid, and the young men are shocked by it into a realization of the
frivolity with which they have abandoned the Lenten view. They are not, however, shocked back into their previous superficial and inadequate attitudes. "For
your fair sakes," says Berowne to the ladies, "have we neglected time, / Played
foul play with our oaths" (V.ii.745–46). But their reason for so doing—the
love of woman's beauty—is a good reason, and they will not abandon it. So
the king and Berowne urge the serious claims of the love they have already
declared.

The princess, however, will not admit the validity of those claims:

> We have receiv'd your letters full of love;
> Your favours, the ambassadors of love;
> And in our maiden council rated them
> At courtship, pleasant jest, and courtesy,
> As bombast and as lining to the time.
>
> *(V.ii.767–71)*

The young men's love has been declared in time of Carnival, in that unending
"now" when anything goes and nothing counts. But now "now" has ceased to
be unending and has become the end of something. "Now," says the king, "at
the latest minute of the hour, / Grant us your loves" (V.ii.777–78). The princess has her reply:

> A time, methinks, too short
> To make a world-without-end bargain in.
>
> *(V.ii.778–79)*

This is a kind and charming way of saying no, but the princess's lighthearted echo of the prayer book—*world without end, in secula seculorum*—is an indication of how serious a thing love is for her. The young men's Carnival love must prove itself capable of eternity by enduring for a bit in Lenten time. Love must, at least, be able to survive

> until the twelve celestial signs
> Have brought about the annual reckoning.
>   *(V.ii.787–88)*

But it must also survive other Lenten claims. The princess and Rosaline impose penance on their loves. For the king, this means the loneliness and self-denial of a hermitage. Berowne must "jest a twelve-month in an hospital," matching his Carnival wits against the Lenten facts of death and suffering.

This imposition of penance results in the substitution for the usual end of comedy by the usual beginning, in which lovers are separated by a task imposed upon the hero. Berowne is aware of the anomaly:

> Our wooing doth not end like an old play;
> Jack hath not Jill: these ladies' courtesy
> Might well have made our sport a comedy.
>   *(V.ii.864–66)*

The king is characteristically optimistic: "Come, sir, it wants a twelvemonth and a day, / And then 'twill end." Berowne, as usual, sees the practical objection: "That's too long for a play." Berowne's line is the cue for Armado to enter and announce the lyric dialogue which ends the play:

> *Spring.*   When daisies pied and violets blue
>   And lady-smocks all silver-white
>   And cuckoo-buds of yellow hue
>   Do paint the meadows with delight,
>   The cuckoo then, on every tree,
>   Mocks married men; for thus sings he,
>   Cuckoo;
>   Cuckoo, cuckoo: O word of fear,
>   Unpleasing to a married ear!
>   When shepherds pipe on oaten straws,
>   And merry larks are ploughman's clocks,

> When turtles tread, and rooks, and daws,
>   And maidens bleach their summer smocks,
> The cuckoo then, on every tree,
> Mocks married men; for thus sings he,
>   Cuckoo;
> Cuckoo, cuckoo: O word of fear,
> Unpleasing to a married ear!

Winter. When icicles hang by the wall,
>   And Dick the shepherd blows his nail,
> And Tom bears logs into the hall,
>   And milk comes frozen home in pail,
> When blood is nipp'd, and ways be foul,
> Then nightly sings the staring owl,
>   Tu-whit;
> Tu-who, a merry note,
> While greasy Joan doth keel the pot.
> When all aloud the wind doth blow,
>   And coughing drowns the parson's saw,
> And birds sit brooding in the snow,
>   And Marian's nose looks red and raw,
> When roasted crabs hiss in the bowl,
> Then nightly sings the staring owl,
>   Tu-whit;
> Tu-who, a merry note,
> While greasy Joan doth keel the pot.

                                                    (V.ii.884–919)

Twelve months may be too long for a play, but they are not too long for a lyric.

One function of the songs is to bring us, in our imaginations, to the expiration of the year of mourning which separates us from the play's truly comic ending. The spring will pass, winter will come and go, and spring will come again. Jack will have Jill and all shall be well.

But in addition to compressing the revolution of the twelve celestial signs into a series of brilliantly precise seasonal images, the songs function more importantly in striking a balance between the forces which I see in conflict in *Love's Labour's Lost*. The reassertion of the Lenten view has been extremely powerful. Carnival attributes, like wit and sexual appetite, have been firmly curbed. Love has been identified as one of those things, like honor and fame, that must be achieved within a period of linear time. Life is something that will come to an end and so is time, and before time passes it can be measured mathematically as if with a ruler, cut into segments and doled out. The princess's phrase for the year is "the annual reckoning," a Lenten concept indeed with its suggestion of clerks and factors totting up profit and loss and its light reminder of the heavy reckoning which all of us will face ultimately. The dialogue of the owl and the cuckoo does not deny the truth of this apprehension of time. It does deny, by its existence, that the Lenten view is the whole truth. The songs' images, simply by being, mean; and one of the things they mean is that whatever else it may be, time is also cyclical. Spring flowers will paint the meadows with delight and birds will sit brooding in the snow and spring flowers will paint the meadows with delight and birds will sit brooding in the snow—in spite of "cormorant devouring Time." The resolution which Shakespeare is attempting to engineer for the conflict in *Love's Labour's Lost* is not a victory for one side or the other. Rather he is trying to create an alliance that will combine the seemingly irreconcilable strengths of both. The song of the owl and the cuckoo is his final tactic for achieving this complex apprehension of life, love, and time.

Postscript

The editor of *Shakespeare Studies* has very kindly permitted me to add a note to this essay directing the reader's attention to a document relevant to my argument which has just been published, namely "An Epilogue Possibly by Shakespeare" by William A. Ringler, Jr., and Steven W. May, *Modern Philology*, 70 (November 1972), pp. 138–39. The epilogue in question is entitled "to ye Q. by ye players 1598" and was probably delivered at the end of a Lord Chamberlain's Men's play when they performed before the queen and her council on Shrove Tuesday, February 20, 1599 (New Style). The poem begins:

> As the diall hand tells ore/
> yᵉ same howers yt had before
> still beginning in yᵉ ending/
> circuler account still lending
> So most mightie Q. we pray/
> like yᵉ diall day by day
> you may lead yᵉ seasons on/
> making new when old are gon.

The combination of a holiday occasion with the necessity for flattering Elizabeth has prompted the author to attempt the same reconciliation of linear, Lenten time with circular, Carnival time that I have tried to show Shakespeare achieving in *Love's Labour's Lost* and particularly in the concluding songs. The anonymous poet's success is, in my opinion, comparable to Shakespeare's, and the poem's theme, I think, supports the conclusion reached by Ringler and May that "it is at least possible" that Shakespeare wrote the epilogue they have discovered.

Notes:

This paper was originally delivered to the Shakespeare section at the Modern
Language Association Meeting, December, 1970.

1. *The Vocal Songs in the Plays of Shakespeare: A Critical History* (Cambridge,
   Mass., 1967), p. 25.
2. "The Dialogues of Spring and Winter: A Key to the Unity of *Love's Labour's
   Lost*," SQ, 17 (1967), 119–27.
3. "Berowne and the Progress of *Love's Labour's Lost*," ShakS, 4 (1969), 40–72.
4. *Shakespeare's Festive Comedy* (Princeton, 1959), 118.
5. All quotations from *Love's Labour's Lost* are cited from the New Arden edition,
   ed. Richard David (London, 1951).

The Folk Background of Petruchio's Wooing Dance: Male Supremacy in *The Taming of the Shrew*

MICHAEL WEST

As Richard Hosley has remarked of *The Taming of the Shrew*, "it is a curious fact that the play rates higher with directors, actors, and spectators than it does with critics, teachers, and readers."[1] Why? A conspectus of the criticism suggests that a partial answer lies in a common tendency to intellectualize and so misconstrue the play's treatment of women's rights. Thus George Bernard Shaw praised the play's "realism," but found the last scene "altogether disgusting to the modern sensibility" and fumed, "No man of any decency of feeling can sit it out in the company of a woman without being extremely ashamed of the lord-of-creation moral implied."[2] Likewise Mark Van Doren finds the play "curious" since it "leans . . . on a doctrine which Shakespeare must have adopted in cold blood, for on the evidence of the other plays it was not his own . . . the doctrine of male superiority."[3] It is with an air of surprise that he goes on to confess, "Yet the resulting play, as its popularity attests, is strangely and permanently interesting." Defenders of the play are often tempted to ironize the last scene, arguing that "otherwise it is an unaccountable exception and regresses to the wholly un-Shakespearean doctrine of male superiority."[4] Others like Hosley have emphasized that the play's attitude was characteristically Elizabethan and was expressed more humanely by Shakespeare than by some of his sources.[5] But such defenses fail to explain the strange and permanent interest that Van Doren noted, fail to explain why audiences of ordinary men and women continue to respond to the play with indecent enjoyment, as Shaw would have it, from the first scene through the last.

Actually, Shaw's and Van Doren's ambivalent responses point toward the real sources of the play's imaginative appeal. Upon his first appearance Petruchio, in a nodal image, describes his wanderings to Hortensio: "I have thrust myself into this maze, / Haply to wive and thrive as best I may" (I.ii.53–54). Though not usually so glossed, *maze* probably refers to the Elizabethan dance pattern; for when Hortensio goes on to mention a rich heiress, Petruchio promptly professes his intention to marry her, "As wealth is burden of my wooing dance" (I.ii.66). Hortensio's reply may even faintly echo this governing metaphor: "Petruchio, since we are stepped thus far in, / I will continue" (I.ii.81–82). The initial scene has dramatized Kate as threatened by spinsterhood: " 'Mates,' maid, how mean you that? No mates for you / Unless you were of gentler, milder mold" (I.i.59–60). Throughout the play Petruchio's brusque pursuit of her is to be viewed as a kind of mating dance with a spirited partner whose sexual appeal he frankly acknowledges: "Now, by the world, it is a lusty wench" (II.i.160). One critic has casually but aptly noted that "his demonstrations of physical exuberance, wit and bawdry are provocative court-ing plumage."[6] A sixteenth-century theorist like Thoinot Arbeau could justify dancing as necessary to preserve a hierarchical social order, functioning as a means whereby lovers explored each other's health and strength.[7] Thus the elaborately patterned verbal strutting of Petruchio's first conversation with Kate leads to his command "O, let me see thee walk. Thou dost not halt" (II.i.258) and his praise for her "princely gait" (II.i.261), while the lack of a bridegroom makes Kate complain bitterly that she "must dance barefoot" (II.i.33) on her sister's wedding day. As Renaissance theologians disapprov-ingly stressed, weddings were often distinguished by dancing of an exuberant and cheerful sensuality: "For the bryde must be brought in to an open dauncy-ing place. Then there is such a renninge / leapinge / and flynging amonge them / then there is such a lyftinge up and discoueringe of damesels clothes and of other wemens apparell / that a man might thinke / all these dauncers had cast all shame behinde thẽ."[8] Despite Kate's seeming disdain for her brisk partner, she has glimpsed a happier alternative to the *dump,*[9] the melancholy dance that Baptista uses to characterize her sullen solitude: "Why, how now, daughter Katherine? In your dumps?" (II.i.286).

As Hosley predicted, recent scholarship has done much to illuminate the play through the discovery of new sources and analogues. In an important ar-ticle Jan Harold Brunvand convincingly demonstrates that the Petruchio-Kate plot in *The Shrew* contains elements common to folk versions of the story but not shared by *A Shrew,* which must thus be regarded as a derivative of Shake-speare's play and not its original.[10] The plot's roots in folk tradition are further explored by W. B. Thorne, who rightly suggests that Petruchio's boasting is deliberately reminiscent of the fool in the mummers' wooing plays, and that elements from these have been consciously combined with "May games, pas-times, and popular ballads . . . to lend additional meaning to a familiar plot. As a result of the parallels with folk wooing sequences . . . the action of the plot has connotations which the Elizabethan audience could not help noticing."[11] Thorne's parallels are easily supplemented. There were half-a-dozen fertility festivals celebrated from Twelfth Night to the wooing games mentioned by Perdita in *The Winter's Tale:* "Methinks I play as I have seen them do / In Whitsun pastorals" (IV.iv.133–34). Hocktide, in particular, involved "a contest between the men and women of a community" and featured "the capture of . . . women by the opposite sex, with 'lifting,' removal of shoes, or the imposition of a tax."[12] Surely such a ritual underlies the stage tradition that has Petruchio carry Kate off on his shoulders after their wedding, ironically assuring her, "Fear not, sweet wench; they shall not touch thee, Kate. / I'll buckler thee against a million" (III.ii.234–35). Wooing dramas like *The Nut Brown Maid* formed a part of the seasonal festivals,[13] and this fact lends particular point to Petruchio's assertion that "Kate like the hazel-twig / Is straight and slender, and as brown in hue / As hazelnuts and sweeter than the kernels" (II.i.255–57). Indeed, in the induction Shakespeare clearly alerts his audience to the way in which Elizabethan drama drew upon its folk antecedents. Greeting the strolling players who come to the inn, the lord singles out one of their number: "This fellow I remember / Since once he played the farmer's eldest son; / Twas where you wooed the gentlewoman so well" (Ind.i.83–85). As Baskervill notes, this reference suggests that professional actors consciously adapted Lincolnshire folk drama, or, indeed, that "Shakespeare may have been describing the plays of the villages like Barton-on-the-Heath and Wilnecote from which the characters of his Induction hail."[14]

Song-and-dance drama of the folk portrayed a clownishly wanton wooer's pursuit of a pert, scornful maiden, and this theme is pervasive in Elizabethan popular balladry. Its hold upon Shakespeare's imagination may be gauged from *Henry V*, where in order to court his Kate the king must assume the role of the bumpkin wooer, to the dismay of Dr. Johnson, who wondered why in the last act Hal should suddenly be given the character of Hotspur, as it seemed to him. Johnson's intellectual puzzlement is understandable, for the transformation ignores the logic of character development and is fully explicable only in terms of deep-seated and rather primitive feelings about the nature of physical courtship. Dialogue ballads on this theme even more directly influenced Elizabethan drama, for they were a mainstay of the stage jig, the song-and-dance performance that customarily concluded an afternoon at the theater. Indeed, Shakespeare's own company had pioneered in exploiting the vogue for such afterpieces, and the actor Will Kemp was particularly renowned for his skill in them. Some ballads were mainly satirical, like "The devil is dead," from which Grumio quotes a snatch (IV.i.36–37). The shrewish wife was a favorite satirical theme, and there was "a fairly extensive group of dialogue ballads in the nature of conjugal brawls or flytings" (p. 171), which probably were utilized as stage jigs.

In *The Taming of the Shrew* Shakespeare has blended their influence with that of the even larger number of dialogue ballads comically portraying a sensual courtship. The prevalence of such song-and-dance upon the stage is suggested in *Much Ado About Nothing* when Beatrice, herself "so shrewd of . . . tongue" and "too curst" (II.i.17–18), informs Hero that "wooing, wedding, and repenting is as a Scotch jig, a measure, and a cinque-pace: the first suit is hot and hasty like a Scotch jig (and full as fantastical)" (II.i.63–66). Wooing jigs were so notorious for their obscenity that there were "a large number of vulgar puns on 'jig' in the Renaissance" and the word appears to have had "in some form a sexual connotation among the people" (p. 12, n. 1). Thus Hamlet ironically claims that Polonius can only appreciate "a jig or a tale of bawdry" (II.ii.488). Significantly, in his courtship scene with Kate Petruchio first quotes the refrain of the popular ballad "I Cannot Come Every Day to Woo," very likely an early stage jig: "Signior Baptista, my business asketh haste, / And every day I cannot come to woo" (II.i.114–115). Then, when his antics have reduced a bewildered but secretly dazzled Kate to tacit consent, he exits singing a snatch from another dialogue wooing ballad: "And kiss me, Kate, 'We will be married a Sunday' " (II.i.326). Again, this old popular song probably derives from a song-and-dance drama of the folk and may have been staged as a jig (pp. 213–15).

Likewise, Kate's situation as the unchosen maiden waiting for a suitor is consciously parallel to singing games played by Elizabethan and modern children, like the one mentioned by Beatrice in *Much Ado*: "I may sit in a corner and cry, 'Heigh-ho for a husband' " (II.i.286–87). Freed from isolation by her brisk rescuer, her relation to Petruchio follows the general pattern of country dances such as the one called "Sweet Kate," which was varied, spontaneous, dramatic, and called for kissing (p. 350). Indeed, we must consider in the light of popular song-and-dance Petruchio's three triumphant requests for kisses, not only the one quoted above but the conclusion to Act V, scene i, and his climactic final command "Why, there's a wench! Come on and kiss me, Kate" (V.ii.185). These merely echo "the plea for a kiss . . . popular in early wooing song" (p. 189). "Joan, come kiss me now" was not only a widely known Elizabethan song but gave its name to a familiar dance tune. Thoinot Arbeau describes a similar kissing song, *Baisons nous belle*, as proper accompaniment for a galliard (p. 89). Variant verisions are common, such as "Come kys me Johan grammercy Ione" and "Come hither, sweet, and take a kiss," while a similarly phrased motif in the mummers' wooing plays points to the currency of such pieces as song-drama (pp. 20–21). Thus Petruchio's busses are ritualistic and resonate with meanings reinforced not only by social pastimes like kissing games but ultimately by seasonal fertility festivals.

There is an abundance of evidence in Shakespeare and other Elizabethans to show that jigs were not the only dances that could be interpreted as miming the sexual impulses of animals. In fact, this was one of the charges in the Puritan crusade against all dancing.[15] The pavane took its name from the peacock, and the mating dance of that bird was proverbial: Sylvester's *Du*

Bartas speaks typically of "a Peacock, prickt with loues desire, / To woo his Mistresse, strowting stately by her."[16] The galliard, as Sir John Davies informs us in *Orchestra*, was "a gallant daunce, that lively doth bewray / A spirit and a vertue masculine,"[17] qualities reflected in the etymology of its name, which combines connotations of bravery with gaiety and high spirits. Davies describes its function in a courtship where the male "like a reuellour in rich aray, / Doth daunce his galliard in his lemman's sight" (xxxix). The dance was particularly distinguished by "lofty turnes and capriols in the ayre, / Which with the lusty tunes accordeth faire" (lxvii), and like most educated Elizabethans Davies was etymologist enough to associate the dance's *capriols* with the proverbially lustful behavior of the goat. So was Shakespeare, to judge by *Twelfth Night*, where Sir Toby encourages Andrew Aguecheek to dance galliards with capers as a way of courting Olivia (I.iii.107–27). Touchstone's leering pursuit of Audrey among her goats in *As You Like It*, together with his slyly punning comparison of himself to "the most capricious poet, honest Ovid" (III.iii.6), confirms Shakespeare's understanding that cutting capers was emblematic of lustful desires.

If Petruchio's conquest of Kate is a kind of mating dance with appropriate strutting and biceps-flexing, she in turn is a healthy female animal who wants a male strong enough to protect her, deflower her, and sire vigorous offspring. Petruchio's elemental force differentiates him from the numerous old pantaloons who people the comic world of the play, especially the Bianca plot. Alexander Barclay's *Mirror of Good Maners* was characteristic of the Renaissance in pinpointing where the inadequacy of an aging suitor was revealed: "Not well presentith he the wower in a daunce, / But very ill he playeth the volage amorous / Which fetered in a gine woulde gambalde leape & praunce, / Attached to a chayne of linkes ponderous."[18] The animal imagery in which the play abounds is a prime reason for its disfavor with the critics, who find such terms degrading to Kate and to the concept of matrimony. True, Petruchio undertakes to "woo this wildcat" (I.ii.196) and punningly vows "to tame you, Kate, / And bring you from a wild Kate to a Kate / Comfortable as other household Kates" (II.i.278–80). Likewise, there is the nodal metaphor of hawk taming, and at the end he wagers on her obedience as on his horse or his hound. But these images are less the mark of the master than his tribute to the animal spirits that they both share. He is perfectly willing to style himself "a combless cock, so Kate will be my hen" (II.i.229). If she can be compared to the jennet in *Venus and Adonis*, inwardly eager but coyly standoffish, Petruchio's behavior recalls the stallion's in that poem: "Anon he rears upright, curvets, and leaps, / As who should say, 'Lo, thus my strength is tried, / And this I do to captivate the eye / Of the fair breeder that is standing by'" (279–82). Shakespeare's easy acceptance of the facts learned in Warwickshire barnyards, his evident sympathy for all animal life, should forestall any critical squeamishness on our part. His Elizabethan audience, after all, could cheerfully look for guidance to a marriage manual like Pierre Viret's *The Schoole of Beastes, intituled, the good Housholder* (London, 1585), where behavior proper to husbands and wives is approvingly illustrated with a host of euphuistic comparisons drawn exclusively from the animal kingdom. We should remember that when Hamlet eulogizes man as angelic in action and godlike in apprehension, he is at the same time perfectly capable of viewing him as "the paragon of animals."[19]

It has been conjectured that like many other Stratfordites Shakespeare once kept doves.[20] He must have known as well as other Elizabethans that "the females . . . will endure and abide their emperious males. . . . Then shall ye hear the cocks grumble in the throat, quarrel and complain, and all to-rate the hens: then shall ye see them peck and job at them cruelly with their beaks; and yet soon after, by way of satisfaction and to make amends again for their curst usage, they will fall to billing and kissing them lovingly, they will make court unto them and woo them kindly, they will turn round about many times together by way of flattery, and as it were by prayers seek unto them for their love."[21] Although Shakespeare was familiar with Pliny's *Natural History*, where he might have encountered this observation, he scarcely needed the Roman author to confirm the evidence of his own eyes. Like his contemporaries he was prepared to acknowledge a parallel in human affairs: "Lovers at first, / before each know another, / Will uncouth seeme, the one unto the other. . . . / And peece and peece as they see goe the guise, / Step back, or forward, in their wooeing wise."[22] Moreover, his experience probably familiarized him with the old truth embodied in Pliny's observation that among animals sexuality is healthier and less debasing than among human beings, for whereas they all have a limited breeding season and are essentially temperate, "we only are insatiable that way" (p. 121), "are given to excess and superfluity infinitely in everything, and shew the same in every member that we have" (pp. 70–71).

Far from degrading Petruchio and Kate, then, animal imagery is profoundly appropriate for a play the major action of which takes place on a honeymoon. Somehow, most criticism has contrived to ignore the fact that Kate's handling by her husband represents among other things a spirited young creature's sexual initiation by a handsomely qualified male animal. However, in this connection we must note that Shakespeare is very careful not to have Petruchio wrest conjugal rights from an unwilling bride, as one suspects the authors of some of the analogues would cheerfully have permitted. As his punning with her name suggests, Petruchio regards his "super-dainty Kate" as a choice piece, a sensual morsel, "for dainties are all cates" (II.i.188–89). Yet Kate is scarcely diminished through being eyed frankly as a sexual object, for a similar appetite is presumed to underlie her interest in him. Thus in the play's poetic pattern the starvation training that Petruchio inflicts upon her functions as a theatrical symbol for appetite denied. Instead of raping his bride, Petruchio teases her by deliberately postponing the consummation of their marriage. Their first night at their new home finds him, as Curtis informs us, "in her chamber, making a sermon of continency to her" (IV.i.170), to her stunned amazement. Tantalized with the possibility of a satisfied appetite, sleep, and the wifely garb emblematic of full-blown womanliness, Kate must learn to behave in a way that will allow the sexual act to take place properly, *ille supra, illa subter*. Indeed, there is a profound sense that only with this act is the marriage fully valid.[23]

From this felt necessity the climax of the play derives its poetic force. Kate's long speech of feminine submission is not primarily ironic—a morally obnoxious notion that would forbid us to admire domination based on honest force while sanctioning manipulation based on guile. On the other hand, her speech is not primarily a recipe for the male's domestic and social tyranny. Although the overt terms are domestic and social, and as such can be paralleled by similar Elizabethan pronouncements, within the poetic pattern of the play the speech functions mainly as a token of Kate's acquiescence to the demands and joys of sex. Her willing capitulation thus fulfills a rhythm fundamental to much comic drama. Petruchio can scarcely be expected to tup Kate onstage; Elizabethan censorship would not have tolerated an *Oh Calcutta*. But such explicitness was scarcely necessary for the men and women in Shakespeare's audience. They could be relied upon to interpret Kate's speech of submission with imaginative responsibility. They knew what to make of a tableau where she kneels to embrace Petruchio's foot and then both promptly and explicitly hustle offstage to bed. With a reigning queen on the throne, they were in no danger of taking literally Kate's extravagant verbal endorsement of male superiority, any more than one can imagine the grocer's wife in Beaumont's *Knight of the Burning Pestle* espousing such an attitude toward her husband. Indeed, to thwart any misconception on this point Shakespeare begins with Christopher Sly's bumbling, graphically illustrating the difficulty of translating what is essentially a poetic vision of male sexual supremacy into everyday reality.

In sum, criticism has generally misconstrued the issue of the play as women's rights, whereas what the audience delightedly responds to are sexual rites. When Shaw fumed that no man of decency could witness the play's end in the company of a lady without feeling embarrassment, he was preoccupied with women's suffrage when he should have been thinking of the sundry damsels whose sexual conquest he devoted himself to with frank relish. While he stayed up to write his review, one suspects that some of the couples in that turn-of-the-century audience had found a better way of reconciling their differences, at least temporarily. Petruchio and Kate's relationship is less a model for the domestic and social subjugation of women than a theatrical metaphor for a kind of male dominance often expressed in erotic contexts and not necessarily elsewhere. Indeed, properly understood, the play's ideals may not be so hostile to those of a modern feminist.[24] Far from idealizing the wishy-washy, stereotypically feminine subservience of a Bianca, Shakespeare's play is suffused with the sense that spirited and independent women like Kate make not only the best bedmates and the best helpmeets, but are simply the most fun to be with as people. In this it is of a piece with the later comedies. Shakespeare would probably have agreed with Sir John Davies in viewing not only courtship but marriage itself as a dance:

> What if by often enterchange of place
> Sometime the woman gets the vpper hand?
> That is but done for more delightful grace,
> For on that part shee doth not euer stand;
> But, as the measure's law doth her command,
>   Shee wheeles about, and ere the daunce doth end,
>   Into her former place shee doth transcend.
>
> (*Orchestra, cxii*)

One may reasonably assume that Petruchio and Kate look forward to a flexible marriage in which both partners are sufficiently secure about their sexual roles to have mastered the "delightful grace" of not being confined to them.

Notes:

1. From his introduction to the play in *Complete Works*, ed. Alfred Harbage (Baltimore, 1969), p. 83. I cite Shakespeare from this edition.
2. *Shaw on Shakespeare*, ed. Edwin Wilson (New York, 1961), p. 188.
3. *Shakespeare* (New York, 1939), pp. 48–49.
4. Harold C. Goddard, *The Meaning of Shakespeare* (Chicago, 1951), p. 68.
5. "Sources and Analogues of *The Taming of the Shrew*," HLQ, 27 (1963–64), 289–308.
6. M. C. Bradbrook, "Dramatic Role as Social Image; A Study of the Taming of the Shrew," *SJW*, 94 (1958), 139.
7. *Orchesographie*, trans. Cyril W. Beaumont (1925; rpt. New York, 1968), p. 18.
8. Henry Bullinger, *The Cristen state of Matrimonye*, trans. Miles Coverdale (Lon-

don, 1541), cited by Chilton Latham Powell, *English Domestic Relations 1487–1653* (New York, 1917), p. 27.

9. See Gerda Prange, "Shakespeare's Aüsserungen über die Tänze seiner Zeit," *SJW*, 89 (1953), 160.

10. "The Folktale Origin of *The Taming of the Shrew*," *SQ*, 18 (1966), 345–59.

11. "Folk Elements in *The Taming of the Shrew*," *QQ*, 75 (1968), 495.

12. Charles Read Baskervill, "Dramatic Aspects of Medieval Folk Festivals in England," *SP*, 17(1920), 42.

13. Baskervill, "Some Evidence for Early Romantic Plays in England," *MP*, 14 (1916–17), 480.

14. Baskervill, "Mummers' Wooing Plays in England," *MP*, 21 (1924), 230. Baskervill's studies of this material culminate in his *The Elizabethan Jig and Related Song Drama* (1929; rpt. New York, 1965), a massive compilation upon which I have drawn heavily in my following account; subsequent page references are to this volume. For additional examples from popular balladry, see R. S. Forsythe, "*The Passionate Shepherd* and English Poetry," *PMLA*, 40 (1925), 693–742; and also H. M. Richmond, "Polyphemus in England: A Study in Comparative Literature," *CL*, 12 (1960), 229–42.

15. See H. P. Clive, "The Calvinists and the Question of Dancing in the Sixteenth Century," *BHR*, 23 (1961), 297.

16. *Bartas: His Devine Weekes and Works*, trans. Joshua Sylvester (1605; facsimile rpt. Gainesville, Fla., 1965), p. 121.

17. *Complete Poems*, ed. Alexander B. Grosart, (London, 1876), I, 187 (st. lxviii).

18. Cited by Baskervill, p. 144.

19. On this subject see Audrey Yoder, *Animal Analogy in Shakespeare's Character Portrayal* (New York, 1947), esp. pp. 27, 34–35, 61. On Viret's manual see Powell, p. 140.

20. Emma Phipson, *The Animal-Lore of Shakespeare's Time* (London, 1883), p. 216.

21. Philemon Holland, trans., *Pliny's Natural History*, ed. Paul Turner (Carbondale, Ill., 1962), p. 117. For Shakespeare's familiarity with Pliny in the original, see T. W. Baldwin, "Shakespeare's Use of Pliny," in *The Parrot Presentation Volume, Essays in Dramatic Literature*, ed. Hardin Craig (Princeton, 1935), pp. 157–82.

22. Zacharie Boyd (1585?–1653), *Joseph Tempted to Adultery*, in *Four Poems from "Zion's Flowers*," ed. Gabriel Neil (Glasgow, 1855), p. 73.

23. On the legal point at issue see, in addition to Powell, pp. 6–7, William G. Meader, *Courtship in Shakespeare* (New York, 1954), p. 182.

24. For a suggestive discussion of the play along these lines, see Germaine Greer, *The Female Eunuch* (New York, 1972), pp. 220–71.

"Dispaire and Dye": The Ultimate Temptation of Richard III

Bettie Anne Doebler

During most of the play Shakespeare's Richard III undergoes little temptation in the usual dramatic sense; in the manner of the conventional dramatic Machiavel, he announces his evil course to the audience and systematically and bloodily carries it out. No audience of any time could doubt the wickedness of Shakespeare's character. Even the twentieth century with its sympathy for the physically deformed instantly recognizes Richard's evil. It is thus not surprising that Mr. Spivack in his *Shakespeare and the Allegory of Evil* can illustrate so copiously the fundamental connection between Richard and the old Vice of homiletic tragedy.[1]

Given the lack of internal conflict in the character, the audience of any time, but especially the Elizabethan audience with its view of life as a Pauline battle, would have a focus for its dramatic interest in the external conflict between Virtue and Vice that runs throughout the play and reveals ultimately the downfall of Vice as embodied in an evil king. Familiar to critics and scholars are the bloody Senecan conventions of ghosts, dreams, murders, and vengeance. Thus far unspecified, however, has been Shakespeare's use of the popular symbolic tradition of the *ars moriendi* to dramatize the example of a wicked king who has lived badly and must be shown to die badly. The conventions of the *ars moriendi* tradition are most clearly illustrated in the famous third scene of Act V, where Richard is visited by a succession of ghosts. Most striking are the psychological and dramatic implications of this scene for a Renaissance audience. These implications emerge, not simply from the obvious references to murder, death, and the supernatural, but from the iconic structure given the scene by its relation to the Temptation to Despair, part of the last battle of Satan for the soul. I do not mean to argue, of course, that the allegorical level accounts for the whole play; indeed, it is Shakespeare's genius that while involving the audience fully in a particular ethical and historical situation he can suggest an elaborate dimension of universals. In this instance, however, the particular scene moves closer to the theological dimension than much of Shakespeare and therefore requires commentary.

Shakespeare, as usual, gives the conventional material new vitality by integrating it into the dramatic context so that it enlarges both the vision of history and that of personal experience. Not only does he place it at the climax of the action, thus drawing upon the natural high feeling to which the audience has been brought, but he incorporates into the staging of the scene the familiar

iconography of the deathbed scene, which supports emotionally the metaphorical language from the *ars moriendi*. A modern audience, however, misses a
good deal of the power of the scene (and thus the play) because it is not
sensitive to the fusion of the iconographical implications of both staging and
language.

Though Shakespeare also makes brilliant and original use of the popular
ars moriendi tradition in both *Othello*[2] and *Hamlet*, his most elaborate and
explicit re-creation of its conventions occurs in the earlier history plays. Dignified by their relation to the history of England, these plays appropriately
contain formal conventions which embody many of the questions and answers
in the allegory of salvation that shaped the Elizabethan attitude toward history. History was to the Renaissance mind, even the popular mind, always
related typologically to biblical truth and was therefore close to the great questions of the salvation of the soul. For a Renaissance man, the four last things
were still important concerns. One should not then be surprised that the theme
of death would be elaborated in *Henry V* and, in parodic form, in the dying of
Falstaff in *The Merry Wives of Windsor*.[3] But the richest and most illuminating use of the art of dying well appears in the above-mentioned scene in the
last act of *Richard III*. The play was often entitled *The Life and Death of Richard the Third*, a title which suggests the powerful Renaissance belief in the
centrality of the moment of death to a man's life and character.[4]

Although the *ars moriendi* tradition on which Shakespeare drew took
various popular shapes in the sixteenth century, the most explicit form of
instruction for the battle between the Good and Bad Angels for the soul of
the dying occurs in a fifteenth-century series of eleven woodcuts published in a
block book about 1450. In addition to the text, the book contains woodcuts of
the five temptations of the dying one by the Devil, the five inspirations by the
Good Angel, and the final receiving of the soul out of the mouth of the dead
by the Good Angel. These woodcuts were at the center of the *ars* tradition
and as such were often reproduced in the sixteenth century. Paintings, also,
often portrayed the same subject matter.[5] It is the second of these temptations
that lies behind Richard's scene.

In Act V, scene iii of *Richard III*, Richard is no longer the demonic aggressor
or the conqueror we have seen in much of the play. Much of the action lies in the
middle. Although he has accomplished all his ends, mainly through the
vices traditionally most closely associated with evil—deceit and murder—
his past sins, namely the murders he has committed, rise up to accuse him
and to bring him to despair. Ironically, his victories have brought him to
defeat. Partly because this is a dream scene, Richard is passive. His passivity,
however, becomes part of the great theatrical image of the familiar deathbed

scene that would have struck the chords of memory in an Elizabethan audience. The night before his actual death, he lies in the posture of the *Moriens* in the woodcuts, a figure of death to the audience as he dreams that he is visited by all those he has murdered, including Henry VI, who lay as a corpse between Richard and Lady Anne in an early scene.

Tom Driver has interpreted this scene brilliantly in terms of the forces of history coming together in judgment upon Richard and England.[6] There is no question that the historical and cosmic cohere, especially since the scene is built upon a broad contrast in which both Richard and Richmond are seen in bed on stage, and the ghosts treat them again in a manner that suggests the old opposition between Virtue and Vice. In this instance, the scene plays up the contrast between the bad king and the future good king, a favorite opposition in the Renaissance and one built firmly upon the literature which deals with the education of the prince. To an audience whose literate members were familiar with Elyot's *Book of the Governor* and Castiglione's *Courtier* (to name only the most influential examples), the godhead working through history must have been seen to pass its inexorable judgment upon such a king as Richard, who had broken many of the laws of political philosophy as well as the laws of nature.

But there is more than the judgment of God in history in this scene; Richard comes to an internal judgment upon himself, or, at least, his mind forces him finally to a judgment which must of necessity include his past. Richard labels this judgment *conscience* in his waking speech.

Before we consider the internal judgment, however, it will be fruitful to examine the dream which culminates in Richard's meeting with conscience. Although concerned with the outward struggle between Virtue and Vice which implies the force of this moral interpretation of history, Shakespeare nevertheless always returns to the more personal allegory of salvation that Miss Tuve has called attention to.[7] It would be foolish in the instance of a history play to argue the superiority of the spiritual allegory which this scene plumbs. Clearly, the moral allegory is most often dominant in the plays that interpret the facts of history. But it is a mark of Shakespeare's dramatic genius that he also goes beyond the historical into the depths of a personal conflict to produce the tragic.[8]

The strength of Richard's personal sense of damnation in this scene is imparted to the audience through the rich adaptation of several aspects of the *ars moriendi* tradition. As indicated above, the visual images of Richard and Richmond in bed on stage with the procession of the ghosts of those murdered by Richard would in themselves have brought immediate associations for the audience with the Temptation to Despair, the most powerful scene in the *ars moriendi* series of temptations and alternating inspirations. As those familiar with the *ars* tradition know, all five of these temptations were believed to be staged by the Devil at a man's end in the last great battle against God for the soul. This scene as portrayed in the woodcuts shows the Devil bringing all the past sins of the dying man to parade before his eyes[9]— including as one of the sins the figure of a man he has murdered—with the intent to lead him to despair of the mercy of God.[10]

Although this traditional image is obviously in the background of the stage image and would undoubtedly have been seen as such by an Elizabethan audience, here, as usual, Shakespeare has selected and adapted his material creatively. The inspirations of the Good Angel in the woodcuts are absent as far as Richard is concerned. Shakespeare seems to say that Richard has already gone so far towards damnation that he cannot see or hear his own Good Angel. The inspirations of the Good Angel, however, which are part of the woodcut series, are drawn upon in Shakespeare's scene; they are so placed to comfort and encourage Richmond. This is obvious, I think, in the visual and rhetorical structure of the scene; but if anyone should miss it, Shakespeare has the ghost of Clarence associate with angels the "wronged heirs of York" by his "Good Angels guard thy battle, Live and Flourish" (V.iii.156), and, later, Buckingham assures Richmond that "God, and good Angels fight on Richmonds side" (V.iii.206). Shakespeare with this adaptation maintains the visual balance of temptations and inspirations that is part of the *ars* tradition. The *ars*, after all, was historically a tradition of comfort, in which the Good Angel through inspirations wins the soul of the *Moriens*, though in *Richard III* Shakespeare reverses the outcome.[11]

In addition to the striking visual use of the *ars moriendi* through the image of Richard lying abed on stage, Shakespeare has structured his scene rhetorically to invoke the powerful emotions associated with the theme of damnation in the Elizabethan mind. The most obvious reference to the Temptation to Despair is the repetition of the refrain "Dispaire and dye" (V.iii) by all those Richard has murdered: the ghosts of Prince Edward, son to Henry VI; King Henry VI; Clarence; Rivers, Grey, and Vaughan in a group; Hastings; the two young Princes; Anne; and Buckingham. The repetition of this refrain, with such minor variations as Edward's "Dispaire therefore, and dye" (V.iii.135) or Grey's "let thy soule dispaire," sounds a somber bell of judgment throughout the scene, especially as it contrasts with the alternative words of comfort and life addressed to Richmond.

It was, of course, commonplace to show the contrast between the death of the virtuous man and that of the wicked man. Here Richmond is not literally upon his deathbed as Richard is at least close to being, but the opposition of

Virtue and Vice, which balances that in the famous courtship scene between Anne and Richard (I.ii), suggests the kind of contrast often shown or discussed in a death scene. One of the earliest, and most clearly allegorical, instances of the contrast appears in the beautiful, early fourteenth-century De Lisle Psalter, now in the British Museum. (It was acquired by Lord William Howard, of Naworth, Cumberland, in the late sixteenth century.) An illumination of the twelve articles of faith shows, also, the soul of Lazarus being received by good angels and that of Dives by bad angels.

Shakespeare's refrain suggests the relentlessness with which Richard's past sins accuse his conscience and ultimately overwhelm him with despair; it also suggests the commonplace revelation of past sins being paraded before the sinner on his deathbed in the Temptation to Despair. The scene has, however, the narrative formality of procession or masque as Shakespeare handles it, rather than the visually simultaneous presentation of the sins as they are shown in the woodcut. The formal liturgical repetition builds gradually to the appearance of the last ghost murdered, who is Buckingham:

> *Ghost to Rich.* The first was I
> That help'd thee to the Crowne:
> The last was I that felt thy Tyranny.
> O, in the Battaile think on Buckingham,
> And dye in terror of thy guiltinesse.
> Dreame on, dreame on, of bloody deeds and death,
> Fainting dispaire; dispairing yeeld thy breath.
>
> (*V.iii.196–202*)

From the numerous allusions to the *ars* tradition one might speculate that Shakespeare did not consider this a unique or unusual dream but an instance of the preparation for death that every man must be concerned with. Though the earliest form of the *ars* might suggest that it is relevant primarily to those calmly dying in bed at home, the tradition was adapted in the hands of preachers and devotional writers to instruct people who lived less safe or stable lives. For example, the popular preacher William Perkins has an *ars* book intended for instruction to "Marriners when they goe to sea; Souldiers when they goe to battell; Women when they travell of childe."[12] And Shakespeare himself in *Henry V* (IV.i.181–89) gives Henry lines on the equal necessity for preparation for death by the soldier and the man who will die at home in bed. In fact, Shakespeare's dream scene in *Richard III* picks up from the devotional tracts the familiar idea that a man's whole life must be a preparation for his death, though the *ars* also insists, of course, that there is always time for repentance on his deathbed. Ironically, Richard's preparation has been a series of heartless murders that can only lead him to the despair the ghosts counsel. Though the *ars* has throughout most of its manifestations insisted that the grace symbolized by the Good Angel is always available to the sinner, Shakespeare's scene, like the end of *Dr. Faustus,* makes the dramatic point that Richard's preparation for death through murder has cut him off from the mercy of God by leading him to a state of despair in which he cannot throw himself upon the mercy of the Christ whom he has rejected throughout his life. He cannot believe that so great a sinner can be forgiven—such is the hopelessness of despair. In short, it is his own state of mind and soul that causes the Good Angel to be absent from his consciousness, for the dream is an image of the state of Richard's soul.

This internal dimension, which is more characteristic of allegory than of Elizabethan drama, is underlined by Richard's waking speech in which he reveals to his audience the judgment of his conscience:

> *Rich.* Give me another Horse, bind up my Wounds:
> Have mercy Jesu. Soft, I did but dreame.
> O coward Conscience! how dost thou afflict me?
> The lights burne blew. It is not dead midnight.
> Cold fearefull drops stand on my trembling flesh.
> What? do I feare my Selfe? There's none else by,
> *Richard* loves *Richard,* that is, I am I.
> Is there a Murtherer heere? No; Yes, I am:
> Then flye: What from my Selfe? Great reason: why?
> Lest I revenge. What? My Selfe upon my Selfe?
> Alacke, I love my Selfe. Wherefore? For any good
> That I my Selfe, have done unto my Selfe?
> O no. Alas, I rather hate my Selfe,
> For hatefull Deeds committed by my Selfe.
> I am a Villaine: yet I Lye, I am not.
> Foole, of thy Selfe speake well: Foole, do not flatter.
> My Conscience hath a thousand severall Tongues,
> And every Tongue brings in a severall Tale,
> And every Tale condemnes me for a Villaine;
> Perjurie in the high'st Degree,
> Murther, sterne murther, in the dyr'st degree,
> All severall sinnes, all us'd in each degree,
> Throng all to' th' Barre, crying all, Guilty, Guilty.
> I shall dispaire, there is no Creature loves me.
> (V.iii.209–32)

I have quoted this speech at length because, as Richard's answer to his dream, it sums up many elements of the tradition. A few lines later, at the actual end of the speech, he makes himself resolute to battle to the death with Richmond, and the final section of the speech moves us forward into the battle itself. But it is this earlier major section that is our concern. We notice, to begin with, that it seems a rather long set speech, following the formal, nearly allegorical structure of the dream itself. Examined internally, however, one sees that the speech is a microcosm of Richard's confrontation with his past sins and is actually the only instance where he seems to have a conscience. The very use of the phrase "O coward Conscience" reveals Shakespeare's sophisticated use of the Temptation to Despair, whereby the ancient allegory of the Devil struggling for the soul of the sinner against his Good Angel may be seen to represent an internalized struggle within the individual soul.

Contained in this struggle are lines which suggest technical or formal elements within the *ars* and which together form a rhetoric through which the speech moves. Line one, of course, suggests that upon waking, the reality of his dream convinces Richard that he is in the battle scene the next day, that he is wounded and in need of a horse, just before his actual (as opposed to psychological) death scene. The immediacy of death gives point to his calling upon Jesus' mercy. From a modern point of view, this appeal to Christ may seem odd in a character who, throughout the play, has been allied obviously with the Devil; but here again Shakespeare's audience would have found commonplace the *ars* convention that recognized the name of Jesus as the most powerful and present help against despair. Time and again, contemporary (and much older) devotional books had insisted that the greatest help for the *Moriens* at his moment of temptation was to fix his eyes upon the crucifix and, indeed, to have the crucifix itself laid upon his eyes.[13] In the woodcuts and in most of the visual representations a crucifix hangs before the eyes of the sinner to remind him that the mercy of Christ through which he suffered the passion is available to the sinner until the moment of his death, specifically the moment at which his soul goes forth out of his mouth.

Richard, however, like Faustus, hears no answer from his Savior, but turns inward to find only himself present. Shakespeare makes the experience dramatically more powerful by portraying Richard's profound sense of aloneness. Unlike the figure in the woodcuts, who is surrounded by companions supernatural and human, Richard wakes to find himself alone. The loss of all companionship is perhaps the strongest foreshadowing of hell. The ghosts have come and gone, the demons have disappeared, and Richard is left with himself: "Is there a murtherer here?" (V.iii.215).

Throughout the rest of the speech he vacillates between despair and the

last shred of self-esteem that keeps him from literal suicide. *Despair* here at
the end of the speech is used in the technical theological sense that was familiar
to Elizabethans. It was not considered simply a state of very deep distress, but
the loss of faith in the mercy of God for one's self that ultimately leads to
suicide. Throughout the speech Richard has battled with himself lest he
revenge himself upon himself. To the Elizabethan this meant a struggle with
the impulse to suicide, the worst of sins because it did not allow time for
repentance before death. The allegorical elaboration of this struggle may
be seen at its most frightening in the "Despair Canto" of the *Faerie Queene*[14]
and at the end of *Dr. Faustus*, but an Elizabethan would not have had to turn
to poetry or drama to be aware of the theological and human implications of
despair. Devotional literature had sounded its dangers, especially in the sixteenth century when the Temptation to Despair had become the most frequently developed of the last temptations by the Devil. So strong, apparently,
was the fear of being overcome by the sense of sin encouraged by the Devil
at the last illness that some devotional manuals for the sick, such as the one
attributed to Luther, had become simply compendiums of comforting biblical
passages which emphasized the unquenchable mercy of God.[15] In the oldest
conventions of the *ars* in the block books, the Inspiration against Despair shows
the angel pointing to Paul and Peter as the archetypes of great sinners who
have found mercy.

Richard, however, though he retains enough of conventional piety to call
upon the mercy of Jesus in the second line of his speech, persuades himself
by the end that the accusation of all his sins, which "Throng all to th' Barre,
crying all, Guilty, Guilty," results in despair. Most damaging of all is his
realization that he can find in himself no pity for himself:

> And if I die, no soule shall pittie me.
> Nay, wherefore should they? Since that I my Selfe,
> Finde in my Selfe, no pittie to my Selfe.
>
> (V.iii.233–35)

The entrance of Ratcliff cuts short Richard's speculations before there is any
indication of suicidal action following the recognition of despair, and the
plotted necessities for battle preparation leave little time for introspection.
The next time Richard speaks of conscience he is seeking to encourage his
forces before the battle. More importantly, however, his desperation remains
clear as he defies the very things that are moving his thoughts. Although he may
seem during the battle heroic to a modern audience, his loss of heaven and the

acceptance of damnation expressed in his speech to Norfolk would mark him as demonic to an Elizabethan audience:

> Our strong armes be our Conscience, Swords our Law.
> March on, joyne bravely, let us too't pell mell,
> If not to heaven, then hand in hand to Hell.
>
> *(V.iii.354–56)*

For it is at this point that Richard is shown by Shakespeare to have turned his back utterly upon his conscience. From a modern point of view we are tempted to see this behavior as a kind of brave whistling in the face of insurmountable obstacles, and certainly I can think of no instance where Shakespeare is totally devoid of sympathy. But the overwhelming force of Richard's speech as prepared for by the Temptation to Despair and its judgment of conscience is to show the desperation in Richard's soul—a desperation which reveals him as utterly lost. The ghosts have urged him to carry in his mind the despair that they have counseled; it is within this context that the battle takes place next day.

It may seem curious that in this very formal ghost scene with its terse speeches and many repetitions, the major one of which is the refrain "Dispaire and dye," the play rises to its emotional climax, culminating in Richard's great soliloquy. It is, indeed, one of the best instances of the way in which formality becomes necessary to contain the most passionate emotions. Vice is finally overcome; the Devil as always is seen to be his own worst enemy. Richard dies later, literally by the hand of Richmond, but the dream scene bodies forth the death of his soul. His death, in the larger sense, has been brought about by the wickedness of his own past. Always within the *ars moriendi* devotional tradition, the *Moriens* is counseled to remember that the death of the soul is far more serious than the death of the body. And just as a good death is dependent on a good life, the life of the soul depends on dying a good death. Horror at the death of the soul is one of the emotions that would be aroused in an Elizabethan audience sensitive to this tradition. At the same time the audience would respond to the justice in the conventional use of the Temptation to Despair, which shows the past sins finally being visited upon their executor. After the capitulation to despair, it would have been no surprise for an Elizabethan audience that Richard is no longer in control. Even the despairing final burst of courage is only to be taken for that. Virtue and Richmond are in the ascendency. Richard is slain without being given a final speech. If the audience thinks at all of him during the final reconciliation of the play, it is only to visualize hellmouth gaping for the hellhound. But that is not in the play.

Notes:

1. Bernard Spivack, *Shakespeare and the Allegory of Evil* (New York, 1958). Mr. Spivack chooses as his major examples of the Vice, Aaron the Moor, Iago, and Richard of Gloucester.

2. For further background on the *ars* tradition in Shakespeare's hands, see Bettie Anne Doebler, "Othello's Angels: the *Ars Moriendi*," *ELH*, 34 (1967), 156–72.

3. See Kathrine Koller, "Falstaff and the Art of Dying," *MLN*, 60 (1945), 383–86. One needs to recall the importance of death in popular Renaissance theology. Dying was seen as the supreme moment of a man's life and the last opportunity for the Devil (the Bad Angel) to ensnare the soul. Likewise, an eternity of bliss or damnation hung upon the outcome of the final battle between the Devil and the Guardian Angel (the Good Angel). Numerous books of popular devotion reiterated these points; they sold for a penny each in London, and many copies were sold every day. See Louis B. Wright, *Middle-Class Culture in Elizabethan England* (Chapel Hill, 1935), p. 235; Helen C. White, *English Devotional Literature 1600–1640* (Madison, 1931); and *Tudor Books of Devotion* (Madison, 1951) for discussion of the popularity and influence of devotional tracts. Several of the more interesting are Thomas Becon, "The Sicke Mans Salve," *The Seconde Part of the Bokes, which Thomas Becon hath made and published* (n.p., 1560); Desiderius Erasmus, *Preparation to Deathe*, no trans. (n.p., 1534); Henry Thorne, *Phisick for the Soule* (London, 1576); Sir Thomas Elyot, *A Preservative Agaynste Deth* (London, 1545).

4. *The Variorum Shakespeare*, ed. Howard Furness, XVI (Philadelphia and London, 1908). All quotations from the play will be taken from this edition. The descriptions of the deaths of great men were one strain within the *ars moriendi*, a part of the general consideration of the importance of death and, especially, the importance of how a man faced his own death. See for examples the account of Essex's last hours in a political sermon by William Barlowe, *Sermon Preached at Paules Crosse* (London, 1601), sig. C7ʳ–8ᵛ, and the more traditional account of the death of John Donne by Isaak Walton in his *Life of John Donne* (London, 1658). Even as late as the middle of the seventeenth century, the traditional interest in the way a man faced his death survived in such a form as William Somner's *The Frontispiece of the Kings Book*, which opened with a poem annexed "the In-security of Princes. Considered in an occasional Meditation upon the King's late Sufferings and Death, 1650."

5. The *Ars Moriendi* (Editio Princeps, circa 1450), facsimile edition, ed. W. Harry Rylands (London, 1881). One example of the numerous reproductions of similar woodcuts is the title page of Wynkyn de Worde's edition of Caxton's *The Book named the Royall* (London, 1506), which reproduces the Temptation to Impatience; also contained in the section on holy living and holy dying (sig. Jvʳ) is the eleventh woodcut in the series, which portrays the soul of the *Moriens* being received by angels in clouds over the bed while the demons speak in scrolls to the effect that they have been foiled again. This book, according to Miss Tuve, in *Allegorical Imagery* (Princeton, 1966), p. 57, is one of the most popular sources of medieval iconography for the Renaissance. Another late example is the painting by Hieronimus Bosch of the "Death of the Miser" in the Andrew Mellon National Art Gallery, Washington, D.C.

6. Tom F. Driver, *The Sense of History in Greek and Shakespearean Drama* (New York, 1960), pp. 87–105. Wolfgang Clemen, *A Commentary on Shakespeare's Richard III* (London, 1968), pp. 202–3. Clemen comments that Shakespeare has substituted a contrast between the two great figures in this, his climactic scene, for the dramatic conflict between persons we should expect. This substitution is perhaps the source of the frequent critical comment this scene has attracted, and it arises, I believe, from the unwillingness to recognize the closeness of the play in form to allegory and the Elizabethan concern with allegory's major theme, the salvation of the soul. See Clemen, also, pp. 203–4, for a discussion of symmetry in the staging of the scene.

7. Though I should agree with Roland Frye that Shakespeare is most concerned with the ethical present, I should also argue that for Shakespeare and his audience the great tradition of allegory provides another dimension to the mimetic mode. The medieval notion that truth is veiled is perhaps even more prominent in the Renaissance than in the medieval period and tends to draw audiences through the particular context to theological implication and back again.

8. I am not arguing that *Richard III* is a full tragedy, but the tragic implications and mood result from this kind of probing of the inner turmoil.

9. The criticism of *Richard III* contains a long argument as to whether the ghosts in the scene have objective or subjective reality, that is, literal reality upon the stage or symbolic reality as existent only in Richard's conscience. I should agree with Clemen that both possibilities are present for Shakespeare: "Shakespeare realizes that an apparition existing outside a conscience-stricken mind may, without losing its reality, at the same time be a symbol for conflicts within the mind of the protagonist." Clemen, *Commentary*, p. 215. See also Hardin Craig, *An Interpretation of Shakespeare* (New York, 1948), p. 74.

10. For a thorough discussion of the sinister aspect of Christianity which concerns attitudes towards the Devil and the Last Judgment and damnation, see Susan Snyder, "The Left Hand of God: Despair in Medieval and Renaissance Tradition," *SRen*, 12 (1965), 18–59.

11. Marlowe as well used the reversed tradition in *Doctor Faustus*. See Beach Langston, "Marlowe's *Faustus* and the *Ars Moriendi* Tradition," *A Tribute to George Coffin Taylor* (Richmond, 1952), pp. 148–67.

12. "A Salve for a Sicke Man. Or a Treatise Containing the Nature, Differences, and Kindes of Death; As also the right manner of dying well," *The Workes of that Famous and Worthy Minister of Christ in the University of Cambridge Mr. William Perkins*, I (London, 1612), 487.

13. Desiderius Erasmus, *Preparation to Deathe*, no trans. (n.p., 1534), sig. F3ᵛ. This text suggests the specific remedy of the crucifix laid upon the eyes, but the injunction to fix one's eyes upon the cross appears in numerous expressions of the *ars moriendi*.

14. See Kathrine Koller's excellent article, "Art, Rhetoric, and Holy Dying in the *Faerie Queene* with Special Reference to the Despair Canto," *SP*, 61 (1964), 128–29.

15. *Every Dayes Sacrifice* (London, 1607).

"Odde Old Ends, Stolne . . .":
King Richard and Saint Paul

JOHN B. HARCOURT

Wolfgang Clemen, remarking upon the distinctive speech patterns of Shakespeare's *Richard III*, suggests that we may find here "the first example of Shakespeare's characterizing a person through language."[1] If this is so—and I am persuaded that it is—attention must be given to Richard's most characteristic expression, his invoking of the Apostle Paul at key moments throughout the play.

> (1) Villaines set downe the Coarse, or by S. Paul,
> Ile make a Coarse of him that disobeyes.
>
> *(I.ii.40–41)*[2]
>
> (2) Aduance thy Halbert higher then my brest,
> Or by S. Paul Ile strike thee to my Foote.
>
> *(I.ii.45–46)*
>
> (3) By holy *Paul*, they loue his Grace but lightly,
> That fill his [Edward's] eares with such dissentious Rumors.
>
> *(I.iii.51–52)*
>
> (4) Off with his [Hastings'] Head; now by Saint *Paul* I sweare,
> I will not dine, vntill I see the same.
>
> *(III.iv.85–86)*
>
> (5) By the Apostle *Paul*, shadowes to night
> Haue stroke more terror to the soule of *Richard*,
> Then can the substance of ten thousand Souldiers
> Armed in proofe, and led by shallow *Richmond*.
>
> *(V.iii.250–53)*

Of this verbal peculiarity, Sisson remarks, "It was, with other personal characteristics referred to in the play, common knowledge,"[3] and other commentators seem at least tacitly to agree. Yet an examination of the sources does not establish "By St. Paul" as Richard's favorite expletive, although a hint for the trick of defining a character through such a habitual turn of speech may have been found in More's reporting of King Edward's words on his deathbed:

Whiche thinges yf I coulde as well haue foresene, as I haue with my more payne then pleasure proued, by Goddes blessed Ladie (that was euer his othe) I woulde neuer haue won the courtesye of mennes knees, with the losse of soo many heades.[4]

On one memorable occasion (the order for Hastings' execution), More reports Richard as invoking St. Paul:

> Then were they al quickly bestowed in diuerse chambres, except the lorde Chamberlen, whom the protectour bade spede and shryue hym apace, for by saynt Poule (quod he) I wil not to dinner til I se thy hed of.[5]

More is followed in this detail by Hall, Holinshed, Legge, *The True Tragedie*, and so on, as well as by Shakespeare. But in the original context, Richard is clearly using an extraordinary rather than a customary expression. He precisely emphasizes his determination that Hastings be presently executed by alluding to a well-known passage in Acts:

> And when it was day, certain of the Jews banded together, and bound themselves under a curse, saying that they would neither eat nor drink till they had killed Paul.
>
> *(Acts xxiii.12; A.V. used as source for all biblical quotes)*

It would appear therefore that Shakespeare's sources provided him with a solitary, though vivid, instance of Richard's swearing by St. Paul. To the best of my knowledge, it is Shakespeare, and Shakespeare alone, who repeats this expression so insistently that we have come to think of it as in some way characteristic of the speaker (and of no other speaker in this or any other play).

But in what way characteristic? Here the commentators are either silent or unsatisfactory. Geoffrey Carnall stresses Marlowe's view of St. Paul as "a Jugler" and concludes that Richard "is positively impersonating, with mischievous exhilaration, the unscrupulous Apostle of the Gentiles."[6] J. D. Wilson suggests that "perhaps Shakespeare adopted this as Richard's habitual oath, because its protestant flavour added a touch to the mock-Puritan piety which is one of the more entertaining masks that his Richard assumes."[7] Yet for all the Reformation's recovery of the main drift of Paul's theology, it would be rash to maintain that Protestants cited him more than Catholics did; and it is most improbable that Puritans would invoke a saint—even a New Testament one— in the first place.[8] In fact, Protestant views on such matters seem to be hinted at in Anne's scruples concerning prayer to the saintly Henry VI in I.ii.11 ("Be it lawfull that I inuocate thy Ghost"), and on a more immediately literary level, it was Catholic, not Protestant, piety that produced the wealth of medieval legend concerning Paul and the many liturgical plays dealing with his conversion. More needs to be said, I feel, about Richard's relationship to that enigmatic figure who could describe himself as "one born out of due time . . . the least of the apostles . . . because I persecuted the church of God" (I Cor. xv.8–9).

We might note, in a preliminary way, that Shakespeare's play has a curiously Pauline atmosphere. Quite apart from the oaths, we learn in I.ii.33 that Henry's body has been "Taken from Paules" to be interred at Chertsey. The Scrivener enters in III.vi, bringing the indictment of Lord Hastings, "That it may be to day read o're in *Paules*." And the curious phrase "Humfrey Hower" in IV.iii (IV.iv in most modern editions) apparently refers to a walk in St. Paul's where impecunious courtiers might be found at dinner time. In fact, "Humfrey Hower" may establish the locale of this scene as being in or near the cathedral church, a likely place of sanctuary for the three mourning women, whose straitened circumstances Richard mocks through his allusion.[9]

Beyond these topicalities, the principal Pauline concept constitutes something of an internal imagery in this play. The word *grace* reverberates from beginning to end, to a degree equalled only by *Henry VIII* in the Shakespearean canon. Often, of course, "grace" is merely a title of courtesy; at other times, it occurs in an explicitly theological context or in some half-consciously ironic usage midway between the two.[10] Richard boasts that his own language is saturated with theological allusion:

> But then I sigh, and with a peece of Scripture,
> Tell them that God bids vs do good for euill:
> And thus I cloath my naked Villanie
> With odde old ends, stolne forth of holy Writ,
> And seeme a Saint, when most I play the deuill.
>
> *(I.iii.350–54)*

But this preoccupation with the vocabulary of religion is an indirect tribute to its residual power, a perhaps involuntary recognition of the traditional moral order. The world that Richard bustles in is essentially the realm of grace. In it, man's will cannot override divine Providence, yet neither is man reduced to insignificance by fate or predestination. Richard can invoke an iron determinism as a means of winning an argument, but Elizabeth effectively counters his "All vnauoyded is the doome of Destiny" with "True: when auoyded grace makes Destiny" (IV.iii.229–30). Man may accept grace or he may reject it; and therein, for Paul, lies his freedom or his misery.

An analysis of Richard's "By Saint Paul" must of course begin by recognizing that many oaths in Shakespeare are mere noises; all the "marry's,"
" 'sdeath's," and the like surely fall within this comprehensive category. But
when an oath dominates a metrical line, it often seems to have some measure
of relevance to the dramatic context. Rainer Pineas has pointed out that in
the Protestant morality plays of the sixteenth century, "the Vice brands himself as a proponent of Catholicism . . . by his use of Catholic oaths,"[11] and an
unpublished dissertation by Walter R. Coppedge finds oaths and imprecations
dramatically significant in twelve Shakespearean plays.[12] Indeed, in a purely
a priori way, it might be maintained that since the Elizabethan playwright had
an almost inexhaustible number of possibilities to choose from in this regard,
some personal habit or associational link must have determined, though often
on a largely unconscious level, his actual selection. Since "By Saint Paul" is
used by no other character in this play or in any other Shakespearean play, we
may safely rule out authorial predilection. The specific contexts need therefore
to be more closely scrutinized, especially since the one instance of Richard's
oath in the chronicle sources is so clearly and deliberately allusive.

A point of difference between the quarto and the Folio texts of *Richard III* is
instructive here. At I.i.149, Richard swears in the quartos by St. Paul and in the
Folio by St. John. Many editors have preferred the quarto reading on the
grounds that St. Paul would obviously have been Richard's choice. But the
argument is unconvincing. The Folio "Now by S. Iohn" is left wholly unaccounted for; and if we agree that the quarto is a memorial reconstruction, it
would seem likely that actors aware of Richard's partiality to St. Paul would
have "remembered" precisely that at I.i.149, whatever the author may originally have written.

The appropriateness of "Now by S. Iohn" to the dramatic situation should
suffice to dispose us in favor of the Folio reading. Just a few moments before,
Richard has been engaged in seemingly innocent joking with Clarence on the
way to the Tower:

> O belike, his Maiesty hath some intent,
> That you should be new Christned in the Tower.
>
> *(I.i.56–57)*

In grim fact, Richard will play the role of baptizer to his brother. And, more
immediately, Hastings has just announced dismal news:

> The King is sickly, weake, and melancholly,
> And his Physitians feare him mightily.
>
> *(I.i.147–48)*

Richard replies, in feigned concern:

> Now by S. Iohn, that Newes is bad indeed.
> O he hath kept an euill Diet long
> And ouer-much consum'd his Royall Person.
>
> *(I.i.149–51)*

Richard, in short, is pleased to speak as the voice of conscience, as one commissioned to preach repentance to those in high places as well as low, to rebuke even a king for the evil of his ways. What prototype, then, might he more naturally—or more diabolically—invoke than John the Baptist?

> For Herod had laid hold on John, and bound him, and put him in prison, for Herodias' sake, his brother Philip's wife. For John said unto him, It is not lawful for thee to have her.
>
> *(Matt. xiv.3–4)*

In the earlier conversation with Clarence, Richard attributes to Edward's women—to his queen and to Mistress Shore—those powers over life and freedom that Matthew gives to Herodias and Salome. And later in the play (III. v.81), as if in continuation of this role, Richard cynically professes scruples regarding the lawfulness of King Edward's marriage.

Other instances of thematically relevant oaths in *Richard III* may be cited. In I.iii, after Margaret is derisively hooted off stage, those who remain register some reaction to her frightening curses. Richard characteristically turns the occasion to his own use by continuing in his pose of pious amiability:

> I cannot blame her, by Gods holy mother,
> She hath had too much wrong, and I repent
> My part thereof, that I haue done to her.
>
> *(I.iii.319–21)*

He thus associates Margaret, fleetingly and no doubt perversely, with the familiar image of the Mater Dolorosa. Later in the play, Buckingham prefaces his report on the assembly at the Guildhall with an angry "Now by the holy Mother of our Lord" (III.vii.3) and then proceeds to summarize his systematic besmirching of the maternal virtue not only of Elizabeth but also of the Dowager Duchess of York. Stanley also articulates his fears to Hastings with an oath:

> You may ieast on, but by the holy Rood,
> I doe not like these seuerall Councels, I.
>
> *(III.ii.84–85)*

Here the reference to the Cross suggests impending betrayal and death and is associated with councils that are reminiscent of the similarly malignant councils of the Passion narratives. Likewise in IV.iii (IV.iv), the Duchess of York, after referring to her difficult travail, counters Richard's "And came I not at last to comfort you?" with an apposite image of torment: "No by the holy Rood. . . .'" At the opening of III.iv, poor blind Hastings addresses the nobles:

> Now Noble Peeres, the cause why we are met,
> Is to determine of the Coronation:
> In Gods Name speake. . . .

Although in this speech God and Richard would appear to have been ironically merged, the play later separates the two when Richmond's "in Gods name march" (V.ii.25) neatly balances Richard's "the rest march on with me" (IV.iii.578).

In this light, let us re-examine Richard's invocation of Paul in Act I:

> Who is it that complaines vnto the King,
> That I (forsooth) am sterne, and loue them not?
> By holy *Paul*, they loue his Grace but lightly,
> That fill his eares with such dissentious Rumors.
>
> *(I.iii.49)*

Here, "his Grace" is quite possibly ambiguous: it refers, in the first instance, to King Edward, yet following directly after "By holy *Paul*," it may also suggest, maliciously, the grace proclaimed by the apostle:

Now the works of the flesh are manifest, which are these: Adultery, fornication, uncleanness, lasciviousness, idolatry, witchcraft, hatred, variance, emulations, wrath, strife, seditions, heresies, envyings, murders, drunkenness, revellings, and such like. . . . But the fruit of the Spirit is love, joy, peace, longsuffering, gentleness, goodness, faith, meekness, temperance. . . .

(Galatians v.19–23)

Or we may recall the false accusations made concerning Paul to Felix (Acts xxiv), or Paul's appeal to Caesar when he was arraigned before Festus:

> Then said Paul, I stand at Caesar's judgment seat, where I ought to be judged: to the Jews have I done no wrong, as thou very well knowest. For if I be an offender, or have committed any thing worthy of death, I refuse not to die: but if there be none of these things whereof these accuse me, no man may deliver me unto them.
>
> *(Acts xxv.10–11)*

These were familiar passages from the Prayer Book lectionary, and Baldwin reminds us that Acts was in common use as a grammar-school text.[13] Thus it may be that Richard, with unerring tactical skill, has chosen to identify himself with a scriptural figure universally recognized as an image of wrongly accused innocence. Somewhat later (II.i.80), he will say, "I thanke my God for my Humility."

But we must also consider the quite different circumstances of Richard's invocation of Paul in I.ii, when, coming on stage as the very embodiment of military energy and Renaissance *virtù*, he halts the royal funeral procession, intimidates the bearers with threats of physical violence, and compels Anne to listen to his plea. Here Richard is a commanding, knightly figure, dominating the scene by the sheer force of his dynamic and ruthless personality.

This is, to put it mildly, far removed from most twentieth-century conceptions of Saint Paul. We think of hairsplitting theological analysis, of hallucinations and raptures to the third heaven, of strange afflictions that were neurotic in origin, unless we prefer—in a diagnosis that fearlessly spans two millennia —to argue for epileptic seizures. If we are heirs to a liberal Protestantism, we think of a disturbed fanatic morbidly concerned with women's hair, who transformed the simple ethic of the Sermon on the Mount into a bizarre Greco-Oriental mystery cult—a Paul who was nothing less than the founder of the organizational church. The emphases may of course have been quite different for Shakespeare and his audiences. To take an extreme example, Marlowe was not conspicuously given to the praising of saints and apostles, yet if Richard Baines's deposition is to be trusted, even the arch-blasphemer could commend Paul's intellectual acumen, however deplorable his social ethics may have been:

> That all the apostles were fishermen and base fellows, neither of wit nor worth; that Paul only had wit but he was a timorous fellow in bidding men to be subject to magistrates, against his conscience.[14]

It may be helpful at this juncture to recall that Paul had been a stage reality long before Richard III or any other English king. The liturgical calendar had from time immemorial commemorated the Conversion of St. Paul on January 25th, and the events leading to the vision on the road to Damascus early lent themselves to dramatic presentation. A Latin liturgical play is preserved in the Fleury playbook (13th century),[15] and Hardin Craig notes that a play on this theme was diffused all over Europe and eventually appeared in English in the well-known "Conversion of St. Paul" from the Digby manuscript.[16] The stage directions of the Latin version indicate an important aspect of the dramatization of the role. At the palace of the High Priest in Jerusalem, a young man "in similitudine Sauli" is found, and with him, a retinue of armed attendants. He begins with menacing words against the Christians (based on Acts ix.1—"And Saul, yet breathing out threatenings and slaughters against the disciples of the Lord, went unto the high priest"). Upon hearing that many of the hated sect have fled to Damascus, he rises, "quasi iratus," from his seat and proceeds to the *sedes* of the High Priest to receive his commission. The dramatic Paul is thus from the beginning a youthful knight, irascible, supercharged with destructive energies.

This delineation is amplified in the English play of the late fifteenth century. After a prologue and dance, Paul makes an impressive entry: "Here entryth Saule, goodly besene in the best wyse lyke an aunterous knyth, thus sayyng":

> Most dowtyd man I am lyuyng vpon the ground!
>   Goodly besene with many a riche garnement!
> My pere on lyue I trow ys nott found.
>   Thorow the world, from the oryent to the occydent,
>   My fame ys best knowyn vndyr the fyrmament.
> I am most drad of pepull vnyuersall;
> They dare not dysp[l]ease me most noble.
>
> Saule ys my name. . . .
>
> (*Adams, p. 212*)

After "threte and menace," he accepts his charge from the High Priest; at this point, the production makes major capital out of the image of Paul as the "Man on the Horse." A stage direction sends him aside "for to make hym redy to ryde," and a low-comedy scene between Seruus and Stabularyus ensues, in a way reminiscent of Shakespeare's hostelry scenes. One of the attendant knights then brings a palfry to Paul, who mounts and prances about the *platea* before setting off to Damascus:

Here Sale rydyth forth with hys seruantes a-bowt the place [and] owt of
the p[lace].

(p. 215)

After an interval, he rides onstage again, the scene now changed to the
Damascus road. Paul repeats his intention to dispose of the Christian sectaries
"with furyous vyolacion":

> Thus shalbe subduyd tho wretchys of that lyfe,
> That non shall in-joy, nother man, chy[l]de, nor wyfe.

(p. 216)

Then the long expected miracle occurs:

> Here commyth a feruent [flame] with gret tempest, and Saule faulyth
> down of hys horse; that done, Godhed spekyth in heuyn.

(p. 216)

The power of this dramatic moment far exceeds the doggerel verse that
articulates it in the English play. Perhaps its impact upon the medieval-Ren-
aissance imagination can best be seen from the iconographic representations.
In Caravaggio's *Caduta di S. Paolo*, a resplendent knightly figure lies on the
ground after a shattering fall from a powerful horse;[17] Taddeo Zuccari shows
a youthful, helmeted figure toppling headfirst from his mount; the Paul of
Niccolò dell'Abate is more mature, with the emphasis on the ramping animal;
Michelangelo subordinates the man to center on the horse plunging toward the
rear of the painting.[18] The scene figured prominently in a humbler pictorial
tradition as we may gather from *Don Quixote* (Part II, chap. lviii): men dressed
like laborers display images of St. George, St. Martin, and St. Paul fallen
from his horse, and the Don accepts the Apostle as a true knight-errant in the
earlier portion of his career.

Those who credit Shakespeare's imagination with the creation—from the
merest hints in the chronicles and in *The True Tragedie*—of "Giue me another
Horse" and "A Horse, a Horse, my Kingdome for a Horse" might ponder the
possibility that Shakespeare is evoking an ironic reminiscence of that scriptural
scene so indelibly impressed upon the mind of Christian Europe. Much as the
custodians of the Elizabethan settlement may have preferred to present Paul
as authority for an unquestioning submission to the ruler's will, the older image
of the "aunterous knyth" maintained its vitality. Some such spirit of a Saul "yet
breathing out threatenings" seems to inform Richard's lines in I.ii:

> Villaines set downe the Coarse, or by S. Paul,
> Ile make a Coarse of him that disobeyes.

and

> Aduance thy Halbert higher then my brest,
> Or by S. Paul Ile strike thee to my Foote.

We are left now with Richard's final Pauline reference, after his terrible dream with its solemn procession of his victims' ghosts. Richard cannot shake off his fears; his words to Ratcliffe suggest how profoundly the midnight visions have disturbed him:

> By the Apostle *Paul*, shadowes to night
> Haue stroke more terror to the soule of *Richard*
> Then can the substance of ten thousand Souldiers
> Armed in proofe, and led by shallow *Richmond*.
>
> *(V.iii.250–53)*

Characteristically, he has picked up a word from his interlocutor ("Nay good my Lord, be not affraid of Shadows") and twisted it to a new meaning in order to emerge successfully from a disadvantageous situation. *Shadows* as "ghosts" or "nocturnal terrors" becomes *shadows* as "illusions," the opposite of "substance," as he boasts that nothing that Richmond can show will affect him even so much as had a silly nightmare. Perhaps an echo of the self-assured, martial Paul is present here. Yet the lines also concede, perhaps unintentionally, that shadows *have* struck terror to his soul, so that the apparitions may be construed as the penultimate stage in Richard's progressive demoralization; since IV.ii, such notes of insecurity and fear have become increasingly more insistent. This impression is continued by the remainder of Richard's speech to Ratcliffe:

> Come go with me,
> Vnder our Tents Ile play the Ease-dropper,
> To heare if any meane to shrinke from me.
>
> *(V.iii.254–56)*

Yet why should the Apostle Paul be associated with this context of fear, with this apprehension of impending death, with the grim visitants from the world beyond?

Here again, there is an aspect of the legend of St. Paul that has almost totally disappeared from our modern consciousness, but which may well have had its residual effect upon a sixteenth-century play. The apocryphal *Visio Pauli*, dating from the second century,[19] had long before developed the hint of eschatological vision in II Corinthians xii.2 into a detailed exploration of the realms of death. Few works had made a deeper impression upon the medieval imagination: in the second canto of the *Inferno*, Dante links Paul with Aeneas as his two most illustrious predecessors in journeys through hell. Theodore Silverstein writes:

> The importance of *Paul* . . . increased from the eighth century, so that it became one of the chief formative elements in the development of the later legends of Heaven and Hell which culminated in the Divina Commedia of Dante, who seems to have known some form of the Apocalypse at first hand. Echoes of it can also be heard in the works of Chaucer, who was influenced indirectly through the Purgatory of St. Patrick, its English-Irish pendent. . . . The Apocalypse of Paul found a ready audience, because it offered a complete Baedeker to the other world, embodying beliefs and legends already familiar to its readers from other current writings, and giving information as to the fate of the soul in a relatively straightforward exposition which avoided the subtleties of theology, and stressed with a concreteness readily comprehensible the justice of God, Christ's mercy, and the simple relationship between earthly morality and the rewards and punishments of the life to come. . . . Of the forty-seven extant manuscripts of the Redactions twenty-one, or nearly one half of the total number, are English; which points, if not to the origins of the abbreviated versions, at least to their special popularity in England. . . . The influence of the Apocalypse of Paul on the popular lore of Heaven and Hell ceased only when, under the influence of the Renaissance, that lore itself lost its popularity.[20]

The official Protestantism of Elizabeth's England had surely driven underground monkish apocalyptic, as it had suppressed the mystery cycles, which likewise had borrowed too heavily from the noncanonical gospels, apocalypses, and the like.[21] Yet Hamlet's swearing by St. Patrick (I.v.136) is usually glossed as a reference to part of this extended vision-literature; the eschatological details of *Lear* IV.vii, *Measure for Measure* III.i, and *Othello* V.ii ultimately derive from such sources.[22] And the greatest poem in *A Mirror for Magistrates*, Sackville's induction to the "Complaint of Henry Duke of Buckingham," had already linked medieval apocalyptic with the events of Richard's reign.[23]

The last act of *Richard III* is pervasively eschatological. Buckingham's reflections on All Souls' Day in V.i would appear to be Shakespeare's invention: there is nothing of this in Sackville, and the chronicles merely mention his day of execution without comment.[24] As Clemen notes, the emphasis is on judgment ironically fulfilled:[25]

> This, this All-soules day to my fearfull Soule,
> Is the determin'd respit of my wrongs:
> That high All-seer, which I dallied with,
> Hath turn'd my fained Prayer on my head,
> And giuen in earnest, what I begg'd in iest.
>
> (V.i.21–25)

The perturbations of his fearful soul point forward to Richard's nightmare-vision on the eve of battle:

> *Hastings*, and *Edwards* children, *Gray & Riuers*,
> Holy King *Henry*, and thy faire Sonne *Edward*,
> *Vaughan*, and all that haue miscarried
> By vnder-hand corrupted foule iniustice,
> If that your moody discontented soules,
> Do through the clowds behold this present houre,
> Euen for reuenge mocke my destruction.
>
> (V.i.6–12)

Scene i of Act V thus functions as prologue to the remainder of the action.

As Buckingham is led off to execution, the play rushes us toward Bosworth Field, so that even though the historical event took place in August, the three All Souls' Day references establish its symbolic time. That day in the church's calendar was peculiarly associated with visitations from purgatory; in fact, its observance is said to date from a vision of Odilo, the eleventh-century abbot of Cluny.[26] When the ghosts of Richard's victims come trooping in to accuse their murderer, we might remember John Dover Wilson's insistence that even for Elizabethans, the purgatory of the old religion still provided the easiest explanation for the apparitions of the dead.[27]

And so, in near hysteria, Richard cries out to Ratcliffe:

> By the Apostle *Paul*, shadowes to night
> Haue stroke more terror to the soule of *Richard*. . . .

Like the other odd old ends stolen forth of holy writ, this invocation may serve to place him, ironically, within the contexts of the religious tradition which he flouts but cannot wholly reject. Awakening from his nightmare, Richard has uttered a reflexive "Haue mercy Iesu." Now, he must try to dispel his fearful dream by remembering one who, preeminently among living men, had experienced the terrors of death's realm.

Notes:

1. Wolfgang Clemen, "Tradition and Originality in Shakespeare's *Richard III*," *SQ*, 5 (1954), 255.
2. Citations from *Richard III* are from the 1908 Furness Variorum.
3. C. J. Sisson, *New Readings in Shakespeare* (Cambridge, 1956), II, 87.
4. *More's History of King Richard III*, J. Rawson Lumly, ed. (Cambridge, 1883), p. 11.
5. More, p. 48.
6. Geoffrey Carnall, "Shakespeare's Richard III and St. Paul," *SQ*, 14 (1963), 186–88.
7. J. D. Wilson, ed., *Richard III* (Cambridge, 1954), p. xx.
8. In the Homilies, Paul's rejection of "worship" (Acts xiv.8–18) is repeatedly commended as a scriptural argument against the veneration of saints. See *The Two Books of Homilies* (Oxford, 1859), pp. 178, 230, 330.
9. The Duchess of York had sent Elizabeth to sanctuary at IV.i.106. Unlike his sources, Shakespeare does not explicitly identify the place as Westminster Abbey. More (p. 29) refers to St. Paul's as the other principal place of sanctuary in the London area. And Margaret's "Heere in these Confines slily haue I lurkt" may refer to a church as well as to the geographical entity of England.
10. As in I.iii.51.
11. Rainer Pineas, "The English Morality Play as a Weapon of Religious Controversy," *SEL*, 2 (1962), 169.
12. Walter R. Coppedge, "Shakespeare's Oaths and Imprecations," Diss. Indiana University; see *DA*, 28 (1968), 2643A–2644A. For the references to Paul, Coppedge can only ask, "Is not Shakespeare calling attention, mockingly, to the total absence of any Pauline charity in his protagonist?" (p. 36).
13. T. W. Baldwin, *William Shakspere's Small Latine and Less Greeke* (Illinois, 1944), II, 645: "If he [Shakespeare] had any Greek, he would have been particularly drilled upon *Acts*."
14. Quoted from G. B. Harrison, *Elizabethan Plays and Players* (1940; Ann Arbor, 1956), p. 120.
15. See Joseph Quincy Adams, ed., *Chief Pre-Shakespearean Dramas* (Boston, 1924), pp. 51–54.
16. Hardin Craig, *English Religious Drama of the Middle Ages* (Oxford, 1955), p. 312.
17. Reproduced in the *Enciclopedia Cattolica* (Città del Vaticano, 1948), IX, 718.
18. See Arnold Hauser, *Mannerism*, Vol. II (New York, 1965): Plate 181 for Zuccari; Plate 116 for dell'Abbate; Plate 23 for Michelangelo.

19. The *Visio Pauli* is most readily found in *The Apocryphal New Testament*, translated by M. R. James (Oxford, 1924), pp. 525–55.

20. Theodore Silverstein, ed., *Visio Sancti Pauli*, in *Studies and Documents*, Kirsopp and Silva Lake, eds. (London, 1935), p. 16.

21. Pollard and Redgrave list a *'Saint Patrick's Purgatory': A Description of the Cave So Called*, which, they tentatively suggest, was printed in London in 1635 (*Short-Title Catalogue* 19474).

22. See John E. Hankins, "The Pains of the Afterworld: Fire, Wind, and Ice in Milton and Shakespeare," *PMLA*, 71 (1956), 482–95.

23. The comments that follow the *Complaint* suggest some degree of self-consciousness about the materials it contains:

> Said one "And although he herein do follow allowed Poetes, in theyr discription of Hel, yet it sauoreth so much of Purgatory, whiche the papistes haue digged thereout, that the ignorant maye therby be deceyued.

   Cited from *The Mirror for Magistrates*, Lily B. Campbell, ed. (Cambridge, 1938), p. 346.

24. "But when he had confessed the whole facte and conspiracye upon Allsoulen day without arreignemente or judgemente he was at Salsburye in the open merket place on a newe skaffolde behedded and put to death": Edward Hall, cited in *Narrative and Dramatic Sources of Shakespeare*, Vol. III, ed. Geoffrey Bullough (London and New York, 1960), p. 284.

25. Wolfgang Clemen, *A Commentary on Shakespeare's Richard III* (London, 1968), p. 199.

26. "All Souls' Day," *Encyclopaedia Britannica*, 11th ed., I, 709.

27. See chapter 3 of *What Happens in Hamlet* (Cambridge, 1935).

"Fie What a Question's That If Thou Wert Near a Lewd Interpreter": The Wall Scene in *A Midsummer Night's Dream*

Thomas Clayton

According to one of the suggestions in so perfidious, yet brave and ridiculous, a literary monster as *Pyramus and Thisbe: The Burlesque Scenes from Shakespeare's Midsummer Night's Dream Arranged in Two Acts with Full Stage Directions and Suggestions*, "Snout, who presents the Wall, may cover himself with lime and dirt and carry a stone in his hand, or he may have a wall painted on card-board and suspended from his shoulders, in the manner in which the sandwich-men carry their advertisements" (p. 8).[1] Well, yes, but in the manner of "*the* sandwich-men" now? And what "stone"? Certainly Wall has somehow to be recognizable as such in order to manage his stage metamorphosis and effect his proper and faltering stage business. But what Wall does, how he or it stands, and how Pyramus and Thisbe stand, kneel, or otherwise "relate to each other" in relation to the Wall seem to me not so certain a piece of stage business as the Wall's-fingers' chink and cranny of most, if not all, productions and all later editions would suggest.

In this essay I mean to argue that Pyramus and Thisbe engage in their secret, black, and midnight conversation in the Wall scene (V.i.154–204), not between Wall's traditionally upheld fingers (they may still be upheld, though for other purposes), but, baldly, between his legs—that is, roughly "at the Y" as the schoolboys' joke used to have it. I cannot prove beyond a doubt that that was Shakespeare's own intended form of stage presentation, but there is much in the text to suggest that this kind of presentation would make effective dramatic and poetical sense. Moreover, the lines that bear on Wall's business make the fullest possible sense only in connection with such a critic's and actor's reading: the language and this enactment fully interpret each other, being at once reciprocally and inseparably revealing.[2]

Bawdry is surely as old as significant gesture and utterance, and double entendre is probably as old as written, and possibly as spoken, language—at any rate ever since taboos and their conventional violation, in conscious entertainment if not in actual practice, became more or less coextensive. Shakespeare in particular and the Elizabethans in general were neither squeamish nor reserved in such matters, but they were also not much given to repetitious and witless four- or *n*-lettered directness in engendering variously copulative, or otherwise erotic, and scatological drolleries. Their occasional use of quadriliterals makes the words the more effective when they *are* used, as in Trin-

culo's "Monster, I do smell all horse-piss, at which my nose is in great
indignation" (*Tmp.* V.i.199–200); or turned upon, as in the French physician
Caius's phonetically founded and anatomically confounded—yet very apt—
malapropisms in "Peace-a your tongue. Speak-a your tale" (*Wiv.* I.iv.73).[3]

The passage that might seem most to argue against my reading of the stance
of Wall, and of Pyramus and Thisbe, in the Wall scene is one that under
scrutiny may well be taken to give it some support; at any rate, the passage
is not inconsonant with my reading. The tradesmen-players are at rehearsal.

> *Quince.*   Yes: it [the moon] doth shine that night.
> *Bottom.*   Why, then may you leave the casement of the great chamber
>   window, where we play, open; and the moon may shine in at
>   the casement.
> *Quince.*   Aye; or else one must come in with a bush of thorns and a
>   lanthorn, and say he comes to disfigure, or to present, the per-
>   son of Moonshine. Then, there is another thing: we must have
>   a wall in the great chamber; for Pyramus and Thisby, says the
>   story, did talk through the chink of a wall.
> *Snout.*   You can never bring in a wall. What say you, Bottom?
> *Bottom.*   Some man or other must present wall: and let him have some
>   plaster, or some loam, or some rough-cast about him, to signify
>   wall; or let him hold his fingers thus [*he stretches out his
>   fingers*] and through that cranny shall Pyramus and Thisby
>   whisper.
> *Quince.*   If that may be, then all is well. [*takes out a book and opens it*]
>   Come, sit down, every mother's son, and rehearse your
>   parts. . . .
>
>   (*III.i.50–69*)[4]

The quartos and the First Folio read "or"—substituted here for "*and* let him
hold his fingers thus" (V.i.64)—an emendation proposed by Collier in his
annotated copy of the Second Folio and subsequently adopted by a number
of editors. New Cambridge notes that "or let" is "an easy misprint after the
twice-repeated 'or' above" (p. 122), but "and" is hardly an emendation of
unquestionable necessity, or even undoubted propriety.

This is, in fact, a crux of lexically and grammatically trivial—but con-
textually considerable—significance. With "or," Bottom seems to suggest that
Wall "hold his fingers thus," as a digital alternative, "to signify wall," instead
of having "some plaster, or some loam, or some rough-cast, about him" so to
signify. This leaves the exact demonstration of "and through *that cranny*"

somewhat uncertain; the "cranny" is not necessarily one represented by the fingers that may be meant to signify a wall. The reading with *"and* let him hold" makes "his fingers thus" differ absolutely in office and significance from the "plaster, or loam, or rough-cast" that "signify wall"; the building materials signify the wall, the "fingers thus" signify the cranny. But "and" is an editor's interpretative emendation; it is not the reading of quartos or Folio, whose "or" prompts further attention to the lines and their possible implications for clear and appropriate stage business, business of a kind perhaps different from that we are accustomed to. Of course, *"he stretches out his fingers"* is an editorial—and still ambiguous—stage direction.[5]

"Fingers thus" (ll. 64–65) tells us nothing about the digital disposition or the figure the fingers are intended to represent; the fingers and thumb might as well form a circle, a somewhat more chink- or cranny-like signification. The location of "that cranny" is uncertain in any event. The want of stage directions in the early texts tells us only that the appropriate stage business was (presumably) regarded as obvious, or perhaps "country-mattersome" enough, whatever it might have been. I see no reason to suppose that the Elizabethan dramatization was unquestionably the one that Capell imposed with his interpolation of the editorial stage direction, "Wall holds up his fingers," which so many editors have adopted after V.i.176 ("Show me thy chink to blink through with mine eyne. / Thanks, courteous wall," ll. 176–77a), and which New Cambridge has condensed to "Wall obeys" and Furnivall has transmuted to "Snout holds up his hand, with his fingers thus <" (p. 57), expanding the explanation of the symbol he had used earlier (p. 25).

Nor do I see cogent reasons to infer that *V*-shaped fingers, rather than circle-making finger(s)-and-thumb, are necessarily entailed in "thus," or that it is beyond reasonable doubt that the fingers are *meant* to signify the chink or cranny, rather than the wall itself, or, even if they are, that they are meant to signify it by being held "up." Why not "down"? The more appropriately, given the double entendre of the dialogue that by such means comes to life directly and appropriately and has no need of upheld fingers to make sense: "through that cranny"—represented by the spread legs—gives a reading, and stage image, of the meeting of Pyramus and Thisbe that realizes all the potentialities of the bizarre, the absurd, the hempen-homespun, the rude-mechanical, and the quaintly symbolic that one could wish of "the silliest stuff that ere I heard"—and saw (Hippolyta in V.i.211). And the easiest and most obvious way "to signify wall," as distinct from chink or cranny, with the fingers is by making them form a *W*. The most obvious way of doing this would be to hold the little finger with the thumb and have the other three "fingers thus"—spread. A somewhat less obvious way would be to express the Elizabethan graphic form, *VV*, by each hand's index and second fingers' forming one of the *V*'s, but, practically speaking, this would be intelligible to virtually none but highly specialized modern audiences.

The Wall scene proper affords a line in wry—and I think essentially and designedly coarse—equivocation and a spectacle of kinetic grotesquerie, that in Shakespeare has perhaps its nearest parallel in the "four legs and two voices" of "a most delicate monster" in *The Tempest* (II.ii.16–105). Formally complementing this kind of lunacy in *A Midsummer Night's Dream*—especially in the Wall scene—is "the most lamentable comedy and most cruel death of Pyramus and Thisbe," a "tedious brief scene" of "very tragical mirth" that commences with not one, but in effect two, prologues, hastes at a snail's pace and a grovelling wit into the midst of small things (but the homespuns' own), and would conclude with an epilogue but that the duke answers the question "Will it please you to see the epilogue? . . ." with an earnest conjuration to "let your epilogue alone" (V.i.126–344, 351–52, 360), sufficient suggestion, perhaps, that country matters are at stake here. The whole "lamentable comedy" has been discussed in most useful and edifying detail by—among others, of course—Kenneth Muir and J. W. Robinson. Muir attends to Shakespeare's sources in "Pyramus and Thisbe: A Study in Shakespeare's Method" (*SQ*, 5 [1954], 141–53), in which he has an especially enlightening discussion of the version of the story in Thomas Mouffet's inadvertently hilarious didactic poem, *Of the Silkewormes, and their Flies* (1599, but "probably circulating in manuscript for four or five years before that date," p. 142; discussion, pp. 147–51). In "Palpable Hot Ice: Dramatic Burlesque in *A Midsummer Night's Dream*" (*SP*, 61 [1964], 192–204), Robinson finds "the target of Shakespeare's dramatic burlesque" to be the "hybrid or transitional plays, with the demonstrative dramaturgy, current within the memory of some of Shakespeare's audience" (pp. 202–3); he arrives at this identification by pursuing the "clues" of "the title, the company, the *dramatis personae*, and the dramaturgy" of *A Midsummer Night's Dream*'s "Pyramus and Thisbe" (p. 193).

Shakespeare needed no assistance to load his "tedious brief scene" with bawdy, rollicking high jinks, but it seems quite likely that he still took some hints from Mouffet, to serve in various ways, in such lines as: "Leauing their ouall bottoms there behind, / To shewe the state of eu'ry Louers mind." Of these two lines Muir remarks that "we can hardly avoid thinking of the alternative meanings of *bottom* and *behind*," and he describes "Where many silken bottoms hangd in piles" as "even more disastrous."[6] Other such lines are: "Pyramus signifieth as much as fiery," and *something*, in "Pyramus and Thisbe," serves "to signify wall" and chink; "If also carelessnesse haue left a rift, / Or chincke vnstopped in thine aged wall"; and, most prominently among others,

When night approacht, they ech bad ech adew,
Kissing their wal apart where it was chinckt,
Whence louely blasts and breathings mainly flew:
But kisses staide on eithers side fast linckt,
Seal'd to the wal with lips and Louers glue:
    For though they were both thick and many eake,
    Yet thicker was the wal that did them breake.

Are the potentialities of such egregiously open and risible bombast resistible in such a "palpable-gross play"?

The second prologue, or Quince as Presenter "to explain the 'dumb-show' which has just entered" (New Cambridge, p. 145), introduces Wall thus:

This man, with lime and rough-cast, doth present
    Wall, that vile Wall which did these lovers sunder:
And through Wall's chink, poor souls, they are content
    To whisper. At the which let no man wonder.

                             (V.i.130–33)

Now "lime and rough-cast" signifies wall, but the chink remains. Shortly after, the Wall scene proper (ll. 154–204) follows, and the players perform, as they had previously rehearsed, their parts (III.i), most "obscenely" (I.ii.100) and now also most outrageously. I give the Wall scene in full to let the lines at first and chiefly speak for themselves; at lines 162 and 176 I call attention, in square brackets, to the fact that editorial stage directions are customarily supplied (and needed), but to "reopen" the context I omit the customary directions. "Wall steps three paces forward" (l. 153 s.d.) and begins to discharge his part.

    Wall. "In this same interlude it doth befall
That I, one Snout by name, present a wall: *155*
And such a wall, as I would have you think,
That had in it a crannied hole or chink:
Through which the lovers, Pyramus and Thisby,
Did whisper very often secretly.
This loam, this rough-cast, and this stone doth show   *160*
That I am that same wall; the truth is so.
And this the cranny is, right and sinister,
                  [Editorial stage direction: 162 s.d.]
Through which the fearful lovers are to whisper."

Theseus. Would you desire lime and hair to speak better?   *165*
Demetrius. It is the wittiest partition that ever I heard discourse, my lord.

Pyramus steps three paces forward

Theseus. Pyramus draws near the wall: silence!
Pyramus. "O grim-looked night! O night with hue so black!
  O night, which ever art when day is not: *170*
O night, O night, alack, alack, alack,
  I fear my Thisby's promise is forgot.
And thou, O wall! O sweet, O lovely wall!
  That stand'st between her father's ground and mine,
Thou wall, O wall! O sweet and lovely wall!   *175*
  Show me thy chink to blink through with mine eyne.
                              [*Editorial stage direction:* 176 s.d.]
Thanks, courteous wall. Jove shield thee well for this!
  But what see I? No Thisby do I see.
O wicked wall, through whom I see no bliss,
  Cursed be thy stones for thus deceiving me!"   *180*
  Theseus. The wall, methinks, being sensible, should curse again.
  Pyramus. No, in truth, sir, he should not. "Deceiving
me" is Thisby's cue: she is to enter now, and I am to spy
her through the wall. You shall see, it will fall pat as
I told you. Yonder she comes.   *186*

Enter THISBY

Thisby. "O wall! full often hast thou heard my moans,
  For parting my fair Pyramus and me.
My cherry lips have often kissed thy stones;
  Thy stones with lime and hair knit up in thee."   *190*
  Pyramus. "I see a voice: now will I to the chink,
    To spy an I can hear my Thisby's face.
Thisby!"
  Thisby. "My love! thou art my love, I think."
  Pyramus. "Think what thou wilt, I am thy lover's grace;
And, like Limander, am I trusty still."   *195*
  Thisby. "And I like Helen, till the Fates me kill."
  Pyramus. "Not Shafalus to Procrus was so true."
  Thisby. "As Shafalus to Procrus, I to you."
  Pyramus. "O! kiss me through the hole of this vile wall."
  Thisby. "I kiss the wall's hole; not your lips at all."   *200*

Pyramus. "Wilt thou at Ninny's tomb meet me straightway?"
Thisby. " 'Tide life, 'tide death, I come without delay."

                                              exeunt Pyramus and Thisby

Wall. "Thus have I, Wall, my part discharged so;
And being done, thus Wall away doth go."

                                                        exit Wall

According to J. W. Robinson, "by dropping three persons" from the earlier dramatis personae "and adding two personifications, the actors have joined their play to that large class of Elizabethan interludes and plays, conveniently labeled 'hybrid,' which contains a mixture of historical persons and abstractions or personifications," the most notable example of such plays being *Cambises*. "Wall, of course, is a degree more absurd as a personification than, say, [*Cambises*'] Proof, since it is so concrete" (p. 198). As *lime and hair* ("a kind of plasterer's cement, which added hair binds closely together" [*SOED*]; see V.i.164–65), Wall is indeed somewhat concrete, and resplendently absurd. Whether or not we accept Robinson's ingenious and well-argued interpretation of "Pyramus and Thisbe" as so specific and historical a burlesque, a wall played by a person and showing more of the character of the player than of the thing played is at once a preposterous spectacle and a staggeringly ill-founded conception—by the "interior" playwrights, that is, not by their creator. Wall is, at any rate, decidedly substantive, as person, place, and thing all at once. He, or it, is perhaps less a personification in the strict general sense, however, than he is one of its species, still further altered, which might be called, in this context, a "bathetic phallusy." Snout-Wall, or Wall-Snout, is at the least a piece of very free, indeed licentious, masonry and, as lines 203–4 playfully suggest, nearly the converse of the biblical "any [man] that pisseth against the wall."[7]

Wall's role seems well conceived allusively to confuse the relative and reciprocal functions of walls and persons, after the hint of the curious biblical idiom quoted. It is apt also, perhaps, that Wall is played by "one Snout" (a "nozzle"), a tinker, and as a tinker (though Snout is dutiful enough) proverbially a botcher, an idler, and a waster; and perhaps the equally proverbial "tinker's curse," or "damn," gives part of a particular point to Theseus's "The wall, methinks, being sensible, should curse again" (182).[8] Among the proverbs establishing the Renaissance "character" of tinkers are: "As lazy as the Tinker who laid down his budget [sack] to fart," "A Tinker and a Piper make bad music together," "A Tinker stops one hole and makes two (three)" (cf. T 351), "As rough as a Tinker's budget," "A Tinker's budget is full of necessary tools" (s.v. "Contemptus" in John Clarke's *Paroemiologia Anglo-Latina*, 1639), and "As merry as Tinkers" (T 345–50). A number of these Tilley records from collections printed after Shakespeare's death, but most proverbs have a considerable currency—virtually by definition—long before they find their way formally into the collections, and a group of—even "later"—proverbs attests to the currency of a constellation of conventional notions. Snout, as a tinker, is at once well- and rough-cast as Wall.

Shakespeare's conception of the dramatis persona Wall probably also owes something to proverbial lore, as well as to the biblical idiom, in such formal expressions as "Farther than the Wall we cannot go," "Look on the Wall and it will not bite you" (of the nip of hot mustard), "To be driven (To go) to the Wall," "To look upon a Wall" (that is, "To make water"; inferentially related to the biblical idiom), "A white Wall is a fool's paper," "Bare Walls make giddy housewives," "Walls . . . have ears (eyes)" (as in V.i.205), not to mention mouths, and in *A Midsummer Night's Dream* the whole of human anatomy (Tilley W 12, W 14–19), and "The Weakest goes to the wall" (W 185), which Shakespeare "quotes"—or formulates—in that form in *Romeo and Juliet*, I.i.17.

Of the prologues and the like of "Pyramus and Thisbe," New Cambridge very rightly observes that "the explanations . . . are as long as the play itself," and that, when Quince as Presenter (in V.i.126–50) "has finished, the play itself is seen to be superfluous" (pp. 144, 145). At the beginning of the Wall scene, Wall introduces his selves by paraphrasing at length and in detail (154–61) the presentation he has just been given by Quince (130–33), but he also enlarges upon his role, stance, and character by adding further specifications, to the effect that "this the cranny is, right and sinister, / Through which the fearful lovers are to whisper" (162–63). Between those two lines, Wall, according to Furnivall's editorial stage direction, "holds up his fingers thus <"; according to the New Cambridge edition "he stretches forth his fingers." The quartos and the Folio have no stage direction, and, while use of the fingers to signify a chink or cranny is reasonable, it is within the prospect of reasonable inference that the "chink" or "cranny" is the space between Wall's (not yet spread) legs; such a vertical aperture is no less appropriate, though somewhat differently so, than a horizontal one (or perhaps a bilateral pair) to be described in this homespun play as "right and sinister": "right and proper" is wanted, but "sinister" is a necessity for what New Cambridge aptly refers to as "an exquisite rhyme!" (p. 145). "Right" is forced by the primary Latin sense of "sinister" ("left") to take on a passing—and I think deliberately irrelevant—spatial sense. But "right and sinister" together also make the pointedly oxymoronic jar of simultaneous "upright and base," and other "unequal yoke-fellows" of the kind.

After Pyramus, like Wall before him, "steps three paces forward" (167 s.d.), he addresses a passionately repetitive apostrophe to the "O sweet, O lovely wall" (173, 175), which in overdue course is sufficiently moved to answer his request and is given an expression of well-mannered gratitude in Pyramus's "Thanks, courteous wall. Jove shield thee well for this!" (177). Before the line of thanksgiving, Furnivall interpolates—where quartos and Folio have no direction—the stage direction, "Snout holds up his hand, with his fingers thus <" (p. 57; "Wall obeys" in New Cambridge, p. 66). The major alternative to variations of Furnivall's (traditional) editorial stage direction is something like "Wall moves from 'attention' to 'parade rest,'" or "Wall spreads his legs," which gives a particularly bizarre and preposterous turn to the courtly Pyramus's "Thanks, courteous wall." Pyramus's earlier "wall / That stand'st between her father's ground and mine" (173–74) makes sense enough as a higher model of the "orchard wall" of Romeo's leaping (*Rom.* II.i.5), but the descriptive clause also has—appropriately for the homespuns and their play—all the terms that would as well describe not only a "sundering" wall but also an outdoor, closeting privy-chamber in the form of a jakes. Such overtones, though they cannot be insisted upon, are suitably misfitting.

Most of the rest of the argument I leave to a reading of, especially, lines 180 and perhaps 181, 189–90, 191 indirectly, 199–200 (which suggest, according to this line of interpretation, the placing of Pyramus, fore, and Thisbe aft, relative to the Wall), and 203–4. The lines speak for themselves in this connection, and, though they are somewhat coarse of tongue read so, I do not think that they are un-Shakespearean, especially in a fabric of such crudely homespun art. The last two lines of the Wall scene, 203–4, which constitute Wall's concluding couplet, are customarily followed by the editorial, and unquestionably apt and obvious, "exit Wall" and then by the much-vexed line that reads "Now is the Moon vsed between the two neighbors" in the quartos, "Now is the morall downe . . ." in the Folio (the lines are quoted from Furnivall, p. 58), and "Now is the Murall downe . . ." according to Pope's ingenious and frequently adopted emendation (second edition). Wall's concluding couplet needs little comment to call attention in general to the obvious double entendre, but it is worth emphasizing that the real force and wit of the lines seem to turn quite specifically on the—biblically and otherwise—conventional relationship between man and wall: "Thus have I, Wall, my part discharged so; / And being done, thus Wall away doth go." This is a metaphorical, dramatic, and ontological reversal of which one might well say "How wild a Hysteron Proteron's this, which Nature crosses, / And far above the top the bottom tosses" (Joseph Beaumont, *Psyche*, 85), and, with Jonson, "And [may] his Title be long foole, / That in rearing such a Schoole, / Was the founder"—

with a characteristically arch and labored Latin pun on *ars*—*arse* as English "ass" or "fool"—*longa, vita brevis* ("A Fit of Rime against Rime," 58–60).[9]

"Now is the *moon used* between the two neighbors" (Theseus, V.i.205) is surely the right reading; R. G. White and Henry Johnson argue for it (see Variorum, p. 221), and the New Cambridge reading is based on much the same grounds as Johnson's argument. Johnson and New Cambridge both call attention to the presentation of Moonshine earlier (ll. 134–37):

> This man, with lantern, dog, and bush of thorn,
> Presenteth Moonshine. For, if you will know,
> By Moonshine did these lovers think no scorn
> To meet at Ninus' tomb, there, there to woo.

Wall's departing couplet immediately follows Pyramus and Thisbe's temporarily concluding stichomythic agreement: to Pyramus's "Wilt thou at Ninny's tomb meet me straightway?" Thisbe replies, " 'Tide life, 'tide death, I come without delay" (201–2). ". . . Wall, who had served between the two neighbors, makes his explanation and leaves the stage"—reversing the terms of "go-between," it might be noted. "Thereupon the Duke says that now, in accordance with the statement of the Prologue, the Moon will be used between the two neighbors, probably in some such ingenuous way as the wall had been" (Johnson, as quoted in the Variorum, p. 221). New Cambridge asks, "Has Theseus some other meaning also? Demetrius' words—'No remedy, my lord, when walls are so wilful to hear without warning' (Tilley W 9)—seem to be a reply to a jest of some kind" (p. 146).

The points seem to me to be, first, that, now that the Wall has served his turn, the Moon will be used between the two neighbors Pyramus and Thisbe to facilitate their way to Ninus's tomb, as promised in the Presenter's précis, as Johnson says and New Cambridge agrees. Second, that, when the Wall has lost its function by being anthropomorphized ("when walls are so wilful to hear without warning") and can no longer be counted on to perform its office of wall (or jakes) between the two neighbors in standing still "between her father's ground and mine" (V.i.174), the Moon can as well be expected to perform the Wall's office, in so arbitrarily and abruptly metamorphic an atmosphere: when the man in the Wall resigns his wallhood and goes, "no remedy," perhaps, but the Moon may be a man in the Moon impersonating a wall. It is worth quoting the prologue to Lyly's *Endymion*: "we must tell you a tale of the Man in the Moon, which, if it seems ridiculous for the method, or superfluous for the matter, or for the means incredible, for three faults we can make but one excuse: it is a tale of the Man in the Moon," and "we hope in our times none will apply pastimes, because they are fancies; for there liveth none under the sun that knows what to make of the Man in the Moon. We present neither comedy, nor tragedy, nor story, nor anything but that whosoever heareth may say this: Why, here is a tale of the Man in the Moon." So with the tail of the Wall scene, and the whole tale of "Pyramus and Thisbe," for that matter.

An appropriate stance for Wall and the stone-crossed lovers that is consonant both with what is said by Wall, Pyramus, and Thisbe, in Act V, scene i, and what was set in type by the printer of the First Quarto and was retained unaltered by the editors of the First Folio is, simply and in short, and sweatly if not sweetly, thus: Wall holds up three fingers of one hand (or the three fingers of both hands) to form a *W* (or a pair of *W*'s) "to signify wall" (this is only loosely countenanced); his spread legs represent the chink, or cranny, through which Pyramus and Thisbe whisper. I find it difficult not to suppose that Shakespeare intended the Wall scene to be played approximately in this manner and saw to it that it was played so. According to what seems most directly countenanced by the text in this interpretation, the editorial stage directions—to paraphrase—should read something like:

162 s.d. Wall points to the parting between his legs (which are not spread)

or

162 s.d. Wall holds his spread fingers at the parting between his legs (which are not spread)

176 s.d. Wall spreads his legs slightly

Whether strictly Shakespearean or not, this is stage business eminently suitable for a modern production. From a strict, if ribald, Shakespearean point of view, it also makes full sense of Rabelaisian causes of guffaw implicit in the text and suggested situation without a critic's jot of textual or interpretative license more than has become "traditional" in the years' rationalizing of the same context. It is perhaps significant as well as noteworthy that the conventionally edited texts provide at once the more "modest" and the less "theatrical," and for the context, I think, less "poetical," reading. In the reading suggested here, the play's emphatically the thing. Bowdler did none but Nunnerists a service, and that a frozen. One would hope that none does the Bard a disservice by enchasing and dis-chastening him at one and the same time and custom, and that only sometimes the weakest goes to the wall: *durior lectio preferenda est*—especially when it also has, perhaps, the heartier art.

Notes:

1. *Pyramus and Thisbe* is by Frank Raymond Harris (Franklin, Ohio: Eldridge Entertainment House, 1912). The quotation of the title is from *MV*, III.iv.79–80.

2. It is an interesting measure of the tempo of the changing temper of spectator and spectacle in our time that this interpretation, which first occurred to me several years ago, seemed then, to many, almost radically "indecent" but must seem now, to most, quite decorous, and even, by the standards of current *Theatre à Nu*, pretty tame.

3. In connection with the Wall-stones of *MND* it is worth taking note of Dr. Caius's threat to "teach a scurvy jack-a-nape priest to meddle or make. . . . By gar, I vill cut out all his two stones; by gar, he shall not have a stone to trow at his dog" (I.iv.99, 100–102). Trinculo's shock-word was of course somewhat less "impolite" in Shakespeare's day than it has since become, as *SOED*'s notation "not *now* in polite use" implies.

4. Except as otherwise specified, I quote from the New Cambridge edition of *A Midsummer-Night's Dream*, ed. Sir Arthur Quiller-Couch and John Dover Wilson (Cambridge, England, 1924); both the edition and the editors are referred to as "New Cambridge." There is unfortunately no facsimile available of the quarto of 1600, the primary substantive text, but I have made use of *The Old-Spelling Shakespeare: A Midsommer Nights Dreame*, ed. F. J. Furnivall (New York, 1908), which is based on the quarto and has complete collations; *A Midsommer Nights Dreame: Facsimile Reprint of the Text of the First Folio, 1623*, ed. Henry Johnson (Boston and New York, 1888), "With Foot-notes giving every Variant in Spelling and Punctuation occurring in the two Quartos"; and also two reprints of the New Variorum edition of 1895, ed. Horace Howard Furness (the first, New York, 1963; the second, with a supplementary bibliography by Louis Marder, New York, 1966).

5. Furnivall's square-bracketed symbol, "[<]," very neatly and economically represents the usual stage business of V-spread index and second fingers on a horizontally held arm, with forearm up or out, to represent the chink.

6. Muir's note (14, p. 148) is well worth adding in this connection: "Another stanza must be given in the decent obscurity of a footnote:

> Yea, when all other creatures looked base,
> As mindful onely of their earthly foode:
> Or else as trembling to behold the place,
> Where iudge eternall sate, and Angells stood:
> Then humane eyes beheld him face to face,
> And cheekes vnstain'd with fumes of guiltie bloud,
>   Desir'd no maske to hide their blushing balles,
>   But boldly gaz'd and pried on heau'nly walles.["]

7. See I Sam. xxv.22, 34; I Kings xiv.10, xvi.11, xxi.21; and II Kings ix.8 (Authorized Version of 1611, closely modeled on the Bishops' Bible of 1568 that Shakespeare is supposed to have used most for his earlier plays, while he drew on the Geneva Bible of 1560 for his later).

8. "Tilley" gives, as A 4, "He swears like an Abbot (falconer, lord, tinker)," making no explicit reference to a "tinker's curse," in Maurice P. Tilley, *A Dictionary of the Proverbs in England in the Sixteenth and Seventeenth Centuries* (Ann Arbor, Mich., 1950).

9. In his edition of *The Complete Poetry of Ben Jonson* (Garden City, N. Y., 1963), William B. Hunter, Jr., notes the pun (p. 168n).

A Midsummer Night's Dream:
Analogous Image

RICHARD HENZE

Robert W. Dent, James L. Calderwood, and C. L. Barber leave one little doubt that imagination in love and art is the major theme of *A Midsummer Night's Dream*.[1] Much of the play is, as Dent says, Shakespeare's defense of poetry, presented indirectly and without emphasis on "strictly moral edification" (p. 129). One might expect that theory to repeat the common Renaissance hybrid of Aristotelian imitation and Platonic inspiration that one encounters everywhere, from Scaliger, Mazzoni, and Tasso to Puttenham, Sidney, and Harington. William Rossky very well summarizes that hybrid: "poetic feigning is a glorious compounding of images beyond life, of distortions which are yet verisimilar imitations, expressing a truth to reality and a higher truth also, controlled by the practical purpose, the molding power, and, in almost every aspect, by the reason and morality of the poet."[2] Shakespeare's defense, however, is notable in that its emphasis is not on higher truth, ideal image, and the author's moral intention so much as it is on credible images analogous to the images of life. Without following in the footsteps of Dent, Calderwood, and Barber any more than necessary, I want to show that, while Shakespeare's dramatized theory of the imagination resembles somewhat that of Sidney and his colleagues, it reveals itself finally to be a theory of the creative imagination unfettered by either Platonic frenzy or Aristotelian ideal imitation as it demonstrates the selective imitation that will proceed from observation of life, experience with common images, and awareness of the nature of the audience's relationship to a play.

Sidney's description of the poet's art, known by his English colleagues and dependent on his Italian fellow theorists, is characteristic of Renaissance theory of the imagination in its blend of Aristotelian and Platonic ideas about the imagination. Sidney describes the poet's golden world where the wit wings unfettered and where the poet is a maker, as Puttenham says, "such as (by way of resemblance and reuerently) we may say of God."[3] But Sidney also recommends, as do his Italian precursors, Aristotelian ideal imitation of this less than golden world. The hybrid blend pervades Sidney's essay. The poet may with "learned discretion" create "formes such as neuer were in Nature, as the *Heroes, Demigods, Cyclops, Chimeras, Furies*, and such like" as parts of a properly imaginative whole, and the poet's only limit will be the "Zodiack of his owne wit" (p. 156), his ability, as Theseus says, to roll his eye from heaven to earth; but the poet's "learned discretion" is a "diuine consideration of what may be, and should be" (p. 159); and the poet's freedom to create is the freedom to ideally imitate: "that the Poet hath that *Idea* is manifest, by deliuering them forth in such excellencie as hee hath imagined them. Which deliuering forth also is not wholie imaginatiue, as we are wont to say by them that build Castles in the ayre: but so farre substantially it worketh, not onely to make a *Cyrus*, which had been but a particular excellencie, as Nature might haue done, but to bestow a *Cyrus* vpon the worlde, to make many *Cyrus's*, if they wil learne aright why and how that Maker made him" (p. 157).[4] Here Sidney disagrees with Theseus's statement in *A Midsummer Night's Dream* that the poet creates from thin air and that the vision that results is insubstantial pageant, incredible and soon faded, hardly a nearly divine creation or even an imitation of what should be and may be.

Theseus, however, is not the spokesman for Shakespeare's doctrine of the imagination. Critics have noted the inadequacy of his rather commonplace Platonic description of the imagination, with his poet in a "fine frenzy" compact with lunatic and lover.[5] But so strong is the impact of his words that even those critics who find his words neither illuminating nor distinguished are liable to admit that his words on the poet do "bear witness to the poet's power to unite the divine and worldly and to the power, in impressing form on airy nothing, of his creative imagination,"[6] or that the dreamer is, after all, "one of the company of the lunatic, the lover, and the poet, for like them he gives to airy nothing a local habitation and a name."[7] Theseus does describe the lunacy of lovers' fantasies accurately; one only has to remember Titania's transposition of Bottom into lover to agree with him. But the very distrust of imagination that makes him a rational, if overbearing, critic of lovers' fantasies makes him an inept critic of the products of poetic inspiration. He echoes the old phrases and old criticisms: his poet, like Plato's in *The Phaedrus*, is in a "fine frenzy" and creates visions from nothing.[8] A rational and gracious man, especially the duke of Athens, will be able to enjoy the most uninspired dramatic efforts of his most unimaginative subjects, for, after all, good drama is no different from bad drama; all poetic visions are bushes turned bears, incredible shadows of the substantial real, and Theseus has imagination enough to amend them all.

When Theseus and Hippolyta disagree about the credibility of "fairy toys," their disagreement indicates not so much a conflict between basically Platonic and Aristotelian concepts of imaginative matter, as Howard Nemerov suggests (p. 641), as it indicates the distance between Theseus's distrust and Hippolyta's trust of imaginative matter. Theseus is more gracious toward imaginative efforts shortly when he opposes Hippolyta's sensible but ungracious condemnation of Bottom's play, but even there his attitude, as Nemerov points out, is confidently contemptuous toward imaginative material in general. But Theseus's contempt fails to answer Hippolyta's remark that all the tales of the night seem credible, and Theseus's confident "imagination" fails to "amend" the efforts of Bottom. The play, finally, not Theseus, has the authoritative last word about imagination.

Theseus's assertion that "fairy toys" and, by implication, poetic creations in general, are false and should not be believed, is, like most of his statements about imaginative material, an ancient objection, given authority by Plato in *The Republic* where he accuses even Homer of falsehood, and encouraged by both Aristotle's and Plato's location of the imagination in the lower soul, a belief echoed by many a medieval mind and finally taken up by the Puritans. The answer to that objection that Shakespeare furnishes is similar to Sidney's, which, in turn, echoes that of the Italians Castelvetro and Fracastoro.[9] Sidney says that poets are not concerned with facts, that "of all Writers vnder the sunne the Poet is the least lier, and, though he would, as a Poet can scarcely be a lyer. . . . he nothing affirmes, and therefore neuer lyeth. For, as I take it, to lye is to affirme that to be true which is false" (p. 184). Then Sidney adds the Aristotelian touch: the poet tells, not what is, "but what should or should not be: and therefore, though he recount things not true, yet because hee telleth them not for true, he lyeth not" (p. 185). Sidney's answer, popular before Sidney, remains popular after. Sir John Harington, for example, agrees with Sidney, whose essay he knew: "but Poets neuer affirming any for true, but presenting them to vs as fables or imitations, cannot lye though they would."[10]

A Midsummer Night's Dream's answer to Theseus's objection goes beyond Sidney even while it agrees with him that poets, effective poets at least, do not affirm or lie. Rather than being a liar, the poet is an artist and craftsman who makes use of observation and experience as well as imagination, who need not be literally realistic but is imaginative enough to recognize the likeness between fairy and Mustardseed and ass and Bottom, who is not so much unique in his imaginative vision as he is like other men, who differs from other men not in imaginative perception but in the ability to express an image so that it will awaken imaginative perception on the part of his audience, and who, in this rather complex imaginative ability, is greatly unlike the lunatic, lover, or dreamer.

Both Shakespeare and Sidney emphasize the poet's ability to deliver an image. But Shakespeare, unlike Sidney, modifies Theseus's skeptical Platonism without alluding to Aristotle's doctrine of ideal imitation, even though Shakespeare was surely aware both of contemporary trends in the theory of imagination and of the limitations of that theory, particularly in its insistence on the poet's nearly divine creative power and his need to achieve ideal or verisimilar imitation. *A Midsummer Night's Dream* lacks the Aristotelian insistence on ideal imitation of the artist's imagination. The artist is distinct from other men not in his ability to give form to airy nothing, nor in his ability to ideally imitate, but in his ability to express imaginative forms that all men see.

Puck describes the process whereby one arrives at an image of a fairy. He points out that it is a mortal tendency to imagine that fairies exist: the gossip who spills her drink; the aunt who misses her stool; the average Elizabethan afflicted by any apparently mischievously caused mishap likes to blame fairies for his own slips:

> And sometime lurk I in a gossip's bowl
> In very likeness of a roasted crab,
> And when she drinks, against her lips I bob
> And on her withered dewlap pour the ale.
> The wisest aunt, telling the saddest tale,
> Sometime for three-foot stool mistaketh me;
>
> (II.i.47–52)[11]

Titania too points out the tendency of mortal men to blame fairies' brawls for bad weather: because Oberon and Titania have quarreled, "the green corn / Hath rotted ere his youth attain'd a beard" (II.i.94–95). Shakespeare's fairies act as mischievous or quarrelsome fairies are commonly thought to act, and the very congruity between poetically expressed image and common image makes the fairies acquire the appearance of reality that Bottom's Pyramus lacks. That appearance of reality results from neither frenzy nor divine vision; it results from the artist's ability to express a common image. Puck has, as his fellow fairy notes, the very shape of Puck (II.i.32).

Shakespeare is not, then, as Ernest Schanzer says, doing "something that he had never done before" by creating fairies from "airy nothing";[12] instead he illustrates the common tendency to give human attributes to mysterious forces and describes small, mischievous, and anthropomorphic fairies like the commonly experienced image.

That dependence of image on experience Aristotle, too, points out in his psychology of the imagination;[13] *A Midsummer Night's Dream* seems more dependent on Aristotle's rather old-fashioned psychology than on his more new-fashioned and popular *Poetics*. In order to imagine a bush a bear, Aristotle points out, one needs to have seen a bush and a bear. Imagination does not have the exact dependence on experience that memory has; we may imagine what we have not experienced—a purple cow, for example—but, in order to imagine the purple cow, we need to have experienced both purple and cow. Whether or not we consider the fairies more than poetic dream depends on our power to imagine their reality, and that power depends on the poet's success in presenting an image that accords with our experience and expectations. Theseus would have it that, for drama to be effective, only the audience need be imaginative. Sidney emphasizes, as Shakespeare does also, that the poet, to be effective, needs to be able not only to imagine, but also to deliver his image in such a form that others, who are not poets, will be able to share in the poet's vision; the poet, unlike the lover or lunatic, can deliver his visions in such "excellencie as he hath imagined them" (p. 157) that he can keep the old men from the chimney corner and the children from play, not because his visions are fairy toys, but because they are credible and substantial.

Part of the substance of Shakespeare's fairies is given them by Bottom by the very fact that he sees the fairies, and, his asininity notwithstanding, lends them a credibility that they would not have if he were not to see them. Bottom lends them that credibility exactly because we imagine him to be a very reasonable, literal-minded, simple creature who demands facts and refuses to be fooled into any imaginative tremors: "I shall desire you of more acquaintance, good Master Cobweb. If I cut my finger, I shall make bold with you" (III.i.185–87). Yet Bottom's literal-mindedness is itself a vision constructed by the dramatist out of nothing but words that describe an image of an asinine man analogous to the common image of such. The fact that Bottom sees the fairies is not, therefore, an affirmation that fairies exist; rather that fact proves, once again, that fairies exist insofar as we imagine that they exist, and Bottom aids that imaginative process by being apparently reasonable and seeing the fairies, even though he never admits that they are fairies, and, therefore, encourages us to imagine that they do, indeed, exist. But first we have to imagine that Bottom exists, for Bottom is part of the midsummer night's dream too, and as part of that dream, his existence is just as questionable or just as real as that of the fairies or even of Pyramus.

As the playwright presents congruous images of fairies, lovers, Theseus, and Bottom, the images acquire credibility. For Bottom surely is as an ass should be, unimaginative, overbearing; we can readily imagine him with an ass's head, for with such he has that congruity that Pyramus lacks. But the fairies, lovers, Theseus, and Hippolyta all have that congruity too. Puck points it out for the fairies; Hermia, Helena, and Lysander prove once again that the course of true love never did run smooth; gracious Theseus is gracious; self-controlled Hippolyta is self-controlled; all of Shakespeare's creations are sufficiently analogous to the common image to be credible.

Bottom, on the other hand, who insists on affirming that Pyramus is real and believes that a man in a lion's skin will frighten the ladies because they will indeed think he is a lion, does not present credible images. The distinction that Bottom does not make, and that Theseus fails to make also, is that between judgment and imagination, a distinction that Aristotle, Sidney, and *A Midsummer Night's Dream* all carefully indicate. Plato, in *The Republic*, lacks that distinction too: when the soul, says Plato, like an eye, turns away from truth "towards the twilight of becoming and perishing, then she has opinion only, and goes blinking about, and is first of one opinion and then of another, and seems to have no intelligence."[14] Opinion and image are the same. Aristotle, on the other hand, separates conception and imagination, for "imagination is under our control, and can be stimulated when we wish. . . . Conception, on the other hand, is not under our control. For it must be either false or true."[15] Imagination and judgment do occur together, but they are not the same: we imagine the sun "to be a foot in diameter, whereas we believe it to be larger than the inhabited earth."[16]

Images can be false, but only if we, like the lunatic or dreamer still asleep, judge things really to be as we imagine them to be. Otherwise, imagination deals not with the true or false, but with the possible. Everyone except a child knows the difference, says Sidney, between imagining that the stage is Thebes and believing that it is Thebes, but not everyone in *A Midsummer Night's Dream* perceives that difference.

Bottom can himself distinguish imaginary from real; he knows that fairies belong in poems, not in the Athenian woods. His problem is not that of a lunatic like Don Quixote, who destroys a puppet show in order to save "brave Don Gaiferos and the fair Melisendra" even though they are just pasteboard figures.[17] Don Quixote, unlike Aristotle, would not be able to continue to think the sun larger than the world when it seems just a foot in diameter, for he is exactly the lunatic described by Theseus. The distinction that Don Quixote cannot make, a poet must perceive, as an audience must also, if it is a sane audience. While Bottom is not a lunatic like the Don, he does not allow his audience to be as sane as he is: "for the more better assurance, tell them that I Pyramus am not Pyramus, but Bottom the weaver. This will put them out of fear" (III.i.21–23). That will put them out of imagination. Bottom thinks that the audience will consider Bottom dead and that the lion will become to the audience a real lion. He fails to allow the audience to distinguish for themselves between Thebes and the stage and, lacking that allowance, destroys the audience's ability to imagine the stage to be Thebes. Theseus's problem is as bad as Bottom's but not the same. Theseus, thinking that the poet intends the stage to be Thebes, allows the audience sanity but makes the poet a lunatic.

Since Bottom insists on pointing out the unreality of his production, he forces us to judge it to be unreal, and once our common sense tells us that it is silly stuff, its credibility is lost. The credibility of the lion depends on its being enough like a lion and roaring enough like a lion to enable one to imagine for a moment that it is a lion even though one knows that it is only Snug, the joiner. As the Canon says in *Don Quixote*, "fiction is all the better the more it looks like the truth, and gives the more pleasure the more probability and possibility there is about it,"[18] and poetic truth, Shakespeare indicates, is no more than the commonly perceived image. If Bottom were to play the lion and "roar you as gently as any sucking dove," the power to imagine would be lost, for the lion would be so obviously not a lion that even a child's imagination could not be fooled. Likewise, we can overlook the fact that Flute has "a beard coming" if Flute can act enough like a woman generally and Thisbe particularly to allow us to ignore the obvious fact that Flute is a man and imagine, for the moment, that he is indeed Thisbe. The audience should be able to imagine that, for, after all, the actor playing Helena, as well as the actor playing Flute, perhaps had a beard coming; Flute accords with the common image to that extent.

As Flute points out, actors do intervene between audience and playwright. The play clearly indicates that intervention, and, as Bottom demonstrates in his failure as an actor, the actor, like the playwright, must be able both to perceive and to express the imaginative idea if the play is to be successful. For Bottom's audience to imagine a credible Pyramus, Bottom the actor's Pyramus, as well as Bottom the playwright's Pyramus, must be credible. If the playlet is to succeed, both the playwright's and actor's Pyramuses must be believably dead. Long before Bottom rises with his assurances that he is alive, the imaginative expression has been so disrupted that the audience's imaginative perception is prevented. Imagination cannot amend the matter; judgment takes over, and judgment tells us that this is the silliest matter that we have ever heard.

If we are able to reject *A Midsummer Night's Dream* as easily as Theseus rejects fairy toys and Hippolyta dismisses Bottom's efforts, then we become so suspiciously reasonable that we no longer enjoy the specifically imaginative participation in the drama that Theseus describes. The only "imagination" that remains will be Theseus's grace, no imagination at all; and grace may fail too, as it does in Theseus's case. If the matter on stage is Bottom's "Pyramus and Thisbe," Pyramus and Thisbe will be so improbable that one's common sense will not allow one to imagine them to be real; they may be very funny as burlesque, but one will not imagine them to be credible as Pyramus and Thisbe. If, on the other hand, the matter on stage is Oberon and Titania, we may well agree with Hippolyta that it is credible. Of course, our relationship to Bottom and his fellows is not the same as Theseus and Hippolyta's relationship to Pyramus and Thisbe. While Hippolyta finds it difficult to force her imagination to amend the production as Theseus recommends because of its incongruity and her judgment, we are able to suspend such judgment of Bottom himself and to imagine the reality of Bottom even as we reasonably recognize burlesque of Pyramus to be burlesque. In fact, the success of the reason in recognizing burlesque for what it is makes easier the success of imagination in accepting Bottom's reality, for Bottom's unconscious burlesque is exactly the touch that we expect of Bottom. Because Bottom seems so credible, his Pyramus seems so incongruous; because Pyramus seems so incongruous, Bottom seems credible. Reason recognizes the incongruity, imagination decides the credibility.

Theseus does not recognize, as Hippolyta does, how thoroughly bad drama prevents imagination and awakens judgment. When he judges the acceptability of drama by the simple motives of the workmen instead of by the quality of the art itself, Theseus erases all standards and transposes "to form and dignity things base and vile," a transposition no more acceptable in art than in love.[19] The play is, as Hippolyta points out, silly stuff. The worst in this kind are worse, and imagination alone will not amend them and make them equal to good art. We cannot "imagine no worse of them than they of themselves," for they are simply not "excellent men" as far as acting and playwriting go. Where the best drama will encourage imagination as well as grace, the worst drama will awaken common sense with a recognition of incongruity. And, with the return of judgment, imagination's power to amend will be lost.

The love plot, on the other hand, itself a play within the play, is not such silly stuff, partly because it accords with common images, partly because its actors—Hermia, Lysander, Helena, and Demetrius—are able to act.[20] Under the influence of imagination, they pass easily from one role to the next. Bottom, on the other hand, remains always Bottom.

Yet that is what one expects of Bottom; thus he is credible, and he is credible because the poet in *A Midsummer Night's Dream* is well aware that the process of turning Bottom into ass or Mustardseed into fairy depends on the poet's ability to imagine and present a Bottom and a fairy analogous to the images of Bottom and fairy that all men may have. Thus, Shakespeare, without repeating the contemporary hybrid theory of the imagination, answers Theseus's account of the poet's "fine frenzy" that turns bush into bear.

Shakespeare does allow the poet a creative imagination, creative not in its divineness or frenzy, but creative in its very workmanlike ability to deliver an image analogous to the images of most men yet unique as an artistic expression of that image. The emphasis is on the artist's expression; and in placing the emphasis squarely on that, Shakespeare emphasizes the poet's art rather than his inspiration and imitation of common images instead of ideal imitation of the truth. Through such art, the poet does attain truth or whatever one wants to call the poet's expression of common images, the image of a Bottom as an ass forever, not just for two hours' traffic of the stage; the image of Theseus, properly gracious and rational, but no satisfactory drama critic; the image of mischievous Puck. All these images are credible while imagination rules in the theater or in the study, even if they seem like far-off mountains when one has other things to judge or imagine. Uniquely able to deliver such credible images, Shakespeare's poet is less a divine creator than Sidney's, less frenzied than Theseus's, but he is just as surely a poet.

Notes:

1. Robert W. Dent, "Imagination in *A Midsummer Night's Dream*," *Shakespeare 400*, ed. James G. McManaway (New York, 1964), pp. 115–29; James L. Calderwood, "*A Midsummer Night's Dream*: The Illusion of Drama," *MLQ*, 26 (1965), 506–22; C. L. Barber, *Shakespeare's Festive Comedy* (Princeton, 1959), pp. 139–62.

2. "Imagination in the English Renaissance: Psychology and Poetic," *SR*, 5 (1958), 73.

3. "The Arte of English Poesie," in *Elizabethan Critical Essays*, ed. G. G. Smith (London, 1904, 1967), II, 3.

4. "An Apologie for Poetrie," in *Elizabethan Critical Essays*, I, 150–207.

5. See, for example, Howard Nemerov, "The Marriage of Theseus and Hippolyta," *KR*, 18 (1956), 633–41; Ernest Schanzer, " 'A Midsummer Night's Dream' and 'Romeo and Juliet,' " *NQ*, NS 2 (1955), 13–14; D. F. McKenzie, "Shakespeare's Dream of Knowledge," *Landfall*, 18 (1964), 40–48.

6. McKenzie, p. 46.

7. Schanzer, "The Moon and the Fairies in *A Midsummer Night's Dream*," *UTQ*, 24 (1955), 245.

8. See William A. Nitze, " 'A Midsummer Night's Dream' V.i.4–17," *MLQ*, 50 (1955), 495–97.

9. See J. E. Spingarn, *A History of Literary Criticism in the Renaissance*, 2nd ed., rev. (New York, 1925), p. 34.

10. "A Briefe Apologie of Poetrie," in *Elizabethan Critical Essays*, II, 201.

11. Citations from Shakespeare are to *The Complete Works of Shakespeare*, ed. George Lyman Kittredge (Boston, 1936).

12. " 'A Midsummer Night's Dream' and 'Romeo and Juliet,' " p. 13.

13. "On Dreams," in *Aristotle's Psychology*, trans. W. A. Hammond (New York, 1902), p. 239.

14. *The Republic of Plato*, trans. B. Jowett, 3rd ed. (Oxford, 1892), III, 209.

15. Aristotle, "On the Soul," in *Aristotle's Psychology*, p. 106.

16. "On the Soul," in *Aristotle's Psychology*, p. 108.

17. *Don Quixote*, part II, chap. 26.

18. *Don Quixote*, part I, chap. 48.

19. McKenzie, p. 47.

20. See Calderwood, pp. 513–14.

Prince Hal: Mirror of Success

NORMAN COUNCIL

The idea that Shakespeare arranges the three principals of *1 Henry IV* in a quasi-Aristotelian paradigm of the theme of honor has been so often iterated and has so dominated the teaching of the play that it has become a virtual truism. Hotspur, the argument goes, represents the excess, Falstaff the defect, and Hal the virtuous mean of the honorable man.[1] This has been an appealing idea, I suspect, partly because it is a convenient scheme and partly because if it were valid it would help to demonstrate either that Shakespeare had read his Aristotle or that the humanist revival had made the Aristotelian ethic so commonplace as to be dramatically useful. Unfortunately, this reading of the play does not bear scrutiny.

The difficulty is that Falstaff's and Hotspur's behavior in no way resembles any of the definitions of defective and excessive desire for honor which a wide variety of late sixteenth-century books on honor provide. *The Nicomachean Ethics* had defined honor as the "reward of virtue" and had clearly established that the desire for honor is to be judged excessive, moderate, or defective according to desert:

> honour may be desired more than is right, or less, or from the right sources and in the right way. We blame both the ambitious man as aiming at honour more than is right and from wrong sources, and the unambitious man as not willing to be honoured even for noble reasons. . . .[2]

This statement of the idea was accepted with no substantial modification by most of the writers on honor of the 1580s and 1590s.[3] Robert Ashley, a faithful Aristotelian eager to lay claim to his "Peripatetike" authority, whose essay *Of Honour* is likely to have been precisely contemporary with Shakespeare's play, makes it clear that Shakespeare's contemporaries think of a man's "deservings" as the mark by which he is to be judged ambitious or base minded. "The ambitious ys blamed because he hunteth after honour . . . more greedilie than he ought," Ashley argues, and "contrariwise the abject or base minded ys . . . reprehended bicause that notwithstanding his good deservings he refuseth honour . . ." (pp. 41–42). Half a dozen other books or essays written in the decade surrounding Shakespeare's play deal in more or less detail with the question of an excessive desire for honor; they all rely on the basic assumption that honor is a positive good which man has an ethical responsibility to pursue,

and that his pursuit of that honor is to be judged excessive or defective according to his deserts. John Norden's *The Mirror of Honor* is within a year of being
contemporary with Shakespeare's play, and the danger to true honor which he
remarks is typical. "Among the rest [of the dangers] *Pride* is the most perillous
. . . whereby . . . highest reputation [may be] blemished, and that by assuming
more of it selfe to it selfe, then reason or desert will yeeld, from other men"
(p. 22). *The Courtiers Academie,* translated from the Italian in 1598, defines
honor as "that ardent heate which enflameth the mind of man to glorious enter-
prises making him audacious against enemies, and to vices timorous," a Platonic rather than an Aristotelian definition (see below, p. 133), and the same
work consistently justifies only that desire to acquire honor appropriate to the
virtuous deed performed.[4] The idea is a commonplace of such books as these.
George Whetstone's *The Honorable Reputation of a Souldier,* printed in 1585,
and William Segar's *Honor Military and Civil,* printed in 1602, display the
consistency with which standard opinion judged a man excessive in his desire
for honor only if he sought more honor than he deserved. Whetstone's book
praises nineteen illustrious generals, emperors, and kings who, though of
mean parentage, were justly elevated to such honorable eminence for valorous
and virtuous deeds, but it damns the ambitious desire for unjustified honor.
In one place, for instance, Whetstone describes the honor due soldiers who give
their lives to protect the state, but he warns against "the difference between
rash and necessary bouldnesse." Martial virtue consists in doing the state
service; "willfull falling upon the enemies sword, is reduculous, daungerous,
and very dishonorable."[5] Segar's book is more a codification of the rules of
honorable combat than a definition of the idea, but he expresses the familiar
assumption when he bewails the decadent tendency of the aristocratic young to
"glory in the ancient badges, titles, and services of their Auncestors" even
though they have done nothing to warrant the honor they claim.[6] In as august
a place as Hooker's *Laws of Ecclesiastical Polity* and in as unexpected a place as
Thomas Nashe's bid for epic respectability one can observe the ubiquity of this
basic judgment. In Book 7, Hooker justifies the rewards of honor, even to
ecclesiastics, by arguing that "there is always some kind of virtue beneficial,
wherein they excel who receive honour." "Degrees of honor," he concludes,
"are distinguished according to the value of those effects which the same
beneficial virtue doth produce."[7] And in *Christs Teares Over Jerusalem* Nashe
reverts to a characteristic tone to condemn as ambition the desire for honor
beyond one's—in this case martial—deserts. "Ambition," Nashe asserts, "hath
changed his name unto honor. . . . Not the honour of the fielde (Ambitions
onely enemy) . . . but Brokerly blowne up honour . . . honour bestowed for
damned deserts."[8]

These are only a few instances, of course, but most of these writers are expounders rather than explorers of the orthodox, so they do provide evidence that standard opinion among Shakespeare's contemporaries viewed honor as a positive good—indeed, the "chief good," as Ashley, following Aristotle, defines it—to be pursued, and that those contemporaries judged a desire for honor excessive or defective according to desert. If Shakespeare's intent had been to shape his play according to the Aristotelian paradigm which Tillyard and others have proposed, he would surely have used the widespread understanding of Aristotelian excess and defect which was available to him. He did not, however, create Hotspur as "the ambitious man . . . aiming at Honour more than is right and from wrong sources," Falstaff as "the unambitious man . . . not willing to be honoured even for noble reasons," nor make Hal a resolution of those extremes as the man who desires honor "from the right sources and in the right way."

Falstaff never rejects reward, merely the established honorable ways of getting it; far from unambitiously declining to be honored for noble deeds, he, ambitious to a fault, very much wants to be honored for ignoble deeds. Shakespeare makes the distance between Falstaff's deserts and his desire for reward clear in both the comic and the chronicle scenes. Most explicit are his early exaggerations of the numbers that robbed him and his later demand for reward for killing Hotspur. In the first instance every line he speaks seeks unwarranted acclaim for his presumed swordsmanship and heroism.

> I am a rogue if I were not at half-sword with a dozen of them two hours together. I have 'scaped by miracle. I am eight times thrust through the doublet, four through the hose; my buckler cut through and through, my sword hacked like a handsaw—*ecce signum*. I never dealt better since I was a man. All would not do. A plague of all cowards!
>
> (II.iv.162–68)[9]

In the second instance he demands an honorable title on the pretense of having killed Hotspur.

> There is Percy: if your father will do me any honour, so; if not, let him kill the next Percy himself. I look to be either earl or duke, I can assure you.
>
> (V.iv.138–42)

Compared with Falstaff's, Hotspur's desire for honor is modesty itself, for he quite consciously bases his claim on what he and everyone else in the play, enemies and allies, consider to be noble deeds. Even King Henry sees Hotspur's honor as unstained.

> A son [Hotspur] who is the theme of honour's tongue;
> Amongst a grove, the very straightest plant;
> Who is sweet Fortune's minion and her pride. . . .
>
> (I.i.80–82)

And throughout the play "honour's tongue" sounds Hotspur's name again and again. The emphasis is consistently on the honor his valor deserves, and though Henry will see it as the beginning of rebellion, he never questions that Hotspur deserves the "never dying honor" he has gained "against renowned Douglas!"

If Hotspur and Falstaff do not represent Aristotelian moral extremes for Hal to stand between, clearly the play employs the pervasive theme of honor in a different manner than has commonly been supposed. Reference to sixteenth-century books on honor demonstrates a remarkable similarity between the details of behavior which they describe as the perfect attributes of the honorable man and the behavior which Shakespeare gives Hotspur. This close and consistent similarity makes it clear that Hotspur's role in the play is to embody perfectly the principles of a rigorous and well-defined code of honor; he is a "mirror of honor," as many contemporary "remembrances," exempla, and biographies of illustrious men used the phrase. Conversely, Shakespeare makes Falstaff consciously and explicitly reject the code of honor, the demands of which he understands but repudiates; rather than representing a defective desire for less honor than he deserves, therefore, he dramatizes the nature and consequences of a reasoned rejection of the pervasive code of honor. Shakespeare keeps Hal aloof from the demands of the code, for, rather than accepting or rejecting the code, Hal exploits it for his pragmatic purposes; he is thereby made, much as Shakespeare had done with Bolingbroke in *Richard II*, a mirror of success.

Regarded in this way, the issue of Falstaff's cowardice is moot. At the heart of the code of honor is the principle that honor is more precious than life. Various tracts elaborately codify the forms of honor to be sought and protected through virtuous deeds; virtually all of them begin with the assumptions that honor originates in martial valor done in service of the state and that death is to be preferred before the dishonor caused by defeat or flight. "In any case," Count Romei has Gualinguo remark in *The Courtiers Academie*, "a man of honor should alwaies preferre death, before infamous saftie. . . ."[10] William Segar, in the preface "To the Reader" in *The Booke of Honor and Armes*, lightly makes the same assumption before he goes on to codify the rules of honorable combat. "The matter of content is Iustice and Honor. For love whereof, we shun no care of minde, losse of wealth, nor adventure of life."[11]

This position is familiar enough, and, of course, a number of Shakespeare's characters, with varying degrees of sincerity, maintain it. Shakespeare confronts Falstaff with this honorable demand in both the chronicle and comic scenes and has him consistently and consciously reject it. Falstaff's catechism on honor is in response to Hal's saying, as he exits, that Falstaff "owest God a death." "Well," Falstaff muses, " 'tis no matter; honor pricks me on." But he will have none of the widespread contention, displayed by the books on honor, that honor is more precious than life. It is but a nominal ethic, and clearly not worth dying for.

> What is honor? A word. What is in that word honor? What is that honor?
> Air.

"Insensible" to the dead, unavailable to the living, honor is finally for Falstaff "a mere scutcheon" (V.i.127–41). By having Falstaff place such emphasis on honor's belonging uniquely but only ornamentally to the dead, Shakespeare produces a character who is perfectly aware of the central demand which honor makes but who is unwilling to pay the price. Poins has Falstaff exactly, and distinguishes him from his more simply motivated fellows, when he anticipates Falstaff's flight from Gad's Hill.

> Well, for two of them, I know them to be as truebred cowards as ever turned back; and for the third, if he fight longer than he sees reason, I'll forswear arms.
>
> (I.ii.177–80)

At Shrewsbury, Falstaff's actions represent, as do those of the other major characters, precisely the attitude toward honor which he has maintained throughout, and the "battle" in which he engages there displays the logical conclusion of that attitude. Shakespeare gives Falstaff some very curious things to do at Shrewsbury; none of them furthers the plot, but the substitution of the bottle of sack for his pistol, the ragamuffin soldiers that Falstaff leads to slaughter, and the battle with Douglas all display a character who by rejecting all the principles of honor has become the antithesis of the honorable man. The ragamuffin soldiers and the sack are convenient instances of Falstaff's satisfying his desire for personal gain and his appetites rather than the demands of honor. As one would expect, the tracts on honor provide evidence that the code considered physical appetites a danger to a soldier's valor, and therefore his honor. Whetstone's *Honorable Reputation of a Souldier*, for instance, remarks that "When the body is stuffed with delicates, the mind is dull, and desirous of

ease, which is the undoer of a Souldier . . ." (sig. Dii). One is reminded of the
Antony whom Octavius Caesar admired because he, faced with famine, "didst
drink / The stale of horses and the gilded puddle / Which beasts would cough
at." "And all this," Caesar concludes in comparing the honorable Antony with
Cleopatra's Antony, "(It wounds thine honour that I speak it now) / Was borne
so like a soldier that thy cheek / So much as lank'd not" (I.iv.61–63, 68–71).
When Hal discovers the bottle of sack in place of Falstaff's pistol we are given a
clear if somewhat crude symbol of the deliberate inversion of honorable values
which Falstaff represents: he prefers sack, let alone life, before honor. Hal
throws the bottle at him and exits; Falstaff replies quite explicitly to this protest
at his dishonorable behavior.

> I like not such grinning honor as Sir Walter hath. Give me life, which if I
> can save, so: if not, honor comes unlooked for, and there's an end.
>
> (V.iii.58–61)

Falstaff's counterfeit death is but the logical conclusion of the role he has played
in regard to honor, for, by escaping from Douglas by feigning death, Falstaff
is made quite literally to act out his preference for life before honor. Dead,
Falstaff could anticipate only the "mere scutcheon" which honor can provide,
and the battle with Douglas provides Falstaff with the opportunity to act upon,
and to articulate, his priorities.

> 'Sblood, 'twas time to counterfeit, or that hot termagant Scot had paid me,
> scot and lot too. Counterfeit? I lie, I am no counterfeit: to die is to be a
> counterfeit, for he is but the counterfeit of a man, who hath not the life of
> a man: but to counterfeit dying, when a man thereby liveth, is to be no
> counterfeit, but the true and perfect image of life indeed.
>
> (V.iv.112–19)

If Falstaff be the true and perfect image of life, Hotspur is certainly the true
and perfect image of honor. Seemingly inconsequential details of Hotspur's
behavior, from the outset of the play and in each of the eight scenes in which
he appears, coincide so exactly with schematic descriptions of the honorable
man which had become commonplace in the 1580s and 1590s that there seems
little doubt that Shakespeare was at pains to create Hotspur as the perfect
mirror of honor. This definition of the character represents a consistent modification of the Hotspur who appears in Holinshed. The chronicle characteristically provides the Percys with what little justification for rebellion it allows by
reminding its readers that Henry is a usurper, "for the which [usurpation]

undoubtedly both he, and his posteritie tasted such troubles, as put them still in daunger of their states, till their direct succeeding line was quite rooted out. . . ."[12] Shakespeare, on the other hand, carefully keeps Hotspur distinct from his fellow rebels by making his act of rebellion—and all his other actions —a consequence of his adherence to the principles of honor.

Hotspur's definition as the honorable man begins with King Henry's demand for the Scottish prisoners and his refusal to ransom Edmund Mortimer. Shakespeare develops the definition from a hint found in Holinshed that the king's demand is counter to the code of honor. Holinshed reports the quarrel, noting that only "Mordake, Erle of Fife, the Duke of Albanies sonne" had been delivered to the king in spite of the king's having demanded all the prisoners, and concludes by explaining the reason for the Percys' angry response to this demand.

> Wherewith the Percies [were] sore offended, for that they claymed them
> as their owne proper prisoners, and their peculiar prayes. . . .[13]

The idea that prisoners are a source of honor (the peculiar praise of the captors) and the idea that prisoners, until ransomed, remain the property of their captors unless, as in the case of the earl of Fife, their royal blood requires their being delivered to the king—these had been commonplace enough aspects of the code of honor to permit using the ideas on the stage at least as early as *The Spanish Tragedy*. Half of Kyd's second scene, it may be recalled, debates whether Lorenzo or Horatio deserves the honor and reward of Balthazar's capture. The king, appropriately, adjudicates the issue; Hieronimo pleads Horatio's case, "enforced by nature and by law of arms,"[14] and the king awards the ransom and arms to Horatio, the captor, but the noble prisoner to Lorenzo, the prince. Indeed, Shakespeare returns to the matter of honorable and appropriate disposition of prisoners in the final scene of *1 Henry IV*, so this particular aspect of the codes of honorable behavior is a familiar enough subject for the stage. A. R. Humphreys notes that "the law of Arms" permits Hotspur to keep his prisoners and cites *Pallas Armata* (1683) as authority.[15] He might also have cited William Segar, whose *Honor Military and Civil* details the various rules of honor governing the escape or ransom of prisoners and is more nearly contemporary with the play,[16] though indeed the idea that ransom and other honorable rewards under the law of arms belong to the captor is implicit in most books on the subject. In Shakespeare's first scene, he has King Henry explicitly describe Hotspur's prisoners as "honorable spoil" and has Westmoreland call Hotspur's victory "a conquest for a prince to boast of." It is consequently a clear affront to Hotspur's honor to demand more from him than is the king's due, namely, the royal earl of Fife, whom Hotspur has appropriately agreed to surrender. Shakespeare further develops that affront by introducing Hotspur's account of the popinjay lord into the quarrel. The emphasis has been on Hotspur's "well deserved honor," and Hotspur's description of the arduous battle makes clear the distinction between honor "dearily bought" on the battlefield, as Whetstone's *Honorable Reputation* phrases it (sig. Bv), and the foppish posturings of the popinjay.

Shakespeare's introduction of this curious lord also assists in the resolution of the most troublesome problem implicit in his effort to define Hotspur as a mirror of honor. Honor, in both its tangible and intangible forms, is ultimately dispensed by the monarch, and rebellion is per se a dishonorable act. The popinjay lord provides Hotspur with an honorable excuse for not having delivered his prisoners and thus delays his open rebellion. He is, of course, still denying the king his prisoners when he describes the popinjay's behavior to the king, but again Shakespeare has Henry pursue the matter in a manner designed to affront Hotspur's honor without raising the question of his loyalty. When the king describes Hotspur's brother-in-law as "the foolish Mortimer, / Who, on my soul, hath wilfully betray'd / The lives of those that he did lead to fight . . ." (I.iii.79–81), the insult is clear. This, after all, is what Falstaff does at Shrewsbury.[17] Hotspur's reply implies no disloyalty to the king; it, rather, defends Mortimer's honor. He has "dearily bought" his honor in battle with Glendower, and the honor so gained cannot, for Hotspur, exist side by side with the dishonorable treachery of which Mortimer stands accused.

> He never did fall off, my sovereign liege,
> But by the chance of war: to prove that true
> Needs no more but one tongue for all those wounds,
> Those mouthed wounds, which valiantly he took
>
> . . . . .
>
> In changing hardiment with great Glendower.
>
> . . . . .
>
> Then let not him be slander'd with revolt.
>
> *(I.iii.93–111)*

The king does not argue. He answers Hotspur with a deliberate insult, accusing him of lying and dismissing him with a belittling form of address.

> Thou dost belie him, Percy, thou dost belie him.
>
> . . . . .
>
> Art thou not asham'd? But sirrah, henceforth

Let me not hear you speak of Mortimer:
Send me your prisoners with the speediest means,
Or you shall hear in such a kind from me
As will displease you.

(I.iii.112–20)

It is this affront which arouses Hotspur's celebrated ire, but this is a quite appropriate, not an excessive, response for the honorable man to make. The speech in which Hotspur thinks "it were an easy leap, / To pluck bright honour from the pale-faced moon" is set in a scene which displays Hotspur's irascibility, not his ambition, and sixteenth-century books on honor usually associate anger with honor. This is probably the speech which most occasioned the quasi-Aristotelian reading of the play, but if the urge to see the play as being organized according to a specific philosophical scheme remains overpowering, the Platonic description of man's tripartite soul provides a considerably more satisfactory explanation of Hotspur's outburst—and of Falstaff's sensuality—than does the Aristotelian ethic. In the fourth book of *The Republic*, Plato identifies the desire for honor with "passion or spirit," which combines with the rational and the concupiscent to make up the three principles of the soul. This identification is expressed in the sixteenth century in various places; Robert Ashley is the most explicit:

And seeing (as Plato will have yt) the powre of the mind ys of three partes, whereof one ys named reason, another termed anger, and a third called desire. . . . Honour seemeth to have his root and beginning of the second, for . . . the desire of honour . . . as Plato saieth, cometh out of the angry part of the mind. . . . So we see that men of great mindes are much moved with honour, but that the abject, and baser sort be nothing affected therwith because the sence and feeling thereof ys geven only to those that are of high spirite.

(*Of Honour*, p. 40)

This connection between the irascible passion and the desire for honor is a more likely origin of Hotspur's outburst in Act I than the theory of Aristotelian excess, just as the Platonic idea that concupiscence uncontrolled by reason turns to sloth is a more likely origin of Falstaff's behavior. One has only to recall Pyrochles' ire in Canto 5 and Cymochles' sloth in Canto 6 of Book II of *The Faerie Queene* to observe a more explicitly allegorical use of the Platonic idea and, indeed, to observe how excessive irascibility was apt to be portrayed in a sixteenth-century poem. By having Hotspur respond with this angry outburst to the affronts Henry has leveled against his honor, Shakespeare continues to define Hotspur as a man who perfectly embodies all the characteristics of the honorable man.

The dilemma remains that it is the king who has affronted Hotspur's honor, and disloyalty to the king is itself a source of dishonor. Hotspur, after all, has just asked that Mortimer not "be slander'd with revolt." At the next moment in the play, after King Henry's insult and Hotspur's angry response have been displayed, Shakespeare has Worcester and Northumberland quite illogically tell Hotspur, as though he were ignorant of the fact, that Mortimer has been proclaimed heir to the throne by Richard. This delayed information provides a resolution to the dilemma, even if it be realistically improbable that Hotspur would not know of Mortimer's claim, for Hotspur can now see his virtuous and therefore honorable duty to be the restoration of Mortimer as the rightful king. The long speech that he is given in response to this information emphasizes the injustice of which his father and uncle have been guilty in aiding Bolingbroke and the honor which they have consequently lost.

> Shall it for shame be spoken in these days,
> Or fill up chronicles in time to come,
> That men of your nobility and power
> Did gage them both in an unjust behalf
> (As both of you, God pardon it! have done)
> To put down Richard, that sweet lovely rose,
> And plant this thorn, this canker, Bolingbroke?
>
> (I.iii.168–74)

This justification is as much a part of Hotspur's honorable behavior as his anger. By providing it, Shakespeare allows Hotspur to pursue his honor by righting the wrong which he considers Bolingbroke, with the Percys' aid, to have committed.

> yet time serves wherein you may redeem
> Your banish'd honours and restore yourselves
> Into the good thoughts of the world again;
> Revenge the jeering and disdain'd contempt
> Of this proud king. . . .
>
> (I.iii.178–82)

Restoring their tarnished honor is never, of course, Northumberland's or Worcester's motive. They, rather, are concerned to protect themselves against the king, who they know will find "a time to pay us home." Hotspur's commitment to the principles of honor isolates him from the pragmatic workings of his allies and of his enemies, leaving him with a naïveté which will have disastrous consequences for him at Shrewsbury.

In the first of the scenes at Shrewsbury Shakespeare develops a virtually self-contained dramatic pattern which reflects in small both the nobility and the practical shortcomings of Hotspur's commitment to honor. He enters with Douglas, who calls him "the king of honour," to discover that Northumberland's forces will not arrive. Holinshed had indeed reported wholesale defections from the rebels' cause, and Shakespeare dramatizes these defections as the occasion of a series of choices which Hotspur must make. He responds to the first news in practical fashion; he knows that his father's absence weakens their army, but argues that they now have a refuge should fortune turn against them. "Were it good," he asks, "To set the exact wealth of all our states / All at one cost?" (IV.i.45–47). But Shakespeare has Worcester argue that Northumberland's absence might "breed a kind of question in our cause. / . . . We of the off'ring side," he argues, "Must keep aloof from strict arbitrement, / And stop all sight-holes, every loop from whence / The eye of reason may pry in upon us" (IV.i.68–72). This slur on the justice of their cause touches Hotspur's ruling concern, and Shakespeare gives him a characteristic reply. Northumberland's absence, for Hotspur, now "lends a lustre and more great opinion, / A larger dare to our great enterprise. . . ." Vernon enters to this with his glittering description of the king's forces and of the renascent Prince of Wales, news which fills Hotspur with eager expectation of the honorable actions of war, the same sort of eager irascibility Shakespeare has him display in his response to the king's insult in Act I.

> They come like sacrifices in their trim,
> And to the fire-ey'd maid of smoky war
> All hot and bleeding will we offer them.
>
> .   .   .   .   .
>   I am on fire
> To hear this rich reprisal is so nigh,
> And not yet ours!
>
> *(IV.i.113–19)*

Shakespeare delays Vernon's other news, Glendower's absence, until after Hotspur's compelling desire for honor has been thus brought forward, by which time no deterrent of a merely practical kind can compete. The scene begins with Hotspur's debating the effect on the rebellion of Northumberland's

sickness; it concludes with Hotspur so committed to honor that he can happily
dismiss success—and life—to serve it.

> Doomsday is near; die all, die merrily.
>
> *(IV.i.134)*

Yet this compulsion is but part of the perfect image of honor, corresponding
to Hotspur's outburst in Act I, scene iii. There, Shakespeare has Hotspur justify
his opposition to the king by describing it as a virtuous and therefore honorable
effort to restore Mortimer; he reintroduces that justification into the play in
Hotspur's next scene. After a brief scene which introduces Falstaff's pitiful
soldiers, the action returns to the rebel camp to disclose a Hotspur who, though
eager for battle, is prepared by the end of the scene to send his uncle to negotiate with the king. Much of this scene is taken up by a long speech which
Shakespeare gives Hotspur to rehearse the Percys' role in Bolingbroke's usurpation and the dishonor they have consequently suffered.

> In short time after, he deposed the King,
> Soon after that, deprived him of his life.
>
> .   .   .   .   .
>
> To make that worse, suffered his kinsman March,
> Who is, if every owner were well placed,
> Indeed his king, to be engaged in Wales
>
> .   .   .   .   .
>
> Disgraced me in my happy victories
>
> .   .   .   .   .
>
> Rated mine uncle from the Council board,
> In rage dismissed my father from the Court
>
> .   .   .   .   .
>
> And in conclusion drove us to seek out
> This head of safety. . . .
>
> *(IV.iii.90–103)*

No narrative or expository purpose is served by this rehearsal, for the information it provides is already common property. It does, however, provide the
necessary balance to Hotspur's honor. In his prior scene, Hotspur's honorable
impatience for the glories of battle was emphasized; here his sense of the virtuous intent which justifies his actions and of the dishonor the king has offered
him is the central concern. Hotspur's offer to negotiate a settlement thus balances the grandiose "Die all, die merrily" with which Shakespeare concludes

the previous scene. At the end of the next scene in which Hotspur appears these two aspects of his honor are merged in a single speech. After further characterizing Hotspur by having Worcester assume that he would abandon the war should "the liberal and kind offer of the King" be made known to him, Shakespeare gives Hotspur a speech which precisely states the balance between his eager pursuit of honor and his justification of that pursuit.

> O gentlemen, the time of life is short!
> To spend that shortness basely were too long
> If life did ride upon a dial's point,
> Still ending at the arrival of an hour.
> And if we live, we live to tread on kings,
> If die, brave death when princes die with us!
> Now, for our consciences, the arms are fair
> When the intent of bearing them is just.
>
> (V.ii.81–88)

Hotspur thus enters battle the picture of an honorable man, secure in conscience and indifferent to death if it add honor to an otherwise valueless life. His death is displayed as the logical consequence of this attitude. Hotspur, wishing that Hal's "name in arms were now as great as mine," only regrets that Hal is not a more honorable foe, and his death, immediately juxtaposed with Falstaff's feigning death, is as precisely the true and perfect image of honor as Falstaff's action is the image of life. He dies pronouncing the basic article of the creed of honor.

> I better brook the loss of brittle life
> Than those proud titles thou hast won of me:
> They wound my thoughts worse than thy sword my flesh. . . .
>
> (V.iv.77–79)

As Shrewsbury is the scene where Shakespeare brings Hotspur and Falstaff to the conclusions demanded by the roles in the theme of honor he has given them to play, so it displays the successful consequences of Hal's role. Hal, throughout the play, is kept aloof from the intricate demands of honor that so compel Hotspur and repel Falstaff; Shakespeare makes Hal concerned with honor only as a means to other ends. Hal sounds the theme of honor in his first soliloquy, which, if viewed in terms of the code of honor, is more devious than the "Aristotelian" reading of the play assumes. That soliloquy, the interview with his father in Act III, and his actions at Shrewsbury comprise Hal's explicit part in the theme of honor, though some comic commentary on the theme may be intended by the scenes at Gad's Hill and The Boar's Head. Hal's part in the theme of honor is, then, conspicuously less extensive than Hotspur's, and, though Shakespeare uses extranarrative scenes such as Hotspur's conversation with Kate and argument with Glendower to expand the idea of Hotspur's commitment to honor, he consistently displays Hal in the comic scenes as indifferent to, or even amused by, the sort of honor which Hotspur so thoroughly serves. Success is Hal's motive, and he differs from Hotspur and Falstaff in his capacity to use honor as a means to that success.

Hal's first soliloquy announces his attitude toward honor; he intends, by engaging in low behavior, to delay the acquisition of honor so that, when acquired, his reputation will seem grander than it otherwise would. The soliloquy is familiar, but attention to its metaphoric and literal statements that reputation is but a facade that can be advantageously enhanced demonstrates it to be a thoroughly pragmatic plan to exploit apparent dishonor for advantage, rather than a statement of a sort of nascent nobility awaiting education or maturity. The images all emphasize the effects of unexpected behavior on observers; Hal nowhere considers the inherent worth of the behavior he plans.

> So when this loose behavior I throw off,
> And pay the debt I never promised,
> By how much better than my word I am,
> By so much shall I falsify men's hopes;
> And like bright metal on a sullen ground,
> My reformation, glittering o'er my fault,
> Shall show more goodly, and attract more eyes
> Than that which hath no foil to set it off.
> I'll so offend, to make offence a skill,
> Redeeming time when men think least I will.
>
> (I.ii.203–12)

This attitude toward honor differs from Hotspur's in its intention to exploit, rather than serve, the code of honor. Instead of considering honor an ideal to which life itself must be sacrificed, Hal sees an honorable reputation as a useful political commodity, and he intends to exploit appearances to increase his grip on that commodity. To comprehend the difference between this attitude and the one Shakespeare gives Hotspur, one only need realize that most of the books on honor considered it so demanding a code that they argue that a single dishonorable act irrevocably destroys one's honor. *The Courtiers Academie* addresses itself to the problem with a typical judgment.

The greater sort of men hold their honor so deare, as that they dare not do evill, for feare of the losse thereof, knowing that it once only being lost, can never be recovered.

(Sig. P2)

Nor is the company one keeps to be taken lightheartedly by the man bent on honor. James Cleland's advice to his student reader describes "with what company [they] should converse."

Companie changeth mens manners. . . . Hee that keepeth company with the wicked shal hardly escape without blemish, either in life or credite.[18]

Certainly the jealous and constant protection of honor is a familiar enough characteristic among noble figures of the Elizabethan stage for this manipulation of it to be marked in Hal. This first soliloquy introduces to the audience a unique character who, though no malignant Machiavel, intends to exploit appearances to gain success.

Hal's interview with his father develops the plan. As Falstaff will serve as a contrast, so Hotspur will serve as a means to the reputation Hal intends to acquire. It is an unusual scene. After a series of scenes filled with Hotspur's honorable outbursts or with rapid, witty, and irreverent dialogue between Falstaff and Hal, this scene stands alone with its long, discursive speeches both analyzing the nature and prophesying the effects of Hal's behavior. Save for the single, if major, fact that Henry can after this count Hal as a trusted ally, the scene contributes nothing to the narrative. It is clearly a pause, put right at the center of the play, designed to unfold the basic characterization of Hal which his first soliloquy has implied.

Hal is first and last his father's son, for, though Shakespeare here keeps Henry IV from recognizing the fact, they share the same assumptions and aspirations. Henry has two kinds of complaints about Hal's behavior, and the fact that the first is dealt with perfunctorily and the second at detailed length further defines the sort of response which Shakespeare gives Hal to the code of honor. Henry finds it incomprehensible, unless Hal be divinely sent to punish him, that Hal should match the "greatness of [his] blood" (III.ii.16) with "such inordinate and low desires" (III.ii.12). Hal, discrediting the excessive reports that "base newsmongers" have brought to Henry's ear, admits to the faults of youth and asks forgiveness. They are speaking the language of honor, for throughout sixteenth-century discussions of the idea runs the assumption that those of high birth have a correspondingly greater responsibility to be honorable. Castiglione's *Courtier* is one example.

For it is a great deale less dispraise for him that is not born a gentleman to
faile in the acts of vertue, then for a gentleman. If he swerve from the
steps of his ancestors, hee staineth the name of his family.[19]

William Segar sounds the same note.

And the more highlie he be borne, the worse reputation he meriteth, if
he cannot continue the honor left him by his Ancestors.
                                        (*Booke of Honor and Armes*, sig. F1–F2)

Shakespeare gives only thirty lines to Henry's concern about, and Hal's apology
for, having ignored these basic demands of honor. Hal asks forgiveness, and
Shakespeare has Henry dismiss the issue with a brief "God pardon thee!"
before he turns the scene to its central concern with the practical effects of
Hal's action, a concern which will occupy the next 130 lines.

Henry complains that Hal's actions have ruined "The hope and expectation
of thy time" (III.ii.36) and quite unabashedly asserts that the manipulation of
public reputation is necessary to success. As in Hal's first soliloquy, the terms
in which Shakespeare has the Lancasters express themselves emphasize their
assumption that honor is a useful facade which may be put on or off, like masks,
at will. Hal has there determined that his reformation should "show more
goodly, and attract more eyes / Than that which hath no foil to set it off."
Henry here describes the effects of having "dressed" himself in humility.

> And there I stole all courtesy from heaven,
> And dressed myself in such humility
> That I did pluck allegiance from men's hearts,
> Loud shouts and salutations from their mouths,
> Even in the presence of the crowned King.
> Thus did I keep my person fresh and new,
> My presence, like a robe pontifical,
> Ne'er seen but wonder'd at, and so my state,
> Seldom, but sumptuous, show'd like a Feast. . . .
>   (*III.ii.50–58*)

Conspicuously absent from this is any sense that an honorable reputation,
being the mark of virtuous action, is valuable in itself, an attitude Hotspur is
consistently made to exemplify. And when Henry turns to comparisons between Hal and King Richard, as he then was, and between Hotspur and himself,
as the young Bolingbroke, his description of honor as a means to political ends

becomes more extreme. Richard lost the crown because he did not attend to his reputation, Henry asserts, and he warns that Hal stands in similar danger. Hotspur, Henry most illogically asserts, has more right to the crown than Hal, for he has achieved a more honorable reputation. This last is at once the most extreme conclusion of Henry's attitude toward the practical political effects of an honorable reputation and the clearest instance of the difference between Hotspur's thoroughgoing commitment to the ideals of honor and the Lancasters' exploitation of those ideas.

> Now, by my sceptre and my soul to boot,
> He hath more worthy interest to the state
> Than thou, the shadow of succession:
> For of no right, nor colour like to right,
> He doth fill fields with harness in the realm,
> Turns head against the lion's armed jaws,
> And, being no more in debt to years than thou,
> Leads ancient lords and reverend bishops on
> To bloody battles and to bruising arms.
>
> *(III.ii.97–105)*

Shakespeare delays Hal's response until all of Henry's accusations have been expressed, then in that response gives Hal precisely the same assumptions about the nature of honor. There are alternative responses. The king has concluded by saying that Hal is even able "To fight against me under Percy's pay . . . / To show how much thou art degenerate" (III.ii.126–28); so, were honor at the stake, it would be logical for Hal to profess his interest in maintaining the succession in order to avert civil discord, or his interest in putting down rebellion, or some other manifestly virtuous interest. Indeed, in the sources from which the play is drawn, just such an interest is the prince's motive. In Holinshed and in *The Famous Victories* this meeting is used by the prince to convince his father that he has no intention of usurping the throne, which suspicion Holinshed reports slanderous informants to have planted in the king. In the play, however, Shakespeare modifies the scene to accord with his plan to develop Hal as the pragmatist who, aware of other men's commitment to the code of honor, determines that exploitation of that commitment is the way to success. Consequently, Shakespeare has Hal respond to Henry's complaints by announcing his intention to use Hotspur's reputation for his own gain.

> I will redeem all this on Percy's head
> And in the closing of some glorious day

Be bold to tell you that I am your son;
When I will wear a garment all of blood
And stain my favours in a bloody mask,
Which, wash'd away, shall scour my shame with it. . . .

(III.ii.132–37)

This is precisely the intention Hal has announced in his first soliloquy, and it is an intention which remains fundamentally different from the sort of commitment to honor which controls Hotspur. Hotspur's honorable reputation is useful to Hal, and he means to acquire it.

Hal's first speech at Shrewsbury puts into action his long-anticipated bid to enter the lists of chivalry. The reasons he gives for challenging Hotspur to single combat are beneficent and humane, and there is no evidence that the play intends that he be cynically or ironically understood. That Hal is pragmatic does not mean that he is diabolic. In fact, however, the action demands Shrewsbury, not a single encounter between Hal and Hotspur, so that Hal's offer can only be seen as a definition of character and not as a potential alternative to the narrative line. Hal has planned to make Hotspur exchange "His glorious deeds for my indignities," and Shakespeare appropriately dramatizes that plan by having Hal challenge Hotspur to a trial of arms, the most explicitly honorable act available, to mark Hal's first step in his successful acquisition of an honorable reputation. The effect of this step is quickly seen in Vernon's glowing report to the rebel camp of Hal's challenge. Hotspur, jealous of his honor, asks if the challenge "seemed . . . in contempt," and Vernon does considerably more than reassure him. His account describes a model instance of that honorable balance between the offering of honest praise and the rejection of self-praise which Glendower has so contorted in his argument with Hotspur and which Hotspur and Douglas so carefully maintain.

No, by my soul, I never in my life
Did hear a challenge urg'd more modestly.
 . . . . .
He gave you all the duties of a man.
 . . . . .
Spoke your deservings like a chronicle,
Making you ever better than his praise
By still dispraising praise valu'd with you,
And which became him like a prince indeed,
He made a blushing cital of himself. . . .

(V.ii.51–61)

This and Vernon's other descriptions exaggerate what the audience has already seen, and so exhibit the first successful consequence of Hal's deliberate entry into the honorable life. His plan is succeeding, for, as first described in Vernon's speech, his new reputation does in fact "show more goodly . . . / Than that which hath no foil to set it off." Vernon, who has described Hal, armed, as having risen from the ground "like feather'd Mercury" and who has heard Hal's challenge, explicitly draws the comparison between these things and Hal's earlier behavior.

> but let me tell the world—
> If he outlive the envy of this day,
> England did never owe so sweet a hope
> So much misconstru'd in his wantonness.
>
> (V.ii.65–68)

Hal's victory over Hotspur, with Falstaff lying by feigning death, puts into action the success which Hal has planned and Vernon described. It also dramatizes Hal's essential indifference to honor except as a means to other ends. The epitaph which Hal speaks over Hotspur's body is as much a farewell to the ideals of honor which have so compelled Hotspur's behavior as to Hotspur himself. John Dover Wilson compares Hal's supposed epitaph over Falstaff with Hamlet's over Yorick,[20] but Hal's speech over the dead Hotspur bears even closer resemblance to Hamlet's tracing the noble dust of Alexander until he finds it stopping a bunghole. Hamlet's trials in that play lead more logically to his rejection of human glory and honor as vanity, so in Hal's mouth, by comparison, the speech seems largely a commonplace; however, it is consistent with, and may even be a belated effort to provide a moral basis for, Hal's indifference to honor as an ideal.

> *Hotspur.*   Percy thou art dust,
>   And food for—
> *Hal.*   For worms, brave Percy. Fare thee well, great heart!
>   Ill-weav'd ambition, how much art thou shrunk!
>   When that this body did contain a spirit,
>   A kingdom for it was too small a bound;
>   But now two paces of the vilest earth
>   Is room enough.
>
> (V.iv.84–91)

The Hal who then meets Falstaff with a willingness to gild a lie "with the happiest terms I have" and who elaborately arranges for the honorable release of Douglas is not a different or more educated Hal than the Hal of Act I, nor is he an embodiment of the triumph of moral mediocrity; he is a character in whom is dramatized the successful consequences of the pragmatic plans he has articulated in his first soliloquy and developed in his interview with King Henry. There is in the play no outright condemnation of this pragmatism, and if Hal's response to the world of the play makes him less sensual than Falstaff, less honorable than Hotspur, and less engaging than either, it is the response which, by definition, brings him success.

The structure suggested by the present argument is more characteristically Shakespearean than the supposed Aristotelian paradigm. To dramatize the beginnings of England's civil wars, Shakespeare makes honor a code of behavior central to the play and gives each of the major characters a different response to the demands of that code. Each suffers or enjoys the logical and ethical consequences of his response. Hamlet will, in a few years, call for plays "to hold, as 'twere the mirror up to nature; to show virtue her own feature, scorn her own image, and the very age and body of the time his form and pressure" (III.ii.24–27). The three principals of *1 Henry IV*, and the play itself, are such mirrors.

Notes:

1. David Berkeley and Donald Eidson, "The Theme of *Henry IV, Part 1*," SQ, 19 (1968), 25–31, provide the most recent study. They consider honor only "a prominent subtheme" (p. 25), but in that context agree with the customary interpretation. They cite as proponents of this interpretation Zeeveld, SQ, 3 (1952); Haydn, *The Counter-Renaissance* (New York, 1950); Boas, *Shakespeare and his Predecessors* (New York, 1896); and W. B. Hunter, "Falstaff," *SAQ*, 50 (1951), 86–95 (through error Hunter's article is cited as appearing in *Shakespeare Quarterly*). Hunter, indeed, extends this Aristotelian scheme to assign to the prince the virtues of "liberality," "good temper," "temperance," "a sense of humor," and even "magnanimity," comparing these with appropriate excesses and defects in Hotspur and Falstaff. Curiously, Berkeley and Eidson overlook Tillyard's formulation of this interpretation in *Shakespeare's History Plays* (1944). Cleanth Brooks and Robert Heilman further sanction the idea and give it wide distribution in their text *Understanding Drama* (New York, 1948). A clear indication of the fairly recent but pervasive acceptance of the idea may be gained by comparing Kittredge's introduction to the play (Boston, 1940), where no hint of the "Aristotelian" reading of the play is implied, with Ribner's introduction to the play in The Kittredge Shakespeares series, where Ribner easily assumes that "Shakespeare adopts the Aristotelian principle of temperance, with real virtue as a mean between extremes" (Waltham, Mass., 1966), p. xvii.

2. Aristotle, *Nicomachean Ethics*, IV.4, in *The Works of Aristotle*, trans. W. D. Ross (Oxford, 1925), Vol. IX.

3. Curtis Watson, in the only book-length treatment of the idea to date, recognizes the pervasiveness of the Aristotelian definition, stating that "Aristotle's original definitions are a hidden spring from which flow most of the ideas [about honor] of the writers of the 16th century" (*Shakespeare and the Renaissance Concept of Honor* [Princeton, 1960], p. 66). However, Watson's central concern to isolate honor as belonging uniquely to the ethics of "pagan humanism" and as being in explicit conflict with the ethics of Christianity renders his conclusions suspect, for he fails to consider such Christian uses of the Aristotelian idea as theologians like Richard Hooker make, and he disregards those portions of secular arguments which claim a Christian origin for human honor. Robert Ashley, for instance, easily accommodates the Aristotelian definition to a Christian context, concluding his inquiry into the origins of honor by saying, "so must I fetch the beginning of Honour from God" (*Of Honour*, ed. Virgil Heltzel [San Marino, 1947], p. 27). John Norden, to cite but one more sixteenth-century example, after another discourse on the divine origin of honor, concludes on a more practical note. "True honor is never gotten in the warres without Religion and virtue" (*The Mirror of Honor* [London, 1597], p. 12). Watson, in any case, is not concerned with Shakespeare's dramatic development of the idea of honor in individual plays and makes only a passing reference to *1 Henry IV*.
4. Count Annibale Romei, *The Courtiers Academie*, trans. John Kepers. The copy in the British Museum is not dated, but Valentine Sims had a license to print this title in 1598.
5. George Whetstone, *The Honorable Reputation of a Souldier* (London, 1585), sig. E.
6. William Segar, *Honor Military and Civil* (London, 1602), p. 203.
7. Richard Hooker, *Of the Laws of Ecclesiastical Polity*, Bk. VII, Chap. xvii, Sec. 4, in *The Works of . . . Richard Hooker*, ed. John Keble (New York, 1845).
8. Thomas Nashe, *Christs Teares Over Jerusalem*, in *The Works of Thomas Nashe*, ed. Ronald B. McKerrow (Oxford, 1958), II, 82.
9. All quotations of *I Henry IV* are taken from A. R. Humphreys' Arden edition (London, 1961). References to other plays of Shakespeare's are to *The Complete Works*, ed. G. L. Kittredge (Boston, 1936).
10. Romei, p. 101. Watson, *Shakespeare and the Renaissance Concept of Honor*, cites this passage as evidence to support his disjunction of "pagan humanist" and Christian ethics on the issue of honor. He reads this passage as a justification for suicide, but Gualinguo's remark that the Stoics sometimes permitted suicide in preference to dishonor is intended to emphasize the power that honor has always held rather than to justify present suicide. Watson does, however, cite several other instances where the assumption that honor is more precious than life is expressed (pp. 157, 215, 217, 219, and 361).
11. William Segar, *The Booke of Honor and Armes* (London, 1590), sig. A2.
12. Raphael Holinshed, *The Last Volume of the Chronicles of England, Scotlande, and Irelande . . .* (London, 1577), p. 1138.
13. Holinshed, p. 1136. The *OED* lists *prayes* as a sixteenth-century variant spelling of *praise* and provides a definition appropriate here: "That for which a person . . . is, or deserves to be, praised." The second edition of Holinshed (1587) substitutes *preies* for *prayes. Preies* is not among the variants listed for *praise*, but

one form of *prize,* or *price,* is *preis.* This may be the meaning the second edition intended.

14. Thomas Kyd, *The Spanish Tragedy,* ed. J. R. Malryne (*The New Mermaids,* London, 1970), I.ii.168.

15. Humphreys, p. 8, note to ll. 91–94. Humphreys further remarks that Holinshed does not mention Hotspur's justification under the law of arms. However, Humphreys uses the 1807–8 reprint of the second edition (1587) of Holinshed for his editorial purposes, which edition does not record Holinshed's original description of the Percys' claiming the prisoners as "their peculiar prayes." (Cf. fn. 13.)

16. *Honor Military and Civil,* Bk. 1, Chaps. 31–32, *passim.*

17. Cf. Humphreys' note to V.iii.36 for citation of various sixteenth- and seventeenth-century statements which condemn betrayal by a commander of his men as particularly dishonorable.

18. James Cleland, *The Institution of a Young Noble Man* (Oxford, 1607), pp. 191–92.

19. Baldassare Castiglione, *The Book of the Courtier,* trans. Thomas Hoby (1561), ed. Ernest Rhys (London, 1928), pp. 31–32.

20. John Dover Wilson, *The Fortunes of Falstaff* (Cambridge, 1943), pp. 67–68.

The Intemperate Knight and the Politic Prince: Late Morality Structure in *1 Henry IV*

ALAN C. DESSEN

To argue for the debt of *1 Henry IV* to the morality tradition is apparently to belabor the obvious. For the first such suggestion, in fact, the literary historian can cite no less an expert than Prince Hal himself, who described Falstaff as "that reverend vice, that grey iniquity, that father ruffian, that vanity in years."[1] Using Hal's analysis as a point of departure, modern scholars have offered detailed accounts of Falstaff's dramatic bloodlines, including considerable reference to the morality Vice and the allegorical tradition. The reader with a genealogical bent can thereby choose among such formidable figures as Gluttony, Riot, Sloth, and Vanity (alone or in various combinations) for the honored spot at the top of the fat knight's family tree.[2]

With such allegorical possibilities already at hand, it is an easy leap to seeing Hal, the Vice's companion, as a *Humanum Genus* figure, an Every Prince with a psychomachia conflict.[3] Thus John Dover Wilson argues that *Henry IV* is "Shakespeare's great morality play." Since the plays and tales involving the Prodigal Son invariably contain "the same three principal characters: the tempter, the younker, and the father with property to bequeath and counsel to give," Wilson treats Hal as younker, Falstaff as tempter, and Henry IV as the father figure whose property to be bestowed is the kingdom itself. Such a formulation neatly ties together many thematic strands of the two plays and is basic to Wilson's thesis "that the reign of this marvellous Lord of Misrule must have an end, that Falstaff must be rejected by the Prodigal Prince, when the time for reformation came."[4]

Although this approach has been accepted and reaffirmed by many subsequent critics, Wilson himself admitted that his account of Shakespeare's dramatic plan did not include many "alluring stretches" and several significant figures, particularly Hotspur (p. 15). To be sure, many readers have regarded these two plays solely in terms of Falstaff and Hal, but these two characters do not dominate the dramatic time of *1 Henry IV*. If one eliminates the overplot scenes (for example, I.i., parts of Act V) and other expository moments (for example, II.i, IV.iv), the prince and his circle are allocated I.ii, II.ii (the robbery), II.iv (the famous tavern scene), III.ii (Hal's interview with his father), III.iii (the second tavern scene), IV.ii (Falstaff and his ragged army), V.i (Hal's challenge), the battle scenes, and the concluding V.v. But the rebels are allotted equal time: in the long latter part of I.iii (the plot), in II.iii (Hotspur with the letter, then his wife), in III.i (with Glendower and Mortimer), in the pre-battle scenes (IV.i, IV.iii), and in V.ii when Hotspur receives the king's supposed message. To describe Hal as Every Prince and *1 Henry IV* as analogous to *Mankind* or *Lusty Juventus* or *Wit and Science* is therefore to simplify and distort Shakespeare's carefully wrought dramatic structure, to ignore the evidence because of a preconceived pattern.

To note such limitations is not necessarily to deny the basic insights and fruitful results of Wilson's formulation or the presence of morality play elements in *1 Henry IV*. In many ways Shakespeare here does make use of the structure and techniques of the native morality tradition. To understand this indebtedness without distorting Shakespeare's play, however, the modern reader must go beyond the limited and often misleading concept of "morality play" assumed by many scholars. In particular, close attention should be paid to scholarly assumptions about what constitutes such a "morality play," especially assumptions about the absence or presence of an Everyman figure as protagonist.

I

According to one representative account, the fifteenth-century moralities were "mainly intent upon grasping human nature in some form of abstraction standing for mankind as a whole"—an Everyman, a Mankind, a *Humanum Genus*—but the protagonist of the sixteenth-century plays "tends to lose the abstract quality of *Humanum Genus*." The author's conclusion is that "the morality in Elizabeth's reign is obviously drawing near the end of its service as a literary form. With few exceptions it shows distinct loss of ability to attain unification in a central character, and it shows a related tendency to rambling diffuseness."[5] Even though a few such heroes may still be noted (Impatient Poverty, Moros, Wit), representative moralities of the 1560s and 1570s clearly do not exhibit the structure typical of the plays of the previous century.

But then why should they? With what justification has "unification in a central character" been made an essential criterion for a morality play? General Elizabethan literary practice, for example, exhibits no such emphasis upon unity and simplicity of structure. As Madeleine Doran reminds us:

> multiplicity is one of the first things that strikes us as characteristic of sixteenth century literary art. Rabelais, Ariosto, Cervantes, Spenser, and Shakespeare saw beauty in multiplicity of detail. Abundant variousness was a way of seeing the world in the sixteenth century that no longer had the same meaning or value at the end of the next century.[6]

As a preface to his discussion of early Elizabethan dramatic practice, David Bevington observes:

the fallacy of enforcing classical precept upon late medieval structure is not so much the invidious comparison of greater and lesser as it is confusion of incommensurate qualities. One cannot account for these plays by aesthetic laws of unity, correspondence, subordination, and the like, because they were not composed with such ideas in mind. If some contemporary had had occasion to speak for the critically inarticulate authors of these plays, and had extracted a pattern or series of patterns from their work, he might have spoken quite differently of repetitive effect, multiplicity, episode, progressive theme.[7]

If then Everyman or Youth or Wit is no longer the protagonist of the intermediate or late morality, can the literary historian safely ignore what may be a development rather than a degeneration of an earlier dramatic form? Since one reference work lists roughly fifty moralities between 1558 and 1590[8] (including extant plays that encompass a wide variety of themes, structures, and techniques), to ignore such evidence is to flirt with the danger of imposing modern tastes and expectations upon a crude but nonetheless viable and lively Elizabethan dramatic form, a form accurately described as "the dominant mode of popular dramatic expression for about a century."[9]

Let us consider then some alternatives to "unification in a central character" found in the Elizabethan morality play. The avowed purpose of Ulpian Fulwell's *Like Will to Like* is to demonstrate "NOT ONLY WHAT PUNISHMENT FOLLOWETH THOSE THAT WILL RATHER FOLLOW LICENTIOUS LIVING, THAN TO ESTEEM AND FOLLOW GOOD COUNSEL: AND WHAT GREAT BENEFITS AND COMMODITIES THEY RECEIVE THAT APPLY THEM UNTO VIRTUOUS LIVING AND GOOD EXERCISES."[10] Granted this homiletic goal, what type of dramatic plan does Fulwell employ? Certainly he does not resort to a *Humanum Genus* figure and a psychomachia conflict. Rather, he offers a host of characters, including six vicious figures who are corrupted by the Vice and consequently serve as "moral exhibits."[11] The victims of the Vice, in fact, provide "an inventory of social evil: vile language, rioting, heavy drinking, thievery, and beggary."[12] The alternative way of life is posited dramatically through Virtuous Living, who, never in any danger of succumbing to evil, stands firmly (a modern reader might say woodenly) in opposition to Tom Tosspot, Cuthbert Cutpurse, and the other fallen figures. The same general dramatic method is to be found in George Wapull's *The Tide Tarrieth No Man*,[13] where again the emphasis is upon the Vice and his many victims (a grasping landlord, a greedy usurer, an aspiring courtier, an extravagant young married couple) and where again the dramatist supplies the homiletic alternative, here Faithful Few, who per-

severes and ultimately rescues Christianity. In both plays, the dramatists have
chosen to preach their dramatic sermons by means of an emphatic contrast
between a series of degenerate figures drawn from contemporary society and
their virtuous, godly counterparts who are given less dramatic time but are
expected to carry a good deal of moral freight. The absence of a *Humanum
Genus* figure as the dramatic focus does *not* necessarily indicate the absence
of form or structure. There *is* a plan in both plays, although not one that might
appeal to Sir Philip Sidney.

W. Wager's *Enough is as Good as a Feast*[14] has much in common with the
two plays already cited but significantly offers, not a wide range of degenerate
figures, but rather a dramatic structure built upon dual protagonists—one
virtuous and one vicious. The long opening scene presents the confrontation
between Worldly Man and Heavenly Man, the former for the moment being
converted. When Worldly Man next appears, he is accompanied by and satisfied with Enough. But the Vice (Covetous) and his henchmen quickly succeed
in winning Worldly Man away from Enough and lead him into various abuses
of his earthly possessions. At the height of his prosperity, Worldly Man denies
his debts and obligations, ignores the Prophet's message of impending doom,
is struck down by God's Plague, and is finally carried off by Satan, who encourages all worldly men in the audience to follow the same path. Although the
dramatic emphasis is upon this vicious figure, Heavenly Man does play a major
role in the opening scene and makes at least a token appearance (lines 949–69)
after Covetous's successful temptation of his counterpart. In the final scene,
Heavenly Man, Enough, and Contentation devote seventy-five lines to analysis
of Worldly Man's errors and praise of the life that pursues heavenly treasure
and is satisfied with enough. Heavenly Man is then rewarded with Rest rather
than with God's Plague and damnation. Even though dramatic time is not
equally distributed, the homiletic thesis is conveyed primarily through the
contrast between these two protagonists who act out alternative ways of life.
In addition, Covetous—who places much emphasis upon his cap, gown, and
chain—and Enough—who is plainly dressed—are set off against each other,
both in costume and as choices open to Worldly Man. In short, the play contrasts two ways of life through allegorical protagonists, each with a set of
companions who can appropriately epitomize the choices made.

An even better example of this dramatic structure is to be found in the
anonymous *Trial of Treasure*.[15] Thus the opening scene provides a confrontation between Just and Lust, which starts with recriminations and culminates
in a wrestling match in which Lust appears *"to have the better at the first"*
(p. 266) but is eventually cast down and driven off stage. Allegorically, we have
been shown "the conflict of the just, / Which all good men ought to use and

frequent"; every man in this way should strive against Lust: "And though, at the first, he seem sturdy to be, / The Lord will convince him for you in the end" (pp. 266–67). Through this verbal and physical confrontation, the dramatist has begun his play with a working definition of the two ways of life basic to his thesis, here emphasizing the short-term strength of Lust but the ultimate triumph of Just based upon "the might of his sprit that dwelleth in me." In the second scene, the way of Lust is further defined when this already corrupted character accepts the Vice (Inclination) and his allegorical henchmen as servants. A summary speech tells us:

> This Lust is the image of all wicked men,
> Which in seeking the world have all delectation;
> They regard not God, nor his commandments ten,
> But are wholly led by their own inclination.

To ensure the audience's awareness of the simple yet basic dramatic contrast, the scene concludes: "Thus see you how men, that are led by their lust, / Dissent from the virtuous, goodly and just" (p. 275).

In the third and fourth scenes the dramatist provides the first of the two visual analogues basic to the structure of his play. First Just and Sapience discuss "treasures here gotten" which are "of a vanishing kind" as opposed to "treasures of the mind" that "do continually remain." With Sapience as his guide, Just then shows his mastery over the Vice by bridling him. The moral is clear:

> Thus should every man, that will be called Just,
> Bridle and subdue his beastly inclination,
> That he in the end may obtain perfect trust,
> The messenger of God to give sight to salvation.
>
> *(p. 279)*

Moments later, Lust unbridles the Vice who promises to bring him to Lady Treasure. In simple homiletic terms, the bridling of Inclination allows man to "obtain perfect trust," while the unbridling is associated with the hope for treasure that (in spite of the Vice's assurances) will obviously not "continually remain" (p. 282). This bridling and unbridling in consecutive scenes has thereby heightened the contrast between these two ways of life through economical yet visually effective means.

The dramatist achieves a similar effect by bringing on stage in consecutive scenes the only two female figures in the play along with their attendant satisfactions. First Just appears with Trust, "*a woman plainly [apparelled,]*" and Contentation to provide a lengthy analysis of "true trust" and "celestial treasure." This heavenly alternative is countered by Lust's appearance with Treasure, "*a woman finely appareled*" (p. 288), and Pleasure, who "will be always with Treasure in sight" (p. 291), a figure analogous to Contentation (a relationship that could easily be heightened through costuming or blocking). To drive home the allegorical parallel, the Vice lists for Lust and the audience what he has "won":

> Marry, now you are well indeed, Master Lust:
> This is better, I trow, than the life of the just:
> They be compelled to possess contentation,
> Having no treasure but trust of salvation.
>
> *(p. 290)*

Again the dramatist has set up a visually heightened contrast between the ways of Just and Lust, this time by means of analogous figures and comparable situations.

The conclusion of the play comes as no surprise. Lust ignores God's Visitation (who takes away Pleasure) and persists in his foolish trust in Treasure; finally, he is taken off by Time, who returns with a similitude of dust and rust to indicate the ends of Lust and Treasure. In contrast, Just bridles the Vice a second time, receives a crown from Trust, and earns Consolation (defined as "joy or comfort in this life transitory"). Admittedly, the dramatist's message is no different from that found in *Enough* or in other didactic, anti-materialistic works of the sixteenth century. What *is* significant and distinctive here is the tightly knit dramatic structure built around dual protagonists, each representing a way of life, each accompanied by analogous allegorical companions (Lady Trust and Lady Treasure, Contentation and Pleasure, even God's Visitation and Consolation). The center of the play consists of episodes which neatly (if a bit obviously) establish revealing contrasts in consecutive scenes, whether through the bridling and unbridling of the Vice or through the presence of visually analogous figures. Here then is a morality performed during Elizabeth's reign with a carefully wrought dramatic structure well suited to its homiletic message, a structure that is certainly an offshoot of the *Humanum Genus*-centered morality but a branch with significant variations and therefore distinct advantages over the original stock. If the reader can isolate structure and technique from content, here is a dramatic form with a decided potential for comparing two attitudes or characters or ways of life, a form that could prove fruitful for a dramatist concerned with issues other than the fall of

Worldly Man or Lust. "Unification in a central character" is decidedly *not* the sole means by which the morality, particularly the late morality, achieved its goals.[16]

II

Dramatic historians have argued for a firm connection between the morality tradition and the history plays that burgeoned in popularity at the end of the century. Thus Irving Ribner has pointed out that

> the morality drama contained elements admirably suited to the dramatic presentation of history in such a way that the didactic ends of Tudor historiography might be served. There was first a sense of form by which the elements of history could be related to one another and made to constitute a meaningful whole. The stock morality device of *Humanum Genus* torn between good and evil angels, for instance, could easily be translated into terms of a king torn between good and evil counselors, as we have so clearly illustrated in *Woodstock* and *Richard II*. The dramatic pattern of the morality play became a part of the greatest history plays of the age of Elizabeth, where it is perhaps most perfectly and strikingly evidenced in *Henry IV*.[17]

Ribner's formulation, although fruitful in many ways, does not make allowances for any "dramatic pattern" other than "the stock morality device" inherited from the fifteenth century, for his argument precludes any later developments in the morality play which might have brought about some concomitant evolution in the history play. But such dramatic evolution *is* to be found during the second half of the sixteenth century. *Trial of Treasure*, to be sure, is scarcely a household word, even among historians of the drama; nonetheless, the plays cited above are quite representative of the moralities which have survived from the first part of Elizabeth's reign. Although unfamiliar to the modern reader, such plays may well have been known by the succeeding generation of dramatists and can offer suggestive evidence about the nature of other plays now lost.[18] Even though there is, to my knowledge, no evidence that *Trial of Treasure* served as a direct source for later plays, the presence of dual protagonists and related techniques suggests that such a dramatic structure may have been one recognized means for achieving the homiletic goals announced by Fulwell. If so, the morality tradition bequeathed to later dramatists a greater legacy than has usually been granted or, in Ribner's terms, "the sense of form by which the elements of history could be related to one another and made to constitute a meaningful whole" could include a good deal more than "the stock morality device of *Humanum Genus* torn between good and evil angels."

Before discussing this legacy further, one important qualification is necessary. In spite of any evidence adduced from the earlier drama, the modern reader certainly cannot assume that every set of contrasting characters to be found in a history play or comedy is to be attributed to morality influence. Common sense, rhetorical training, or even the source materials used by the dramatists could easily lead to such a device. So *Sir Clyomon and Sir Clamydes*, a knightly romance with two heroes, has little in common with *Trial of Treasure*, while plays like *Old Fortunatus*, *The Dutch Courtesan*, and *Eastward Ho!* are at best distant cousins. Rather, the descendants of the type of play best represented by *Trial of Treasure* will exhibit not only dual protagonists (admittedly only a limited link) but also symbolic companions, parallel groupings, and analogous situations in consecutive scenes, all of which taken together develop the dramatist's thesis. The essential criterion is the entire dramatic mode, not merely the presence of two contrasting heroes.

Several early historical plays have at least some affinities with this dramatic pattern. Peele's *Battle of Alcazar*, for example, is structured around the two claimants to the throne, Abdelmelec and Muly Muhamet, each of whom has analogous companions and significantly divergent attitudes towards Heaven and Fortune. The central theme of the play—the virtues of a rightful title and the attendant perils of ambition and usurpation—is set forth largely through the continuing dramatic contrast between two protagonists who embody opposed ways of life. Similarly, Lodge's *The Wounds of Civil War* depicts the struggle between Marius and Scilla, each with a sharply defined point of view. Through various parallel actions and through the alternating scenes of Act III, Lodge develops his distinction between Fortune's conqueror and Fortune's fool.

Perhaps most interesting is the manner in which the anonymous author of *The Life and Death of Jack Straw*[19] has structured his play around his titular figure and Richard II. Here the alternation of scenes between the two protagonists or their supporters is consistent and basic to the fabric of the play. Both Jack Straw and the king clearly embody opposing attitudes on major questions (for example, personal gain versus the good of the kingdom); each, moreover, has something to learn about himself and his role if he is to realize his goals and not be manipulated by others. Also of interest are the companions of the two protagonists; thus Parson Ball, the prime spokesman for rebellion, is a rebel equivalent first for the Archbishop, a contrasting figure of religion at the side of Richard II, and later for the Lord Mayor, who in his exhortation to his soldiers echoes Ball's words to the rebels.[20] At the climax of the play, the rebel captain, who has placed his trust in false companions, is destroyed, while the king, who has wisely trusted Newton and the Lord Mayor, is victorious and can announce to the rebels that he "will be your Captaine and your friend" (963). In its dual protagonist structure, *Jack Straw* offers interesting evidence of how the emerging history play could find a dramatic pattern in the late morality tradition without recourse to a central *Humanum Genus* figure.

III

To turn from *Trial of Treasure* and *Jack Straw* to *1 Henry IV* is to move from dramatic possibilities to artistic realization. The reader not led astray by the *Humanum Genus* will-o'-the-wisp can recognize how an alternative concept of morality structure, one that can encompass dual protagonists and analogous companions, sheds interesting light upon Shakespeare's dramatic strategy. Thus, as C. L. Barber observes: "We are invited, by the King's unfavorable comparison in the opening scene, to see the Prince in relation to Hotspur,"[21] for here Henry IV echoes the public assumptions of the play—that Hotspur is "so blest a son," "amongst a grove the very straightest plant," "sweet Fortune's minion and her pride," while "riot and dishonour stain the brow / Of my young Harry" (I.i.79–85). An alert listener might perceive that Hal's riot and dishonor arise from "looking on the praise of him," not necessarily from viewing the reality; nonetheless two public value judgments have been made in this opening scene, judgments which award Hal lower if not failing grades when judged by Hotspur's standard.

The evidence provided by the next two scenes, however, calls into question these initial judgments upon the two young men, one of whom has had his age drastically changed in defiance of history to enhance the parallel.[22] First in I.ii Shakespeare shows us how Hal has been spending his time. The prince's opening speech indicates his total awareness of Falstaff's way of life, in which "to demand the time of the day" is superfluous; Sir John's assertion that "I must give over this life" (92–93) is then immediately tested ("Where shall we take a purse tomorrow, Jack?") and exposed as a pretense. Hal is obviously *not* the archetypal morality hero (Youth, Wit, Lusty Juventus) led astray by Riot and Dishonor, for Riot (if one accepts that equation with Falstaff) is not in control but rather is tolerated and enjoyed. The famous (or, to some, infamous) soliloquy that ends the scene reinforces our impression of Hal's self-awareness. The prince sets up a revealing analogy, citing "the base contagious clouds," which "seem to strangle" the sun but which, in reality, are only permitted to "smother up his beauty from the world" until that moment that he (sun-son) may "please again to be himself." Hal exhibits his awareness of how "this loose behaviour" appears to the world and to his father but goes on to argue that "when" (not if) he throws it off, such a "reformation" will "show more goodly, and attract more eyes / Than that which hath no foil to set it off." If nothing else, Hal's self-conscious control over his present and future image to the world should prevent the audience from underestimating him as do his father, his companions, and his antagonists.

In sharp contrast to Hal's control of himself and his surroundings, despite his apparent immersion in vice, we next see Hotspur's lack of such control and awareness, despite his impressive credentials. With the angry departure of the king in I.iii, Shakespeare emphatically establishes the analogous pattern basic to the structure of this play. In the latter part of I.ii, two figures were on stage (a youth and an old man) when a third figure arrived with a plot (the Gadshill robbery). Here in I.iii the audience sees before it Hotspur and Northumberland, rather than Hal and Falstaff, with Worcester, rather than Poins, entering with his plot against the king's crown, rather than the king's money (or crowns). Each of the plots, moreover, is centered around the respective young man whose participation is essential for the ultimate effect (to expose Falstaff, to gain the necessary support for the rebellion).

As in *Trial of Treasure*, such parallel staging calls attention to a contrast basic to the play. In I.ii Hal showed us his control of himself and his situation, including the old man who accompanied him; in fact, the plot accepted by the prince was directed *at* Falstaff. But Hotspur shows no such control over his plot or his old men. Rather this second young man is rash, hot-tempered, and lacking in any subtlety or craft, as demonstrated by his anger at the king's dismissal of Mortimer's cause, his enthusiasm for danger that can lead to honor, and his excitement over the "noble plot." The two old men are thereby forced to wait for the subsiding of the "woman's mood" that ties "thine ear to no tongue but thine own" (234–35). But the staging of the scene should make clear that Hotspur's outbursts are, in reality, under the control of the two old men who are subtly manipulating this tempestuous figure. Thus, during Hotspur's first tirade, Worcester and Northumberland carefully redirect and reinforce the young knight's anger by blandly conversing about Richard II's proclamation that Mortimer was to be "the next of blood" (144). Hotspur, a warrior rather than a politician, has a sudden insight into the king's motives, an insight that the audience has seen implanted by figures seeking to use him. Although this young knight had earlier mocked the courtly popinjay, he fails to recognize the much more insidious danger to be found at Court, the political and social manipulation that can destroy the self-hood and self-control of the individual. The ringing speeches on that honor which must be worn "without corrival"

(205) become suspect in a context in which Hotspur is reacting to stimuli supplied by figures with questionable motives (particularly Worcester, an old man who has been singled out for criticism by both the king and Westmoreland). Meanwhile, the many verbal echoes of the previous scene (for example, "time," "debt," and "redeeming"), the parallel staging, and Hotspur's mocking of "that same sword-and-buckler Prince of Wales," who could be "poison'd with a pot of ale"—all call attention to Hal as the alternative young man. Although most of the dramatis personae would undoubtedly accept Hotspur's public image, the audience has both heard Hal's soliloquy and seen his superiority to *his* old man. To the heroically minded reader, Hotspur's initial stance may have greater appeal than the prince's calculated biding of his time, but Shakespeare is testing such heroic assumptions by placing Hotspur's statements and gestures in a murky political context in which a naive warrior may end up losing his battle before it is waged. By stressing the alternative path followed by this second young man, Shakespeare is emphasizing what Hal is *not* and further defining those qualities (not always the most appealing or idealistic ones) necessary for the effective ruler. As in *Trial of Treasure*, the dramatist is using alternating scenes, analogous companions, and parallel staging to distinguish between his dual protagonists—here a politic prince and an intemperate knight.

The same dramatic strategy can be found in Acts II and III. In II.iii Hotspur finds only cowardice in a letter which, in fact, offers a perceptive critique of the intended rebellion ("The purpose you undertake is dangerous, the friends you have named uncertain, the time itself unsorted, and your whole plot too light, for the counterpoise of so great an opposition" [10–14]), thereby revealing his inability to accept any truths that do not fit with his heroic code. This knight's immersion in a self-contained world places him at the opposite extreme from Hal, who could rightly state: "I know you all" (I.ii.190). This question of communication is then picked up at the beginning of II.iv where Hal's speech to Poins is his equivalent to Hotspur's reaction to the cautious letter. Instead of the fiery knight's contempt, the prince announces that he has "sounded the very base-string of humility" (5–6) with the drawers and "all the good lads in Eastcheap" (14) and has, in the process, learned their language ("good boy," "dyeing scarlet," "Hem!" and "Play it off!") and won their hearts. Hal can conclude: "I tell thee, Ned, thou has lost much honour that thou wert not with me in this action" (19–21), a use of *honor* and *action* that Hotspur would certainly not understand. In contrast to Hotspur's self-induced deafness, Hal has again shown his ability to play a part (a truant, a robber in a buckram suit, a drinking companion) and learn languages other than his own to achieve his goals. An actor need only brandish a piece of paper (containing the new words Hal has learned) to drive home the parallel to Hotspur and his letter.

The contrast between the two young men is further heightened through the practical joke played upon Francis the drawer. So Hal's offer of money and his testing of Francis's bond to the vintner is played off against first Poins's and then Hal's use of the drawer's name as a stimulus to elicit a mechanistic response (verbally—"Anon, sir"; physically—a movement towards the speaker), a response that causes the prince to conclude: "That ever this fellow should have fewer words than a parrot, and yet the son of a woman!" (II.iv. 96–97). The stage business portrays Francis as a puppet jerked by two competing strings until *they both call him; the Drawer stands amazed, not knowing which way to go"* (77 s.d.). To the audience, Prince Hal is the obvious puppetmaster who can control Francis's reactions because of his knowledge of what makes the puppet work, whereas no one else understands the purpose of the test case (Poins can ask: "But hark ye, what cunning match have you made with this jest of the drawer: come, what's the issue?" [87–89]). Of those on stage in Act II, only Hal grasps the essential nature of the figures who surround him and is thereby able to use that knowledge to manipulate others, to be a controller rather than one of the controlled. Francis, on the other hand, by being so easily manipulated, calls into question his credentials as a "son of a woman" and serves as a comment upon Hotspur's subjection to the promptings of the two old men in I.iii. In particular, the young knight's heroic code may be his loftier equivalent to Francis's "Anon, sir," his version of a predictable response which can be manipulated by some other figure. To heighten this parallel in production, a director need only have Francis's scurrying about the stage visually echo Hotspur's frenetic movements in II.iii[23] or have the drawer, between Hal and Poins, correspond to the young knight caught between Worcester and Northumberland in I.iii.

The exuberant baiting of Falstaff then gives us more evidence of Hal's superiority. Falstaff's "coward on instinct" may be a brilliant comic improvisation, but it certainly does not deceive the prince who twits his old man (II.iv. 277–78), successfully cross-examines Bardolph when Falstaff is off stage, and toys with "instinct" (351, 367). The old man's claim: "I knew ye as well as he that made ye" (263) only stresses again how no one in the play truly "knows" Hal, whether because of a vizard and buckram suit or a supposed stain of riot and dishonor on his brow, while Hal is the sole figure, here or elsewhere, who can claim with any force: "I know you all" (ironically echoed by Falstaff's "I know not what you call all" [182]). Even granted the enormous disparity between Francis and Falstaff as comic butts, Hal's roles as controller, puppetmaster, and stage manager in both instances are quite similar. Unlike Hotspur in the previous scene, Hal here can listen to, observe, and learn from those around him, whether the lads of Eastcheap, Francis, Falstaff, or Bardolph.

The first part of the famous play extempore that follows shows us Falstaff in the role he would like to be playing toward Hal—father figure and controller to his young man. The stage image of Falstaff above, with his chair, dagger, and cushion, and Hal below, as subject and son, acts out the view of the supposed truant prince held by Henry IV, Hotspur, and England as a whole. Here, in addition, is a visual emblem for the potential trap awaiting both of the youthful protagonists, a trap associated with subjection to the control of an old man. But significantly in the second act of this interlude Hal reverses the roles and plays father figure and controller to his old man, a reversal of roles for which there is no equivalent in Hotspur's dramatic career. Especially pertinent is Hal's description of Falstaff in terms befitting a morality play tempter: "that villainous abominable misleader of youth" (II.iv.456), "that reverend vice, that grey iniquity, that father ruffian, that vanity in years" (447–49), and "a devil" who haunts the prince "in the likeness of an old fat man"[24] (441–42). But Hal, unlike Hotspur (or Youth or Wit), is not in any way misled by his old man. Rather Shakespeare makes it clear that the prince's summary comment ("I do, I will") is based upon accurate knowledge of his companions (emphasized again through the papers from Falstaff's pockets), complete control of himself (in evidence since I.ii), and total awareness of the debt that remains to be paid, the role that must be assumed, and the world that must eventually be banished. Hal's four revealing words are in themselves enough to explain his ultimate victory over Hotspur if only in the vision that allows him to see the future in the present (as in his soliloquy) and steer his own independent course through uncharted political and moral waters.

In keeping with the consistent dramatic strategy of *1 Henry IV*, this major display of Hal's abilities is followed by the most revealing exposure of Hotspur's limitations. Thus the first half of III.i presents Hotspur's baiting of Glendower, first through his scoffing at the magician's claims to supernatural powers, then through his proposal to change the course of the Trent, and finally through his mocking of poetry and the Welsh language. All these nonhistorical incidents[25] heighten Hotspur's headstrong, blunt nature which cannot make allowances for the idiosyncrasies of others, even his own allies. In the previous scene Hal had learned the language of the lads of Eastcheap; controlled Francis, Falstaff, Bardolph, and even the Sheriff; and shown his understanding of both his present surroundings and his future role ("I will"). But Hotspur, in contrast, does not truly grasp either his own role in this rebellion or the tenuous bonds that tie his allies to him ("the purpose you undertake is dangerous, the friends you have named uncertain . . .") and consequently can allow personal pique to triumph over politic control.

With Glendower off stage, both Mortimer and Worcester chide Hotspur for his willful, impolitic behavior. Unlike the young man, the Welshman has been exercising considerable restraint, for "that man is not alive / Might so have tempted him as you have done /Without the taste of danger and reproof" (III.i.167–69). Worcester adds an important political context:

> In faith, my lord, you are too wilful-blame,
> And since your coming hither have done enough
> To put him quite besides his patience;
> You must needs learn, lord, to amend this fault.
> Though sometimes it show greatness, courage, blood,
> —And that's the dearest grace it renders you—
> Yet oftentimes it doth present harsh rage,
> Defect of manners, want of government,
> Pride, haughtiness, opinion, and disdain,
> The least of which haunting a nobleman
> Loseth men's hearts and leaves behind a stain
> Upon the beauty of all parts besides,
> Beguiling them of commendation.
>
> _(III.i.171–83)_

Even though Hotspur's "greatness, courage, blood" on the battlefield are unquestioned, the shrewd politician still argues that heroic virtues out of control can become politic vices that lose men's hearts. While Hal is moving to erase the stain of riot and dishonor supposedly on his brow, Hotspur stands accused of staining the beauty of "all parts besides" through his "wilful-blame" behavior.

The latter part of the scene further heightens Hotspur's inadequacies by displaying the language barrier between Mortimer and his wife. Here again Shakespeare calls our attention to the problem of communication, for Mortimer's inability to understand Welsh corresponds to Hotspur's inability to fathom Glendower's language, superstitions, and habits of mind. Unlike Hal, who has mastered the language of Eastcheap, both Mortimer and Hotspur are symbolically isolated from their surroundings and from those companions of whom they most have need. When the much maligned Glendower does call for ethereal musicians who "hang in the air a thousand leagues from hence" (III.i.219), _"The music plays"_ (223 s.d.), a supernatural response that enhances the magician's claims and counters the gibes of the incredulous Hotspur (50–52).

Taken as a whole, this scene effectively displays Hotspur's failings in the political rather than the chivalric arena. As in II.iii, this irascible yet charming young knight is totally committed to his personal heroic code and to his no-nonsense attitudes toward superstition, poetry, oaths, and language, a situation which at critical moments can prevent him from understanding a figure like Glendower who may be essential to his cause. Like Francis, Hotspur too can fall short of his potential as "son of a woman" because of such semiautomatic responses based upon hair-trigger reflexes and simple assumptions about the world around him. Although in the world's view Hotspur, with his military credentials, appears better prepared for the confrontation ahead, to the audience it is Hal who has been schooled into an awareness of what is demanded of him and how he must rise to those demands—through language, control, and vision, not through scoffs, self-isolation, and subjection to others. In consecutive scenes both young men bait their companions (another parallel that could easily be heightened by analogous blocking), but Hal's handling of Francis and Falstaff proves his control and superiority while Hotspur's mishandling of Glendower only stresses his inadequacy.

Shakespeare takes this pattern of alternating scenes yet one step further, for the confrontation in III.i between a young man and an old man who is a potential ally is followed by Hal's confrontation with another highly significant old man who is already antagonized by his apparently dissolute life. Henry IV, like Worcester, is much concerned with the political repercussions of his young man's image, here the supposed "inordinate and low desires" that have made the prince "almost an alien to the hearts / Of all the court and princes of my blood" (III.ii.12, 34–35). According to this master politician, Hal (like Richard II) "hast lost thy princely privilege / With vile participation" (86–87). But in spite of his acknowledged shrewdness, the king's critique of his son cannot be accepted by an audience that has seen repeated demonstrations of Hal's control of himself and others. Similarly, that same audience should by now look askance at Henry IV's comparison between Hotspur (a "Mars in swathling clothes" who has gained "never-dying honour") and his son ("my nearest and dearest enemy"). The king's long disquisition on political image-making that can "pluck allegiance from men's hearts" (52) does not take into account evidence the audience has seen and heard—how, for example, the prince has won the right "when I am King of England" to "command all the good lads in Eastcheap" (II.iv.13–14). Unlike the audience, Henry IV has not heard Hal's first soliloquy nor his "I do, I will."

The king's judgments upon Hotspur and Hal, whether here or in I.i, have been based upon the concept of honor as understood by "all the world" (III.ii. 93), an honor that can be affected "by smiling pickthanks, and base newsmongers" (25). In the pivotal moment in this scene, when the prince defends his past and makes his promises for the future (129–59), Hal does not reject this hollow honor accepted by the king and Hotspur but rather uses that concept and its adjuncts as a common language between himself and his father, the common language missing for Hotspur and Glendower or Mortimer and his wife. So the prince, referring to the supposed stain of dishonor upon his brow, promises to "redeem" all past offenses so that, "in the closing of some glorious day," he "will wear a garment all of blood, / And stain my favours in a bloody mask, / Which, wash'd away, shall scour my shame with it." In a revealing passage, Hal then invokes the honor that is little more than a commodity. Hotspur, in this view, becomes the prince's "factor," engaged "to engross up glorious deeds on my behalf," an agent under contract who eventually will be called "to so strict account / That he shall render every glory up" or else Hal "will tear the reckoning from his heart." Just as the prince has understood and thereby controlled both Francis and Falstaff, here he can grasp and use the assumptions of his father to cancel out his apparent truancy and rejoin the public world of the play. In contrast to Hotspur's linguistic deficiency with Glendower, Hal has mastered the public language of "glorious deeds" (III.ii.146, 148), "glorious day" (133), "glory" (150), "honour" (142), and "honour and renown" (139). Whether or not he is truly an orthodox adherent to such a chivalric code, the prince can use such terms to win over the most significant old man in the play. The series of alternating moments that started as early as I.ii here reaches a climax when Hotspur's political lapses of III.i are countered by Hal's politic victory. As in the latter part of the play extempore, Hal again transcends his old man (perhaps standing over the seated king)[26] while Hotspur never really fathoms Glendower or Worcester.

Since the paths chosen by the two protagonists are now quite clear, Shakespeare can demonstrate the implications of such choices without resorting to the same emphatic alternation of scenes. Thus Hotspur in IV.i must face the reality he has so far failed to admit. The first rebuff, the news of Northumberland's illness, does not daunt him, because he can argue that his father's absence "lends a lustre and more great opinion, / A larger dare to our great enterprise, / Than if the Earl were here" (IV.i.77–79). As in III.i, Worcester provides the politic view: that "the quality and hair of our attempt / Brooks no division"; that "it will be thought" by outsiders "that wisdom, loyalty, and mere dislike / Of our proceedings kept the Earl from hence"; and consequently that "this absence of your father's draws a curtain / That shows the ignorant a kind of fear / Before not dreamt of" (IV.i.61–75). Hotspur, however, is concerned, not with politics and men's hearts, but with his heroic code, "a larger dare," honor waiting to be plucked from the pale-faced moon. Similarly, when Hotspur's snide question about "the nimble-footed madcap Prince of Wales" (IV.i.95) elicits Vernon's glowing description of the new Hal (97–110), the fiery knight impatiently cuts off the description ("this praise doth nourish agues" [112]), again showing his unwillingness to hear unwelcome truths. The final news, that Glendower "cannot draw his power this fourteen days" (126), is the most telling indictment of Hotspur's impolitic course of action; although Shakespeare is by no means explicit, the elaborate Welsh-baiting of III.i is surely designed to offer some explanation for Glendower's failure to appear at Shrewsbury. Mocking the advice of the letter in II.iii, ignoring Worcester's politic vision here and in III.i, and failing to see the strings controlling him, this angry young knight is acting out the blindness and impetuousity that distinguish him from the alternative young man who does succeed in the same hostile, debilitating world. Falstaff's antiheroic comments in the next scene, especially his description of his "pitiful rascals" as "food for powder" (IV.ii.64–67), can then spell out the ugly reality behind the chivalric rhetoric so confidently set forth by Hotspur, another captain leading his men to their deaths. Significantly, it is Hal who cross-examines the false captain in IV.ii and thereby demonstrates his superiority to such suspect captaincy in any form.

Hotspur's delegation of his authority to Worcester and Vernon leads to his absence from the meeting between the rebels and the king in V.i, an absence that points to his isolation from the realities of the play. The confrontation between the two shrewd old men,[27] Henry IV and Worcester, is followed by the public emergence as a chivalric hero of another young man, who can grant his counterpart full honors as "active-valiant," "valiant-young," "daring," and "bold" (V.i.85–92), yet nonetheless assert himself and his own future, thereby creating for himself a new image that Hotspur is unable to recognize or accept. Hal's proposal "to save the blood on either side" by trying "fortune with him in a single fight" (99–100) is his alternative to Hotspur's "die all, die merrily" (IV.i.134) or Falstaff's "food for powder," for the prince, who realizes that "in both your armies there is many a soul / Shall pay full dearly for this encounter / If once they join in trial" (83–85), can posit the value in the human life to be lost. Hal's rising to the occasion is more than an admission of having "a truant been to chivalry" (94); rather, it involves an insight and depth of understanding rarely found in this factional, short-sighted world.

Even granted several ringing speeches and a moving call to arms, Hotspur has no equivalent opportunity to rise to the occasion, because his old man never reveals to him "the liberal and kind offer of the King" (V.ii.2). Since the suspicious, politic Worcester lacks faith in Henry IV's guarantees (at least for those without Hotspur's "excuse of youth and heat of blood" [17]), this young man is never made aware of the options available to him. The hotheaded warrior, who has continually rebelled against his uncle's politic advice (how to handle Glendower, when to fight), has had no combat experience in dealing with such a deception—unlike Hal, who has seen through his old man in II.iv. As a captain and a leader, the Hotspur who is about to take his men into an apparently unnecessary battle is disturbingly similar to the Falstaff of IV.ii with his bedraggled army of little life expectancy.

The young man's failure to perceive Worcester's treachery is followed by his inability to accept the image of the new Prince Hal. Vernon's speech (V.ii.51–68) not only provides an account of Hal's challenge, but also emphasizes how the prince gave to Hotspur "all the duties of a man," setting forth his opponent's "deservings like a chronicle, / Making you ever better than his praise," and thereby showing the world that he has been "much misconstru'd in his wantonness." But Hotspur scoffs at this report ("Cousin, I think thou art enamoured / On his follies"), asserting that "never did I hear / Of any prince so wild a liberty" (69–71). Although in his challenge Hal could give his opponent full honors, Hotspur is unable or unwilling to accept an eyewitness report and go beyond the world's limited view of the prince. Within a brief dramatic moment, Hotspur has shown his inability to evaluate accurately both a supposed friend and a known foe, thereby demonstrating a major reason for his ultimate downfall.

The young knight's subsequent call to arms, like his speeches on honor in I.iii, provides a highly theatrical rendition of his chivalric appeal, but the full dramatic meaning of this speech involves far more than what this heroic figure thinks he is saying. The heart of his statement (V.ii.81–88) is based upon a warrior's view of the relationship between time and heroic action. If "the time of life is short," the hero's major concern should be not "to spend that shortness basely." In the forthcoming battle, according to Hotspur, the man seeking to use his time heroically has the worthy options of either treading on kings or suffering "brave death when princes die with us." In conclusion, the young knight can argue that "the arms are fair / When the intent of bearing them is just"; but Shakespeare has carefully placed this exhortation in a context that belies such heroic values. To be sure, Hotspur's inability to grasp the truth about his major antagonist is understandable, but his blindness to Worcester's machinations and his failure to see the pointlessness of the coming battle cannot be passed over so lightly. His simple assumptions about the honorable use of time, moreover, come about ninety lines after Falstaff's incisive catechism

(V.i.127–41), a cynical speech that calls into question the essence of Hotspur's code and concludes that "Honour is a mere scutcheon." Through such dramatic context, Shakespeare is forcing his audience to weigh carefully Hotspur's claims and assumptions. Can the hero be truly honorable when not fully aware of the cause (or lack of cause) for which he is fighting? Is the "intent" of bearing arms "just" in this instance? Can Hotspur, symbolically isolated from the king's offer and Hal's challenge, make meaningful statements about time and honor, especially with Worcester, the old man who has deceived him, standing by his side? While Hal as sun-son is emerging from behind "the base contagious clouds," Hotspur's lack of control and self-knowledge is leading him to a captaincy and a battle that can only be self-defeating. Once again the dramatist has offered us comparable examples in consecutive scenes of how these two young men are using their time in a demanding arena that includes war and politics, vaunts and sophistries, heroic ideals and ugly realities. Through a range of dramatic devices comparable to those found in *Enough* or *Trial of Treasure*, Shakespeare has fully explored for his audience the divergent paths chosen by the two protagonists as they move toward their climactic meeting.

Not surprisingly, the pivotal figure in the battle scenes that follow is not Hotspur but Prince Hal. It is Hal who once again in temporal terms shows his superiority to his old man ("What, is it a time to jest and dally now?"), who refuses to be escorted from the field because of a shallow scratch ("Lead me, my lord?"), and who saves his father's life by driving off Douglas ("It is the Prince of Wales that threatens thee, / Who never promiseth but he means to pay"). Through "this fair rescue" Hal has, in the eyes of his father and the world, "redeem'd thy lost opinion" and fulfilled the promises of I.ii and III.ii. The prince's emergence from behind his cloud, not the many marching in the king's coats, has preserved the life of Henry IV.

In both *Enough* and *Trial of Treasure*, the two protagonists confronted each other in the opening scene and then pursued their divergent paths. The climax of Shakespeare's dual protagonist structure, on the other hand, is the first and only meeting between Hal and Hotspur. Typically, the initial talk is of honor. Although Hal can grant Hotspur his due ("a very valiant rebel"), the latter wishes that the prince's "name in arms were now as great as mine," so that the current possessor of honor would have more to gain and less to lose. Again honor is seen as a commodity that can be engrossed up by a factor and called to account. With his defeat, time once more becomes an issue for the dying warrior, who admits that "thoughts, the slaves of life, and life, time's fool, / And time, that takes survey of all the world, / Must have a stop." Significantly, Hotspur's heroic code can "better brook the loss of brittle life / Than those proud titles thou hast won of me." In striking contrast to Falstaff's two recent prose speeches, Hotspur values honor over life and, according to his rigorous interpretation of his own heroic code, can envisage no honor for himself now that he has once been defeated (thereby making a mockery of the "never-dying honour" cited earlier by Henry IV). Ironically, Hotspur's evaluation of his own honor seems to substantiate Falstaff's claim that honor is only "air," "a trim reckoning," and "insensible . . . to the dead." Although the young knight's final broken phrase ("and food for—") is completed by his opponent in the conventional way ("for worms, brave Percy"), the audience may well remember Falstaff's "food for powder" and the disturbing connection between the fate of the ragged army of IV.ii ("not three of my hundred and fifty left alive" [V.iii.37]) and this chivalric hero.

Hal's epitaph suggests a different concept of honor and chivalry, for in the midst of his comments upon "ill-weav'd ambition" the prince can still refer to "brave Percy," "great heart," and "so stout a gentleman." If Hotspur were still "sensible," Hal would not be free to "make so dear a show of zeal" or indulge in such "fair rites of tenderness," here the combination of final tribute and covering the dead knight's face with his favors. In a suggestive way, Hal's evaluation of his defeated opponent shows an ability to "know" the strengths and weaknesses of his enemy, to measure accurately the world around him, and to separate private truths from public rhetoric. By suggesting, moreover, that Hotspur "take thy praise with thee to heaven! / Thy ignominy sleep with thee in the grave, / But not remember'd in thy epitaph!" Hal gives the dead knight more honor in defeat than the latter would have claimed. The prince, who has defeated his antagonist in combat and now stands over his prostrate body, is not only physically but also intellectually superior; he has transcended his opponent's limited notion of honor in favor of a more realistic, inclusive definition that can encompass both "praise" and "ignominy." Hal's triumph is manifold.

But to appreciate the full impact of this dramatic moment, one must consider the total stage image, particularly the presence of two and perhaps three prostrate bodies. Hal, whom the audience has just seen as an erect figure standing over the body of Hotspur, now assumes a similar position over the recumbent body of Falstaff, who is "counterfeiting" death. Hal's second epitaph is certainly less weighty than the first, especially to Falstaff-lovers, but more important than the actual words spoken is the visual effect presented to the audience. Before he exits, this successful young man has stood over and addressed two of his symbolic antagonists—both his obvious foil, Hotspur, and the old man who sought to control him (the potential equivalent to the Worcester who led another young man into this unnecessary battle that cost him his life). Hal's erect posture over such recumbent figures is therefore a visual summary of his total triumph, not only as a warrior who has won honor but more important as a controller rather than one of the controlled, as *the* young man who has learned to transcend the machinations of others and the deceptive surfaces around him to achieve his own goals. If, moreover, the body of Sir Walter Blunt dressed in the king's coat is also still in view, the prince's visual triumph could include a symbolic victory over his father as well.

Falstaff, needless to say, is very much alive; like Henry IV, he has sought to protect himself by "counterfeiting." In II.iv Falstaff momentarily placed himself above Hal as a father-king figure of control, but the prince then reversed their roles (as he has done again here on the battlefield). But Hotspur has shown no such control over his old man, a point emphasized once more by Henry IV's critique of Worcester's treachery at the beginning of the final scene. So, fittingly, our last view of the redoubtable Harry Percy is of his body being first wounded, then picked up, and eventually carried off stage by an old man whose speeches on honor have placed him at the farthest possible remove from the young knight's heroic code. Falstaff's gaining of honor at Hotspur's expense is perhaps the most devastating comment in the play upon the hollowness of this chivalric abstraction. Just as Worldly Man had been carried off on Satan's back or Moros had been carried to the Devil on Confusion's back (*The Longer Thou Livest, the More Fool Thou Art*), so here the young man who has failed in his worldly quest for honor is borne off by a symbol of the forces that have destroyed him.

As a final irony, Falstaff's one-sided combat with Hotspur yields the honor which has eluded the dead knight. Even though the strange tale delivered to the two princes is scarcely believable, Hal assures his old man that "if a lie may do thee grace, / I'll gild it with the happiest terms I have." The action of the play has clearly demonstrated that the honor frantically sought by Hotspur, accepted by the king, and catechized by Falstaff is only a sham or counterfeit —in short, a lie. Since Hal, more than any other figure, has transcended this superficial concept of honor, he can not only see through that lie but even control or manipulate it. Consequently, it is Hal in the final scene who can recognize Douglas's heroism ("his valours . . . have taught us how to cherish such high deeds, / Even in the bosom of our adversaries") and who can give the honors of the day to Prince John, just as he had earlier awarded due honor to Hotspur and the lie to Falstaff. Since the prince, unlike Hotspur, is not obsessed with wearing his honor "without corrival," he can create honors for others without himself being limited by such surfaces. Here again one is struck by the force of the two visual images presented at the end of the battle—the erect Hal standing over the prostrate bodies of both Hotspur and Falstaff, and

then the puffing Falstaff, wounding and then carrying off the body of Hotspur
and the honor that is a lie. The alternative paths chosen by the two young
protagonists, choices defined in I.ii and I.iii and orchestrated as the play has
developed, have here led to their dramatic and thematic conclusion, with Hotspur subject to Falstaff's sword and Hal unaffected by the vanities that corrupt
or mislead others.

IV

What then does this complex and highly original play owe to the native morality tradition? Certainly there is evidence in the text for Falstaff's association
with the Vice. To treat Hal as Every Prince is not to exaggerate that young
man's importance for this play and for the second tetralogy. But from I.ii on,
Falstaff, unlike Inclination or Riot or Courage, is quite unsuccessful as a
tempter-controller (at the end the fat knight carries off on his back Hotspur,
not Hal), while the prince's control of and superiority to his surroundings
distinguish him from most morality play protagonists (with the notable exception of Just and Heavenly Man, whom the critics do not have in mind). Since
the Hal-Falstaff scenes, moreover, account for only part of the play's dramatic
time, to see the young man and his tempter as the dramatic center is to over-
simplify Shakespeare's theatrical strategy. Clearly, if *Mankind* or *Wit and
Science* or *Lusty Juventus* is to be the yardstick, the morality play has only
limited relevance to this history play.

But if the reader's conception of "morality play" includes *Trial of Treasure*
and *Enough*, he *can* note a revealing link between *1 Henry IV* and the morality
tradition. Admittedly, Shakespeare's play provides no such obvious homiletic
contrast as that between a Lust and a Just or between a Worldly Man and a
Heavenly Man, for missing here are any black-and-white alternatives on an
absolute moral scale. Nonetheless, in performance in the theater both *Trial of
Treasure* and *1 Henry IV* offer their audiences a similar evolving pattern built
around two contrasting figures, each epitomizing a different set of attitudes
towards the play's central questions, each with an appropriate set of companions, each undergoing analogous experiences. Thus in nonallegorical terms,
Falstaff and Worcester (or Glendower and Henry IV) play much the same roles
for their young men as had Inclination and Sapience or Covetous and Enough;
in a sequence of moments ranging from II.iii to III.ii, Hal and Hotspur display
their politic (or impolitic) natures in a manner analogous to the much simpler
bridling and unbridling of Inclination; the results of the choices made by these
two young men allow them to act out in Act V their complex versions of the
winning of Lady Trust and Lady Treasure. Shakespeare's alternating scenes,

symbolic companions, and visually analogous moments are superior in quality and complexity, but not necessarily different in kind, from their equivalents in the moralities. Rather, in both morality play and history play, themes, images, contrasts, and parallels are set in motion through a sequence of scenes built around two protagonists, a sequence which develops the dramatist's point of view through all the verbal and visual means available.

The morality legacy bequeathed to *1 Henry IV* does not then consist of any one character or relationship or set of ideas. Rather, that legacy involves an entire dramatic mode of putting concepts into action on stage, a mode that could be used for both a relatively simple theatrical sermon against materialism and a highly complex exploration of moral and political questions. Such dramatic strategy, in fact, represents the most significant contribution of the morality tradition to mature Elizabethan drama. *1 Henry IV* is not a dramatic sermon, nor is it allegorical in the morality fashion. But its characters, its issues, its relationships are *structured* according to a pattern apparent in some earlier plays which *are* didactic, allegorical, and obvious. Here then is further evidence in the morality tradition of a "sense of form by which the elements of history could be related to one another and made to constitute a meaningful whole." To understand tradition and the individual talent, to appreciate Shakespeare's skill as both an innovator and a traditional craftsman who knew the work of his former guild members, the modern reader can start with no better primer than *1 Henry IV* and its morality heritage.

Notes:

1. II.iv.447–49. The text used is the New Arden edition, ed. A. R. Humphreys (London and Cambridge, Mass., 1961).

2. See, for example, John Webster Spargo, "Interpretation of Falstaff," *Washington University Studies, Humanistic Series,* 9 (1922), 119–33; John W. Shirley, "Falstaff, An Elizabethan Glutton," *PQ,* 17 (1938), 271–87; Daniel C. Boughner, "Vice, Braggart, and Falstaff," *Anglia,* 62 (1954), 35–61; Bernard Spivack, "Falstaff and the Psychomachia," *SQ,* 8 (1957), 449–59; and Eben Bass, "Falstaff and the Succession," *CE,* 24 (1963), 502–6. See also Humphreys' introduction, pp. xlii–xliii.

3. So over fifty years ago Sir Arthur Quiller-Couch argued that Hal "is poised on the balance. In the one scale is Hotspur, challenging him to honour with a provocation purposely made exorbitant: in the other, packed into Falstaff, all that is sensual—this also exorbitant, the very bulk of the man helping our impression of the weight that would drag the Prince down." He concludes that "the whole of the business is built on the old Morality structure, imported through the Interlude" and "might almost be labelled, after the style of a Morality title,

Contentio inter Virtutem et Vitium de anima Principis" (*Notes on Shakespeare's Workmanship* [New York, 1917], pp. 125–27). See also Spargo, pp. 130–33, and Robert Adger Law, "Structural Unity in the Two Parts of *Henry the Fourth*," *SP*, 24 (1927), 240–42.

4.   *The Fortunes of Falstaff* (Cambridge, 1943), pp. 14, 22.

5.   Willard Farnham, *The Medieval Heritage of Elizabethan Tragedy* (Berkeley, 1936), pp. 209, 242. For similar views see Irving Ribner, *The English History Play in the Age of Shakespeare* (Princeton, 1957), p. 43; and Bernard Spivack, *Shakespeare and the Allegory of Evil* (New York, 1958), p. 307 and *passim*.

6.   *Endeavors of Art* (Madison, 1954), p. 6.

7.   *From "Mankind" to Marlowe* (Cambridge, Mass., 1962), p. 3.

8.   *Annals of English Drama 975–1700*, ed. Alfred Harbage, rev. S. Schoenbaum (London, 1964), pp. 34–55.

9.   Bevington, p. 4.

10. *The Dramatic Writings of Ulpian Fulwell*, ed. John S. Farmer (London, 1906), p. 2.

11. Spivack, *Shakespeare and the Allegory of Evil*, p. 231.

12. Bevington, p. 158.

13. Ed. Ernst Ruhl, *SJ*, 43 (1907), 1–52.

14. Ed. R. Mark Benbow along with *The Longer Thou Livest* for the Regents Renaissance Drama Series (Lincoln, 1967).

15. *A Select Collection of Old English Plays Originally Published by Robert Dodsley in the Year 1744*, 4th ed., ed. W. Carew Hazlitt (London, 1874–1876), III, 257–301. Because of some seventy-four lines shared by *Enough* and *Trial of Treasure*, some scholars have argued for Wager's authorship of both plays. See, for example, Leslie Mahin Oliver, "William Wager and *The Trial of Treasure*," *HLQ*, 9 (1946), 419–29. Oliver's argument, however, does little with technique and nothing with dramatic structure. The most recent editor of *Enough* (see note 14) argues that the similarities cited by Oliver "are insignificant or traditional characteristics of the moral interlude" (p. x). Benbow finds *Enough* superior to *Trial* in tension and dramatic action, a verdict with which I would disagree.

16. For discussion of another divergent structural pattern found in the late morality, see Alan C. Dessen, "The 'Estates' Morality Play," *SP*, 62 (1965), 121–36.

17. *The English History Play in the Age of Shakespeare*, pp. 40–41.

18. E. K. Chambers has pointed out that although 307 plays are extant for the period between 1586 and 1616, there is reason to suppose that this total "only represents a comparatively small fraction of the complete crop" (*The Elizabethan Stage* [Oxford, 1923], III, 182). The percentage of lost plays is probably even higher for early Elizabethan drama, a situation that forestalls any confident generalizations from the existing evidence. Nonetheless, that evidence must be considered carefully if the modern reader is to understand the native English dramatic legacy to the later drama, for, as Bevington points out (p. 10), "almost all pre-Marlovian plays of the sixteenth century which bear convincing evidence of popular commercial production are in fact moralities or hybrids." The use of dual protagonists in at least two such plays could therefore be quite significant.

19. Ed. for the Malone Society by Kenneth Muir and F. P. Wilson (Oxford, 1957). According to Ribner (p. 76), Jack Straw makes "the same choice as a typical

morality play hero, and he undergoes much the same consequences," pursuing to his destruction a chosen path of rebellion; according to Mary G. M. Adkins, the king, not Jack Straw, is the dramatic focus, for "Richard may be said to dominate the play not only in dramatic conception of character, but also in dramatic emphasis, both in the scenes in which he actually appears and those in which he is talked about" ("A Theory About *The Life and Death of Jack Straw*," U. of Texas *Studies in English*, 28 [1949], 79). Both views share the same fallacy, that unity and emphasis demand a single focus, a king or a rebel.

20. So the parson had told his followers that "God will giue you strength and might, / And put your enemies to flight," assuring them "of mine honestie your quarrels right" (862–65). Moments later the Lord Mayor tells his soldiers that "it is our God that giues the victorie" and assures them that "London wil giue you power and armes, / And God will strengthen you and daunt your foes" (970–74).

21. *Shakespeare's Festive Comedy* (Princeton, 1959), p. 200.

22. For an excellent discussion of Shakespeare's adaptation of his sources in this play see Humphreys, introduction, pp. xxi–xxxix. On Hotspur's "unhistorical youthfulness" see pp. xxvi–xxviii.

23. Thus John Shaw argues that Lady Percy's speech in II.iii "is long simply so that Hotspur can ignore it! No other reason will suffice to account for the astonishing protraction of details. The speech, then, is a kind of stage direction for Hotspur: MOVE ABOUT." To Shaw, it is this arbitrary movement "that Francis unknowingly mimicks in the next scene," thereby establishing an analogy between the two figures ("The Staging of Parody and Parallels in '1 Henry IV'," *ShS*, 20 [1967], 71).

24. For a thorough analysis of these terms and their associations see Humphreys' notes on pp. 80–81 and his general comments on pp. xli–xlii. See also Falstaff's reference to "a dagger of lath" (II.iv.134) and Humphreys' note on p. 64.

25. This scene is of particular value in assessing Shakespeare's dramatic plan for this play, for it represents his imaginative expansion upon a neutral, unprepossessing sentence in Holinshed (for the passage, see Humphreys, pp. 170–71). In the chronicles, these negotiations were carried out by agents, not by the principals, while Northumberland, not Hotspur, was to gain a third of the kingdom.

26. For a detailed treatment of the potential relationship between II.iv and III.ii, see Shaw, "Parody and Parallels," pp. 63–67.

27. The age of both Henry IV and Worcester is clearly established here in V.i.13, 23–25. On the king's age, see Humphreys, p. xxviii.

"Division 'tween Our Souls":
Shakespeare's Stoic Brutus

MARVIN L. VAWTER

After many years of being relegated to a secondary position among Shakespeare's tragedies, *Julius Caesar* has, in the last decade or so, received new interest and scholarly attention. As we gradually discover its complexity, Shakespeareans are treating *Caesar* with new respect. While we have always recognized its power and magnetism on the stage, we have often been less than eager to deal with it in the graduate seminar. Fortunately, that reluctance is disappearing as closer scrutiny is given to the intellectual fabric of the play. But much remains to be done.

In a seminal study, John Anson recently emphasized the importance of the Stoic doctrine of impassivity in the play by examining *Caesar* in an anti-Stoic context.[1] Pointing to the constriction of emotional feeling especially apparent in Caesar, Anson argues convincingly that Shakespeare was familiar with neo-Stoic works, such as Du Vair's, and was at odds with their stress on emotional repression. Anson's article probes the boundaries of fertile but complicated material that deserves further exploration. Perhaps because Anson relies on a modern commentator's synopsis of Stoicism,[2] his reading of *Caesar* misses many crucial elements. Impassivity, in fact, is but one symptom of the disease devouring mankind in Shakespeare's vision of Stoic Rome.[3]

I

Most critics agree that the pivotal character in *Caesar* is "the noble Brutus." To decipher him is to begin unraveling the play's complexity; and, as Brutus's critical fortune rises and (most recently) falls in scholarly disputes, so the drama changes from a tragedy of heroic struggle against tyranny to an ironic portrait of a misguided idealist. In nearly every discussion, however, one infers that somehow Brutus must be salvaged from outright condemnation. He is either hero or pathetic victim; to accuse him of moral corruption is to commit heresy.[4] Yet with so much depending on our understanding of Brutus, there has been no thorough study of the "idealism" he is alleged to possess. Brutus is, after all, the only major character in Shakespeare's plays professedly identified with a particular "philosophy" (IV.iii.144, 193; V.i.101ff.).[5] No one has disputed the assumption that the "philosophy" is Stoicism, but only a few studies, all severely limited in scope and emphasis, have brought that fact to bear on Shakespeare's characterization of Brutus and on events in the play.[6]

173

Even the historical validity of Shakespeare's portrayal of Brutus as a Stoic has never been adequately considered.[7] For all of his fidelity to Plutarch, Shakespeare could not have known of Brutus's Stoicism from this one source. Brutus's philosophical sympathies, in fact, are left ambiguous by Plutarch when he says that among "the Graecian Philosophers . . . above all the rest, [Brutus] loved Platoes sect best." But Plutarch touches obliquely on Brutus's Stoicism by relating that he "did ever greatly esteeme the Philosopher Antiochus" and that it was "Marcus Cato the Philosopher" whom Brutus "studied most to follow of all other Romans."[8] Shakespeare may have learned that Antiochus was a Stoic from Cicero, who says that Antiochus was with "very few modifications, a perfectly genuine Stoic" (germanissimus Stoicus).[9] The reference to Brutus's idolization of his father-in-law Cato would also have associated Brutus with Stoicism, especially if Shakespeare were familiar with Cicero's De Finibus, in which Cato speaks as the Stoic authority in Book III.

The entire De Finibus, as a matter of fact, is addressed to Brutus, and there Cicero wages an intense attack on Stoicism in his debate with Cato. The debate is an important corrective to the modern commonplace assumption that Cicero was the fountainhead of Renaissance Stoicism.[10] While his philosophical essays provided the Renaissance with elaborate outlines of Stoic doctrine, they also invariably contained astute refutation of the same Stoic principles. Cicero could admire a Cato for his strength of character, could sympathize with the Stoics' pursuit of the absolutely virtuous life, and could respect (to a point) their personal fortitude in the face of private griefs. Nonetheless, he could not be a Stoic; the fundamental premises of their system were illogical, perhaps even dangerous.

Cato, in the De Finibus debate, asserts that the Stoic Wise Man will choose virtue (always synonymous with reason in Stoic doctrine) as the sole good. By eliminating from his plan of life all emotional motives, the Wise Man will allow only his reason to discern the true Good. In his refutation, Cicero states rather bluntly that there is no substance, conviction, or motivation in the Stoic maxims; "they may convince the intellect, but they cannot convert the heart" (IV.iii).[11] Fundamentally, argues Cicero, the Stoics simply do not understand the true nature of human beings.

Stoicism, Cicero points out, begins with the same first principles as those of most other philosophies:

that we must study what we ourselves are, in order to keep ourselves true to our proper character. We are then human beings, consisting of soul and body . . . and out of these we must construct our End, our Chief and ultimate Good. And, if our premises are correct, this End must . . . consist in the attainment of the largest number of the most important things in accordance with nature.

(IV.x)

But at this point—on what man's "nature" is—the Stoics go their separate way from all other schools. The Stoics conceive the "nature" of man to be, in the state of perfected and self-sufficient virtue, a disembodied mind. Mocking the pious Cato, Cicero describes this wonder for us:

By what means or at what point did you suddenly discard the body, and all those things which are in accordance with nature . . . and lastly duty itself?

Why is it, he continues, "that so many things that Nature strongly recommends," such as love, friendship, duty, and bodily sustenance, "have been suddenly abandoned by Wisdom?" What the Stoics have for so long revered is "some living creature that consisted solely of a mind," but "it is impossible even to imagine a self-consistent picture of what such a creature would be like" (IV.xi–xii). Naturally, the highest good for "a creature consisting solely of . . . intellect" *would* be total rationalism; conversely, if the creature "is nothing but a body, the chief things will be health, freedom from pain, beauty and rest." But neither of these descriptions fits man:

as a matter of fact the creature whose Chief Good we are seeking is man. Surely then our course is to enquire what has been achieved in the whole of man's nature.

(IV.xiii–xiv)

Such an effort cannot fail to prove that the "whole" man naturally possesses emotion and feeling as well as reason. Nature adds reason to control desire and emotions, not to eliminate them. Indeed, even virtue and duty exist in man *first* at the emotional level, and without the power of these emotions man will have no accurate motive force toward these goals:

virtue is an absolute impossibility, *unless* it holds to the objects of the primary instincts. . . . [If you] grant the ultimate Good that I am now upholding, it becomes clear at once what one's duties are and what actions are prescribed. But you, who have no other standard in view but abstract right and morality, will not be able to find a source and starting point for duty and for conduct.

(IV.xv–xvii)

In his summation, Cicero asserts the fundamental contradiction of Stoicism in any political context:

> To maintain that the only Good is Moral Worth is to do away with the care of one's health, the management of one's estate, participation in politics, the conduct of affairs, the duties of life, nay, to abandon that Moral Worth itself, which according to you is the be-all and end-all of existence. . . . Wisdom had no ground to stand on when desires were abolished.

(IV.xxv)

When the Renaissance, therefore, turned to Cicero as an authority on, but *not* a member of, the Roman Stoics, it also found in his essays substantial and forceful reasons for rejecting Stoicism as an ethical foundation. What is important for our purposes here is that many of these essays, including *De Finibus* and *Paradoxa Stoicorum*, were dedicated to the Stoic Brutus, almost as if they were an attempt by Cicero to persuade his friend to abandon this murky and potentially dangerous philosophy. In his *Tusculan Disputations*, a work Shakespeare seems to have known well,[12] Cicero addresses Brutus on the occasion of Brutus's treatise on virtue-reason (*De Virtute*, now lost). The *Disputations* several times recognize Brutus as a Stoic Wise Man and cite him as an authority for Stoicism's severest maxims on virtue, especially on the "Stoic vintage" that "virtue can be sufficient for leading a happy life" (V.v). Significantly, in the opening of the fifth book, Cicero speaks directly to Brutus:

> This fifth day, Brutus, will bring the Tusculan discussions to an end, and on that day we discussed the subject which of all subjects meets with your warmest approval: for from the book you have written . . . as well as from the numerous conversations I have had with you, I have realized the strength of your conviction that virtue is self-sufficient for a happy life.

But Cicero—and I believe Shakespeare found this illuminating—expresses grave doubts about the Stoic precept. "I begin to lose confidence in this opinion of yours and feel exceeding fear of the weakness and frailty of mankind" (V.i). All of Book V, therefore, is devoted to the reverse proposition: that "virtue alone seems to be insufficient for leading a happy life."[13]

The real possibility exists then that Shakespeare would have identified Brutus not merely as a Stoic but as one of its chief authorities on the self-sufficiency of virtue-reason, in other words, as a Stoic Wise Man. Specifically, Shakespeare's portrait of Brutus evokes a severe Stoic Wise Man who, in his private *and* public roles, ironically demonstrates the *insufficiency* of virtue-reason; indeed, Brutus is a dramatic illustration of the hollowness, presumption, and moral sickness inherent in the secular concept of virtue-reason's sufficiency. For this characterization, Shakespeare fused dogma from orthodox Stoics with satiric-ironic materials in the, by then commonplace, anti-Stoic tradition with which Shakespeare was familiar.[14]

II

In symbolic statement and dramatic action throughout *Caesar*, Shakespeare forces us to consider the nature of man. Of what is he made? What parts go together to form the ideal, inherited from Cicero and others, of the "whole man"? In the composition of the human soul and body—as in the politic soul and body[15]—what mixture results in harmony? What in disharmony? What force in man binds the elements together? What perversion creates a rupture in the bond?

The "state of man," says Brutus, is "Like to a little kingdom," composed of two parts, the "genius and the mortal instruments" (II.i.66–68), the mind and the body. Similarly, Caesar defines man as a physical and rational dualism: "men are flesh and blood, and apprehensive" (III.i.67); and, less abstractly, Antony alludes to the same sensitive and rational composition when speaking to the populace: "if I were dispos'd to stir / Your hearts and minds . . ." (III.ii. 123–24). Within these statements is implied the commonplace Christian definition of man's soul as a unity of rational and sensitive halves. Like Cicero, Augustine viewed man as an inseparable composition of mind and body and warned that only as a unity could man achieve the true good. Rejecting the fragmented creatures that Stoicism and Epicureanism held up as ideals—the one deifying mind at the expense of body, the other elevating flesh to the detriment of mind—Augustine argued for a cooperative bond between man's emotions and his reason, between the flesh and the soul. The "whole human nature," he says, "is composed of flesh and soul," not just one or the other. And the man who abjures his own body is a living contradiction and a fool:

For he who extols the nature of the soul as the chief good, and condemns the nature of the flesh as if it were evil, assuredly is fleshly both in his love of the soul and hatred of the flesh.

(*The City of God, XIV,* 5)[16]

Milton, centuries later, conceived of the same bipartite organism in which the soul has two different but inseparable elements. The "whole man," he asserts, is "not compound or separable, not . . . made up and framed of two distinct and different natures, as of soul and body." Instead, man is a "substance individual, . . . sensitive, and rational" (*The Christian Doctrine*, I.vii).

No such view of the harmonious and dynamic interaction of man's halves was allowed by the Stoics' definition of human nature. In their view, as Cicero pointed out, the ideal man is a disembodied mind, ruling over his body as a tyrant does his bondslave. Thus, when the Renaissance neo-Stoic Justus Lipsius rehearses the Stoic doctrine, his terms are equally severe.[17] In his work on *Constancie*, only mind and soul are equated; the body is but an unruly servant for menial labor but otherwise disdained:

> Man consisteth of two parts, Soule and Body. That being the nobler part, resembleth the nature of a spirit and fire: This more base is compared to the earth. These two are ioyned together, but yet with a iarring concord, as I may say, neither doe they easily agree, especially when controversie ariseth about soverainty & subiection.[18]

To be "constant" in the Stoic sense, then, is to attain a mental disengagement from the body and its emotions, to make the mind the supreme "soverainty" and to relegate the body to "base . . . subiection."

These conflicting definitions of man are materials with which Shakespeare was working when he wrote *Caesar*. Knowing the historical Brutus was a Stoic who believed in the self-sufficiency of virtue-reason, Shakespeare portrays Brutus as a cultural elitist shutting out communication with the communal body of his loved ones and countrymen and subjecting his physical body to the totalitarian authority of his mind. In Brutus the "iarring concord" of which Lipsius speaks becomes a full-scale battle: "poor Brutus, with himself at war, / Forgets the shows of love to other men" (I.ii.45–46). As Brutus's "genius" plans "the acting of a dreadful thing," the murder of a man he says he loves, his "mortal instruments," the emotional and physical half of his soul or "state," resist this hideous deed. Brutus "suffers then / The nature of an insurrection" (II.i.64–69). But the sensitive half of Brutus's soul is no match for his tyrannous mind.

As I have suggested elsewhere,[19] tyranny in what Hooker calls "the soul of a politic body" obtains when the political head severs its bond with the communal body because it has become "prodigious grown" (I.iii.77) on the "meat" of flattery, on the self-debasing bodies of fawning noblemen such as Brutus and

Cassius who unwittingly create their own "bondage." We are meant to see, I am certain, a similar state of bondage in the soul of Brutus. Because he is a Stoic, his inflated mind tyrannizes over his body and the emotional feeling within that body. That is, his mind is the tyrant, and his heart is the bondslave.

One thing is manifestly evident about Brutus: due to the complete neglect of his bodily needs, his mental obsessions have left him physically ill. In the first few scenes of *Caesar*, Brutus's illness is foreshadowed by a marked change in his behavior to others. Showing no interest in the Lupercalian celebration, he remains on stage while all but Cassius depart. Interested, Cassius inquires as to the cause of his friend's detachment, to which Brutus replies, "I am not gamesome: I do lack some part / Of that quick spirit that is in Antony." Without this "part" of his "spirit," Brutus has been remiss, Cassius tells him, in affection for his friends:

> I have not from your eyes that gentleness
> And show of love as I was wont to have.
> You bear too stubborn and too strange a hand
> Over your friend that loves you.
>
> *(I.ii.27–34)*

But Brutus has little reply. All that he will reveal of his troubled state is that he contains an inner "war" in which one part of him is enemy to another: "I turn the trouble of my countenance [head or forehead] / Merely upon myself" (I.ii.37–38).

The remainder of the play, of course, gives the lie to Brutus's remark: whatever his disturbance, it has profound implications for others. Not only does he neglect "the shows of love" to Cassius—and later to Caesar—he has also forgotten how to love Portia. In his scene with her, we see the extent of his physical degeneration. As he had shown no "gentleness" to Cassius, so Portia tells him, "Y' have ungently, Brutus, / Stole from my bed. . . . You star'd upon me with ungentle looks" (II.i.237–38, 242). She then describes something "enkindled" (II.i.249) in Brutus, some mental fever, and its results on his body have been ravaging:

> It will not let you eat, nor talk, nor sleep;
> And could it work so much upon your shape
> As it hath much prevail'd on your condition,
> I should not know you Brutus.
>
> *(II.i.252–55)*

Now if we read the play rather than see it, we do not know until this moment how accurate Cassius was when he described himself as Brutus's "reflection" and "glass" (I.ii.67). Caesar gave us a detailed description of Cassius:

> Let me have men about me that are fat,
> Sleek-headed men, and such as sleep a-nights.
> Yond Cassius has a lean and hungry look;
> He thinks too much: such men are dangerous.
>
> *(I.ii.190–93)*

Clearly, Portia has described a remarkably similar man in Brutus. Moreover, the absence of "quick spirit" and of interest in physical pleasure that Brutus admits is also foreshadowed in Caesar's analysis of Cassius and in terms that Shakespeare had elsewhere associated with Stoicism:[20]

> He loves no plays,
> As thou dost, Antony; he hears no music.
> Seldom he smiles, and smiles in such a sort
> As if he mock'd himself, and scorn'd his spirit
> That could be mov'd to smile at any thing.
>
> *(I.ii.200–204)*

Also unsmiling, dispirited, and "not gamesome," Brutus is evidently even leaner, hungrier ("It will not let you eat," says Portia), and more of an insomniac ("nor sleep") than Cassius;[21] and his sickness has progressed so far as to prevent him from communicating except by frenzied, quaking gestures. Portia tells him,

> You scratch'd your head,
> And too impatiently stamp'd with your foot;
> Yet I insisted, yet you answer'd not,
> And with an angry wafture of your hand
> Gave sign for me to leave you.
>
> *(II.i.243–47)*

Brutus has obviously distorted his nature, his "condition," and is physically wasting away. "Enkindled" in him is a destructive fire, consuming his love for Portia, now becoming his "harlot," and destroying his own body. Unable to see himself, however, Brutus says he is "not well in health, and that is all"

(II.i.257), as if he were suffering from nothing more serious than a bad cold. But Portia, also in a "weak condition" (II.i.236) and thus another "reflection" of Brutus, pinpoints the diseased part of Brutus. It is not his body that hinders him, she says; indeed, his body is the victim:

> Brutus is wise, and were he not in health,
> He would embrace the means to come by it.
>
> . . . . . .
>
>   What, is Brutus sick?
> And will he steal out of his *wholesome* bed
> To dare the vile contagion of the night,
> And tempt the rheumy and unpurged air
> To add unto his sickness? No, my Brutus;
> You have some sick offence within your mind.
>
>   *(II.i.258–59, 263–68; my italics)*

What we have learned from Portia is crucial: his sick mind is brutalizing his body with the result that there is nothing "wholesome" about him. The fire in his obsessed mind (recalling the "fire" of the Stoic mind to which Lipsius alluded) was first noted in Brutus by Cassius: "I am glad / That my weak words have struck but thus much show / Of fire from Brutus" (I.ii.173–75). After Cassius had flattered Brutus's name (I.ii.140) and his lineage (I.ii.157–59), the fire began to burn; and thus Cassius identifies Brutus as one of the "noble minds" (I.ii.308). Similarly, Cassius refers to Brutus as an abstracted mind when speaking to Casca: "I have mov'd already / Some certain of the noblest-minded Romans" (I.iii.121–22). Cassius's vision of Brutus seems never to include a whole man. Brutus spoke of himself in terms of "parts," and Cassius echoes his words: "three parts of him /Is ours already" (I.iii.154–55). Casca too, repeating Brutus's self-image of a "countenance" "turned" on the rest of his body, describes Brutus as a "countenance" which can change an "offence" into a "virtue" (I.iii.158–60). In addition, there is Portia, unable to separate her mind from her body, yet desperately trying to emulate the Stoic rationalism of Brutus. Try as she may, her emotions and instinct still rightly warn her of disaster; and the divisive tension within her is driving her to suicide:

> O constancy, be strong upon my side;
> Set a huge mountain 'tween my heart and tongue!
> I have a man's mind, but a woman's might.
>
>   *(II.iv.6–8)*

Finally, we have Brutus's own self-abstraction as a disembodied mind. Speaking in third person, a self-detaching viewpoint, he tells Cassius,

> No, Cassius, no: think not, thou noble Roman,
> That ever Brutus will go bound to Rome;
> He bears too great a mind.
>
> (V.i.111–13)

Thus, when we recall Artemidorus's letter to Caesar about the conspirators, we should view it in a new and symbolic light. There is, he says, "but one mind in all these men" (II.iii.4–5). That mind, "bent against Caesar," is of course the disembodied and unfeeling mind of Brutus.

Integrated into this pervasive portrait of an obsessively cerebral man are Brutus's countless references to "reason." He is concerned, for example, lest Caesar's "reason" be "sway'd" by his "affections" (II.i.20–21); he gives Caius Ligarius "reasons" to join the conspiracy (II.i.219); to Antony, Brutus offers assurance that "Our reasons are . . . full of good regard" for slaying Caesar (III.i.224); he mounts the pulpit to "show the reason of our Caesar's death" (III.i.237); and to the populace he promises "public reasons" for the assassination (III.ii.7), though he never reveals them. Momentarily persuaded by Brutus, even the crowd envisions him as only a head or mind to be set on the headless body of Caesar: "Caesar's better parts / Shall be crown'd in Brutus," shouts one plebian (III.ii.52–53).[22]

Transcending his spiritual dualism by annihilating the sensitive half of his soul—the half that once responded with "shows of love to other men"—Brutus unleashes his demented mind upon the already sickened world by killing the man he professes to love. In Cicero's words, "Wisdom had no ground to stand on when desires were abolished."

Montaigne, in the context of attacking the Stoic Wise Man's pretensions to "constancy," provides an important Renaissance point of view on such men as Shakespeare's Brutus. Constancy, Montaigne asserts, is a presumptuous myth: "there is no constant existence, neither of our being nor of the objects." In fact, attempts at Stoic constancy may corrupt the very virtue it seeks to preserve:

> for how much the more he shall close and press that which, by its own nature, is ever gliding, so much the more he shall loose what he would hold and fasten.

A constancy, in other words, that constricts human feeling is tantamount to stagnation and death.

> It is for our Christian faith, not for his Stoike vertue, to pretend or aspire to this divine metamorphosis.[23]

Stoic constancy, says Montaigne, is destructive because the nature of man is a dynamic organism that achieves its highest state of being in the interaction of its parts:

> The body hath a great part in our being, and therein keeps a speciall rancke. . . . Such as goe about to sunder our two principall parts, and separat them one from another, are much to blame: They ought rather to be coupled and joyned fast together. The soule must be enjoined not . . . to despise and leave the body . . . but ought to combine and cling fast unto him. . . . Christians have a particular instruction concerning this bond, for they know that Gods justice . . . embraceth this conjunction of body and soule. . . . God beholds the whole man.
>
> (II.xvii)

Condemning the man whose mind is obsessed with "dissociating hir selfe from the body," Montaigne issues a significant warning:

> It is meere folly, insteade of transforming themselves into Angels, they transchange themselves into beastes: in lieu of advancing, they abase themselves. Such transcending humours affright me.
>
> (III.xiii)

If Montaigne is frightened by such men, so too is Shakespeare's Caesar; and we must not limit his warning to Cassius alone. Brutus, even more than Cassius, "thinks too much: such men are dangerous" (II.ii.193).

Though mentally and morally sick, Brutus nonetheless believes Fate has chosen him to be physician to a political body corrupted by a malignant head.[24] As he prepares to "cut the head off" (II.i.163), Brutus, only a partial man himself, can yet speak of performing "A piece of work that will make sick men whole." Caius Ligarius, seizing the other half of the paradox, retorts, "But are not some whole that we must make sick?" (II.ii.327–28). Ligarius's rejoinder exposes the shallowness of Brutus's medicinal metaphor. The emphasis on wholeness should also recall the opening scene of the play. When the Tribunes question the cobbler as to his profession, he answers that he is "a mender of bad soles." The cobbler reminds us that when the "sole" is "bad," the shoe need not be destroyed: "when they are in great danger I recover them." How are they mended? "Truly, sir," answers the simple craftsman, "all that I live by is with the awl" (I.ii.13–21). This seemingly comic excresence on the plot actually rings with symbolic puns that form a miniature paradigm of the play's central thesis: there must be unity in a man, as in a state, before the good is achieved. Failing to live by their "awl"—their entire spiritual being, sensitive and rational—Brutus and Caesar have "bad soles" that should be mended, not destroyed.

Caesar gorging his ego on the self-debased bodies of the noblemen and Brutus devouring his own body through mental disengagement from his own needs and feelings really amount to different views of the same symbolic actions. But, while all of Brutus's mirrors—Cassius, Portia and Caesar himself —reveal images of sickness, Brutus can see only the sickness of Caesar. And against that infirmity Brutus brings the antidote of his Stoic constancy:

> Let not our looks put on our purposes
> But bear it as our Roman actors do,
> With untir'd spirits and formal constancy.
>
> (II.i.226–28)

Just prior to the assassination, when Cassius shows signs of fear, Brutus again urges him to suppress his emotions: "Be constant" (III.i.22). At the moment of the murder, Brutus becomes a dramatic image of constancy; while all around him are in complete turmoil, he remains unmoved: "People and senators, be not affrighted. / Fly not; stand still" (III.i.82–83). And just before his suicide —the ultimate assertion of Stoic constancy—he again appears as an image of the unmoved man, sitting on a "rock" (V.v.1) in the midst of battle. But there have been too many times in the play when Brutus's "constancy" has been undercut for us to accept his self-proclaimed firmness. Portia's description of a rattled and sickened man evokes anything but constancy; neither do his angry attacks on Cassius support his claims. Indeed, we have watched Cassius earlier "move" Brutus (I.ii.165) and remark afterward that even Brutus's "mettle may be wrought" because no one is so "firm that cannot be seduc'd" (I.ii.306, 309). Everyone is susceptible to movement here: "all the sway of earth / Shakes like a thing unfirm" (I.iii.3–4). For all of Caesar's pretensions to being "Constant as the northern star" and "Unshak'd of motion" (III.i.60, 70), Decius easily changes his mind with flattery.

The issue here, then, is not *whether* men are "mov'd," but *how* they are moved. For a man to believe himself insusceptible to emotional persuasion makes him all the more liable to it because of his presumptuous pride. "But when I tell him he hates flatterers, / He says he does, being then most flattered," says the clever Decius. Similarly, can a man move himself to right action purely by reason without calling upon his instincts, emotions, and will to aid in determining the true good? Can an orator move his audience without also moving their hearts and feelings? Brutus, in the pulpit, alludes to "reasons," but the people are "mov'd" (III.i.234) by Antony's appeals to both their best and worst feelings, their love for Caesar and their lust for money; for the people "are not wood," they "are not stones, but men" (III.ii.144). Obviously, emotion without reason, as dramatized in the maniacal cruelty of the mob, is perversion of man's soul. But no less a perversion occurs when pure reason, in contradiction to love and feeling, moves a man to kill his friend. In Brutus's own words, the "abuse of greatness is when it disjoins / Remorse from power" (II.i.18–19). This is what he says "might" occur in Caesar (II.i.13), but it is manifestly what does happen to Brutus.

A "constancy" that suppresses love (for Cassius, for Portia, and finally for Caesar) is clearly evil and results in spiritual death. Amidst the imagery of sickness that pervades the second act of *Caesar*, one important dramatic image must persuade us that Brutus, far from being the healer of the state, is rather a carrier of the disease. In a crucial sequence, Brutus first sees himself as the physician who will cure with constancy (II.i.180, 227). Immediately thereafter, we watch as he infects Portia with the constancy that will eventually cause her death. Portia appeals to their "vows of love," but Brutus shows no signs of being moved by Portia's feelings for him. I find it difficult to understand why critics feel this scene is "tender" and mitigates Brutus's later cruelty.[25] On the contrary, if viewed as a central symbol of Brutus's constancy —the same constancy that could allow him to say he loves Caesar (I.ii.81 and III.ii.22) and yet carve him into pieces—this scene displays Brutus's deranged mind with terrifying force.

Initially, Portia begs Brutus to "unfold" to her the source of his "grief." She kneels and invokes their "bond of marriage"; still Brutus does not respond. As a woman and the feminine half of their union—corresponding to the sensitive half of Brutus's soul—Portia desperately tries to reach him. She pleads

> By all your vows of love, and that great vow
> Which did incorporate and make us one,
> That you unfold to me, your self, your half. . . .
>
> *(II.i.271–75)*

But Portia is Brutus's other "self," the "half" of him that is now reduced to bondslave. Having severed the bond of his own soul, Brutus is no longer capable of participating in any healthy union of reciprocal affection and sustenance. Brutus abrogates, in fact, his contract with every natural social unit: with his friends, with his state, and with his wife. Not until Portia indicates her willingness to repudiate her own sensitivity and pervert her feminine nature, not until she brutalizes her own body, can she enter the counsels of the Stoic Wise Man:

> I grant I am a woman; but withal
> A woman well reputed, Cato's daughter.
> Think you I am no stronger than my sex,
> Being so father'd and so husbanded?
> Tell me your counsels, I will not disclose 'em.
> I have made strong proof of my constancy,
> Giving myself a voluntary wound
> Here, in the thigh: can I bear that with patience,
> And not my husband's secrets?
>
> (II.i.294–302)

Only by transcending her own flesh as proof of her Stoic constancy does Portia move the hardened Brutus. Then and only then with Portia bleeding in front of him—just as "Caesar must bleed for it"—does Brutus raise her in rank. From his "harlot," she now becomes "this noble wife!" (II.i.303). The quality of "constancy" and the impulse to self-destruction are visually equated at this moment.

Upon seeing the open wound, Brutus promises that "by and by thy bosom shall partake" of his "secrets" (II.i.305–6). Three scenes later, after Brutus has apparently disclosed the plot to Portia and has gone "sickly forth" (II.iv. 14) to murder Caesar, the disease of unnatural constancy eats away inside the bosom of Portia, corrupting her judgment and speech as it had in Brutus. Now a companion in that sickness, half out of her senses, barking incoherent orders to Lucius, Portia wars with herself to maintain Brutus's Stoic standards. She begs "constancy" to "Set a huge mountain 'tween my heart and tongue" (II.iv.6–7); and as the "mountain" of constancy, like a cancerous tumor, intrudes between the halves of her soul, the honesty she had begged from Brutus is now annihilated in herself. Horribly ill, she yet says,

> Run, Lucius, and commend me to my lord;
> Say I am merry; come to me again,

> And bring me word what he doth say to thee.
>
> *(II.iv.44–46)*

The culmination of Portia's infection with constancy is her suicide. Brutus had argued that the "virtue" of the conspiracy bore "fire enough . . . to steel [make firm and constant] with valour / The melting spirits of women" (II.i. 120–22). But the metaphor becomes gruesome reality when Brutus describes Portia's death:

> Impatient of my absence,
> And grief that young Octavius with Mark Antony
> Have made themselves so strong; with this she fell distract,
> And, her attendants absent, swallow'd fire.
>
> *(IV.iii.151–55)*

Spreading through Rome, the fever of self-sufficient reason that disrupts the elemental balance in mankind and burns out all human feeling literally consumes Portia. Yet what an ironic comment on Brutus's moral obtuseness that he should view Portia's attempt *to be constant* as a sign that she was incapable of it.

Clearly, the perverting sickness has its source in Brutus, and, as it destroys the bodies of Brutus and Portia, so it comes to work on Caius Ligarius, who enters "a sick man" (II.i.310) as Portia exits. Ligarius's sickness is inserted here as a reinforcement of the ironic image of Brutus as a miraculous healer. At Brutus's wish that Ligarius "were not sick," he is instantly cured by a faith in the sufficiency of Brutus's Stoic virtue to heal him:

> By all the gods that Romans bow before
> I here discard my sickness. Soul of Rome!
> Brave son, deriv'd from honourable loins!
> Thou, like an exorcist, hast conjur'd up
> My mortified spirit.
>
> . . . . .
>
> And with a heart new-fir'd I follow you,
> To do I know not what; but it sufficeth
> That Brutus leads me on.
>
> *(II.i.320–24, 332–34)*

Like Portia, Ligarius has come under the spell of the "exorcist" who frees Ligarius's rational spirit from its bodily confines. But always the exorcism requires physical mutilation. The abstract and self-deceiving language must not dispel the hard reality of the action: two sick men ignoring their physical needs and a sick woman, in perverse imitation, stabbing herself and swallowing hot coals.

All of Brutus's professed "constancy," "patience," and "endurance" is pure form. Nothing so clearly illustrates this as his actions in the quarrel scene. According to Stoic doctrine, the self-sufficient Wise Man must absolve himself of all emotional ties to humanity and

> raise himself above his human lot, [so] that he can view with unconcern pains and losses, sores and wounds, and nature's great commotions as she rages all around him, [and] can bear hardship calmly. . . .
>
> *(Seneca,* On Firmness, *v–vi.)*[26]

And indeed, Brutus is an apparent model of Stoic endurance at the announcement of Portia's death. But a persistent charge against the Stoic Wise Man is that he is able to "view with unconcern" the loss of his friends and family (Seneca's Wise Man watched as his house burned down, his daughters were abducted and his country pillaged, and yet could declare, "my holdings are all intact and unharmed") precisely because he is incapable of loving them in the first place. In the belief that his own personal sense of virtue-reason is "self sufficient for a happy life" the Stoic Wise Man deliberately cuts himself off from all ties with a less perfect humanity. He is an absolutist: virtue-reason is wholly sufficient for his existence, and he believes himself incapable of mis-judgment or moral error. Conversely, in accordance with the Stoic paradox that "all offences are equal,"[27] he has no forbearance for the faults or shortcomings of others. Horace says of the Stoic Wise Man:

> When you look over your own sins, your eyes are rheumy and daubed with ointment; why, when you view the failings of your friends, are you as keen of sight as an eagle?
>
> *(Satire* I.3*)*[28]

Erasmus repeated the criticism: "wise men . . . are eagle-sighted into their friends' faults, but so blear-eyed to their own."[29] In other words, we must not view Brutus's reaction to Portia's death in isolation, for Shakespeare has provided us with an objective test by which to measure Brutus's ability to "bear" the hardships of this world.

In the quarrel between Brutus and Cassius, which occurs immediately before Portia's suicide is revealed, Brutus piously accuses Cassius of taking bribe money—money he will demand from Cassius minutes later for his own uses. At this moment, we can understand how "the eye" of the Stoic Wise Man "sees not itself." "You love me not," says Cassius in response to Brutus's undocumented charges. "I do not like your faults," retorts Brutus. But Cassius replies, "A friendly eye could never see such faults." Echoing the attacks on "hearts" we have seen Brutus make elsewhere, Cassius laments,

> Brutus hath riv'd my heart.
> A friend should bear his friend's infirmities.
>
> (IV.iii.84–89)

The unmistakable emphasis on Brutus's inability to "bear" the shortcomings of his friends is repeated several times in the scene. We are first told that "every nice [that is, trivial] offence" seems to "bear his comment" (IV.iii.7). Having reminded Brutus that being a friend means being able to "bear his friend's infirmities," Cassius asks pointedly, "Have you not love enough to bear with me . . . ?" (IV.iii.117). His penetrating question strips away much of Brutus's thin facade of mental fortitude and prepares for the entrance of the simple-minded poet.

To underscore the essential contradiction in Brutus's professions of constancy, Shakespeare brings on an inept but sincere poet whose doggerel rhymes contain an enormous truth that Brutus will not heed:

> For shame, you generals! What do you mean?
> Love, and be friends, as two such men should be;
> For I have seen more years, I'm sure, than ye.
>
> (IV.iii.129–31)

Cassius's reaction to the poet's well-meaning verse is tolerant laughter, but Brutus angrily shouts, "Get you hence, sirrah!" Cassius urges, "Bear with him, Brutus; 'tis his fashion." The comment, however, means nothing to Brutus: "I'll know his humour, when he knows his time," he says haughtily (IV.iii. 133–35). Ignoring the poet's thought, Brutus rebukes the awkward form ("time") of the poet's speech. Like all cultural elitists, Brutus is always concerned with form: the archaic form of his ancestral namesake, the frenzied form of a tribal "sacrifice," the deceptive form of the conspiracy, and the empty form of words such as *noble, virtue, honor, patience,* and *constancy.* Later, Brutus will ask his servant Lucius to "Bear with me, good boy, I am much forgetful" (IV.iii.254), but he has already clearly illustrated the extremely short threshold of his own patience and forbearance. And yet, when Messala tells Brutus that he must "like a Roman bear the truth" of Portia's death, he replies with chilling calmness,

> Why, farewell, Portia. We must die, Messala,
> With meditating that she must die once,
> I have the patience to endure it now.
>
> *(IV.iii.189–91)*

Indeed, we all know that death is a natural event; Portia's death, however, is hideously unnatural. Cassius, whose reaction surely represents normal human feeling, replies,

> I have as much of this in art as you,
> But yet my nature could not bear it so.
>
> *(IV.iii.193–94)*

No, nor could any man's "nature" except that of the Stoic Wise Man, whose definition of man's nature prohibits tolerance for the imperfections of others and eliminates the emotion of love.

When Cassius says that a friend should "bear his friend's infirmities," he adds, "But Brutus makes mine greater than they are." Brutus stiffly answers, "I do not, till you practise them on me" (IV.iii.84–87). As a matter of fact, however, Brutus judges Cassius strictly on hearsay evidence and has no concrete proof of his perfidy whatever. But the most important aspect of this scene is the extent to which Brutus's attack on Cassius mirrors his indictment of Caesar. He admitted that he knew "no personal cause to spurn" Caesar (II.i. 20–21), but, to justify the assassination in his own mind, Brutus also makes Caesar's "infirmities greater than they are" by saying to himself: "what he is, augmented, / Would run to these and these extremities" (II.i.30–31). Furthermore, he does not kill Caesar because he has seen Caesar "practise" an offense; he murders him *"lest* he may" (II.i.28, my italics).

The quarrel between Brutus and Cassius turns on the meaning of "friend." Beneath the argument is the question "What is the duty of a friend?" Cicero's *De Amicitia*, a treatise on friendship well known during the Renaissance, is of significance here. In this work, Cicero assails the Stoics for believing that the Wise Man can rely "upon himself and is so fortified by virtue and wisdom that he is dependent on no one and considers all his possessions to be within himself."[30] When the self-sufficient man destroys the bond of natural benevolence between men ["*rerum natura benevolentiae coniunctionem*"] then, says Cicero,

the social pillars of the universe crumble (VII). If "distress of mind befalls a
. . . man, as it certainly does unless we assume that human sympathy has been
rooted out of his heart," then a man most needs a commiserating friend. "For
when the soul is deprived of emotion, what difference is there . . . between man
and a stock or stone? Nor are we to listen to those men who maintain that virtue
is hard and unyielding and is . . . something made of iron" (XIII). But perhaps
the crucial remark from Cicero concerns how a man should have forbearance
for his friend's faults:

> You should love your friend after you have appraised him; you should not
> appraise him after you have begun to love him. . . . If we deliberate after
> the event . . . we do what the ancient proverb forbids—we argue the case
> after the verdict is found.
>
> *(XXII)*

Precisely that mode of reasoning, arguing "the case after the verdict is found,"
informs Brutus's syllogism in Act II which begins, "It must be by his death"
(II.i.10ff.); after he has passed sentence on Caesar, Brutus constructs an elaborate argument to rationalize the verdict. Then, after murdering Caesar, he
reasserts his friendship for him: "So are we Caesar's friends, that have abridg'd
/ His time of fearing death" (III.i.104–5). Once more we must trust the plainspoken responses of lesser men to illuminate the twisted logic of the Stoic
Brutus. When he later requests Volumnius to help him commit suicide, Volumnius restores moral meaning to friendship: "That's not an office for a friend"
(V.v.29).

   Always hiding his own "monstrous visage," never allowing his "looks" to
reveal his "purposes" (II.i.225), Brutus remains until the last a charlatan of
words:

> *Brutus:*   Words before blows: it is so, countrymen?
> *Octavius:* Not that we love words better, as you do.
> *Brutus:*   Good words are better than bad strokes, Octavius.
> *Antony:*   In your bad strokes, Brutus, you give good words;
>   Witness the hole you made in Caesar's heart,
>   Crying, 'Long live! hail! Caesar!'
>
> *(V.i.27–32)*

Shakespeare's portrait of the "wordy" Brutus bears a striking similarity to
Cicero's description of Stoic orators:

the Stoics hold a different view of good and bad from all their fellow-citizens . . . and give a different meaning to "honour," "disgrace," "reward"[;] . . . if we were to adopt their terminology, we should never be able to express our meaning intelligibly about anything.

(De Oratore, III.xviii)[31]

Just such a man is Shakespeare's Brutus, a cultural elitist who keeps reality at word's length, cut off from the baser reality to which a part of himself belongs but to which he no longer listens. Cassius's parting words to Brutus after the quarrel symbolically describe what has happened to the Stoic Brutus:

> This was an ill beginning of the right.
> Never come such division 'tween our souls!
>
> (IV.iii.234)

From the literal level of political and social turmoil to the symbolic depths of the human soul, Shakespeare shows us the ravages of division in either the politic body or the human body and the utter desperation and inevitable failure to which it leads. The perpetual human myth of individualism and self-reliance—succinctly dramatized by focusing on the elitist impulses inherent in Stoicism—collapses under the strain of its own egoistic weight.

In the communal theater, a dramatist can, momentarily at least, restore the universal bond by forcing all men to feel the same emotions. When verisimilitude replaces mysticism, when the body is hacked into bloody pieces, the word confronts reality. The difference between the contemplation of the mystical rite of exorcism and the brutal butchering of a human being is a difference past rational comprehension, a difference that can only be viscerally understood. In Julius Caesar, Shakespeare attempts to reunite the sensitive and rational souls of his audience so that they will realize that Brutus commits, not a sacrificial ritual of cultural salvation, but a savage felony of cultural assassination. Even though his Stoic philosophy makes him a man alone, his disembodied mind brings chaos to an entire social order. In the disparity between Brutus's claim, "let no man abide this deed / But we the doers" (III.i.94–95), and the actuality that Shakespeare dramatizes—the destruction of Cinna the poet, of Portia, and of Rome itself—lies the truth of Stoic self-sufficiency and the reality of the "noble Brutus."

Notes:

1. "Julius Caesar: The Politics of the Hardened Heart," ShakS, 2 (1966), 11–33. Anson traces what he conceives to be an image of hand against heart and the

suppression of emotion reflected in the images. His main concern is Caesar himself; thus Brutus is curiously subordinated. Anson also misconstrues Antony's involvement in the Stoic imagery, arguing that Antony, Brutus, and Caesar are parallel in their attempts to harden the people. Clearly Antony's approach to the populace must be discriminated from Brutus's, but a full defense of the point would require a separate study.

2. Herschel Baker, *The Image of Man* (Cambridge, Mass., 1947), pp. 301–12. Anson cites Baker as his authority for neo-Stoicism, as if neo-Stoicism is the only consideration here. Anson seems unwilling to grant the possibility that Shakespeare could have been familiar with original Stoic doctrine or the tradition of anti-Stoic criticism. What anti-Stoic material Anson does bring to bear refers only to emotional repression.

3. Shakespeare, like any other educated Elizabethan who had read Cicero's works, would have associated Rome with only two major philosophical systems exclusively: Stoicism and Epicureanism. Despite Cicero's own affinity for the Academics, he makes it clear that Stoicism and Epicureanism held the Roman field to the detriment of all other Hellenistic schools.

4. There are two exceptions: John Palmer, *Political Characters of Shakespeare* (London, 1945, 1957), pp. 22ff.; and Gordon R. Smith, "Brutus, Virtue, and Will," *SQ*, 10 (1959), 367–79. Yet even here there are qualifications directed at mitigating Brutus's errors. Palmer argues that Brutus is good but dangerously ineffectual, and Smith inserts final reservations about his own conclusions by doubting that Shakespeare "understood" his ironic portrait of Brutus (379). In an article of my own, soon to appear in *JEGP*, I have argued that Brutus commits unmitigated acts of savagery as a result of his having broken all ties with humanity ("*JC*: Rupture in the Bond").

5. All citations from *JC* are from the New Arden Shakespeare edition, ed. T. S. Dorsch (Cambridge, Mass., 1955).

6. A complete bibliography on Stoicism and Shakespeare's drama is available in John W. Velz, *Shakespeare and the Classical Tradition: A Critical Guide to Commentary, 1660–1960* (Minneapolis, 1968). See also Joseph Chang, "Shakespeare and Stoicism," Diss. Univ. of Wisconsin, 1965. While Chang's study deals directly with *JC*, it is very misleading and, at times, in error about Stoic doctrine. In addition, Chang takes no account of anti-Stoic commentary that may have influenced Shakespeare.

7. Two studies are relevant here: Robert Ornstein, "Seneca and the Political Drama of *Julius Caesar*," *JEGP*, 57 (1958), 51–56; and Frank L. Schoell, *Etudes sur l'humanisme continental en Angleterre à la fin de la renaissance*, *BRLC*, 29 (1926). Ornstein, because he judges Shakespeare's source to be Seneca's *De Benificiis*, imposes Seneca's judgment that Brutus was an ineffective Stoic; in slight contradiction, Schoell argues that Brutus's Stoicism derives from Epictetus.

8. North's translation as reprinted in Geoffrey Bullough, *Narrative and Dramatic Sources of Shakespeare* (London and New York, 1964), V, 90.

9. *Academica*, trans. H. Rackham (London and New York, 1933), II.xliii.

10. See, for example, Rudolf Kirk's introduction to *Joseph Lipsius, TVVO BOOKES of Constancie*, trans. John Stradling, London, 1594 (New Brunswick, 1939), pp.

15–16. Throughout his introduction, Kirk refers casually to Cicero as a Stoic.

11. *De Finibus Bonorum et Malorum*, trans. H. Rackham (Cambridge, Mass., 1951).

12. Trans. J. E. King (Cambridge, Mass., 1950). On Shakespeare's familiarity with the work in reference to Hamlet, see M. H. Addington, "Shakespeare and Cicero," *N&Q*, 165 (1933), 116–18.

13. See especially V.xxxi, where Cicero suggests that the Stoics deceive themselves in pretending to ignore pain and anguish.

14. The anti-Stoic tradition begins with Cicero, but by Shakespeare's time many authors were parodying the Stoic Wise Man (or his modern equivalent). Bodin, Erasmus, Montaigne, Bacon, Marston, and Burton were among those who were extremely skeptical, if not contemptuous, of Stoicism's pretensions to moral piety and wisdom, particularly in a political context. Shakespeare was certainly familiar with the criticism and used the most common wordplay on "Stoic" when he had Tranio in *The Taming of the Shrew* say, "while we do admire / This virtue and this moral discipline, / Let's be no stoics nor no stocks . . ." (I.i.29–31).

15. I discuss Brutus's role in the politic body in more detail in my forthcoming article in *JEGP*. The present study focuses on the moral defects of Brutus but argues for a close parallel between Brutus the politician and Brutus the human being.

16. Trans. and ed. by Marcus Dods (New York, 1948).

17. A similarly severe distinction between mind and body is made throughout Guillaume DuVair's *The Moral Philosophie of the Stoicks*, trans. Thomas James (1598), reprinted with notes and introduction by Rudolf Kirk (New Brunswick, N.J., 1939).

18. *TVVO BOOKES*, p. 80.

19. "*Julius Caesar*: Rupture in the Bond," *JEGP* (forthcoming).

20. Tranio, in counseling Lucentio to abjure the Stoic philosophy, argues that instead of this ascetic creed, "Music and poesy use to quicken you"; and he adds, "No profit grows where is no pleasure ta'en" (*Shr.*, I.i.37, 39).

21. The typical separation of Cassius as Epicurean and Brutus as Stoic is not justified. A "lean and hungry look" can in no way be associated with a philosophy which has always (rightly or wrongly) been identified with fleshly indulgence. Cassius mentions Epicurus only in the context of omens. Otherwise, physically and intellectually, he becomes more and more the mirror image of Brutus as the play progresses. A recent production of *JC* by the Stratford-upon-Avon players (1968) was attacked in a review for casting Barrie Ingham, a very thin actor, in the role of Brutus. Ingham portrayed Brutus, says the reviewer, as "the most neurotic Roman of them all" and "leaner and hungrier than Cassius"—a scheme the reviewer found "perverse." Clearly, the Stratford director was more faithful to Shakespeare. See Phillip French, "Marcus, Marcus, Marcus," *New Statesman*, 12 (April 1968), 492.

22. There is no evidence to believe that this line indicates the people are trying to make Brutus a king, as many critics, reading the word "crown'd" literally, have argued. Within the scheme of the head-body imagery, the line should be read as symbolic of the politic body's instinctive need for a head. The previous line

says, "Let him be Caesar," not "Let him be king." The repeated use of the word *let* may also be significant.

23. *Essays*, trans. John Florio (1603), reprinted in the Everyman edition (London, 1910), II.xii.

24. It was because the Stoics revered Fate that they tried to divine Fate's will through all forms of divination, augury, and prophecy. Cicero says that the "stoics . . . defended nearly every sort of divination," and he lists the many treatises on the subject written by Stoics. See *De Divinatione*, I.iii. In this light, the impact of the soothsayer's prediction on Brutus may be important. After the assassination, Brutus shouts, "Fates, we will know your pleasures" (III.i.98).

25. Mildred Hartsock, "The Complexity of *Julius Caesar*," *PMLA*, 81 (1966), 60.

26. *Moral Essays*, trans. John W. Basore (New York, 1928).

27. See Cicero's *Paradoxa Stoicorum*, "Paradoxon III."

28. *Satires, Epistles, and Ars Poetica*, trans. H. Rushton Fairclough (Cambridge, Mass., 1951).

29. *The Praise of Folly*, trans. John Wilson (1688; Ann Arbor, Mich. 1958), p. 31.

30. Trans. William Armistead Falconer (Cambridge, Mass., 1950).

31. Trans. H. Rackham (Cambridge, Mass., 1950).

Hamlet, Hecuba, and Plutarch

James A. Freeman

> What's Hecuba to him, or he to Hecuba,
> That he should weep for her?
>
> . . . . .
>
>   I have heard
> That guilty creatures sitting at a play
> Have by the very cunning of the scene
> Been struck so to the soul that presently
> They have proclaimed their malefactions.
>
>   (II.ii.585–86; 617–21)

Hamlet is so chagrined by the actor who weeps for Hecuba that he castigates his own sloth and determines to "catch the conscience of the king" by restaging his father's murder in front of Claudius. Hamlet's justification for the mousetrap is that killers in the past, seeing crimes enacted at a theater, have been moved to reveal their own guilt publicly. In order to substantiate Hamlet's claim, commentators point to three works in which a similar tactic appears: *A Warning for Fair Women* (1599), Thomas Heywood's *An Apology for Actors* (1612), and Philip Massinger's *The Roman Actor* (1629). Because of its date, only *A Warning for Fair Women* may be put forward as a source for Shakespeare's statement. But a careful reading of the anonymous play certainly disqualifies it from any but a marginal relationship to *Hamlet*. Indeed, none of the incidents in any of the other works explains the collocation of "a fiction" of Hecuba to a weeping confession by some guilty king so well as does an episode in Plutarch's *Pelopidas*.[1]

Even if Shakespeare had seen or read *A Warning for Fair Women*, he would have had to go to improbable lengths in order to enlarge one unemphatic stage maneuver into the Hecuba soliloquy. The pedestrian plot of this play, which was acted by the Lord Chamberlain's company, concerns the passion of George Browne for a married woman, Anne Sanders. He enlists his servant Roger and a go-between, Anne Drurie, in order to win Mrs. Sanders. The predictable sequence of lust, murder, detection, and punishment is enlivened by three dumb shows which are introduced by Tragedie and function as previews of coming action. In the first, Lust embraces Anne Sanders while Chastitie vainly tries to intervene. After Anne Drurie pushes aside Chastitie, Browne hugs Mrs. Sanders, Roger hugs Anne Drurie, and "the Furies leape

and imbrace" (sig. D1). The second dumb show is only slightly more imaginative. A tree springs up between Browne and Anne Sanders. Lust hands an axe
to her which she declines; Browne accepts it and cuts down the tree. Chastitie
enters and points out for Mrs. Sanders a picture of her husband, an action
which "seemes to tell her, that that is the tree so rashly cut downe" (sig. E3ᵛ).
Neither of these vivified plot summaries, of course, can be related to *Hamlet*.
But they are typical of the technique of *A Warning for Fair Women*: a straightforward tale is retold by its main characters who indicate their moral choices
by symbolic acts. Since the dialogue of the play is generally quite ordinary,
the presence of personified abstractions in the dumb shows helps to give a
slight air of profundity, not to mention of melodrama.

Only the third dumb show bears the slightest claim on *Hamlet*, and that
a tenuous one. It takes place after Browne and Roger have killed Mr. Sanders:
Chastitie tells her woeful story to Mercy, who wakens sleeping Justice. The
latter dispatches officers who return with Mr. Sanders's body. The printed
stage directions at this point are remarkably tepid when compared to Hamlet's
assertion: "Mistris *Sanders, Drury,* and *Roger,* led after it, and being shewne
it, they al seeme very sorrowful, and so are led away" (sig. G3). Even Tragedie's
words which are spoken immediately after the dumb show do not claim the
power of lie detection so important in Hamlet:

> The dead body brought for instance forth,
> Strait inquisition and search is made,
> And the offenders as you did behold,
> Discouer'd where they thought to be unseene.

There is no need to labor the differences between *A Warning for Fair Women*
and *Hamlet*. The main point of the Lord Chamberlain's dumb show is that
murder will out; the point of Hamlet's words is that murder can be detected by
"cunning." The anonymous play directs actors to "seeme very sorrowful," not
to admit their guilt. In fact Browne's guilt is established by John Bean, a servant
of Mr. Sanders who has lived through the assassination attempt. During the
trial only Roger confesses and he is in no way influenced by a stage play. Hamlet's numbed will is animated by recollections of another more memorable
example of crime detection.

Far worthier for encouraging the Wittenberg student is an episode told
in Plutarch's *Pelopidas* about Alexander of Pherae. The character of Alexander
is so thoroughly denigrated that he would seem to be immune to any claim of
conscience. He is hated by his own wife since he "besides all other infamous
actes of his detestable life, committed Sodomy with her youngest brother."[2]
Neighboring cities help Alexander's enemies because they are "marvelous glad

for the hope they had, quickly to see the tyran have his deserved hyer, for all his former wicked deeds" (sig. DD6ᵛ). Even though Alexander neglects his noble prisoner Pelopidas, Epaminondas is hesitant about attempting a rescue since he knows

> the daunger and crueltie of [Alexander's] beastly rage. . . . He was a cruel man, and one that neither regarded reason, nor justice in any sorte, consideringe howe he made some man to be buried alive, and others to be put in the skinnes of beares and wilde bores, and then to set houndes apon them to teare them in peeces, or else him selfe for his pastime would kill them, with shootinge or throwinge of dartes at them.
>
> *(sig. DD6ᵛ)*

This sadist killed allies, children, and his own uncle. Plutarch is careful to include details about Alexander which imply that he is impervious to any human responses. For example, he worships the spear with which he murdered his uncle. And yet the plight of Hecuba moves him to tears:

> An other time being in a Theater, where the tragedy of *Troades* of *Euripides* was played, he went out of the Theater, and sent word to the players notwithstandinge, that they should go on with their playe, as if he had bene still amonge them: saying, that he came not away for any mis-liking he had of them or of the play, but bicause he was ashamed his people shoulde see him weepe, to see the miseries of *Hecuba* and *Andromacha* played, and that they never saw him pity the death of any one man, of so many of his citizens as he had caused to be slaine. The gilty conscience therefore of this cruell and heathen tyran, did make him tremble at the only name and reputacion of Epaminondas.
>
> *(sig. DD6ᵛ, EE1)*

For Shakespeare's purposes, this incident has several useful qualities. Plutarch's Alexander furnishes a prototype for Claudius, whom Hamlet carica-tures as "bloody, bawdy villain! Remorseless, treacherous, lecherous villain" (II.ii.609–10). Strictly speaking, these traits fit Alexander more closely than they fit Claudius, but in Hamlet's eyes his uncle *is* an Alexander. Both are "lecherous" villains. From Hamlet's first soliloquy where he imagines Claudius to be an incarnation of bestial appetite ("a satyr" in I.ii.140), to his final words when he executes Claudius, the accusation of unbridled sexuality is similar to that leveled at Alexander. Even the specific charge of incest which Plutarch raises reappears in Shakespeare. Throughout the play Hamlet associates Claudius with "incestuous sheets" (I.ii.157) and "the incestuous pleasure of his bed" (III.iii.90). The ghost's curse on "that incestuous, that adulterous beast" (I.v.41) is satisfied when his son executes Claudius:

> Here, thou incestuous, murderous, damned Dane,
> Drink off this potion. Is thy union here?
> Follow my mother.
>
> *(V.ii.336–38)*

A second trait which both Alexander and Claudius share is the murder of a close male relative. Hamlet imputes to Claudius the same unrepentant gloating which marks Alexander as a hardened killer. He fails to discern that Claudius only seems unmoved by his crime and is, in his futile attempt to pray, tormented by guilt. This guilt complicates the character of Claudius as well as negates the one-dimensional picture which Hamlet has created. With grim irony the man who claimed "I know not 'seems'" (I.ii.76) accepts the surface of Claudius to be a true indication that he is a latter-day Alexander, impervious to remorse.

Another of Plutarch's attractions is that, unlike the bourgeois characters in *A Warning for Fair Women*, *Pelopidas* reveals the intrigues of state rulers in extraordinary moments at court. The discomfiture which a nameless actor playing Hecuba caused Alexander is in line with those innumerable stories of kings who fell from high estate because of unusual accidents. A memory of Alexander's fall remains in Hamlet's mind until the graveyard scene:

> *Hamlet*: Dost think Alexander looked o' this fashion i' the earth?
> *Horatio*: E'en so.
> *Hamlet*: And smelt so? pah!
> *Horatio*: E'en so, my lord.
> *Hamlet*: To what base uses we may return, Horatio!
> Why may not imagination trace the noble dust of
> Alexander, till he find it stopping a bung-hole?[3]

Not only are the themes of incest, cold-blooded family murder, and courtly tragedy common to Plutarch and Shakespeare, but so is the general situation of Pelopidas and Hamlet. Both are nobles who find themselves unjustly detained by monsters. With typical subtlety, Shakespeare expands the motif of confinement until it becomes a metaphor for all life:

> *Hamlet*:   Denmark's a prison.
> *Rosencrantz*: Then is the world one.

Hamlet: A goodly one; in which there are many confines,
               wards and dungeons, Denmark being one o' the worst.

                                                   (II.ii.251–53)

Yet the Hecuba speech functions in *Hamlet* as it does in Plutarch: it initiates
the release of a prisoner. Awakened by the actor, Alexander's "gilty conscience" prompts him to free Pelopidas. Presumably the tyrant views
Epaminondas as an embodiment of Nemesis who has come to punish his
crimes. In Hamlet's case, the feeling of impotent confinement changes to one
of hope because the actor arouses a chain of thoughts which culminates in
Hamlet's command "About, my brain" (II.ii.617). As soon as his memory
recalls "that guilty creatures" may lose their apparently unshakable self-
control "at a play," he is able to initiate his own liberation. The example of
Alexander allows Hamlet to begin his own regeneration. By staging the play
he can change from prisoner to judge, from "John-a-dreams" (II.ii.595) to
avenging agent and from spectator to cunning director.

Notes:

1. The strong attraction which North's Plutarch had for Shakespeare seems to
   have inspired no imitators in the matter of "guilty creatures sitting at a play."
   Both Heywood and Massinger mention people who reveal their crimes while
   at the theater. But the two women in Heywood's *Apology* are notable only because they support his defense of the stage as a socially useful medium. Heywood's first example is typical of the folktale tone of the entire tract: *Fryer
   Francis* plays without interruption in Norfolk until "a townes-woman (till then
   of good estimation and report) finding her conscience (at this presentment) extremely troubled, suddenly skritched and cryd out Oh my husband, my husband"
   (sig. G1ᵛ). Massinger slightly alters this commonplace about plays and women
   with secrets. Most of *The Roman Actor* III.iii is devoted to a court play in which
   Empress Domitilla acts the part of Anaxarete in front of her suspicious husband
   Domitian. By her enthusiasm she reveals her love for Paris, an actor playing Iphis.
   Neither of these later authors deals with guilty men, nor with incest, nor with
   imprisonment, nor with Hecuba, nor, finally, with the same situation as Plutarch
   and Shakespeare.
2. Plutarke of Chaeronea, *The Lives of the Noble Grecians and Romanes*, trans.
   Thomas North (1579), sig. DD6.
3. V.i.218–26. Alexander of Pherae ruled 369–358 B.C., while his more famous
   namesake Alexander the Great lived 356–323 B.C. Both were vilified by historians,
   but the tradition of an ignominious death belongs to the Macedonian. It is likely
   that Shakespeare merges the two figures here. See references to other works
   (including Shakespeare's) in Leslie George Whitbread, *Fulgentius the Mythographer* (Columbus, Ohio, 1971), pp. 226–27.

More on the Search for Yorick's Skull;
or, The Goths Refuted

A. P. STABLER

Scholars of Germanic and Scandinavian literatures have long patriotically attempted to claim for their authors more of the credit for source contributions to Shakespeare's *Hamlet*, despite the fact that it is already universally conceded that the basic framework of the story was originally furnished by the Danish historian, Saxo Grammaticus, in his *Gesta danorum* . . . .[1] Recently, however, an attempt has been made to go much further and to deny altogether the claims of Belleforest,[2] generally recognized as the intermediary source, and to suggest that Shakespeare (or his predecessor, the author of the putative *Ur-Hamlet*)[3] needed to go no farther for his raw materials than to Saxo, or to a new contender, the German, Albert Krantz.[4] This is the position of Yngve B. Olsson in his "In Search of Yorick's Skull: Notes on the Background of Hamlet," in *Shakespeare Studies*, 4 (1968), 183–220. The present note seeks to refute Olsson's thesis.

In order to challenge successfully Belleforest's position as principal *immediate* source of *Hamlet* (or of the *Ur-Hamlet*), there are two quite simple, but quite definite, requirements: to show (1) that there is in the derived versions a body of material, *clearly not in Belleforest*, and *clearly present* in Saxo and/or in Krantz; and conversely (2) that there is *not anything* in the derived versions (Shakespeare, for the present discussion) *which necessarily must come from Belleforest* rather than from other sources. I submit that Olsson has fulfilled *neither* requirement, and that his demonstration thus collapses from want of a valid foundation.

It is perhaps most saving of time to begin with the second of the two propositions. Olsson, basing himself on one discussion of *Hamlet* sources published in 1957, and ignoring later work on the subject, mentions "the *two* [italics mine] details in Belleforest which are missing in Saxo but which have been found to be in agreement with Shakespeare's *Hamlet* . . ." (p. 214). This view of the relative paucity of Belleforest's original contributions to *Hamlet* has, I hope, been exploded in a number of articles I have published since 1962,[5] and to which I refer those interested in the details: suffice it to say that Belleforest has contributed to the Shakespearean *Hamlet* not only a number of important features (for example, the ghost and the more developed characterization of Queen Gertrude), but even specific turns of phrase (for example, "suits of inky black," and "fruitful river in the eye"; "Sir, I lack advancement") —features totally lacking in either Saxo or Krantz.[6] The burden of proof,

therefore, shifts to those who would seek to show that Shakespeare (or the
author of the *Ur-Hamlet*) went elsewhere for items which, after all, *do* appear
in Belleforest's version—such as the "melancholy" and the "adultery"—
whether or not they are treated in precisely the same way in Shakespeare,
whether or not they occupied a "prominent place" in Belleforest's text (cf.
Olsson's argument, p. 214), or whether Krantz's account, for example, is
"clearer and simpler" (p. 206). It has been abundantly shown, indeed, that
Shakespeare (or whoever) read Belleforest with quite an eye to detail, since
a number of relatively obscure items, even from Belleforest's long-winded
"further adventures of Hamlet," appears in the derived versions.[7]

Olsson's principal suggestion, then, that the English *Hamlet* might not
necessarily be derived, *even in part*, from Belleforest's version, is patently
incorrect. Let us now see if there is any reason to be obliged to suppose that
Hamlet may have been partially derived from the version of either Saxo or
Krantz, on the basis of the features which Olsson alleges to be present in the
latter authors, but not in Belleforest.

On pages 203–4 the matter of the eavesdropping counselor in the closet
scene is discussed. Olsson's contention is that Krantz's version differs from that
of Saxo, and possibly from that of Belleforest, in that Krantz has the eavesdropper hide under the bed, rather than merely under the bedcovers (or behind
the arras), with his feet showing, although he has attempted to conceal them
by pulling the covers down over himself. Olsson also contends that neither
Belleforest's nor Shakespeare's accounts necessarily contradict this under-the-
bed interpretation, which he finds generally superior to a behind-the-arras one.
This latter leg of the conclusion I find farfetched, if not impossible; but I
should also like to suggest that Krantz's account does not necessarily imply
that the counselor was actually under the bed, or that his feet were showing. In
order to buttress this interpretation, indeed, Olsson has actually mistranslated
one of the passages from Krantz which he quotes: he renders "stratum lecti
superinduxit delitescenti sibi" (he pulled the covers of the bed over himself
for concealment) as "he crept under the bed and pulled down the counterpane
in order to conceal himself" (pp. 195, 196). There then follows the matter of
the feet: Krantz says "latus defodit latentis, quem pedibus sub lectulo de-
prendit," which Olsson believes equivalent to "pierced the side of the eavesdropper, whom he detected under the bed by his feet" (pp. 196, 197): the
question here being, by *whose* feet? Both Saxo and Belleforest tell us that
Amlethus, jumping onto the bed beneath the covers of which the eavesdropper
lay concealed, felt him there;[8] Saxo specifies, *as a lump beneath his feet.*
Krantz's account is practically identical, and the simple word *pedibus* (used,

as in Saxo, as an ablative of means) gives no clue to the owner of the feet; even Olsson's translation could be construed with the *his* referring to Amlethus. True, there is the *sub lectulo* to explain; and here I would maintain that "under the bed" may by a sort of synecdoche just as well mean "under the bedcovers" as Olsson's suggestion that in Belleforest "under the covers" could mean "under the bed." In any case, if the man's feet were showing, why the necessity for Amlethus to detect him by jumping onto the bed?

Olsson concludes this section by wondering, in view of the essential similarity in the Krantz and Belleforest accounts, whether Krantz may not be Belleforest's source (presumably, rather than Saxo). Closer investigation would have revealed that Belleforest indeed acknowledges Krantz as a source in several of his *Histoires tragiques* (for example, in Vol. IV, no. 2); but there is no indication that he did so in the case of his *Hamlet.*[9]

Next, on pages 206–9, we find a lengthy treatment of the problem of Gertrude's adultery, which does not appear to add anything to the many discussions in previous studies. Olsson's conclusions seem to be that (1) Belleforest evidently alleges adultery on the part of the queen during the lifetime of her first husband; (2) Krantz may or may not imply the same; and (3) Shakespeare's stand is equally ambiguous, so that nothing can be proved one way or the other as to what source was used, by referring to this feature. One can only agree!

On pages 201, 211, and 213–14, Olsson discusses the matter of the "epitaphs" provided for Hamlet in Saxo, Krantz, Belleforest, and Shakespeare. His general conclusion is that the "grandiloquent" epitaph of Saxo/Krantz prepares Fortinbras's *envoi* at the conclusion of Shakespeare's play, whereas "Belleforest's epitaph of Hamlet reads as if he grieved not a hero but a fool . . ." (p. 213). Olsson here has either inadvertently or deliberately confused Belleforest's "epitaph" (Gollancz, p. 306)—which is in essential accord with that of Saxo/Krantz—with his estimate of Hamlet's "fatal flaw" (Gollancz, p. 308).[10] With respect to this latter, Olsson also states (p. 213) that Belleforest's identification of the flaw (an "amitié trop véhémente" which he bore his wife and which caused him to lose his "admirable prudence") is "totally different from the flaw in Hamlet's character that Saxo attributes to him. . . ." I am unable to find any statement in Olsson's text identifying Saxo's version of the "flaw," but referring to Saxo's text itself, just preceding his own tirade on the "frailty thy name is woman" theme, we read: "Tanta autem Hermutrudae charitate tenebatur: ut majorem futurae ejus viduitatis, quam propriae necis solicitudinem animo insitam gestaret," which Saxo's translator renders as: "Yet he was enchained by such love for Hermutrude, that he was more deeply concerned about her future widowhood than about his own death" (Gollancz, pp. 160, 161). Again, one finds no significant difference in the versions of Saxo and Belleforest.

On page 209, Olsson suggests Saxo's "caetera silere memineris" (Gollancz, p. 114) as the possible source of Shakespeare's "the rest is silence." Whatever may be the merits of his demonstration, again Saxo is unnecessary as an immediate source, since Belleforest in the corresponding place has Hamlet instruct his mother: ". . . au reste . . . que le Roy, ny autre ne soit en rien informé de cecy, et me laissez faire au reste . . ." (for the rest . . . let not the King, nor anyone else hear aught of this, and leave the rest to me . . .; Gollancz, p. 218).

On his page 211 Olsson has, I believe, found a good hint for the source of Claudius's *fear* of Hamlet, in the fact that Amlethus was popular with the "general gender"; but Krantz's phrase was hardly necessary to furnish this hint, in view of the fact that, after his harangue to the Danes (Gollancz, pp. 132–41, and pp. 264–83), Amlethus was *elected king by general acclamation*, as is reported in all the sources.[11]

Further efforts are made to promote Saxo/Krantz and to disinherit Belleforest on page 212, where we learn that the colorfully misogynistic material from the former authors "breaks through" into the nunnery and closet scenes of Shakespeare's *Hamlet*; Belleforest is not here mentioned, even though he has even more of the same material (misogyny is one of his specialities) in all the corresponding places. Olsson does allude to this later (p. 213).

Olsson's arguments and demonstrations, then, are in part erroneous, and elsewhere inconclusive, winding up with statements such as "therefore, even if the name [Hercules] occurs in both [*sic*] Saxo, Krantz, and Belleforest, it would seem that the sense in which it was used in Shakespeare's *Hamlet* agrees more with the two Latin texts than with Belleforest" (p. 201); or, (after his lengthy treatment of Amlethus's harangue to the Danes [pp. 209–11]) "if the . . . motif is not Shakespeare's own invention, it cannot be attributed to one source to the exclusion of any of the others" (p. 211). Olsson is also quick to concede to Shakespeare considerable originality, and transformation of his raw materials when he differs from Saxo or Krantz; but he seems to feel that material from Belleforest, to be considered as having influenced the play, should have come across intact (see, for example, pp. 214–15). One must also deplore the procedure of the author, who exposes himself to the suspicion of having developed a subjective bias against the French writer, in prefacing his observations with such remarks as "Belleforest stoops to . . .", or "is not content to tell the straightforward story." One such observation is, however, particularly inappropriate: "Belleforest goes out of his way to give a discourse on Hamlet's powers of divination" (p. 202; see also discussion, pp. 214–15). Unfortunately for Olsson's point here (Belleforest's undeniable prolixity), this discourse on divination has proved to be particularly rich in Belleforest contributions to *Hamlet*: note especially "O my prophetic soul!" and all the material on the ability of the melancholiac to receive preternatural information regarding hidden past events, and the danger of being "abused by the devil."[12]

Finally, one may observe that the various minor and vague resemblances between Saxo/Krantz and Shakespeare, in the absence of any clear use, prove nothing; every feature of any work is going to resemble something else, somewhere. Granted that Shakespeare (or whoever) in *Hamlet* used subsidiary sources in addition to his central source; but there is no need to seek further than the central source for items which are clearly to be found therein. By the same token, Olsson's introductory material (however interesting it may be in itself) stressing "the connection between *Hamlet* and the Scottish royal family [King James and his Danish queen]" (p. 185), the non-availability of Belleforest's version in English, and so forth, becomes quite irrelevant in view of the refutation of the main thesis.

Olsson's suggestion, therefore, that the versions of Saxo and/or of Krantz "may have contributed to the play besides, or instead of Belleforest" (p. 184) stands, as to the first of the two requirements I have considered, as not proved, and as to the second, disproved. The existing evidence points to an ever closer connection between Belleforest and Shakespeare.[13]

Notes:

1. Ed. J. Olrik and H. Raeder (Copenhagen, 1931). The *Hamlet* stories of both Saxo and Belleforest (see next note) are most conveniently to be consulted in Sir I. Gollancz's *The Sources of Hamlet . . .* (London, 1926)—hereinafter referred to as Gollancz.
2. François de Belleforest (1530–83), whose *Hamlet* story is to be found in Vol. V of his *Histoires tragiques . . .* (Paris, 1572).
3. There are a number of late sixteenth-century references to an English Hamlet-play probably antedating that of Shakespeare; for bibliography see any modern critical edition of the play.
4. His version of the *Hamlet* story appears in his *Chronica regnorum aquilonarum: Daniae, Suetiae, Norvagiae . . .* (Argentorati, 1546). For additional bibliography on Krantz, see the article of Yngve B. Olsson discussed in the present note.
5. "King Hamlet's Ghost in Belleforest?" *PMLA*, 77 (1962), 18–20; "The Sources of *Hamlet*: Some Corrections of the Record," *RS*, 32 (1964), 207–16; "Elective Monarchy in the Sources of *Hamlet*," *SP*, 62 (1965), 654–61; "Melancholy,

Ambition, and Revenge in Belleforest's *Hamlet*," *PMLA*, 81 (1966), 207–13; "The Source of the German *Hamlet*," *ShakS*, 5 (1969), 97–105.

6. For Belleforest's contributions to the role of the queen, see the article in *RS* cited in n. 5; for the phrases cited, see the article in the June, 1966 issue of *PMLA*, p. 209 n.

7. E.g. the name Gertrude, which, as Olsson points out (p. 212), is a conflation of *Gerutha* (Amlethus's mother) and *Hermetrude* (his second wife); and more especially the "epitaph" (discussed below); see also p. 212 n. 22 in the last article cited in note 5 above.

8. Olsson takes no account of scholarly discussion of the "straw" with which Saxo is alleged to have furnished the bedchamber of Queen Gerutha; even Gollancz, in 1926, read *stramentum* as "quilt," (see his p. 319); see the article in *RS* cited in n. 5; p. 209 n.

9. In support of the possibility of Krantz being Belleforest's source, Olsson furnishes lists of the dates of the editions of the two authors; in these, and also on p. 187 he indicates that the first edition of Belleforest's *Hamlet* appeared in 1576, thus perpetuating an error of Gollancz and others, rectified many times both before and since the time of the latter: for the record let it be known that the first edition (now lost) of Belleforest's *Hamlet* was of 1570, and the second (and best surviving) in 1572. For a rather complete bibliography, see my diss., "The *Histoires Tragiques* of François de Belleforest . . ." (Univ. of Virginia, 1958).

10. On the matter of the epitaph, see p. 213 in the last article cited in note 5 above.

11. See article on elective monarchy cited in note 5 above for detailed discussion.

12. See pp. 207–8 in the last article cited in note 5 above.

13. After the original completion of the present note, it occurred to me that I had not spoken to Olsson's last point, that Shakespeare, if he had consulted Krantz, might have gotten the idea for Yorick's skull from the death's-head pictured in the woodcut of the initial *W* (reproduced by Olsson on p. 214 of his article) of Krantz's chapters 20 and 21. While attaching no great weight to this speculation (see for example the treatment of the skull in Harry Morris's "*Hamlet* as a *Memento Mori* Poem," *PMLA*, 85 [1970], 1035–37) I did ask myself if on the other hand there might be anything in Belleforest's version which might—in Olsson's words—have triggered a similar association. It immediately came to my mind that the name *Yorick* is but one letter off from that of Gerutha's father, King *Rorick* (in Belleforest *Rorique*), who is mentioned in all the source versions. For a dramatist in search of a name for a minor (deceased) character, with Belleforest's tale before him, the invention of the name *Yorick* would be entirely natural; and, on further check, I find that the same suggestion was made as early as 1872 by a Mr. Magnusson, as cited by H. H. Furness in his *Variorum Hamlet . . .* , Vol. I, p. 395, n. 170.

Desdemona Unpinned:
Universal Guilt in *Othello*

Julian C. Rice

The linking and parallelism between individual characters in Shakespearean drama is nowhere more prevalent than it is in *Othello*. As Barbara Everett has expressed it, the characters are all "forced by the 'elements that clip us round about' into a perpetual sense of, or straining toward, community. The 'net shall enmesh them all' is made at the instant the play begins, and is a condition of common need and common imperfection, so that a character can only define itself through other characters."[1] This linking may have serious thematic implications. Is Othello responsible for his actions, or does he perhaps represent a common human vulnerability to Iago's destructive powers? The idea that all men share the responsibility for the acts of any individual human being is suggested when Desdemona paradoxically accuses herself of her own murder: "*Emilia*. O, who hath done this deed? / *Desdemona*. Nobody—I myself."

Although the abstract idea of universal guilt, stemming from the Fall, has been connected with the play, the criticism almost unanimously excludes Desdemona from participation. Most frequently, she is viewed as a Christ-figure, a morally perfect and entirely innocent victim. If it can be shown that Desdemona resembles Othello in more ways than she transcends him, however, the drama may be said to be less a tragedy of individual character than of human nature itself. Evil is most terrifying when it is performed with the conviction of goodness and moral necessity. But the archetypal evildoer, like Oedipus, is not himself as malicious as he is, ultimately, blind. It is the "blood and baseness" of Othello's nature which leads him to "preposterous conclusions," but the same blood and baseness is present in the most outwardly virtuous of human beings—even in Desdemona.

Brabantio's disillusion with Desdemona foreshadows the play's more subtle revelations. Just as Desdemona's last speech in the play indicates that, being human, she shares the responsibility for her own murder, so her first lines in the play force Brabantio to face the reality that "she was half the wooer." Significantly, Brabantio says that he will forswear retributive justice upon Othello, if Desdemona turns out to be guilty. The realization that if all do offend, none do offend, is a traditional concomitant of the very logical Christian response of compassion toward human frailty.

> I pray you hear her speak,
> If she confess that she was half the wooer

> Destruction on my head if my bad blame
> Light on the man!
>
> (I.iii.175–78)[2]

But Brabantio is as foolish as King Lear temporarily is, when, faced with human imperfection, he condemns generation: "I had rather adopt a child than get it." No child of Adam and Eve can be any better than Desdemona proves to be, but even she is morally vulnerable.

Her first major motive in the play, to accompany Othello to Cyprus, occasions a plea for sympathy from the "gracious Duke." Her speech may also be taken as a Christian plea for charity from the audience:

> Most gracious Duke,
> To my unfolding lend your prosperous ear,
> And let me find a charter in your voice,
> T'assist my simpleness.
>
> (I.iii.239–42)

As her true nature and simultaneous naïveté are "unfolded" in the course of the play, so are the same qualities shown in her husband. To hold Othello or Desdemona morally responsible or "damned" for the unfolding tragedy would presumably not be the response of a "prosperous" or "gracious" auditor. Her next speech expresses her love for as well as her resemblance to Othello. Being married, they are of the same family, and more symbolically they have always been married members of the human family: "My heart's subdued / Even to the very quality of my lord." In their Platonically proud denial of the body's claims (like Othello's earlier refusal to promote Iago), they are exactly alike.

While Othello and Desdemona may consider their union to be a marriage of true minds, many members of Shakespeare's audience were probably not Neoplatonists. A denial of sexual reality may have been as obviously naïve to devout "married" Protestants in Shakespeare's audience as it would be today to commonplace psychological perception. After Desdemona insists that she wants to go to Cyprus for reasons other than sexual desire ("I saw Othello's visage in his mind") Othello himself puts what he comically considers to be first things first:

> Let her have your voice.
> Vouch with me, heaven, I therefore beg it not
> To please the palate of my appetite,
> Nor to comply with heat—the young affects

In me defunct—and proper satisfaction;
But to be free and bounteous to her mind;

(I.iii.261–66)

His next lines ominously and ironically foreshadow the tragic action:

No, when light-winged toys
Of feathered Cupid seel with wanton dullness
My speculative and officed instrument,
That my disports corrupt and taint my business,
Let housewives make a skillet of my helm,
And all indign and base adversities
Make head against my estimation!

(I.iii.263–69)

A base adversary does indeed suborn Othello's noble sentiments and psychological naïveté to his own purposes. A new tragic "estimation" of human nature is a major aspect of the play's development. The audience will have to reassess the appearance which the noble Moor presents in Act I. To neglect this and to accept Othello's and Desdemona's own definitions of themselves is to be fooled as they are by flattery, that is, an overly optimistic or Neoplatonic view of the human condition.

In II.i Desdemona listens disapprovingly to Iago's pessimistic view of women:

You are pictures out of door,
Bells in your parlors, wildcats in your kitchens,
Saints in your injuries, devils being offended,
Players in your housewifery, and housewives in your beds.

(II.i.110–13)

Such a slanderous view disturbs Desdemona, and she needs to reassure herself that she does not resemble the universal woman which Iago describes. In effect she dares him to define her:

Desdemona. What wouldst write of me, if thou shouldst praise me?
Iago.   O gentle lady, do not put me to't,
                 For I am nothing if not critical.

(II.i.118–20)

The whole scene is an example of her need for self-justification, perhaps to repress a subconscious guilt. An audience need never have heard of Freud to sense that in this scene "the lady doth protest too much." In her aside, she even justifies her participation in the conversation. She feels that she should be more concerned for Othello's safety than for her own need to be reassured. She cannot face this need and thinks of the whole conversation as simply a diversionary means of passing the time. But her aside itself is the real diversion:

> *Desdemona.* I am not merry; but I do beguile
> The thing I am by seeming otherwise.—
> Come, how wouldst thou praise me.
>
> (*II.i.123–25*)

Iago's answers comprise an accurate and unflattering description which is corroborated by the rest of the scenes in which Desdemona appears. The language of his answer resembles the riddling responses of a fool character, and such language intentionally invites speculation and explication. In the repartee which follows Desdemona's invitation, there is a significant pun on "white" and "wit." Desdemona asks how Iago would praise a woman who is black (unattractive) and witty:

> *Iago.* If she be black, and thereto have a wit,
> She'll find a white that shall her blackness fit.
>
> (*II.i.133–34*)

Just as Iago has mocked the human need to justify action, when he flippantly speaks of his "motives" for destroying Othello, so he is mocking Desdemona's use of her "wit" to "fit" or to cover the inner "blackness" of her psyche. Similarly, to complete the pun, human beings have little difficulty finding a "white" reason to cover a black sinful impulse. A wit in fallen man is only a device to whitewash the reality of insistent desires.

It is, symbolically, the inner blackness which both Othello and Desdemona try to deny. Desdemona is not unfaithful to Othello, but, like Othello, she is unfaithful to herself. When she insists that Iago describe "a deserving woman indeed—one that in the authority of her merit did justly put on the vouch of very malice itself," she is obviously thinking of herself. Ironically she is asking Iago to "vouch" for her virtue. And his response, being that of "very malice itself," another quality which the single Vice may personify, is maliciously candid. In each line of his speech, he mentions an abstract quality of moral perfection which does not match the reality of human capability. In the last line he suggests that such a "wight" is a human impossibility. Again there may be a pun on Desdemona's being white. Nothing is all white or all black, as it were. A pure "wight" is impossible. All human beings are "black," or fallen, within. When Desdemona asks Iago to describe one who is "black and witty," good and evil, or sinful and self-deceiving, she is asking for the description of herself which he then extensively supplies:

> She that was ever fair, and ever proud;
> Had tongue at will, and yet was never loud;
> Never lacked gold, and yet went never gay;
> Fled from her wish, and yet said "Now I may";
> She that being angered, her revenge being nigh,
> Bade her wrong stay, and her displeasure fly;
> She that in wisdom never was so frail
> To change the cod's head for the salmon's tail;
> She that could think and ne'er disclose her mind,
> See suitors following, and not look behind:
> She was a wight (if ever such wights were)—
>
> .   .   .   .   .
>
> To suckle fools and chronicle small beer.
>
> (II.i.149–61)

Desdemona's primary virtue in the play is her ability to forswear revenge, to bid "her wrong stay, and her displeasure fly" and to transcend the "frailty" of hasty and useless retributive action, or changing the "cod's head for the salmon's tail." Emilia tempts her to precisely this sort of "womanly" revenge in IV.iii. Such virtues, however, are no panacea for curing folly, as Iago's last line suggests. Folly is an inherent and permanent frailty, passed on to children, and existing within even the most virtuous individuals. Desdemona perhaps exhibits some of the most important virtues mentioned in Iago's speech, but she also reveals some of the faults which he catalogs. Most obviously, the words "never proud" do not accurately fit Desdemona. Both she and Othello are as complacently confident as Adam and Eve were before Eve encountered the serpent, although it is the male half of "mankind" who most directly confronts the devil in this play. And in *Othello* the Fall occurs without any explicitly reassuring hope of redemption, as Desdemona's lines ironically suggest. The heavens are not clearly protecting mankind against evil here:

Desdemona.   The heavens forbid
                   But that our loves and comforts should increase

Even as our days do grow.
Othello.   Amen to that, sweet powers!
I cannot speak enough of this content;
It stops me here; it is too much of joy
And this, and this, the greatest discords be [*Kissing her*]
That e'er our hearts shall make!
Iago. [*Aside*] O, you are well tuned now!
But I'll set down the pegs that make this music,
As honest as I am.

(II.i.195–203)

What Bradley called "fate" seems to be the unconscious combination of contradictory good intention gone awry, furthered by unlucky chance incidents and blind human optimism or pride. Tragically and unwittingly, Desdemona contributes to her murder with her idealistic zeal. Her overconfidence in the power of virtue to triumph, often taken to be an example of her pure faith, may be simply a self-righteous obliviousness to sin and frailty. It is really her own power to move Othello that she repeatedly assures Cassio of when he entreats her intercession. The scene reveals her vanity and her susceptibility to flattery, qualities of Eve rather than Christ:

Desdemona. Be thou assured, good Cassio, I will do
All my abilities in thy behalf.

.   .   .   .   .

Do not doubt, Cassio
But I will have my lord and you again
As friendly as you were.

.   .   .   .   .

And be you well assured
He shall in strangeness stand no farther off
Than in a politic distance.

.   .   .   .   .

Do not doubt that; before Emilia here
I give thee warrant of thy place.

(III.iii.1–2, 5–7, 11–13, 19–20)

Desdemona's faith in the power of virtue to triumph may foreshadow the play's skepticism concerning Providence as well as her psychological naïveté. Although Othello might be particularly prone to insecurity because of the racial

differences emphasized in the opening scenes, Desdemona's idealistic Neoplatonism makes her impervious to his vulnerabilities.

> Assure thee,
> If I do vow a friendship, I'll perform it
> To the last article. My lord shall never rest;
> I'll watch him tame and talk him out of patience;
> His bed shall seem a school, his board a shrift;
> I'll intermingle everything he does
> With Cassio's suit.
>
> *(III.iii.20–26)*

Othello then enters and Cassio leaves in spite of Desdemona's request that he
stay and hear her speak, a request dictated by her desire to demonstrate her
power over her husband to an admiring audience. Sans audience (on stage, at
least) she confidently approaches Othello and begins almost peremptorily,
"How now, my lord? / I have been talking with a suitor here, / A man that
languishes in your displeasure." As she continues, her references to "grace and
power to move" are marks of feminine vanity, the desire to have the "maistrye,"
rather than genuine Christ-like attributes. Her power to move is ironically
limited to her ability to sexually attract. It is really this power which she is,
very normally and inevitably, playing upon. Her description of Cassio is really
a description of herself. Although both Cassio and Desdemona have faults, the
play repetitively and indirectly invokes a compassionate response toward them.

> For if he be not one that truly loves you,
> That errs in ignorance and not in cunning,
> I have no judgment in an honest face.
> I prithee call him back.
>
> *(III.iii.48–50)*

Her lack of judgment allows her to aggravate Othello's incipient suspicion. She
presses on, more because Othello is refusing her than out of genuine concern
for Cassio. The comic repetition of her insistent questions suggests this:

> *Desdemona.* . . . Good love, call him back.
>   *Othello.* Not now, sweet Desdemona; some other time.
> *Desdemona.* But shall't be shortly?
>   *Othello.*   The sooner, sweet, for you.

> Desdemona. Shall't be tonight at supper?
> Othello.   No, not tonight.
> Desdemona. Tomorrow dinner, then?
> Othello.   I shall not dine at home;
>   I meet the captains at the citadel.
>
> (III.iii.54–59)

She offers a pretext of wifely demurral to her husband's wishes, but her specific request is a paradoxical combination of entreaty and command:

> Why then, tomorrow night, on Tuesday morn,
> On Tuesday noon, or night, on Wednesday morn.
> I prithee name the time, but let it not
> Exceed three days.
>
> (III.iii.59–63)

When Othello inadvertently hits upon Desdemona's real motive of intercession ("Let him come when he will! I will deny thee nothing"), she strongly "denies" that she is testing Othello's devotion and her own power over him. There is an inherent comic quality in her insistence that the "boon" is for Othello's sake rather than her own. Othello's lines about denial are repeated again after Desdemona's speech, which is, with dramatic transparency, a psychological denial of her own selfishness:

> Othello. . . . I will deny thee nothing.
> Desdemona.   Why, this is not a boon;
>   'Tis as I should entreat you wear your gloves,
>   Or feed on nourishing dishes, or keep you warm,
>   Or sue to you to do a particular profit
>   To your own person. Nay, when I have a suit
>   Wherein I mean to touch your love indeed,
>   It shall be full of poise and difficult weight,
>   And fearful to be granted.
> Othello. I will deny thee nothing!
>
> (III.iii.76–83)

She reveals herself entirely, when she petulantly answers Othello's request to be left to himself: "Shall I deny you? No. Farewell my lord." As she exits, she speaks a couple of lines, which bear more ironic implications:

> Emilia, come. Be as your fancies teach you;
> Whate'er you be, I am obedient.
>
> *(III.iii.88–89)*

The decorous obedience which a wife was supposed to offer her husband has been only a thinly disguised veil over Desdemona's words which reveal the traditional feminine vice of desiring the "maistrye." Desdemona is not obedient to the ideals of generosity and charity, in regard to Cassio, any more than she is truly obedient to her husband. She is in reality obedient, as all mankind must frequently be, to her pride, her fallen nature, and her "fancies." Both Othello and Desdemona are as their "fancies teach" them. The line is a foreshadowing of Othello's surrender to his own jealous fancies, externalized in the personified Vice, Iago. "Whate'er" Othello is by nature, Desdemona must also be.

But Desdemona certainly does not wish to believe in her own frailty, judging by her responses to Othello's direct accusations in IV.ii. Before Desdemona's entrance, Othello, although referring literally to Emilia, unwittingly describes both himself and Desdemona:

> This is a subtle whore
> A closet lock and key of villainous secrets,
> And yet she'll kneel and pray; I have seen her do't.
>
> *(IV.ii.21–23)*

The same irony continues as he identifies Emilia's "mystery" in a way which ironically describes his denial of his own inherent sin:

> *Othello.* *[To Emilia]* Some of your function, mistress:
> Leave procreants alone and shut the door;
> Cough or cry hem if anybody come.
> Your mystery, your mystery! Nay, dispatch!
>
> *(IV.ii.27–30)*

When he confronts Desdemona, Othello is especially concerned with the indignity of his imagined situation: "But, alas, to make me / The fixed figure for the time of scorn / To point his slow and moving finger at." Actually, both accuser and accused are guilty of the same sin and the same falseness here. This is implied in Desdemona's self-exonerating question, which is simultaneously an ironic indictment of herself, "Alas, what ignorant sin have I committed?" The sin of ignorance can be committed by anyone, regardless of social identity. Desdemona believes that because she is a Christian, she cannot possibly be a strumpet:

> *Othello.*   Are not you a strumpet?
> *Desdemona.*   No, as I am a Christian!
>
> (*IV.ii.82*)

Her refusal to face the reality of her nature and of the Fall is suggested further in the next scene. When Emilia asks how she is, Desdemona accurately defines her awareness: "Faith, half asleep." She restates her naïveté within a few lines. Her words consciously imply that she deserves no chiding, but they also describe an old habit of self-righteousness, an imperviousness to self-chiding:

> Those that do teach young babes
> Do it with gentle means and easy tasks.
> He might have chid me so; for, in good faith
> I am a child to chiding.
>
> (*IV.ii.111–14*)

As she cannot face her own feminine frailty, she cannot bring herself to pronounce the word "whore"—"Am I that name, Iago?" She reiterates her image of herself by dramatizing her virtue for Iago and Emilia:

> Here I kneel:
> If e'er my will did trespass 'gainst his love
> Either in discourse of thought or actual deed,
> Or that mine eyes, mine ears, or any sense
> Delighted them in any other form.
>
> (*IV.ii.151–55*)

Her reference to her "discourse of thought" and to her "senses" as having been perfectly pure is another example of pride, since the mind and the senses were notoriously fickle from the Skeptical and Calvinistic points of view. The line foreshadows Desdemona's becoming guilty of just these "sins" in the next scene. A virtuous person was expected to acknowledge and thus control his sinful impulses (thought and sense) rather than try to deny them as Desdemona does. But for Desdemona the fallen nature within her is literally an unspeakable horror: "I cannot say 'whore,' / It does abhor me now I speak the word." The presence of Bianca in the play suggests that all women are sisters. Desdemona shrinks with horror from, or "abhors," the word "whore." The obvious pun also suggests that she shrinks from the reality of the whore within her, the potential whore which exists within all women. Just as Cassio runs from the external, literal whore, Bianca, so Desdemona psychologically flees or abhors a part of her inner self. Cassio is in a sense "married" to the whore without, and Desdemona is bound to the whore within.

The courtesan, Bianca, is an important character for what she reveals to the audience about the other less "honest" women in the play. She does not appear in Cinthio's novella, and Spivack has a number of explanations for her presence in *Othello:* 1) "a married Cassio would have been less tractable a subject for Iago's intrigue"; 2) "with two respectable wives already inside a play dealing with matrimony, a third would have had no dramatic virtue at all compared with the opportunity to stage a harlot," especially given "the theatrical fashion in prostitutes . . . during the early years of the seventeenth century"; and 3) Iago is able to increase Othello's anger by saying that Cassio looked upon Desdemona with no more respect than he did "his whore." He emphasizes that practical dramaturgic considerations were the major reasons for unmarrying Cassio, and that these took precedence over a morally accurate picture of the lieutenant, whose "daily beauty" would have gained from a wife "a degree of enhancement that the courtesan does not altogether supply."[3] The point that Spivack has minimized suggests that Shakespeare did not neglect moral considerations by including Bianca but may actually have enhanced them. Her presence in the play serves to reveal the hypocrisies of Cassio and Desdemona rather than their "daily beauty." Bianca is a "fallen" woman, but she is generous and loving to Cassio. If she is dishonest in the sense of being unchaste, she is at least psychologically honest about her feelings and her identity. Othello's wife is literally honest or chaste, an "honest" woman, but like her husband and like Cassio, she is, in her pride, psychologically dishonest. Emilia stands between the other two women. More psychologically honest about herself and human nature than Desdemona, she nevertheless is not ready to admit to herself that she could be as bad as Bianca.

Although Emilia admits that she would not commit adultery by the "heavenly light" Desdemona swears by, her humorous rejoinder echoes the mocking but disturbingly truthful comments of Iago:

> *Desdemona.* Wouldst thou do such a deed for all the world?
> *Emilia.*   Why, would not you?
> *Desdemona.*   No, by this heavenly light!

> Emilia.   Nor I neither by this heavenly light;
>   I might do't as well i' th' dark.
>
> (IV.iii.64–67)

She goes on to distinguish herself from a courtesan, however, with a humorous sort of moral doublethink:

> Marry, I would not do such a thing for a joint-ring, nor for measures of lawn, nor for gowns, petticoats, or caps, or any petty exhibition; but, for all the whole world . . . ?
>
> (IV.iii.72–74)

She then plays the Vice to Desdemona as Iago plays it to Othello. Emilia tempts Desdemona to evil by preaching a gospel of justice and logical retribution. If Emilia is not so purely an incarnation of evil as Iago, the Iago-presence within her is strong enough. The illusion of justice and repayment for wrong accompanies moral evil as tenaciously as Iago serves Othello. Emilia is so specific in cataloging "wrongs" that although she shows admirable courage and loyalty later, she may here be playing the bawd. Courage, loyalty, and sexual promiscuity are not contradictory qualities, especially if Shakespeare is as psychologically sophisticated as the critical tradition considers him to be:

> And have not we affections?
> Desires for sport? and frailty? as men have?
> Then let them use us well; else let them know,
> The ills we do, their ills instruct us so.
> Desdemona. Good night, good night. Heaven me such uses send,
>   Not to pick bad from bad, but by bad mend.
>
> (IV.iii.101–6)

Desdemona's response is a human emulation of Christ-like behavior, not necessarily that of a spotless soul. It is the only psychologically possible answer for her to make at the moment, although her moral hypocrisy is not as crude as that of Emilia. Emilia makes a fine distinction between adultery for a gown and adultery for the whole world, but she is comically self-righteous later when she berates Bianca, who has been falsely accused of complicity in Roderigo's death and Cassio's injury:

> Iago.   This is the fruits of whoring. Prithee, Emilia,
>   Go know of Cassio where he supped tonight.
>   [To Bianca.] What, do you shake at that?

Bianca. He supped at my house; but I therefore shake not.
Iago.   O, did he so? I charge you go with me.
Emilia. O fie upon thee, strumpet!
Bianca. I am no strumpet, but of life as honest
        As you that thus abuse me.
Emilia.   As I? Fie upon thee!

                                      (V.i.116–23)

But the play carefully and subtly expresses what the characters strenuously attempt to deny. And if IV.iii reveals certain aspects of Emilia's character, it also seems to me to reveal more about Desdemona than many critics have been willing to admit. In the scene, Desdemona is preparing for bed, and during a section of about thirty lines she is shedding articles of clothing while she speaks. The scene employs the conventional *topos* of clothing to symbolize the psychological exposure of Desdemona, which is simultaneously occurring. As she takes off articles of clothing, the lines reveal previously concealed qualities of her psyche. She tells Emilia that Othello has dismissed her, and Emilia replies that she wishes Desdemona had never seen Othello. Desdemona disagrees:

    So would not I. My love doth so approve him
    That even his stubbornness, his checks, his frowns—
    Prithee unpin me—have grace and favor.
                              (IV.iii.19–21)

Her love for Othello has never admitted the possibility of human fault, and she can only turn the reality into an illusion. Her speech is, however, punctuated by a significant request that Emilia "unpin" her. The request foreshadows the revelation of the next few lines. Desdemona's next speech suggests a traditional truth she had never accepted: "All's one. Good Father, how foolish are our minds!" Although "all's one" is literally a reference to the unimportance of Emilia's having laid out the wedding sheets, in another sense the words along with what follows suggest the universal inclusiveness of human folly, which inevitably includes the "divine Desdemona." The story of her maid, "Barbary," whose love proved mad and did forsake her, also suggests that Desdemona is not meant to be a unique exemplar of virtue. The maid's name recalls Othello's nationality, and Iago's earlier mocking reference to him as a "Barbary horse." If Desdemona parallels "Barbary," who by implication is a Moor like Othello, she and Othello are interchangeable in their possession of the same human weaknesses. When, a few lines before, she says her love "approves" Othello, another Renaissance meaning of "approve" as "resemble" suggests that she, like Othello, sees faults (such as "stubbornness") as virtues. This is, in a sense, a "song" which Desdemona dies singing:

> She had a song of "Willow";
> An old thing 'twas, but it expressed her fortune,
> And she died singing it.
>
> *(IV.iii.28–30)*

In saying that she feels like hanging her "head all at one side" and singing "like poor Barbary," there is the implication that she, like Barbary and like Othello, has faced only one side of her character and of human identity.

Another shocking revelation occurs after her second request to be "unpinned." In an unguarded utterance Desdemona reveals that she is not above normal human impulses. In IV.i Iago fed Othello's jealousy by implying that Lodovico, as well as Cassio, was involved with Desdemona: " 'Tis Lodovico, / This comes from the Duke. See, your wife's with him." When Othello strikes Desdemona, Lodovico defends her and tells him to "call her back." Othello's reaction implies further jealousy: "*Othello.* What would you with her sir? / *Lodovico.* Who? I, my lord? / *Othello.* Ay! You did wish that I would make her turn." Othello then speaks bitterly of his wife, directing the speech to Lodovico. Thus Lodovico is established in Othello's mind as a potential threat or rival. This is obviously, in a literal sense, as preposterous as his accusation of Cassio. But in a more subtle psychological sense Othello's jealousy may be unwittingly accurate. Desdemona has been repeatedly abused and checked by her husband. She has been defended by a handsome young emissary from Venice. Desdemona's momentarily "unpinned" words to Emilia suggest that she is a descendant of Eve, and, however pure, a sister of the Wife of Bath and Bianca. Emilia's more basic response simply places Desdemona's inner character into sharper relief for the audience:

> *Emilia.*   Shall I go fetch your nightgown?
> *Desdemona.* No, unpin me here.
>   This Lodovico is a proper man.
> *Emilia.*   A very handsome man.
> *Desdemona.* He speaks well.
> *Emilia.*   I know a lady in Venice would have walked barefoot to Palestine for a touch of his nether lip.
>
> *(IV.iii.34–40)*

Being unable to face the implications of what she and Emilia have just said, she sings her willow song, which itself suggests that Desdemona refuses to face undeniable natural realities. The first two lines contain a contradiction. Although the "poor soul sat singing by a sycamore tree," she sang "all a green willow." Although Desdemona lives in a world which is undeniably and by nature composed of good and evil elements, she has admitted only the good. This is as foolish as sitting next to a sycamore tree, while "singing" that "all" trees are "green willows." After giving Emilia her clothes ("Lay by these"), she repeats the chorus, and with her literal and symbolic clothing removed, her line suggests her own limitations of insight within the play: "Sing all a green willow must be my garland." In her next line she repeats her "approval" of Othello's "scorn." She then stops singing momentarily, because she feels that she is not singing accurately. Why should she approve Othello's scorn, unless the insistent knocking of a repressed truth might make her feel that Othello's jealousy is somehow justified? Only a few lines before she had spoken admiringly of Lodovico. She fears that her song, or her soothingly idealistic view of herself and of life, will be interrupted. But the knocking or potential interruption is being sounded only in her own mind:

> Let nobody blame him, his scorn I approve—
> Nay, that's not next. Hark! Who is't that knocks?
> *Emilia.* It is the wind.
>
> (*IV.iii.52–54*)

The song then concludes with the sort of skepticism Desdemona has always fled from. The disparity between the prettiness of the sound of the singing and the reality of the words' meaning is, in the theater, a dramatic perspective on the pathetic attempt at denial which consistently characterizes Desdemona. Her natural human impulses attract her to Lodovico and make her potentially, if not actually, unfaithful to Othello. It is this view of human nature that neither she nor Othello can accept. But the voice of psychological reality is growing so loud in her mind that she "approves" Othello's scorn, although in a literal sense it is unjustified. When the song itself becomes cynically real, Desdemona attempts to dismiss Emilia, a personification of this cynical reality (as Othello had dismissed her earlier).

> "I called my love false love; but what said he then?
>   Sing willow, willow, willow:
> If I court moe women, you'll couch with moe men."
> So, get thee gone; goodnight.
>
> (*IV.iii.55–58*)

But Emilia does not leave, and Desdemona can only ask her a desperate question. The question is necessary, since she fears the encroachment into her consciousness of a hidden part of herself. If she can deny that women are naturally promiscuous, she can more effectively deny the urgings she senses knocking in herself. But Emilia's response, like those of her husband to Othello, expresses the tragic reality rather than a romantic dream:

> *Desdemona.*   O, these men, these men.
>   Dost thou in conscience think, tell me, Emilia,
>   That there be women do abuse their husbands
>   In such gross kind?
>
> > *(IV.iii.59–63)*

Emilia's longer speech of definition, previously quoted, appropriately concludes the scene's revelation that women are more like men than angels: "And have not we affections? Desires for sport? and frailty? as men have?"

Although Desdemona may not be naturally superior to the other characters in the play, there are at least two instances where she seems to distinguish herself favorably. At the end of the scene just discussed she refuses to cynically capitalize on the definition of human nature with which Emilia has just provided her: "Heaven me such uses send, / Not to pick bad from bad, but by bad mend." And in the scene immediately preceding, IV.ii, she reacts to Othello's abuse without vengeful anger. Thematically, the following speech suggests that Desdemona is asserting the bond between human beings rather than exaggerating the division. In so doing she is departing from the retributive and angry actions which possess Othello and most of the rest of humanity. Thus, as Emilia unthinkingly remarks, Desdemona's reaction is both a change indeed and, as the line's double entendre suggests, a change in deed:

> *Desdemona.*   Prithee tonight
>   Lay on my bed my wedding sheets, remember
>   And call thy husband hither.
> *Emilia.*   Here's a change indeed!
>
> > *(IV.ii.104–6)*

On the other hand, it may actually be Desdemona's inability to face reality which accounts for her "virtue" here. She can only reply to Emilia with a trite proverb in IV.iii, and she would prefer to return to her Edenic honeymoon rather than admit the state to which her marriage has fallen. Her "sacrifice," whether consciously virtuous or psychologically necessitated, does not evoke the heaven-sent "uses" to which she had earlier referred.

The play ends with the "bloody period" of Othello's final stab. Iago's contemptuous references to humanity's destructive foolishness cannot be glossed over or evaded as unduly cynical. Desdemona is not a living contradiction of Iago's demonstration of human nature. His cynicism does not "break down upon the rock of her truth." As the Vice he has caused the other characters to exhibit the various vices he personifies. And the picture is not heroically tragic in any sense. The self-destructive urges are not understood. Man knows no more at the end of the play about why evil occurs than he did at the beginning. No Providential revelation explains the tragic action. The ritual quality of the last act arises from the use of the traditional familial convention.[4] Man can be counted upon to behave recurrently in the same basic ways. He loves, sexually, and he murders. The human race exists perpetually bound in a marriage of love and of death. The implied sexual puns on "die" in the speeches of Othello before he kills Desdemona suggest the tragic basicity of these two human actions:

> *Othello.*   Sweet soul take heed,
>   Take heed of perjury; thou art on thy deathbed.
> *Desdemona.* Ay, but not yet to die.
> *Othello.*   Presently.
>   Therefore confess thee freely of thy sin,
>   For to deny each article with oath
>   Cannot remove nor choke the strong conception
>   That I do groan withal. Thou art to die.
>   (*V.ii.50–56*)

Othello's final words at the end of the play also reveal the parallelism between sexual love and murder: "I kissed thee ere I killed thee. No way but this? Killing myself, to die upon a kiss." His words imply the question of the play. Must the blind continue to slaughter the blind? Must man be as much at the mercy of his impulses to destroy for a "cause" as he is compelled to express his sexual nature? No very reassuringly redemptive note is sounded at the end. Lodovico compares Iago's cruelty to other natural threats. Human evil is as powerful as "anguish, hunger, or the sea!" And Cassio, a man who has many of the same faults which characterized Othello and Desdemona, now has the task of governing the "city" and of dealing with Iago. There is no progressive feeling that the new governor, or the new generation, so to speak, will be any more successful in dealing with the problem of Iago than the old one was:

"No way but this?" *Othello* is decidedly not a comedy of redemption. The futures of Othello and Desdemona in another life and the future of the human race in this life are frighteningly and tragically ambiguous.

Notes:

1. Barbara Everett, "Reflections on the Sentimentalist's Othello," *CritQ*, 3 (1961), 128–29.
2. All *Othello* citations are from *The Complete Plays and Poems of William Shakespeare*, ed. William Allan Neilson and Charles Jarvis Hill (Cambridge, 1942).
3. Bernard Spivack, *Shakespeare and the Allegory of Evil* (New York, 1965), pp. 417–18.
4. The plot is an allegory of what in modern speech would be called "man's inhumanity to man" or a violation of the "brotherhood" of man. A relatively literal age like ours retains only the metaphor of opposing brothers. But the familial convention in an older tradition was used more broadly. In Euripides' tragedy, *The Bacchae*, an Iago-like god named Dionysus provides the impetus and the illusion of justice which culminates in the ritual murder of Pentheus at the hands of his mother, Agaue. Oedipus kills his father, and the "unnatural" children in *King Lear* think themselves justified in the cruelty they inflict upon their father. In *Hamlet* brother kills brother, and the meaning is more immediately clear to a modern perception. But the murder of a wife may have carried the same metaphorical meaning for Shakespeare's audience as the murder of a brother does for us.

"In Every Corner of the Stage":
Antony and Cleopatra, IV.iii

JOHN SHAW

One of the most unusual scenes in Shakespeare occurs in *Antony and Cleopatra*, Act IV, scene iii. This is that curious episode, set the night before the land battle at Alexandria. The stage directions require the actors (probably five or six of them) to place "themselves in every corner of the Stage," after which the "Musicke of the Hoboyes . . . under the Stage" is heard, coming from "under the earth" and "i ' th ' air." At this point, a soldier says

> 'Tis the god Hercules, whom Antony lov'd,
> Now leaves him.

His fellows seem to agree with this interpretation of the noise, speaking of the sounds as ominous and "strange." On best authority the stage directions are undoubtedly Shakespeare's own.[1]

Few critics have commented on this episode; those who have, have not connected any special significance to the staging.[2] But some aspects of the scene have seemed worth investigating, particularly its possible derivation and its implications.

First of all, one cannot doubt that the staging derives from the traditional emblematic stage of the Middle Ages, the platform representing earth, with heaven above and hell beneath. Maurice Charney and Thomas Stroup have both pointed this out, as well as others.[3] It would seem that Shakespeare, in sending the soldiers to the four corners of the platform, then, evidently wished to signify that the stage, for a moment, did indeed represent "earth," the world, and not Alexandria. Precedence for this kind of symbolic stage action can be found in the tournament, when the marshal typically "at the fower cornars of the listes" issues formal proclamations, as if to the four corners of the world.[4] But more to the point, occurrences similar to Shakespeare's can be found, for example, in Thomas Heywood's *The Silver Age*, in which "the Devils appear at every corner of the stage with fireworks" in order to establish that the location represented by the platform, for the moment, is hell, and not some place on earth.[5]

Now in "abstracting" his stage to represent generally earth, instead of Alexandria, Shakespeare is deliberately reshaping his source in order to stress an important idea. Plutarch had shown not Hercules but Bacchus leaving Antony, and leaving apparently in the direction of Caesar's camp:

. . . it is said that sodainly they heard a marvelous sweete harmonie of sundrie sortes of instrumentes of musicke, with the crie of a multitude of people, as they had bene dauncing, and had song as they use in Bacchus feastes, with movinges and turninges after the maner of the Satyres: and it seemed that this daunce went through the city unto the gate that opened to the enemies, and that all the troupe that made this noise they heard, went out of the city at that gate. Now, such as in reason sought the depth of the interpretacion of this wonder, thought that it was the god unto whom Antonius bare singular devotion to counterfeate and resemble him, that did forsake them.[6]

Thus, Shakespeare has made two slight changes in his source. He changes Bacchus to Hercules, and he dramatizes a departure that is specifically not toward Caesar's camp. The reasons for these alterations in Plutarch are not difficult to understand. Taking the second change first, we can see that Shakespeare did not wish his audience to see in the departure of the god from Antony a mere shift of allegiance. When the god "unto whom Antonius bore singular devotion to counterfeate and resemble him" leaves, Shakespeare wishes to make it clear that this god is leaving the world. Hercules is not going out of the city at "the gate that opened to the enemies": he is leaving earth altogether.

As for the second shift, from Bacchus to Hercules, probably the dramatist wished to draw a clear distinction between the character of Antony, which was supported by and which did "counterfeate" the greatness of Hercules, and that of Caesar, which was supported merely by Fortune. We recall the soothsayer's comment to Antony:

> Thy demon, that thy spirit which keeps thee, is
> Noble, courageous, high, unmatchable,
> Where Caesar's is not. But near him thy angel
> Becomes a fear, as being o'erpow'red . . .
>
>   .   .   .   .   .
>
> If thou dost play with [Caesar] at any game,
> Thou art sure to lose; and of that natural luck
> He beats thee 'gainst the odds.
>
> *(II.iii.19–27)*

J. Leeds Barroll, after examining the meaning of Hercules to the Renaissance audience, writes:

. . . the Hercules who deserts Antony is meant to be construed as that heroic figure who, in the face of temptation at the fork of the road, chose virtue and rejected *Voluptas*. Consistent with this point is the continual commentary by Enobarbus immediately preceding the Hercules scene on the increasing degeneration of Antony's reason and judgment into fool-hardiness, and also the picture of a boasting Antony, in the scene follow-ing, preparing for great personal exploits in a battle which even Cleopatra can see as futile. Furthermore, to conclude the point, it must be remembered that seldom in the Renaissance is Hercules a mere god of battle; he is always a figure of morality, however ambivalent.[7]

An audience, therefore, schooled in emblematic meaning would experience in the peculiar staging of Act IV, scene iii, a dramatization of the departure of a certain kind of strength, or virtue, symbolized by Hercules, heralding the demise of Antony and the end of greatness on earth. Now Cleopatra can say, "the odds is gone, / And there is nothing left remarkable / Beneath the visit-ing moon" (IV.xv.66–68), and "the world . . . is not worth leavetaking" (V.ii.296–97). Shakespeare wanted his audience to feel this sense of empti-ness: hence, the ceremonial bit of staging in which Hercules is sent off from earth, leaving "this dull world . . . / No better than a sty" (IV.xv.61–62).

But the situation would seem to be more complicated than this. In an article published in 1946, Ethel Seaton pointed out a number of parallels between phrases from the Book of Revelation and details and images from *Antony and Cleopatra*.[8] And more recently Helen Morris has argued convincingly that in these same passages, Shakespeare might also have been influenced by a tradition of illustrative interpretations of the Apocalypse inspired by Albrecht Dürer.[9] Among others, the chief relationships mentioned by Miss Seaton and Miss Morris are the falling star references (in *Antony and Cleopatra*, III.xiii. 145–47 and IV.xiv.106–13; in Revelation viii.10 to ix.6; and in Dürer, *Die Sieben Engel*) and Cleopatra's dream of Antony (V.ii.79–86; in Revelation x.1–6; and in Dürer, *Die Verteilung der weissen Gewander*).

Now, surely one of the most vivid and memorable of all passages in Revela-tion is the opening of Chapter VII:

And after these things I saw four angels standing on the four corners of the earth, holding the four winds of the earth, that the wind should not blow on earth, nor on the sea, nor on any tree. And I saw another angel ascending from the east having the seal of the living God. . . .

This passage, of course, also receives treatment by Dürer. His woodcut por-trays the faces of the four winds blowing in the upper part of the illustration, as though at the four corners of the sky, with four angels, sword in hand, standing back to back in the left foreground. Each angel looks up at one of the four winds, intending to hold it back. At the same time, at the very top center, an angel ascends, having "the seal of the living God" in his hands.[10]

I think we might see in the passage from Revelation another instance supporting the theory of Miss Seaton, that Shakespeare's imagination, when he was at work on this play, was influenced if not inspired by Revelation. As for the Dürer illustration, though it does not depict the four angels at the four corners of the picture, it does suggest this arrangement by their back-to-back position and by the four winds in the upper corners of the sky. Moreover, the vision of the ascending angel is the most compelling part of the illustration. In Shakespeare the soldiers place themselves in the corners of the platform; strange music is heard beneath the stage and in the air; Hercules is known to be leaving Antony, "ascending" from earth. Could not Revelation, and perhaps Dürer, too, have inspired the slight change Shakespeare makes from the Plutarch, sharpening up the distinction already being developed in the play between Antony-Hercules and Caesar-Fortune? In this case, the inspiration is not so much the borrowing of an image or detail as it is the conception of some staging.[11]

Of course, the medieval conception of the stage as representing the world is ultimately derived from biblical cosmology, according to which the earth was considered to be a square having angelic watchers at each corner. Thus, four angels standing at the four corners of the earth, or a marshal blowing his trumpet at the four corners of the tiltyard, or soldiers placing themselves "in every corner of the Stage": these actions are all visualizations of the same basic world view. It is little wonder the vivid biblical passage from Revelation vii, the one that inspired one of Donne's best known sonnets, could so easily have helped form the imaginative vision of Shakespeare, as he worked with his source from Plutarch. Hercules leaves, but he leaves more according to Revelation or Dürer than according to Plutarch.

What can we make of all this? Aside from the point already mentioned, that Shakespeare wished to emphasize the contrast between Antony and Caesar, we can be certain of very little. Miss Seaton and Miss Morris are reluctant to conclude more than that Revelation and Dürer served as a "possible source of inspiration" or "illuminated Shakespeare's working thought." Miss Seaton adds,

The lovers themselves undergo a purification of their passion; and it may well have been brought about by their creator's self-submission to the poetry and the mystery of the *Book of Revelation*.[12]

But was Revelation the immediate source, or Dürer? Could Shakespeare's use of images from Revelation in these passages in *Antony and Cleopatra* in the last two acts derive from accounts other than Revelation? The tradition of Roman history in the Renaissance, which has been studied by Professor Barroll in some detail, is mingled with medieval biblical conceptions going back to the Book of Daniel and the succession of four monarchies.[13] "Medieval chroniclers . . . would regard the death of Cleopatra, the last of the Ptolemies, as the end of the Alexandrian monarchy and the accession of Augustus as the beginning of the Roman."[14] But why, then, the apocalyptic imagery in the demise of Antony and Cleopatra? And what was the imagery supposed to suggest to Shakespeare's contemporaries? I suspect the references meant more to them than the "self-submission to the poetry and the mystery" that Miss Seaton mentions. But the full import will no doubt remain unknown, like the mysterious working of Shakespeare's creative genius.[15] The apocalyptic details and images may simply serve to undercut the victory of Caesar over the lovers, suggesting faintly the ironic futility of Caesar's triumph by placing his conquest in the context of the doom Revelation predicts awaits Rome. The fascinating parallels between the play and Revelation, and Dürer, astonishing as they may be, are certainly there; and the staging of Act IV, scene iii may very possibly be one of them. If it is, it is probably the only instance in Shakespeare where a literary or pictorial source proved the inspiration of a conception of staging.

Notes:

1. See W. W. Greg, *The Shakespeare First Folio* (London, 1955), p. 399.
2. The only extended discussion is the very interesting digression in J. Leeds Barroll's article, "Enobarbus' Description of Cleopatra," *Texas Studies in English*, 37 (1958), 61–78, where the meaning of Hercules' departure in this scene is considered. M. Charney, *Shakespeare's Roman Plays* (Cambridge, 1961), refers briefly to the episode, saying that "this scene is in the symbolic tradition of the medieval pageant wagon" and that it gives Hercules' departure a "mythological compulsion" (p. 138). D. Traversi, *Shakespeare: The Roman Plays* (Stanford, 1963), p. 159, speaks of the scene as "evoking the sense of human life against a background of fatality" and as "conveying the pathos which accompanies, in Antony's approaching tragedy, the dissolution of his heroic integrity." The most recent book-length study of *Antony and Cleopatra*, by Julian Markels, *The Pillar of the World: "Antony and Cleopatra" in Shakespeare's Development* (Columbus, 1968), does not discuss the scene.
3. See Charney, p. 138; T. Stroup, "The Structure of *Antony and Cleopatra*," *SQ*, 15 (1964), 289 ff.
4. See the description of the Elizabethan tournament of 1571 in *Antiquarians Repertory*, ed. F. Grose, Vol. I (London, 1807), 181 ff. Thomas Duke of

Gloucester's rules for tournament procedure are given on pages 154–57. G. Wickham, *Early English Stages*, Vol. I (London, 1959), 15, and Vol. II (London, 1963), 230, speaks of the influence of the tournament on cultural thought and artistic expression.

5. *Shakespeare Society Reprints*, ed. J. P. Collier, Vol. XLVI (1851), 169. A similar instance would be from Heywood's *The Golden Age*: "Thunder and tempest. Enter, at four several corners, the four winds. Neptune riseth disturbed. The Fates bring the four Winds in a chain, and present them to Æolus, as their King." *Ibid.*, p. 81.

6. *Narrative and Dramatic Sources of Shakespeare*, ed. G. Bullough, Vol. V (London, 1946), 308.

7. Barroll, *op. cit.*, pp. 72–73. The concept of Fortune has been much discussed. The most comprehensive and recent review of the Renaissance interpretation of Fortune may be found in Russell A. Fraser, *Shakespeare's Poetics* (Nashville, 1966), chapter 4. Fortune in relation to Caesar and Antony is discussed by Markels, *op cit.*, 147–49.

8. "*Antony and Cleopatra* and the *Book of Revelation*," RES, 22 (1946), 219–24.

9. *ShakS*, 4 (1968), 252–62. Miss Morris discusses which Bibles Shakespeare might have used and what chances there would be for versions of the Dürer woodcuts to appear as illustrations in these Bibles.

10. *Dürer's Apocalypse*, with an introduction by Erwin Panofsky (London, 1964), 6th illustration: The Four Angels Holding the Winds.

11. See Barroll, pp. 70–73. Another interesting point: in Plutarch no land battle is described as taking place the day after the "straunge noises heard, and nothing seene" episode. In Shakespeare, however, Antony has a great victory on that day, even though Hercules has left him. Could this alteration of his source have been inspired by the conception of the angels holding back the winds of destruction while the chosen are sealed? The point of the episode in Revelation is that the chosen will be exempted from the general doom, to come later. In the meantime, there is a lull.

12. Seaton, p. 224.

13. "Shakespeare and Roman History," *MLR*, 53 (1958), 327–43.

14. *Ibid.*, p. 331.

15. An interesting letter from J. Lindsay to *RES*, 23 (1947), 66, points out that "the apocalyptic imagery to which his poetic intuition drew him was in fact closely related to those historical events." Lindsay then quotes W. W. Tarn to the effect that much of the apocalyptic material was composed during the war between Rome and Cleopatra, so that Shakespeare apparently by "intuitive insight" made the correlation between Plutarch and Revelation. Professor Roy Battenhouse in *Shakespearean Tragedy* (Bloomington, 1969), 176–81, also discusses the imagery of Revelation in *Antony and Cleopatra*.

Disguise and New Guise in *Cymbeline*

JOHN SCOTT COLLEY

W. W. Lawrence felt that the central problem of dramatic characterization in *Cymbeline* could be resolved in only one way. Modern readers must imagine the play as the Elizabethans understood it, "as they saw it on the stage":

> Posthumus and Imogen and Iachimo are too often treated as if they were persons of the nineteenth century, and their acts interpreted like those of characters in a modern realistic novel, instead of a tale the outlines and spirit of which had been determined by centuries of literary and social tradition.[1]

Lawrence's conclusions about *Cymbeline* have not proved as convincing as his critical methodology. His designation of Posthumus as an essentially "blameless" hero, completely justified in his jealousy and attempted revenge, has met with strong opposition.[2] Yet even if Lawrence was mistaken about the relationship of *Cymbeline* to certain literary traditions, he was quite correct in insisting that modern audiences attempt to understand the play as did Shakespeare's original audience. And the Elizabethans must have felt that Posthumus had learned his "lesson" in the play and had indeed earned the love and loyalty of the delightful Imogen. Otherwise, the long reconciliation scene at the end of the play would have proved dramatically unsatisfying. But to modern students of the play, Posthumus's dramatic growth, and his ultimate penitence, have proved unconvincing: "The puppet is plastered over with the cynicism of Edmund, the pessimism of Lear and the violence of Timon, and rants with the incoherence of Coriolanus."[3] And presumably, Posthumus lacks the very attributes that give Edmund, Timon, Lear, and Coriolanus magnitude, or dramatic life. Posthumus seems a hero without a play, or an unlikely hero for the play in which he does appear.

How did the Elizabethans view this raging, jealous husband who manifests so little faith in his wife, who herself is a model of fidelity? Certainly *Cymbeline* is no tragedy, and Posthumus would have been viewed differently from Timon or Lear. And while the play may have recalled the "problem" comedy, *Much Ado About Nothing*, Posthumus certainly reveals neither the youthfulness nor wit that gains sympathy for Claudio. In any period Posthumus must present difficulties for his audience. Indeed, his arresting and memorable qualities are too often presented only verbally, while his unfortunate characteristics are most vividly represented. The audience learns of his goodness by report, but sees his volatile anger visually portrayed. After an absence of two acts, he is brought onstage at the end of the play, and the audience is expected to be moved by his grief, convinced of his new vision of his wife's fidelity, and satisfied with his furious, warlike purgation. But how many students of the play today are convinced by Posthumus's rapid and seemingly effortless change of character?

Perhaps the problem of the "heroic" Posthumus can be traced to his emblematic role in the plot. His is not a moving, psychological portrait, but is rather a pictorial one. His shifts of attitude, his inner turmoil, and his eventual triumph, are represented not in terms of action, but in terms of verbal and visual signs. His characterization owes more to Everyman than to Hamlet. Posthumus is a puppet in a strange morality-romance puppet show, and both his initial rage and eventual "transcendence" are dramatized in an uncharacteristic, un-Shakespearean manner. Posthumus is certainly no character from a "modern realistic novel." He is more of an "emblem" that figures importantly in a drama of reconciliation and forgiveness. The Elizabethans were more prepared than we to accept Shakespeare's manner of dramatic characterization in the drama of Posthumus, Imogen, and Cloten. For in *Cymbeline* Shakespeare returns to a method of "schematic" characterization, in which moral states are suggested through costumes and costume changes. An Elizabethan viewing the play may have seen in Posthumus's various "guises" sufficient indication of moral growth so that the "comic" conclusion of Posthumus's personal drama would have been artistically convincing.

Costuming had always been an important element of characterization in early English drama. Everyman's new spiritual awareness is indicated by his adoption of the "garment of sorrow," and when he is clothed, he can say "now have I on true contrition." Similarly, Lear's pilgrimage from folly, to insanity, and finally to a momentary understanding, is marked by a significant series of costumes: kingly robes, nakedness on the heath, and finally, simple new clothing supplied by Cordelia. Hamlet's melancholy is reflected in his plain, dark garments, which contrast with the resplendent court dress of those around him. The usurper Macbeth constantly speaks of borrowed or ill-fitting clothing, for he has wrested the garments of power from the rightful wearers.[4]

In no play does Shakespeare so fully rely upon costume and disguise as in *Cymbeline*. In this play not only characterization, but almost every complication in the action, every dimension of the theme, is related to uses of costume and disguise or repeated references to garments. Although Shakespeare employs costume and disguise extensively in *Cymbeline*, he puts them to predictable uses.[5] Good people are found dressed humbly, while the evil swagger about in finery. Developing, dynamic characters are seen going through a series of costume changes, while static characters remain in their ordinary dress. What makes *Cymbeline* unique is the length to which Shakespeare goes to realize his dramatic ends through visual and poetic uses of garments and changes of garments. The audience is constantly asked to note contrasts and ironies that are reflected in a character's appearance. At the same time, viewers are moved to conceive of certain situations in terms of clothing imagery. Reversals and conflicts are described as well as pictorially displayed through the visual and poetic impression derived from an emblematic use of garments. Shakespeare conceives of character largely in terms of clothing, and a full interpretation of the role of Posthumus, as well as the roles of Imogen and Cloten, is dependent upon an appreciation of the significance of costume, disguise, and comments about costume and disguise.

At the opening of *Cymbeline*, Shakespeare immediately introduces themes of deception, artifice, hidden motives, and mistaken identity in terms of "clothing," or disguise. The Princess Imogen has displeased her parents by marrying the poor but worthy Posthumus Leonatus, and the gentlemen of the court share reports of the king's reaction to the match:

> *First Gent.* You do not meet a man but frowns: our bloods
> No more obey the heavens than our courtiers
> Still seem as does the King's.
>
> . . . . .
>
> But not a courtier,
> Although they wear their faces to the bent
> Of the king's looks, hath a heart that is not
> Glad at the thing they scowl at.
>
> (I.i.1–15)

The men of the court "wear their faces" as a type of disguise in order to mask their true feelings about the match and the king's insistence upon Imogen's marriage to the horrible Cloten.

The well-dressed character of Cloten represents a parodoxical truth about human nature. He is as tall and well-proportioned as is Posthumus, and in his clothing, probably exceeds all of the courtiers at the court of Cymbeline. But he is known to be a clownish brute. He is presented as a complete opposite of his noble rival in love. When he seeks out Imogen at her chamber, he is intercepted by a lady who notes that his rather striking garments contradict his true nature:

> *Lady.* Who's there that knocks?
> *Clo.*   A gentleman.
> *Lady.*   No more?
> *Clo.*   Yes, and a gentlewoman's son.
> *Lady.*   That's more
>   Than some whose tailors are as dear as yours
>   Can justly boast of.
>
> > *(II.iii.78–81)*

In the brief exchange the lady shows she has more wit than the dull prince, and she also points to an aspect of his personality. Cloten is noble in name, elegant only in his rich, tailored dress. The irony of the lady's words becomes clearer as Cloten continues to woo Imogen. He cannot conceive why she would prefer the lowly, banished Posthumus to a man of his own rank and "dignity":

> The contract you pretend with that base wretch,
> One bred of alms, and foster'd with cold dishes,
> . . . it is no contract, none;
>
> .   .   .   .   .
>
> Yet you are curb'd from that enlargement, by
> The consequence o' th' crown, and must not foil
> The precious note of it; with a base slave,
> A hilding or a livery, a squire's cloth,
> A pantler; not so eminent.
>
> > *(II.iii.114–25)*

To Cloten, Posthumus is a lowborn rascal, and he fittingly visualizes his thoughts on the subject with a contrast between his own fine dress and station and Posthumus's "squire's cloth" and poor fortune. Imogen recognizes Posthumus's innate worth, however, and values it more than Cloten's superficial characterization of his own rank and appearance. Of Posthumus, she says:

> His mean'st garment,
> That ever hath but clipp'd his body, is dearer
> In my respect, than all the hairs above thee,
> Were they all made such men.
>
> > *(II.iii.134–37)*

Cloten can only sputter in reply: (1) " 'His garment!' Now the devil—"; (2) " 'His garment!' " (3) " 'His meanest garment!' " and (4) "I'll be reveng'd:

'His meanest garment!' Well." Cloten has been struck in a vulnerable spot. His pride, his vanity, his sense of superiority have been challenged by the sharp-tongued Imogen. Now he can do no worse than threaten to tell her father what she has said. After her disappearance from the court in Act III, however, he chances upon a clearer notion for revenge. Forcing Pisanio to bring him a suit belonging to Posthumus, Cloten announces to the audience what is on his mind:

> She said upon a time (the bitterness of it I now belch from my heart) that she held the very garment of Posthumus in more respect than my noble and natural person, together with the adornment of my qualities. With that suit upon my back, will I ravish her: first kill him, and in her eyes; there shall she see my valour, which will then be a torment to her contempt . . . (which, as I say, to vex her I will execute in the clothes that she so prais'd).
>
> (III.v.136–48)

Wearing the discarded clothing of Posthumus, Cloten plans to kill his rival and ravish the princess (who will be made to watch the murder): "She hath despis'd me rejoicingly, and I'll be merry in my revenge" (III.v.149–50).

Later standing alone in Posthumus's clothing, Cloten ruminates upon the garments, Imogen, and his revenge:

> How fit his garments serve
> me! Why should his mistress who was made by him that made
> the tailor, not be fit too? The rather (saving reverence
> of the word) for 'tis said a woman's fitness comes by fits.
> Therein I must play the workman, I dare speak it to myself,
> for it is not vain-glory for a man and his glass to confer
> in his own chamber; I mean, the lines of my body are as
> well drawn as his; no less young, more strong, not beneath
> him in fortunes, beyond him in the advantage of the time,
> above him in birth, alike conversant in general services,
> and more remarkable in single oppositions; yet this
> imperseverant thing loves him in my despite. What
> mortality is! Posthumus, thy head (which now is growing
> upon thy shoulders) shall within this hour be off, thy
> mistress enforced, thy garments cut to pieces before thy
> face: and all this done, spurn her home to her father, who

may (haply) be a little angry for my so rough usage: but
my mother, having power of his testiness, shall turn all
into my commendations.

(IV.i.2–24)

Besides the amusing quibbles on "fits" and "fitness," and the malicious tone
Cloten introduces into the new act, the speech represents another of Shakespeare's evocations on the theme of the "inner" versus the "outer" nature of
man. Cloten is a thorough villain, yet, as he tells us, in the lines of his body he is
no less attractive than Posthumus (as Imogen's later confusion will prove).
He is like Posthumus in other particulars, but as the audience can see, Cloten
is quite different inwardly. Cloten is so concerned with superficial trappings
of nobility and elegance that he conceives of victory in terms of garments and
clothing, the outer signs of what is supposed to be the inner condition. He
speaks of victory over Posthumus in terms of cutting his garments to pieces
before his face. Earlier he had thought of Posthumus as being dressed in
"squire's cloth." In each instance, the differences between himself and his
rival are put in terms of clothing: superiority means better apparel; victory
means "garments cut to pieces." Unfortunately for Cloten, though, the real
world is not organized with such artificial distinctions. Cloten finds out too
late: he stumbles upon the "lost" Prince Guiderius and asks him, "What slave
art thou?" In a parody of Cloten's previous soliloquy, Shakespeare has the
true prince return the challenge: "What art thou? Have not I / An arm as big
as thine? a heart as big?"

> Clo.   Thou villain base,
>   Know'st me not by my clothes?
> Gui.   No, nor thy tailor, rascal,
>   Who is thy grandfather: he made those clothes,
>   Which (as it seems) make thee.
> Clo.   Thou precious varlet,
>   My tailor made them not.
> Gui.   Hence then, and thank
>   The man that gave them thee. Thou art some fool . . .
>   .   .   .   .   .
> Clo.   To thy further fear,
>   Nay to thy mere confusion, thou shalt know
>   I am son to th' Queen.
> Gui.   I am sorry for't: not seeming
>   So worthy as thy birth.

> *Clo.*   Art not afeared?
> *Gui.* Those that I reverence, those I fear: the wise:
>   At fools I laugh: not fear them.
>
> (IV.ii.80–96)

Guiderius's humorous reply to Cloten's reference to his courtly attire is that the clothing evidently makes a better man out of him than he really is. Since men are "made" by their forefathers, Cloten's grandfather must be his tailor, for his tailoring is all that there is to him. The stupid Cloten takes the words quite literally and protests that his tailor did not make the clothes, for these are the garments that formerly belonged to Posthumus. Such quibbling makes no difference to Guiderius, for the true prince knows nothing of Cloten's disguise. He does perceive, however, that Cloten does not behave as nobly as his attire suggests he should, and there is nothing in Cloten's manner that he should respect: "Those that I reverence, those I fear: the wise: / At fools I laugh: not fear them." Guiderius's reply to Cloten would have been an apt one no matter how the villain was attired, but in this instance the irony of being and appearance is doubly striking. Cloten is wearing the noble garb of a nobler person, a person who, like Cloten himself, has not been acting a role befitting a costume. Guiderius addresses Cloten directly, but the audience could perceive a relevance in his remarks that applies to the sadly misled Leonatus. When Posthumus leaves Imogen and Britain, he assumes the dress of Italy and takes on some of the vice and deception of that locale. He is easily duped by Iachimo, and as a result assumes a role that is baser than the elegant garb he wears. Now Cloten, wearing the cast-off garments of his rival in love, represents a similar deception in appearance, an appearance that hardly fazes the naturally noble, though rudely dressed, Guiderius. Cloten draws his weapon and, with no courtly lords to save him from his rashness, is vanquished by the angry "rustic." The pretender to the crown and to the nobility it entails is defeated in combat by the true heir and true possessor of the grace of kingship.

After Guiderius has "sent Cloten's clotpoll down the stream" and has discovered his brother with the "dead" Fidele, he is reminded by Belarius that "reverence . . . doth make distinction / Of place 'tween high and low." Cloten is nobly born and should be buried as befits his station. Guiderius assents, though adding characteristically, "Thersites' body is as good as Ajax' / When neither are alive." He will bury the prince, yet he implies that it is the inner nature of men that makes one better than another: when the soul has fled the body, skin, bone, and garments mean nothing. Earlier Arviragus has spoken to Fidele:

> *Arv.*   Brother, stay here:
>   Are we not brothers?
> *Imo.*   So man and man should be;
>   But clay and clay differs in dignity,
>   Whose dust is both alike.
>
>   *(IV.ii.2–5)*

There is a difference between men, but in the context of *Cymbeline*, all of the participants are nobly born, and some naturally act as they should while others never reach the ideal of their heritage. If Cloten had lived, there is little chance he ever would have met any standard of rank; there is yet chance for Posthumus. But the two lost princes vividly illustrate how dignity of birth can lead naturally to dignity of action. Their appearance as crudely dressed peasants underscores the very high dramatic irony of the sequence.

The two missing princes, whom we see on the stage dressed in rough garb, are in exaggerated contrast to the courtiers in the world of Cymbeline and Cloten. In soliloquies, Belarius, himself banished by "wicked Queens" and "Clotens" of his own generation, repeatedly tells the audience:

> How hard it is to hide the sparks of Nature!
> These boys know little they are sons to th' king.
>
>   .   .   .   .   .
>
> I' th' cave wherein they bow, their thoughts do hit
> The roofs of palaces, and Nature prompts them
> In simple and low things to prince it, much
> Beyond the trick of others.
>
>   *(III.iii.79–86)*

Imogen too, when she comes on the scene, remarks how noble these mean boys are. She calls them "brothers," and remarks that the courtiers lie when they "say all's savage but at court." The audience enjoys the unconscious irony of her statements; her innocent "recognition" of her brothers and their natural nobility is preparing her for a joyous reunion with them at the end of the play. One valid reason the king has in opposing Imogen's marriage with Posthumus is that Imogen is the only heir to the throne. The queen complicates the situation, certainly, but with the return of the true heir, the princess is more free to choose a less royal mate. The "recognitions" of this scene work both ways. Belarius and the boys perceive that Fidele "hath had / Good ancestors": presumably, good breeding is prelude to greatness in *Cymbeline*. The play is no celebration of the common man. The play rather celebrates the innate goodness that can be found in people of high rank and illustrates how a perversion of nobility leads to the dire consequences it does.

Shakespeare could have pictured the baseness of Cloten and the simple nobility of the mountain princes without any references to costume or disguise. Of course, dramatic irony is heightened by disguise, and the encounter of Cloten and Guiderius is especially striking because of the garb in which the two appear. But the characters are portrayed so directly that their roles depend less upon visual images than do the roles of the more problematic characters such as Imogen and Posthumus.

It is the problem of Posthumus's character and the nature of his growth and development as a person worthy of the rewards given him at the end of the play that cause many of the enigmas of the structure of *Cymbeline*. Yet clothing imagery and the changes of costume that are associated with Posthumus have great relevance for an understanding of his appropriate role in the drama. The initial views of Posthumus are supplied by commentary of several gentlemen of the court. Of Posthumus they say: "I do not think / So fair an outward, and such stuff within / Endows a man, but he" (I.i.22–24).

> A sample to the youngest, to th' more mature
> A glass that feated them, and to the graver
> A child that guided dotards. To his mistress,
> (For whom he now is banish'd) her own price
> Proclaims how she esteem'd him; and his virtue
> By her election may be truly read
> What kind of man he is.
>
> (I.i.48–54)

Handsome and wonderfully endowed with all the traits of nobility, Posthumus is said to be both outwardly and inwardly a fine match for the princess. Not only is he great in his own person, but he is greater to be valued so by Imogen. Posthumus is, in short, everything that Cloten is not. He is soon driven from his wife, however, and is barely allowed to make an independent impression on the audience before he reaches Italy. This is the source of one of his problems. He is constantly spoken of in hyperbolic terms, but, when his role is dramatized, he appears choleric and unreasonable. The "gentlemen" are given over twice as many lines to describe him as Posthumus is given to characterize himself. Indeed, when he arrives in Italy, there is another lengthy prologue supplied to catalog his merits and his exploits, and again Posthumus is spoken of before he has an opportunity to speak for himself.

Iach. Believe it, sir, I have seen him in Britain; he was then of a crescent note, expected to prove so worthy as since he hath been allowed the name of. But I could then have look'd on him without the help of admiration, though the catalogue of his endowments had been tabled by his side and I to peruse him by items.

Phi. You speak of him when he was less furnish'd than now he is with that which makes him both without and within.

(I.v.1–7)

Iachimo is immediately suspicious of the hyperboles that accompany any discussion of Posthumus and declares that the Briton is worthy only because he had the good fortune to marry Imogen, and that good fortune was purely a matter of luck.

Iach. This matter of marrying his king's daughter, wherein he must be weighed rather by her value than his own, words him (I doubt not) a great deal from the matter.

French. And then his banishment.

Iach. Ay, and the approbation of those that weep this lamentable divorce under her colours are wonderfully to extend him; be it but to fortify her judgment, which else an easy battery might lay flat for taking a beggar without less quality.

(I.v.14–23)

Iachimo begins to prepare the audience for his verbal assault upon Imogen that is immediately to follow, a series of cutting remarks that are designed to annoy and infuriate the visiting Briton. The Italian is pictured as a villain ready to attack any virtuous person, and the fine reputation of Posthumus especially maddens him. Iachimo is thoroughly wicked, and his designs are only evil, but his words have a strangely disturbing effect. It is true that Posthumus has exhibited nothing of his supposed greatness, and, as the Italian observes, his qualities and his values are deemed only in terms of exaggerated praise. Posthumus was expected to prove worthy, but he really is not so impressive after all. Iachimo's words are prompted by malice, but there is a disquieting truth to his observations.

Iachimo has little trouble engaging Posthumus in the well-known wager, and the results of that wager provide the major complications of the play. There is much scholarly attention given to the validity of the romance hero's testing of his wife or sweetheart,[6] but whatever conventions Shakespeare was employing, he was careful to include warnings of the folly of Posthumus's actions. Philario warns Posthumus repeatedly to restrain himself and then refuses to even arbitrate the proceedings: "I will have it no lay" (I.iv.138). There is no fear that Imogen will fall before the Italian's advances, but in the early scenes of *Cymbeline*, deception and deceit are rampant, and it is certain that Iachimo will attempt to disguise the truth in order to triumph over the confident Briton. Indeed, the deception does succeed, and Iachimo is easily able to convince Posthumus of Imogen's readiness to betray her love. To Philario's protest that Iachimo may have bribed some of Imogen's maids to supply the evidence, Posthumus gives only perfunctory attention:

> *Phi.*   Have patience, sir,
> And take your ring again, 'tis not yet won:
> It may be probable she lost it: or
> Who knows if one of her women, being corrupted,
> Hath stol'n it from her?
> *Post.*   Very true,
> And so, I hope, he came by't. Back my ring,
> Render to me some corporal sign about her
> More evident than this: for this was stol'n.
> *Iach.* By Jupiter, I had it from her arm.
> *Post.* Hark you, he swears: by Jupiter he swears.
> 'Tis true, nay, keep the ring, 'tis true. I am sure
> She would not lose it. Her attendants are
> All sworn and honourable:—they induced to steal it?
> And by a stranger? No, he hath enjoyed her.
>   (II.iv.113–26)

The noble Posthumus, once aroused to anger and distrust, is more inclined to believe the oath of his tormentor, to trust in the "sworn and honourable" attendants to Imogen, than to rely on his faith in his wife. He finds it impossible that the maids could be induced to steal "by a stranger," while finding it quite likely that in a space of twelve hours or less his beloved Imogen would succumb to the overtures of a man she had never seen before. Given the hyperbolic mode of *Cymbeline*, given the romance models for the tale, given the tradition of the fidelity test, it would still be hard for any audience to find much to admire in Posthumus at this point in the play. He is fooled by a clever knave, but he is fooled easily, even before Iachimo has an opportunity to present his most damning piece of evidence—his description of the mole under Imogen's breast. Iachimo's designs could betray any man, but Posthumus's rage is too rapid and too full of ironies to seem moving to an attentive viewer.

Posthumus disappears until the last act of the play. He has instructed Pisanio to murder Imogen, and at the beginning of Act V he comes on holding the bloody handkerchief, the sign that the revenge has been completed. The realization that his lady is "dead" shocks him into a change of heart. He realizes that Iachimo was false and his lady true, and he wonders why he ever commanded Pisanio to murder "the noble Imogen." As a sign of penitence, he will die for his wife and for his country. And he will die as an emblem of the truth that is often perverted and twisted by deceivers:

> Let me make men know
> More valor in me than my habits show.
> Gods, put the strength o' th' Leonati in me!
> To shame the guise o' th' world, I will begin,
> The fashion less without, and more within.
>
> (V.i.29–33)

Here is the first sign that Posthumus is indeed the man described in the first act of *Cymbeline*, "So fair an outward and such stuff within / Endows such a man but he." Now, finally, the hero has lived up to expectations and is able to deserve the vision, and the reunion, of the last act. He then throws off his "Italian weeds" and suits himself "as does a Briton peasant." He has perceived the guise of the world, and wishes to start a new fashion in opposition to the deception of the world. More inner strength is required, and less outward show. Dressed in his new simplicity, he immediately meets his old tormentor, Iachimo, and vanquishes him. The Italian is shaken and immediately feels that he is thus being punished for what he did to Imogen's name.

> *Iach.* The heaviness and guilt within my bosom
> Takes off my manhood: I have belied a lady,
> The princess of this country; and the air on't
> Revengingly enfeebles me, or could this carl,
> A very drudge of Nature's, have subdued me
> In my profession? Knighthoods and honours, borne
> As I wear mine, are titles but of scorn.
> If that thy gentry, Britain, go before
> This lout, as he exceeds our lords, the odds
> Is that we scarce are men and you are gods.
>
> (V.ii.1–10)

The two speeches by Posthumus and Iachimo, delivered within moments of each other, draw the audience's attention forcibly to the import of Posthumus's declaration upon "habits" and "fashion." Iachimo thinks he has been overwhelmed by a rustic and thus is deceived. Ironically the rustic is really his equal in rank and his better as a man. But the shock of defeat and the remorse for his earlier crimes cause Iachimo also to muse that titles "worn" as he wears his are a mockery. He thinks he is being punished for his crimes, for otherwise a man of high rank could surely defeat one of lowly station. It is this revelation that prepares Iachimo for the general reconciliation at the end of the play. His repentance, like Posthumus's, is expressed in terms of fashions and guise, and, with the shedding of an old guise, he is ready to wear honor and nobility inwardly as well as outwardly.

In the ensuing battle, the rudely dressed Posthumus joins the "lost princes" and Belarius in repulsing the Roman attack. Posthumus marvels at the country lads who are "charming" the British to counterattack with their own "nobleness." Contrasting with the fierceness and natural courage of the rudely clad youths is the nobly appointed "Briton Lord" who has retreated before the Roman onslaught. The lord asks Posthumus to recount the miraculous deed of the battle and, in his insistent questioning, angers the noble hero. Rather than speak to an "angry" carl, the lord continues his flight from the field. Posthumus then exclaims, "Still going? This is a lord! O noble misery, / To be i' th' field and ask 'What news?' of me!" (V.iii.64–65). On the battlefield, the seemingly noble are vanquished, and the seemingly plain and crude are victorious.

Having fought valiantly for Britain in his disguise as a humble peasant, Posthumus has not found "the penitent instrument to pick that bolt"—death. He therefore resumes his Roman dress, hoping to be killed by the rallying British.

> No more a Briton, I have resumed again
> The part I came in. Fight I will no more,
> But yield me to the veriest hind that shall
> Once touch my shoulder. Great the slaughter is
> Here made by th' Roman; great the answer be
> Britons must take. For me, my ransom's death:
> On either side I come to spend my breath,
> Which neither here I'll keep nor bear again,
> But end it by some means for Imogen.
>
> (V.iii.75–83)

His penitence will be death: "For Imogen's dear life take mine" (V.iv.22). His wish seemingly will be granted, for he is captured and led off to jail. However, while he sleeps, his father and brothers appear to him in a dream; even Jupiter descends from the heavens to promise that Posthumus and Imogen will be "happier much by this affliction made." Jupiter leaves a prophecy on the sleeping hero's breast, and Posthumus soon awakens to find the solution to his dilemma:

> A book? O rare one,
> Be not, as in our fangled world, a garment
> Nobler than that it covers. Let thy effects
> So follow, to be most unlike our courtiers,
> As good as promise.
>
> (V.iv.133–37)

His preliminary hopes seem unjustified; the prophecy is senseless to him. Fortunately, though, he decides to keep the tablet in his possession, "if but for sympathy." The words will be given meaning later in the play. What is immediately interesting is Posthumus's image of a garment "nobler than that it covers." Here his words are a concise evocation of one of the primary concerns of the play. In the fangled or contrived world of Cymbeline's court, and Iachimo's Italy, deceptions and errors are masked by the gentle cloak of civility. The vain, wicked Cloten dresses in fair courtly garb, while the two lost princes are clothed in rustic weave. The smooth, confident Iachimo is a scheming liar, who undermines a husband's faith in his unrivaled wife. Posthumus himself has presented false appearances up to this point, and it is by means of his metaphor and his previous long speeches that he shows the audience that he has returned to the ideal of true nobility and has abandoned the deceptions and failings of the rotten world of Clotens and Iachimos. With the Jupiter scene the action turns and all wrongs begin to be righted. In the next few hundred lines all of the characters are brought together, and the king, Imogen, and the others slowly and impatiently learn what has been happening around them. The masked are unmasked. The young step forward to replace the old. The natural nobility of the princes and the reformed Posthumus triumphs over the false, deceitful nobility of the queen, Cloten, and Iachimo. It is with Posthumus's recognition in the last act that complications cease and order can be restored at court.

Therefore, when Posthumus initially leaves Britain, he is prey to deception and despair. He returns to his homeland, contrite, and presents his new vision of truth in terms of a number of costume changes. He maintains his "disguise" until the last moments of the play, and it is only after a long, penitent period that he is rewarded with the reunion with Imogen. As Belarius says of Posthumus's masked exploits on the battlefield:

> I never saw
> Such noble fury in so poor a thing;
> Such precious deeds in one that promised nought
> But beggary and poor looks.
>
> *(V.v.7–10)*

Belarius is speaking of Posthumus as he fought disguised as a rude peasant. The ironic quality of the speech points to a truth about Posthumus's role in the entire drama. After Act II, scene iv, few viewers would expect such "precious deeds" from the raging, jealous, deceived Leonatus, truly "one that promised nought / But beggary and poor looks." Posthumus's transcendence is dramatized in terms of a combination of good deeds and good looks, a combination of a strong inner character and fine exterior garments. But his great deeds are performed while wearing humble "weeds"; when he is dressed the best, he acts the basest. Once he experiences growth, he presumably will be able once again to adopt the garb of a prince, for only then will it be a garb that will not belie his true nature.

Another of the great problems with *Cymbeline* as a romance-morality is the character of Imogen. While the other characters really belong to a drama of types and abstractions, Imogen manifests moments of dramatic life that associate her with the witty heroines of Shakespeare's previous romantic comedies. Yet she too shares a role in this drama of deception, and she too suffers as a result of misleading impressions. She happens to be the most interesting and sympathetic character in the play, and when she "falls" as Posthumus, Cymbeline, and others fall, the figure of deception becomes even more frightening and powerful than before. Early in the play, a lord tries to calm the disappointed Cloten by saying of Imogen that "her beauty and her brain go not together. She's a good sign, but I have seen small reflection of her wit" (I.iii.28–30). The words are ironic, of course, for the princess is both witty and beautiful. Yet in Act III, after Pisanio has lured her to Milford Haven, she begins to feel the pressure of mystery and puzzlement and begins to exemplify the type of blindness that her banished husband had been prey to. Pisanio shows her the letter from her lord and announces that he has been ordered to kill her.

> *Imogen.* I false? Thy conscience witness: Iachimo,
>   Thou didst accuse him of incontinency;
>   Thou then look'dst like a villain; now, methinks,
>   Thy favour's good enough. Some jay of Italy
>   (Whose mother was her painting) hath betrayed him:

> Poor I am stale, a garment out of fashion,
> And, for I am richer than to hang by th' walls,
> I must be ripp'd:—to pieces with me!
>
> (III.iv.46–53)

Imogen, who has left the splendor of the court to meet her beloved and has adopted a riding suit, "no costlier than would fit / A franklin's housewife," now envisions herself as an out-of-fashion garment, tossed aside in favor of something newer. Moreover, her betrayal makes her think of old clothing being ripped to pieces, an expression that recalls Cloten's previous image of his intended murder of Posthumus. She is soon calmed by Pisanio, however, and is convinced that some deception is involved in Posthumus's rage. Pisanio persuades Imogen to disguise herself as a boy and take up service under the Roman Lucius, so that she might hear directly about Posthumus and decide for herself if he has deceived her. Imogen agrees and adopts her third costume of the play. Imogen's great love, even at a moment of anger and distress, drives her to try something at least before she loses faith in her husband. Posthumus never gave Imogen the benefit of the doubt and, as suggested, hardly required much convincing at all from Iachimo.

Imogen's dress in the play is quite significant. Her quest for her lover leads her, symbolically, down the steps of social rank from princess, to franklin's housewife, to a wandering pageboy. Yet, in actuality, she acts more nobly with each change of costume and "rank." With each new stage in her quest, she finds herself farther and farther from the protection of the court, until she is left alone in the wilds with only a shadow of a hope of reaching Rome and her husband. Yet with each step away from civilization, security, and established levels of status and dress, she approaches more closely to a quality of mind and spirit that no other character in the play matches. Each phase of her lowering of status brings her nearer to reunion with her brothers and her husband and earns her the sympathy and affection of the audience.

Having adopted her last disguise, Imogen meets her brothers, eventually takes the drug that the queen had given Pisanio, and is discovered "dead" by her new comrades. Later regaining consciousness next to the trunk of Cloten's body, she suddenly believes that her experience with the cave-keeper had been but a vision or a dream: " 'Twas but a bolt of nothing, shot of nothing, / Which the brain makes of fumes. Our very eyes / Are sometimes like our judgments, blind" (IV.ii.299–302). Yet her thoughts about the nature of deceiving impressions are sadly ironic, for once she spots Cloten's body, still clad in the cast-off clothing of Posthumus, she is immediately fooled by appearances:

> The garments of Posthumus?
> I know the shape of's leg: this is his hand:
> His foot Mercurial: his Martial thigh:
> The brawn of Hercules: but his Jovial face—
> Murder in heaven! How?—'Tis gone.
>
> *(IV.ii.309–12)*

Here is the ultimate irony in the play. Imogen, the wittiest and most admirable person that can be found in the world of *Cymbeline*, is cruelly fooled by deceiving impressions. The very best person in a dissembling world is not able to see through the duplicity of sensory impressions. The body looks like Posthumus's: the shape of the limbs, the garments, everything. Yet how different is the reality of a Cloten from the reality of a Posthumus. Posthumus has fallen from an ideal state, but he never becomes a Cloten. Posthumus is blinded, but he learns to see again. Cloten, however, is the very opposite of the worthy Leonatus. As Belarius warns his "sons" later in the play: "forbear. / Creatures may be alike." Superficially creatures can often be confused, but man's true nature resides deep within. Garments, titles, appearances are all meaningless without an inner, noble essence.

Imogen takes up service as a "page" to the Roman commander and is forced to remain in ignorance until the last scene. Meanwhile the British triumph, Posthumus experiences his "transcendence," and the audience is prepared for the final awakening. After the masque of Jupiter comes the judgment scene in which all of the surviving characters are united. Slowly and painfully one mystery after another is cast aside, disguises are taken off, superficial trappings are shed before the assembled court. Cornelius supplies the first revelation when he announces the queen's death and her terrible confession. She was the cause of all of the evil and had been slowly poisoning the king so that she and her son could reign alone. Cymbeline is astounded.

> Mine eyes
> Were not in fault, for she was beautiful:
> Mine ears that heard her flattery, nor my heart
> That thought her like her seeming. It had been vicious
> To have mistrusted her.
>
> *(V.v.62–66)*

The king himself recognizes finally that he has been deceived by beauty and flattery, that his trust in appearances has been unfounded. The queen was, in effect, in a disguise, a disguise she maintained until her dying moments. Suddenly Cymbeline's perplexity is interrupted by the arrival of the Roman prisoners accompanied by the disguised, and mutually ignorant, Imogen and Posthumus. Imogen immediately catches the king's eye: "Boy / Thou has looked thyself into my grace / And art mine own" (V.iv.94–96). He unknowingly "recognizes" her birth and station and promises her any demand. She uses the opportunity to challenge Iachimo, who immediately confesses his part in the complicating series of deceptions. He even manages to contribute more lines to the already excessive catalog of Posthumus's virtues:

> the good Posthumus
> (What should I say? He was too good to be
> Where ill men were, and was the best of all
> Amongst the rar'st of good ones).
>
> *(V.v.157–160)*

The audience has further impetus now to accept Posthumus's "conversion" and repentance; Imogen too has heard all she needs to hear, and she rushes to her husband as he steps forward. In his ignorance, Posthumus casts her to the ground, calling her a "scornful page."

> *Pis.*   O, gentlemen, help!
> Mine and your mistress: O, my lord Posthumus!
> You ne'er kill'd Imogen till now. Help, help!
> Mine honour'd lady!
> *Cym.*   Does the world go round?
>
> *(V.v.229–32)*

In this most "theatrical" of moments, many sophisticated viewers would tend to puzzle with Cymbeline, who can hardly comprehend the fantastic series of unmaskings and recognitions. Yet the entire Posthumus-Imogen plot is recapitulated vividly in this last spectacle of the mutual disguising and mutual misunderstanding. Neither lover had recognized the truth about the other; neither could see beyond misleading impressions, disguises, deceptions. Posthumus, in ignorant rage, throws the boy "Fidele" to the ground; still unable to recognize the faithfulness of his wife, Posthumus reacts with unwarranted violence. He rejects "faith" because it appears shrouded in a disguised exterior. Imogen still lives in ignorance herself and immediately denounces Pisanio as a murdering traitor, for it is he who supplied her with the evil queen's drug. Both husband and wife react as they had earlier in the drama. Posthumus is deceived by "garments," appearances. Imogen again is fooled by veils of illusion. Of course, it is significant in the final little drama of misunderstanding that it is Imogen who embraces her lord and is cast aside by him. But both share a type of blindness, and only with renewed sight can the two experience reconciliation.

Eventually Cloten's disappearance and the identity of Belarius and the princes are explained. The soothsayer interprets Posthumus's vision, and a grand future for Britain and Rome is predicted. Wrongs are righted, crimes are forgiven, families are united: "Pardon's the word to all" (V.v.423). The last vision of the world of *Cymbeline* is a vast panorama of British, Roman and Italian, the courtly and the simple, the true and the false, the fair and the foul. In the center stands Cymbeline, who represents British royalty. At his side stand his heirs Guiderius and Arviragus, humbly dressed, but of great promise and great natural nobility. To another side are Roman battle tunics and the garb of Italian gentlemen. And dominating the entire scene are Imogen and Posthumus, one in the suit of a lowly page, the other in the guise of an Italian warrior. The two lovers have met trials, have changed their clothing and their states of mind, and have grown to better deserve each other and to better deserve the king's blessing. In this setting, the characters out of their suitable costumes are the greater characters; the men dressed as they "should" remain morally ambiguous. While they speak movingly in the last act, Iachimo and Cymbeline do not experience the growth of the protagonists. They do not change from an old suit into a new one and, in the context, appear removed from the realm of truth and understanding. The princes Guiderius and Arviragus have not "changed" as much as they have "emerged." They prove that their rude dress was but a cover that obscured their inner "sparks." And the lovers, of course, are now ready to resume the costume of husband and wife, princess and nobleman. They have changed from a lowly state into a superior one. The final change of costume is not shown; it is only intimated. The lost princes and Posthumus will again adopt courtly British dress; Imogen will clothe herself as a woman and as a princess. But before changes can be made, the last panorama of *Cymbeline* reflects one important theme of the play. The sight of courtier, king, peasant, Italian and Roman, suggests the paradoxical quality of appearances, appearances that are now recognized as being often deceptive and insubstantial.

While Posthumus is no "blameless" hero, he certainly does experience a type of redemption during the last act of the play. He originally falls into error within the cloak of Italy, that seat of deception and villainy. Yet he overcomes his wrath and jealousy and, in a series of costume changes, signals his emergence as a husband worthy of Imogen.

Shakespeare goes to some lengths to reestablish sympathy for Posthumus.

Besides the emblems of change, his garments, there are other means by which the heroic Posthumus is characterized. His folly, and his greatness, are reflected in both likeable and detestable characters. Indeed, the drama of Posthumus may be said to be mirrored in the several dramas of Cloten, Imogen, and Guiderius. Posthumus originally acts like a Cloten but grows into a Guiderius. The "courtly" Posthumus is a raging, jealous beast, but the "beggarly" warrior Posthumus earns the protection of the gods. In Imogen, too, there is an image of Posthumus's folly. Upon receiving damning evidence, she curses her lord, as he had cursed her. She is fooled by familiar-looking garments, as he had been fooled by Iachimo's deceit. But she transcends illusion and is united with her husband. Similarly, Posthumus undergoes trials of remorse and penitence before he is rewarded with reconciliation. Hence, Posthumus is ultimately a sympathetic hero because his metamorphosis is displayed through his various garbs, especially his "garment of contrition." Moreover, he shares his guilt with the lovely Imogen, and eventually he shares unadorned greatness with the gruff, plainspoken Guiderius. Once the Cloten in Posthumus is "cast off," he becomes a hero worthy of the princess and of the play.

Notes:

1. W. W. Lawrence, *Shakespeare's Problem Comedies* (New York, 1931), p. 179.
2. Homer Swander, "*Cymbeline* and the Blameless Hero," *ELH*, 31 (1964), 259–70.
3. J. M. Nosworthy, "Introduction," the Arden *Cymbeline* (Cambridge, Mass., 1955), p. lxi. I use Nosworthy's edition as my text.
4. For a general discussion of the uses of disguise in pre-Shakespearean drama, see T. W. Craik, *The Tudor Interlude* (Leicester, 1962), pp. 49–92. For the dramatic significance of clothing in other Shakespearean plays see Dean Frye, "The Context of Lear's Unbuttoning," *ELH*, 32 (1965), 17–31; and Cleanth Brooks, "The Naked Babe and the Cloak of Manliness," *The Well-Wrought Urn* (New York, 1947), pp. 21–46.
5. For an intelligent survey of conventions of clothing and disguise, see M. C. Bradbrook, "Shakespeare and the Use of Disguise in Elizabethan Drama," *EIC*, 2 (1952), 159–68.
6. See Lawrence and Swander, above.

"Unless I Be Reliev'd by Prayer":
The Tempest in Perspective

D'Orsay W. Pearson

Almost without exception, the critical tendency has been to see in *The Tempest* Shakespeare's positive glorification of the theurgist's art. Prospero, it has been claimed, accrues to himself none of the guilt which attaches itself to evil magic; his power comes from his studies—his books—which distance him from guilt and make his "art" totally acceptable and even sacrosanct.[1] That such views are in direct opposition to the legal and religious attitudes toward any kind of magic during the early seventeenth century is ignored in favor of casting over both character and action in the drama the romantic twilight of imagination, which has distanced Prospero and Ariel even further from reality than their island setting distanced them from Shakespeare's audience. To see Prospero, as Gervinus saw him, as "mild and merciful" in his use of power throughout the drama,[2] or to claim, with Coleridge, that anything disagreeable about Prospero's magic is "reconciled and shaded in the humanity and natural feelings of the father"[3] is to violate both the text of the play and the context of ideas in which it must be approached.

W. C. Curry's attempt, in the 1920s, to justify such positive evaluations of Prospero's role by identifying the philosophical pattern upon which *The Tempest* is structured had at least the merit of allying scholarship with the impressionistic evaluations of the past. Curry, who claimed for Shakespeare a firsthand knowledge of various Neoplatonic writers and their translator-disciples of the Italian Renaissance, concluded that the dramatist drew upon his readings of them to the extent that the play is "formalized by traditional Neo-Platonic conceptions and may be considered, therefore, as being essentially classical and pagan in spirit."[4] He went on to say that "Prospero is evidently a theurgist of high rank," whose "soul is not yet completely assimilated to the gods because he has not yet freed himself from all human passions and from interest in personal affairs," though "his ability to command rational demons ... proves beyond doubt that he must energize in the sphere of at least ethereal demons, whose province in the natural order is to govern rational and through them irrational demons" (p. 188).

Throughout his study, Curry consistently assumed a positive pagan ethic for the play, as his evaluation of the "Epilogue" reveals: "Understanding these principles [the methods by which the theurgist achieved union with the gods] Prospero would now engage in that prayer which frees from all faults and fits man to be alone with the gods. Thus he still adheres to theurgical principles in

attempting to achieve the utmost reach of which the human soul is capable"
(p. 197). Such claims as these both spawned and perpetuated pronouncements
which continue to be in violation of text and context. Critics since Curry appear
to have engaged in competition to see who can create for Prospero a reputation
as a divine or quasi-divine figure, possessed of qualities which enable him to
bring about goodness or render true justice or function within some allegorical
framework as a divine Providence who through affliction brings men to repentance.

Typical of such pronouncements is Sisson's claim that the magician is "the
learned and philosophical ruler, working justice, righting wrongs, defeating
rebellion . . . a visible providence, a conception that would be grateful to the
learned and philosophical King James the First,"[5] or Spaight's assertion that
Prospero has "borrowed the divine prerogatives" and is "a quasi-sacerdotal
figure,"[6] or Frye's notion that "his motives being good, his magic is in tune with
the higher order of nature."[7]

Curry and the other critics who see that within *The Tempest* Prospero must
be regarded as a theurgist and not a goetist are certainly correct. Such a distinction is of utmost importance in determining the full significance of the
theme of usurpation which pervades every level of action in the tragicomedy;
it is of equal importance in understanding the pattern of forgiveness in the play
and, in particular, in determining the characterization which Shakespeare
achieves in Prospero. The goetist harbored no illusions about the nature of his
power, which normally involved an explicit or implicit pact with the agents of
evil; he operated with the full awareness that his power was secondary, deriving from his temporary control over his demon agents. The theurgist, on the
other hand, saw his power as deriving from his union with divine essence,
which allowed him to manipulate the spirit world and the elements spirits controlled in the same manner as did the controlling One—a definite presumption
of divine prerogatives which the orthodox Renaissance thinker would not allow
to man standing in the shadow of Adam's fall.

The fallacy of *Tempest* criticism which sees Prospero as a theurgist, then,
lies not in the problem of identification, but in two related assumptions which
critics tend to make as a result of that identification. The first of these is that
Shakespeare was familiar with the writings of such Neoplatonists as Proclus,
Plotinus, and Iamblichus, and that, as Curry indicates, he was attempting to
structure his characterization of Prospero within the framework of purification
and contemplation which theoretically enabled the theurgist to achieve, through
his own will, union with and participation in godhead. Whitaker correctly identifies the weakness of such an assumption when he writes that in Elizabethan
England "no satisfactory theoretical basis for a beneficent magic ever became

a part of general learning," and that Shakespeare "seems to have reflected this Renaissance confusion rather than the pure form of theurgy or white magic."[8] But Whitaker continues to support the second and more serious assumption, which develops from the first. He says, "In contrast to his considerable knowledge of conventional demonology, Shakespeare's acquaintance with white magic and the system of ideas that it postulated was therefore slight. His failure to resolve the conflict between his view of Prospero and his account of Ariel— that is, to explain how a good character could control demons—is in striking contrast with the care with which he worked out the implications of the ghost in *Hamlet* or the witches in *Macbeth*" (p. 323). By continuing to accept Prospero as a "good character" Whitaker joins the numbers who support the graver error—to wit, that like such Renaissance figures as Ficino, Agrippa, and Dr. John Dee, Shakespeare (and presumably his audience) accepted theurgy as a lawful practice and the theurgist as a beneficent figure. By accepting this second corollary, Whitaker fails to recognize the care with which the theurgic implications are worked out in *The Tempest*. For not only did no theory of beneficent magic ever become a part of general learning in Elizabethan England, but also— and of even greater importance for *The Tempest*—no general acceptance of a beneficent magic as lawful is evident during the period. Both church and state condemned it, and, if the actions of the general populace in destroying John Dee's library at Mortlake in 1583 are any indication, so did the average Englishman.

Shakespeare's treatment of Prospero throughout *The Tempest*, the mass of current criticism notwithstanding, is not conditioned by a positive view of the theurgist's art. On the contrary, his treatment of his protagonist throughout the play is confined by the attitude of both church and state that theurgy is a damnable, unlawful art which is sometimes more dangerous to the practitioner than is the obviously damnable and unlawful practice of goety. James I, in his *Daemonologie*, chose to make no distinction between the theurgist and the geotist, but grouped them together as magicians and necromancers whom he distinguished from the vulgar witch by noting that, while the witch was an acknowledged servant of the devil, the practitioner of "magie" believed himself to be the devil's commander.[9] Of the power wielded by magicians, James wrote, "they blindlie glorie of themselves, as if they had by their quicknes of ingine, made a conquest of *Plutoes* dominion, and were become Emperours over the *Stygian* habitacles. Where, in the meane time (miserable wretches) they are become in verie deede, bond slaues to their mortall enemie: and their knowledge for all that they presume thereof, is nothing increased, except in knowing evil . . ." (pp. 10–11). Sir Walter Raleigh, despite his Neoplatonic orientation, was another of Shakespeare's contemporaries who stressed the damnable un-

lawfulness of theurgy and the blind self-delusion of which the practitioner was
guilty. He wrote,

> There is another art besides the aforementioned [necromancy and goetia]
> which they call *Theurgia* or *White Magicke;* a pretended conference with
> good Spirits or Angels, whom by Sacrifice and Invocation they draw out
> of heaven and communicate withal. But the administering Spirits of God,
> as they require not any kind of adoration due unto their Creator, so, seeing
> they are most free spirits, there is no man so absurd as to think (except the
> Devil have corrupted his understanding) that they can be constrained or
> commanded out of Heaven by threats. Wherefore let the Professours
> thereof cover themselves how they please by a professed purity of life,
> by the ministry of Infants, by fasting and abstinence in general; yet all
> those that tamper with immaterial substances, and attract natures, either
> by Sacrifice, Vow, or Inforcement, or men of evil faith, and in the power
> of *Satan.* For Good Spirits or Angels cannot be constrained; and the rest
> be devils, which willingly obey.[10]

These representative contemporary claims[11] would not only deny Prospero's
beneficent status, but also point toward another factor which is important in
evaluating the protagonist of *The Tempest:* the sinful degree of self-deception
and presumption the theurgist is prone to. The real issues of *The Tempest* can
be resolved only in these Christian and orthodox terms, by recognizing in
Prospero something much more ominous than the priestly theurgist, and in his
actions something infinitely more malevolent than a positive godlike manipulation of men and elements. The theurgy Shakespeare incorporates into his play
is not the theurgy of Iamblichus, Porphyry, and Plotinus, but the theurgy of the
orthodox detractors of the art. There is nothing in *The Tempest* which Shakespeare could not have drawn from contemporary, and orthodox, vernacular
sources, for example, from Thomas Lodge's *The Divell Coniured,* Thomas
Nashe's *Knight of the Post* and *Pierce Penilesse,* James I's *Daemonologie,* and
Thomas Healey's 1610 translation of St. Augustine's *The City of God.* Shakespeare's attitude toward the theurgic elements of *The Tempest* is exactly the
attitude of the orthodox. Converse with demons is presumptuous and damnable, and the individual who presumes to godhead through theurgic practices is
himself blindly deceived both about his own power and his own nature.

Recognizing Prospero as a type of the potentially damned sorcerer is essential to any realization of the full scope of *The Tempest.* It is his potentially
damned state which provides the most intense ironic tension in the play; out
of his own blind regard for his art and the powers it brings him arises the

hamartia which could so easily culminate in the tragedy of a Macbeth or a Dr. Faustus. What Battenhouse says of the protagonist of Christian tragedy is equally true of Prospero: "Disgraceful error and painful effort: Are not these the hallmark of every tragic hero? What Augustine helps us to see is that their root is not ignorance alone but an ignorance resulting from a misplaced love. Love of some temporal good in preference to God. . . ."[12] Only his recognition of his error and of its relationship to his planned revenge against those who have injured him (an obvious attempt to gratify his self-love) prevents the play from becoming an exposition of Prospero's tragedy. Prospero's blindness to his own condition through the first four acts of the play would not have been shared by either Shakespeare or a Jacobean audience familiar with the orthodox attitudes toward magic black or white, however much they may have been fascinated by his powers. Prospero's vision of those powers as licit and limitless in potential would not have been their vision. Whatever claims he may make, implicitly or explicitly, about his own powers would have been recognized for what they were—unlawful violations of his human condition. Prospero's actions proclaim that he accepts the theurgic belief that "he commands these powers, because through arcane symbols, he, in a certain respect, is invested with the sacred form of the Gods."[13] It is because he is unable to see his theurgy as a human attempt to usurp divine power that he, like Lear, views himself as more sinned against than sinning. He cannot recognize that his is the exemplary usurpation, one which is far more serious than the usurpation of temporal dukedoms or island kingdoms.

The negative aspects of Prospero's position are all too closely allied to his blindness to his own un*kind*ly behavior. From the moment he admits to Miranda his own part in the shipwreck and identifies himself as the sometime duke of Milan, one becomes aware of a disparity between his account of events or his conception of his powers or his view of his actions and the actual evaluation one must make of them within the dramatic context Shakespeare has established. The dramatist maintains a constant tension between Prospero as *humanum genus*, that creature who of himself can will no spiritual good, and Prospero as he envisions himself, the respository of divine prerogatives. As a civil magistrate, for example, Prospero is both obligated to punish breaches in civil conduct and limited to extending that punishment to the body; Prospero the theurgist sees punishment as a personal vendetta which, the play suggests, would extend to the spirit as well. Shakespeare points repeatedly to the errors in Prospero's self-concept. He establishes the inefficacy of Prospero's learning, continually suggests the demonic nature of his agents, and depicts his lack of compassion, that particularly human virtue, throughout the first four acts of the play. The dramatist employs the subplot of the fools to suggest the real nature of Prospero's planned revenge, and he structures the play as a whole upon the archetypal pattern which Greene had employed earlier for *Friar Bacon and Friar Bungay*, a pattern in which the evil sorcerer (however clever or amusing his actions) is blind to his own error until some traumatic event awakens him to an awareness of his potentially damned state and to repentance.

Prospero's misfortunes began, as his tale of the usurpation of his dukedom shows, with his own defection from his human, social role. His account of the loss of his position, despite his legitimate right to rule, would not have struck Shakespeare's audience as being quite so complimentary to the theurgist as some critics would have us believe. Early seventeenth-century English political theory had no sympathy for the philosopher-king who abdicated his duties to dwell in the ivory tower of contemplation. When Prospero seeks to portray himself as the innocent victim of "unnatural" perfidy, what he actually reveals is that he himself furnished the opportunity, and was in large part responsible, for his own political downfall. He tells Miranda,

> My brother, and thy uncle, call'd Antonio—
> I pray thee, mark me—that a brother should
> Be so perfidious!—he whom next thyself
> Of all the world I lov'd, and to him put
> The manage of my state; as at that time
> Through all the signories it was the first,
> And Prospero the prime duke, being so reputed
> In dignity, and for the liberal arts
> Without a parallel; those being all my study,
> The government I cast upon my brother,
> And to my state grew a stranger, being transported
> And rapt in secret studies.
>
> *(I.ii.66–77)*[14]

As though this single admission of defection from his proper role were not stress enough, Shakespeare allowed Prospero to repeat himself:

> I, thus neglecting worldly ends, all dedicated
> To closeness and the bettering of my mind
> With that which, but by being so retired,
> O'er-priz'd all popular rate, in my false brother,
> Awak'd an evil nature. . . .
>
> *(I.ii.89–93)*

Here, Prospero depicts himself as the selfless seeker for knowledge, recalling Raleigh's "professed purity of life" the damned theurgist affected. His portrait of a "perfidious" brother and a "false uncle" with an "evil nature" is balanced by his own double admission that the quest for "secret" knowledge had for him become more important than his role as a respected head of state; it becomes apparent that his failure to fulfill his proper role had furnished the opportunity and fed the appetite which resulted in Antonio's seizure of power.

Prospero thus reveals himself, however inadvertently, as less than a perfect ruler. For Sisson to have suggested that such a portrait of the philosopher-king would have pleased James I is belied by the king's own advice to his heir, Prince Henry, in the *Basilikon Doron*. Prospero violates not one, but several strictures included in the king's advice to his son. The first violation occurs in Prospero's definite association with the magic arts. In the *Basilikon*, as in the *Daemonologie*, James had inveighed against all magic arts; witchcraft, the father advised, was one of the crimes "ye are bound in conscience neuer to forgiue."[15] Second, instead of advising withdrawal from the burden of rule, James had urged active participation, including a visit throughout the domain once every three years to allow the ruler to hear "your selfe their [the citizens'] complaintes," rather than depending upon the reports of "Vice-roies" (p. 55). The third violation occurs in Prospero's involvement in his studies, which he first associates with the liberal arts and later classifies as "secret." James had advised: "Therefore, besides your education, it is necessarie ye delight in reading and seeking knowledge of all lawfull thinges, but with these two restrictions: that ye choose idle houres for it, not interrupting therewith the discharge of your office; and next, that ye study not for knowledge nakedly, but that your principall end be, to make you able thereby to use your office, practicing according to knowledge all points of your calling . . ." (p. 88). In withdrawing from the world of action to pursue his studies and in choosing to involve himself in "unlawful" magical practices, Prospero violated an inclusive stricture: "Think not, therefore, that the highness of your dignity deminisheth your faults (much lesse giveth you a license to sinne) but by the contrarie, your fault shall be aggrauated, according to the height of your dignitie; and any sinne that ye committe, not being a single sinne procuring the fall of one; but being an exemplare sinne & therefore drawing with it the whole multitude to be guiltie of the same" (pp. 2–3). Prospero's exemplary usurpation of power which did not properly belong to him as man is mirrored on every level of society in *The Tempest*. Antonio and Sebastian plot to usurp Alonso's kingdom; Caliban claims that Prospero has usurped his island and he, Stephano, and Trinculo plan to re-usurp it. Antonio, aided by Alonso, has already usurped Prospero's dukedom. There is even the possibility that Prospero himself considers a form of usurpation in Naples, allowing Ferdinand to think his father dead so that the son and Miranda may occupy the throne.

Prospero, in portraying himself to his daughter and to the audience as more sinned against than sinning, reveals his inability to grasp the analogy between his search for power above nature, power not intended for man, and his brother's seizure of temporal power he cannot legitimately claim. This lack of self-knowledge is a fitting prologue to his exile on an island inhabited only by demons and Caliban, an exile which can be viewed as an emblem of his presumption since it represents an alienation from his own kind and a fitting correlative of his own corrupt spiritual state. His presumption of divine power exiles him methaphorically from the world of man as effectively as geographical displacement separates him from Milan.

For how little Prospero sold his kingdom can be seen by examining the effectiveness of the power his secret studies gave him. Reduced to ruling a kingdom made up of the hagseed Caliban and a troop of elemental spirits, he achieves his ends through fear of the pain produced by the power of his art. Prospero's learning has enabled him to teach Caliban, but, as Prospero himself observes,

> Abhorred slave,
> Which any print of goodness wilt not take,
> Being capable of all ill! I pitied thee,
> Took pains to make thee speak, taught thee each hour
> One thing or other. When thou didst not, savage,
> Know thine own meaning, but would gabble like
> A thing most brutish, I endow'd thy purposes
> With words that made them known. But thy vile race,
> Though thou didst learn, had that in't which good natures
> Could not abide to be with; therefore wast thou
> Deservedly confin'd into this rock,
> Who hadst deserv'd more than a prison.
>
> (I.ii.351–62)

And when Caliban himself replies,

> You taught me language: and my profit on't
> Is, I know how to curse,
>
> (I.ii.363–64)

it becomes apparent that Prospero has indicted his own studies in his attempt to indict Caliban and has defined their limitations. All his power and all his learning have not been able, despite good intentions, to bring about a regeneration of Caliban's naturally concupiscent tendencies; only grace, a divine gift, could effect this end: "For it is the Holy Ghost, and no other thing, that doth quicken the minds of men, stirring up good and godly motions in their hearts, which are agreeable to the will and commandment of God, such as otherwise of their own crooked and perverse nature they should never have."[16] Prospero could not change the brutish nature of the unregenerate spawn of Sycorax and the devil; he could not even ascertain that his gift of language would assure lip service to goodness. Neither his attempts to tutor Caliban nor his kindness to him had the power to make him good, as the "slave's" attempt to violate Miranda and his cursing prove. Nor did the afflictions showered on Caliban by the magician make him repentant or meek. On the contrary, he assures his master that but for the force which prevented him, he had "peopled else / This isle with Calibans" (I.ii.350–51). Caliban curses the theurgist even as threats of pinches and cramps and aches coerce him into obedience. For him, the only difference between the art of Prospero and the art of "the damned witch Sycorax" is one of degree, not kind. Prospero's art

> is of such power,
> It would control my dam's god, Setebos,
> And make a vassal of him.
>
> *(I.ii.373–75)*

Caliban does not see, nor does his condition show, Prospero as a gracious ruler who is the source of all benevolence; he is a tyrant and a usurper, an individual who, without his magic books, would be "but a sot, as I am" (III.ii.101).

Like Caliban, Ariel and his fellows appear to obey Prospero through fear rather than the love which traditionally should motivate the service of elemental spirits to both God and man. Ariel, when called upon by Prospero to perform "more work," considers his master's commands "toil" and reminds him,

> Since thou dost give me pains,
> Let me remember thee what thou hast promis'd,
> Which is not yet perform'd me.
>
> *(I.ii.242–44)*

Prospero replies angrily to Ariel's reminder that he has been promised his freedom. The theurgist points out that upon his arrival he had found Ariel pinned in a "cloven pine" where the spirit had been imprisoned by his former mistress, Sycorax, adding,

> Thou best know'st
> What torment I did find thee in; thy groans
> Did make wolves howl, and penetrate the breasts
> Of ever-angry bears. It was a torment
> To lay upon the damn'd. . . .
>
> (I.ii.286–90)

If Ariel "more murmur'st," Prospero threatens,

> I will rend an oak
> And peg thee in his knotty entrails till
> Thou hast howl'd away twelve winters.
>
> (I.ii.294–96)

Sycorax's punishment, Prospero says, though it was a "torment / To lay upon the damn'd," is mild compared to what the spirit can expect if he does not co-operate with the theurgist. The soft wood of the pine had been exquisite torture; the oak, tough and hard, promises a torment even greater. Small wonder, then, that Ariel immediately promises,

> Pardon, master;
> I will be correspondent to command
> And do my spriting gently.
>
> (I.ii.296–98)

Like Caliban, Ariel could have concluded that the only difference between the power of his former mistress Sycorax and the power of his present master lay in the latter's superior strength, not in kind, since it promised similar but more torturous punishment.

In this interchange between magician and attendant spirit, Shakespeare managed to suggest two facts about Ariel which would point toward his being a demonic rather than a beneficent spirit. First is Ariel's reminder that Prospero had promised to grant him his freedom a year before his time was due to expire —a reminder that suggests the traditional blood pact of goety rather than the divine manipulation of beneficent spirits by a figure who had managed to unite himself with the gods. Good spirits, within orthodox pneumatological theory, could not be constrained; whatever services they performed for man were done through love and as the agents of God, not through fear or force. Second is the fact that Ariel had been controlled and punished by the admittedly evil Sycorax; his punishment had shown him so completely in her power that she could imprison him for refusing to obey her. Ariel's subjection to Sycorax, an evil figure, would support the conclusion that the spirit himself is demonic. In consequence, the character of his present master becomes correspondingly less positive. Perhaps the fact that the "pact" between Ariel and Prospero never reaches a Faustian conclusion tends to mitigate his demonic orientation and at the same time to lessen the theurgist's eventual guilt, making his recognition and reversal viable. Yet these are only the first two of many suggestions that Ariel and his fellows are demonic spirits, and, in the orthodox scheme of things, their demonic qualities reflect on Prospero in a negative rather than a positive manner.

Despite his Puckish charm, Ariel displays from the beginning of *The Tempest* talents which were frequently connected with demons. The missions he carries out for Prospero include the creation of a storm, the provision of a banquet at which he assumes the shape of a harpy, and the tormenting of the three fools and the "three men of sin," all of which had their analogues in contemporary devil lore. For example, despite the efforts of such writers as George Gifford and Reginald Scot, who insisted that to attribute manipulation of the weather to demons was superstitious—to fail to attribute to the Author of all things his just due—belief in demonically contrived storms was a sixteenth- and seventeenth-century commonplace. James I himself had been in a storm similar to the one Ariel raises in *The Tempest* to disrupt the journey of the court party homeward after having attended the wedding of Claribel, the king's daughter, to the king of Tunis. James I was also en route home after attending a wedding, his own, in Denmark, and his ship was buffeted by a storm which was believed to have been contrived by the North Berwick witches, in whose trials he later took an active part. The incident, recounted in the *Newes from Scotland,* occurred thus:

> Againe it is confessed, that the said christened Cat was the cause that the Kinges Maiesties Ship at his comming out of Denmarke, had a contrary winde to the rest of his Ships, then being in his companye, which thing was most strange and true, as the Kinges Maiestie acknowledgeth . . . and further the saide witche declared, that his Maiestie had neuer come safelye from the Sea, if his faith had not preuailed aboue their ententions.[17]

Ariel's activities during the storm—he "flamed amazement" over the ship so that, as he himself declared, Ferdinand jumped overboard on the theory that "all the devils in hell are here" (I.ii.214)—were, as Ferdinand's speech revealed, definitely associated with the demonic. The spirit's role as the fire which flew over the rigging is that of the *ignis fatuus*, St. Elmo's fire or, on land, foxfire, of which Burton wrote, "Fiery Spirits or Devils such as commonly work by blazing stars, firedrakes, or *ignes fatui* . . . they signify some mischief or other to come unto men . . . St. Elmo's fires they commonly call them, & they do likely appear after a sea storm."[18]

If the storm, and Ariel's part in it, has clear demonic associations, the same is true of the banquet scene, which at least one critic has seen fit to view as the communion table from which the men of sin are kept by Prospero and Ariel because they are not fit to partake of it.[19] On the contrary, however, Prospero's function in directing this scene and Ariel's performance in it again serve to suggest for both a demonic rather than a divine orientation. The belief that demons could, at the command of their masters, supply dainties from the farthest points of the globe at a moment's notice was as widespread as the belief that they could contrive storms. James I, in the *Daemonologie*, mentioned it briefly in his preface to the reader; later in the same work he wrote, "And he [Satan] will make them to please Princes, by faire banquets and daintie dishes, carryed in short space fra the fartherest parts of the worlde" (p. 22). In the prose history of Dr. Faustus, the doomed sorcerer twice entertained friends and patrons by serving viands brought from distant lands; once he entertained fellow scholars, and once he procured grapes out of season for the pregnant wife of an influential patron.

In the banquet scene, Shakespeare once again allowed a member of the play world to call attention to the demonic associations of the action. This time Prospero, rather than a member of the court party, cites the diabolic connections of the servitors. Gonzalo had judged,

> though they are of monstrous shape, yet, note,
> Their manners are more gentle, kind, than of
> Our human generation you shall find
> Many, nay, almost any.
>
> *(III.iii.31–34)*

Prospero's reply,

> Honest lord,
> Thou hast said well; for some of you there present
> Are worse than devils,
>
> *(III.iii.34–36)*

suggests that he regards his spirit attendants as devils, not "good" essential creatures.[20]

Prospero's association with the evil sorcerer of orthodox tradition is further suggested by the effect which the banquet scene has upon the "three men of sin" and by the torment which he and Ariel together shower upon the three fools. Contrary to claims that he had from the beginning intended to forgive those who had wronged him, there is really very little in the text of *The Tempest*, prior to Act V, to warrant such suggestions. The punishment of the court party began in the first scene of the play, a scene which may be called the prologue to a drama directed by a man who is indifferent to the suffering he creates and who cannot, like Miranda, summon up the virtue of compassion for the actors. It is true that in response to his daughter's "piteous" reaction, he calms her with,

> Wipe thine eyes; have comfort.
> The direful spectacle of the wreck, which touch'd
> The very virtue of compassion in thee,
> I have with such provision in mine art
> So safely ordered that there is no soul—
> No, not so much perdition as an hair
> Betid to any creature in the vessel
> Which thou heard'st cry, which thou saw'st sink.
>
> (I.ii.25–32)

Yet, when Ariel recounts the reaction of the mariners to the wreck, telling his master,

> Not a soul
> But felt some fever of the mad, and play'd
> Some tricks of desperation. All but mariners
> Plung'd in the foaming brine, and quit the vessel,
> Then all afire with me. The King's son, Ferdinand,
> With hair up-staring—then like reeds, not hair—
> Was the first man that leap'd; cried, "Hell is empty
> And all the devils are here,"
>
> (I.ii.208–15)

he receives a strong mark of approbation from Prospero, who praises him with "Why, that's my spirit!" (215). Prospero is equally satisfied with the results of the banquet scene, when the three men of sin, led on by Ariel's speech to them, run from the stage in a state of despairing madness, if Gonzalo's evaluation is correct:

> All three of them are desperate. Their great guilt,
> Like poison given to work a great time after,
> Now gins to bite the spirits. I do beseech you,
> That are of suppler joints, follow them swiftly
> And hinder them from what this ecstasy
> May now provoke them to.
>
> *(III.iii.104–9)*

Yet of this spiritually dangerous state which, if perpetuated, would lead to damnation, Prospero expresses only satisfaction:

> My high charms work,
> And these mine enemies are all knit up
> In their distractions. They are now in my power;
> And in these fits I leave them, while I visit
> Young Ferdinand, whom they suppose is drown'd,
> And his and mine lov'd darling.
>
> *(III.iii.88–93)*

Thus it would appear, not only from Prospero's reference but from Gonzalo's as well, that the magician's plot is to push the three nobles toward the ultimate sin of despair. Within the pneumatological framework of the period, Prospero thus can be seen as a type of Satan, working through his spirit agent Ariel to achieve his end. That magicians employed their spirit familiars for such damnable purposes was again a well-known tenet of Renaissance witchcraft theory; during the 1612 trial of the Lancashire witches, for example, one witness against those accused cited as evidence against them the appearance of a spirit which tempted her to drown herself.[21]

Despite the spiritually dangerous consequences of the banquet scene, it is nevertheless the scene toward which critics turn when stressing the sacerdotal character of Prospero. Here they rely upon Ariel's speech to Alonso, Ferdinand, and Sebastian and upon Prospero's claim that in delivering it his agent had "nothing bated." Ariel's speech is, in fact, ambiguous, and its very ambiguity is intensified by his own nature and by the position Prospero has presumed for himself. Ariel tells Prospero's enemies:

> You are three men of sin, whom Destiny,
> That hath to instrument this lower world

And what is in't, the never-surfeited sea
Hath caused to belch up you; and on this island
Where man doth not inhabit; you 'mongst men
Being most unfit to live. I have made you mad,
And even with such-like valour men hang and drown
Their proper selves.

(III.iii.53–60)

As Ariel's speech is the product of Prospero's prompting, it presents the theurgist's concept of himself as Destiny, or the divine force that "instruments"
events upon the earth. Prospero, through Ariel, claims responsibility, not only
for the storm which cast Alonso, Antonio, Sebastian, and the others ashore,
but also for the madness of the three men of sin, a state in which, the speech
notes, men do violence upon themselves. The same implication—that Prospero
presumes for himself a divine power—is present in Ariel's later statement that
the "powers" have only delayed punishment, not forgotten the crimes of which
they are guilty. The spirit continues,

But remember—
For that's my business to you—that you three
From Milan did supplant good Prospero
Expos'd unto the sea, which hath requit it,
Him and his innocent child; for which foul deed,
The powers, delaying, not forgetting, have
Incens'd the seas and shores, yea, all the creatures
Against your peace. Thee of thy son, Alonso,
They have bereft; and do pronounce by me
Lingering perdition, worse than any death
Can be at once, shall step by step attend
You and your ways, whose wraths to guard you from—
Which here, in this most desolate isle, else falls
Upon your heads—is nothing but heart's sorrow
And a clear life ensuing.

(III.iii.68–82)

Through Ariel's speech, Prospero implies a divine right to judge, to punish, and
to set up the criteria for avoiding punishment. On one hand, a careful examination of the text reveals that the entire scope of what is to happen to the three
members of the court party—what they are threatened with—is temporal.
They have been cast up on an uninhabited island; Alonso has been bereft of
Ferdinand; "lingering perdition" will follow them "in this most desolate isle"

unless they experience repentance and reformation. And they have been driven to madness.

This latter fact is perhaps most important of all in evaluating the nature of Prospero's function as "Destiny." For despite its surface declarations of temporal punishment deriving from a "divine" figure for wrongs he has suffered, the speech resounds with theological overtones. Alonso, Sebastian, and Antonio are more than civil offenders; they are "three men of sin." Their punishment is viewed as "perdition," or damnation, which is certain unless they experience repentance, in terms of both sincere contrition and amendment of life. But the measure of Prospero's "divine prerogative" in this instance rests not in the temporal or spiritual content of the speech itself, but in its effect. The three nobles to whom it has been directed run mad, and in this state they remain through Act IV and into Act V.

In participating in a drama with such results, Ariel has functioned, on one level, as the devil's advocate, leading Alonso, Sebastian, and Antonio not only to an awareness of their own evil deeds but into a madness which, as he suggests, often ends with the madmen committing suicide, a suggestion which Gonzalo seconds. If this eventuality is included in Prospero's plan for the fate of his enemies, then his presumption is supreme. His revenge upon his enemies extends to damning not only their bodies but also their souls, for if madness was a punishment for the sins of the reprobate, suicide was the visible sign of religious despair. Within the cause-and-effect pattern of madness and suicide, the divine attribute of mercy is absent; the madman, bereft of reason, is incapable of repentance. And if repentance is what Prospero seeks, this pattern, in which his victims are "all three distracted" (V.i.12), does not provide for it. Nor does the text of *The Tempest* suggest any alternative aim for Prospero the theurgist. It suggests instead, through Caliban, Stephano, and Trinculo, their plotting and their fate, that the torments of hell are exactly what Prospero has in mind for his fellow nobles.

This inability to keep counsel blooms into fully plotted evil when Caliban meets Stephano and Trinculo. Finding himself at last with allies who can aid him in effecting his revenge upon his usurper, he suggests a plot whereby the three will kill Prospero, place Stephano upon the throne, and marry the new king to Miranda. Or, in more general terms, his plot calls for deposing through murder the present ruler, installing a new one in his place, and marrying the new ruler to Miranda.

Despite his vagueness about his own intentions, Prospero's plot as it develops in action has salient similarities to the fully defined plot of the three fools. Like Caliban, he seeks vengeance upon those who have taken part in his usurpation. He has separated Ferdinand from his father, and Ferdinand believes that his father is dead and he is king of Naples. Nor does Prospero offer any sincere objections to the growing love between Ferdinand and Miranda; though he uses no charms to further that love, he deliberately brought them together and agrees to their marriage. And his saving of the ship and crew provides a means for returning to Naples. In general terms, Prospero appears to have deposed Alonso, set Ferdinand up in his place, and approved of the marriage of the new king to Miranda.

If, as I suggest, the subplot both mirrors and foreshadows the action of the main plot,[22] that subplot throws further doubt upon Prospero's intended punishment of Alonso, Antonio, and Sebastian. Because of the theurgist's more sophisticated and intricate approach to vengeance, and because of his more cerebral and devious character, his ability to keep his counsel about those intentions actually makes them more frightening than Caliban's proposed revenge. That Caliban can suggest to Stephano and Trinculo that he will

> yield him thee asleep,
> Where thou mayst knock a nail into his head, . . .
>   (III.ii.68–69)

would suggest that some fate more exquisitely horrible than a quick death awaits Prospero's victims.

Once the three fools become, like the three sinners of the court party, enemies of Prospero in a related pattern of usurpation, their fate begins to suggest the possible fate Prospero has in store for his more noble victims, the ones who have succeeded in wronging him. Prospero's exacting of "justice" for the wrongs the three fools intend to inflict upon him—notably the destruction of his magic books, his murder, the usurpation of his island kingdom, and the mating of Miranda with Stephano—is not so subtly exquisite as that he wreaks upon his noble usurpers. It is, however, very much in keeping with his identification with the evil sorcerer of orthodox tradition. The comic quality of the chasing of the three fools through mud and fen and briar may in one way appear nothing more than the exacting of a sort of poetic justice. Yet it is exactly the sort of punishment one finds associated with figures who in Shakespeare's time had become identified as prototypes of the doomed magician. In the prose chapbook of *The Famous History of Friar Bacon*, the friar ordered one of his attendant spirits to lead one of his enemies just such a pixilated, frustrating chase; and the prose account of Dr. Faustus includes several episodes in which the obviously evil magician employs his skills to create discomfort for those who oppose him. In one instance, Faustus changes the head of a nobleman into a stag's head, which gets stuck in a window; in another, he changes a bottle of hay into a horse to confound a thieving horse dealer, and when the horse wades into water, it becomes hay once again. The presence of such comic elements in contexts that were essentially serious and tragic appeared in no way to contradict the damned nature of the sorcerers; and it is in this spirit that Ariel's *joie de vivre* in leading the fools a merry chase must be regarded.

Caliban in many ways is a debased analogue of Prospero himself. Both are the victims of usurpation, and Caliban,in describing the loss of his island adopts much the same self-excusing tone which Prospero had employed in relating his story to Miranda. Caliban recalls, as did Prospero, his generosity to his usurper, but he goes further in voicing his curse for the man against whom his own malice is directed:

> This island's mine, by Sycorax my mother,
> Which thou tak'st from me. When thou cam'st first,
> Thou strok'dst me and made much of me, wouldst give me
> Water with berries in't, and teach me how
> To name the bigger light, and how the less,
> That burn by day and night; and then I lov'd thee,
> And show'd thee all the qualities o' th' isle,
> The fresh springs, brine-pits, barren place and fertile.
> Curs' be that I did so! All the charms
> Of Sycorax, toads, beetles, bats, light on you!
> For I am all the subjects that you have,
> Which first was mine own king; and here you sty me
> In this hard rock, whiles you do keep from me
> The rest o' th' island.
>
> (I.ii.331–44)

As Prospero had done earlier, both in recounting his usurpation to Miranda and in chastising Ariel, Caliban points to actions which should have bred gratitude and did not. The difference here between master and slave, usurper and usurped, is simply that Prospero can keep counsel and Caliban cannot. Caliban, in his naïveté, insists upon voicing his intentions for revenging himself upon his victim, though at this stage nothing better comes to hand than an inefficacious mouthing of the evil charms of his dead mother.

Shakespeare, however, succeeds in imprinting a more than usual degree of diabolical association upon the torments which are visited on the three fools. In Act IV, as Sebastian and Trinculo plunder Prospero's goods, they are set upon by "divers Spirits in shape of dogs and hounds," urged on by Prospero and Ariel. Prospero charges Ariel,

Go charge my goblins that they grind their joints
With dry convulsions, shorten up their sinews
With aged cramps, and more pinch-spotted make them
Than pard or cat o' mountain.

(IV.i.259–62)

As the three exit, Prospero enjoins Ariel to "Let them be hunted soundly"
(263), and then concludes,

At this hour
Lies at my mercy all mine enemies.
Shortly shall all my labors end, and thou
Shalt have the air of freedom.

(IV.i.263–66)

The unanswered question, at this point, is how Prospero intends for his labors
to end. If the "mercy" he plans for the three men of sin is anything like the
mercy he has shown the three fools, their fate would appear wholly unenviable.
To be chased like beasts by spirit hounds which recall the folk belief in the
hounds of hell[23] is hardly a merciful fate. "Mercy" in this context does not
appear to carry any implication of forgiveness. Prospero is simply saying that
his enemies lie in his power, and as the final act of the play begins, he is still
working his charms so that his "project gathers to a head" (V.i.1). That his revenge was not designed to stop at this stage is suggested by his statement that

Though with their high wrongs I am struck to th' quick,
Yet with my nobler reason 'gainst my fury
Do I take part. The rarer action is
In virtue than in vengeance. They being penitent,
The sole drift of my purpose doth extend
Not a frown further.

(V.i.25–30)

This decision results from Prospero's own recognition of his error, however; he
is speaking at this point as Prospero the sometime duke of Milan, not as Prospero
the theurgist. Except that Ariel had succeeded in reminding him of his true nature, the text of the play suggests that, far from intending from the beginning
to forgive his enemies, Prospero had planned to exact the ultimate spiritual
punishment—damnation—from those by whom he had been wronged.

Prospero's recognition of his error and the reversal of his planned revenge are both bound up with the question of his own position and with the degree of power he possesses. Up to Ariel's appearance in Act V, Prospero has presumed he has the power not only to control spirits but to judge and to punish his fellow man as a participant in godhead, not just as a civil magistrate. Yet it is Ariel, acting not as Prospero's agent but as an agent of some higher power, who awakens the theurgist to an awareness of his own exemplary sin. Reporting on the plight of the court party, Ariel tells his "master,"

> Your charm so strongly works 'em
> That if you now beheld them, your affections
> Would become tender.
>
> *(V.i.17–19)*

Prospero responds, "Dost thou think so, spirit?" (V.i.19), to which the spirit replies, "Mine would, sir, were I human" (V.i.20). Into this two-line exchange Shakespeare has poured the essence of Prospero's error; the two words, *spirit* and *human*, imply the vast distinction between what is proper to man and what is possible for essences. Prospero is, after all, human and not divine. His potential excellence lies not in the power to know the secrets of the universe or to manipulate both elements and man as a result of knowing those secrets, but in his ability to "passion with" his fellow man and to seek, to the best of his human ability, to know God. Spirits, on the other hand, even fallen spirits, knew secrets of nature and even truths which man might never know, but they were incapable of passioning with either their fellows or with man. It is this distinction which lies at the heart of Prospero's own exemplary sin, and it is this distinction which awakens him to an awareness of it. As he is struck by the validity of Ariel's statement, Prospero says,

> Hast thou, which art but air, a touch, a feeling
> Of their afflictions, and shall not myself,
> One of their kind, that relish all as sharply,
> Passion as they, be kindlier mov'd than thou art?
>
> *(V.i.21–24)*

With this realization, Prospero can then go on to decide that the rarer action is in virtue and not in vengeance, thus acknowledging the Augustinian theory that man was capable of excelling the spirits in piety. Sending Ariel to bring his victims to him, he then repudiates his control of the spirit world, a control which had been the outward sign of his presumption. In resigning his "rough magic" (V.i.50) and promising to break his staff and drown his book, Prospero moves from what the homilies consider the "spirit of the devil" to the spirit of Christ:

> But to conclude, and make an end, ye shall briefly take this short lesson; wheresoever ye find the spirit of arrogance and pride, the spirit of envy, hatred, contention, cruelty, murder, extortion, witchcraft, necromancy, &c. assure yourselves that there is the spirit of the devil, and not of God, albeit they pretend outwardly to the world never so much holiness. For as the Gospel teacheth us, the spirit of Jesus is a good spirit, an holy spirit, a sweet spirit, a lowly spirit, a merciful spirit, full of charity and love, full of forgiveness and pity, not rendering evil for evil, extremity for extremity, but overcoming evil with good and remitting all offense even from the heart.
>
> (p. 516)

Until Ariel stressed the distinction between what was proper to man and what was proper to spirits, Prospero appeared certain to have rendered evil for evil, not in a pattern of positive theurgy, but as an individual whose desire for revenge and involvement in magic practices marked him as being imbued with the spirit of the devil.

It is customary, in keeping with the view of Prospero as a positive character, to negate the deeply moral and religious nature of his recognition and reversal. Dover Wilson found in them "no hint of moral compunction, no reminder, as in Portia's speech, of the promptings of religion;"[24] other critics have suggested that, having achieved his ends, having done all he could as a theurgist, Prospero has no need to continue his magical practices and so discards them.[25]

Yet the text of the play will not bear out these claims. At the point where Prospero repudiates both his art and the vengeance toward which he had been directing it, nothing of value had been accomplished. Caliban remains the unregenerate character he was in Act I, still unrepentant and fearful of Prospero's power, and still tormented by his spirits. Antonio, Sebastian, and Alonso have been reminded of their sins, but they are mad, incapable of either contrition or amendment of life; the best any one of them has felt is the remorse Alonso exhibited just before he ran mad. The final resolution of *The Tempest* comes about not through any sacerdotal ability on Prospero's part to engender a change of character in his victims, but rather because he foregoes his pretensions to godhead and assumes his proper role as man. Once he discards his magic robes and clothes himself as the sometime duke of Milan, a man within a world of men, his exemplary actions are reflected in the actions of his former enemies. Alonso, confronted with "The wronged Duke of Milan, Prospero" (V.i.107), declares,

> since I saw thee,
> Th' affliction of my mind amends, with which,
> I fear, a madness held me. This must crave,
> An if this be at all, a most strange story.
> Thy dukedom I resign and do entreat
> Thou pardon me my wrongs.
>
> (V.i.114–19)

The effect of Prospero's forgiveness on Sebastian and Alonso is less easy to gauge. Prospero tells these two villains that he could "pluck his Highness' frown upon you" (V.i.127), but "At this time / I will tell no tales" (V.i.128–29): and, when Sebastian declares that "The devil speaks in him" (129), the duke answers with a brief "no" which could indicate his awareness of his own merciful attitude. Prospero then proceeds to tell Antonio,

> For you, most wicked sir, whom to call brother
> Would even infect my mouth, I do forgive
> Thy rankest fault,—all of them; and require
> My dukedom of thee, which perforce, I know
> Thou must restore.
>
> (V.i.130–34)

Sebastian's reversal of intent is made obvious through his dialogue, however brief, during the remainder of the scene, but not so with Antonio, whose almost total silence throughout the remainder of the action has often been remarked upon. This silence can, as has been suggested, denote his lack of repentance, but again, in dramatic action, repentance can be conveyed by more than words. Antonio's action in usurping his brother's dukedom has been no more vicious than Caliban's intent to drive a nail into his master's head to kill him, and even Caliban is not untouched by the new attitude Prospero has adopted. Brought back on stage with the belief that "I shall be pinched to death" (V.i.276), he is told by his master that "As you look / To have my pardon, trim it [Prospero's cell] handsomely" (V.i.291–92). Prospero's reference to "pardon" here contrasts sharply with his earlier insistence that Caliban "deserved" even stronger punishment than he had received in being imprisoned, enslaved, and tormented by spirits. Caliban's reaction to his master's mercy is,

> Ay, that I will; and I'll be wise hereafter,
> And seek for grace.
>
> (V.i.294–95)

"Wisdom" and "grace" are both divine gifts; Caliban is saying here that he has at last been given the insight to realize what his true aim should be. And this awareness has not come, nor had it come earlier, through Prospero's theurgic efforts. Rather it has been achieved because Prospero the earthly ruler has acquired the self-knowledge which enabled him to temper justice with mercy in the pattern which every Christian ruler, in his analogous relationship to the state, was to practice in imitation of God's dispensing both justice and mercy in the universe.

To argue that Prospero's theurgical potential does not bring about the resolution of the problems of *The Tempest* is not, however, to deny that he possessed magical powers. Rather, such a claim necessitates examining those powers within the orthodox pneumatological framework which existed during Shakespeare's time. There are, in fact, two schemes of causation operable in *The Tempest*: the scheme adopted by Prospero when he presumes to control spirits, create storms, and punish sinners, and the scheme implicit in his recognition and reversal and the final resolution of the action, a scheme which places Prospero in the position of instrument rather than final cause.

It was a doctrinal truism of witchcraft that the practitioner of magic, be he goetist, theurgist, or the unpretentious witch, only thought he controlled his spirit agents. Although he appeared their master, he was in reality their servant. The magician who appeared to command was, in fact, the instrument in a line of command which ended in God himself. Whatever malice or whatever apparent good he worked through the aid of his spirit agents was permitted by God and was used by God for some end, normally to punish sinners, to bring about their reform, or to confirm them in either their faith or their reprobation. James I had written in the *Daemonologie*, "where the deuilles intention in them is euer to perish, either the soule or the body, or both of them, that he is so permitted to deale with: God by the contrarie, draws euer out of that euill glorie to himselfe, either by the wracke of the wicked in his justice, or by the triall of the patient, and the amendment of the faithful, being awakened vp with that rod of correction" (p. xiv). Thus, even though Ariel in carrying out Prospero's commands may act as a demon, and though Prospero may believe Ariel works at his command, neither could proceed against his victims without God's permission.

That Ariel is capable of action not specifically commanded by Prospero is suggested by Shakespeare early in *The Tempest*, when he embroiders upon Prospero's awareness that Antonio and Sebastian will try to murder Gonzalo and Alonso and prevents the action, concluding that "Prospero my lord shall know what I have done" (II.i.236). Later, it becomes apparent that Ariel's actions in discovering the plot of the three fools (he declares "this will I tell my

master" [III.ii.124], which belies Prospero's total omniscience) and later his
leading them through mud and briar and fen were his own idea, not Prospero's.
For Prospero must ask Ariel, in Act IV, what he has done with the fools, and he
replies to Ariel's story, "This was well done, my bird" (IV.i.185).

Unless one can accept that Ariel is capable of action apart from that which
Prospero commands, it would be difficult to accept his role in Act V, where it is
his performance which brings Prospero to an awareness of his own guilt. For
though Ariel does not afflict Prospero with physical punishment as a means of
awakening him to his own sinful condition, he nevertheless does act, not as
Prospero's agent, but as an agent of a power concerned not only with the sins
of the court party and the three fools, but also with Prospero's own sin of presumption. Within *The Tempest*, then, Ariel becomes, not Prospero's agent, but
an agent of divine Providence working to bring about ends that transcend
Prospero's own personal end of revenge.

Such a dual vision of causation is present within *The Tempest* itself. Prospero
attributes to "Providence divine" (I.ii.159) the fact that he and Miranda did
not die at sea but reached the island on which they have lived; he had earlier
said they were "blessedly holp hither" (I.ii.63). Again, in Act V, Ferdinand
declares that Miranda is his "by immortal providence" (V.i.189), a claim which
gains support from the fact that aside from bringing the two young things
together, Prospero employed no charms or enchantments to further their love.
Yet on the other hand, Prospero sees "most bountiful Fortune / Now my dear
lady" (I.ii.178–79) as the power which has placed his enemies at his command,
and claims,

> I find my zenith doth depend upon
> A most auspicious star, whose influence
> If now I court not but omit, my fortunes
> Will ever after droop.
>
> *(I.ii.181–84)*

Prospero's insistence upon power conceived in pagan terms as an affiliate of
his own actions is equally obvious in the banquet scene, where Ariel, speaking
the speech Prospero has prepared, identifies himself as agent of *Destiny, Fate,*
and *Powers*. Ironically, however, these terms during Shakespeare's time were
capable of a dual interpretation which mirrors the dual vision of causation in
The Tempest. From Prospero's point of view, such terms define his concept of
his assumed role, rooted as it was in the pagan tradition of Neoplatonism. From
the point of view of a Christian scheme of causation, however, *Destiny, Fate,*
and *Powers* become synonymous with the divine Providence with which God

instruments this lower world, a scheme in which all things work, not by accident or blind chance, but within a pattern which transcends any individual will and actually employs the perverted individual will to bring about good instead of evil. Calvin, for example, had written:

> let us be assured that all creatures above and below are ready at his service, that he may employ them in whatever way he pleases. Hence we infer, not only that the general providence of God, continuing the order of nature, extends over the creatures, but that by his wonderful counsel they are adapted to a certain and special purpose.
>
> Those who would cast obloquy on this doctrine, calumniate it as the dogma of the Stoics concerning fate. The same charge was brought against St. Augustine. . . . We are unwilling to dispute about words, but we do not admit the term Fate, both as it is of the class which Paul teaches us to shun, as profane novelties (1 Tim.vi.20), and also because it is attempted, by means of an odious term, to fix a stigma on the truth of God. But the dogma itself is falsely and maliciously imputed to us. For we do not with the Stoics imagine a necessity consisting of a perpetual chain of causes, and a kind of involved series contained in nature, but we hold that God is the disposer and ruler of all things,—that from the remotest eternity, according to his own wisdom, he decreed what he was to do, and now by his power executes what he decreed. Hence we maintain that, by his providence, not heaven and earth and inanimate creatures only, but also the counsels and wills of men are so governed as to move exactly in the course which he has destined. What, then, you will say, does nothing happen fortuitously, nothing contingently? I answer, it was a true saying of Basil the Great, that Fortune and Chance are heathen terms; the meaning of which ought not to occupy pious minds. For if all success is blessing from God, and calamity and adversity are his curse, there is no place left in human affairs for Fortune and chance.[26]

It is within this larger scheme of causation that *The Tempest* is resolved. Such a scheme provides not only for Prospero's presumptuous actions but for his own reformation as well. It provides for an understanding of Ariel's role both as agent for Prospero and as agent for Prospero's reform. And in providing Shakespeare with these explanations, it provided him as well with an orthodox explanation for the fully reintegrated society, which gives the play its comic ending: order within the state is itself a divine gift. It comes not from Prospero's presumptuous powers, but as a result of his recognition of his presumption and his repudiation of it.

Prospero's full reconciliation to his role as man is evident in the epilogue of *The Tempest*. Here, the drowning of his book and the breaking of his wand are in the past, and he declares:

> Now my charms are all o'erthrown
> And what strength I have's mine own,
> Which is most faint. Now, 'tis true,
> I must be here confin'd by you,
> Or sent to Naples. Let me not,
> Since I have my dukedom got,
> And pardon'd the deceiver, dwell
> In this bare island by your spell;
> But release me from my bands
> By the help of your good hands.
> Gentle breath of yours my sails
> Must fill, or else my project fails,
> Which was to please. Now I want
> Spirits to enforce, art to enchant,
> And my ending is despair
> Unless I be reliev'd by prayer,
> Which pierces so that it assaults
> Mercy itself, and frees all faults.
>> As you from crimes would pardoned be,
>> Let your indulgence set me free.

Despite the obvious elements of the *plaudite* here, the epilogue is both conclusion to and summation of *The Tempest*. In the first three lines, Prospero repeats the essence of his recognition and reversal; he is, after all, but a man, one whose strength as man is faint; it was, by implication, his presumption of theurgic powers which gave him strength beyond anything man has the right to acquire. In the last lines, he indicates his awareness of the sinful nature of his presumption: except that he be the recipient of "mercy," his ending will be "despair." Warburton, in the eighteenth century, suggested that these lines mirrored the traditional repentance of the evil sorcerer, a suggestion which has frequently been repudiated since. Yet this is exactly what Prospero is doing, restating the repentance included in Act V and indicating how he hopes to avoid the damnation he deserves for his sin. The plea for mercy from the audience and the stress upon his own exemplary "mercy" to those who have wronged him emphasize his plea for the divine mercy which will free him from his faults. Prospero's last words are an echo of Friar Bacon's:

> Yet, Bacon, cheer thee, drown not in despair;
> Sins have their salves, repentance can do much,
> Think mercy sits where justice holds her seat. . . .[27]

The Prospero of the first four acts of the drama demanded justice untempered by a suggestion of mercy. The Prospero of Act V tempers human justice with human mercy in imitation of the pattern in which he prays divine mercy will be shown to him, just as Prospero the actor prays the audience will show the play the "mercy" of its favor.

In order to see Prospero as a positive theurgist throughout *The Tempest*, it would be necessary to eliminate much within the drama. If Shakespeare's audience had not been able to view him as a type of the doomed sorcerer, his repentance and his resumption of his human condition would have been unmotivated and superfluous, and much of the last act and the epilogue confusing, to say the least. Prospero, like Friar Bacon and the magician Asterius in Lodge's *The Divell Coniured*, had been caught up by the fascination and the power which magic offered. As Asterius said, "for so delightful is the emperie ouer nature, the knowledge of the stars, the commanding of spirits, the manner of exorcisme, that instead of forsaking them, men rather earnestlie affect them" (p. 20). This desire for power, this fascination, was what writer after writer during Shakespeare's era sought to control by pointing out how dangerous such activities were to the soul's health. Prospero, like Bacon and Asterius, recognized the error of his unlawful command and repented. His repentance brings him not only his dukedom and the marriage of his daughter to Ferdinand, but the reestablishment of old friendships and a fuller integration of the social order than would have been possible if he had continued to insist upon justice without mercy. The final society can provide not only for Antonio, Sebastian, Alonso, Stephano, and Trinculo, but for Caliban as well; and he in his wisdom will seek for grace, a pattern which the exemplar Prospero also follows. Prospero the duke of Milan succeeds to a degree which Prospero the magician could not have achieved, making an effective and orthodox commentary upon the validity of his art. True to his age, Shakespeare did not deny the existence of the occult arts. He only denied their positive value in creating, of themselves, anything of value in a world of men. Only the truly divine could bring good out of evil; Prospero, as he achieves good, is the agent of that will and not the prime mover, the will itself.

Notes:

1. See, for example, H. Littledale's "Folklore and Superstition, Ghosts and Fairies, Witchcraft and Devils," in *Shakespeare's England* (London, 1950), II, 542. An

interesting, if inaccurate, attempt to exonerate Prospero occurs in Frank Kermode's introduction to the Arden edition of *The Tempest* (Cambridge, Mass., 1958). He urges that either Shakespeare or a scribe capitalized "Art" in the play to indicate it should be understood in a "technical" theurgical sense (p. xli). Even a cursory familiarity with treatises dealing with magic arts—either reprints or original publications—during the period reveals that the term "Art" was frequently capitalized when used to refer to any occult practices. See, for example, Thomas Nashe, *Pierce Penilesse, His Supplication to the Devil* (1592), *The Works of Thomas Nashe* (Oxford, 1958), I, 228 and 240; Lambert Daneau, *A Dialogue of Witches . . .* (London, 1575), sig. Kv^v, or Thomas Potts, *The Wonderful Discoverie of Witches in the Countie of Lancaster* (1612), in *The Trial of the Lancaster Witches*, ed. G. B. Harrison (London, 1929), p. 52.

2.   *Shakespeare Commentaries* (London, 1883), II, 792.

3.   Quoted in *The Tempest: A New Variorum Edition of Shakespeare* (New York, 1966), p. 22n.

4.   *Shakespeare's Philosophical Patterns*, 2nd ed. (Baton Rouge, 1959), p. ix. In disagreeing with Curry's interpretation of Prospero's character and the positive nature of his power, I do not deny that the magic of Prospero follows a Neoplatonic pattern. In practicing the unlawful magic of the theurgist, Prospero works wonders, but never miracles, a fact which has led N. S. Bushnell, "Natural Supernaturalism in *The Tempest*," *PMLA*, 47 (1932), 684–98, to argue that the element of magic in the drama could be totally eliminated, since everything that happens could have a rational or logical explanation.

5.   "The Magic of Prospero," *ShS*, 9 (1959), 450.

6.   *Nature in Shakespearean Tragedy* (London, 1955), p. 157.

7.   *A Natural Perspective* (New York, 1965), p. 150. For similar claims, see Robert Reed, *The Occult on the Tudor and Stuart Stage* (Boston, 1965), p. 124; Philip Brockbank, "*The Tempest*: Conventions of Art and Empire," *The Later Shakespeare*, Stratford-Upon-Avon Studies VIII (London, 1966), 188.

8.   *Shakespeare's Use of Learning* (San Marino, 1953), pp. 321–22.

9.   (Edinburgh, 1593), p. 22.

10. *The History of the World*, 2nd ed. (London, 1677), I.ix.4.

11. See also Thomas Lodge, *The Divell Coniured, The Complete Works*, 4 vols. (New York, 1963), III, 20; Jean Weir, *Histoires, Despvtes et Discours des Illusions et Impostures des Diables . . .* (1579), Libraire Diabolique (Paris, 1885), p. 166, or Nashe, *Pierce Penilesse*, p. 235. The Weir citation is particularly pertinent, since Weir is so frequently cited as a "sceptic" because he argued in sympathy with the vulgar witch, indicating she deserved merciful treatment because she suffered from delusions or melancholy or illness and often was not what she claimed to be. In actual fact, scholars who cite Weir's scepticism about witches forget that a great portion of his work (four of the six books) was devoted to condemning the practices of the learned occultist.

12. *Shakespearean Tragedy: Its Art and Its Christian Premises* (Bloomington, 1969), p. 220. Battenhouse also observes that the Christian connotations of *hamartia* included "godlessness, presumption, idolatry, injustice" (p. 218), all of which can be associated with Prospero as theurgist. The magician was considered an

"idolater" because he turned to false gods rather than to the true God to attain his ends.

13. Iamblichus, *On the Mysteries of the Egyptians and Chaldeans*, trans. Thomas Taylor (London, 1895), p. 207.

14. *The Complete Plays and Poems*, ed. W. A. Neilson and C. J. Hill (New York, 1942), p. 542. All citations within the text are from this edition, although any potentially controversial passages have been collated with other editions, including *The First Folio of Shakespeare: The Norton Facsimile*, ed. Charlton Hinman (New York, 1968).

15. (Edinburgh, 1603), p. 31.

16. "A Homily Concerning the coming down of the Holy Ghost and the Manifold Gifts of the same," *Sermons or Homilies Appointed to be Read in Churches in the Time of Queen Elizabeth of Famous Memory* (London, 1825), pp. 505–6.

17. (London, 1591), sig. Ci^r.

18. *The Anatomy of Melancholy* (London, 1932), I.ii.1.4. A similar association of demons and storms is found in Regius, *A Homilye or Sermon of Good and Evill Angels* (London, 1583), sig. Cv^v.

19. Robert G. Hunter, *Shakespeare and the Comedy of Forgiveness* (New York, 1965), p. 234. I also disagree with Hunter in seeing Prospero's presumption as the exemplary sin of the play and in identifying the subplot of the three fools as a mirror of Prospero's plot. Hunter would see the exemplary sin as Alonso's (p. 229) and the subplot of the three fools as a mirror of the action of the court party (p. 231).

20. The appearance—and disappearance—of the demonic banquet in *The Tempest* should also be judged by two literary analogues which come from the second half of the seventeenth century: Satan's temptation of Christ in the wilderness in Milton's *Paradise Regained*, II.337–404, a banquet served by beautiful demons which Christ recognizes as a type of the temptation of concupiscent man; and the demonic banquets in Dryden's redaction of *The Tempest*. In Dryden's version, not one but two demonic banquets are served; the banquet placed before the court party disappears, and Gonzalo, a comic figure, comments that someone must have said grace, so that "This comes on't, when Men will be godly out of season." See the *Variorum Tempest*, p. 492. Dryden was of course working with the orthodox theory that demons could not tolerate prayer or any truly pious utterances and so fled them.

21. *The Wonderful Discoverie*, pp. 87–88.

22. Shakespeare had earlier employed his subplots in a similar manner, as a means of defining, evaluating, and commenting upon the action of the major plot and at the same time of foreshadowing action on that level. For example, in *Love's Labor's Lost*, the unnatural quality of the vows taken by the king of Navarre and his nobles is thrown into its proper perspective when Costard and Don Armado, both more "natural" because the one is a rustic and the other a fool who is therefore less constrained by custom or reason, break the part of the oath involving conversation with women. At the same time, their involvement with the wench Jaquenetta foreshadows the eventual forswearing of vows by the four young noblemen when they woo the princess of France and her maidens.

23. Pierre Le Loyer, *A Treatise of Spectres and Straunge Sights* (London, 1605), sig. Diii^r, wrote of "the infernall Hagge," Hecate, who "did send dogges vnto men to feare and terrifie them. . . ." See also Jacob Grimm, *Teutonic Mythology*, 4 vols., trans. James J. Stallybrass (London, 1882), III, 996–97.

24. "The Meaning of *The Tempest*," in *His Infinite Variety: Major Shakespearean Criticism Since Jonson*, ed. P. N. Siegel (New York, 1964), p. 407.

25. See, for example, Herbert R. Coursen, Jr., "Prospero and the Drama of the Soul," *ShakS*, 4 (1968), p. 326. An interpretation nearer my own is that of Theodore Spencer, *Shakespeare and the Nature of Man* (New York, 1961), pp. 197–99.

26. *Institutes of the Christian Religion*, trans. Henry Beveridge (Grand Rapids, Mich., 1966), I.xvi.7–8. A similar statement can be found in "The Sermon for the Second Part of Rogation Week," *Certain Sermons or Homilies*, pp. 532–33. Another clearcut example of the Renaissance tendency to identify fate and destiny with the will of the Christian God can be found in *The Mirrour for Magistrates*, ed. Lily B. Campbell (New York, 1960), p. 214, where Henry VI says,

> If likewise such as say the weken fortune warkes,
> Take Fortune for our fate, and sterres thereof the markes,
> Then destiny with fate, and Gods wil al be one:
> But if they mean it otherwise, skath causers skyes be none.
> Thus of our heavy happes, chief causes be but twayne,
> Whereon the rest depende, and vnderput remayne.
> The chief the wil diuine, called destiny or fate,
> The other sinne, through humours holpe, which God doth highly hate. . . .

27. *The Honorable Historie of Friar Bacon and Friar Bungay*, sc. xii.99–101, in *English Drama, 1580–1662*, ed. C. F. Tucker Brooke and N. B. Paradise (New York, 1933).

The Audience of Shakespeare's Plays:
A Reconsideration

Ann Jennalie Cook

Shakespeare's Audience by Alfred Harbage[1] has stood for thirty years as the standard work on its subject. With astonishing success, Harbage redeemed the audience from the low esteem it suffered at the beginning of the century, largely by marshaling evidence to show that the majority of the playgoers were good, sensible, working-class people rather than coarse ruffians. Such a redemption was long overdue and was achieved with remarkable success. But now that Harbage's conclusions have been so widely accepted and so thoroughly digested, perhaps it is time to see if any exceptions need to be noted and explored.

Even after thirty years, it would be hard to take issue with the chapters on the evidence, the probable size of the audience, their behavior, and the appraisals accorded them both then and now. However, the theory that the majority of the spectators were working-class people invites a closer look. The central argument is stated most clearly in the summary at the end of chapter 3, which deals with the class composition of the audience:

> All that we can say of the composition of Shakespeare's audience, other than that it was a cross section of the London population of his day, is that youth may have predominated somewhat over age, male over female, the worldly over the pious, and, of course without the "perhaps," the receptive over the unreceptive. Although the more leisured classes would have been better represented than by their pro rata of the population, *it was predominantly a working class audience because of the great numerical superiority of the working classes in the London area and because theatrical tariffs had been designed largely for them* [italics mine].
>
> (p. 90)

The analysis of the composition of the audience might have been restricted to the various sorts of persons known to have been in attendance without claiming the predominance of a particular group. Why press the point of the preponderance of the working class? The answer, I think, lies in a larger thesis concerning the audience and its relationship to Shakespeare, as set forth in the last three chapters of this book and carried to its logical conclusions in *As They Liked It*[2] and *Shakespeare and the Rival Traditions*.[3]

Struck by the fact that no other age has produced a Shakespeare and that none of the Elizabethan entertainments directed at specific classes attained the excellence of Shakespearean drama, Harbage looks to the heterogeneity of the audience for an explanation. This timelessly human, truly universal audience sat for a portrait of "man in the large" (*Audience*, p. 163) painted by Shakespeare in his plays. And to the collective mind of the audience, Shakespeare addressed the vast scope and complexities of his dramas, captured in full by no one spectator but "caught in the mesh of a thousand minds" (p. 161).

From this perspective, the caricature of the vulgar rabble, so contemptuously sketched by earlier critics, cannot stand unchallenged or serve as an explanation for the greatness of Elizabethan popular drama and Shakespeare's genius. Thus the groundling is elevated from barbarity into the working class and is endowed with the universal good taste of all Elizabethans, with either education or much common sense, with an average income, and with the skills of a craftsman. The cruder sort must have gone off to drink and bait bears. This common workman becomes the representative patron of the theater:

> We may say in the present case, quite apart from Beaumont's satirical use of them as the spectators in *The Knight of the Burning Pestle*, that a grocer, his wife, and their young apprentice form as acceptable an epitome of Shakespeare's audience as any the facts will warrant us to choose. If Shakespeare did not write to please such a little cockney family as this, he did not write to please his audience. But if he did so write, then *there must be some correspondence in quality between the plays and our sample three—the grocer, his wife, and their young apprentice* [italics mine].
>
> (p. 155)

The full power of the mystique of the common man is displayed in *As They Liked It*, which argues for the soundness of his moral sensibilities, and in *Shakespeare and the Rival Traditions*, which discusses the pernicious effects of drama aimed at a morally decadent, avant-garde coterie. The logic of this wider thesis rests upon the establishment of a particular kind of ordinary workingman as the typical spectator at the public theater and the demonstration of his numerical preponderance in the audience.

My purpose in the following analysis is a limited one. I do not propose to show that the working classes were absent from the theater or that some other group was in the majority. Instead, I would like to re-examine the hypothesis of a working-class majority in light of certain evidence not considered in *Shakespeare's Audience* and also in light of the evidence cited there. Basically, the hypothesis contends that the working classes must have been in the majority for two reasons: (1) they made up the majority of the population in the London area, and (2) the admission prices were designed largely for them. I shall raise three basic questions in dealing with these contentions: (1) Were the working classes in the majority in London? (2) Were theater prices designed largely for the working classes? (3) Even if the workers constituted a majority of the population and even if the price scale suited their pocketbooks, were they necessarily in the majority in the theater audience?

I

Whether or not the working classes were in the majority in London involves two central considerations. The first concerns the definition of the working classes. On the one hand, the basic groups *Shakespeare's Audience* begins with and later calls working classes do not seem to conform to an inherently twentieth-century use of the term. On the other hand, restricting the group to the modern meaning of wage earner would eliminate a sizable number of the original groups and thus raise doubt about the numerical preponderance of the remaining groups. The second consideration entails a closer look at other groups in London society to determine whether or not the working classes were necessarily in the majority, even if one accepts the given definition in its most inclusive form.

One difficulty is that this book never really defines the term "working class." On the basis of a 1608 muster roll, men are divided into five classifications as follows:

Gentry, professional men, and officials	6.3
Dealers and retailers	19.3
Craftsmen	52.0
Laborers, carriers, etc.	c.15.0
Servants and miscellaneous	c.7.4

(p. 54)

The construction of a majority begins with the largest group, the craftsmen. But instead of adhering to the original term, "craftsmen," there are continual substitutions of other terms—"workers," "workmen," and "wage earners." The craftsmen seem to be equated with a twentieth-century social class. With regard to salaries, for example, the chapter states, "The most appropriate figure to use for equation is the average weekly wage of the millions of contemporary industrial workers" (p. 56). Thus the largest group in Elizabethan society is transformed into the largest group in twentieth-century society. "Dealers and retailers" are eventually included in the majority as well, since most shopkeepers made only about 12½ percent more money than craftsmen (p. 61). The authority here is Gregory King's census for 1688, even though the figures are not necessarily valid for 1595–1615. Nonetheless, the two groups are combined in this summary statement: "We must conclude . . . that audiences were composed largely of shopkeepers and craftsmen, people of low income taking advantage of the almost unique opportunity to get their money's worth" (p. 64). From that point on, the "craftsmen" and the "dealers and retailers" are never again distinguished but simply become the "working classes in the London area" (p. 90).

Significantly, *Shakespeare's Audience* never deals with the last two categories of "laborers, carriers, etc.," and "servants and miscellaneous." By exclusion of the lower echelons, the working class is similar in size yet in many ways superior to its modern counterpart, as is obvious from statements like this one: "Skilled craftsmen, such as earned 16d. a day in Shakespeare's London, no longer form a large percentage of wage earners; they are now, deservedly, a highly paid aristocracy" (p. 56). And later the group is described in these terms:

> Many were highly skilled, performing functions now allotted to the chemist, architect, and engineer. Let us not be too much influenced by contemptuous allusions to how the "barmy Jacket of a Beer-brewer" contaminated the public theatres. Those at the Globe had chosen playgoing in preference to boozing and animalbaiting.
>
> *(pp. 60–61)*

By now it should be clear just what sort of working class is involved here. The group is comparable in size to the modern industrial working class, with the same relative uniformity of wages. It is broadly inclusive of everyone from the merchant to the apprentice, although it excludes laborers and servants. At the same time, this class is highly skilled and is possessed of innate good taste, as witnessed by its preference for the theater—just exactly the sort of playgoers required to support that broader thesis concerning the Shakespearean audience's superiority to the coterie audience.

But how closely does this construct of the working class conform to the available evidence on the Elizabethan craftsmen and retailers? And how closely does this sort of working class resemble the modern working class? To begin with, the Elizabethan groups outlined in *Shakespeare's Audience* simply will not be pressed into the uniformity of income and life style that the work presupposes. George Unwin's classic study breaks down the group in question into large merchants, large and small shopkeepers, merchant-employers, large masters, small masters, and journeymen.[4] Additionally, there were the apprentices, an unknown number of workers in unskilled positions, as well as aliens and others who practiced various crafts and trades without having formal membership in the guilds or companies.[5] At the top of the heap, the great London merchants, numbering about eight hundred at the close of the sixteenth century,[6] were among the richest and most powerful men in the kingdom. Social distinctions in the ranks of the guilds and companies were clearly marked, with a limited membership in the controlling body of the livery; a larger membership in the yeomanry (many of whom were wealthy younger sons on their way up to power in the company); ever-growing ranks of journeymen, who did not yet have their own establishments; and the apprentices.[7] The same sorts of distinctions were shown in the apprenticeship system itself, with the common limitation of three apprentices to a member of the company's governing body, two to a member of the livery, and one for an ordinary member.[8] Even apprentices ranged from vagrants and children of the poor, who were forcibly sent into service under the Poor Law of 1597,[9] to the apprenticed sons of wealthy merchants. The latter group of apprentices were often well educated and possessed of so much money that those who "did affect to go in costly apparel and wear weapons and frequent schools of dancing, fencing and music" were finally dealt with by an order of the Common Council.[10] To have an apprentice at all, under the 1562 Statute of Artificers, a man had to be a householder, and that involved the ability to support a good many people. A baker's household recorded in 1618 included the baker, his wife, three children, four journeymen, two apprentices, and two maids.[11] Furthermore, there were distinctions throughout England among the various crafts. In 1582 the fees charged craftsmen who came to Great Grimsby to set up practice ranged from 3s. 4d. for a married shoemaker, tailor, or tinker to 20s. for a merchant-adventurer.[12]

Thus, if one truly includes all craftsmen, dealers, and retailers in the working classes, then the group embraced everyone from Sir Francis Drake, who was an honorary member of the Drapers Company,[13] to the children of paupers. That such a group comprised a majority of the London population may be true, but one cannot accurately call this group the working class, he cannot validly equate them with the twentieth-century industrial working class, and he cannot fairly claim that they composed the vast majority of the groundlings.

On the other hand, if one restricts the group in question to wage earners, then he must omit apprentices, small and large masters in many trades, employer-shopkeepers, and of course the great merchants and the most powerful guildsmen. With laborers and servants already excluded, what remain are the journeymen and the artisans who worked for wages. And it may be seriously doubted whether they composed a majority or even a plurality of the London population, much less a majority of the theater audience.

But even if one accepts the craftsmen and retailers in their entirety as the working classes, there are still sound reasons for doubting that they constituted a majority of Elizabethan Londoners. The lack of trustworthy demographic information about sixteenth-century England is noted by every writer on the subject. It is not until the end of the seventeenth century that fairly reliable records and surveys, such as Gregory King's, become available. There are Elizabethan figures for baptisms, deaths, tax assessments, parish rolls, muster rolls, and the like, but even the best estimates are calculated guesses. Moreover, the population and the distribution of occupations in London, then the largest city in Europe, stand in a unique position with respect to other English cities. Estimates of its population range from 140,000 to more than 250,000, with a steady mushrooming throughout Shakespeare's career. *Shakespeare's Audience* sets the figure at 160,000 (p. 41). (This can be compared with Norwich, the second largest city in England, with a population of about 17,000.[14]) How many of the 160,000 were members of the working class would be difficult if not impossible to determine.

Lacking any figures for London, *Shakespeare's Audience* relies upon "a muster roll of 1608, classifying the men between twenty and sixty years of age in the towns of Gloucester, Tewkesbury, and Cirencester" (p. 54). A. J. and R. H. Tawney, who discovered the muster roll, are well aware of its defects. A large but unspecified number of men avoided the survey or refused to be surveyed at all. Out of a total of 19,402 men, 11.5 percent gave no occupation at all, and 3.6 percent are listed only as sons or brothers of various occupations. Furthermore, the city of Bristol, with a population of 10,549 persons, is not included. All the men surveyed in Gloucester, Tewkesbury, and Cirencester total only 1,367, less than 1 percent of the population of London.[15] Even if the survey were completely accurate, it seems questionable to assume any great consistency between the occupational distribution of three small towns and that of the great city of London.

While the difficulty is recognized and to some extent allowed for, the figures are just too useful to abandon altogether.

The classification is only suggestive, even as applied to the towns of Gloucester county, and has no authority for London; nevertheless, it gives us a starting point. In the London area, the presence of the court with all

its administrative offices—particularly the law courts and their append-
ages, the Inns of Court and Chancery—and the standing of the city in
the world of fashion would have raised the proportion of "Gentry, professional men, and officials" perhaps to as high as 10 percent. At the other
end of the scale there is a category wholly unaccounted for in the muster
roll—what Gregory King was later to call "Transitory People"—
cashiered soldiers and seamen ashore, as well as vagrants, paupers,
thieves, and peddlers. Shakespeare's London probably succeeded in sub-
merging more than the traditional tenth.

But when all adjustments are made, the group remaining by all odds the
largest, although not so large as 52 percent of the whole, will be the
"Craftsmen."

(pp. 54–55)

On the basis of the suggested adjustments, the revised chart looks like this:

Gentry, professional men and officials	10.0
Dealers and retailers	19.3
Craftsmen	36.3
Laborers, carriers, etc.	15.0
Servants and miscellaneous	7.4
Transitory people	12.0

Considering these revised figures, and considering the exclusion of laborers,
servants, and transitory people from the working classes, and in view of the
enormous range of income and social rank within the craftsmen's groups,
one may perhaps question whether craftsmen "must have composed the vast
majority of the 'groundlings'" (p. 60). Indeed, the three lower categories on
the revised scale total 34.4 percent, a percentage comparable with the 36.3
percent for craftsmen.

A closer look at some of the social groups in London during the period may
cast doubt on these revisions and suggest the possibility of still further revisions. The nobility, for instance, bulked larger in the greater London area
than anywhere else in England. Chapter 3 refers to 1,500 courtiers in attendance on the queen (p. 76), many of whom had their families nearby in
London residences during much of the year. In addition, there were the
foreign ambassadors and emissaries and their retinues. The great lords and,
to some extent, the lesser gentry surrounded themselves with big entourages
and large numbers of servants. The earl of Derby's embassy to France in
1584 included a train of 130 gentlemen in liveries of purple and gold lace and

black satin and taffeta. Seventy of these gentlemen were members of his personal retinue, even though he had none of his council or country men with him. In his country house at Latham alone he had 118 servants in 1587, and they had increased to 140 by 1590—for a family of five.[16] Granted, these are extravagances, but if the percentage of the nobility in London is increased, then there should be corresponding allowances for servants and well-born attendants—and that whittles down still further the percentages of craftsmen and retailers.

As for the legal colony of London, there were close to 1,000 in residence at the Inns of Court and Chancery in 1574, plus many others unorganized outside (Rowse, p. 525). *Shakespeare's Audience* lists 769 for the Inns of Court in 1574, rising to about 1,040 in the reign of James I (p. 80), but there is no allowance for the Inns of Chancery or for those unorganized outside the inns. At any rate, the numbers in the legal fraternities grew so constantly that despite much building, the chambers had to be divided because of the crowding. In 1588, Lord Chamberlain Hatton said, "There are now more at the bar in one house than there were in all the Inns of Court when I was a young man."[17] Added to the legal professionals were persons from all over England who had pleas before the courts, their attendants and servants, plus the numerous servants and associates of the inns and their residents.

Still other professions included the clergy, many of whom did not attend the theaters but who nevertheless comprised a certain number of that group of "gentry, professional men and officials." It would be hard to determine just how many served the hundreds of pulpits in the city in an official and semi-official capacity. There were also the teachers at the eleven schools in London and their pupils, numbering some 1,500,[18] in addition to the servants required for the religious and educational institutions. It is even more difficult to calculate the number of officials in London not included in the above groups or to know just how many professionals, subprofessionals, and servants they required. In any case, the increase of "gentry, professional men and officials" from 6.3 percent in three small towns to only 10 percent in London may be open to question. Likewise, the failure to adjust the 7.4 percent of "servants and miscellaneous" is questionable also. And any further enlargement of other categories means a corresponding shrinkage of the proportion of "craftsmen" or "dealers and retailers."

Another major category has perhaps been underestimated, that of "transitory people," which is admitted to include more than the "traditional tenth." Here, one must be particularly cognizant of the social changes of the period.[19] The population as a whole was rising at a steep rate, while the available land was being consolidated into a smaller number of holdings, thus forcing large numbers off the land and a great many of the uprooted into London. At the same time, prices increased sixfold between 1500 and 1600, while wages only doubled.[20] Consequently, at a time when wages would purchase a third less than a century earlier, more and more people were totally dependent on earnings alone. To complicate matters, the disestablishment of the church and the dissolution of the monasteries, along with the political and military difficulties between 1500 and 1590, all combined to erode traditional methods of caring for the poor. By 1594, after five straight years of bad harvests, prices were so high, food was so scarce, and unemployment so general that famine and starvation threatened. A planned uprising led by a carpenter named Bartholomew Steere was discovered by the Privy Council, and some twenty ringleaders were executed. In 1594, the lord mayor complained to the Privy Council that the suburbs on the south side of the river were such breeding places for the beggars swarming over the city that the justices of Surrey and Sussex should either banish them from London or bar them from crossing the bridge. He estimated their numbers at 12,000,[21] almost 8 percent of the entire population of London, according to Harbage's estimate. Even allowing for exaggeration by the lord mayor, by the time one considers the poor in the rest of the city—those who were cared for in the numerous almshouses and other charitable institutions, the aged and infirm, the whores and thieves and other criminals, plus the discharged seamen and soldiers complained of everywhere—the estimate of "more than the traditional tenth" begins to seem a rather conservative adjustment. Furthermore, the equation of the working classes with wage earners means the ranks of the poor were swelled and the ranks of the workers diminished at just such times as these, when those dependent upon wages were often without employment. The Poor Law of 1597 was a masterful instrument designed to cope with the massive problems of unemployment and poverty, but its provisions did not begin to have full effect until near the end of Shakespeare's career.

There is one final difficulty with the assertion of a large numerical superiority of craftsmen-retailers. From time to time, the demographic information of Gregory King compiled in 1688 is used, with such covering statements as, "I assume that the proportion at the end of the century . . . held good for the beginning" (p. 76n). I would not agree that the 1688 census is valid for 1600, particularly in view of the political, social, and economic upheavals of the seventeenth century. However, if the validity of Gregory King's 1688 figures is assumed, then one must consider the implications of some of King's other figures which are reproduced in chapter 3. In the discussion of the probable ratio of ten men to thirteen women in London, there is a footnote on the following population breakdown supplied by King:

Group	Percentage
Husbands and wives	37
Widows and widowers	
(mostly widows then as now)	9
Children	33
Servants	13
Sojourners, etc.	8

(p. 76n)

From these figures can be derived certain information that sheds further light on the probable percentages of working-class persons in the population of London as a whole. First, as I have already suggested, the percentage of "servants and miscellaneous" was much greater than the chapter has allowed (21 percent), if the 1688 situation holds true for 1600. Second, something considerably less than a majority of the London population was available to fill the ranks of the working classes. Even if one includes half the children as being old enough to enter apprenticeship or to work, the breakdown for potential workmen, drawn from the male population exclusive of servants and sojourners, comes out like this:

Group	Percentage of Male Population	Percentage of Total Population
Husbands	37	18.5
Widowers (allowing for more widows than widowers)	6	3.0
Children	17	8.5
	60	30.0

In other words, out of 60 percent of the male population (or 30 percent of the total population) must come the male members of the nobility, gentry, professionals, officials, dealers, retailers, craftsmen, and laborers. The size of the working classes gets smaller and smaller.

In my opinion, the assertion that the audience was predominantly working class because of their "great numerical superiority" will not stand a close analysis. If all craftsmen, dealers, and retailers are included in the working class, then the term no longer retains the twentieth-century meaning assigned to it. If the term is used to denote only wage earners, then it excludes so many that it no longer constitutes a majority. But even if the term "working class" is defined to include all the craftsmen, dealers, and retailers, there is evidence to suggest that this class was not necessarily in the majority.

II

Shakespeare's Audience also claims the playgoers were predominantly working class "because theatrical tariffs had been designed largely for them" (p. 90). There is general agreement with Thomas Platter's 1599 account that the initial admission to the yard was only a penny, with an additional penny for a seat in the gallery and a third penny for a better seat.[22] There were also sixpenny and twelvepenny rooms. When *Bartholomew Fair* was presented in 1614 at the new Hope theater, the induction stated, "It shall bee lawfull for any man to iudge his six pen'orth, his twelve pen'orth, so to his eighteene pence, 2. shillings, halfe a crowne, to the value of his place."[23] Even as early as 1592, Henslowe recorded selling the lords' room for 10s. and 13s.[24] Thus the price range was always wide and tended to grow wider as time went by.

The range might well suit the wide variety of incomes represented by all the London craftsmen and retailers. But *Shakespeare's Audience* persistently refers to the average wages of London workmen. Such wages were set by law and applicable only to those who were neither apprentices, independent shopkeepers, nor employers. Furthermore, most of the working-class audience is specifically tied to the groundlings and thus to the penny admission. Therefore, in order to determine whether or not the admissions were really designed largely for the working class, I shall first examine the degree to which the penny prices correspond with the incomes of craftsmen and dealers. Then I shall consider whether or not there were other groups in London who might have been restricted to the price of a penny. And finally, I shall follow the same procedure for the more expensive prices.

First comes the moot question of whether or not the incomes of the working classes can safely be tied to the penny paid by the groundlings. If it is possible—or probable—that for many the penny was too low and for many others the penny too dear, then one is not on safe ground in saying that craftsmen and shopkeepers must have constituted the vast majority of the groundlings. As already indicated above, many of the craftsmen and merchants ran large businesses, ranging from the comfortably prosperous to the enormously wealthy. For instance, the cost of admission into the livery of the Drapers Company was raised in 1602 from £6 13s. 4d. to £26 13s. 4d., and the revenues of the company arising from rents, leases, fees of enrollments, fines, and the like amounted to £6,700 that year.[25] The baker's household of 1618 referred to above gives a bit more information on the kind of weekly income it took to run a craftsman's or retailer's business.

Expenditure   £. *s. d.*

House rent at £30 per annum 11 6

Diet of man & wife, 10s., of three children,
   7s. 17 0

Diet of 4 journeymen, 2 apprentices, 2 maids
   @ 4s. 1 12 0

Clothing of man, wife, and apprentices at
   £20 per ann. 7 8

Clothing and schooling of 3 children 3 0

Wages of 4 journeymen at 2s. 6d.; of 2 maids
   at 10d. 11 8

Yeast 10s., wood 12s., coal 1s. 4d., sacks
   1s., salt 1s., boulters 1s., garner rent 2s.,
   baskets 3d., water 8d. 1 9 3

Miller's toll 15s., porter's fees 2s. 17 0

Parson, poor rate, scavenger, watch 1 0

Total expense of baking 6 quarters 6 10 1

(Unwin, "Commerce," p. 308)

Any man who could maintain four journeymen, two apprentices, and two servants, pay £30 a year for rent, send three children to school, and pay at least a shilling per week in assessments was not limited to standing in the yard at the theater nor even to the twopenny and threepenny seats, if he cared for something more luxurious. Not all bakers or tailors or haberdashers were so prosperous. However, as I have already indicated, to have even one of the thousands of London apprentices, a man had to be a householder—with all the expenses that that responsibility entailed.

But perhaps the focus of attention should be shifted away from the one master baker to his four salaried journeymen. They were true wage earners in any sense of the term. Journeymen had to complete apprenticeship and purchase their freedom in order to practice their trade. The fees for freedom were set by law at 3s. 4d. (Dunlop, p. 59) but were often higher; in addition, guild, craft, or company membership meant assessments for benevolences, gifts, and dinners. By the seventeenth century, a guild membership was further restricted by the "masterpiece," a costly and elaborate work for which the ordinary journeyman lacked both time and money (Unwin, *Gilds,* p. 265). And to set up in business for himself, he had to have tools, equipment, and often a shop. Thus the 2s. 6d. weekly wage marks a big gulf between him and the prosperous members of his trade—a wage, incidentally, which the employer could not raise or lower under penalty of a five-pound fine and ten days imprisonment.[26] And lest one think the journeyman was a lucky fellow with so much money to squander on himself each week, while his employer provided his food and clothing, it would be well to remember that apprenticeship lasted until the age of twenty-four and that most journeymen had families of their own to feed and clothe and house (Dunlop, p. 65). Unless other members of the family worked (and this was usually the case), 2s. 6d. simply would not support a family. The baker paid 4s. per week per employee for food alone. That the rate for food and the rate for wages is not out of line for the entire period is substantiated by a 1588 assessment in London, which set the wages for the "best and most skillful" journeymen in the crafts at 6d. to 9d. per day with meat and drink, 10d. to 14d. per day without meat and drink (Unwin, "Commerce," p. 321).

Though the salary figures I have just given were available, *Shakespeare's Audience* illustrates wages with those paid to masons working on London Bridge between 1593 and 1602—14d. to 16d. per day.[27] According to this source, masons were more highly paid than roughmasons, bricklayers, or other construction workers, and even the mason's high earnings declined sharply in purchasing power. The 16d. figure remained unchanged from 1571 to 1612, while real earnings (purchasing power) declined by about one-third (Knoop, p. 213). Again, what is being presented is a man with a 7s. weekly income, a man with a high degree of professional skill, a man who could very easily spare a penny to stand in the pit. I would not claim that the journeyman-baker is more typical than the mason, but the discrepancies in salaries do indicate the fallacy of generalizing about wages for the working classes strictly on the basis of the mason's 16d. per day. A penny laid out at the theater was perhaps more of a luxury for some wage earners than is admitted. Moreover, during the hard times of economic recession in the 1590s, when unemployment was so rampant, many wage earners found themselves altogether out of work and in the ranks of the paupers. Even if the unemployed man had a penny to spare for an afternoon at the Globe, he could no longer qualify for membership in the working classes but would then belong to the "traditional tenth" that included the poor.

Now what of the apprentices, the lowest rungs of the working classes? Contemporary documents testify to their presence at the plays, so obviously they came. The restrictions on dress and other luxuries, as well as the family background of some apprentices cited earlier, also indicate that a few had plenty of money to come to the theater. The question remains as to whether large numbers of them had no pennies at all—or had them very rarely. Significantly, perhaps, the baker lists no salaries for his two apprentices. According to Dunlop, apprentices were not supposed to receive any wages, although "the boy sometimes received small sums of pocket-money, or a small lump sum, clothes or tools, at the end of his term, to help him make his start in life. . . . Such conditions, however, do not seem to have been so general at this time as they were in the seventeenth and eighteenth centuries; at any rate, there are few recorded instances of their payments" (p. 55). The forcibly apprenticed vagrants and children of paupers had no money of their own and could expect none from any but the most generous of masters. And in their cases, masters had to forego the customary fees paid at the enrollment of apprentices— legally 2s. 6d., but often much more (Dunlop, p. 59). Besides, there are several regulations surviving which specifically prohibited masters from permitting their apprentices to attend performances at the theaters, even on holidays.[28] Therefore, it may be doubted whether most apprentices had either money or permission to be frequent playgoers.

It should now be clear that many of those in the working classes could afford any seat in the theater with ease and thus cannot be safely identified with the groundlings. On the other hand, many apprentices, journeymen, and marginal craftsmen and dealers might have been hard-pressed to spare even a penny to stand in the yard, especially in view of the rampant unemployment and the steady squeeze of rising prices against stable wages.

But there is no necessity for supposing that most of the penny patrons had to be workmen. *Shakespeare's Audience* lists a good many groups who would have found the cheapest admissions suitable to their purses, pointing out that teachers, for instance, made less than artisans (p. 61). Though lawyers were the most prosperous professionals, there were hundreds in residence at the Inns of Court and Chancery who were serving out the six to nine years of education or the five-year term as utter barrister before they could charge fees and practice in the Westminster courts (Rowse, p. 523). There were also the 1,500 or so students in the London schools (Stowe, pp. 188–89). Such young students and lawyers may have found a penny's standing to their liking, particularly if pocket money were limited or debts pressing. "The twopenny gallery, for all its bourgeois flavor, might well have been considered expensive by the younger or lesser gentry. Money was scarce among the majority of all classes" (Harbage, p. 62). Servants, who are excluded from the ranks of the working class, could have afforded only the cheapest place in the theater, if they could manage to get away for an afternoon's entertainment. In addition to these respectable groups, there was a host of the disreputable who probably would have taken penny places. To read the statements of the Puritans and the London officials, one would suppose the yard to be entirely filled with vagabonds, whores, thieves, beggars, paupers, and rabble-rousers, with scarcely a place for a majority of workmen. At one point, chapter 3 limits the numbers of the poor because they could hardly afford even a penny (p. 63) but states a couple of pages earlier, "It is possible, however, that the high cost of living worked in favor of the theatres in one way: if the penny spent on food meant only an additional cucumber or two, one might as well squander it on a play" (p. 60). If this argument holds true for the bricklayer, then there is no reason why it will not hold true for the beggar. It should be fairly clear by now that the penny prices could have been designed for plenty of people other than the working classes.

But were the higher prices in the theater also designed largely for the working classes? The question may be answered negatively if one can show, first, that many workmen could not afford seats in the gallery and, second, that the more expensive places could have been or were occupied by groups other than craftsmen and merchants. This is not to say that no one in the working class occupied any of the rest of the theater but only to ask whether they constituted the majority of the audience and whether prices were primarily aimed at their purses.

Shakespeare's Audience estimates that the places in the galleries outnumbered those in the yard by a two-to-one margin (p. 30). Moreover, it cites the watermen's suit of 1613, which asked that the actors be forced to abandon the Middlesex theaters and return to Bankside because "every day in the week they do draw unto them three or four thousand people, that were used to spend their monies by water" (p. 37). This figure is relied on absolutely as a measure of daily attendance. But if the watermen's figures are correct, then there were three or four thousand in the audiences who could afford the price of admission plus the cost of a boat across the Thames—a fee listed at 3d. (p. 59). Obviously, if there were large numbers of workers who could scarcely afford a penny to stand in the yard, they could not have doubled or tripled their outlay, much less have hired a boat. And this fact is tacitly admitted when craftsmen are identified with groundlings and when it is pointed out that 160,000 Londoners were within *walking* distance of the theater (pp. 53–54).

At the other end of the scale from the penny-shy wage earner was the well-to-do merchant or craftsman, ranging from the 16d.-a-day mason, perhaps, to the baker of 1618, and on up to the wardens of the livery. They could well have paid out 2d. and more. But were there sufficient numbers of them to fill up twice as many places as there were in the yard? And were other groups known to have occupied the galleries? Again, the evidence presented seems to contradict the argument. On the one hand, there is the flat statement "Playhouse prices were not designed for earls" (p. 63). And yet that same page quotes from the personal expense account of the earl of Rutland, listing boathire and theater admission for a whole party of "his Lordship and his men" on October 1, 1598; another hired boat and a play on November 18; and still a third entry for boathire "to the play howse sondry tymes" (p. 63). Even if prices were not designed for earls, this particular earl still attended the theater. The prices at the Fortune were not beneath the dignity of such foreign dignitaries as Chaplain Busino of the Venetian embassy, who made the following report: "The best treat was to see such a crowd of nobility so very well arranged that they looked like so many princes listening as silently and soberly as possible."[29] There is also the testimony of Philip Gawdy, who described a sudden descent upon a playhouse in 1602 ordered by the Privy Council to apprehend loose and idle persons for impressment into the army. Embarrassingly, "they did not only presse Gentlemen, and sarvingmen, but Lawyers, Clarkes, country men that had lawe cawses, aye the Quens men, knightes, and as it was credibly reported one Earle" (p. 91). The foregoing examples of well-born patrons of the public theaters are selected from dozens included in *Shakespeare's Audience* and are drawn from many more available in the Elizabethan dramatic records. There were plenty of people—lawyers, scholars, courtiers, foreigners, travelers, officials, gallants, and courtesans, to name a few—for whose purses the higher prices might have been intended besides those of the more comfortable members of the working classes. In view of the preceding evidence concerning both high and low prices, it seems reasonable to doubt that the audience was predominantly working class "because theatrical tariffs had been designed largely for them" (p. 90).

III

Even if the working classes did constitute the major proportion of the London population, and even if theater admission prices were specifically tailored for their incomes, it would still have to be demonstrated that they filled the majority of the places in the playhouses. On this point I shall first consider whether the working classes really had sufficient leisure and opportunity for theatergoing, as compared with other groups. Then I shall consider certain contradictory implications deriving from attendance figures and from contemporary audience descriptions.

The true working classes in Shakespeare's London had their hours of labor and leisure set by law. *Shakespeare's Audience* declares that the workday ranged from eight to twelve hours (p. 67). The law was quite specific. From March to September employees worked from five in the morning until seven or eight in the evening and from dawn to dusk the rest of the year (about 5:30 A.M. to 6:30 P.M. in fall and spring, 8:10 A.M. to 4:00 P.M. at the winter solstice). During the day a total of two hours was allowed for meals, with an extra half hour for a midday nap from May to August. A penny was to be deducted from the wages for every hour of work missed.[30] Just how strictly the law was enforced or how uniformly it applied to all workers is not clear. Harbage says a man might pool his free time and use it to go to the theater but offers no evidence to support this possibility (p. 67). The law made no such provision. If the workers had to walk to the theater, then more than one day's total free time would be required to see a play. City officials and preachers complained that the plays drew apprentices and others from their work, but because of their general hostility toward the theater, it would not be safe to accept their statements at face value. Some workers may have risked a fine or forfeited half-a-day's wages to see a play, but one cannot conclude that most of them did or that the audiences were largely composed of such persons. In hard times this entertainment would have been costly indeed.

As for legitimate times of leisure, chapter 3 states: "The leathersellers agreed that work was to cease early on Saturdays, vigils, and festivals. Vigils and festivals were many, and they varied for various crafts" (p. 67). However, Dunlop, the source for this statement, is referring to a regulation of 1482, a century before Shakespeare's day. Furthermore, the leathersellers' rule actually states that "on Saturdays, vigils, and festivals work was to cease at three o'clock" (Dunlop, p. 56)—too late an hour for a performance beginning at two o'clock. According to the figures derived from Henslowe's diary, Saturday netted less money than any other day in the week (Harbage, p. 174). Knoop and Jones, the authority for the masons' wages, indicate that the number of holidays actually declined during the period. Weekly income between 1301 and 1540 was equivalent to five days' wages on account of holidays, but between 1541 and 1701 the weekly income represented six days' wages because of the relative absence of holidays (Knoop, p. 213). When there were holidays, with huge crowds of workers thronging the streets in search of amusement, theater attendance was 35 percent to 100 percent larger than usual (Harbage, p. 175). However, new plays, with their doubled prices, were never given on holidays. Now if large numbers of workers were avid theatergoers, surely they would already have seen the plays. It seems curious that the acting companies would pass up a chance to pack the house at twice the profit, unless, perhaps, the troupes were catering to a group so little acquainted with playgoing that any piece in the repertoire would serve, so long as the price of admission was not too steep. As for Sundays, the theaters were legally closed early in the period. After that time, the number of sermons castigating the playhouses for drawing decent people away from worship diminished markedly.[31] In short, the slim Saturday receipts, the declining number of holidays, the fare provided for the holiday crowds, and the ban on Sunday performances all point toward the Elizabethan worker as an occasional rather than a habitual frequenter of the theater. Certainly there is little evidence here in favor of a predominantly working-class audience except on special occasions.

By contrast with the workingmen, there were many groups in London who were at leisure in the afternoons. Shopkeepers could shut down their businesses, if they did not mind the loss of income, and employers might leave the work to their employees if they wished, but *Shakespeare's Audience* does not press this possibility too hard or offer any evidence to support it. Others in London society seem to have been entirely at leisure, with "the afternoone beeing the idlest time of the day; wherein men that are their owne masters (as Gentlemen of the court, the Innes of the Courte, and the number of Captaines and Souldiers about London) do wholy bestow themselves vpon pleasure."[32] As we have already seen, there is abundant mention of the courtiers at the theater. Court schedules provided ample time off for practicing barristers. Law students attended readings and exercises in the morning, moots and bolts in the evening. One Elizabethan wit suggested that "the lawyers should be obliged to the players for giving them something to do of an afternoon."[33] The Inns also had a tradition of lively dramatic interests, as did the court. As for the "Captaines and Souldiers," one might remember that after the defeat of the Armada, hordes of discharged and vagrant soldiers plagued London (Aydelotte, pp. 71–72). To their numbers can be added other idlers, such as whores, thieves, rogues, vagabonds, and beggars. Enough of all such persons came to the theaters to make them the subject of continuing complaints by city officials: "To which places allso doe vsually resort great numbers of light & lewd disposed persons, as harlotts, cutpurses, cuseners, pilferers, & such lyke, & thear, vnder the collour of resort to those places to hear the playes, divise divers evill & vngodly matches, confederacies, & conspiracies."[34] Because so many people from various levels of society had free time during the afternoons and because the performances conflicted with working hours, there is considerable doubt that workers formed a majority of the audience, regardless of their numbers in the population.

In creating a working-class majority, *Shakespeare's Audience* sets up another difficulty in its treatment of theater attendance figures. After a rather complicated statistical analysis, chapter 2 concludes that "only a minority of Londoners were habitual playgoers and the majority were not playgoers at all" (p. 44). A further refinement states that only two of every fifteen Londoners were weekly patrons and that sixty to seventy thousand adults plus another forty thousand children never attended.

The explanation of that phenomenon lies in the one factor not hitherto examined. It is obvious enough. Many people stayed away from the theaters because they did not care for plays. A dramatic and poetic age confers no universal taste for poetry and drama. Elizabethans could be Philistines, and thousands of them were.

(p. 83)

This passage, set down in the middle of the discussion of the composition of the audience, seriously damages any claim for predominance of the working classes on the basis of their numerical superiority in the population. No principle is offered for judging which persons did not care for plays, and there is no reason to assume that Philistines were evenly distributed throughout all segments of the population. The working classes may well have had less than their pro rata share of the taste for poetry and drama. If more than a hundred thousand people never set foot inside the theater, then theoretically the entire working class could have stayed away from the playhouses without affecting attendance in the least. Such was not the case, I grant. But without a sound egalitarian basis for distributing the love of or distaste for the drama, one need not assume that the majority of the population became a majority of the theater audience.

Finally, the contemporary descriptions of the audience, selected as representative of the span of Shakespeare's career, require a close scrutiny, since it is claimed that "the descriptions fused into one composite portrait give us, I believe, the truth about the kind of people in Shakespeare's audience" (p. 86). Here are the descriptions:

Anno 1582

the common people which resorte to Theatres being but an assemblie of Tailers, Tinkers, Cordwayners, Saylers, olde Men, yong Men, Women, Boyes, Girles, and such like. [*Stephen Gosson, Playes Confuted in Fiue Actions, in William C. Hazlitt, ed., The English Drama and Stage (London, 1869), p. 184.*]

Anno 1583

Mentioned as killed, injured, or miraculously saved when Paris Garden collapsed while a thousand people were watching a bearbaiting on Sunday:

Adam Spencer, a felmonger of Southwark.
William Cockram, a baker of Shoreditch.
John Burton, a clerk of St. Marie Wolmers in Lombard St.
Mathew Mason, a servant with Master Garland of Southwark.
Thomas Peace, a servant with Rob. Tasker of Clerkenwell.

Alice White, a servant to a pursemaker without Cripplegate.
Marie Harrison, daughter to John, a water-bearer of Lombard St.
Mrs. Webb, wife of a pewterer of Limestreet.
An unidentified woman and her small child. [*John Field*, A Godly Exhortation, *in Chambers*, Elizabethan Stage, *IV, 220.*]

Anno 1595

For, as we see at all the play-house doores,
When ended is the play, the dance, and song,
A thousand Townesmen, gentlemen, and whores,
Porters and serving-men together throng.
[*Sir John Davies, "In Cosmun," Epigram No. 17, in Alexander B. Grosart, ed.,* Complete Poems *(London, 1876), II, 18.*]

Anno 1597

They are the ordinary places for vagrant persons, Maisterles men, thieves, horse stealers, whoremongers, Coozeners, Conycatchers, contrivers of treason and other idele and daungerous persons to meet together. . . . They maintaine idlenes in such persons as haue no vocation & draw apprentices and other seruants from theire ordinary workes and all sorts of people from the resort vnto sermons and other Christian exercises to the great hinderance of traides & pphantion of religion. [*"Dramatic Records of the City of London: the Remembrancia," in* Malone Society Collections, *I, Part I, 80.*]

Anno 1608

The wise, and many headed Bench, that sits
Upon the Life and Death of playes, and Wits,
Compos'd of Gamester, Captain, Knight, Knight's man,
Lady or Pusill that wears mask or fan,
Velvet, or Taffata cap, rank'd in the dark
With the shops Foreman, or some such brave spark.
[*Jonson's commendatory verses to* The Faithful Shepherdess.]

Anno 1609

[Dramatic cakes]
fit for ladies: some for lords, knights, squires,
Some for your waiting wench, and city-wires,
Some for your men, and daughters of white-Friars.

[*Prologue,* Epicoene *(1609), in Herford and Simpson, eds.,* Ben Jonson, *V, 163.*]

Anno 1624

I doubt not but you have heard of our famous play of Gondomar, which hath been followed with extraordinarie concourse, and frequented by all sorts of people old and younge, rich and poore, masters and servants, papists and puritans, wise men *et ct.,* churchmen and statesmen as Sir Henry Wotton, Sir Albert Morton, Sir Benjamin Ruddier, Sir Thomas Lake, and a world besides; the Lady Smith wold have gon yf she could have persuaded me to go with her. I am not so sowre nor severe but that I wold willingly have attended her, but I could not sit so long, for we must have ben there before one a clocke at farthest to find any roome. [*Chamberlain to Carleton, August 21. See* Letters of John Chamberlain, *ed. Norman E. McClure (Philadelphia, 1939), II, 577–78.*]

(*pp. 84–85*)

The 1582 selection does describe a predominantly working-class audience, although the date is too early for Shakespeare, the writer prejudiced, and the categories of workers balanced by more general age and sex groupings. Furthermore, there is at least a hint in the syntax that the "common people" who go to plays are to be distinguished from the elite who go to plays. The 1583 description, also early, is not relevant. It concerns a bearbaiting, not a play, and takes place on a Sunday, when all workers were at leisure. In the 1595 selection, only the townsmen are possible candidates for the majority, and they are not clearly identifiable as members of the working classes. Of all those mentioned in the 1597 diatribe, the apprentices alone belong to the supposed majority. Likewise, the shop's foreman is the single contribution of the 1608 piece. The prologue of 1609 mentions no one who could definitely be tied to the working class. And both the 1608 and the 1609 selections refer to audiences at private rather than public theaters. Only the masters in the 1624 letter directly correspond to the major group, and they are at least rich enough to have servants. Besides, all three of the last descriptions refer to plays very different from any Shakespeare ever wrote for his audience. A final selection, dated 1641, is entirely too late for Shakespeare's career and lists no workers. In short, this composite portrait which gives the "truth" about Shakespeare's audience does not seem to substantiate the theory of a working-class majority.

The foregoing calculations of attendance and compilations of audience descriptions, as well as the Elizabethan conditions of labor and leisure, indicate that even if the working classes formed a majority of Londoners, and even if theater prices were designed largely for them, they were not necessarily in the majority in the theater audiences. Despite the undeniable soundness of *Shakespeare's Audience*, even after thirty years, it does need to be revised on the issue of a working-class majority. Either no group dominated the audiences, or else a new group can be proposed as preeminent. However, establishing a new majority is a task demanding enough for a separate study.

Notes:

1. (New York, 1941).
2. (New York, 1947).
3. (New York, 1952).
4. *Industrial Organization in the Sixteenth and Seventeenth Centuries* (Oxford, 1904), p. 12.
5. O. Jocelyn Dunlop, *English Apprenticeship and Child Labour* (New York, 1912), p. 96; see also Thomas Girtin, *The Golden Ram* (London, 1958), p. 63.
6. Penry Williams, *Life in Tudor England* (New York, 1964), p. 55.
7. A. L. Rowse, *The England of Elizabeth: The Structure of Society* (London, 1950), p. 210.
8. Unwin, *The Gilds and Companies of London* (New York, 1908), p. 265.
9. *39 Eliz., c. 3.*
10. John Stow, *Survey of London* (1633), ed. John Strype (London, 1720), II, 328–29.
11. *Analytical Index to Remembrancia*, 1878, p. 386, as cited by Unwin, "Commerce and Coinage in Shakespeare's England," *Studies in Economic History* (London, 1927), p. 308.
12. *Historical MSS. Report*, Great Grimsby, p. 278, as cited by Unwin, *Industrial Organization*, p. 73.
13. Girtin, *The Triple Crowns* (London, 1964), p. 184.
14. W. Hudson and J. S. Tingey, *Records of the City of Norwich*, cxxvi–cxxvii, as cited by Rowse, p. 159.
15. Tawney and Tawney, "An Occupational Census of the Seventeenth Century," *Economic History Review*, 5 (1934–35), 25–64.
16. *The Derby Household Books*, ed. F. R. Raines (Manchester: Chetham Society, 1853), pp. li, 23–27, 88, as quoted by Rowse, pp. 253–54.
17. F. A. Inderwick, *Calendar of Inner Temple Records* (London, 1896–1901), p. lxxxiii.
18. J. H. Brown, *Elizabethan Schooldays* (Oxford, 1933), p. 7; A. M. Stowe, *English Grammar Schools in the Reign of Queen Elizabeth* (New York, 1908), pp. 188–89.
19. For an analysis of the sociological and economic changes and their effect on the poor, see John Clapham, *A Concise Economic History of Britain* (Cambridge, 1951); W. K. Jordan, *Philanthropy in England 1480–1660* (New York, 1959); Frank Aydelotte, *Elizabethan Rogues and Vagabonds* (New York, 1913).
20. Clapham, pp. 186–87. For a fuller interpretation of this phenomenon, see E. H. Phelps Brown and Sheila W. Hopkins, "Seven Centuries of Building Wages,"

Economica, 22 (1955), 195–206; "The Price of Consumables, Compared with Builders' Wage Rates," *Economica,* 23 (1956), 291–314; "Wage Rates and Prices: Evidence for Population Pressure in the Sixteenth Century," *Economica,* 24 (1957), 289–99.

21. *Remembrancia,* II, 74, as cited by Aydelotte, p. 74.

22. E. K. Chambers, *Elizabethan Stage* (Oxford, 1923), II, 364–65, 531–38.

23. C. H. Herford, Percy and Evelyn Simpson, eds., *Ben Jonson,* VI (Oxford, 1938), 15.

24. W. W. Greg, ed., *Henslowe's Diary* (London, 1904), I, 10; Chambers, II, 535.

25. Girtin, *Triple Crowns,* pp. 196, 198; see also *Golden Ram,* pp. 63–81; Guy Parsloe, *Wardens Account of the Worshipful Company of Founders of the City of London, 1491–1681* (London, 1964), pp. 222–54.

26. Muriel St. Clare Byrne, *Elizabethan Life in Town and Country* (New York, 1926), pp. 142–43.

27. Douglas Knoop and G. P. Jones, *The Medieval Mason* (New York, 1967), p. 211.

28. See Lord Mayor's precept of April 3, 1582, Chambers, IV, 287; Ordinance of the Clothworkers' Company for July 2, 1587, and By-Laws of the Vintners' Company for June 3, 1594, *Malone Society Collections,* III, 165, 167.

29. "Diaries and Despatches of the Venetian Embassy at the Court of King James I, in the Years 1617, 1618," *Quarterly Review,* 102 (1857), 416.

30. *5 Eliz., c. 4.*

31. Except for Henry Crosse's *Vertues Common-wealth* of 1603 and William Rankins's *A Mirrour of Monsters* of 1587, documents denouncing the theater on religious and moral grounds stop abruptly in 1584, according to the compilation in Chambers, IV, Appendix C. Thereafter, the city government is the chief source of complaint.

32. Thomas Nashe, *Pierce Penilesse, his Supplication to the Divell* (1592), in *Works,* ed. Ronald B. McKerrow (London, 1904–1910), I, 212.

33. G. M. Young, "Shakespeare and the Termers," *Proceedings of the British Academy* (1947), p. 5. Young is probably referring to John Earle's *Microcosmographie* of 1628, though the jest was a common one.

34. Lord Mayor to Archbishop Whitgift, February 25, 1592, *Remembrancia,* I, 635.

Shakespearean Tragedy and the Problem of Transcendence

René E. Fortin

The sessions of critical thought about Shakespeare's metaphysics are anything but sweet and silent. On the one side we hear the theologizers of Shakespeare argue their case, insisting that every rift in the plays is loaded with Christian ore, that indeed the tragedies should be recognized as quasi-allegorical adumbrations of the Christian mysteries. Thus, G. Wilson Knight's assertion that "each of Shakespeare's tragic heroes is a miniature Christ"[1] has been, for better or worse, extensively explored in subsequent criticism, while Roy Battenhouse, probably the most conspicuous and most influential of today's theologizers, has recently argued that "the ultimate archetype for the tragic hero [is] a figurative Adam," and that tragic heroism in Shakespeare is, in fact, a *parody* of the Christ story:

> Adam is related to Christ by analogy, in the way in which the Old Adam in every man is related to the potential new Adam in him: the first is but the mistaken shadow-version of the second. From this point of view, the agony and "sacrifice" we see in a typical tragic hero is not at all identical with Christ's but rather its rival analogue.[2]

But the secularizers of Shakespeare resist this theological treatment of Shakespeare's work, countering that Shakespeare's tragedies, and indeed all tragedies, are pervasively secular, essentially Manichaean or agnostic.[3] Sylvan Barnet's defense of the secularist position is representative of this view:

> Shakespeare was a writer of, among other things, tragedies, and his tragedies show the material fall of heroes. In the great plays this fall is generally accompanied by an increased awareness of the nature of life, but such profit is gained at the expense of life. Shakespeare had an Anglican education, and the ethics in the plays partake of Christian ethics, but they are not based, as Christian ethics in fact are, upon the eschatology of the Christian system.[4]

Those critics who choose not to be perplexed in the extremes are left to choose the labyrinthine middle ground, where things are but are not, where the critic giveth and the critic taketh away. In this middle ground, the reader, after being assured that Shakespeare's plays have no religious or philosophical dimensions,

is more than likely to be solemnly initiated to the *real* religious and metaphysical meaning of the plays. Bradley, for example, argues that Shakespeare
"practically confined his view to the world of nontheological observation and
thought" but then adds that the ultimate power in the tragic world is a cosmic
moral order "which shows itself akin to good and alien to evil."[5] And, despite
his conviction that the tragic question cannot be posed or answered in religious
terms, Bradley comes embarrassingly close to describing *Hamlet* as a religious
drama.[6]

Roland Frye is no surer guide. Though he is convinced that "the weight of
evidence and of critical opinion is in favor of the secular analysis of Shakespeare," he nevertheless states that "a familiar understanding of Christian doctrine in historical perspective . . . contributes to a fuller understanding of
Shakespeare's art. . . ."[7] The convolutions of Frye's argument can best be
appreciated by noting that the authorities he marshals to "furnish a theological
validation of [Shakespeare's] primarily secular approach to literature" are,
remarkably, Luther, Calvin, and Richard Hooker.[8]

This critical befuddlement provides ample testimony that the place of religion in Shakespeare cannot easily be determined. The historical test, which
would bear witness to Shakespeare's tragic meaning by establishing the religious expectations of his audience, is called into question by nothing less
than history itself. However much the historical critic would like to take refuge
in the residual medieval pieties of the Renaissance world, he runs afoul, if he is
at all thorough, of disconcerting counter-evidence—the growing anxiety about
the "trepidation of the spheres" and about the New Philosophy which finds
expression most prominently in the poetry of John Donne. The Shakespearean
moment, we are told in *Hamlet*, is a "drossy age" in which man acts as if "the
world were now but to begin, / Antiquity forgot, custom not known . . ."
(V.ii.181; IV.v.103–4).[9] It is, most significantly, an age uncomfortable with
myth and miracle:

> They say miracles are past, and we have our philosophical persons, to
> make modern and familiar, things supernatural and causeless. Hence is it
> that we make trifles of terrors, esconcing ourselves into seeming knowl-
> edge when we should submit ourselves to an unknown fear.
>
> (*AWW*, II.iii.1–6)

If the historical test is at best inconclusive, the contextual test is no more
satisfactory. Certainly we can affirm by counting images that Shakespeare
used a religious idiom familiar to himself and his viewers, and by tracing image
patterns we can even establish that these image patterns have dramatic sub-

stance, that is, that they are to be taken seriously. But we cannot assume that they necessarily point to a religious interpretation of the action. When Richard II describes himself as a Christ-figure, we must, for example, consider first, that he is a medieval king who would naturally resort in his ordeal to the semantic of Christianity, and secondly, that he is by personality prone to self-dramatization and self-exculpation. Thus his image of himself as a Christ-figure would be emotionally uplifting for him but would nevertheless invite the sceptical appraisal of the viewer. Richard's appeal to the mysteries of Christianity, one could argue, says nothing about the Christian mettle of the character or the play, much less of the playwright. And so with such other religious manifestations as the several "miniature Christs" who, in the words of Roland Frye, "appear in such weltering profusion as almost to crowd all other actors from the stage."[10]

On the other hand, it is equally hard to dissolve the imagery and language of the plays into some miraculous manna that satisfies everybody's craving for meaning without having a taste or character of its own. The religious imagery of many plays is far too insistent, precise, and coherent to be dismissed as mere dramatic artifice or as a *lingua franca* of the Shakespearean theater. The involved reader of *Hamlet* or *Othello* will inevitably feel that the religious questions dwelt upon in the plays are of some moment, that Hamlet's anxiety about resolving the religious ambiguities of his experience is somehow an integral part of the play's meaning, just as the dark vision of damnation imagined by Othello is more than a merely poetic consummation of the play's action. The intuition of a supernatural reality seems, in short, to be an indissoluble part of the tragic hero's—and, by extension, the audience's—experience.

How are we then to get beyond this perplexity? I would suggest as a first step that the controversy about religious meanings be recognized as the result of naive theologizing (engendering an equally naive anti-theologizing). The crux of the problem seems to be that the religious significance of the tragedies is often approached as "given," with the result that the critic establishes prematurely the ethical and metaphysical bases of judgment. Thus a religious symbol occurring in a key passage is seen as validating the Christian significance of a tragedy, allowing the critic then to read theological meanings back into any passage of the play. Conversely, the absence of overt Christian references (as in *King Lear*) is often seized upon as decisive evidence of the secularity of the plays. What seems needed, many readers will agree, is an approach that will do justice to the evidently valid perceptions of both the humanists and the theologizers.

Perhaps it would be profitable for critics to follow the lead of contemporary students of religion and to recognize the possibility of an *inductive* theology, such as that expounded in Peter Berger's recent *Rumor of Angels*.[11] This inductive theology could be described as a thoroughly unbiased anthropology ready to take into account all of the dimensions of human life and consciousness; it would begin with the facts of human experience and strive to discern "signals of transcendence within the empirically-given human situation."[12] Berger goes on to describe these signals of transcendence as "phenomena that are to be found within the domain of our natural reality but that appear to point beyond that reality."[13]

What is especially important from the critic's point of view is that this concept of inductive theology offers the possibility of acknowledging religious experience in the tragedies without compromising the integrity of secular experience. Accordingly, Shakespearean tragedy, while remaining "this-worldly" in its utter fidelity to perceptible human experience, may nonetheless uncover within the heights and depths of this experience signals of transcendence, phenomena which point to a religious dimension in human life. In this tragic world it is not the religious symbols that reveal the significance of the dramatic action, but the dramatic action that validates (or often invalidates!) the "revealed" symbol. Theological insight is earned rather than given, for the heroes of the tragedies as well as the critics. Moreover, because of the anthropological (that is, humanistic) basis of these tragedies, we are offered at best only intimations of a meta-empirical reality, the probability but not the certitude that a Something Other exists. We are offered not a theological confession of faith but a dramatic world which admits of, without compelling, belief.

Indeed, the prominence of two related patterns of thought in the great tragedies invites us to read Shakespeare's tragedies as a deliberate search for an inductive theology. The first of these patterns is a preoccupation with paganism in its various manifestations, particularly in its interaction with traditional Christianity. In *Hamlet* Shakespeare, by deliberately introducing Christian elements into the originally pagan narrative, creates a tension between a pagan Teutonic ethos and the Christian ethos. In *Othello*, Othello's conversion to Christianity must withstand the pressures put upon it by the paganism of his own background as well as the neo-paganism of Iago. In *King Lear* the originally Christian source is purged of all Christian references and transformed to an austere paganism, while in *Macbeth* the Christian world is invaded by the occult in the form of the demonic witches. The intention of this strategy seems to be to explore the relationship between "natural man" and "religious man," to penetrate as deeply as possible into the concept of Natural Man in order to determine whether man is indeed sufficient unto himself, whether he is indeed the measure of all things.

The second major pattern I would describe as the progressive penetration of the tragedies into negative transcendence. From *Hamlet* on, what we observe is a penetration into the mystery of evil, with each tragedy bringing us progressively closer to the springs of evil. We are gradually encouraged to believe that the natural explanation of evil is inadequate, that some supernatural hypothesis must be resorted to in order to account for the iniquity of man. Paradoxically, it is this affirmation of the mystery of evil, expressed in the imagery of diabolism, that lends credibility to the companion mystery, the mystery of good. For the barriers of reason, once breached, cannot be reconstructed, and the unsentimental affirmation of negative transcendence, that is, of metaphysical evil, prepares one to believe in a positive transcendence. It is thus the uncanny evil of Iago that authenticates the virtue of Desdemona, as it is the perversity of Goneril and Regan that testifies to the transcendent goodness of Cordelia. In this intuition Shakespeare anticipates Wallace Stevens, who writes in his "Esthétique Du Mal":

> The death of Satan was a tragedy
> For the imagination. A capital
> Negation destroyed him in his tenement
> And, with him, many blue phenomena.

It is an intuition voiced also by Chesterton:

> The world can be made beautiful again by viewing it as a battlefield. When we have defined and isolated the evil thing, the colours come back into everything else. When evil things have become evil, good things, in a blazing apocalypse, become good. There are some men who are dreary because they do not believe in God; but there are many others who are dreary because they do not believe in the devil.[14]

II

Shakespeare begins the journey to the heart of darkness with *Hamlet*. A remarkable feature of *Hamlet* is Shakespeare's manipulation of his sources to introduce Christian elements into an erstwhile pagan setting. Belleforest, well aware that revenge was inconsistent with the "official" Christian ethos of the Renaissance, was careful to insist in his very first paragraph that the Hamlet narrative was based upon a pagan ethic:

> You must understand, that long time before the kingdome of Denmark received the faith of Jesus Christ, and imbraced the doctrin of the Christians, that the common people in those dayes were barbarous and uncivill,

and their princes cruell, without faith or loyaltie, seeking nothing but murther, and deposing (or at the least) offending each other, either in honours, goods, or lives. . . .[15]

By this appeal Belleforest offers an easy way out of the ethical difficulties, allowing the Christian viewer to suspend moral judgment of Hamlet's revenge motive and lend his sympathy to the hero. But Shakespeare, while maintaining the pagan atmosphere of the revenge story, seems to go out of his way to introduce into this story a relatively developed Christian ethos. The *Hamlet* that emerges is not, to be sure, a Christian play, but it is certainly no longer a pagan play. Rather, it is a play in which two incompatible moral contexts are held in tension.

The Christian elements in the play have been so well elaborated elsewhere that I shall limit myself to a few observations. They include a ghost that is decidedly more Christian than Senecan—that indeed describes itself as a purgatorial spirit "confined to fast in fires" (I.v.11)—and a multitude of references to Christian eschatology and Christian liturgy, ranging from the "angels and ministers of grace" (I.iv.39) invoked by Hamlet to the "churlish priest" who is berated by Laertes for the maimed rites accorded to Ophelia:

> I tell thee, churlish priest,
> A minist ring angel shall my sister be
> When thou liest howling.
>
> (V.i.227–29)

They significantly include Hamlet's own Christian perceptions, particularly after his "change of heart" in Act IV, where he expresses belief in a "special providence," in a "divinity that shapes our ends, / Rough-hew them how we will" (V.ii.208–10; 10–11). *Hamlet* is unquestionably among the most Christian of the tragedies in language and imagery.

And yet, it cannot be described as unequivocally Christian because each Christian element seems to be neutralized by a corresponding pagan element. The ghost, for all of its Christian credentials, imposes upon Hamlet a mission that is totally incompatible with the Christian moral system. And Hamlet, though he does entertain severe doubts about the nature of the ghost, wondering whether it is a "spirit of health or goblin damned" (I.iv.40), never once explicitly questions the mission of revenge, though revenge is abhorrent to Christian thought. Any suggestion that he is repelled by the task on moral grounds can only be inferred from his several vague remarks about conscience and scruples as causes of his delay. Moreover, Hamlet, despite his association with Wittenberg (in Shakespeare's—though not in the original Hamlet's—time a citadel of Lutheran thought), is remarkably inconsistent in his eschatological views, to the extent that we cannot determine whether or not he believes in God and immortality. If in one instance he can refer to a God who has "fixed / His canon 'gainst self-slaughter" (I.ii.131–32), he is equally capable in another instance of questioning the existence of an afterlife:

> To sleep—perchance to dream: ay, there's the rub,
> For in that sleep of death what dreams may come
> When we have shuffled off this mortal coil
> Must give us pause.
>
> *(III.i.65–68)*

He elsewhere utters a statement that seems to be an explicit confession of unbelief:

> this most excellent canopy, the air, look you, this, brave o'erhanging firmament, this majestical roof fretted with golden fire—why, it appeareth nothing to me but a foul and pestilent congregation of vapours.
>
> *(II.ii.296–99)*

Even the redeemed Hamlet who returns from his sea voyage to speak so confidently of a special providence, of a heaven ordinant in his good fortune, cannot be comfortably accepted by the audience. For it is possible to interpret his quietism as a submission to pagan fatalism rather than to the will of God. Bradley, for one, finds that Hamlet's statements at this point "seem to express that kind of religious resignation which, however beautiful in one aspect, really deserves the name of fatalism rather than that of faith in Providence...."[16] The strongest support for this view is Hamlet's mood in the graveyard scene, where we seem to have a concrete re-statement of Hamlet's view of man as a "quintessence of dust" (II.ii.304); a spiritually renewed Hamlet would presumably view death in the light of his Christian faith, but Hamlet's macabre humor about the final absurdity of death reveals nothing whatever of a Christian hope in resurrection:

> ... Alexander died, Alexander was buried, Alexander returneth to dust; the dust is earth; of earth we make loam; and why of that loam whereto he was converted might they not stop a beer barrel?
>
> *(V.i.196–99)*

Even more disconcerting is his rejoicing over the killing of Rosencrantz and
Guildenstern, whom he has had executed "not shriving time allowed" (V.ii.47)
and therefore placed in jeopardy of eternal damnation. This action, made possible—according to Hamlet—by divine intervention, is inconceivable as the
action of a morally sensitive person and severely undercuts Hamlet's pretensions of spiritual renewal.

The ambivalence which surrounds Hamlet is maintained to the very end.
Whatever the arguments forwarded to find religious meaning in his "the rest
is silence" (V.ii.347), it is hard to dispel the sense of an awesome finality in the
lines. Ironically, our chief source of consolation in the final scene is Horatio,
who has hardly impressed the viewers as a religious person, in his "Good night,
sweet prince, / And flights of angels sing thee to thy rest" (V.ii.348–49). It is
the sceptic in the play who most strongly endorses belief in Christian immortality.

The world of Hamlet, we must conclude, is in fact two worlds, a Christian
world, and a pagan world that affords man little sign of a benevolent Providence
or hope of an afterlife, a world in which man is nothing but a quintessence of
dust or a plaything of mysterious agencies. Hamlet's crucial question "What
should such fellows as I do crawling between earth and heaven?" (III.i.127–28)
expresses the hopelessness of this pagan vision. But the play does suggest,
however vaguely, that there is something more than natural in man's experience and even that the mystery of evil is somehow more present to man than
the mystery of good. The question of transcendence, however negative, is
posed most insistently by the irreducible ghost; but the ghost's precise meaning is engulfed in darkness, and we no more than Hamlet can come to a
reliable conclusion about its significance. As Mack has stated, what the play
finally dramatizes is

> man in his aspect of bafflement, moving in darkness on a rampart between
> two worlds, unable to reject, or quite accept, the one that, when he faces it,
> "to-shakes" his disposition with thoughts beyond the reaches of his soul
> —comforting himself with hints and guesses.[17]

In *Othello* the confrontation between the pagan world and the Christian
world is embodied in the conflict between Othello, the baptized pagan, and the
cynical Iago. Othello's tragedy stems from the fact that his love for Desdemona
is undermined by Iago, who rejects the possibility of altruistic love, considering
love "a sect or scion" (I.iii.331) of lust, that is, a mere sublimation of biological
urges. Othello, whose love for Desdemona is based upon an intuitive faith in
her goodness, is finally persuaded to share Iago's cynicism.

Like *Hamlet*, *Othello* is conspicuously Christian in language and imagery, and Othello's loss of faith in Desdemona is equated with the loss of his Christian faith. After Iago's subversion has succeeded, Othello is ready, as Iago had predicted, "to renounce his baptism, / All seals and symbols of redeemed sin" (II.iii.326–27); and when Othello discovers his tragic error, he naturally reverts to the semantic of Christianity, vividly picturing his own damnation for throwing away "a pearl . . . / Richer than all his tribe" (V.ii.347–48). Moreover, he reads his fall as the result of a diabolical plot, portraying himself as an Everyman seduced by the Devil:

> Will you, I pray, demand that demi-devil
> Why he hath thus ensnared my soul and body?
>
> *(V.ii.300–301)*

There is indeed warrant for believing in the diabolism of Iago, who is—despite his mask of secularity—surrounded throughout the play with images of the diabolical and is, in fact, quite fond himself of using such imagery; the following is but one of many examples:

> Divinity of Hell!
> When devils will the blackest sins put on,
> They do suggest at first with heavenly shows,
> As I do now.
>
> *(II.iii.333–36)*

Moreover, his "motiveless malignity," the fact that none of the motives he offers for his malice toward Othello is convincing, is entirely consistent with his status as a quasi-allegorical figure of metaphysical evil. The implications of the kind of imagery used by Othello and Iago are, it seems to me, quite clear: on one level the action of *Othello* approximates that of the medieval morality play, with Desdemona, as Iago's mighty opposite, becoming a Mercy-Good Angel figure vying for the soul of Othello-Everyman.

These are familiar arguments, and, within certain limits, they are quite convincing. But again, as in *Hamlet*, the play offers another equally convincing possibility—that the tragedy of Othello is entirely imputable to natural causes. From this perspective Iago is a realistic character who, impelled by a spirit of cynicism, probes latent weaknesses in Othello to effect the destruction of his love. The love of Othello can be said to fail, not because of supernatural forces, but because of its own radical deficiencies. From the very beginning of the play Othello seems himself to be aware of these deficiencies—the differences of race, age, and class, as well as the military occupation which prompts Roderigo to describe him as "an extravagant and wheeling stranger" (I.i.135). It should be noted that Othello is curiously defensive from the very start; he stresses in his first major speech the services he has done for the state and points out his noble descent, "from men of royal siege" (I.ii.22). Later, confronted by hostile senators, he insists that lust has nothing to do with his marriage, "the young affects / In me defunct" (I.iii.263–64). And, as Iago's plot develops, Othello again broods about differences in social background, race, and age:

> Haply, for I am black
> And have not those soft parts of conversation
> That chamberers have, or for I am declined
> Into the vale of years. . . .
>
> *(III.iii.263–66)*

It is this exposed nerve that Iago attacks in his temptation scene, when he reminds Othello of the "country disposition" (III.iii.201) of Venetian women and dwells upon the theme of "clime, complexion, and degree" (III.iii.230).

Thus Othello's loss of faith in Desdemona seems prepared for; the tragedy of Othello is not, in this reading, that product of metaphysical forces represented by Iago—nor is it even caused by Iago. Rather Iago serves only to catalyze social pressures inherent in Othello's situation from the beginning. The romantic love simply cannot withstand the pressures placed upon it by reality.

What I have described, in fact, are the two extreme positions in the contemporary debate about *Othello*.[18] Briefly stated, the question is whether the natural forces ranged against Othello are necessary and sufficient causes for his fall, or whether it is necessary to postulate supernatural agencies. Is, in fact, the religious world view constantly referred to in the play, like love, merely a sublimation of grosser realities, a projection of purely human intuitions? Or is the symbolic aura surrounding both Iago and Desdemona an intimation that natural human experience in its most intense moments reaches out to supernatural dimensions? The answer in *Othello* is, I think, noncommittal; as in *Hamlet* we are given two worlds, discrete and self-sufficient, but we are denied any decisive judgment.

King Lear seems to be a further step in this direction. Inverting the procedure he followed in *Hamlet*, Shakespeare carefully excises every overt trace of Christianity from an originally Christian story.[19] His object seems to be to explore further the question raised in the earlier tragedies, whether it is possible or necessary to discover supernatural dimensions in human experience. More specifically, the basic question seems to be whether man's evil can be attributed to natural causes; it is Lear himself who, in the mock-trial of Goneril and Regan, most directly approaches the question:

> Then let them anatomize Regan. See what breeds about her heart. Is there any cause in nature that makes these hard hearts?
>
> (III.vi.74–76)

The ordeal of King Lear impels him to re-examine the traditional conceptions of man. It is important to note that even in *Lear*, despite the pagan setting, the world view is initially religious. Lear, for example, swears by Apollo and by Jupiter (I.i.160, 178), expresses confidence that the heavens will love old men (II.iv.184–85), and refers to "high-judging Jove" (II.iv.223). Similarly Kent, pitying Cordelia, prays "The gods to their dear shelter take thee, maid" (I.i.182), and even Edmund, despite his own unbelief, appeals to Gloucester's faith in a transcendent moral order:

> . . . I told him the revenging gods
> 'Gainst parricides did all the thunder bend.
>
> (II.i.45–46)

But we are, I think, to interpret these as facile appeals to transcendence and therefore doomed to be disappointed. As G. Wilson Knight has said, "the 'gods' so often apostrophized are, however, slightly vitalized; one feels them to be figments of the human mind rather than omnipotent ruling powers—they are presented with no poetic conviction. And exactly this doubt, this questioning, as to the reality and nature of the directing powers, so evident in the god-references, is one of the primary motives through the play."[20] Thus a significant phase of Lear's ordeal is his crisis of confidence in his pagan gods, in the benevolent moral order that will vindicate him. Despite his prayers and curses, the rain and thunder torment, not Goneril and Regan, but Lear himself, and his easy reliance upon benign gods is frustrated:

> I tax not you, you elements, with unkindness.
> I never gave you kingdom, called you children;
> You owe me no subscription. . . .
>
> .   .   .   .   .
>
> But yet I call you servile ministers. . . .
>
> (III.ii.16–18, 21)

From this awareness of an indifferent cosmos Lear moves to his next phase, an acceptance of a purely natural definition of man, a concept of man as no more than a clever animal with a capacity for sophistication or guile:

> Is man no more than this? Consider him well. Thou ow'st the worm no silk, the beast no hide, the sheep no wool, the cat no perfume. Ha! here's three on's are sophisticated. Thou art the thing itself; unaccommodated man is no more but such a poor, bare, forked animal as thou art.
>
> (III.iv.97–102)

This is essentially an acceptance of Edmund's Nature, the "goddess" who is a hypostatization of a world whose fundamental law is the law of the jungle, self-interest; it is a world in which virtue and altruistic love are inconceivable. Lear's "unbutton here," his stripping of his clothing, formalizes his intuition that there is no discontinuity between men and animals.

But this is an intermediate stage quickly bypassed as the action progresses, for we notice the gradual emergence of two kinds of villainy: the "natural" villainy of Edmund, motivated by resentment of his state and ambition for self-advancement, and the almost gratuitous villainy of Goneril and Regan. Where Edmund is amoral, almost cavalier in his villainy, Goneril and Regan practice an aggressive immorality, disclosing a viciousness that surpasses normal selfishness. Despite G. Wilson Knight's judgment that "the good and bad elements [in *Lear*] are . . . natural, not, as in *Macbeth*, supernatural,"[21] what we are finally compelled to acknowledge is precisely that the cruelty of Goneril and Regan is inconceivable in animals, that the human capacity for evil surpasses even the bitter logic of the jungle. This progression of understanding can be located specifically in the reactions of Albany to the deeds of Goneril and Regan:

> Tigers, not daughters, what have you performed?
> A father, and a gracious aged man,
> Whose reverence even the head-lugged bear would lick,
> Most barbarous, most degenerate, have you madded.
>
> (IV.ii.40–43)

> See thyself, devil:
> Proper deformity seems not in the fiend
> So horrid as in woman.
>
> (IV.ii.59–61)

> Howe'er thou art a fiend,
> A woman's shape doth shield thee.
>
> *(IV.ii.66–67)*

It is not enough for Albany to consider the daughters as predators; the intensity of their cruelty begs for a more metaphysical explanation.

Albany has at this point accepted the intuition of evil first offered by Edgar as Tom o' Bedlam, whose insane ramblings dwell obsessively upon the presence of diabolical powers. Despite some critical scepticism regarding the significance of Tom's semantic of hell,[22] it seems probable to me that the imagery of diabolical possession that pervades his speeches, from his initial "Away! the foul fiend follows me" (III.iv.45), overtly states what seems to be a central intuition of the play—that rational and natural explanations of evil are inadequate. Edgar, like Albany, prepares us to accept the metaphysical depths of the deeds of Goneril and Regan. Thus if Lear's early religiosity is shattered by his experience, his suspicions of negative transcendence—of "darkness and devils" (I.iv.243)—are confirmed.

But we are not left with this counsel of despair, for if the insistent evil in the play has broken down the pales and forts of reason, it has thereby provided access to good. It is not necessary to see Cordelia as a "Christ-figure" (though there seems warrant enough for granting her some such anagogical significance) to recognize that her love has in it something more than natural, that indeed, all love and altruistic behavior is incomprehensible unless the mystery of the human condition is acknowledged. As West has suggested,

> Does Cordelia, as an exception to natural evil, draw Lear's understanding of nature somehow beyond nature? Lear's understanding rises—as it touches Cordelia, anyway—toward a conscious remission of self-interest, a conscious community with the beloved, that in natural creation only man seems persistently capable of. This feeling concern for another, this surpassing love, is a kind of doubling on nature's tracks, is a transformation of nature's law of self, a departure from the predation so constant in unalloyed nature and a rising superior to it. Through love we can put up with one another's natural faults and filths better than an impartial observer might expect. Is this a kind of supernature, of spirituality, in us and from beyond us? Several higher religions have said something of this sort. [23]

But Cordelia is only the highest and clearest manifestation of what the perceptive viewer has detected throughout the play, the perdurance of simple human goodness in a world apparently overwhelmed by evil. Fully as important as the monstrosity of the sisters is the theme of "unpublished virtues" (IV.iv.16), given dramatic substance by the loyalty of Kent and the Fool, the humane reactions of Cornwall's servants to the blinding of Gloucester, and the moral regeneration of Albany and Gloucester. It is true that these virtues are inconspicuous—Edgar and Kent, significantly, are in disguise, while Cordelia's presence is for a time kept secret—but we are nonetheless given favorable indications, even before evil has achieved full dominance, that virtue is only temporarily eclipsed. The "unpublished virtues," rising beyond self-interest and even reaching at times the splendid absurdity of sacrifice, point to a dimension of grace in human behavior, to some kind of discontinuity between man and nature—a motiveless benignity as incomprehensible as the motiveless malignity of the villains.

If Lear is at all redeemed, it is in these terms, that his penetration of the evil of Goneril and Regan makes it possible for him to come to terms with the inexplicable love of Cordelia; and growing from this perception, Lear is willing again to take upon himself the mystery of things. G. Wilson Knight describes Lear's regeneration in these terms:

> Slowly, painfully, emergent from the *Lear* naturalism we see a religion born of disillusionment, suffering, and sympathy: a purely spontaneous, natural growth of the human spirit, developing from nature magic to "God."[24]

However, *King Lear* cannot be said to affirm unequivocally the traditional Christian world view. Despite the anagogical intimations of Cordelia and the other unpublished virtues and despite the fact that the evil forces have been defeated with the deaths of Goneril, Regan, and Edmund, "the bounty and the benison of heaven" (IV.vi.221) is called into question by the gratuitous death of Cordelia. Is Lear's final "Look there, look there—" (V.iii.312) then to be read as an intuition of human immortality which would redeem all human suffering, or should we construe it as a final desperate lament? No decisive answer to the questions posed by the tragedy is given; instead, as Stampfer has pointed out,

> Certainly almost every possible point of view on the gods and cosmic justice is expressed, from a malevolent, wanton polytheism . . . to an astrological determinism. . . . from an amoral, personified Nature-goddess . . . to "high-judging Jove." But the very multitude, concern, and contradictory character of these references do not cancel each other out, but rather show how precarious is the concept of cosmic justice. . . . Despite

the pagan setting, the problem of theodicy, the justification of God's way with men, is invoked by so many characters, and with such concern, that it emerges as a key issue in the play.[25]

What the play has suggested more strongly than ever is that the religious hypothesis is at least as convincing as the natural hypothesis, which seems incapable of accounting for the mystery of human vice and virtue.

In *Macbeth*, the last phase of his penetration into evil, Shakespeare is finally able to posit the existence of supernatural agencies. Though it would have been possible to present Macbeth's tragedy as a fully secular fall, as the tragedy of a great man undone by his ambition, Shakespeare introduces into the plot the demonic witches whose presence unequivocally establishes the metaphysical dimensions of evil.

The witches have long been an acute source of embarrassment to many of Shakespeare's critics; Samuel Johnson, for one, was appalled by their crudity:

A poet who should now make the whole action of his tragedy depend upon enchantment, and produce the chief events by the assistance of supernatural agents, would be censured as transgressing the bounds of probability, be banished from the theater to the nursery, and condemned to write fairy tales instead of tragedies. . . .[26]

But however embarrassing this residual Gothicism may be to enlightened critics, the witches resist being exorcised; other manifestations of the "supernatural" in *Macbeth*, such as the dagger or the apparition of Banquo's ghost (which are seen by Macbeth alone), may be explained as mere projections, as images of guilt welling up from Macbeth's fevered imagination, but the witches, especially since they were also seen by Banquo, must be accepted as embodiments of supernatural evil somehow distinct from the inner evil of Macbeth. Their indissoluble reality, whatever their precise identity, confirms beyond any reasonable doubt the several intuitions of diabolism voiced in, for example, Macbeth's reference to "night's black agents" (III.ii.53), in Lady Macbeth's reference to "murd'ring minsters" (I.v.46), and in the porter's description of himself as "porter of hell gate" (II.iii.1).

Shakespeare is careful, however, to protect the human dimensions of Macbeth's crime; the witches' powers are so circumscribed that they cannot compel Macbeth to perform his deed, nor, it seems clear, have they even inspired it. The witches, despite Macbeth's reference to their "supernatural soliciting" (I.iii.130), seem more to "wait upon nature's mischief" (I.v.48) than to take the initiative. Bradley's assessment of their role is still most convincing:

> while the influence of the Witches' prophecies on Macbeth is very great, it is quite clearly shown to be an influence and nothing more. There is no sign whatever in the play that Shakespeare meant the actions of Macbeth to be forced on him by an external power, whether that of the Witches, or of their "masters," or of Hecate. It is needless therefore to insist that such a conception would be in contradiction to his whole tragic practice. The prophecies of the witches are presented simply as dangerous circumstances with which Macbeth has to deal. . . .[27]

And yet, though the witches do not *cause* the actions of Macbeth, they are more intimately related to these actions than Bradley suggests. They seem, indeed, to body forth what the ambiguous ghost in *Hamlet*, the inscrutable enigma of Iago, and the moral horror of Goneril and Regan have adumbrated in the earlier plays—that the intensity of evil requires a metaphysical hypothesis. Macbeth's sins, in this dramatic embodiment of the mystery of evil, are at once his own and the product of diabolical forces, the inner and outer evil existing in some mysterious relationship incomprehensible to man. With more assurance than ever before, the tragic world of Shakespeare is able to reassert the traditional conception of evil as simultaneously the evil within and the evil without.

Again, in *Macbeth*, the defeat of this conspiracy of evil is inexplicable. Perhaps no one understood better than Shakespeare that virtue is intrinsically undramatic and unconvincing, for once more in this play the "unpublished virtues"—the seemingly bland and impotent good people such as Malcolm and Macduff—are the implausible agents of the defeat of Macbeth's titanic evil. Despite the imagery of holiness that surrounds their cause (for example, the saintly aura of King Edward), we are prepared to believe in the transcendence of goodness, in the "grace of Grace" (V.viii.72) only because we have believed in the deep damnation of Macbeth.

An important feature of the tragic pattern I have tried to describe is that it is comprehensive enough to include both secular and theological approaches to Shakespeare. To speak of Shakespeare's tragedies as theological in their ultimate reaches requires, however, an understanding of theology as something more than a deductive system of truths pertaining to supernatural dimensions of human experience. Roland Frye, who has, in my opinion, presented the most formidable challenge to the theologizers of Shakespeare, implicitly defines theological drama as drama in which supernatural religious concerns are directly and overtly given dramatic form. The following questions which he poses are indicative of this concept:

> does a play's inception, its development through crucial or pivotal incidents, and its ending accord in some meaningful way with the structures of theological doctrine? Are the conflict and "competition" of the play related to the divine order with sufficient consistency and force to make the divine references a major influence, or are such references more accurately described as rhetorical and supportive? Is the divine presence in rejection and acceptance, judgment and mercy sufficiently strong in the play to shape or even to affect the major actions of the plot and of the characters? Are the internal struggles of the characters directly and meaningfully related to God? Is guilt directly and primarily associated with a character's relations to God through his relations with others, or is that guilt primarily concerned with his relations to society and to himself? Is conscience kept within a framework which is primarily social and personal, or is that primary framework meaningfully and consistently embraced in the larger order of divine will?[28]

On the basis of these questions we may accept Frye's verdict that Shakespeare's plays are not—in his sense of the word—theological. But the concept of an inductive theology allows us to see more clearly the implications of Shakespeare's tragedies. In such an approach, the theological structure is not given or assumed; if it is initially present, it is placed in tension with the plot—as a hypothesis to be tested rather than an a priori solution to the problem of existence. The theological thrust of Shakespeare's tragedies is inquisitive rather than affirmative and apodictic; briefly stated, the recurrent questions in the tragedies are whether or not the religious hypothesis is valid or necessary, whether or not the Christian faith in a benevolent Providence can be corroborated by the hard facts of life.

Shakespeare's relentless exploration of secular experience in his tragedies, along with his attention to signals of transcendence, to intimations of meta-empirical reality, suggests that his understanding of Christianity was profoundly humanistic; for the Christian experience revealed in the tragedies, though ultimately transcendent, is primarily, to use Frye's words, social and personal. Moreover, the remoteness of God in the tragedies, noticed by Frye and Clifford Leech,[29] among others, seems rather the result of this humanistic conception of the Christian experience than of a secular purpose. If God is not for most Christians precisely Pascal's *deus absconditus*, he is certainly less immediately present to them than Frye implies. As Schillebeeckx has stated:

Even human history does not show us God. Precisely because he demonstrates his effective presence in this world in his own way, he seems to be
absent. . . . Man can thus reach out to God only as to someone who is
absent from the normal totality of created things. . . . Thus all appearances
speak against the existence of God. Our human insight finds it impossible
to justify his providence.[30]

Shakespeare's tragedies are secular because they faithfully depict a Christian
experience that is itself tentative and secular; we are denied our theophanies,
burning bushes, or pillars of fire, being given at best only the shadowy outlines
of a pattern that vindicates human striving. Yet from this human striving, in its
moments of peak intensity, issue signals of transcendence.

Notes:

1. G. Wilson Knight, *Principles of Shakespearian Production* (1936; rpt. Baltimore,
    1949), p. 166.
2. Roy W. Battenhouse, *Shakespearean Tragedy: Its Art and Its Christian Premises*
    (Bloomington, Indiana, 1969), p. 91.
3. I. A. Richards, *Principles of Literary Criticism* (New York, 1928), p. 246; Clifford
    Leech, *Shakespeare's Tragedies and Other Studies in Seventeenth Century
    Drama* (London, 1950), p. 18.
4. Sylvan Barnet, "Some Limitations of a Christian Approach to Shakespeare," in
    Approaches to Shakespeare, ed. Norman Rabkin (New York, 1964), p. 222—
    the article was first published in *ELH*, 22 (1955).
5. A. C. Bradley, *Shakespearean Tragedy* (1904; Greenwich, Conn., 1965), pp. 30,
    37. See also Battenhouse, pp. 68–69, for a commentary on Bradley's incon-
    sistencies regarding the metaphysical or religious implications of Shakespeare's
    tragedies.
6. Bradley, p. 147.
7. Roland Mushat Frye, *Shakespeare and Christian Doctrine* (Princeton, 1963),
    pp. 60, 51.
8. Frye, p. 60.
9. All references to the plays are to *William Shakespeare: The Complete Works*,
    ed. Alfred C. Harbage (Baltimore, 1969).
10. Frye, p. 34.
11. Peter Berger, *A Rumor of Angels* (Garden City, N.Y., 1969).
12. Berger, p. 65.
13. Berger, pp. 65–66. In order to support his claim for the validity of religious
    experience, Berger attempts to "relativize the relativizers," that is, to neutralize
    the sceptical Feuerbachian argument that all religious experience is merely a
    projection of man's own "better nature"—see esp. pp. 57–59.
14. G. K. Chesterton, *Charles Dickens: The Last of the Great Men* (New York,
    1942), p. 204.

15. "The Hystorie of Hamblet," in Sir Israel Gollancz, *The Sources Of Hamlet* (1926; rpt, New York, 1967), p. 179.

16. Bradley, pp. 122, 123; see also Battenhouse, pp. 157, 158; Battenhouse, far less ambivalent than Bradley, states that "Hamlet has become resigned to a fatalism. He would view his own human condition as that of a person not responsible for his madness, although we have heard him praise rashness only a moment before. Hamlet's reasoning harbors contradictions which he is too confused to fathom."

17. Maynard Mack, "The World of Hamlet," in *Shakespeare: Modern Essays in Criticism,* ed. Leonard F. Dean (New York, 1961), p. 241.

18. For representative arguments for either position, see M. R. Ridley, New Arden *Othello* (Cambridge, Mass., 1962), p. lx; and Leah Scragg, "Iago—Vice or Devil," *ShS,* 21 (1968), pp. 61–62.

19. See William R. Elton, *King Lear and the Gods* (San Marino, Calif., 1966), pp. 63–67.

20. G. Wilson Knight, *The Wheel of Fire* (1930; New York, 1957), p. 187.

21. Ibid., p. 187.

22. Ibid., p. 188; see also Elton, pp. 92–93.

23. Robert H. West, *Shakespeare and the Outer Mystery* (Lexington, Ky., 1968), pp. 158–59.

24. *Wheel of Fire,* p. 191.

25. Judah Stampfer, "The Catharsis of *King Lear,*" in *Shakespeare's Tragedies: An Anthology of Modern Criticism,* Laurence Lerner, ed. (Baltimore, 1963), p. 153. Stampfer, however, finds that the issue is flatly resolved by the denouement of the play, which "destroys any basis for providential justice." (p. 155). The essay first appeared in *Shakespeare Survey,* 13 (1960).

26. *Samuel Johnson on Shakespeare,* ed. W. K. Wimsatt, Jr. (New York, 1960), p. 99.

27. Bradley, p. 285.

28. Roland M. Frye, "Theological and Non-Theological Structures in Tragedy," *ShakS* 4 (1968), pp. 146–47.

29. Ibid., pp. 136–38; Leech, p. 11.

30. E. Schillebeeckx, O.P., *God and Man* (New York, 1969), p. 22.

The Importance of Manningham's *Diary*

Jarold Ramsey

The diary and commonplace book that John Manningham of the Middle Temple kept in 1602 and 1603[1] remains best known for its two vivid allusions to Shakespeare—one an eyewitness account of a performance of *Twelfth Night* in the Middle Temple on Candlemas, 1601/2, the other that rather endearing anecdote of Shakespeare as a wenching "William the Conqueror." None of Manningham's other entries is so arresting as these, but—more than has been generally recognized—the *Diary* as a whole is a uniquely rich resource for students of later Elizabethan and early Jacobean literature, history, and culture, and it is well worth consulting in its entirety.

Unfortunately, the only available edition of Manningham (by John Bruce for the Camden Society in 1868) is seriously incomplete, the text having been thoroughly expurgated by the editor, who assures his readers that much of the language of the *Diary* is "of course entirely indefensible" and that a number of passages have been omitted "as unfit for publication." It was, to his high-Victorian taste at least, "the slough of a coarser generation, which our ancestors had not then entirely cast off."[2] In what follows, without meaning to mock Bruce, who was, his prudery aside, a careful transcriber and editor, I restore the most significant of his deletions of Manningham's jottings, and I attempt to make the *Diary*'s three main areas of interest more accessible for scholarly use. These three areas are (1) literary gossip and allusions; (2) Manningham's extraordinary attention to sermons and what it suggests about late Elizabethan attitudes toward the spoken language in the playhouse as well as in the church; (3) evidence that Manningham is a more representative Inns of Court man in his sensibility and interests than the roistering, cynical figure of the Elizabethan law student now generally accepted in theories about Shakespeare's reading and playgoing public.[3]

I

Manningham's allusions to Shakespeare have been so widely cited and discussed that there seems little to add. One writer, noting that the *Diary* manuscript passed after its discovery through the hands of John Payne Collier, has surmised that the story of Shakespeare's amorous upstaging of Burbage is a forgery,[4] but internal evidence and scholarly opinion generally support its authenticity, as coming from Manningham's pen. Perhaps the chief unresolved question is about the story's immediate source: in Manningham's tiny and

sometimes blotted script, the attribution given in the manuscript could be to
Mr. Curle or to Mr. Touse; the configuration of letters is just about identical.
Bruce queries *Touse*, others have read *Curle*. Both are frequently cited for
entries in the *Diary*, and each one raises interesting possibilities about the
authenticity of the story itself. William Towse, who clearly supplied the diarist
with an anecdote about Spenser's poverty only a month after the entry in question, was a prominent Bencher in the *Inner* Temple but evidently circulated
amongst the younger members of the other Temple; Manningham cites him as
a source on six occasions. As for Manningham's associations with Edward
Curle, they were extensive and of long standing. The diarist had become a
roommate of Curle's only a month before recording the story;[5] subsequently
there are frequent attributions to "my chamberfellow" and to other members
of the Curle family, and around 1607, having been called to the bar, Manningham married his roommate's sister Anne.

In the face, then, of what seems like wholly ambiguous paleographic evidence, I conclude that the circumstantial evidence strongly supports Curle as
the source of the Shakespeare wenching anecdote. Again and again, Manningham cites him as the source of some pungent, even racy, story about some
prominent contemporary. There is one about the Puritan Thomas Cartwright's
fatal powers of condemnation (p. 77), another about the Bishop of London's
profanity while bowling (p. 81), and a third about the widow-snaring means
by which Sir Thomas Bodley, founder of the great library, came by his wealth.
In the Shakespeare anecdote, the playwright is described as being "at his game"
with Burbage's admirer; interestingly enough that expression occurs again in
Curle's story about Bodley and nowhere else in the *Diary*: ". . . he found the
widdowe in a garden, courted, and obteined his desyre; soe he played his game,
while an other held his cardes" (p. 63). (Evidently a real card game with another suitor was involved, but the reference becomes metaphorical in this passage.) All in all, Curle would seem to be the likelier source of the Shakespearean gossip—whatever its actual relation to the playwright might be. (The
possibility of a more direct line from Manningham to Shakespeare cannot be
discounted: around the time of the "William the Conqueror" entry, William
Combes of Stratford was admitted to the Middle Temple. He was the son and
nephew respectively of Shakespeare's close neighbors and associates Thomas
and John Combes. Manningham does not name him, but in a house of around
two hundred men, it seems likely that they would meet.)

In his entry of February 2, 1601/2, describing a special performance of
Twelfth Night, Manningham started to write *mid-* for the title, as if thinking of
an earlier festive comedy, then canceled it. It is noteworthy that he goes on to
compare the play to the only other play by Shakespeare known to have been

presented at the Inns of Court, *The Comedy of Errors* (at Gray's Inn in 1594). The *Diary's* summary of the action is as observing and appreciative as we can hope for; Manningham doesn't name the characters, but the account makes it clear that he had a good laugh at the bamboozling of Malvolio, calling it "a good practice" (p. 18). Bruce, I believe, miscopies one line dealing with the joke: instead of the counterfeit letter "prescribing his gesture in smiling, his apparaile, etc.", the line seems to read "prescribing his gesture in *suiting*, his apparaile, etc."—*suiting* having the old meaning of paying court to a lady, and making better sense than the rather odd "gesture in smiling."

A year later, just after the death of Queen Elizabeth, Manningham records a reminiscence of the old queen that almost certainly tallies with an episode in *Twelfth Night*. Quoting Francis Curle, probably one of his roommate's brothers, he tells how

> one Dr. Bullein, the Queens kinsman, had a dog which he doted on, soe much that the Queene understanding of it requested he would grant hir one desyre, and he should have whatsoever he would aske. Shee demaunded his dogge; he gave it, and "Nowe, Madame," quoth he, "you promised to give me my desyre." "I will," quoth she. "Then I pray you give me my dogge againe."
>
> (*pp. 148–49*)[6]

In the play, Feste plays the same trick in V.i on Fabian, who asks to see Malvolio's letter, and, being put off, remarks rather cryptically, "This is to give a dog, and in recompense desire my dog again." The witty doctor Shakespeare and Manningham are both referring to here is Dr. George Boleyn, a cousin of the queen, Bishop of Lichfield, who died himself in 1603.

Considering Manningham's literary allusions more generally, we find mention of the following English authors besides Shakespeare in the *Diary*: Launcelot Andrewes, Francis Bacon, the Venerable Bede, Thomas Sackville, William Camden, Thomas Campion, Chaucer, Sir John Davies, John Donne, Robert Greene, Sir John Hayward, Richard Hooker, John Hoskyns, Ben Jonson, John Marston, Richard Martyne, Sir Thomas More, Sir Thomas Overbury, Sir Walter Raleigh, Samuel Rowlands, Spenser, John Stowe, Richard Tarlton, Aurelian Townshend, William Warner—an interesting range of reading and acquaintance to find in a young law student's casual journal for fifteen months.

Of the names on this list, it is worth mentioning that John Hoskyns, the lawyer-poet-rhetorician, was Manningham's first roommate when he entered the Middle Temple.[7] The reference to another sometime Inns of Court man, John Donne, dated December 1602, is noteworthy as a piece of current news

about the poet's disastrous secret marriage; Manningham couches it in a rue-
ful pun used by Donne himself on occasion: "Dunne is undonne; he was lately
secretary to the Lord Keeper, and cast of because he would match himselfe to a
gentlewoman against his Lords pleasure" (p. 99). A few months later, in February and March 1602/3, Manningham jotted down a series of selections, slightly
garbled as if heard rather than read, from Donne's paradoxes, epigrams, and
"The Storme"—some of the earliest known allusions to the poet's work.[8] One
of the quotations is actually attributed in the manuscript to Donne, but Bruce
miscopied his name as "drunk";

> Of a beggar that lay on the ground [Dun]
> He cannot goe, nor sitt, nor stand, the beggar cryes;
> Then, though he speake the truth, yet still he lyes.
>
> *(p. 156)*

At least one of the paradoxes, "He that weepeth is wise," though identifiable
as Donne's, was not included in early editions; apparently Manningham's
manuscript was more complete than that eventually used by the printer.

The mention (on November 21, 1602) of John Marston, a fellow Middle
Templar, sorts well with the mordantly sarcastic tone of the plays he was writing about this time:

> Jo. Marston the last Christmas he daunct with Alderman Mores wives
> daughter, a Spaniard borne. Fell into a strang commendacion of hir witt
> and beauty. When he had done, she thought to pay him home, and told
> him she though[t] he was a poet. "Tis true," said he, "for poets fayne and
> lye, and soe dyd I when I commended your beauty, for you are exceeding
> foule."[9]
>
> *(p. 86)*

Of references to that fantastical character, Sir John Davies, author of *Orchestra, Nosce Teipsum,* and the like, the *Diary* is particularly full. Manningham
clearly knew him and despised him for his vanity, and although the *Diary* does
not mention Davies's notorious ambush in 1598 of a fellow Middle Templar
and rival wit, Richard Martyne, which led to his expulsion from the house,
Manningham evidently was friendly with Martyne (as was Ben Jonson) and
quotes an anagram by him against his attacker:

> Davis
> Advis.   Judas.
>
> *(Manningham, p. 18)*

Elsewhere the diarist offers his own fond anagram of Martyne's name, which Bruce for some reason omits: "Martyne / myne art" (fol. 27, p. 36) Likewise Bruce omits Manningham's slanderous description of Davies's outlandish appearance and gait—likely the most vivid image of the poet we have, and all the more interesting coming in part from Thomas Overbury the "character"-writer.

> J. Davys goes waddling with his arse out behynd as though he were about to make every one that he meets a wall to pisse against. / B. Rudyard, Th. Overbury / He never walks but he carries a cloke bag behind him, his arse sticks out so farr.
>
> *(fol. 128, p. 168)*

For someone who was in the company of "gay and dissolute benchers" and therefore, according to the accepted notion, a devotee of plays, Manningham reveals, alas, surprisingly little interest in the drama of his time. Shakespeare's plays are the only ones he mentions; and his literary interests, while extensive, run more towards poetry, and most of all towards the sermon, as will be seen below. But two passing remarks by him on drama are worth quoting together for the way they underscore the growing controversy in his time over the moral value of plays. On the one hand, he reports in April 1602 that his friend Dr. Henry Parry, one of the queen's chaplains, "told how his father was Deane of Salisbury, kept a sumptuous house . . . used to have showes at his house, wherein he would have his sonne an actor to embolden him" (p. 52). On the other hand, on December 12, 1602, he quotes from a sermon at St. Clement's by "a plaine plodding fellow" (a Puritan?) who argued that Abraham "was called, therefore every one must [take] upon him some calling and profession, and this calling must be allowed of God; therefore the trade of stageplayers unlawefull" (p. 100). The irony here, of course, is that much of the sermonizing of the time was nothing if not histrionic, and, as we shall see, worshipers like Manningham evaluated a preacher's performance in part in dramatic terms.

II

Manningham's *Diary* has been widely cited by scholars of the Elizabethan sermon; one writer speaks of it as "one of the great sources of information for details concerning preaching"; another calls the diarist "the prince of note takers, whose deft and often remarkably full summaries . . . provide evidence of the breadth of appeal which sermons commanded at that time."[10] Something of his devotion to the art of pulpit oratory can be seen in the fact that during the approximately fifteen months he kept the *Diary*, he recorded notes on fifty-three sermons—sometimes two per Sabbath, often in great detail. One guesses that Manningham's interests were as much critical as pious, but, whatever his motives for churchgoing, no one has left us a more vivid set of impressions of what an Elizabethan sermon was like as delivered and what an educated worshiper expected it to be; and those impressions are worth considering, I think, for what they may reveal about the kind of auditory attention Elizabethans brought to another and indeed rival form of public spectacle, the drama.

With (so to speak) God's plenty of preachers to choose from in London, Manningham apparently strove to sample the field, and he often begins his notes with an impression of the figure a preacher cut in his pulpit, very much as one might comment critically on the style of an actor. One is merely "a plaine plodding fellowe" (p. 100); another is "a blacke fellowe, with a sower looke, but a good spirit, bold, and sometimes bluntly witty" (p. 105); a third seems almost to have stepped straight from the Globe to St. Paul's, with his "long browne beard, a hanging looke, a gloting eye, and a tossing leering jeasture" (p. 104).

Perhaps a law student like Manningham, preparing for a career of pleading and "courtroom drama," would naturally be attentive to a preacher's gestures, elocution, and choice of words; at any rate, he is sharply critical of rhetorical affectations and inadequacies. A preacher should not fail to live up to the rhetorical advantages of the pulpit, but by the same token he should not overdo it. Of a sermon by one Marbury in the Temple, he protests: "I may not write what he said, for I could not heare him, he pronounces in manner of a common discourse. We may streatche our eares to catch a word nowe and then, but he will not be at the paynes to strayne his voyce, that wee might gaine one sentence" (p. 95). One of the queen's own chaplains, Dr. Thompson, speaking at Whitehall after her death, does not escape censure: "He hath a sounding laboured artificiall pronounciation; he regards that soe muche, that his speach hath no more matter than needes in it" (p. 166). Similarly condemned is a young preacher at St. Paul's who "made a finicall boysterous exordium, and rann himselfe out almost drye before he was halfe through" (p. 132).

But Manningham reserves his deepest contempt for the showy gestures of a Dr. Dawson of Cambridge, holding forth at Paul's Cross: "All the while he prayd he kept on his velvet night cap untill he came to name the Queene, and then of went that too, when he had spoken before both of and to God with it on his head" (p. 84). And of a famous Oxford divine who was ostentatiously fond of quotations and of homely speech, he jeers,

> Reynolds esteemes it his best glorie to quote an author for every sentence, nay almost for every syllable; soe he may indeede shewe a great memory but small judgment. Alas, poor man! he does as yf a beggar should come and pouer all his scraps out of his wallet at a rich mans table. . . . He takes

a special grace to use an olde worne out sentence, as though anie would like to be served with cockcrowen pottage, or a man should take delight to have a garment of shreeds.

(pp. 85–86)

Having heard on October 31, 1602, a preacher at Paul's condemn a fashionable brother-divine, Dr. Egerton, for catering to rich ladies and allowing them to parade their finery, Manningham went to see and hear for himself on December 12. His description of Egerton's style—at once disapproving and intrigued —emphasizes how much *ad hoc* drama could attend the ritual of the service, especially when it was held next to a theater!

At Blackfriars—Mr. Egerton, a little church or chappell up stayres, but a great congregacion, specially of women. After "God be merciful," reade after the second lesson, having sat a good tyme before in the pulpit, willing them to sing to the glorie of God and their owne edifying the 66 Psalme 2 part; after he made a good prayer, then turned the glas, and to his text.

(p. 101)

One wonders what Manningham would have made of Donne's pulpit dramas. Certainly he would have approved of his daring command of metaphor; frequently the *Diary*'s shorter reports on sermons consist of little else than lists of the figures the preacher used as he strained to relate heaven and earth—ambitious men are like little children chasing butterflies, honor is like a spider web or a craggy rock, before Christ's intercession on behalf of humanity "was like a man in prison, could not gett forth to sue for pardon," and so forth.

All in all, though Manningham in his critical bent is not given to praising the preachers he heard (not even the famous Launcelot Andrewes and John King), one can surmise that he was looking for sermons like the one he heard his friend Dr. Parry give at Richmond during the queen's last sickness: "It was a very learned, eloquent, religious, and moving sermon" (p. 145). A dramatic presence in the pulpit there should be, evidently, joined with clarity and a heightened use of language—in short, the pulpit rhetorician should be ruled by a dramatic decorum much like what Hamlet urges on the players.

So far I have been discussing the diarist's *impressions* of preachers; but in fact many of his entries are detailed précis of sermons, clearly outlining the structures of the works, and often listing the speakers' subheadings in series of ten items and more. His digest of a sermon by John King at Paul's Cross on

October 24, 1602, covers thirteen pages in the manuscript. How was this done? By feats of memory, by assiduous note-taking, or by means of some form of shorthand like Dr. Timothy Bright's "Charactery"?

No question but that some Elizabethans had incredible powers of memory, perhaps through mnemonic training of the sort described by Francis Yates in *The Art of Memory*. Manningham himself notes that his kinsman and benefactor, Richard Manningham, at age sixty-two could recite verbatim most of the first two books of the *Aeneid* (p. 143). But to memorize on only one hearing whole sermons like King's seems beyond anybody's powers of recall, no matter how well trained. And even if Manningham had mastered the new art of shorthand, it seems not unreasonable to think that the *Diary* would show some evidence of it, but there is none. After all, in a journal kept only for himself, why would he invariably translate his shorthand notes back into intelligible English? I conclude that, probably like many other educated churchgoers who hoped to enrich their command of the language as well as their souls, Manningham came to church prepared to take extensive notes on the sermon, especially on its logical structure, and supplemented this stenography with a very alert memory for the preacher's most crucial and provocative statements. In other words, his practice was roughly that of a college student taking notes of a lecture course—recording the outline of the lecture and registering, less faithfully, the wording of the professor's bon mots and pithy assertions.[11]

As luck would have it, at least one sermon Manningham recorded in detail was subsequently printed, allowing us to test these conclusions. On June 20, 1602, Robert Wakeman of Balliol College preached on Jonah at Paul's. When the sermon was printed in 1606, Wakeman justified himself on the grounds that "many copies of it, as they were taken by note, are scattered abroad in London and elsewhere" in "unperfect" form. He goes on to declare that the printed text is faithful to the sermon as originally written and delivered— "not adding, or detracting, any one worde in the whole"—even to the extent of sharply condensing the second half of the original text just as he was forced to do in the cathedral because of a severe storm.[12] Now one might well suspect such a claim, on the grounds that the printed text of a celebrated sermon could be made to sell better if it were claimed to be wholly authentic, whether it was or not. Most Elizabethan preachers, in fact, seem to have spoken from notes, not written texts.[13] But there is such a consistent agreement both of ordering and of wording between Wakeman's text and Manningham's précis that the former's claim really does appear to be honest.

Manningham begins his entry with an exact point-by-point outline of the sermon, suggesting, I think, that the preacher himself offered some sort of prefatory synopsis, as he does index-fashion at the beginning of the printed text. When, early in the sermon, Wakeman discourses on St. Bernard's condemnation of divines who are *non correptores sed corrosores* and goes on to refer to Pliny's tale of dog-headed Indians who bark instead of speaking as a metaphor illustrative of this vice, Manningham records the gist of the quotations exactly. And when the preacher turns to censure flattering and time-saving ministers, who "sow pillowes under men's elbowes," likening them to the sun-following flower *Heliotropium*, Manningham records:

> But as he misliked those sharpe biters, soe must he neede speake against such preachers as flatter greate men, and sowe cushions under their elbowes. They are like Heliotropium. . . .
>
> *(p. 37)*

Having denounced these preachers for using "soft and silken words," Wakeman compares their behavior to the sinuous course of the river Jordan—"so do these time-serving preachers turne and winde themselves in their sermons to the multitude." Manningham, reversing this order (as one might do when drawing on memory as well as on notes), writes that they are "like the river Jordan, turnes and windes every way; speake nothing but silken wordes . . ." (p. 38).

Turning to Jonah's sermon to the city of Nineveh, warning of its destruction, Wakeman humbly questions St. Augustine's interpretation that the city itself is not meant but rather the sins of the people, arguing instead that Jonah's words have "a condition implied in them, as if he had said: 'The Lord your God is a patient God, he will not wound you before he warne you.'" Yet, the text continues, "the longer the Lorde heareth and forebeareth to punish the sins of men, the heavier will his punishment be in the end." Manningham's digest runs:

> Nineveh, as St. Augustine in his booke *De Civitate Dei*, signifieth not the citie but the synns of the people; and soe the prophecy verryfied, for that synn was destroyed by their repentaunce with in 40 dayes. But he rather inclined to expound it by way of an implyed condicion, that they should be overthrowen unles they repented . . . God is slowe in punishing, yet *tarditas poenoe gravitate pensature.* . . .
>
> *(p. 38)*

At this point, just as he is drawing dire parallels between Nineveh and London and preparing to move from the first half of his outline—Jonah's sermon

—into the second half, on the circumstances of Nineveh's repentance, Wakeman acknowledges the "sodainely unseasonable" weather and promises to abridge his text. And at just this point, without referring to the Nineveh-London equation or the storm, Manningham ends his notes—fleeing, it seems clear, an equinoctial London downpour! His enthusiasm for listening to sermons must not have been dampened, however, for that same afternoon, close to home in the Temple Church, he took notes on a preachment by Dr. Buckridge.

Obviously it would be rash to erect a whole theory about the way in which Elizabethans listened to sermons on this one set of preacher's text and worshiper's notes; perhaps other sets can be found. But in these details of Manningham's method of following one sermon, as in his entries on pulpit oratory generally, I think we can grasp a little more firmly the really extraordinary appetite of educated people in Shakespeare's time for all the public uses of language, something of their consuming interest in the way men—lawyers, divines, actors—rose dramatically to their public occasions. Through acquaintance with such documents, we are better able, perhaps, to inquire how writers like Shakespeare might have been influenced in their use of language by having auditors at least as rhetorically alert as Manningham.

III

All told, Bruce excised, not always with acknowledgment, about forty-five passages from the *Diary*, most of them to some degree off-color. It would be an act of extreme smugness to restore them all simply because a Victorian editor once took them out. In the following partial restoration, I have tried to include entries that seem to have real historical, cultural, or linguistic significance, in addition to what they can tell us about that delicious and still uncharted subject, the Elizabethan taste for dirty jokes and bawdry. Actually, coming from a law student in his twenties, Manningham's bawdy stories seem rather tame, even childish. It would be imprudent to flatly reject the going assumptions about the high state of sexual sophistication and dissoluteness of Inns of Court men on the basis of this sampling alone, but the possibility does seem more cogent, I think, that their worldliness has been overestimated, if the *Diary* is any index. (In the following listing, the first pagination refers to the manuscript, the second to the page in Bruce's edition where the passage should appear.)

> *fol. 2, p. 2: n.d.*
> on Luce Morgan
> I say that Luce's bodie's chast
> Downe from hir head unto hir wast,

But to hir wast up from hir thyes
Whoe says she's chast I say he lyes.

fol. 9, p. 11: n.d.
Offer noe Love nights, but lett your wife still seeke them,
For when they come unsought they seldome like them.

fol. 12, p. 16: Jan. 1601/2
Rashness ridiculous / One had fouled his finger with [stercorem?], and
would have shaken it off in great haste but in his haste he stroke his
finger against a bord, and then as many use in such cases, forgetting
where his finger had bin, clapt it presently in his mouth to have easd the
payne. Mr. Danvers

fol. 12, p. 17: Jan. 26, 1601/2
They say London stones are proud, but I made them kisse myne arse, q.
the country man when he had a falle.

fol. 25, p. 34: June 7, 1602
Where is your husband said Mr. Reems to a girl. He is a building said shee.
The worse luck for you q. hee a bilding in [Wiltsh?] signifies a male with
one stone. Ch. Da.
   [The bracketed word, though clearly specifying a language or region,
   is indistinct in the text. I have not found *bilding* in any dictionary;
   gelding, of course, is close. *Hilding* formerly denoted a poor horse
   of either sex; *OED* has *bilder*, "a kind of horse, a nag."]

fol. 25, p. 35: June 9, 1602
Georgius Savile
Egregious vile ass
   [It seems impossible to determine which member of the numerous
   Savile family this anagram points to—possibly Sir George, Sheriff
   of Yorkshire, who died in 1622.]

fol. 27, p. 36: June 15, 1602
Lahy doth keepe his sister and his whore
Lahus doth keepe his sister and noe more. G.M.

fol. 30, p. 39: March 11, 1601/2
Sergeant Yelverton and Serg. Heale being upon a tyme in the companie of
gent. [women] which were merrly disposed Yelverton began to take exception against Heale that he went not oftner then once by the year to pay
his wife hir duty. Heale said that the gentlewomen were fittest judges in

this controversie, and therefore he would but put the case and refer it to them. If a man be to pay you a good round summe whether had you rather receive it by dribbles or the whole togither. After the gent. had strayn'd courtesie who should breake silence at last one of them made him this answer, Lett me be paid as I neede it. Mr. Ed. Curle

> [This jest, definitely from Edward Curle, smacks in its language and substance of the bawdy tale about Shakespeare; I conjecture that the diarist got both from his roommate.]

fol. 44, p. 59: Oct. 11, 1602

At Guildhall once long since Sergt. Heale went to move a cause which he said was betwixt the cuckold and the cuckold maker, but his client was the honester man for he came to prove himselfe the cuckold. His mayd in hir answers to my Lord upon his examination said still, And it like you my Worship.

fol. 44, p. 60: Oct. 10, 1602

Mr. Tanfield speaking of a knave and his queene said he was a little to inward with hir.

fol. 44, p. 61: Oct. 12, 1602

[On the earl of Sussex] It is conjectured that Captain Whitlocke, like a base pander, hath incited the Earl to followe his sensuall humour, by preferring strange flesh before his owne, as he did the Earl of Rutland. . . . I would be loath to come after him to a wench for feare of the pox, sd. Mr. Curl of E. of Sus.

> [Here Manningham records some choice current gossip about one of the decade's chief scandals. The unfortunate lady, Bridget, was a patron of Robert Greene, among others. Capt. Whitlocke's career as a rogue and instigator of strife continued into James's reign; he was at first a chief suspect in the Gunpowder Plot. His other victim mentioned, the earl of Rutland, was Roger Manners, fifth earl; *his* rejected wife was none other than Elizabeth, Sir Philip Sidney's daughter.]

fol. 45, pp. 61–62: Oct. 1, 1602

[Bruce transcribes a few lines of and comments on Samuel Rowland's Chaucerian poem, *Tis Merry When Gossips Meet*,[14] but then omits twenty additional lines jotted down by Manningham as he read through the poem—some of them, like the following, mildly risqué:]

> She ply'd him with the wine in golden cup,
> Turning the liquor in, the bottom up. [of Dido and Aeneas]

Wine and virginity kept stale drink flatt.

Taurus so rules and guides your husbandes heads
That every night they sleepe in hornework cap.

I know tis better to take wrong than do it
But yet in such a case flesh leades us to it.

[Rowland's poem was published in 1602, and Manningham seems to have copied quite carefully from the printed text, apparently adding to his growing store of bawdy quips and trifles.]

fol. 57, p. 77: Nov. 5, 1602

One said Nel [Freingeham?] kisseth like a neetes foote, she turns him inside out. [Franklin]

fol. 57, p. 77: Nov. 5, 1602

Ch. Danvers told me he would tell me a jest how that a young gent. after long suit having obtained a gent. woman the first night they were married after he had performed his duty and taken that he soe long had longed for, And is this all, said he, I so much desyred: fayth I wish I were un-married again. And is this all your *wo.* she said, fayth you might have kept to your selfe.

fol. 59, p. 81: Nov. 6, 1602

Mrs. T. because hir brother would have crost hir lascivious love toward hir man H. shee would have practiced to hang him for a thief had not Mr. S. professed the contrary. So violent and unnaturall a womans malice. Hir owne daughter knowes her *luxurio quam incaute quam inepte quam indigne.*

fol. 60, p. 83: Nov. 12, 1602

The callender of women saynts was full long agoe. There are fewe nowe that will not yield to opportunity yf they be importuned.

fol. 71, p. 92: Nov. 27, 1602

A wenching gent. desirous to put an opinion on some that he spent his tyme well: told them he laid close and did nothing but look on his booke. One told him, that his booke was a fayre volume, but it had but two leaves (legs) to open, and he was a bad scholler could doe nothing without his fescue (: his *p.*)

[A fescue was a rod or pointer used for teaching children their letters. This usage and most of Manningham's other bawdy euphemisms are not recorded in Partridge's *Shakespeare's Bawdy* and similar glos-saries; the subject deserves more attention.]

fol. 75, p. 98: Dec. 7, 1602

Mr. Irving held while he was reader at Paules that yf a man and his wife lye together after either of them knowes the other hath committed adultery, this is adultery in them. Mr. Colebrand.

fol. 98, p. 129: Feb. 8, 1602/3

One told Toplife that he could tell him of papists that frequented mass: and would bring him where he could take them at it: but he brought him where he took a gent. in bed with his daughter at it. (Ch. Danvers)

fol. 98, p. 130: Feb. 9, 1602/3

I offered Mr. Kedgwyn as being myne auncient in the house to sit before me. He rose with this phrase, Nay, I regard not men as women doe, for their standing.

fol. 98, p. 130: Feb. 8, 1602/3

One told Sergt. Harrys howe many there were nowe prikt sergaunts. Would I were now prikt to q. he it would be better for my wife then.

fol. 104, p. 138: Feb. 28, 1602/3

A whore is noe worse than a catt: for shee plays with hir tayle / and the whore dost noe more: / one in the tiltboat as I came from London

> [The tiltboat was a capacious wherry with a "tilt" or awning, plying chiefly from London to Gravesend—OED]

fol. 109, p. 145: June 8, 1603

My cosen told me the strange manner of the wolves in their generation. The bitche when she growes proud gathers a companie of the dogs togither, and runnes before them so long, that having tyred them and her self, she lyeth down, and they fall asleepe about hir, then she rises alone and singles out one which she likes best, and he does the deede, but instantly after all the rest fall upon him, and teare him in pieces for it. Observe: the wolfe dyes with getting his young, as the viper doth by bearing hir young ones. An old man that kills himselfe to get a child.

fol. 118, p. 156: March 31, 1603

Two were going to washe them selves, one spies the other properties discovered, I pray you be covered, q. he.

fol. 118, p. 156: March 31, 1603

A wench complained that she was ravished in a chamber, and being asked how chaunced she cryed not, why there were some in the next roome said shee, and they would have heard mee. An other said she could not cry for laughing. Mr. Howe.

Manningham's fondness for such wretched stories seems to lessen as the *Diary* progresses into the momentous year of 1603; more and more his entries reflect concern over the old queen's decline and the state and future of the realm. His accounts of Elizabeth's last days and death are as vivid and soberly affecting as any we have; most of their details seem to have come firsthand from Dr. Henry Parry, who was praying with her when she died.

> This morning about three at clocke hir Majestie departed this lyfe, mildly like a lambe, easily like a ripe apple from the tree, *cum leve quadam febre, absque gemitu.* Dr. Parry told me that he was present, and sent his prayers before hir soule; and I doubt not but she is amongst the royall saints in Heaven in eternall joyes. . . .

> The proclamacion [of James' succession] was heard with greate expectacion and silent joye, noe great shouting. I thinke the sorrow for hir Majesties departure was soe deep in many hearts they could not soe suddenly showe anie great joye, though it could not be lesse then exceeding for the succession of soe worthy a king. And at night they showed it by bonefires, and ringing. Noe tumult, noe contradiction, noe disorder in the city; every man went about his busines, as readylie, as peacably, as securely, as though there had bin noe change, nor any newes ever heard of competitors. God be thanked, our king hath his right! *Magna veritas et prevalet.*
>
> (pp. 146–47)

Bawdy stories and gossip in close alternation with detailed criticism of sermons, sober citations of apothegms, and eloquent accounts like these of the end of an era and the beginning of a new—the composite image of Manningham in his *Diary* is an appealing and plausibly human one, and his rather unstructured, unwitty, low-level but acute perspective on the times is of considerable value and deserves to be better known. Certainly no one formulating a theory about the literary public in Shakespeare's heyday, especially that important segment identified with the Inns of Court, can afford not to test his theory against Manningham's ordinary and, I think, representative point of view. The pleasure and the special value of the *Diary* lie in just that, its ordinariness—the way the trivial and the momentous, the everyday and the consequential, come together in its entries. Nothing is more typical of Manningham's outlook, and nothing could be more revealing of how a patriotic but uneasy common Londoner viewed the approach of his new monarch from the North, than this note on March 27, 1603, three days after the old queen's death:

I saw this afternoon a Scottishe Lady at Mr. Fleetes in Loathesbury; she was sister to Earl Gowre, a gallant tale gent., somewhat long visage, a lisping fumbling language.

(p. 154)

Signs of the time: in such telling small manifestations and responses, rarely recorded, do new ages begin.

Notes:

1. Harleian 5353. I am grateful to the British Museum, especially to its Photographic Service, for providing a photocopy of the *Diary* and to the University of Rochester Library for commissioning the photocopy.

2. John Bruce, preface to *The Diary of John Manningham*, Camden Society First Series No. 99 (Westminster, 1868), pp. xvi–xvii.

3. Among the numerous writers who accept the stereotype and allow it to color their interpretations of Shakespeare's plays, see O. J. Campbell, *Comicall Satyre and Shakespeare's "Troilus and Cressida"* (San Marino, 1938); Peter Alexander, "Troilus and Cressida, 1609," *The Library*, 4th Ser., 60 (1928–29), 278 ff.; Leslie Hotson, *Shakespeare's Sonnets Dated* (New York, 1949). In "The Provenance of *Troilus and Cressida*," *SQ*, 21 (1970), 223–40, I offer reasons for rejecting the Inns of Court theory of the play's origins and discuss the critical consequences of accepting it.

4. Sydney Race, "Manningham's Diary: The Case for Re-examination," *N&Q*, 199 (1954), 380–83.

5. *Middle Temple Records*, Vol. I, ed. Charles H. Hopwood (London, 1905), p. 418.

6. The identification has been made by G. B. Harrison in a note for his complete edition of Shakespeare (New York, 1952), p. 875.

7. Middle Temple Records, II, 382.

8. R. E. Bennett, "John Manningham and Donne's *Paradoxes*," *MLN*, 46 (1931), 309 ff.; W. Milgate, "The Early Reference to Donne," *N&Q*, 195 (1950), p. 229.

9. Several writers have doubted the authenticity of the story, but in *N&Q*, 202 (1957), pp. 243–44, Gladys Jenkins confirms that Alderman John More indeed had a Spanish stepdaughter, one Mary Perez, who would have been twenty-two (and marriageably wealthy!) when Marston met her at the Christmas dance.

10. W. Fraser Mitchell, *English Pulpit Oratory from Andrewes to Tillotson* (London, 1932), p. 36; Millar Maclure, *The Paul's Cross Sermons 1534–1642* (Toronto, 1958), p. 144.

11. Another late-Elizabethan diarist, Lady Margaret Hoby, seems to have used the same recording methods when, in London during the winter of 1600–1601, she attended sermons by some of Manningham's preachers, including the ladies' favorite, Egerton. On Nov. 30 she writes: "After privat praier, I went to the Minster, wher I hard a good sarmon by one of the prebendes: after I was come home and had dined, I went to the blake friers, from whence I returned hom and set downe in my testement the chieffe notes delivered by Mr. Egertone." Unfor-

tunately her notes are not extant. *The Diary of Lady Margaret Hoby 1599–1605,* ed. Dorothy M. Meads (Boston and New York, 1930), p. 49.

Further, in his *Autobiography,* Sir Simonds D'Ewes tells how, as a fourteen-year-old scholar in 1616, he was directed at school "to take notes in writing at sermons, and so to become a rational hearer; whereas before, I differed little from the brute creatures that were in the Church with me, never regarding or observing any part of Divine Service." Evidently to this end young D'Ewes devised a rudimentary shorthand which, as a grown man, he was still using. *The Autobiography and Correspondence of Sir Simonds D'Ewes, Bart.,* ed. J. O. Halliwell (London, 1845), I, 84.

12. Robert Wakeman, *Jonahs Sermon and Ninevehs Repentance* (London, 1606).

13. Alan F. Herr, *The Elizabethan Sermon: A Survey and a Bibliography* (Philadelphia, 1940), p. 82.

14. In *The Complete Works of Samuel Rowlands,* Vol. I (Glasgow, 1880), 11 ff.

Structure in Shakespearean Tragedy

J. Leeds Barroll

Among the many generalizations which can be helpful in differentiating the various approaches to "tragedy" throughout the history of literature, inquiries into the concept of tragic structure would seem to be one useful kind of formulation. In the case of Shakespeare, this kind of discussion would seem to be an especially important consideration, because if we can evolve useful statements about the subject of "tragedy," taken in itself, we can perhaps clarify our understanding of other aspects of his formidable creative outflow. The problem, however, is that we are never quite certain of what we mean when we speak of "tragic structure" or "tragic form." Even though the concept itself has been the subject of numerous essays and books on Shakespeare, discussions about the matter so often modulate into speculations on the sociological question of "the tragic in life" or of man's "sense of the tragic" that, as laudable and as important as such musings may be, they are too seductively successful in drawing our attention away from the main question.

I

"Tragedy," we may assume, is in some sense a process (a "sequence"? of what?). This process presumably differs from another kind of process which we are in the habit of calling "comedy." From this point, our own dialectic may most usefully proceed in the form of commentary on a popular line of reasoning illustrated by the writing of Willard Farnham upon the subject.

> Finally, Gothic tragedy is in nothing more patently different from Greek tragedy than in the structural forms evolved for its own peculiar purposes and given most subtle fitness for those purposes by Shakespeare. The two tragic arts may far more readily be united upon some general technical principle of function, even the purgation of pity and fear, than upon some general technical principle of unity.
>
> In its nondramatic beginnings the tragedy of Christian Europe finds that what it has to say often falls by nature into a biographic form. In stories of ambitious human careers notable for the violent contrast of their rise and fall it finds that the full blow to a mortal pride involving attachment to the world and its transitory prizes is best delivered by recording both rise and fall with circumstantiality and making them equally vivid to the reader. Never far from the mind of author or reader

is the figure of Fortune and her wheel. Frequently Boccaccio and his followers in *De Casibus* story quite obviously think of the scope of tragedy as the whole round of Fortune's wheel—the subject's attachment to the ascending side and his climbing thereby, his perilous enthronement after the ascent (emphasized as the turning-point of the tragedy), his decline upon and final precipitation from the descending side. The full untrammeled sweep of this biographic form is often seen in Elizabethan tragic drama, sometimes with the simplest ascetic implication to be found in *De Casibus* narrative. Shakespeare eventually takes the tragedy of ascent and descent into the realm of supreme art.

In two of the four tragedies which have been commonly accepted as embodying his genius at its highest, Shakespeare builds a pyramid of rise and fall and balances its sides with delicacy and exactitude. They are, of course, *Hamlet* and *Macbeth*. If *Antony and Cleopatra* is to be made a fifth in the roll of honor, it must be grouped with *Hamlet* and *Macbeth* as another example of the same structural principle. Each of the three plays has a protagonist who is driven by an ambition or by a powerful impulsion toward some highly difficult accomplishment in a theater of worldly action. He aspires toward his desire and climbs step after step of ascent through almost exactly half the play. . . . The end is ruin and death accomplished through the gathered momentum of his fall. In the outline of the pyramid one may see the round of Fortune's wheel with a difference. For in these plays Shakespeare is certainly not occupied with any such wholly mysterious tragic reversal as might be attributed to the averting of Fortune's face. . . . He partly gives the reversal a grimly logical causation—as we look back we can see that it was being prepared for in the ascending action—and never for a moment does he allow to the tragically aspiring spirit a sense of complete achievement.[1]

The passage has been quoted at some length to illustrate the typical development of this popular line of thought which, in Mr. Farnham's study, has been preceded by such an extensive survey of the "Fortune" motif both in Boccaccio and in the *Mirrour for Magistrates* that the survey itself tends to lend historical validity to the author's otherwise purely critical remarks. For this reason, it is important to review these concepts of Fortune, if Farnham's tracing of a *De Casibus* tradition through Boccaccio and the *Mirrour* does have some relevance to the development of tragedy, to determine whether they indeed do inevitably lead to such a theory as Farnham has promulgated. Elsewhere he has observed that "Poets, theologians, and all manner of men in the Middle Ages were to picture Fortune's feminine whimsicality, revile her ways, dispute with her as they would dispute with the inexplicability of life itself. They

were to create the image of Fortune's wheel and imagine Fortune as governing the round of worldly routine, elevating men to the 'sweet fruition of an
earthly crown' and casting them down into ruin, all without reason" (p. 29).
Gradually, says Farnham, they penetrated her realm and took much of it away,
transferring what they had won from her rule to the rule of justice. The
history of Fortune in the "Gothic world" includes the history of her enfeeble-
ment by "a new order of philosophic unity," a new explanation of the world.
And as Fortune was deposed, "the Gothic spirit" discovered that "heroic
misfortunes" were not to be merely bewailed as inexplicable falls from high
to low degree, but were to be plotted with the subtlety of tragic poesy. Yet the
Gothic spirit continued to "pay lip service" to Fortune even as it learned to
cast off her yoke. Fortune had to be subdued "before the Shakespearean
tragedy which issues out of human character could be created."

If we accept this version of the development of tragic theory throughout
the Middle Ages and into the Renaissance, we do, of course, come to the concept of any Shakespearean tragic process with a number of assumptions having to do with the inherent nature of an age-old process. It seems well, therefore,
to briefly revisit the scenes from which such theorizing has been derived to
determine whether there is historical validity in Farnham's reasoning and,
further, to determine how much the concepts of "elevation" and "casting
down" have to do with the process of Shakespearean tragedy itself. From the
historical point of view, we must recall, in the first place, that when we speak
of "Fortune" we allude to a rather ancient concept which shades into a number of distinctions. Vincenzo Cioffari has traced the role of the concept in
Aristotelian thought, reminding us of the philosopher's definition in the
Nicomachean Ethics of the "goods of Fortune" as being wealth, political
power, friends, beauty, good birth, and good children. This position was subsequently to appear in the Stoic views.[2] Then, to simplify, the Christian position,
as represented by Augustine, was that fortune did not exist at all except as an
aspect of divine Providence. This was a position reinforced by other writers
who themselves also referred back to Aristotle for general authoritative justification. Boethius also utilized Aristotle's distinction concerning the "goods"
of Fortune. The consistency of this tradition may be noted when we observe
that these distinctions were preserved by Aquinas, who himself adduced not
only Boethius but also Aristotle's *Magna Moralia* to make the point.[3]

In the early Renaissance, we observe the continuity of this mode of thought
in the remarks of Ludovico Vives, who speaks of the "gyftes of fortune, or
of body" and adopts the Senecan position espoused by Boethius that such
goods are merely lent to men, who must therefore expect to have them taken
away. Sir Thomas Elyot covers these same points, as does Erasmus, whose
summary will be useful here to illustrate the general point.

A mans owne maners doe shape him his fortune. Men commonlie when anie aduersitie chaunce, accuse fortune, or when they see other men to prospere well in theyr matters, they say it is theyr fortune. So they key all together vpon fortune, thinking there is such a thing called Fortune that ruleth all. But surely they are highlie deceiued. It is theire owne maners, their own qualities, touches, condicions, & procedinges that shape them this fortune, that is to say, that cause them, eyther to be sette forwarde or backeward, either to prospere or not to prospere.[4]

Vives, Elyot, and Erasmus, of course, all wrote prior to the printing of the *Mirrour for Magistrates*, and they were joined in their views by Palingenius, Calvin, and William Baldwin, who himself was to assume primary responsibility for the production of the *Mirrour for Magistrates*. Thus, when later figures such as Bodin, Francis Bacon, and Gentillet took the same line, they were not necessarily representing new movements of skeptical thought; rather, they were writing in a climate of opinion shared by Philemon Holland when he commented on his translation of Plutarch's *Moralia*, especially on Plutarch's essay on divine justice. Some contemporaries who shared these views were such diverse figures as La Primaudaye, John Norden, Jeremias Bastingius, Philip de Mornay, Guillaume de la Perrière, Gui du Faur as translated by Joshua Sylvester, Sir William Cornwallis, Vincenzo Cartari, I. Boissard, R. Niccols, and Du Bartas.[5]

If the *Mirrour for Magistrates* itself is then to be regarded as a *locus* for an early Renaissance subscription to some concept of "blind fortune," no matter the ubiquity of other concepts as seen in the foregoing thinkers to whom we have alluded, we should take warning, before resting in this position, from the fact that even as early as the 1559 edition of the *Mirrour*, not only is there lacking any reasoned exposition of a "fatalistic" attitude in any of the "tragedies" contained therein, but there are also three of them which approach the concept of Fortune in terms consonant with those views which we have been examining. Lord Mowbray notes of Fortune that "She gydeth goods, she hampreth not the harte," while Henry Percy, Earl of Northumberland, quotes "Morall Senec" and his view about fortune as pertaining to "worldly welth." Jack Cade, in fact, offers an extremely full and traditional exposition lasting for forty-two lines, the nucleus of which is that

> Skyl is not weake, but wyl strong, flesh is soft
> And yeldes it selfe to pleasure that it loueth,
> And hales the mynde to that it most reproueth.

"Now if this happe wherby we yelde our mynde / To lust and wyll, be fortune, as we name her, / Than is she iustly called false and blynde, / And no reproche can be to much to blame her"

> Yet is the shame our owne when so we shame her,
> For sure this hap if it be rightly knowen,
> Cummeth of our selves, and so the blame our owne.

It is interesting that this lengthy exposition which distinguishes the concept of "fortune" from the concept of the will is full enough for Baldwin, the interlocutor, to comment afterwards, "Howe notably and Philosopher like hath he discrybed Fortune and the causes of worldly cumbraunce."

In the 1563 edition, published a year before Shakespeare was christened, we can also observe that Lord Hastings in his tragedy devotes three stanzas to the idea that "A heathen god they hold, whoe fortune keepe."[6] In the 1575 edition, Irenglas also expends three stanzas urging the reader: "Let vs not then complayne of Fortunes skill: / For all our good, descendes from goddes good will," and Guidericus in the 1578 edition concludes on the same note. In the 1587 edition, we hear from Bladud and from Claudius Tiberius Nero that Fortune is the situation into which the worldly throw themselves out of human blindness, while Sir Nicholas Burdet devotes three stanzas to an elaboration on the point that "God sends to euery sorte these tempests sad"; "Fortune," in these circumstances simply is a form of expression[7]—an observation that historians of the drama might do well to consider, as they also study Renaissance theories of rhetorical embellishment.

With this background, we will not be overly surprised then if we observe motifs in such a drama as Dekker's *Old Fortunatus* whereby Fortune, though awarded the dominion of the world, must itself yield to Virtue, or if we note Gonzago in Marston's *Fawne* saying that "vertue & wisedom are not fortunes giftes." In Garnier's *Cornelia*, as translated by Thomas Kyd, the Chorus to the second act observes that "All fortunes" depend upon the "will of Heauen," while Sir Thomas More, to adduce another sampling, enters his play stating that

> It is in heaven that I am thus and thus
> And that w[ch] we prophanlie term o[r] fortuns
> Is the provision of the power aboue
> fitted and shapte Iust to that strength of nature
> w[ch] we are borne.[8]

If the general theory seems clear enough, as well as a widespread subscription to and understanding of it not only in the dramatists but in the
authors of the *Mirrour*, one might nevertheless argue that the use of the
figure of "Lady Fortune" would seem to show quite a different viewpoint. Lady
Fortune, however, was not so much a concept as a literary device used in
several ways to make a general ethical point by transcendentalist approaches
to the problem of causation and responsibility in those human affairs about
which it was argued that God refrained from exerting any special aspect of his
general providential plan for mankind. The pagan cult of the goddess and some
of the traditional imagery surrounding her have, of course, been extensively
discussed by H. R. Patch, cited by many but read by few. In the late medieval
and early Renaissance context, however, the figure of Fortune, especially with
her "Wheel," was not nearly so profound or widespread a concept as it has
been assumed and did not affect later theories of dramatic structure in any
profound way.[9] In fact, it is very important to note that it was not the "Wheel"
at all which was the salient metaphorical device illustrating the role of Fortune;
rather, we must pay attention to a much more important visualization, that
presented by the *Tabula* of Cebes.

"Cebes the Theban" figures in Plato's dialogues and was thus said to have
been a pupil of Socrates, having been, in the *Phaedo*, present at his death. The
Tabula, which is now regarded as a product of Roman Stoical thought, was
attributed to this shadowy figure, and this *Table of Cebes* appeared variously
and copiously throughout the Renaissance,[10] the most elaborate, and possibly
the earliest depiction of interest to us being a woodcut executed by Hans Holbein the Younger. This woodcut was first used, significantly, for a Latin
edition of the New Testament by Erasmus in 1521; it appears subsequently
in various other works.[11]

It is well to recall the plan of this *Table*, for which the British Museum
Catalogue lists more than forty different editions in six different languages
before 1600 alone. If we are prone to think of Fortune and her wheel either
as aesthetically definitive of a quasi-modern Stoicism or as symbolic of a
vestigial organization from which Elizabethan tragedy took its shape, rec-
ollection of the *Table* is especially useful. It presents three concentric rings
of walls, each of which surrounds a park. The ethic of the plan is that
according to which the outside parks are places of false and seductive pleasures
distracting the mind from the inmost circle wherein truth is to be found. Various figures people the outside parks, including two contrasting women.
One of them "stands vpon that round stone, seeming as though shee were
blinde, and carrying a semblance of madnesse in her gesture." This is Fortune,
whose blindness "is not single, but accompanied with madnesse, and deaf-

An undated oil depicting the *Table of Cebes*.

nesse." She wanders about, taking from this person, giving to another, eventually taking back what she has just given and bestowing it upon still a third person "without all reason and constancie." She is depicted as standing upon a round stone because "her gifts are neuer secure nor certaine. For hee that buildeth vpon them, shall bee sure one day to pay deerely for his credulity." Furthermore, the people to whom Fortune is busy bestowing her gifts have a collective name. They are "Fooles": the laughing fools are Fortune's favorites, while those who are wailing and wringing their hands are those from whom Fortune has taken back the gifts which she had previously bestowed upon them.

The gifts themselves are termed *"Reputed goods"*: they are riches, nobility, children, glory, sovereignty, empire, "and such like." If a man manages to ignore such gifts and this woman as well as the other attendant evils in the pageant of this life within these outer circles, he can, with the aid of Confidence and Fortitude, make his way to encounter that other woman, a modest figure "standing vppon a stone not round but cubike, and directly square." Her name is Instruction; her handmaids are Truth and Persuasion. Instruction stands upon a fixed cubic stone to show that the path leading to her is fair and firm and that her gifts "doe blesse the receiuer with fruits of security," for she gives confidence, security, and *"Acquittance from troubles."*

When a man has successfully learned from Instruction, he is then in the position of attaining to the inmost circle. This circle is filled with the figures of women representing in general the Aristotelian virtues. Thus the *Table of Cebes* reinforces the usual prose statements about Fortune by showing Fortune as the agency which dispenses the Aristotelian external goods, the acquisition of which does not depend upon virtue. The roundness of the stone obviously represents the uncertainty of chance in contrast with the constant and firm square that virtue represents.

The relevance of the *wheel* to all this is a complex one. In a sense, Christian historiography would deny cyclical theorizings about life, even though the poets themselves could allude to the metaphor of a Fortune turning a wheel. At the same time, Boethius, who seems to have been largely responsible for the spread of that conceptual innovation according to which Fortune turns a wheel instead of being upon it herself, will not allow the goddess any ultimate power. Hence, as Patch has observed, one must differentiate among visual traditions. Even Lydgate, who translated Boccaccio's *De Casibus*, observes that Fortune "turneth as a bal," and if the authors of the *Mirrour* chose to follow the wheel of Boethius, they may have done so bearing in mind his own ethical context.[12]

Barnabe Barnes sums up one intellectual attitude towards the general idea of the "wheel" in the Renaissance, for in his *Four Bookes of Offices* he alludes to the "harmonious consent or concordance" of Temperance, Prudence, Justice, and Fortitude by the following long parenthesis, in which he further describes what he intends by this "consent" or "concordance." It is an entity

> whose ground in vnison consisteth of a *medium*, which is the moderator or nauel-string of this vnspeakeable musicke, representing the concealed and misticall accord of the numberlesse starres and planets continuing by the ineffable power of the most Almightie God in number and Symphonie; by which sacred force he worketh his will in all creatures: from fatall influence of which diuine torches of light, by the most miraculous power of the most mightie mouer, all worldly chaunces happen; which some not well aduised haue called the wheele of fortune.

James I also points a way to our understanding of the difference between metaphor and that which is represented by a wheel when he tells us to read histories because

> ye shall learne experience by Theorick, applying the by-past things to the present estate, *quia nihil novum sub sole:* suche is the continuall volubility of things earthlie, according to the roundnesse of the worlde, and revolution of the heauenly circles: which is expressed by the wheeles in Ezechiels visions, and counterfaited by the Poets *in rota Fortuna.*[13]

The reference to Ezekiel is itself no innovation, for Calvin took Ezekiel's wheel as a symbol of Fortune as did Thomas Wilson and others; we should bear in mind, however, that they assumed such a "wheel" to represent mutability in general, not some goddess. Spenser does, of course, later place Mutability in its correct position, subordinate to God.[14]

Thus, on the whole, when characters in Renaissance dramas complain about Fortune, we cannot assume that this reveals necessarily fatalistic proclivities in the authors of those dramas. Dod (sig. G7) is to the point when he observes that God's providence and wisdom are abused "when one frets, and speakes grudgingly against Gods worke, vnder the name of fortune, and chaunce: Oh what ill luck was that? what misfortune." As Montaigne put it (I. 35): "those exceed all follie, (forsomuch as impietie is joyned unto it) that will wreake themselves against God, or fortune, as if she had eares subject to our batterie. . . . But we shall never raile enough against the disorder and unrulinesse of our minde."

It is, of course, difficult to state flatly that characters in a drama who rail against Fortune are not to be taken as speaking for the author, for where is the proof? Nevertheless, as far as Shakespeare is concerned, we should view with interest the identity of those of his figures who state that "all is but Fortune." One is the drunken Stephano in *The Tempest*; the other is Malvolio before he finds the "letter" from Olivia in *Twelfth Night*: " 'Tis but Fortune, all is fortune" (1039).[15] Yet in the former case, Stephano becomes subject to the quasi-providential overseeing of Prospero, while Malvolio, too, moves in a somewhat more regulated universe whose particular (comic) causations may be attributable, not to Fortune, but to Maria.

Shakespeare's own specific frame of reference in these respects is perhaps best suggested by the conversation of Fluellen with Pistol, the former a somewhat pedantic moralizer, the latter a retailer of poetic tritenesses and bombasts.

> *Pist.* *Bardolph*, a Souldier firme and sound of heart,
>   and of buxome valour, hath by cruell Fate,
>   and giddie Fortunes furious fickle Wheele,
>   that Goddesse blind,
>   that stands upon the rolling restlesse Stone.
> *Flu.* By your patience, aunchient Pistoll:
>   Fortune is painted blinde, with a Muffler afore
>   his eyes, to signifie to you, that Fortune is blinde;
>   and shee is painted also with a Wheele, to signifie
>   to you, which is the Morall of it, that shee is
>   turning and inconstant, and mutabilitie, and
>   variation: and her foot, looke you, is fixed upon
>   a Sphericall Stone, which rowles, and rowles, and
>   rowles: in good truth, the Poet makes a most
>   excellent description of it: Fortune is an excellent
>   Morall.
>
> *(1475–87)*

We may, trying manfully, gather that the *Table of Cebes* is the basic concept here. The wheel, however, is alluded to, and perhaps the conversation of Rosalind and Celia will expand on this aspect of Shakespeare's view.

> *Ros.* What shall be our sport then?
> *Cel.* Let us sit and mock the good housewife
>   *Fortune* from her wheele, that her gifts may
>   henceforth bee bestowed equally.

> *Ros.* I would wee could doe so: for her benefits
> are mightily misplaced, and the bountifull blinde
> woman doth most mistake in her gifts to women.
>
> *Cel.* 'Tis true, for those that she makes faire,
> she scarce makes honest, & those that she
> makes honest, she makes very illfavouredly.
>
> *Ros.* Nay now thou goest from Fortunes
> office to Natures. Fortune reignes in gifts of the
> world, not in the lineaments of Nature.
>
> *(210–11)*

The duke in *Twelfth Night* will acquiesce in this distinction as he sends Caesario again to Olivia.

> Tell her my love, more noble then the world
> Prizes not quantitie of dirtie lands,
> The parts that fortune hath bestow'd upon her:
> Tell her I hold as giddily as Fortune:
> But 'tis that miracle, and Queen of Iems
> That nature prankes her in, attracts my soule.
>
> *(967–72)*

But in the previous sequence from *As You Like It* the conversation continues for another moment as Celia answers Rosalind's distinction by saying

> *Enter Clowne.*
>
> *Cel.* No; when Nature hath made a faire
> creature, may she not by Fortune fall into the
> fire? though nature hath given us wit to flout
> at Fortune, hath not Fortune sent in this foole
> to cut off the argument?
>
> *Ros.* Indeed there is fortune too hard for
> nature, when fortune makes natures naturall,
> the cutter off of natures witte.
>
> *(212–19)*

The distinctions seem clear enough as they emerge from the jesting. Ultimately, the words of Lucrece may guide us to Shakespeare's particular concept of a turning wheel, for in her famous lamentation against Time, a recurrent theme in Shakespeare's lyric poetry, she speaks of one of Time's functions as being to "turn the giddy round of Fortune's wheel"—we may recall the context of Ezekiel.

Shakespeare, in any event, adheres to the distinctions inherent in the *Table of Cebes*. He is familiar with the notion of Fortune's "fools"; indeed, Romeo displays such awareness as, having just killed Tybalt, he observes "O! I am Fortunes foole" (1574). More specific—but more allusive—is the series of jokes, again in *As You Like It,* where Jacques describes Touchstone and his remarks.

> A Foole, a foole: I met a foole i'th'Forrest,
> A motley Foole (a miserable world:)
> As I do live by foode, I met a foole,
> Who laid him downe, and bask'd him in the Sun,
> And rail'd on Lady Fortune in good termes,
> In good set termes, and yet a motley foole.
> Good morrow foole (quoth I:) no Sir, quoth he,
> Call me not foole till heaven hath sent me fortune.
>
> (985–92)

In terms of Cebes, Touchstone's answer draws upon an obvious and obtrusive concept.

In *Timon of Athens,* Shakespeare demonstrates his familiarity with still another pictorial concept, that of Fortune's "Hill," which was also in this tradition. The poet describes his poem (81–82) wherein Fortune sits enthroned on a height while men strive upwards, sometimes being kicked back down again, while Lady Fortune is herself envisioned as having an "ivory hand." Considering then the evidence for the conventionality of these concepts, we can state that even in the *Mirrour for Magistrates* we find a concern not so much for a structure of wheeled fatalism as for the relation of the classical idea of Fortune to the concept of the freedom of the will and the intellectual operations of the mind. And since Shakespeare himself shows every evidence of familiarity with these received ideas, there is no real substance to any notion that for him the concept of Fortune's wheel was a heritage in moral or aesthetic structure from which he deviated or which he had to modify. Rather, the evidence seems to point in other directions.

II

With these conclusions in mind, then, we may now consider the other problem inherent in Farnham's suggestion. When one looks at a concept of tragic "process" from the point of view of the Wheel of Fortune, it becomes possible to speak of tragic "story" as a rise and a fall, but we must ultimately consider the aesthetic validity of this manner of speaking, which implies the abstraction of a graphic line indicating, as it were, the "shape" of a "plot." There are difficulties in these terms, for to derive a meaningful theory of structure, or even of sequence, from the metaphor is to become entangled in a number of theoretical qualifications.

When we think of a "rise" and a "fall" in tragedy, we risk stumbling into problems which have to do with ethics rather than with the isolation of a concept of sequence. After all, when rising and falling refer especially to a "motion" from the bottom of "Fortune's Wheel" to the top, and then "over and down the other side," each of these three states can only be defined according to sociological criteria. If there is a rise, a pinnacle, and a fall, the "pinnacle," by some ethical evaluations, could actually be a nadir, one man's "good fortune" easily being regarded by others as ill fortune, and so forth. Thus if the configuration of the wheel is at all illustrative of "sequence," it suggests an ethical one or, at most, the sequence of a character's states of mind.

Clearly, in the Elizabethan experience, there were analogies to some 360-degree turn of a wheel—"dust to dust" or the seven ages of man (in which man becomes a child again)—but the application of such a cycle to "process" in tragedy was another matter. Madeleine Doran in chapter 10 of *Endeavors of Art* maintains that the tendency to construct sequences *ab ovo* was only one kind of approach, and we will, of course, remember the epic tradition of "beginning" *in medias res*, which indicated preferences other than those dictated by historical analogy. And even if we look at the *Mirrour*, we observe that the concept of turning wheels has only a limited relevance, for some of the *Mirrour* stories ask the reader to contemplate not some 360-degree sequence, but simply a "fall." If we take the story of "Richard II," it is clear that in "wheel" terms the character stands at the "top" in the beginning, and the tale describes his descent, thereby recalling a form already extant, for instance, in Seneca's *Oedipus* (translated by Neville in 1562). By these terms, then, are we not being forced to think in the metaphor not of a turn, but of a "half-turn" of Fortune's wheel as early as 1559, when this story first appeared? We might also do well to note that, in the final analysis, the *Mirrour for Magistrates* merely presents "ghosts" who hypothetically walk across the stage of life and tell the reader their stories. Hence, by definition, it is difficult to compare the form of these tales to some form of theater, since we are presented with what must ultimately be called "chorus" without complementary stage action. And if the purely ethical commentary of these figures may tend to draw on the concept of "Fortune," the structure of the tales themselves tends to vary. A Cardinal Wolsey may, like Richard, begin his tale when he is at the *top* of Fortune's wheel, but Jack Cade begins at the beginning. In fact, might we not generalize to observe that the various writers who created the *Mirrour* were united merely by a common use of the word *fortune*? Otherwise, the bents of these same writers are in various directions. Their characters describe their own doleful cases as products alternately of the will, of society, or of the universe. Some have begun *ab ovo* in their narrations, some have begun at the point when they were happiest or richest or most powerful. They "fell" through the reactions of political opposition, through chance, or through sins, depending on the ethical premises presented by the narrator.

Such is a "historical" justification for the application of a "rise-and-fall" configuration to the concept of process in Shakespearean tragedy. But the same configuration reappears in criticism, in discourses which utilize not history but the form of Freytag's pyramid.[16] By these terms, it becomes acceptable to state that in, say, *Antony and Cleopatra*, the "structure" is one according to which Antony "rises" until he reaches the "pinnacle of his fortunes" by marrying the sister of Octavius, after which time the hero declines into his "fall." From such a remark we thus abstract a graphic line which indicates the "shape" of the "plot" as "pyramidal" or, in other terms, as having a "turning point." But if we called upon our own familiarity with *Antony and Cleopatra*, we could object that Antony, already owning a third of the world, could hardly rise higher in "fortune" unless we adduce some rather specialized definitions. We must constantly bear in mind the fact that when we make the a priori decision of searching for the "pyramid," we are invoking the far-reaching assumption that in any Shakespearean tragedy there is indeed some "pinnacle of fortune" to which the hero must inevitably "rise" and from which he must inevitably "fall." We must, furthermore, define just what constitutes "good fortune"—whether we refer to riches or to a state of mind. After all, one could make a plausible argument for the possibility that, in *Julius Caesar*, Brutus's "line" rises continually until he reaches that "pinnacle" which is, for example, the peace he attains through his suicide.

There is, then, a dialectical as well as a historical naïveté in employing concepts either of "Fortune's wheel" or of any other system of rise and fall, because both "Fortune" and "rise and fall" suggest valences rather more complex than are usually assumed: they embody notions implying unanalyzed ethical values. Let us therefore attempt to speak of tragic process in some other way to determine the "structure" of tragedy, a way which would not necessarily be anachronistic. It might, in fact, be somewhat closer to the spirit, if not the letter, of the concept of Fortune as suggested by *The Table of Cebes*, although it is not an analogy upon which we would insist.

III

It is possible to discern two kinds of "progressions" or "action-sequences" in Shakespearean tragic structure. One kind of "progression" is a "plot" (I prefer the term *character-action*) which depicts three phases. The protagonist is shown planning the initiation of some activity towards a goal. He is then shown in the process of attaining the goal. Finally he is shown in some kind of *reaction* to that attainment. We indeed must describe this final phase in such ambiguous terms, for the shape of this phase often depends on whether the poet is interested in presenting thereby further characterizations or in delineating an ethical statement. For instance, Brutus could be said to "fall" after his "rise" to power in the Roman state, but, as we would phrase it, the *process* we see is that of Brutus seeking a goal, attaining it, and then reacting to the implications of his attainment—implications not only for the political situation but also for his own state of mind. His quarrel with Cassius would thus emerge, not as "falling action"—one popular phrase—but as a way of revealing characteristics in Brutus to the audience and also as a way of presenting to Brutus the implications of his own attainment of his goal. In one sense, that is, his success at assassinating Caesar has resulted in his contemplation of Cassius's briberies. Thus, the last phase, the depiction of the protagonist in some kind of reaction, allows for variations.

The situation in *Macbeth* is illustrative and is similar to that in *Julius Caesar* insofar as "process" is concerned. The hero is depicted as wishing to attain kingship, as attaining it, and then as reacting to his attainment through the agonizing unrest which makes his reign a tyranny. A similar situation exists in *Richard III* and in *Romeo and Juliet*, our criterion for such identification always being the presence of a demonstration of initial desire on stage: we know quite soon what Richard III wants. A play such as *Hamlet* is perhaps more complicated, but it is still in the class of "process" to which we have been alluding. The protagonist is depicted as pursuing his desire throughout the tragedy, and at the moment of its attainment, he is then pictured in his reaction to killing Claudius by those death-speeches in which he exhibits more of a sense of self-justification than of regret. *Hamlet*, of course, always tends to be an exception: we must discuss it again later. What we would observe at this juncture, however, is that the other tragedies named above do have in common with each other their manner of presenting the relationship of their protagonists to a goal. I would further argue that such shaped sequences influence the arrangement of characters in relationship to each other—in other words, the configurations in the "plot."

In tragedies of this class which we have been discussing, for example, the protagonist is almost always prompted to his planning by a tempting agent. We of course recall Cassius, the ghost of Hamlet's father, the witches, and Lady Macbeth. But variations in the agency of temptation stress a possibly less obvious point, that the tempting agent itself is not always necessarily to be evaluatively taken as a "villain." From the structural point of view, this is understandable, for it is typical of such plots that the protagonist is depicted in response to the *goal*, not necessarily to the person of a tempter. It is therefore the function of the tempter not to present the protagonist with a goal but with a specific formula for action with respect to that goal. And it is then the formula which "tempts" the protagonist.

When this temptation begins to occur, we then begin to observe motivational soliloquies as the protagonist attempts to arrive at some specific decision with respect to attaining his goal. As a consequence, an audience tends to see such protagonists as "thoughtful" and thus to view them, erroneously, even as spokesmen for the ethical problems inherent in the tragedy itself. Brutus may serve as an example; even Macbeth's speeches about "life" are often quoted. "Tomorrow, and tomorrow, and tomorrow," and so forth.

It is a further characteristic of such plots that when the protagonist has suddenly made his decision—when he has accomplished his assassination or his other crucial activity—interestingly random factors are then brought forward by the author to end the protagonist's life. It is a significant approach to the concept of tragic "process." The chanciness of the final battle in *Julius Caesar* is made the plausible precipitator of Brutus's latent despair. And who is to say, besides the three witches, that the mighty warriorship of Macbeth can "logically" be defeated by a MacDuff in single combat, or that Laertes will believably manage to get the poisoned tip into Hamlet's skin, considering Hamlet's obvious superiority at swordplay? If we are interested in tragedies of the "will," are not these deaths of a peculiarly different order than Othello's suicide or Cleopatra's final choice?

Let us consider this particular matter more closely. Whatever our ultimate judgments about Shakespeare's theory of tragedy, it is obvious that the character-actions of such plays as *Macbeth* make plausible the *mistaken* release of an "avenging agent." Polonius, once Hamlet has made a decision, is killed *mistakenly*, and Laertes, hitherto an extraneous factor, overturns Hamlet's calculations. MacDuff, by some prescience known only to himself, rather arbitrarily leaves Scotland and his family. Furthermore, he has been allowed to leave despite what we know of Macbeth's watchfulness. This refugee happens to have been the crucial product of a Caesarean birth and serves as the avenging agent against Macbeth. Antony's motives for not cooperating with the new power structure in *Julius Caesar* are never as closely investigated as the motives of Brutus and Cassius, which are obviously depicted with subtlety and thoroughness.

If we were to generalize further, it should be said that while the desire of the protagonist to make his decision and plan his goal may be stressed in this kind of plot, the grounds for the protagonist's death must be ascribed not to his character plausibilities, but to what we must term "ethical" plausibilities. The protagonists die as a result of immediate and perhaps random factors, but the forces arranging these random factors arise from a kind of ethical determinism. For example, Brutus and Cassius are somehow driven from Rome by a riot that might have been contained by an efficient police force—surely Cassius would be up to anticipating this—and subsequently Octavius and Mark Antony materialize with an army. We have not been shown their ability to effect such a result, however. Rather, the presence of the proscription scene merely tells us that it is in the very nature of Roman politics that Antony and Octavius, with the help of the mobs, have been able to become so powerful as to determine the fates of their political enemies and to raise a force sizable enough to threaten the lives of Brutus and Cassius. How else, ultimately, is the fact of a final battle "plausible"? In history, all would depend on the power structure, organization, and ingenuity of Octavius and Antony, but in the tragedy it is as if mob action must raise such figures as Antony to the top, just as it must make Cassius and Brutus flee the city.

Again, in *Macbeth*, although witnessing only the death of MacDuff's family, we are to gather that all Scotland groans under the tyranny of the protagonist, the people being so demoralized as ultimately to allow Malcolm's army to defeat Macbeth's with ease. And if this "fact" is a plausible one, is it so in terms of "characterization" or of . . . something else? After all Macbeth did manage to persuade the killers of Banquo that Banquo was their real enemy, and it would therefore be at least plausible for Shakespeare to have MacDuff bring Malcolm news that Macbeth rules, not by terror, but by snaking his way into the hearts of the people, turning them against each other only when he wants to commit a political murder. Instead, we are asked to accept the proposition—which must be termed "ethical" in that it is an evaluation—that a murderer will "naturally" be an evil ruler who terrifies his people, and the people in turn will "naturally" not fight for him in any final showdown. It is as if such Shakespearean tragedies as *Macbeth* analyze the protagonist's desire for his goal but then bring forward factors other than these character-elements to make plausible his fall, as if tragic characterization were finally pitted against the playwright's version of "the nature of the world." Thus, in this kind of tragedy, the death of the protagonist is manipulated by the author through an ethical determinism.

Let us finally consider Hamlet's death in this particular context. In the duel
he is winning well at first. But Laertes, perhaps plausibly, pinks him—plausibly
for Laertes. But where is Horatio? He has suspected foul play all along. And
then, in this same scene, Gertrude, for the first time in the play, suddenly becomes insistently thirsty, drinking the poison meant for Hamlet. Finally, we
have the arrival of Fortinbras which makes the point about "accident" in another way: as a "result" of Hamlet's death Denmark falls under the Norwegian
yoke—by the accident of Fortinbras's arrival at the propitious time. Thus, a
series of highly random events has linked together a number of biter-bit murders with the fall of the kingdom to the old enemy. We will certainly not argue
against the proposition that Hamlet himself has made quite plausible the circumstances through which he is exposed to death, but if we judge the character-
action—the "plot"—in terms of a pseudo-achievement of Hamlet's goal—the
mistaken killing of Polonius—it is possible to regard the tragedy as depicting
temptation, planning, achievement, and reaction to achievement, with random
factors (including the attack of the pirates) dictating, however, the chances of
Hamlet's own death. Such chances include, among other things, our being
asked to accept the rather violent change in the behavior of Laertes via the
very natural proposition that a young man can be unhinged by the death of
his father. Yet we can ask, from the viewpoint of plausibility, whether a
Laertes really could stir up such a mob as would attain to the very throne of a
king. To accept Hamlet's death, we are asked to assume a great deal, to embrace a number of values according to which certain activity will seem
"inevitable." At the same time, in other spots in the tragedy we are not asked
to accept Hamlet's character without the subtlest kind of character-exposition.

IV

The second kind of tragic "process" to be found in Shakespeare would
appear to be the poet's normal way of working, if mere enumeration is the
criterion for normality. We can define the form by comparing it with the
mode we have previously been studying. In this second class of structure the
protagonist is *not* presented as planning for, as attaining, and then as reacting
to the attainment of, a goal. If we refer to the wheel of fortune as analogy,
it could be said that we witness only half a turn, "from top to bottom," as
it were. Such structuring is most obvious perhaps in a tragedy with a specifically
political subject, where, for instance, a king is reigning at the beginning of
the tragedy and thus, in a sense, may, as if by definition, have nothing to plan
(except conquests as with *Henry V*). In *Richard II*, for example, the span of the
tragedy depicts Richard's "fall"; yet it has never depicted his "rise." The words
become cumbersome, and it might be well to revert to our own phraseology

of "planning"; for, as we have implied, the social rank of the protagonist in the tragic structure is largely irrelevant. We can see this from the story of Prince Hal, who, though not a protagonist in the tragic sense, shows in the Henriad how someone who is already of princely rank may be depicted nevertheless as in the evolution of a plan for some attainment.

Richard II, on the other hand, is never really depicted as planning anything; instead, he is constantly "prodded," constantly pushed off balance by activity which may indeed have a "logical" basis, but which from the protagonist's own viewpoint seems merely inexplicable or random, perhaps even unnatural because unexpected. Richard is constantly elated or stung, shoved or nudged, the "plot" depicting his behavior primarily as reaction to stimuli. Bolingbroke and Mowbray quarrel before Richard's very presence: he reacts. Then there is the tournament: again there is Richard's reaction. John of Gaunt's long, prophetic speech provokes from the king a hot reply. Later, during Richard's sojourn in Ireland, the political situation in England is turned into a shambles ready for his return.

To be fanciful for the sake of illustration, it is as if a Macbeth were to have left Scotland for several months while, at home, various political activities altered the situation to such an extent that when we saw Macbeth again he would be confronted with a change to which he would have to react. The fact that Macbeth is seldom put in this position illustrates the difference in the two structures between which we are trying to differentiate. A Richard finds himself forced to give up his crown, to leave his queen, to adjust to prison, to listen to music—all of these sequences being stage activity where stimuli are presented almost randomly from the king's viewpoint. In such an organization, it is irrelevant to ask *why* Richard has not been depicted at some specific point as planning a counterattack or as trying to analyze the political situation. Bring it to that, and one could suggest that there must have been some point at which Richard decided to leave Ireland—planned to return to England. But such a theoretical moment is not depicted on stage, and, in such omissions, we can sense the emphasis of this second kind of tragic process or "plot." Whatever the possibilities in life, it would seem to be the structure of this kind of tragedy that the protagonist be pictured, not by means of motivational soliloquies demonstrating his personality by acts and by modes of winnowing different kinds of plans, but in response. The stimuli may be theoretically provocative of many kinds of reaction, the author choosing them so that by their qualities, in their totality, and compared to each other, the audience may eventually fit together the segments of a larger knowledge about the protagonist. If there is "process," in other words, it is a process of discovery of character by the audience.

It would follow that in such "plots" we may expect no "tragedies of decision" such as some critics tend to associate with *Julius Caesar,* and perhaps with *Hamlet.* "Events" are rendered, rather, as the "challenge" of vague or inexplicable universals. Indeed, a consideration of *Coriolanus* will indicate to us how far removed this kind of tragedy is from any concepts of decision making. We will agree that there are at least three extremely crucial "decision-points" which we could imagine the neo-Senecans rendering as instances of considerable rhetorical soul-searching. Early in the tragedy Coriolanus is hustled off to face the populace in his bid for the consulship, and his subsequent behavior in the situation obviously serves to make him manipulatable by the tribunes. Therefore, his "decision" to face the people, to stand for the office, might theoretically be quite an appropriate occasion for soliloquy, for decision-soliloquy. We may argue that he is a hasty man, but surely Shakespeare was not. Even the walk from some house to the marketplace would furnish plausible time. In a second instance, the decision actually to turn against Rome militarily is a momentous one, and it might, in theory, warrant something more than a muttered decision to join the Volscians. Even granted that Coriolanus acts hotly, the poet need not. Nor is hotheaded decision necessarily a function of the brevity of soliloquy, Othello's action being a case in point. Finally, when Coriolanus's mother prevails on him not to attack Rome, why does Coriolanus not return to his home instead of going back with the Volscians? Surely all talk of banishment is ludicrous at this point; the plebeians themselves have already been shown as regretting the exile when they received news of the invasion.

We may argue that so the story goes in Plutarch, but often, when Shakespeare has source-facts to deal with, he either changes them or makes them sufficiently plausible so that such questions do not necessarily present themselves. Why was Antony spared in the assassination of Caesar? It is so in the source, but the seed for this sparing in the tragedy lies in the careful motivation according to which Brutus can fancy an ethical difference between one murder and five. Coriolanus, on the other hand, participates in few such argumentations preceding his own acts. He discusses with his mother the matter of exhibiting his wounds, it is true, but he simply assents. He may be the "hasty, impetuous" type, but it was, in theory, a long walk from Rome to the Volscians, and was there not then time enough to anticipate the problem of the destruction of his family if Rome were to be sacked? We could aver that each of his crucial acts is potential food for endless motivational speculation.

We can alter the direction of our queries in a useful manner if we see *Coriolanus* as a structure similar to the structure of *Richard II,* that is, as a structure rather different from what the activity of *Coriolanus* may most obviously *seem* to suggest. The tragedy is superficially prone to the Freytagian pyramid, Coriolanus reaching his "highest point" at his assumption of his new name, and so on. If we apply a slightly different standard, however, the emphases in this tragedy become clearer, for we can observe that although Marcius does indeed receive his highest honor after the battle of Corioli, this is, importantly, not an honor which he has been depicted as *planning for* since the beginning of the tragedy. Rather, can we not say that things "simply happen to" Coriolanus?

If we do recall the shape of the plot of *Richard II*, the parallels with *Coriolanus* are clear enough. Our protagonist is constantly ambushed into reaction along his subjective course by the "motivated" activities of others in the drama. At the very beginning of the tragedy, Coriolanus is depicted, not as one planning to quell the mutiny, but as one instantly reacting to the presence of the starving citizens who suddenly confront him. As the drama proceeds, Shakespeare then alternately characterizes the crowd, Menenius, Volumnia, the Roman soldiery (following Titus but not Marcius), and the servants of Aufidius so that each of these elements "plausibly" and "characteristically" presents stimuli to which Coriolanus then responds. In fact, his death arises from this very device, for Aufidius prompts Coriolanus into reacting with a display of temper which allows his enemy a specious pretext for assassination. Thus, even if Marcius rises to a "height" by gaining his name at the middle of the tragedy, the structure of the character-action, the "plot," is understandable, not in terms of *Julius Caesar*, but in terms of *Richard II*. After all, can it really be said that Marcius becomes prouder and less sociable after the victory at Corioli? The initial scene with the mob seems to prevent this conclusion, since the protagonist is even more abusive there than later.

Timon of Athens exhibits the skeleton of a similar tragic process, and if the play does not please us, it may instruct us, because it shows its "bare bones" rather more clearly than do similar tragedies. The Poet, the Painter, and various servants present diverse situations to which Timon reacts so as to show his generosity. Timon then confronts a loss of money, which is not explained in the fiscal detail offered by *The Merchant of Venice;* the loss simply "happens." Next the protagonist is placed in a cave where he can be stimulated into reaction by various visitors. This kind of activity has been depicted from the very beginning.

The unpopularity of the tragedy with audience and reader is instructive too. Such a lack of appeal suggests some of the necessities inherent in the form of this particular kind of tragic process, which *Timon of Athens* shares with *Coriolanus* and with *Richard II*. One such necessity is this. If the tragic "process" to which we allude is the gradual revelation of traits through incremental stimuli, there seems to be a concomitant demand, in tragedies so constructed, for immediate motivational plausibility in those agents who present the "challenge" to the characterized protagonist. In *Timon*, man is generally ungrateful, almost unbelievably so, and an audience must acquiesce in this very generalized trait, which serves as the structural instrument working towards a result: Timon's loss of credit, which pushes him off balance and precipitates him into further reactions to the individual interviews. But other such tragedies—*Lear*, for example—are careful to endow such agents with "reasons." Edmund does not gratuitously order Lear and Cordelia killed. If the result of this order is the exhibition of Lear's grief over Cordelia's dead body, this scene nevertheless appears as a plausible result of Edmund's prior activity. The contrast is sharp when we compare Bolingbroke's dealing with Richard II. The latter is perhaps the "richer" character, but it is Bolingbroke who has the more carefully delineated "motivation" for precipitating those events which ultimately serve to characterize, not him, but Richard. In *Timon*, it is perhaps the absence of such complementary motivation in the "prodding" agents that makes the drama seem extravagant; Alcibiades alone emerges as the most "logical" character to visit Timon, bringing motivations which require a slightly more complicated response on Timon's part. Timon cannot merely call the soldier a greedy ingrate.

Another necessity suggested by *Timon* is the requirement of this kind of tragic structure for an activator. Such "activators" we often tend to regard as "villains" in very much the way we regard the "tempting agents" as villains in tragedies like *Julius Caesar*. We think of Edmund and call him a "villain," just as we call Cassius a "villain," but for different reasons. The shape of such a distinction can be observed in *Coriolanus* where Menenius, the crowd, Volumnia, and others actually serve as composite stimuli to Coriolanus. The focusing of such activity, however, into one character in the other tragedies (rather than into some group of characters as in *Coriolanus*) precipitates in us the sense of a "villain." The term is obviously misleading. Shakespeare could easily have constructed a "villain" for *Coriolanus* simply by giving to one character all those activities which serve to stimulate Coriolanus. A Bolingbroke focuses the activity to which Richard must react. Is he a "villain"? If so, he does not resemble Cassius and Edmund; he is an Octavius Caesar, or a Claudius. Rather than speak of "villains" at all, the term being essentially a structural assumption, I would suggest instead that there are stimulative roles requisite to certain kinds of tragic structures and that Shakespeare sometimes gives these roles to single characters and sometimes spreads them throughout a group, as in *Timon,* and in *Lear* too, where Kent, Goneril, Regan, and then Edmund are, if we wish, a "composite villain" evoking Lear's response-pattern.

The fineness of such distinctions is indicated by an *Othello*, which is often taken as a classic example of temptation and reaction. Yet *Othello* is a structure, not like *Macbeth* or *Julius Caesar*, but typical of the second kind of tragedy which we have been discussing. Indeed the many critical remarks regarding the "implausibility" of Othello's quick rage at Desdemona reflect the possibility that in this drama, as in *Coriolanus*, the rendering of "motivated" decision may not be the object of depiction at all. If we were to think of *Othello* primarily in terms of "decision," after all, the most pressing theoretical question might be what "motivated" Othello to break custom by eloping with Desdemona in the first place. Othello, according to his own words, was welcome in her father's house, and so forth. But, as it stands, the tragedy offers us *faits accomplis* of the order which we observe in *Lear*. Othello is married. He is chosen general. Ultimately, too, the wars against the Turks are irrelevant enough to allow the Turkish navy simply to be dispersed in a tempest, and thus, in terms of the strategy of structure, Othello is left static, to be the target of various stimuli embodied by Iago, Desdemona, and Cassio, among others.

If we say that Iago "caused" such activity, we are again perhaps prey to historicist analogy, for we may contrast the situation again with that in *Julius Caesar*. There, Cassius exerts his personality on Brutus, but Brutus must then go his own way dramatically, to make his own decision and to react. Iago, on the other hand, serves to manipulate stage action by which Othello is confronted with Desdemona, with Cassio, and with scenes—all of which are to elicit reaction from the protagonist so as to characterize him. In fact, eliciting has been Iago's most important structural function in the first two acts of the drama. And if there is any true analogy of the Cassius/Brutus kind, it is Iago's dealing with *Roderigo*, not with Othello.

Let us again consider Othello's progress. Suddenly he is accosted on stage by Brabantio and his party with torches, then by Cassio, and then by the emissaries of the duke. Later he is on trial before the senate. Again, in Cyprus, he reacts to seeing Desdemona for the first time since the voyage; he faces the drunken riot; he faces Emilia and Desdemona. And, to demolish "logical cause" utterly, Othello faces the news that Cassio, for some reason, is to replace him as governor of Cyprus. The parallel to *Richard II* is clear. Where such structuring may differ from that of a *Lear* is that the agency of such seemingly random stimuli in *Othello* is focused largely into one character. Even Iago, however, is not sufficient: this may be gathered from the granting of the governorship to Cassio as still another stimulus for Othello. The mechanics of the situation, otherwise, have forced on Shakespeare the interesting problem of uniting all his causations into Iago, who has himself, significantly for our point here, been accused of "inadequate motivation." Shakespeare did not attempt this device again, for an Edmund shares with others the activities which must have an effect on Lear.

Ultimately, then, *Othello* may stand as the most difficult distinction which our definition of two different processes in the structure of Shakespearean tragedy must make. The drama by some tokens could be taken as a "rise-and-fall" play, but from the viewpoint advanced here, we would not call it so since it is Iago, not the protagonist, who is depicted in the planning for a goal, the attainment of it, and the reaction to it, throughout the play. Othello himself is subject to the same characterization-maneuvers typical of those accorded to King Lear: they precipitate "reaction-scenes." And if Rowe objected to the plausibility of the plot, he might equally have objected to the plausibility of *Coriolanus*. Motivated decision in such tragedy is never the "precipitation" of characterization; it is *illustration* of character.

King Lear presents the kind of structure we now discuss. The old king becomes a subject almost immediately and is forced merely to react for the rest of the tragedy. He has not been presented in motivation—trying, as it were, to decide whether he should indeed give up his kingdom, attempting to determine how to divide it. All this he simply does in a moment on stage, and what follows is the serial presentation of stimuli, as Lear reacts to the speeches of each daughter and then to the protestations of Kent. Provocations even to insanity arise from these early situations, and, as we have observed, it is only at a very late date that Edmund, who never, in fact, speaks to Lear, himself has any stimulus-effect on the old king. Clearly, Shakespeare is using a *Coriolanus* structure: multiple provocations of the protagonist by variously motivated agents. If Edmund has a structural role at all, it is confined largely to the level of his family situation, as Gloucester himself imitates the purely reactive stance of his king.

If Edmund plays Iago to Gloucester's Othello, it is interesting to note that, in the tragedy as a whole, Edmund's structural function is, curiously, to precipitate symbol. He makes possible not a Brutus-like soul-searching, but a "poor Tom," as he drives Edgar into exile; he precipitates a "blind Cupid" as he tricks and betrays his father into mutilating punishment as well as attempted suicide. He finally precipitates, too, the ceremonial tournament by which Edgar wins back his status. It is interesting to note this change in structural function for such a "tempter"-figure. Not stimulating Lear's character-reactions, he populates the pageantry of the drama, manufacturing material, not for the primary characters, but for those figures whose function may be ethical commentary.

Other aspects of *Lear* suggest how Shakespeare was generally moving in this kind of tragic plotting as a whole, for Lear's madness is itself almost a complete negation of the importance of demonstrated decision making to this kind of structure. If we term Coriolanus "impulsive" as he makes his own hasty but crucial decisions, Lear, simply by being "mad," can himself move through many characterizing activities and reactions. He requires no more "plausible" motivations than the random directions that madness might take from casual encounters with any stimuli. We err if we simply assume that the old king's mad speeches are necessarily ethical pronouncement by which we are to understand the values implicit in the drama, for that has not been satisfactorily demonstrated. And if the presumption is that Lear speaks so as to characterize himself, it is clear that the difficult use of madness as a mode, while psychologically delicate as an artist's job, does allow a dramatist relaxation in the task of structuring the many kinds of "plausible" stimuli. We may contrast the tragedy with *Timon* again, for the protagonist there sits in his cave merely angry; hence he cannot "believably" ramble too much.

The dilemma of whether Lear's mad speeches indeed are characterization or ethical statement raises a further observation about the kind of tragic structure with which we deal here. When balancing the speeches of the Fool and of Poor Tom against those of Lear (wondering as we do so whether Tom and the Fool have been presented to allow us to distinguish between "mad" ethical commentary and "mad" self-characterization, as in the old king), we note that such problems are precipitated by the form of a *King Lear*. If the "provoking" of the protagonist is not to be the concentrated result of the activities of one character, but the function of *many* figures, then the multiplicity of the "provoking" agents has its own effect. Agents "provoke" in terms of viewpoints, and thus a complex of purely ethical commentary and counter-commentary comes into being. We are thus led to debate values.

We can contrast *Timon* with a *Julius Caesar*, wherein Brutus, in his attempt to make a decision, is given much of the burden both of pondering ethical pros and cons, and of indicating the possible ethical ramifications of his choice. But in the second kind of tragic structure, in a *Timon*, the protagonist reacts merely to exhibit his own character. The ethical issues are presented only when this protagonist acquires a group of figures who, through value statements, urge him on or try to prevent him from some kind of action. He is "fought over," as it were, by contending forces who enunciate their own bases for action. We recall the steward in *Timon*, or the debate between Brabantio and the Venetian Senate, although there is little debate in Othello himself at this point. In *Lear*, the texture of such commentary thickens enormously, perhaps because the definitive mistake of the protagonist is made at the very beginning of the play, and is rendered as irretrievable. If *Coriolanus* widens the possibilities of stimuli by the use of several persuading characters, *Lear* presents a king who, with no power at all, does not need to be plotted against. Rather, his role is to move from figure to figure trying to reclaim his lost power and being taught by their reactions why his power is lost. He has nothing to do but to wonder at the change which began the tragedy and to be led through situations which themselves have been made plausible and which will elicit reaction from him. For such situations to be possible, material which seems "independent," as events are not in *Macbeth*, has to be manufactured.

The exceptions, of course, test the rule, but if the foregoing suggestions about the basic mode of structure in Shakespearean tragedy seem to have some accuracy, we have in our possession a way of talking about certain of the poet's other dramas which we have not mentioned. *Richard III* is an example. At first glance this tragedy has many of the elements of structure characteristic of *Macbeth* and of *Julius Caesar*. We find a protagonist desiring a goal, planning how to attain it, attaining it, and reacting to this attainment. But there are differences. Richard has no one "tempting" him; in fact, he serves as tempter to others. The form easily produces the motivational soliloquies so characteristic of such process, but to be rigorous, Richard, when deciding to be a "villain," becomes, from our point of view, his own "tempter." Shakespeare did not repeat the experiment.

V

Were we to speculate about Shakespeare's structural development, we could follow it in the terms which we have been discussing. If we risk speaking of "early Shakespeare" we will note that an early tragedy such as *Titus Andronicus* belongs to the *Lear* type, essentially. We have all the earmarks: an Aaron who organizes and funnels to Titus stimuli for reactive histrionics. If in later tragedies such stimuli will elicit "character," they do not do so in *Titus* because the provoking acts are in a monotone. Horror is their keynote, and a reaction to horror produces character-manifestation in only one segment of the spectrum. In how many ways can one react when horrible things happen to one's various children or to oneself? Titus may ultimately evolve his own plan for revenge, but the majority of the drama has been consumed in the spawning of activity-sequences in various other figures whose behavior provokes reaction in Titus. Shakespeare utilized—more successfully—the same form in *Richard II*; this fact leads us to assume that perhaps the playwright worked most easily around such a structure. But at the same time—specific dates being confused and therefore, at this juncture, necessarily irrelevant—we have *Richard III*, and perhaps *Julius Caesar* too. *Romeo and Juliet*, however, begins rather like a tragic structure of the *Coriolanus* mode, does it not? What is established at the beginning is a series of societal "facts" occurring independently of Romeo but to which Romeo himself will be asked to react in his first entry on stage. And for much of the early part of the tragedy it is Romeo's character which is the chief issue. His friends speak of his preoccupation with Rosaline, and Romeo himself is exposed to jokes, to feuds, and ultimately to Juliet. His troubles are essentially induced upon him. He wanders into a duel with Tybalt just as he wanders into old Capulet's party, and his reactions are solicited not so much, as in comedy, by any difficulty in winning Juliet, but by a network of "motivated" happenings which exist independently of him, the feud and its ramifications being the most obvious example. But then Juliet begins to enter the structural picture. She too has soliloquies and perhaps a "tempting agent" in the person of the nurse. Nevertheless character-emphasis on Romeo continues, for when he is on the floor in Friar Laurence's cell, he is presented in reaction to news. Juliet's own role is subordinated by the comment of the nurse who observes merely that Juliet is in the same condition, a fact that the audience is not allowed to see for itself.

Ultimately, we would agree that we can "understand" Romeo's activity, but that Juliet's must be accepted on faith. This is a queer fact, which suggests where the basic emphasis may lie in the play—on the character of Romeo—but the presentation of an independent life of Juliet, even if she only evokes remarks from the nurse, from her father, and from Romeo, offers the possibility of another kind of structure, one similar to that of *Julius Caesar*. We could suggest that Juliet herself acts as "tempter" to Romeo, but such an observation would merely be verbal; it would be more accurate to suggest that, as in *Titus*, there is in *Romeo* a beginning which strongly argues for the *Coriolanus* kind of play, while the ending suddenly presents planning—the revenge in *Titus*, the tomb-plot in *Romeo*—which imparts a different kind of activity. What may be significant in both tragedies, however, is that there are not any motivational soliloquies debating the ethical pros and cons when the "planning-points" finally come.

Let us return to *Richard III*. In such a dialectical context, this play occupies a rather interesting place artistically. If it is an attempt at the kind of structure which we have associated with *Julius Caesar* and certain other tragedies, and if *Richard III* predates *Caesar*, then *Richard III* is Shakespeare's first attempt at presenting a pattern where the protagonist plans via soliloquy to a rendered attainment and to a reaction to this attainment. But we have noted that the role of tempter has not yet been utilized there by the author, and, because of this omission, rather interesting sequences result. Because Richard himself is not tempted by someone else, his motivational soliloquies will not ponder pros and cons of ethics. On the other hand, Richard is not given one specific character upon whom to work; therefore, although in personality like Iago, Richard must move in a completely different kind of structure as a protagonist. Lacking tortured self-searching, and lacking the ambition to demolish only one person— an ambition which, structurally, would perhaps remove him from the role of protagonist—he, or Shakespeare, is forced into a structure which is almost the obverse of the poet's normal mode of operation. Richard, in effect, becomes a provoker of many other characters, rather than the target of the activity of those characters towards him. Hence, in soliloquy, he can gloat, but he cannot exhibit too many traits, for he is not stimulated. He is a Macbeth without wife and witches. The situation precipitates him into an imitation of the Vice, a role which many scholars have observed established for him. Richard deviates from the Vice, however, in that he is, after all, presented as an imitation of a human being, endowed with human motivations. If he operates as Vice, it is the dramatist's structure which has prevented other kinds of stimulus to character-presentation: Richard himself has been deprived of a tempter and also of a specific single enemy. Do we not continually say that Richard is either evil, or wickedly amusing—the compleat villain? We speak in terms of ethical evaluations: we do not often argue that Richard is "complex." He is complex, but only to a point. The character-information is ultimately not there in as much abundance as it will be with Iago, who is furnished with a Roderigo, or with Edmund, who will be furnished with Goneril, Gloucester, Regan, and Edgar, all of whom require Edmund to *react* in various dimensions. The form of *Richard III* leads, not to questions about character, but to questions regarding values.

Hamlet, in Shakespeare's development, allows for further speculation along these lines. From one point of view, the outline of the structure of the tragedy may seem sufficiently clear in that the ghost obviously influences Hamlet to formulate a goal, introducing him to it in a more definite manner than does Cassius whose prompting of Brutus has the fertile grounds of Brutus's own specific uneasiness regarding Caesar. Hamlet, however, had no suspicion about murder, despite his formless depression. We also observe motivational soliloquies and the "random events" which make the protagonist's death plausible. Nevertheless, certain exceptions suggest that *Hamlet* does not completely embody the "attainment" form of structure. For we have to determine whether "attainment" lies in the mistaken killing of Polonius or in the final killing of Claudius. We have previously argued how *Hamlet* resembles *Macbeth* if we take the killing of Polonius as the attainment of Hamlet's (structural) goal. If we move this concept of "attainment" to later in the drama, if we view the "structure" from a different perspective, we can, however, make another set of observations. Hamlet is already, in effect, dead, when he kills Claudius. With little opportunity to reflect on the attainment of his goal it is as if, on the "top" of fortune's wheel, he plummets down, in a split second, to the bottom. *Hamlet* could thus be viewed simply as a lopsided play of attainment.

However, other oddities in the "structure" are suggested by comparison with *Macbeth*. In the latter play, we begin with a supernatural agency of temptation in the witches, but Shakespeare, in effect, "transfers" this role to Lady Macbeth, so that a human character becomes tempting agent who can operate, like Cassius, through personality-interplay with the protagonist. Hamlet's only confidant is indeed a human being—Horatio—but he remains neutral, almost rigorously so, if we recall his cautious reaction to the effects of the mousetrap play. Accordingly, Hamlet is not forced to accommodate himself to a personality trying to tempt him. He is held to the necessity of dealing with a supernatural manifestation. This manifestation, the ghost, ultimately takes the shape, not of a character with personality, but of the abstract form of an ethical proposition. If we envisioned the possible appearance of the ghost of Lady Macbeth for the purpose of persuasion, we would by the contrast agree why Hamlet's father could never be regarded as a "character." The audience is always kept from any firsthand knowledge of his traits. Thus, if he urges Hamlet, he ultimately appeals, not to a character-relationship, as do Cassius and Lady Macbeth, but to a relationship-in-principle. The result is that the ghost operates rather as an idea which Hamlet must constantly recall and examine, the questions he asks himself being illustrative: is the ghost good or is he evil? These are questionings concerned with ethics, not the Macbeth-like reactions to a Lady Macbeth who is always present to quell any falterings. In other words, *Hamlet* suggests the kind of structure that we see, not in *Macbeth*, but in *Richard II*.

It could be argued that unlike a Richard II, Hamlet at least has a goal towards which he points and that in this sense he structurally resembles Macbeth. But we must also then reckon with the fact that many character-stimuli appear in *Hamlet*, in virtual parade. The blandishments of Claudius at the very beginning, the ghost itself with the terrible news, the "rejection" by Ophelia, the actor speaking of Hecuba, the sight of Claudius kneeling, the encounter with Gertrude, the passage of Fortinbras, the conversation with the gravediggers, the appearance of Ophelia's coffin (Horatio having presumably "forgotten" to inform Hamlet of this minor occurrence)—all constitute an astounding number of specific stimuli repeatedly aimed at pushing Hamlet into a state of mind differing from that he is in when he first appears in the given scene. The strongest example may be the total unexpectedness (to Hamlet) of the murderous enmity of Laertes at the grave. It is thus the presence of these situations which argues a structure reminiscent of *Richard II* or of *Lear*. In this regard, it is possible, furthermore, to observe agents in this tragedy who organize these stimuli, just as Bolingbroke does for *Richard II*. We have suggested previously that Claudius and Polonius are partners in this structural act, the former by his manipulation of Rosencrantz, Guildenstern, and Laertes, the latter not only in his arrangement of Ophelia's activities, but by his various encounters with Hamlet and ultimately by his presence behind the arras to startle Hamlet into murder. And finally, if we think of *Lear*, we observe that Hamlet's madness, whether real or feigned, allows him the opportunity of displaying reaction to random stimuli. Structurally, it is much the same whether Hamlet is really mad or not: the mode itself allows for subtler and far-ranging essays in characterization through stimulus.

In sum, then, by viewing the structure of *Hamlet* from a different angle, we can discover all the characteristics of the *Coriolanus* plan according to which the protagonist is constantly "attacked" by character-stimulators, so that the questions which we are forced to ask have to do, not with a decision, but with what constitutes the "true" personality of the protagonist. Decision, although it seems so important in *Hamlet*, does not really exist. Any time that Hamlet acts, he is not led through a Macbeth- or Brutus-like sequence of decision making. His "decisions" are rather like those of Coriolanus, ultimately symptoms of character rather than an answer to the question, "Given this dilemma, what did this character finally decide to do?" Thus we have in *Hamlet* a combining of two structures not repeated by the poet again. The combining of tempter-soliloquy-planning-goal sequences with the purely reactive structures of the *Coriolanus* organizations may, in fact, account for the difficulty of the play. By abstracting the temptation into a supernatural agent whose existence raises revenge-suggestion to teleology or reduces it to an *idée fixe* not discussable at length with any tempter, does not Shakespeare make the "temptation" operate rather as a theory in the character's mind than as a result of personality interrelationships? Finally, the fact that we speak of Hamlet's various "opportunities" for revenge seems in itself sufficiently revelatory.

We might test the utility, if not the accuracy, of our theory of structure by recourse to a play such as *Troilus and Cressida*, which scholars tend to argue about, if only to discover whether or not they are supposed to consider it a tragedy. The question can possibly never be answered, especially since any theory as to what constitutes a "Shakespearean tragedy" works from given data, which are fed back into the object of discussion. The limitation of our own theory lies in the fact that it assumes that the dramas described are indeed "tragedies"; therefore it could not properly answer the question of whether *Troilus* is one. We could for the moment, however, hypothesize that it is a tragedy and see how our theory of structure might apply.

We are in some doubt as to who is the protagonist. Hector seems an obvious choice: on the other hand, we cannot ignore Troilus who is presented in a *"Julius Caesar"* sequence complete with a "tempter" in the person of Pandarus. And certainly it would not be too inaccurate to describe the play as Troilus's formulation of a goal, his attainment, and his reaction to his "attainment," if by that last term we imply the simple physical attainment of Cressida with her latently dubious loyalties. We could also suggest that a number of seemingly random forces are mobilized to vitiate Troilus's attainment, since the exchange of prisoners, significantly for our point, is not worked out in terms of character-motivations. We could stretch matters, suggesting that Troilus is going to die in battle and that his "future" death is made plausible by the recklessness which follows his loss of Cressida, but then we move out of consistent theorizing into *ad hoc* conjecture. We therefore suggest, given this situation, an emendation to theories about a "double plot." Perhaps there is a "double structure," since it is Hector who is presented, as was Richard II, by means of character-stimuli and with no definite plan for any specific goal. Hector is primarily reactive. Troilus is a "Macbeth" type, with plans, temptations, soliloquies, and other paraphernalia characteristic of a certain tragic process. We can thus speak of a "double structure" rather than of a "double plot" by alluding to the separate structural necessities engendered by Shakespeare's way with Troilus on the one hand and with Hector on the other.

Finally, *Antony and Cleopatra* is interesting because, like *Macbeth*, it lacks a "villain," and it also lacks a "tempter," no matter what is fabled about Cleopatra in history and in folklore. According to the terms which we have previously constructed, it is clear that Antony is not tempted to contemplate an action, bring it to fruition, and observe its effects. Basically, he is presented in much the same manner as an Othello, to adduce a similar character-type drawn through a similar kind of sequence: Antony "rises" nowhere and "falls" nowhere, for by the wheel analogy, he moves, as Lear moves, merely from "top" to "bottom." Constantly provoked, stung, pushed, he is in perpetual imbalance, answering perpetual challenges; he never sits down, as it were, and formulates a plan. The same can be said of Cleopatra whose scenes are obviously a series of character-stimuli, so much so that we often hear her infinite variety spoken of, when, in reality, we should speak of the infinite variety of the characterization-efforts. And if Caesar focuses events for the purpose of presenting an external opposition to which both Antony and Cleopatra must react, it is interesting that, as in *Coriolanus,* this role of focusing is shared by other characters such as Sextus Pompeius and Enobarbus. From this viewpoint, it can be said that the battle of Actium itself resolves little. Antony has not "pointed" towards it: he merely reacts to it. No matter how definitive Actium was for the forces of Octavius in Roman history, Actium in the play is only as definitive, say, as is Edmund's power to have Cordelia hanged. What follows both incidents is certainly plausible, but the plausibility is used to stimulate character-reaction or ethical equation. Antony and Cleopatra cope with the *idea* of defeat; Lear copes with the *idea* of Cordelia's death.

Antony's characterization, in another way, resembles Shakespeare's work with Coriolanus, for the lover of Cleopatra is endowed with certain theoretically crucial points of decision, which, however, are not made the subjects of debate. Is not Antony's decision to marry Octavia one such crux? His resolution to leave her after he has married her would seem another such. The decision to fight with Caesar would seem the most important crux of all, just as the decision to fight Caesar by sea and the impulse to follow Cleopatra from Actium clearly have enormous relevance to the political issues. But like Coriolanus, Antony is simply conducted so as to be *imagined* as having made these decisions, which do not really determine what "happens" to characters as much as they elicit further reaction by furnishing a background of plausibility. Shakespeare is clearly more interested in showing Antony's agonized reaction to his own cowardice than in showing him in the process of deciding whether or not to declare war on Caesar. Thus, to say that Antony is "impulsive" is to beg the question, for we have been over similar ground in the case of Coriolanus.

The fact that three characters are considered instead of one does present interesting complications, for three sets of substructures are used to provide the stimuli—one set for each character—and from this artistic decision an audience may derive its subjective sense of "worlds": the world of Egypt, the world of Rome, and the world of the soldiers and servants.

If there is a "hero" at all, a protagonist, it is, structurally, not one that can be compared to the phenomenon termed "protagonist" in other plays. In those terms, we have here a "triple protagonist," and this "protagonist" can neither be measured in terms of "movement" from temptation to attainment—and the contemplation thereof—nor in terms of movement through stimuli which gradually reveal the totality of a characterization. We have, instead, as it were, a slowly circular system in which three characters operate so as to reveal each other, all of them moving around through stimuli produced by their reactions to each other in the first place. Thus Caesar's final speech, as he leaves the play alive, is not a pronouncement about events, but a final gesture of self-characterization; his exit is the last inch of rotation, not of a wheel of fortune standing upright, but of a wheel lying flat viewed from its side, presenting in its turning the various faces of another kind of system until Caesar himself is finally phased out of the play.

These remarks about "plot" in Shakespearean tragedy must obviously be regarded as heuristic. They derive from a particular critical point of view which assumes artistic intent, and this view itself has often been challenged. Further argument is therefore irrelevant to the point and summary may serve as a useful mode of conclusion. We have urged that any discussion of "plot" in terms of the concept of Fortune's wheel is simplistic as regards our knowledge of ideas current in the Renaissance, and naive from the viewpoint of desiderata for any systematic critical epistemology. We have considered the larger implications of Renaissance concepts of Fortune and we have also argued for a structural approach to the concept of tragic process. "Plot" or tragic process, I believe, is usefully discussed only outside of a context of ethical presuppositions. We would not thereby deny the relevance of ethics to tragedy. Rather, we insist on refining notions of what may constitute "structure" itself when we speak of Shakespearean tragedy.

Notes:

1. Willard Farnham, *The Medieval Heritage of Elizabethan Tragedy* (San Marino, 1936), pp. 446–48.
2. For Vincenzo Cioffari, see *Fortune and Fate from Democritus to St. Thomas Aquinas* (New York, 1935), chap. 2. For Seneca, see Epistles XVI, XCVIII.
3. *Summa contra Gentiles*, III. 92.
4. For Vives, see *An Introduction to Wysedom*, trans. R. Morsyne (London, 1540), sigs. C4, E6ᵛ–E7, F6; for Thomas Elyot, see *Of the Knowledge which maketh a Wise Man* (London, 1533), sigs. M2–M4ᵛ; for Erasmus, see *Proverbes*, trans. Richard Taverner (London, 1569), sigs. E3ᵛ–E4.
5. See Palingenius, *Zodiak of Life* (London, 1588), Bk. 8, *passim*; William Baldwin, *A Treatise of Morall Philosophie* (London, 1549), II.8, III.3; Jean Bodin, *Six Bookes of a Commonweale*, trans. R. Knolles (London, 1606), sig. 2Z6; Bacon's essay "Of Fortune"; I. Gentillet, *A Discourse upon the Meanes of Wel Governing*, trans. Simon Patericke (London, 1608), sigs. N3 ff.; Plutarch, *Morals*, trans. Philemon Holland (London, 1603), sig. 2Y5ᵛ; La Primaudaye, *French Academie*, trans. T. B. (London, 1586), I.44; John Norden, *The Labyrinth of Mans Life* (London, 1614), sigs. F2ᵛ ff.; J. Bastingius, *Exposition . . . upon the Catechisme* (Cambridge, 1595), sig. G5 ff.; Mornay, *A Discourse of Life and Death* (London, 1592), sigs. I3 ff.; Guillaume de la Perrière, *The Theatre of Fine Devices*, trans. Thomas Combe (London, 1614), sig. A3ᵛ and Emblem 28; Gui du Faur, *Quadrains*, trans. J. Sylvester (London, 1605), sig. 2Y7; Sir William Cornwallis, *Discourses upon Seneca* (London, 1601), sig. E2; Du Bartas, *Divine Weekes*, trans. Joshua Sylvester (London, 1605), sig. F6; I. Boissard, *Emblematum Liber* (Frankfurt, 1593), the last emblem; R. Niccols, *The Furies* (London, 1614), epigram 21; "Megara"; Vincenzo Cartari, *The Fountaine of Ancient Fiction*, trans. R. Linche (London, 1599), sig. Z4–2A4.
6. See *The Mirror for Magistrates*, ed. L. B. Campbell (Cambridge, 1938), pp. 102, 132, 170 ff., 178, 287–88. For E. M. W. Tillyard, see *Shakespeare's History Plays* (New York, 1964), pp. 76–77.

7. See *Parts Added to the Mirror for Magistrates*, ed. L. B. Campbell (Cambridge, 1946), pp. 212–13, 231–32, 303–4, and *Mirror*, p. 465.

8. For *Sir Thomas More*, see Addition III in the Malone Society Reprint, ed. W. W. Greg (Oxford, 1911), Cf. Jonson, *The Poetaster*, V.i.54.

9. See H. R. Patch, "The Tradition of the Goddess Fortuna in Roman Literature" and "The Tradition of the Goddess Fortuna in Medieval Philosophy and Literature" in *Smith College Studies in Modern Languages*, III (1922); *The Goddess Fortuna in Medieval Literature* (Cambridge, Mass., 1927).

10. *The Table of Cebes* (STC 4891) is tentatively dated 1530 by Pollard and Redgrave. We should also note John Healey's translation of Epictetus to which *The Table* is appended (four eds. between 1610 and 1636). We may also add Plutarch, *Howe One may take Profit of his Enmyes* [De Capienda] (London, 1557). See also *Simplicii Commentarius in Enchiridion Epicteti . . . cum Versione Hieronymi Wolfii et C. L. Salmasii* (Leyden, 1640), *passim*. See also H. Green, *Shakespeare and the Emblem Writers* (London, 1870), pp. 12–13, 68, and Mario Praz, *Studies in Seventeenth Century Imagery* (London, 1947), II, 38. For the general popularity of the *Table* see also T. W. Baldwin, *William Shakespere's Small Latine*, I, *passim*, and II, 73, 649. For a study of the manuscript tradition, see C. C. Mueller, *De Arte Critica Cebetis Tabulae Adhibenda* (Virceburgi, 1877), chaps. 1, 2, and *Cebetis Tabule*, ed. C. Praechter (Leipzig, 1893).

11. See Wilhelm Waetzoldt, *Hans Holbein the Younger*, trans. F. B. Aikin-Sneath (Zurich, 1939) where a reproduction of the woodcut, used for an edition of Strabo, is to be found on p. 126. I have also found an excellent painting of the *Table* by an unknown artist in the Rijksmuseum in Amsterdam. This is reproduced on p. 351.

12. See Patch, *The Goddess Fortuna*, chap. 5, and p. 153 with n. 3.

13. See Barnabe Barnes, *Foure Bookes of Offices* (London, 1606), sig. A3ᵛ. For James I, see *Basilikon Doron* (London, 1603), sig. H7. La Perrière (op. cit., sig. A3ᵛ) does demonstrate knowledge of James's attitude here by Combes, who remarks "But that your Maiestie may not blame me, in that (following the errour of the Gentiles and Ethnickes) I attribute to Fortune that which (as a Christian writing to a Christian Princesse) I ought to attribute to Gods prouidence."

14. For Ezekiel's wheel as a "Fortune" motif, see Calvin, "Commentaries on the First Twenty Chapters of the Prophet Ezekiel" in *Commentaries*, trans. Thomas Myers (Edinburgh, 1849), I. 67–68. Thomas Wilson, *A Christian Dictionary* (London, 1612) alludes to the association under the entry, "wheel." The association of Fortune with Mutability is discussed by Raymond Chapman, "Fortune and Mutability in Elizabethan Literature," *Cambridge Journal*, V (1952), 374–82.

15. All references to Shakespeare are to the Norton Facsimile of *The First Folio of Shakespeare* edited by Charlton Hinman (New York, 1968). Line-references accord with the lineation system used therein: the "through line numbering" described by Hinman in his introduction.

16. See Gustav Freytag, *Die Technik des Dramas* (Leipzig, 1863).

REVIEWS

Mysteriously Meant: The Rediscovery of Pagan Symbolism and Allegorical Interpretation in the Renaissance by Don Cameron Allen. The Johns Hopkins University Press, 1970. Pp. x + 354. $12.00.

Reviewer: Philip Rollinson.

This is an impressive work of scholarly investigation. Every student of the Renaissance, whether his interest be in drama or nondramatic literature, should read it. Few scholars have realized or will ever realize at first hand the vast acquaintance with the classical, patristic, Renaissance, and later writers whose allegorical explications Allen patiently summarizes and whose popularity and influence he carefully details.

Of the ten chapters the first three are basically introductory. They consider the broad problem of Christian adoption and adaptation of pagan learning. Chapters 4, 6, and 7 survey the rise, flourishing, and decline of allegorical explication of, respectively, Homer, Virgil, and Ovid. Chapter 5 takes up the Renaissance interest in the mysterious wisdom of the ancient Egyptians and chapter 9 the broader subject of significances found in ancient coins, statues, miniatures, and other archaeological remains. Chapter 8 surveys the mythographers, and chapter 10 turns to creative writers (especially Milton) as well as commentators to illustrate the death of the allegorical tradition.

Allen's preface should be noted carefully, because in it, as nowhere else in the book, he announces the purpose and indicates the scope and method of his study. *Mysteriously Meant*, he remarks, is intended to be the companion piece to some of his earlier work in that it surveys generally and comprehensively the sources from which the evidence of specific metaphorical and allegorical traditions was gleaned, especially in his *Image and Meaning*. Allen also observes that he has deliberately chosen simply to present the evidence with little evaluation and only the most rudimentary organization. Hence he casts an extremely detached, but very comprehensive, empirical survey against the recent flood of highly speculative and theoretical investigations of medieval and Renaissance allegory, with the intention of letting the reader draw his own conclusions.

Admirable as this intention—which he does fulfill—is, especially to those who have puzzled over Edwin Honig, Angus Fletcher, or Michael Murrin, the facts will not, after all, in every case adequately speak for themselves. Indeed the first impression from following Allen's survey will probably be that medieval and Renaissance explicators are even more confusing and probably confused than their modern counterparts. Allen could have aided his reader tremendously simply by systematically categorizing his evidence and in the process venturing to indicate more frequently what the evidence means and in what context it achieves significance. For example, when he turns to Ovid's *Metamorphoses* (chapter 7), Allen pauses to comment on the relatively great number of allegorical commentaries on Ovid in the Middle Ages as opposed to the few on Virgil (p. 163). The possible cause of such a phenomenon remains a mystery to the reader, unless he happens to know that the two works were prime examples of what were construed in late antiquity and the Middle Ages to be two quite different and distinct kinds of narrative: the *Aeneid* being historical fiction with an exemplary lesson embedded in its literal text, and the other a collection of *fabulae* with no meaningful significance whatsoever in its literal sense. If one were going to read Ovid's fables at all, one had to look for concealed meanings. Hence probably arose the great number of Ovidian commentaries.

There are numbers of such problems which Allen's evidence presents but which are not, and presumably intentionally not, resolved. I suppose the main reason, though, that Allen declines to enlighten his reader with some basic guidelines for understanding his evidence is that he has chosen not to present or take any account of medieval and Renaissance theories of allegory and myth (he explicitly eschews theory as uninteresting compared to the practice of allegorical exegesis, pp. 282–83). Theory is only discussed in connection with such important explicators as Landino (pp. 145–54) or Boccaccio (pp. 215–18), who have also speculated on the assumptions behind their interpretations. In these instances Allen's evidence is most useful in illustrating for the modern reader how the allegorist arrived or thought he arrived at his interpretive conclusions. Such an understanding is, after all, one of the more important, if not the most important, realizations of such a study. In the main, however, Allen's evidence only shows what was done, by whom, and when.

I would admit the cavilling nature of objecting to the lack of attention to critical theory were it not that the tremendous influence of sixteenth-century Italian poetics is consequently ignored. The result is that sometimes the implication of evidence speaking for itself is a bit distorted. For example, at the end of both the chapter on mythographers (8) and that on the demise of allegory (10), Allen's evidence leads him to observe that the revival "of the old patristic problem of whether or not a Christian poet should use pagan myth" (p. 247) was instrumental in chilling the allegorical exuberances of the Renaissance. He cites, as "an early example," a work by J. V. Andreae (1619), leaps to another appearing in 1709 (p. 247), and in chapter 10 calls for support on Addison (p.

308) and a letter published in 1742 by William Melmoth (pp. 310–11). What this evidence ignores, of course, is that the issue of Christian poets using pagan myth was not only revived considerably earlier than 1619 but was indeed one of the great critical issues of sixteenth-century poetics, early and late. Furthermore only those who are familiar with J. C. Scaliger's comments on allegory and myth (some of the most intelligent remarks ever made on the subject) will recognize the *Poetices*, first published in 1561, as the probable authority behind both Addison's and Melmoth's observations.

With this warning that some of Allen's evidence will not stand alone, I should add that Allen's own conclusions, when they do occur, are once or twice rather carelessly expressed. For example, discussing the decline of mythography, he remarks:

> It can be assumed that when the mystical interpretations of the Bible were increasingly held in doubt, similar readings of Homer, Virgil, Ovid, and the Greco-Roman mythologies were in the same state.
>
> *(p. 244)*

Curiously enough this remark contradicts the evidence of the section (vii) which it concludes. Allen has just noted the sixteenth-century Protestant reaction (Luther, Calvin, and others) against traditional Roman exegesis of the Bible. One has, however, only to observe the dates of the works discussed in chapters 4 through 9 to realize that at the very time (and indeed considerably after) when the Reformers were protesting the excesses of traditional biblical exegesis, allegorical explication of pagan gods, antiquities, and literature was flourishing in its most excessive manner, even among the Protestants. Indeed on the same page (244) Allen immediately observes that although Francis Bacon, following earlier Protestants, disowned much of the traditional biblical exegesis, he was nonetheless "the best English allegorizer of mythology." The subsequent review of Bacon the mythographer confirms Allen's remark that "Bacon's sensitive views on biblical exegesis became much bolder when he read ancient poetry and fable."

Such an occurrence is rare, and Allen is, of course, essentially nonevaluative. One of the evaluations which he does make in passing (for example, on pp. 261, 277–78, and 281) and which several of the later commentators he discusses make (including More, p. 243, and Warburton, pp. 304–5) needs special emphasis. It is that the practice of allegorical interpretation he surveys is manifestly arbitrary, intuitive, and not really interpretation at all. It involves a creative rather than interpretive use of images and passages in ancient literature, myth, and art as suggestive points of departure for various reflections (ethical, theological, and so on) which pertain to the culture and interests of the exegete without much concern for the culture, interests, or intentions of the ancient artist. Consequently agreement on the meaning of a specific image or passage is realized only with and through traditional acceptance. Such traditional agreement, although certainly not rare, on the other hand generally occurs only in the cases of the most commonplace images and the most familiar passages. Even for these the ubiquitous habit of interpreting *in bono* and *in malo* necessitates considerable caution in the modern reconstruction of meanings in a Renaissance poem or play which are only apparent in terms of traditional allegorical significances and not apparent from the poem or play itself. Allen's own method in *Image and Meaning* seems to me to be an admirable example of the use of carefully documented evidence to support interpretations not immediately obvious in Renaissance texts.

Certainly the materials surveyed in *Mysteriously Meant* contribute significantly to the study of meanings in Renaissance poetry and drama. Allen has done an immense service in showing the scholar-critic both where to look and what kind of thing his investigation will probably uncover.

The Friar as Critic: Literary Attitudes in the Later Middle Ages by Judson Boyce Allen. Vanderbilt University Press, 1971. Pp. xii + 176. $11.50.

Reviewer: Kurt Olsson.

The subject of Judson Boyce Allen's book is the group of scholars whom Beryl Smalley some years ago called the "classicizing friars." Mr. Allen sees in the writings of Robert Holkot, John Lathbury, Thomas Ringstead, John Ridewall, John Bromyard, and Thomas Waleys a unique application to the reading of fiction of exegetical methods commonly used in medieval biblical studies. The issue is fashionable in medieval circles, but Mr. Allen, by approaching it through these works, most of which are still unedited, has made important distinctions which both enrich and make more precise our understanding of medieval literary theory.

Chapter 1 begins to work toward a definition of the basic term in the inquiry, "the spiritual sense of fiction"—for medieval exegetes who follow St. Augustine, not only scriptural words, but the things to which those words refer can mean. Mr. Allen finds in this principle a potential for two kinds of allegory, an allegory of the letter and an allegory of the spirit. Traditionally, fictional allegories tend to be literal: such is the case in both reading and writing, in Arnulf of Orléans's commentary on the *Metamorphoses* and in the *Roman de la Rose*. In these examples, the author argues, the allegory exists referentially on but one level. Spiritual allegorizing, on the other hand, involves a real doubleness: "The letter, whatever it is, must remain intact, . . . and the spiritual sense must exist in parallel to it" (p. 9). Traditionally, this sort of allegorizing is reserved for the Bible. With the friars, however, comes a mixing of fictional and biblical figures. Richard Lathbury, for example, reads the mistress of the Gentiles in Lamentations i.1 not only as the Church or the soul, but as Philosophy and Nature, allegorical personae from Boethius and Alan of Lille. By lifting such figures to the level of things, by using pictorial realism and introducing emotive elements in his portrait, Lathbury marks the interpretative tendencies of the classicizing group.

Chapter 2 treats the traditions out of which the spiritual sense of fiction evolves. By the fourteenth century, Allen argues, commentaries on the Bible and the school *auctores* had reached a stage of apparent completeness. Out of these writings, spiritual meanings were commonly gathered for the use of the preacher. In both sorts of writing, illustrated on the one hand by *distinctiones* in Hugh of St. Cher's *Biblia Sacra* and on the other by interpretations of the third Vatican mythographer, meanings are compiled which in turn achieve the status of convention, easily transmitted from author to author. The two traditions are distinct; yet, they are linked by a common language—that of biblical exegesis—and later in the Middle Ages by a companion use in preaching. The assimilation of materials from school authors and biblical commentators in sermons in the later Middle Ages has long been known to medievalists in the form of the exemplum, often taken from the *libri gentilium,* but Allen points out that the friars not only promulgated the classical tale but created the "picture," a form which in special ways yoked the two traditions. This is a focal consideration in chapter 3.

In this chapter Mr. Allen concerns himself with the spiritual sense more specifically. He begins by noting two assumptions with which the friar commentators approached their reading of fiction. First, by a principle of inspiration, a book in some measure becomes independent of its author, allowing the reader to see Christian truths, for example, in classical texts. Second, while originally the spiritual sense had to be based on the truth of the letter, for later commentators historicity itself becomes "a very dubious criterion for distinguishing between the spiritual sense and the allegory of the literal sense" (p. 68). To be sure, "the spiritual sense of fiction is possible only when truth and fiction look much alike" (p. 64), but convenience, authority, and meaningfulness, not historical fact exclusively, become cogent grounds for interpreting fiction spiritually. Hence, the methodology of the friars, when they approached a literary text, was essentially the same as their technique in exegesis and preaching. The procedure included division of the text, interpretation, and confirmation. Division was essential to their mode of analysis: it "implies that connection between letter and spirit which is isomorphic, hieratic, and analogous detail by detail" (p. 70). The parts of a text are interpreted separately, for each carries spiritual meaning. Thus the friars elaborate the popular form of the *distinctio*, a catalog of senses *in bono* and *in malo* of a specific word or phrase, by making the predicable a collection of objects and meanings which add up to a pictorial whole. Robert Holkot, for example, describes the various features of Cupid—he "is painted like a boy with a quiver, fiery of face, naked, winged, and bound with bonds of adamant" (p. 73)—and interprets *in malo* each term of the love represented. Much of Holkot's description is conventional. Yet, here and elsewhere, the trend to portraiture and the evolution of the spiritual sense of fictional materials makes the accomplishment of the friars distinctive. Unlike the earlier commentators, who attempt to justify their literal allegorical interpretations by arguments from etymology or physical nature, the friars simply state the spiritual sense meanings and add concordant authorities, often drawing the same meanings from the Bible. According to the author, then, fiction comes to mean what the Bible means.

Originally the spiritual sense is sought in the Bible because the Bible is literally true. When stories are rendered "true" or realistic, however, there is greater likelihood that the spiritual sense can be seen in them. Toward the end of this third chapter, Mr. Allen works out a plausible connection between the rise of realism late in the Middle Ages and the invention of the spiritual sense of fiction. While the friars do not rework the literal level of narrative fiction realistically, they do invent realistic detail for their pictures. Such is the case with Holkot's Fortune, which bears little resemblance to the conventional Boethian persona. In the writer's words, "an original meaning demands a new incarnation" (p. 110). This example is but one of many in the author's demonstration of how language, for a specific group of medieval scholars, shapes experience, or more concretely, how exegetical technique alters what is perceived.

Since the general aim of *The Friar as Critic* is historical criticism, since the book is an attempt to discover some of the definitions "under which literature is presumed to operate, and through which, therefore, it is heard," specifically "from the point of view of fourteenth-century England" (p. vii), it might have been wished that Mr. Allen then show how the friars' peculiar approach affected writers and hearers in their own period. He chooses rather in the final chapter to return to his general distinction between the senses of the letter and the spirit and to apply them generally to a wider spectrum of medieval literature. The friars' mode is a technique of reading. Mr. Allen's concern in the fourth chapter, "Applications," is with writing. Which poets sought no more than simple literalism? Which in one way or another deliberately incorporated the spiritual sense? The author's interpretation in chapter 4 is not inherently invalid; often it is quite perceptive. Yet, it is a task which might better be undertaken in another place, for by using authorial purpose as a criterion of application, by dividing medieval literature into five categories of relationship between letter and spirit, by making "organic" as opposed to serial interpretation his mode of operation, the writer has abandoned the theme of his book, the mode of reading that the friars made distinctive. Although Mr. Allen is faced with the problem of limitation, since "in the light of the practice of the friars, any interpretation of any poem or story, if it conformed in content to orthodoxy and depended on the spiritual language of exegesis, would be an acceptable and valid interpretation" (p. 117), the question of the specific historical consequences of their technique might form a significant topic of investigation.

Whatever question one might have about the strategy of the final chapter, *The Friar as Critic* forms an important contribution to our knowledge of the relationship between exegesis and fiction. Often by long excerpts from unedited manuscripts, often by sensitive, clear interpretation, Mr. Allen has made more accessible the thinking of this important group of fourteenth-century critics. More generally, the author is to be commended for his lucid, judicious handling of the vexed problem of allegorical interpretation in the late Middle Ages.

Macbeth and the Players by Dennis Bartholomeusz. Cambridge University Press, 1969. Pp. xv + 276. $11.50.

Reviewer: Herbert Berry.

As he writes in his introduction, Dr. Bartholomeusz has studied performances of *Macbeth* from the beginning to the 1960s "to test the proposition that players achieve special insights into a text" which critics and scholars do not (p. xi). Having tested, he concludes at the end of his book that "there is some truth in the claim made for the special insights of the actor," but not, it seems, a great deal, because many actors have "obscured the text of *Macbeth*" (p. 272).

It is a curious conclusion to a curious quest which, in a sense, Dr. Bartholomeusz has not pursued. For despite the stance he takes up in his introduction and in many other places, he has really written a thorough and closely studied history of *Macbeth* (mostly of the part of Macbeth) on the English stage.

Perhaps it is just as well, because the critical difficulties lying in the way of his ostensible purpose are enormous. The contest between actor and critic, first of all, must be judged by the critic. That critic must have a reliable reading of the play against which to judge the insights of actors from the beginning, which for any of Shakespeare's tragedies must itself be a dubious event. (Dr. Bartholomeusz thinks the play is a struggle between mighty opposites in Macbeth's character.) Then when the actor differs from that reading, the critic must chalk up one score for a special insight or one for obscuring the text. If it is a score for a special insight, does the reliable reading then expand to include that insight against which subsequent actors must perform? Does the reliable reading begin as a simple thing and so grow increasingly complex? If so, what is the value of the original reading? Because, for instance, Sir Ralph Richardson and Eric Porter, among others, do not share Dr. Bartholomeusz's view that the play is about mighty opposites, are they really obscuring the text, as Dr. Bartholomeusz says, or advancing a special insight? Moreover, can the actor who has no special insights, but acts the play well according to Dr. Bartholomeusz's standard, be regarded as important? Despite his ostensible purpose, fortunately, he regularly thinks so.

Barry Jackson and Eric Maturin's interpretation, for instance, was inadequate because they blurred "the struggle between essential good and evil in the play" and in the character of Macbeth (p. 232), and Tyrone Guthrie's was inadequate because he lost some of "the conflict between essential good (imaginatively apprehended) and essential evil (unimaginatively grasped)" (p. 239). The line of criticism here seems rather tenuous, probably because the two interpretations were quite different.

This critical wet ground is forever bedeviling Dr. Bartholomeusz's footwork. He must rely on eyewitnesses who wrote down their impressions of performances, most of them professional critics for newspapers and other journals. When they differ, which of them is he to prefer? Not surprisingly, he has a tendency to accept all the writing about a performance, often about a series of performances, and even about an actor's work over twenty or thirty years, as though it were a consistent comment by one reliable witness. In the end, therefore, he finds that "The most successful," not the best, "interpretations" were Garrick's and Olivier's of 1955 (p. 275), because the critical opinions which he cites were nearly unanimously favorable for those two—if Garrick's work in many performances over thirty years is an "interpretation." One result of this method is that Dr. Bartholomeusz is sometimes unable to make discriminating statements to distinguish the work of one actor clearly from that of another. An exception is Charles Kean, for whom the critical writing was rather single-minded. Kean's wife, however, is not an exception. When she acted Lady Macbeth in 1853, Dr. Bartholomeusz's evidence has her as "not at all deficient, as might have been expected, in the requisite physical force"; "in no scene was she weak; in the sleep-walking scene she was terrific"; and "if her luring on of Macbeth had an appalling intensity, her sleep-walking was calm and dignified, 'the incarnation of agony.' " Dr. Bartholomeusz accepts all these statements as equally true (p. 185).

He is apparently aware of this tendency. He frequently repeats conclusions he has reached about an actor's work as though clinging grimly to distinguishing marks. Henderson, for instance, "fell infinitely short of the admirable model on which he formed himself," Garrick; and an inch or so down the page, "Henderson was not successful as Macbeth. Like other actors before him he was found wanting when judged by the standards that Garrick had established" (pp. 96–97). So, too, was Kean, who had a "limiting approach to the poetry of the play," and a little later, "his grasp of the poetry in the play was inadequate" (pp. 182–83). Irving's cuts "at all times suggest that he was trying to pull everything into line with his conception of the character of Macbeth" and "he liked to pull everything into line with his conceptions" (pp. 199–201). Eric Porter "had a limiting conception of Macbeth's character," and he was "hampered . . . by a limiting view of Macbeth's character," and his "portrayal of Macbeth was strong, closely observed, but limited" (pp. 268–69). Yet even this tenacity can lead Dr. Bartholomeusz into indistinct conclusions. Phelps's "interpretation of the character of Macbeth did not differ radically from Macready's," and "Phelps did not alter the conception of Macbeth's character established by Macready," and "Phelps made no radical changes in Macready's conception of the character," but "his performance was no mechanical imitation of Macready's" (pp. 187–88).

For the early history of the play, his first three chapters, Dr. Bartholomeusz has precious little evidence with which to work. He seems to take, therefore, a rather indulgent view of the evidence he has. He has vastly more faith than most of his readers are likely to have that the Folio text of *Macbeth* represents Shakespeare's intention. He is certain, for example, that the comma in the Folio after the first line of Macbeth's soliloquy, "If it were done, when 'tis done, then 'twer well, / It were done quickly" (I.vii.1–2), is Shakespeare's, rather than, say, Compositor B's. Moreover, he thinks the comma should have the force of a full stop. Garrick "regrettably" omitted it (p. 51), as do nearly all editors. Because he put a full stop there, Kemble twice "had a scholar's eye" (pp. 125, 127) and desired "to interpret what Shakespeare actually wrote" (p. 274). Yet to read the passage so, Dr. Bartholomeusz must next conclude (as he avoids doing openly) that the Folio does not represent Shakespeare's intention when it has a colon after "quickly" and a capitalized "If" after that. Similarly, he assumes as few readers will do that Elizabethan actors put plays through repeated rehearsals before presenting them to the public (pp. 6, 8). He reads Simon Forman's re-mark about a performance in 1611 as meaning that Macbeth actually made his first entry on horseback. "It seems," he adds, "very likely that Shakespeare had instructed the actors" to do it (pp. 3ff.). It will not convince many readers to note that "the rhythm of the scene and the imagery of the play justify an entrance on horseback" (p. 5) despite the lack of a stage direction. Forman actually wrote about "howe Mackbeth and Bancko, 2 noble men of Scotland, Ridinge thorowe a wod, the[r] stode before them 3 women feiries or Nimphes. . . ." Forman then wrote that after the murder of Duncan, Macbeth and his lady could not wash the blood from their hands "by Any meanes." Here, however, Dr. Bartholomeusz says we don't "have to accept the literal view," because Forman "appears to have been thinking and writing metaphorically" (pp. 6–7).

When he gets to Garrick, Dr. Bartholomeusz at last has God's plenty. He applies himself here and later assiduously to primary evidence, much of which is new. One may quibble that he sometimes scants the work of those who have written before him and that he misses at least one obvious source of informa-tion. He ignores a pair of articles by Professor Alan Downer, especially his well-known "Nature to Advantage Dressed" (*PMLA*, 58 [1943], 1002–37), perhaps because Professor Downer's attitude toward Garrick and Macklin is the op-posite of Dr. Bartholomeusz's (when a contemporary prefers, as Professor Downer might, Macklin's dagger scene to Garrick's, Dr. Bartholomeusz re-marks that the contemporary "does not seem to have responded adequately to Garrick's playing in the dagger scene" [p. 87]). The Garrick Club in London has about a dozen prints of Garrick as Macbeth and the original of Zoffany's painting of Garrick and Mrs. Pritchard, a copy of which Dr. Bartholomeusz mentions and a mezzotint of which he reproduces.[1] From Garrick onward, Dr. Bartholomeusz's book is a thorough and often carefully reasoned collection of reports, discussions, and reminiscences of performances of *Macbeth*. If the book cannot give us a satisfactory resolution of Dr. Bartholomeusz's initial proposition, it does give us a very useful history of attitudes toward the play. He always writes clearly, and he rarely lets the mass of his material fatigue the reader.

Notes:

1. Almost anywhere at the Garrick Club one has the uneasy feeling that the same face, Garrick's, is peering at him out of many masks from all directions, so numerous are the likenesses hanging on the walls. It is a feeling which many of Dr. Bartholomeusz's actors knew and know well, for they have been and are members. For my acquaintance with the Garrick Club, I am indebted to another member, Mr. E. K. Timings.

The Dramatic Works in The Beaumont and Fletcher Canon.
Volume II. General Editor: Fredson Bowers. Cambridge University
Press, 1970. Pp. viii + 695. $22.50.

Reviewer: Kenneth Muir.

The second volume of the Fredson Bowers edition of Beaumont and Fletcher contains five plays: *The Maid's Tragedy,* edited by Robert K. Turner; *A King and No King,* edited by George Walton Williams; *Cupid's Revenge,* edited by Fredson Bowers; *The Scornful Lady,* edited by Cyrus Hoy; and *Love's Pilgrimage,* edited by L. A. Beaurline. All five editors were also concerned with the first volume.

It will be recalled that the main characteristics of the edition are the inclusion of textual, but not literary, introductions, the texts with footnotes indicating departures from the copy texts, press variants (if any), emendations of accidentals, and historical collations. The individual editors are given a certain measure of freedom, more, perhaps, than was wise. Four of the editors give the tables of sigla at the head of their historical collations, but Mr. Hoy gives his at the end of his introduction. There seems to be no good reason why Mr. Turner should include collations of the Everyman edition of *The Maid's Tragedy* when Mr. Williams does not collate *A King and No King* from the same volume.

The equally austere edition of Dekker was to have included explanatory notes by the late John Crow. There does not seem to be any intention of providing such notes for the Beaumont and Fletcher volumes. It need hardly be said that such notes would greatly increase the value of the edition. One wonders, indeed, whether it is really possible to establish a reliable text without being able to explain every line of it; and it seems a pity that the knowledge so acquired should not be shared with the reader. In *Cupid's Revenge*, for example, there are five or six words for which the reviewer would have liked assistance, and there must be other Elizabethan scholars almost as ignorant.

The text shows a considerable improvement on that of the Old Cambridge edition, since the quartos are nearer to what the authors wrote than the Folios. But the laudable determination to be conservative does not increase the reader's enjoyment:

> I will find um out
> And utterly destroy them, but they are
> Not to be grasp't: let um be men or beasts,
> And I will cut um from the earth, or townes,
> And I will rase um, and then blow um up:
> Let um be seas, and I will drink them off,
> And yet have unquencht fire left in my breast:
> Let um be any thing but meerely voice.

These *ums* can be defended as a Fletcherian habit; but it is difficult to believe that Diego in *Love's Pilgrimage* (II.ii.108) said "Where my fine Boy" or that Leocadia talked of "a sprighty man" (III.ii.73).

There are two cases where editorial policy is difficult to justify. As the editor of *The Maid's Tragedy* accepts more than 350 readings from the Second Quarto, it would have been wiser to have used that as his copy-text, even though it was sometimes guilty of modernization. The other case is more interesting. The copy of the First Quarto of *A King and No King* in the Dyce collection has some sixty corrections in a contemporary hand, obviously derived from a better manuscript than the one used by the compositor. Mr. Williams recognizes this and quite properly accepts into his text many of these manuscript readings. From his introduction it is apparent that he believes that some readings he has not accepted are what Beaumont and Fletcher probably wrote; but where the manuscript readings are not manifestly superior he retains the readings of his copy-text. This is surely wrong. Where the variants are indifferent, the editor should always give the benefit of the doubt to the manuscript corrections. The differences are comparatively unimportant and this very fact makes it probable that the manuscript readings are all authentic. Whoever was responsible for them was not guessing; he was making a praiseworthy attempt to bring the printed text into line with his manuscript. One would give a lot to have a Shakespeare quarto corrected so meticulously.

There are two obvious misprints on page 570 ("hypo the sizes"; "termina l-*esse*"). It is editorial policy not to give the source of additions to stage directions, and it is not made clear where they all come from.

There have been some signs in recent years of a revaluation of the plays of Beaumont and Fletcher. *The Maid's Tragedy* and *A King and No King*, which were universally regarded as two of their best plays, certainly contain some excellent scenes, but the total effect is one of shoddiness. Aspatia's farewell and Evadne's refusal of Amintor (II.i) and the scene between Melantius and Amintor (III.ii) are admirable. But the killing of the lustful king by the repentant Evadne and the killing of the disguised Aspatia by Amintor are theatrically effective and dramatically false. One cannot assert that the good scenes are by Beaumont and the tawdry ones by Fletcher, for Beaumont seems to have been responsible for the last of these. (It would, incidentally, have been helpful if the editors had done more to assign the scenes to their respective authors and to justify what assignments they make.) The happy ending to Arbaces' apparently incestuous love makes it seem that the authors have aroused our pity and salacity under false pretenses. Little can be said in favor of *Cupid's Revenge*, though the printer declared that he had never read a better. It is the comedies which now appear more satisfying because they are less pretentious. *The Wild Goose Chase* and *The Humorous Lieutenant* are both worth reviving, and, in the present volume, *The Scornful Lady* and *Love's Pilgrimage* are both lively and stage-worthy comedies. In the latter, Theodosia and Leocadia disguise themselves as men for love of the philanderer Mark-Antonio, and their adventures and rivalries are entertaining and charmingly pathetic. It is a pity that the text which has come down to us has been altered, not very expertly, ten years after Fletcher's death. It is much more likely that the reviser, whoever he was, echoed passages in *The New Inn* than that Jonson improved on passages in *Love's Pilgrimage*.

Shakespeare's Dramatic Style by John Russell Brown. Barnes and Noble, 1971. Pp. ix + 191. $7.25.

Reviewer: Robert F. Willson.

The development of a new consciousness in reading Shakespeare is the aim of *Shakespeare's Dramatic Style.* John Russell Brown, whose directorial and acting background have motivated his scholarly work in such books as *Shake-*

speare and his Comedies and *Shakespeare's Plays in Performance*, urges modern readers to create a theater of the mind in order to expand awareness about a number of perplexing questions which criticism generally ignores:" . . . to what extent did Shakespeare allow us to read ourselves and our own concerns into his plays? . . . when are the plays intentionally ambiguous? when are words important, when silence or gesture . . . in what ways, and by what means, is Shakespeare a realistic writer?" While these seem to be divergent and sometimes subjective questions, Brown proposes to answer them by pursuing a discernible method—involving analysis of words and speech rhythms in crucial passages, evaluation of significant action and spectacle, and creation of imaginary performances designed to underscore the demands made on actors for total presentation of "the man"—which will yield approximations to the full dramatic style of the plays. In preparation we readers are encouraged to ask some 115 questions (by my own count) about matters related to textual evidence, the Elizabethan stage, the syntax and grammar of relevant passages ("How long, simple or complicated, are the sentences? Are there many repetitions of words, phrases, or sentence-structures?"), action and performance, and the image of life projected.

This method is applied to five plays—*Romeo and Juliet, As You Like It, Julius Caesar, Twelfth Night,* and *Macbeth*—which are most frequently performed and read; Brown has directed four of them. In spite of this bias we are told not to expect a simple director's manual, since Shakespeare's style is not simple, and that we must be prepared for "complicated explanations" to problems of style. Further, Brown warns that he does not intend to search out meanings or offer interpretations, but "to consider what the words ask the actors to do [his text is J. H. Walter's *The Player's Shakespeare*], and what the enacted drama may do for an audience in performance."

In order to bridge the gap between actors and audience, Brown offers some very practical procedures for the reader who cannot attend an actual performance. (Most of these, it should be noted, have probably been suggested to students by instructors anxious to widen awareness of stage matters.) He should learn by heart a short speech or enter a dialogue with someone else, then try varying the delivery by speaking the lines loudly or softly, slowly then quickly, or by arranging the speech in long phrases, then short. Some action should also be introduced; even a change from standing to sitting position can make a difference in mood. Tape recordings of various readings replayed a week or so later can help the reader-actor decide which rendering sounds best or best fits his conception of the speech and character. This practical experimentation has the added benefit of introducing to the reader the concept of "through-line" or "super-objective" (the terms are Stanislavski's) which another actor may be following in a particular production. Harder to perceive, yet likely to emerge from this experiment, is the existence of a subtext in certain scenes and situations. For instance, Macbeth's exchanges with Banquo (I.iii.87 ff.) center on the truth that he is about to become thane of Cawdor, yet they are only cover for the subtextual reality of his concern for murder and kingship. A capable actor must be able to reveal this undertow of emotion, and a sensitive reader should perceive its relevance to Macbeth's complete character.

Though Macbeth's ambivalence ought to be obvious to any audience, and not veiled in a subtext, other thorny problems of character and motivation in central scenes are illuminated by Brown's approach. His analysis of the balcony scene (II.ii) in *Romeo and Juliet* focuses on the epithet "dear saint" as a kind of password for the second meeting and a sign that the lovers have retained the deep feelings of attachment they experienced the first time they used it at the ball. The phrase also becomes a keynote for a shift in rhythm by which Juliet's replies become more like Romeo's strong and sustained run-on lines in his opening speech. Once they are syntactically engaged, both then proceed to speak in lighter rhythms (ll. 61–62) full of short, simple phrases. "If a member of an audience did not understand a word of English, he could appreciate the excitements, hesitations, assurances, answers and, finally, the shared and almost silent intimacy of this wooing in the very sound of the words that are spoken. . . ." The words, however, must be understood in order to follow the sexual meaning of the encounter; references to dreams, fantasies, levitation, sailing on "the bosom of the air," then falling back to gaze at the "bright angel" Juliet—all suggest a kind of inner necessity which draws the two together but which cannot be expressed directly because of the obstacle of Romeo's name. Clearly, this scene is dominated by words and speech rhythms, movement being kept to an absolute minimum.

Romeo's soliloquy in the Capulet tomb (V.iii.74–120) is also examined carefully and rewardingly to discover the unspoken motivation behind the words. In particular, Romeo's Petrarchan imagery, depicting sea-weary barks wrecked on looming rocks, underscores the strenuous involvement and rapid oscillations of thought the young hero is experiencing. "In this soliloquy Romeo's attention is carried away from himself to his surroundings, to Juliet, to preparation for death, and back to himself; and each movement is made five or six times within the forty-six lines." Further, the audience's knowledge that Juliet is not dead creates in it a half-awareness of his deception and his pointless death. Friar Laurence's hurried entrance with crow and spade, implements held as well by Romeo, reminds us of the helplessness of both urgently involved "pilots."

Brown also displays a sharp-eyed talent for bringing to life sections of the comedies which suffer most in modern readings because of their topicality, obscure puns, and allusions. The metaphoric strain in the speeches of Rosalind and Celia following the wrestling match in *As You Like It* carries on the idea of a battle between the sexes. Orlando, though present, never answers the witty and challenging questions tossed at him by Rosalind; his strong silence proves his ability to overthrow more than his enemies. It provides only a glimpse of his character but enough of a glimpse to prepare us for the laughable result of the strong, silent type's efforts as carver of love poetry. Similarly, the opening scene of *Twelfth Night* awakes only in performance. Shakespeare gives us no sustained explanation of Orsino's character, only a series of sensuous and paradoxical images and puns with sexual overtones. These are enough to prepare us for his later actions, at the same time revealing his deficiencies as ruler of self and state.

Still, Brown's method is generally less successful in a majority of cruxes; he is weakest where he should be strongest—in analyzing the tragedies. By drawing attention to the "silences" in the prince's final remarks *(Rom.,* V.iii.), by narrowing the discussion to hints for meaningful pauses in such lines as "Where be these enemies? Capulet, Montague . . . ," and by noting the use of simple words and the lack of puns, Brown misses the obvious. He overlooks not the meaning but the metaphor of the prince's "I for winking at your discords too / Have lost a brace of kinsmen" (293–94). The ruler's position at the center of the stage and the connection of "winking" with the other planetary references in the play point to this confession as that of an errant planet (monarch) now working to correct its course and assume its proper place in the universe (state). This metaphor also neatly links the conclusion to the prologue (which Brown analyzes in great detail) with its reference to "star-crossed lovers." By searching out the "hidden directions" in the unprinted text, the author has overlooked the ones that are present in the printed speech.

More disturbing is Brown's failure to follow his own instructions about repeated words, a failure that does mar the terminal chapter on *Macbeth.* The hero's "We are yet but young in deed" (III.iv.144) prompts an extended discussion about the line's ambiguity—is Macbeth speaking his pity for Lady Macbeth, and encouragement, or is he, paradoxically, tying his suffering to hers, making it a source of strength? We are told that the full force of these words lies in the way they are spoken and in the changing relationship, physical and psychological, of the actors interpreting them. How the actors leave the stage will be crucial in answering the questions raised here. Yet surely Macbeth's long speech (ll. 130–40) preceding this final line must be taken into account as well. In ten lines he repeats the personal pronoun "I" nine times, a fact which clearly indicates he is now charting his own course of villainy (he has just had Banquo murdered without telling his wife). "We are yet but young in deed," then, could very easily represent Macbeth's conscious invocation of the royal "we" as a way of giving support to his new sense of egoism. In defense of the author's ambiguous reading of the line, one recalls his reluctance to offer interpretations; but, by turning the scene over entirely to the actors and their "super-objectives," has he not abdicated his responsibility as critic and given us what he said he would not—a director's manual?

The book's other flaws—the failure to provide a synthesizing chapter on the plays discussed, a lack of citation for statements about authority of quarto texts, and an annoying habit of asking many questions while answering few—are perhaps not so damaging as the failure of method. Brown's style is generally lucid and congenial, and by isolating certain cruxes he has raised awareness about acting and directorial style. But the matter of Shakespeare's dramatic style remains elusive. One can practice with individual passages as a way of improving perception, yet to apply this detailed but limited approach to an entire play is physically impossible for both reader and audience. Even the most dedicated scholar cannot keep an eye constantly on word choice, syntax, hidden and apparent stage directions, and implied action while reading; even the most avid theatergoer is likely to be struck by a piece of business or some other form of pyrotechnics and then ignore significant parts of the speeches. Finally, one is disturbed throughout by a feeling that Brown is unsure of his audience: is he writing for students, scholars, actors, directors, or all of these? This weakness is particularly damaging since Shakespeare's dramatic style, which Brown takes as fully evident, may be defined and perceived quite differently by each of these groups.

The Evolution of Shakespeare's Comedy: A Study in Dramatic Perspective by Larry S. Champion. Harvard University Press, 1970. Pp. 241. $8.50.

Reviewer: Bertrand Evans.

It is always a pleasure to read a book on Shakespeare that is at once readable and illuminating; it is doubly pleasurable to do so during a prolonged period of dearth, when, alas, the prevailing fashion exhibits chiefly unreadability, obfuscation of the subject, and illumination of nothing else so much as the author's (not Shakespeare's) own personality traits.

Mr. Champion's new book on Shakespearean comedy is forthright and honest, also modest; it announces that it is concerned with a facet of Shakespeare's artistry, a proper subject, and is so to the end. It is a welcome relief after so many books that quite forget the plays themselves except as excrescences of something cultural, social, thematic, or whatever, that always lies outside the plays. To Mr. Champion the plays are what matter; and indeed they do.

Here the plays are divided into "The Comedies of Action," "The Comedies of Identity," "The Problem Comedies," and "The Comedies of Transformation." Mr. Champion concentrates on three plays (*The Comedy of Errors, The Two Gentlemen of Verona, A Midsummer Night's Dream*) in the first category; two (*Much Ado About Nothing, Twelfth Night*) in the second; two (*All's Well that Ends Well* and *Measure for Measure*) in the somewhat purgatorial third; and two (*The Winter's Tale, The Tempest*) in the fourth. His thesis, briefly, is that the evolution of Shakespearean comedy is synonymous with the evolution of comic characterization; Shakespeare moves from characters who do not matter except as creatures of plot to, ultimately, characters whose moral transformation is the *raison d'etre* of the comedy. That is not quite all: Mr. Champion is unswervingly concerned with Shakespeare's growing skill in maintaining, or sustaining, the audience's "comic perspective," or "comic vision," while the key character or characters are in the process of transformation. It is a magic of balancing that Mr. Champion finds to be Shakespeare's ultimate accomplishment, and he finds it only in Leontes (not quite perfectly) and in Alonso, Antonio, Sebastian (perfectly). In the exhibition of the transformation of these latter characters, the dramatist succeeds simultaneously in maintaining the spectators' comic perspective.

The book is thus, primarily, a study of certain key characters along the full route of Shakespearean comedy, and because of its framing idea—the tension between serious character study, on the one hand, and maintenance of comic perspective, on the other—it has much that is illuminating to offer. There are detailed and insightful probings of Bertram, Angelo, Alonso, to name only a few. However, the author will come off scot-free with no Shakespearean: one bridles at what he says of Malvolio; Bottom ought to count for more; he is partly wrong about Angelo; and he is horribly wrong about Bertram (that total rat who "repents" only because the vise is on him). But the passing irritations help, rather than harm, the effect of the book.

The book is a short one; every Shakespearean should read it. The author's acknowledgment of debts along the way is generous and gratifying; unless this reviewer failed to notice, there is no unkind word set down for any current school of critics or for any single wrongheaded Shakespearean. That in itself is an achievement of major proportions and signifies forbearance deserving of approbation if not outright emulation.

Dramatic Character in the English Romantic Age by Joseph W. Donohue, Jr. Princeton University Press, 1970. $14.50.

Reviewer: Dennis Bartholomeusz.

Mr. Donohue tells us that "few better ways exist of understanding the past than by studying its theatre." The assumption that this is indeed so at all times needs examination, for it may work well in the eighteenth century and not work quite so well in the twentieth. For the period dealt with in Mr. Donohue's book, *Dramatic Character in the English Romantic Age,* one suspects that it ought to work well enough. As he suggests, the subjects, the conventions of art in a given time say much about that time as a whole—its delights and aversions, its shared attitudes and tacit preconceptions, its image of itself. Few could object to the principle stated in this way—when the period in mind is the second half of the eighteenth and the early years of the nineteenth century.

The book has a primarily historical concern. Whether the creation and interpretation of character in the Romantic age had a permanent critical value is not within its terms of reference. Critical theory, actors' interpretations, contemporary plays, are looked at for the light they throw on the time. Character in drama is considered useful because it illuminates the age.

The assumption that it could do so is not unreasonable. It is when Mr. Donohue describes the nature of the illumination that one has reservations. There is more than a hint of the handy encapsulation in his use of the word "revolutionary." The book is based "on the premise that a study of the drama, theatre, and criticism in the English Romantic age, and in the period leading up to it reveal innovations that mark it as revolutionary. . . ." "Significant cleavages," we are told, "begin to occur in the late 18th century movement towards subjectivity in the arts, in religion, philosophy and even in government, when a new sense of man's individuality contributed towards revolutions in France and America and to a subsequent series of reforms in England that have determined to a great extent the history of nations since that time." The word "subjective" and the word "revolutionary" are almost synonymous for Mr. Donohue.

It is not irrelevant here to recall that for Lenin the exact opposite was true; the revolutionary spirit demanded an unemotional objectivity. Lenin's response to Beethoven is well known. He was capable of being emotionally stirred by Beethoven's music, but thought that revolutionary objectivity could not afford the luxury of feeling. Mr. Donohue enlists Locke in the cause of revolutionary subjectivism, when Locke, one had always thought, was representative of an objective attitude to life. Locke's psychology of perception was very different from that of the great Romantics. As Yeats saw it, myth and metaphor died when Locke appeared.

> Locke sank into a swoon;
> The Garden died;
> God took the spinning-jenny
> Out of his side.

To believe that subjectivity was an entirely new and revolutionary phenomenon and, working on this premise, to suggest that all acting before Garrick was objective and formal, and that all acting after Garrick became subjective, is questionable. Betterton's acting in the seventeenth century possibly had a subjective dimension. (Steele's account of Betterton's interpretation of Hamlet suggests as much.) And as Bertram Joseph points out, if there were formal patterns of gesture used on the Elizabethan stage in the time of Burbage, they had to be experienced subjectively and afresh if they were to be of real service. The divorce of the objective from the subjective principle was a post-Burbage phenomenon, though the exceptional individual could bring them together again in his art.

The most complete creative artist succeeds in incorporating both dimensions of human experience in his art (Lenin limited himself by not being able to perceive this), just as the great poets of the Romantic period at their best had a firm grasp of the object coupled with a deep subjective and imaginative awareness. One suspects that this is true of the best acting in that age as well.

The fine gradations of the word *subjective* could have been more clearly defined in this book. Mr. Donohue shows that Beaumont and Fletcher, for example, were an important influence on the drama of the Romantic age, but they possessed a special kind of subjectivity, often sentimental in T. S. Eliot's sense of the word, where emotion exists in excess of the object. A good many Romantic plays shared this quality, but not all the poetry nor all the acting was divorced from actuality in this way. We know of the poetry of Wordsworth as of the acting of Mrs. Siddons, that at its best it was distinguished for its firm grasp of the actual. Romanticism at the popular level built its Gothic castles very much in the air. At other levels subjectivity, as in the *Ode to Autumn* by Keats, involved a vivid apprehension of the outer world. For Coleridge the highest imagination demanded a unity of the general with the concrete, the idea with the image, more than usual emotion with more than usual order.

Having made clear my own sense of the limitations of the premise on which this book is based, I would like to add that many of the facts uncovered in the book are useful to us. The chapter on Cumberland's plays is historically informative, and the chapter on the Romantic age and the critical tradition lively and penetrating.

In *The West Indian* Cumberland seems to have wanted to humanize racialism out of existence. It is certainly of interest to know that this kind of social impulse was a motivating force in drama at the turn of the eighteenth century. In *The West Indian*, Cumberland created two characters, each the victim of social prejudice. The conventional stage Irishman, farcically inept and humorously extravagant, re-emerged in all the freshness Cumberland's sympathetic attitude could endow him with. *The West Indian* was given a capacity for a vivacious, giddy dissipation with a generous spirit. Mr. Donohue's remarks imply that *The West Indian* was stage-worthy. It would have been interesting to know whether he believes it can be profitably staged today.

Mr. Donohue's chapter on Shakespearean character in the Romantic age, and the critical tradition (the best in the book, it seemed to me), places critics like Johnson, Whateley, Cumberland, and Coleridge against actors like Garrick and Kemble. Cumberland, we are told, in a critically alert essay published in the *Observer* in 1788, compared Macbeth with Richard III, and pointed out that Macbeth's character grows in the course of the drama while Richard's is fully formed from the moment he announces "I am determined to be a villain." This basic distinction makes Cumberland decide that *Macbeth* is by far the more interesting play. In Richard cruelty flames forth at once, but in Macbeth it seems to dawn gradually in his soul. Macbeth mediates between an attack upon our pity and an attack upon our sense of horror. The essay by Cumberland seems to throw as much light on Shakespeare's text as on the age in which it was written. What surprises when one reads this chapter, thoroughly researched by Mr. Donohue, is the directness and acuteness of some of the lesser known critics of the period.

His study of Kemble's interpretation of Macbeth is equally valuable. Mr. Donohue touches the core of that interpretation and defines it with accuracy and depth. He observes that, while Garrick's performances had anticipated critical views of *Macbeth*, Kemble's interpretation summed up ideas about *Macbeth* which had dominated the thought of his day. As Mr. Donohue shows, despite the imperfect logic and misinterpretations evident in Kemble's pamphlet on *Macbeth*, his conclusion that Macbeth and Richard are as intrepid as men can be, but that Macbeth is both intrepid and a man of feeling, underscores the dual emphasis on courage and agonized remorse in his performance. Kemble achieved a balance between courage and "the last despairing glimmer of original virtue." This chapter contains a balanced summary of Kemble's interpretation, with a clear sense of its depth and range of awareness. What this chapter shows, though Mr. Donohue does not say so, is that Kemble's interpretation is not important merely for the insights it gives into the social and cultural history of the time, but that it throws light on the complexity of the text of Shakespeare's play.

Lyrics from English Airs, 1596–1622, edited and with an introduction by Edward Doughtie. Harvard University Press, 1970. Pp. xxi + 657. $12.50.

Reviewer: Nan Cooke Carpenter.

A strophic song in homophonic style with instrumental (lute) or vocal accompaniment, the English air (ayre) was an important musical form during the late Elizabethan and Jacobean periods. The first printed collection of airs appeared in 1597: John Dowland's *First Booke of Songes or Ayres of fowre partes with Tableture for the Lute: So made that all the partes together, or either of them seuerally may be song to the Lute, Orpherian or Viol de gambo.* (The title is significant of the variety of ways in which each piece might be performed.) John Attey's *First Booke of Ayres*, 1622, closed this chapter in music history. In between were collections by Morley, Pilkington, Coprario, Ferrebosco, and many others. Professor Doughtie has compiled here the lyrics for all these songs, with the exception of the works of Thomas Campion (available elsewhere). This volume, he says (p. viii), "is for those scholars, students, and critics who need more than a modernized text but less than several copies of the originals, and who would be interested in details about manuscript versions, textual matters, and sources."

Preceding the poems is a long introduction, in the first part of which Professor Doughtie distinguishes between the air and other forms (especially the madrigal), delineates the origin and development of the air, and discusses its characteristics. Concluding that the English air "remained a basically native form which changed but stayed within a recognizably continuous tradition," Doughtie explains that "the nature of both the changes and the continuity may be clarified by examining the parallel development of the kinds of poems the songwriters chose" (p. 9).

In the second part of the introduction, Professor Doughtie sets the song-books in the miscellany tradition and proceeds to analyze and describe the poetry of the miscellanies from *The Court of Venus* (1537) through Tottel's *Songes and Sonettes* (1557) to Robinson's *Handful of Pleasant Delights* (1566) and others later in the century, with emphasis upon ballads. Next is a glance at the psalm-singing tradition, which paralleled the cult of the ballad (often an identical tune served for psalm and ballad alike). Sir Thomas More's famous description of *musica reservata* is quoted, leading into a discussion of expres-siveness in music ("one of the main contributions of the Renaissance to later music" [p. 19]) and the development of the consort song (solo song accom-panied by a consort of viols).

Beginning with Byrd's collection of secular music of 1588 (*Psalmes, Sonets, & Songs of Sadnes and Pietie*), representing the native tradition, and con-tinuing into *Musica Transalpina* of the same year (Italian madrigals to English words), and then to later collections, Professor Doughtie analyzes music and verse of the last decades of the century, with attention to French and Italian in-fluences. It is here (p. 26) "that the overlapping between the songbooks and the miscellanies becomes quite noticeable." As publications tended to become more specialized (instead of a collection of verse, a poet might publish a sonnet sequence), miscellaneous lyrics tended to be found only in songbooks (or in plays and romances). "Thus the printed songbooks become more important in a careful historical consideration of the lyric" (p. 27).

The last part of the introduction centers upon characteristics of the poems of the songbooks, special problems connected with setting the lyrics, the uses of imagery and diction, and the conclusion that poetry for songs is necessarily limited to surface effects. "Consequently, songs as poems are generally minor poems—but we would be poorer without them" (p. 41).

There follows a brief section—"The Composers"—consisting of short biographies of the musicians of the songbooks. And a note on editorial pro-cedures explains printing changes made by the author. But the bulk of the book (pp. 51–422) comprises the lyric texts, each set preceded by detailed description of the songbook being considered, including collation, notice of all known copies, *Stationer's Register* entry, *Short-Title Catalogue* date, descrip-tion of the music, plus any significant bibliography. Following the lyrics are variant readings, copious notes, an index of first lines, and a glossarial index, in which some of the words are glossed. (And some, quite noticeably, are not: where, for instance, are *anaphora*, *anadiplosis*, and *exergasia*, mentioned so informally on page 37?)

Slight as they are, for the most part, these poems run the gamut from love

to tobacco (one song, indeed, proves that tobacco is like love [pp. 198–99]) and
contain many curious verses. A battle song echoes Jannequin's famous chanson
La Guerre (p. 198); Gascoigne's "Philip Sparrow" echoes Skelton (pp. 243–44).
Davies's "Twelve Wonders of the World," set by John Maynard, is an embryo
characterbook, wittily describing twelve different types of people (courtier,
divine, soldier, lawyer, the "Phisition" ["The earth my faults doth hide, / The
world my Cures doth see"], and so forth). Among writers of the poems are
some of the leading poets of the age. The first complete poem known to be
by Sir Philip Sidney appeared in a songbook; and one meets here famous
names from Wyatt to Donne. (An index of authors' names would have been
helpful; most of the lyrics are, of course, anonymous.) Finally the composers'
prefaces, letters to readers, and dedicatory epistles also make interesting—and
sometimes curious—reading. Dowland's letters, especially, are filled with
information about music, contemporary musicians, and patrons.

In his preface, Professor Doughtie acknowledges his debt to Hyder Rollins
(whom he never knew). His book is certainly not unworthy of the high editorial standards set by Professor Rollins. One obvious lack, however, stands
out: an explanation of the cutoff with a collection of 1622. The air continued
to be cultivated during the century, although quite changed from the earlier
song (usually declamatory, in the new *stile recitativo*). Doughtie does, in fact,
point out (pp. 8–9) that one of Robert Dowland's collections contains Italian
songs in the new monodic style advocated by the Florentine innovators. And
he does state (p. 22) that "the air was only changed in the work of Lawes
and his contemporaries." But these are offhand statements. A paragraph or so
on the development of the baroque air, with approximate dates and composers
as well as brief stylistic summaries, would have made the otherwise excellent
introduction more meaningful to the newcomer to the history of music as well
as to the scholar primarily interested in literature.

The Shakespearean Grotesque: Its Genesis and Transformations
by Willard Farnham. The Clarendon Press, 1971. Pp. x + 176.
$6.50.

Reviewer: Albert Wertheim.

There is much that will please the reader in Willard Farnham's most recent
study, *The Shakespearean Grotesque*. To understand and appreciate the sub-

ject of this volume, however, one must go beyond the unfortunate title and use of terminology. One might well expect a book entitled *The Shakespearean Grotesque* to include extended commentary on the witches in *Macbeth*, their bizarre incanted anecdotes, their cauldron contents, and their visual prognostications in Act IV. *Macbeth*, however, receives no coverage. One might presume as well the inclusion of such disparate Shakespearean grotesqueries as Kate and Petruchio's wedding ceremony, Imogen's embracing the headless trunk of Cloten, Timon's hurling the dishes of warm water at his guests, the mutilations and Senecan horrors of *Titus Andronicus*, the infamous bear of *The Winter's Tale*, the kissing pole-borne heads of Lord Say and Sir James Cromer in *2 Henry VI*, the interchange between Cleopatra and the clown who brings the basket of asps, or the courtship of Titania and Bottom. With the exception of the last, none of these incidents receives mention in this study. Although a page and a half is devoted to the grotesque relationship between Lear and the Fool, no reference is made anywhere in *The Shakespearean Grotesque* to the well-known "King Lear and the Comedy of the Grotesque" section of G. Wilson Knight's *The Wheel of Fire* (1930 and 1949). These oversights are not accidental, for Professor Farnham's sense of the word *grotesque* is unique.

Grotesque is indeed a vague and vexed term, which has, in recent years, been given considerable and, in some cases, brilliant attention. It seems astounding that Professor Farnham makes no mention of Wolfgang Kayser's monumental study, *The Grotesque in Art and Literature* (English translation, 1963), often hailed as a definitive work. Nor is mention made of Lee Byron Jennings's *The Ludicrous Demon* (1963), a study written and published at Professor Farnham's own university. In fact, the great weakness of *The Shakespearean Grotesque* is that it makes no reference to any study of the grotesque, nor does it take pains to clarify its own singular use of that hazy term. Farnham gives no indication that he recognizes that his use of *grotesque* is not everyone else's or that he is aware that the term has ever given anyone the least bit of hesitation. Though he never gives a definition, Professor Farnham, nonetheless, in his first chapter "Beautiful Deformity" gives the reader a sense of what he means by *grotesque*.

That sense and the title of the first chapter take their cue from St. Bernard's worry about the possible ill effects of sensuous church decoration upon ascetic monks: "For them 'what profit is there in that ridiculous monstrosity, a marvellous kind of deformed beauty and beautiful deformity?' (*quid facit illa ridicula monstrositas, mira quaedam deformis formositas, ac formosa deformitas?*)" (p. 1). What St. Bernard means, Farnham contends, by "beautiful deformity" are the bizarre and clearly secular figures that intrude themselves upon serious Christian art. These include "monsters such as centaurs, other half men, a four-footed beast with a serpent's tail, a fish with a beast's head, a body with many heads, a head with many bodies, and a beast half horse and half goat" (p. 2). After a thirty-two page select survey of pertinent iconography illustrating the appearance of such monstrosities from Pompeiian wall painting to medieval and Renaissance manuscript illuminations and illustrated psalters, Professor Farnham launches into the real subject of his book: the intrusion of what he calls *grotesque*, that is, exaggerated—sometimes comic, sometimes evil, often both—characters into primarily serious plays.

The equation may be a too easy one between the strange shapes hovering on the borders of illuminated manuscripts on the one hand and the comic characters of mystery cycle plays and the witty Ambidexters of serious morality plays on the other. Whether or not the appearances of Mak and Gil in the Towneley *Second Shepherds' Play* and of Meretrix, Huf, Ruf, and Snuf in Thomas Preston's *Cambises* constitute what we may label grotesque also seems open to debate. If, however, one can get beyond these issues and realize what, after all, this book is about, then *The Shakespearean Grotesque* becomes an engaging and intelligent addendum to Professor Farnham's justly famous *The Medieval Heritage of Elizabethan Tragedy* (1936). In the last sections of his first chapter, Farnham astutely points out the singular tone of certain mystery cycle plays. A tone that arises from the addition of what is often low comedy and sometimes gallows humor within the dramatization of Scripture. There are succinct but salient points on the various "Noah" plays and on the Towneley "Slaughter of the Innocents." About the former, Professor Farnham intelligently remarks on the tonal distinction between Noah's attitude toward his wife and hers toward him: "Noah's beating of his wife has the comedy of an ordinary incongruity revealed between high and low, but *her* beating of *him* goes beyond that to the comedy of an extraordinary incongruity in a reversal of the accepted order of things, threatened by the low" (p. 35). About "The Slaughter of the Innocents," Farnham notices the bitter humor of the lamenting mothers' drubbing Herod's soldiers: "Grimness in plenty is present here along with low comedy" (p. 35). An extended section on the Towneley *Second Shepherds' Play* reviews and applauds the readings of this play that posit a dramatic relationship between its low comedy and high religious seriousness. Farnham calls it a "divine comedy" and argues further that it is not enough to contend that the *Second Shepherds' Play* is fractured into two distinct parts that are related to one another by dramatic analogy. The play, rather, functions as a thoroughly integrated totality: there "is an over-all dramatic action that completely absorbs comedy as comedy along with seriousness as seriousness and converts them into the oneness of what may be called a divine comedy" (p. 45). This is a stimulating insight that one wishes could have been carefully explored, but the mystery cycles are not, of course, the subject of *The Shakespearean Grotesque*.

Almost one-third of this book focuses attention upon Falstaff, who is hardly the figure one would have predicted to be the *primary* example of the Shakespearean grotesque. However, when we realize, as we constantly must, that *grotesque* in this study tends to mean the assertive and often satirical "low," then the reasons for the concentration on Falstaff become pellucid. And on Falstaff, Professor Farnham has written two perceptive chapters. The first explores the idea that Sir John is both man and animal at once. He has a rare degree of human wit and reason, but at the same time is a "food- and sex-desirous animal." And this admixture is manifested not only in his action but in his language. *Gravity-gravy* and *waist-waste* puns give us a linguistic measure of the man. As Farnham summarizes, "It is that he wants to be, and joyously is, an animal well endowed with man's mental cleverness, a witty animal, a monstrous animal" (pp. 58–59). The second chapter on Falstaff, "Falstaff and the Codes of High Endeavour," begins with rather a too cursory glance at Falstaff's Shakespearean compatriots. In ten pages Launce, Speed, Costard, and Bottom make their exits and entrances. These are so brief that perhaps they should not have appeared at all. One is genuinely pleased when the discussion returns to Falstaff, for about his place in the Henriad, and particularly in *1 Henry IV*, Professor Farnham has much to say. Falstaff is viewed in the tradition of the medieval Vice and of the mystery cycle devil's advocates like Cain and Mak; and like those characters, Falstaff is, for Farnham, part of a unified dramatic statement. Like those characters, too, he is at once a comic Vice and vicious in the modern sense of the word. His animality may constitute a commentary upon the characters of high seriousness, but no more so than his sharp wit and ready ad hoc rationalizations. These are not particularly novel insights, but they are well put and well argued.

Hamlet carries the pattern of Falstaff one step further. Whereas Falstaff and the "high" characters serve as mutual commentary, Hamlet, who harbors within his nature the matter for both high tragedy and low comedy, internalizes the commentary. He possesses "a double nature, a nature in which a prince and a court fool share alike" (p. 99). This "double nature," this internalization of what Farnham calls *grotesque* and *non-grotesque*, is used to explain Hamlet's vision of man as at once part divine and part brute. In supporting this idea, Professor Farnham has some enlightening things to say about the animal imagery in *Hamlet*. A developed exploration of the thesis in terms of particular passages and scenes, however, would have been welcome. The same may be said for the final section of the book, which, in the main, treats Thersites, Iago,

and Caliban. Here the text provides several brilliant perceptions without following them through. Of Thersites, Farnham comments, "Thersites . . . is very
much for having others suffer just so he may enjoy their suffering" (p. 134);
and of Iago he writes, "Following good Vice tradition he plays fast and loose
in what he tells about himself, to a theatre audience as well as to those he deals
with in the play" (p. 150). Rich and suggestive statements like these almost
always disappointingly go unexplored. One might wish too that *The Shakespearean Grotesque* contained a chapter on *Antony and Cleopatra,* perhaps the
Shakespearean play in which the supposedly lower and higher natures of man
—Farnham's *grotesque* and *non-grotesque*—are seen in their most complex
relationship.

   The Shakespearean Grotesque is not a flawless book. Its title and terminology
are unfortunate, as is its failure to establish clearly its unique definition of
grotesque. Although Falstaff, Hamlet, Thersites, Iago, and Caliban are the principals of this study, only the character of Falstaff is treated with appropriate
scope. The points on Hamlet are unexceptionable, but a longer chapter would
have made them richer. Similarly, Thersites, Iago, and Caliban are the cramped
cohabitants of a final forty-one-page chapter. *The Shakespearean Grotesque* is,
nonetheless, well written and persuasive. It contains many nuggets of singular
insight, any one of which could provide the basis for a meaningful essay or
book. Nearly every passage reflects the author's lifetime study of Shakespearean and Elizabethan drama. Possibly because of this, Professor Farnham is himself so well aware of the implications of what he says that he does not feel the
need to ramify. We can only regret, as we do with any succinct but perceptive
critic, that he did not say more.

Triumphal Forms: Structural Patterns in Elizabethan Poetry
by Alastair Fowler. Cambridge University Press, 1970. Pp. xiii +
234. $11.50.

Reviewer: M. Kay Nellis.

   Alastair Fowler's latest study in numerological criticism is designed, according to his own statement, "simply to arouse interest and to suggest future lines
of exploration," and the structure of the book does in fact reflect this statement
(p. xi). There is a somewhat polemic preface; an introductory chapter discusses
evidence for the existence of numerological patterns; an excellent summary of

the various difficulties involved in numerological criticism forms an epilogue. Previous essays in numerology or symmetry, including studies of classical authors and the Italian Renaissance as background for the Elizabethan period, are reviewed and extensively footnoted. Mr. Fowler's own interests spread from Dante to Pope, from festal poetry to sonnet sequences and *Paradise Lost*, from the complications of symmetry about a central point to the structural and symbolic organization of poems around numbers associated with units of time. Such a range, however, imposes certain limitations: the effect is one of sampling, both in genre and in individual poems where one or two points are brought out but the poem is not considered thoroughly. Conclusions from earlier numerological criticism are cited without the evidence from which they were derived, often with a rather startling effect; background material appears to be representative rather than inclusive, is introduced incidentally (as are most of the symbolic interpretations of numbers), and in the case of visual arts in the Renaissance is distinctly sketchy. The study does indeed raise a number of important issues, including the currently popular question of the analogies between art and literature, and furnishes a variety of examples of numerological criticism of poetry, as well as a guide to past work. Since the book is an introduction to the field, however, it is unfortunate that it does not give equal time to the opposition; relatively few studies arguing against a numerological viewpoint are listed, even in footnotes.

Numerological criticism is based on the principle that structural units extending beyond the line—including groups of lines, stanzas, or groups of stanzas— exist in poetry; the exact number of lines or items arranged in these structural units forms a pattern intentionally devised by the author, often symbolizing or at least connected with the meaning of the poem. The value of the poem is not necessarily correlated with elaborate structure: Chapman's "The Amorous Zodiac," a structurally complex astrological anatomy of his mistress, is a curiosity well worth reprinting, but a poor poem. Numerological organization operates at several levels, from surface pattern (as when an elegy contains one line for each year of the deceased's age) to reinforcement of a theme by suggestive placement of a particular item or by numerological symbolism. Certain difficulties are evident. A "pattern" may be a chance arrangement; numbers in a unit like a stanza may be chosen arbitrarily to form a pattern without symbolic intent. According to Mr. Fowler, though, in the Renaissance "number symbolism was so common an ingredient in public arts and ceremonial that it must have been regarded almost as a necessary aspect of decorum" (p. 20). There was also a common vocabulary of symbolic interpretations, even if several possibilities existed for any one number: "Numbers had certain symbolic meanings as integrally related to them as semantic fields" (p. 20). These meanings are derived from the Renaissance emphasis on number and proportion in the cosmic structure, influenced by Plato and Pythagoras (medieval number symbolism characteristically had a theological basis). Systematic structure, natural to the world, is natural to imitations of the world, so that a numerically organized poem reflects the structure of the world, real or ideal. Such patterns, occurring in the arts as in literature, develop from "the visual ordering of ideas that characterized the period," a concept for which Mr. Fowler is indebted to Father Walter Ong (p. 19).

The first of these basic patterns to be discussed is symmetry, with or without a central stress. One form of symmetry is the triumphal pattern, found in masques and pageants as well as in many Elizabethan festal poems, in which characters are symmetrically grouped around a central figure. For example, in the Masque of Cupid in Book III of *The Faerie Queene*, thirteen preliminaries to love (for example, Ease, Doubt, Pleasure) precede Amoret, led by Despite and Cruelty; Cupid in the central sovereign position is followed by another group of three, Reproach, Repentance, and Shame, then by thirteen feared consequences to love (for example, Strife, Sorrow, Poverty). The structure of the pattern leads Mr. Fowler to suggest that Amoret's feeling, objectified in the masque, is fear of sexual passion and that Busyrane is Amoret's opinion of Scudamour as masterful husband.

In Elizabethan poetry, however, there is a tendency toward more complex types of symmetry in both form and content. "A symmetrical pattern might be left ambiguous, for example, or shared between two centres, or even ironically inverted so as to dignify a figure unfit for the place of honour" (p. 77). In *Venus and Adonis*, the central stanza describes Venus's closest approach, frustrated—a mock climax. Marvell's *The First Anniversary of the Government under O. C.* has Cromwell's fall from his coach as its unexpected center, but this fall, if fatal, would have been inverted into a triumphal ascent to heaven. Several patterns are interwoven in Spenser's *Epithalamion*, among them the popular recessed symmetry, in which the first stanza is paired with the last, the second with the penultimate, and so on to the center.

If number and proportion in the cosmos are a source for Renaissance numerology, then it is logical that astronomical numbers and numbers familiar through their association with units of time should be used to create subdivisions of poetic structure. The number of lines in a New Year's Day poem may represent the interval between January 1 and one of the other dates on which the year was considered to begin, such as the vernal equinox or the civil year. Epithalamiums are often organized by temporal patterns because they traditionally review the wedding day: line or stanza patterns of twelve or twenty-four, reflecting the hours of the day, are common. Spenser's *Epithalamion* contains a much more elaborate astronomical pattern, worked out by A. Kent Hieatt and revised by Mr. Fowler, which pins the poem to a particular date, the longest day in the year; one instance of this complexity is that the 23 ½ stanzas are taken by Mr. Fowler to represent the degrees of the sun's midsummer declination from the ecliptic. The duration of time in a work may have symbolic function, like the week of action in the *Divine Comedy*, but it is difficult to accept that the sudden critical concern with a fixed elapsed time within a work based on its genre (in the drama, unity of time) is a related phenomenon.

The "triumphal forms" of the title refer both to poetic structures with a central point, analogous to the triumph, and to the mannerist preoccupation with intricate poetic structure which Mr. Fowler considers characteristic of the Elizabethan period—form triumphs over content. This partial attempt to correlate literary and artistic styles results in an unusual system of historical categories. Like D. W. Robertson, Mr. Fowler visualizes the Romantic period as a complete change in fundamental patterns of thought: central symmetry, only approximate in Pope, is lost altogether, and stanza form becomes an external decoration because its symbolic function (numerological, of course) is no longer understood. Except for a few instances, this theory of numerological symbolism as the basis for the stanza seems rather improbable; Mr. Fowler does not consider alternative sources like song or dance, or even copying from other periods and languages, and a stanza form may still be functional when no numerical symbolism is involved. "Baroque" is a term borrowed from art history and employed by Mr. Fowler to characterize the simple center and energy of Cowley, Dryden, and the later works of Milton. Earlier poets are mannerist, as far back as Wyatt and Surrey, because their "symmetry has a conceited sharpness or finesse that sets it off from the triumphal style of Dante and Petrarch" (p. 99). Chaucer is left as England's best Renaissance poet.

The value of a classification of historical periods depends on how well it approximates the actual situation and on what additional insights critics may derive from it. An extension of art periods to literature is a desirable if elusive simplification in stylistic theory; difficulties include the selection of qualities representative of the period, the nature of the analogy through which the terms are transferred, and the tendency to impose one set of terms on the other field. Symmetry, proportion, and number symbolism transfer with a minimum of metaphoric imagination; Mr. Fowler's problem is a definition of the point at which form, once fully under control, becomes an objective in its own right, dominating content, and is therefore mannerism. Whether or not the analysis of complex symmetry in Wyatt's "My lute awake" is acceptable, form clearly is not fully under control in the early Elizabethan period, as the crudities of poulter's measure and early dramatic structure demonstrate.[1] One or two mannerist artists do not make a mannerist period. Pressing mannerism back so early also falsifies the relatively consistent critical intuition that a change in mood and technique takes place in Elizabethan poetry around 1600. In short, whether form for its own sake is an objective of Elizabethan poetry must, I think, be left to the judgment of the individual scholar (I disagree), but grouping all Elizabethan poetry under the term "mannerism" is self-contradictory and should be rethought.

The failure to define terms like "spatial" and "mannerism" clearly and immediately creates additional difficulties for the reader. In the preface, the specialized meanings silently attached to "spatial" and to "*ut pictura poesis*" invite misinterpretation and confusion: "spatial" means numerically organized; "*ut pictura poesis*" refers, not to a resemblance in subject matter, but to proportion and arrangement of detail as common principles of composition.[2] This is the way in which mannerism is introduced:

> Thus, I regard it [mannerism] as based partly on external style, partly on ideology, and therefore as delimited in its primary application, even if only loosely and indirectly, by chronological occurrence. It connotes a set of heterogeneous elements including both structural properties (such as formal motifs and stylistic habits) and internal characteristics (such as favorite moods and substantive preoccupations) expressive of ethos or of group psychology. In short, I concur with much of Wellek's position. However, I take *mannerism* to be now firmly enough established to replace *baroque* as a label for the early phase of that style. And I prefer Shearman's account of mannerist style, with his stress of complexity and finesse, to accounts such as Pevsner's that emphasize emotional disturbance or tension. (Thus, for example, the highly patterned rhetorical styles of the sixteenth century are to be regarded as mannerist. . . .)
>
> (*p. 90*)

Very little can be derived from this allusive account without familiarity with the relevant criticism. Wellek's categories are left empty; "complexity and finesse" are defined only by "highly patterned rhetorical styles"; there is no evidence for dismissing Pevsner's viewpoint. The problem is complicated by a failure to footnote at this point: Wellek's article, mentioned by title on the preceding page, is not footnoted until the general footnote on *baroque*, page 116, and does not appear in the bibliography. The implication that Mr. Fowler is in substantial agreement with Wellek is also misleading: the thrust of Wellek's article is toward finding a term to characterize the seventeenth century and distinguish it from the sixteenth, while Mr. Fowler evidently extends mannerism over the sixteenth century. Though the properties of mannerism are eventually brought out in the criticism of various poems, there is no synthesis; the reader must rely on impressions, and the initial confusion is never clarified.

Another problem to be dealt with is that certain types of numerical organization seem less probable than others, or justified in rare instances but not as generally as they have been applied. These must be evaluated for each poem, but it is possible to indicate the areas of greatest difficulty: numbers that approximate another number, like 363 for 365; symmetrical patterns that require the omission of one or more stanzas; the self-referring passage; and the use of number symbolism when there is a competing reason for the number in question. When, for example, Ferrers plans 82 books as the product of 9 times 9, arithmetic error seems more likely and "deliberate finesse" less if it is noted that the number of chapters is also calculated incorrectly—27 times 81 is 2187, not 2177 (p. 4). Self-referring passages, in which some line, usually of scant sense textually, also refers to the numerological structure of the poem, are easily abused, particularly in judging what makes scant sense. The worst analysis in the book, on the structure of Shakespeare's sonnets, depends on taking lines 7–11 of cxxxvi as "pedestrian, overelaborate and obscure, unless they have some further point . . . a secondary reference to the sonnet itself [which] . . . is to be excluded from, yet at the same time included in, the reckoning" (p. 184). The sonnet, not at all obscure, is an attractive paradoxical play on identity: Will as her will is a part of her and as one small part can pass unnoticed, as nothing, in the many parts which compose her. With the sonnet excluded, Mr. Fowler proceeds to calculations based on 153, a well-known symbolic number which is the sum of the first 17 natural numbers, and a pyramidical structure for the sonnets; with the sonnet included, there are three years, each composed of 52 stanza-weeks, allowing for two blank stanzas "mentioned" in lxxvii and found in the parentheses following the six couplets of cxxvi. This hardly needs further comment.

Overextension of number symbolism has a number of facets. All eight-line stanzas, even in epithalamiums, can hardly be attributed to marriage symbolism, as Mr. Fowler acknowledges (and his reasons for connecting eight with marriage at all are unconvincing), but why should a reference to eight at the end of As You Like It have numerological significance when four couples are about to be married? If Mr. Fowler wishes to argue that the fourth couple has been added for symbolic reasons, this would be plausible; as matters stand, no more is involved than a plot reference. "Even" is hardly a key word; it occurs in this sense three times—twice in one speech by Rosalind—and refers, not to "the equity of 8," but to the couples that Rosalind promises to form from the three odd lovers, Orlando, Phoebe, and Silvius (p. 153). That a wedding song happens to be the fifth song in the play and contains a mention of Juno is too probable on other grounds to justify a claim that Shakespeare is writing in a tradition of epithalamic number symbolism. Is equality so strongly associated with justice that the presence of the axe that beheaded Charles at the center of Marvell's *Horatian Ode* (thus dividing the poem equally) symbolizes the justice of the action? Granted that 1:2 is the proportion between the rational and concupiscible faculties in a well-ordered soul according to Pico, how often is this proportion hit on naturally? Numerological interpretations should show substantial proof that they exist.

Although the historical viewpoint and the interpretation of individual works may be open to criticism, the study has a number of contributions to make, not the least of which is the questioning of assumptions about the principles of poetic structure. Emphasis on larger units of composition, the inclusion of interspersed lyrics in the structure of sonnet sequences, as in the analysis of *Astrophil and Stella,* and the possibility of considering poems published with the sequence as part of it should stimulate further study. There is value in the treatment of symmetry, proportion, and number symbolism as concepts moving across different fields in analogous ways and in the investigation of the role of the exact center of the poem. Comments on individual poems are often worthwhile: recessed symmetry in the book structure of *The Faerie Queene;* the symbolism of the garland—circular and endless, reflecting the temporal structure of the poem—in Spenser's *Epithalamion;* Shadwell as the young Ascanius at the inverted center of *Mac Flecknoe.* Finally, I think that for certain festal poems Mr. Fowler has demonstrated that some type of numerical organization was considered appropriate and interesting decoration for a conventional topic.

Notes:

1. In the version published in the fragment *The Court of Venus,* stanza vi is missing; the unusual resemblance between stanzas vi and vii suggests that stanza vi may be a later addition, in which case the original pattern of symmetry is simpler and Mr. Fowler's double pattern the result of revision or accident.

2. A review of the standing of *ut pictura poesis* in the Renaissance may be found in Jean H. Hagstrum, *The Sister Arts: The Tradition of Literary Pictorialism and English Poetry from Dryden to Gray* (Chicago, 1958), pp. 57–65.

The Shakespearean Stage, 1574–1642 by Andrew Gurr.
Cambridge University Press, 1970. Pp. ix + 192. $9.50.

Reviewer: Richard C. Kohler.

We have been in need of this book—a concise and balanced summary of the
basic information and speculation about the Elizabethan, Jacobean, and Caroline stage, including at least portions of many essential documents. Professor
Gurr seems clearly to have recognized the difficulties and dangers of such a
compilation, and his careful initial warning should be taken seriously: "A digest
of eleven volumes of closely-packed information has no value as a reference
work, of course, and the picture which this book tries to paint is therefore
inevitably an impressionistic (not to say Fauviste) one." I cannot speak for the
specialists who may object to specific parts of the book, but I suggest that if it is
recognized as tertiary material, most readers will find it extremely worthwhile
as a "reference outline" and a preliminary guide to the use of staging as a
critical tool.

Hopefully, the convenience of this text will add impetus to an approach to
the drama of the period that is, as Professor Gurr points out, not the same thing
as historical criticism, if what is meant by that is appreciation only in terms
of the response of one of Shakespeare's contemporaries. It is a means of arriv-
ing at a clearer understanding of what these playwrights were attempting to
achieve on stage and from this to gain a deeper comprehension of the plays as
literature. We deal with works written to be performed in theaters of distinctive
design by companies employing a repertory system probably unequaled today,
using conventions of staging substantially different from our own. Although
we still are forced to engage in what may charitably be called "sustained conjecture," surely our appreciation of the full impact of their art must include such
considerations.

The danger of abbreviation is, of course, oversimplification, a danger revealed even in Professor Gurr's title, where "Shakespearean" serves to identify
the period 1574–1642 (from the occasion of first official recognition of the London companies to the closing of the theaters). In six concentrated chapters, we
are provided with an introduction and specific appraisal of "The Companies,"
"The Players," "The Playhouses," "The Staging," and "The Audiences." An
appendix furnishes a select list of plays which, with awkward but advisable
caution, "can reasonably positively be assigned to particular playhouses and

companies," a list derived largely from E. K. Chambers's *Elizabethan Stage*, G. E. Bentley's *Jacobean and Caroline Stage*, and Alfred Harbage's *Annals of English Drama, 975–1700* (revised by Samuel Schoenbaum). The first two of these works are also the main sources for most of the balance of the book and should be consulted regularly by any serious student of the field. Since Professor Gurr leaves critical application entirely to the reader, it is necessary for us, not only to arrive at appropriate techniques, but to reconsider at each step and with each play the factual foundation and the suitable hypotheses. New discoveries and interpretations have already overtaken Gurr's work and are appearing constantly. The book is not, for example, in any sense a comprehensive or even adequate bibliography of the subject, as I will indicate. Nevertheless, these qualifications are not intended to diminish the book but to define it. Professor Gurr is equally precise in declaring it to be a background "useful to this business in a negative way; it minimizes misunderstanding of the plays as they were originally composed."

In the initial chapters, the profit motive is emphasized as the main force behind the creation and operation of the theaters, and indeed, commercial considerations dominate much of Gurr's view of the stage in this period. He goes on to conclude that "traveling seems to have been the great disintegrator" of the companies and that the repertory system was the single most characteristic feature of production. The need for companies of from eight to twelve "sharers" and perhaps ten hired players to produce as many as thirty-eight plays a season, commonly presenting each play no more often than once a month while performing six days a week, is a situation that must have profoundly affected the nature of the plays. It is unfortunate that the sensible appraisal given in this section was not accompanied by mention of the practice of doubling, and in this connection several recent works are suggestive: David M. Bevington's *From Mankind to Marlowe* (1962), Arthur Sprague's *The Doubling of Parts in Shakespeare's Plays* (1966), and William A. Ringler's "The Number of Actors in Shakespeare's Early Plays" (in *The Seventeenth Century Stage*, ed. Gerald E. Bentley, 1968, pp. 110–34).

Appropriate attention is given to the style of acting, which Gurr sees as presumably moving towards a more naturalistic than rhetorical manner (at least by 1600), finding scholastic influence as more likely a characteristic of the children's companies than of the common players in the public playhouses, who appear to have had little formal education. The custom of acting "lines," advocated strongly but not always convincingly by T. W. Baldwin, is treated with admirable caution. We end, I believe, with renewed appreciation of the need for exceptional performers, men and boys whose talents must have included phenomenal memories and remarkable flexibility. Yet more extensive analyses of the subject should be productive, especially when concentrated, as Gurr suggests, on plays written by a company's "resident playwright," such as Shakespeare. Further consideration of acting style should include Bernard Beckerman's observations on what he terms a ceremonious, romantic manner, *Shakespeare at the Globe* (1962); Marvin Rosenberg's measured analysis "Elizabethan Actors: Men or Marionettes," *PMLA*, 69 (1954), 915–27; and J. L. Styan's enthusiastic and stimulating, if not always fully supported, discussion of speech and action in *Shakespeare's Stagecraft* (1967).

It is with the perplexing difficulties of the playhouses and their staging, however, that I believe we come to grips with the material that is most helpful critically. While Professor Gurr adds little to our general knowledge—nor was it his intention to do so—he is both exact and discriminating in his reduction of a mass of data and a plethora of theories. Again, too much emphasis may be placed on commerce (the structure of the theaters is seen as determined largely by the need to control an audience of maximum size), and too little concern may be given to the effect of the "playing place" (on the grounds that the technique of staging was much the same wherever the plays were performed, with flexibility requiring simplicity). I suggest that the seating and standing areas may well have had more of an effect on the production than Gurr recognizes. Seldom (if ever) has there been a modern reconstruction that approximated, much less duplicated, the exact specifications for gallery and yard of which we are certain, from the dirt area to the surrounding three tiers (using, for example, the measurements of the Fortune contract, which was in part patterned after the Globe). Such a reconstruction would provide us with the perhaps unique relationship established when actors were nearly surrounded by probably 2,500 spectators, no one of which was more than fifty feet from a performer at downstage center.

Although Professor Gurr is wise in accepting the Swan drawing as prime evidence of interior characteristics, he continues the practice of slighting the references there to Roman features. Until and unless more substantial proof for classical influence is uncovered, it may be just as well to assume a line of evolution through bull- and bear-baiting arenas and inn yards. Still it would have been more complete to have mentioned suggestions of possible reliance on Vitruvian design offered by Frances Yates (*The Art of Memory*, 1966, and probably too late for consideration, *Theatre of the World*, 1969) and Donald C. Mullin's two articles in *The Educational Theatre Journal*, 18 (1966), 27–33, and 19 (1967), 322–26. Professor Gurr refers to a short essay on the marbling of wood pillars at the Swan (by Richard Southern and C. Walter Hodges, *Theatre Notebook*, 6 [1951–2], 57–58), but curiously he later interprets this as the result of increasing use of Renaissance brick and plaster, partly because wood was becoming scarce (p. 95). Since this feature was noted by de Witt as a painted effect on wood, Gurr's comment appears to be another instance of our general inclination to overlook an obvious fact: an attempt was made to give a classical appearance to the interior of the only Elizabethan public theater for which we have a sketch and a verbal description.

The documentation, here as elsewhere, is of genuine help to the beginning student and to the casual reader whose specialty is elsewhere; teachers will be pleased to find a clear (though necessarily small) reproduction of the Swan drawing and a suitable excerpt from de Witt's commentary; the essentials of both the Fortune and Hope contracts; the Fludd etching of what is perhaps the interior of the Blackfriar's (I. A. Shapiro's interpretation) or the Globe (Frances Yates's); and the Cockpit-at-Court drawings by Inigo Jones, a theater attracting increasing attention, discussed by Gurr using T. J. King's essay in *Theatre Notebook*, 19 (1965), 146–66. Restrictions of space may have forced the exclusion of all exterior drawings of these theaters except the important Hollar "Long View" with its crisp depiction of the second Globe (1614), but it is regrettable that more consideration could not have been given to comparative size. The Hope contract, for example, instructs that it be built "of suche large compasse, fforme, widenes, and height" as the Swan, described by de Witt as the largest of the theaters in ca.1596. Hollar shows the Hope (mislabeled) as surely the same size as the nearby Globe, or more likely as smaller. If so, we have a Shakespearean venue perhaps larger than all the rest of the playhouses (which conflicts with my theory that the Rose and Globe were of much the same size: "The Fortune Contract and Vitruvian Symmetry," *Shakespeare Studies*, 6). Exterior drawings though controversial are not completely useless.

A more serious omission is the lack of any discussion of large stage properties as having had emblematic significance. Nothing is said of George R. Kernodle's discussion of the possible effect of the visual arts on Renaissance theatrical practice (*From Art to Theatre*, 1944) or of Glynne Wickham's contribution (*Early English Stages, Vol. II, Part I, 1576–1660*, 1963), in which he asserts that the practice of multiple staging available at court and in the schools (especially in the plays of the Lylyan school) was not only emblematic but interchangeable with the public theaters. Gurr is right, I believe, in opting for a bare, open stage using a successive rather than multiple technique, but the issue is far from resolved. The most revealing analyses have been those that have focused on plays that can be assigned to specific theaters, such as the studies by G. F. Reynolds on the Red Bull, Beckerman on the Globe, and King on the Phoenix. It may be well to mention two doctoral dissertations (not used by Gurr) on staging at the Rose: Harvey S. McMillin, Jr., Stanford, 1965, and Ernest L.

Rhodes, University of Kentucky, 1958. In the more satisfactory of these analyses McMillin supports Gurr's preference for the successive method.

A few minor objections should be added. Gurr continues the assumption that the Fortune platform (and by analogy, for some scholars, the platforms of the other public theaters) was 27½ feet deep because it extended to the middle of the yard that was contracted to be 55 feet across. But this assumes a tiring-house that occupied none of the platform, and for this we have no evidence. In fact, the Swan drawing (as Wickham seems first to have noticed) displays the tiring-house *on* the platform, perhaps even a separate structural unit resting on the ground of the arena at the rear of the stage, and both of the extant contracts call for construction of the tiring-house and the stage in a manner that suggests separate units. This would, of course, give us a platform substantially more shallow than is usually believed.

The Hope galleries are too easily accepted as duplicating the height at the Fortune on the basis of identical measurements for only the lowest level and a comparable ratio in size (not height) of the pillars. The complex interrelationship between audience and actors explored by such scholars as Anne Righter (*Shakespeare and the Idea of the Play*, 1962) is reduced to mention only of the three-dimensional quality of the stage as a causal factor, neglecting the tradition that extends to the origin of the English drama. And no reference is made to Richard Hosley's complex and, for its method, potentially influential reconstruction of the Swan (with twenty-four sides), "Reconstitution du Théâtre du Swan," in *Le Théâtral à la Renaissance*, ed. Jean Jacquot (1964), pp. 295–316.

The absence of a formal bibliography is frustrating, forcing the reader to search the notes and the introductions to each set of notes (located unhappily at the end of the book) should he wish to recover a work passed over during initial study. While these introductions are concise and with the notes offer many of the essential sources, only the text is indexed. In yet another attempt to help provide a semicomplete list of essential works, let me add James Stinson's brief but thorough survey, "Reconstructions of Elizabethan Public Playhouses," in *Studies in the Elizabethan Theatre*, ed. by Charles T. Prouty (1961) and C. Walter Hodges's excellent second edition of *The Globe Restored* (1968).

Although Professor Gurr has self-effacingly made no claim to have provided us with more than a useful compilation of the work of others, he has made a substantial contribution of his own, in the careful scholarship that such a survey demands and in a number of personal observations. For example, despite my earlier reservations about the emphasis on commercial circumstances, we are made aware, perhaps more clearly than before, of the relative values of the time: a costume might be worth a year's salary for an artisan, who paid about a twelfth of a day's wage to go to the theater. Gurr shows enviable deliberation in handling such vexed issues as that of the inner stage versus the discovery space, although omitting reference to Hosley's extension of his conclusions on the Globe to the majority of the plays of the period: *Renaissance Drama*, 6 (1963), 72–78. He also offers us the most reasonable explanation yet of the strange "structures" beneath the platform in the Swan drawing (an explanation that now seems embarrassingly obvious): he sees them as openings in drapes, the artist or copier failing to complete the appropriate lines at the corners.

In the final chapter, Shakespeare's audience is described as very much the same as our own, and Professor Gurr's discussion here is typical of the comprehensive quality of the entire work, carrying us forward smoothly—although somewhat densely—from the Elizabethans into the 1620s and on to the closing of the theaters. He presents the picture in terms of an evolving set of phenomena: the companies, the theaters, the spectators; both the public and the private playhouses in summer and winter production; the children's companies; and the court and academic productions. As Gurr points out in regard to the London commercial theaters, an average of "as many as a million visits a year" over some seventy years of production prohibits any generalization except one that is "stretched thinly." Seldom has he erred in that direction despite constant opportunity and ample temptation. Seldom, we can conclude, has he seriously misled the new student or violently aggravated the specialist. Both are likely to recognize his difficulties and be thankful for his achievement.

The Plays of George Chapman: The Comedies. A Critical Edition. General editor: Allan Holaday, assisted by Michael Kiernan. University of Illinois Press, 1970. Pp. 594. $20.00.

Reviewer: T. H. Howard-Hill.

Of all the questions which confront the reviewer of a modern edition of an old author, the first and most important to decide upon is whether the job was worth doing. It is also the most difficult question to answer, particularly in the present instance when the editors of *The Plays of George Chapman* have chosen to eschew the critical introductions, commentary, and other exegesis which must preserve Professor T. M. Parrott's 1914 edition of the comedies in the estimation of scholars and students. They have decided to build their texts on new, sounder foundations. The detection and use of variant readings which arose from correction at the press was not new even to Parrott, but the present edition has been able to draw upon a harvest of newly discovered press-variants; this makes the text, in this respect at least, the best text of Chapman's comedies that we have.[1] Parrott's edition has the deficiencies of its time: it gives a modern-spelling text when the current fashion, for editions addressed to scholarly readers, is for texts which follow in the main the orthography of the early printings on which they are based. Further, Parrott's edition, which Professor G. B. Evans judges to be "in many respects a remarkable edition" (p. 561), contains "numerous errors, several of which directly resulted from a decision to correct for the printer a copy of Shepherd's second edition" (p. 2). Those are the words of the general editor of this edition, Professor Allan Holaday, who draws attention to the "inadequacy of Parrott's textual apparatus" (p. 1). For these and other reasons, Mr. Holaday concludes in a sentence of not uncharacteristic ambiguity that Parrott's edition "left unfulfilled the critical need for sound texts" (p. 2): this need Mr. Holaday's edition aims to satisfy.

Mr. Holaday's case for the supersession of Parrott's edition is not so strong as not to invite a close examination of the text and apparatus of his own edition. That the editors have returned to the original spellings is not alone a good reason to abandon an adequate, readable text, unless in this new edition the old texts have been edited with some feeling for language and awareness of the especial requirements of old-spelling editions. The editor himself has directed attention to the apparatus by the comment already quoted above. However, it is above all the *quality* of the readings in which this edition differs from Parrott's, and not their number (especially as the apparatus records mainly accidental or near-accidental emendations) which will determine the superiority of this text. Regrettably, there is not time or space enough to penetrate completely the thicket of minor points which assails and sometimes bewilders anyone who hazards to inspect the apparatus of this edition. That more time in this review is not spent on discussion of substantives is doubtless to its detriment, but, as the whole tendency of Mr. Holaday's edition is to direct attention away from matters of critical, linguistic, and literary significance towards superficial, accidental, and trivial matters, one must be fair to his intentions. I should also say at once that I believe that *no* edition which deliberately turns aside from literary, critical, linguistic exegesis in favor of the establishment of "reliable texts" (p. 4) can reasonably claim for itself the distinction of "definitive" ("having the function of finally deciding; determinative, final"—*SOED*) as this edition does on the dust jacket and in publicity. The most that its editors could claim is that they have produced *texts* which later generations will grace with that distinction. A book as well printed and as attractively designed as this does not need self-awarded laurels.[2] But good texts, all agree, are important, and it is to the texts that attention must turn.

The Plays of George Chapman: the Comedies is subtitled "A Critical Edition" and supplies an apparatus which appears in some respects to have been influenced by the editions of Professor Fredson Bowers. The texts of the several comedies are printed in the spellings of the copy-texts chosen as the basis of the present edition, and they follow the original orthography quite closely. Departures from the readings of the copy-texts are usually recorded; they fall into categories of unequal importance and will be discussed shortly. The textual introductions which precede each text reflect the bibliographical orientation of much modern textual criticism and give what appear to be the best available accounts of the first printings of Chapman's comedies. Besides this, there is a four-part apparatus consisting of a table of press-variants, two collations, and textual notes. The press-variants, the historical collation of substantive and semisubstantive variants "which differentiate the critical text from specified earlier versions" (p. 2), and the textual notes, which provide "a terse commentary on special cruxes and a defense of editorial decisions" (p. 2) follow after the text of each comedy. The other collation, which lists the editor's emendations to the copy-text, is given in notes at the bottom of each page. "These include revision of accidentals as well as substantives, excepting only those covered by a general statement on silent emendations" (p. 2). In Parrott's edition, on the other hand, the notes are together at the end of the volume and include commentary on the meaning and the literary circumstances of the text as well as its graphical forms.

The Blind Beggar of Alexandria was edited by Lloyd E. Berry; the general editor, Allan Holaday, edited *An Humorous Day's Mirth* and *Monsieur D'Olive;* Robert Ornstein, *The Gentleman Usher* and *The Widow's Tears;* G. B. Evans, *All Fools* and *The Memorable Masque;* and *May Day* was edited by Robert F. Welsh. These editors had, no doubt, strong and occasionally conflicting views about editorial practices. When an edition is shared amongst many editors it is essential for the achievement of the common aim that sound rules have been agreed on, and the general editor has a particular responsibility to ensure that the contributing editors have in fact followed the principles and practices which he described in his general introduction when preparing their several texts. Responsibility for default in particulars falls, too, not on their heads but on his, for his name appears on the title page, and his is the ultimate responsibility for the text which is offered to the public. For a judicial examination of his achievement, it is regrettable that Mr. Holaday did not explain rather more fully the reasons for some of his editorial practices. For example, old spelling is assumed to be desirable, but there is no explanation or argument

for the preference of original to modern spellings. Similarly, it is taken for
granted that the reader of this edition will want to find at the foot of each page a
record of departures from the copy-text, substantives and accidentals alike,
rather than information which will assist his reading of the text. Matters of
some significance for an intelligent reading of the plays are relegated to incon-
venient positions whereas a distracting melange of accidental and substantive
readings is given prominence at the foot of each page. A case could be made
for this: it depends on how the general editor sees the function of his edition
and how he expects it will be used. But when an edition departs from familiar
models old and new, it is reasonable to expect the editor to discuss the benefits
he expects his readers will obtain from the arrangement of his apparatus. Discussion is especially necessary when the apparatus directs the reader's attention
so forcibly to the accidents of the text's genesis in the original printings and in
the labors of the present editors.

A possible argument for recording departures from the copy-text at the foot
of the page is that the reader could "reconstruct" the copy-text from the details
recorded in the footnotes. However, Mr. Holaday cannot have intended this,
because, even if it were desirable, it is impossible when some emendations are
made silently and are not recorded in the footnote collations. The silent emendations "include the normalization of speech heads, of wrong-font letters, and
of wrong-font punctuation; correction of turned letters where no ambiguity
exists, of printers' substitutions occasioned by type shortages, and of wrong-
font type for complete words in the stage directions; expansion of the tilde
and ampersand; substitutions of standard types for display capitals and of
lower case for the capitals that usually follow display letters" (p. 3).[3] Mr. Holaday describes these as "without textual significance." However, for the sort of
reader who seeks to recreate in his mind the precise typographical environment
of a reading when he attempts to evaluate a choice of emendations, the normalization of speech prefixes and the expansion of tildes and ampersands, to mention but two of his categories, has significance for "study of the text" if not
for its meaning.[4] Mr. Holaday emends, "to avoid inconvenience to the reader"
(p. 3), words like "loud" to "lou'd," but a reader who, as he assumes, will not
be troubled by the retention of the original u-v, i-j spellings, not to mention
many other more bewildering spellings than "loud," will scarcely be troubled
by "None euer loud but at first sight they loud" (*Blind Beggar*, x.127). Such
unnecessary sophistication seems to take into account one kind of reader, the
silent emendations imply another, and the footnotes, a different kind of
reader. However, Mr. Holaday's decision to retain u-v, i-j is praiseworthy, even
though it is difficult to argue a consistent case for this when long s is (rightly)
dispensed with.

When one turns from the general introduction to the texts themselves, one pauses to consider how well the editors, and particularly the general editor, have done their work. There seems to be no generally agreeable standard for an appraisal. Editors are human and, hence, fallible; critical editions are complicated and charged with opportunities for editorial error. How much error is tolerable is difficult to say. Perhaps all that can be said finally is that although the reviewer might have wished that certain things had been ordered otherwise, the task has been carried out within acceptable limits of accuracy. For the present edition, however, it is very hard to decide how accurate the editors are; they are so inconsistent that it cannot be determined whether they are in error or have consciously changed their practices as the edition proceeded. Two plays have Malone Society reprints edited by Sir Walter Greg. I have checked portions of the present text with these reprints and the facsimiles which Greg prints. It is possibly unfair to the editors of *The Blind Beggar* and *An Humorous Day's Mirth* to particularize their work, but where there is no fault, there can be no blame. There are some general and detailed points which arise from examination of these plays in particular which should be made, especially if there is a chance that the comedies volume will be published in a second edition. For reasons of time and space these notes are based on a partial and sometimes cursory inspection of the text and apparatus. Because Mr. Berry's text of *The Blind Beggar (BB)* comes first in the volume, a large part of the discussion will start from that text.

Although the general editor has written in his general introduction that "correction of turned letters where no ambiguity exists" is an emendation which will be made silently, at i.52 there is "your] yonr"; this is followed in the footnotes (to give only a sampling) by i.169 "leaue] leane," i.175 "masters] mastrs," i.276 "richest] rihcest," i.292 "round] ronnd," iv.SD "Count.] Coont," v.124 "And] and," vi.SD "*with] wiuh,*" vi.65 "knaue] knane," vii.7 "thus] thous," vii.90 "house] honse," vii.96 "dishonor] dshonor," ix.31 "murmering] murmerrng," and x.108 "for] fot." Among these I have included misprints which do not involve turned letters but which are equally dispensable, particularly as many other of the numerous quarto misprints are not listed in the apparatus, for example, ii.40 "dispositon," ii.75 "āre," iii.10 "fosaken," and vi.5 "bc" (for "be"). Similar instances can be found almost at random in the footnotes to the other texts: *An Humorous Day's Mirth(HDM)* V.ii.72 "With] Whith," V.ii.128 SD "*then his] tben his,*" *The Gentleman Usher (GU)* III.ii.198 "Let] Ler," V.i.97 "eminent] eniment," V.iv.187 "Presumptuous] Presumptuons"; *All Fools (AF)* I.i.227 "looke] lookee," I.ii.20 "haue] hane" (see also *MDO* IV.ii.136), I.ii.144 "countenaunce] conntenaunce," II.i.20 "Our] Gur," II.i.117 "thinke] thiuke," II.i.237 "prettie] pretrie"; *May Day (MD)* III.i.182 "good] goodd," IV.iii.6

"hand] haud," IV.iii.14 "remaine] remnine," IV.vi.37 "owne] owne owne";
Monsieur D'Olive (MDO) II.ii.142 "But] Bur," II.ii.295 "Ambassador] Anbas-
sador"; *The Widow's Tears (WT)* V.v.137 "but] bur"; *The Memorable Masque
(MM)* Description 176 "obseruances] obseɹuances." One need not conjecture
what a reader feels when editors direct his attention to this kind of "information." If details like these are to be recorded at all, it should be modestly and
obscurely in an appendix, and, if they are recorded, to be consistent there should
be fewer kinds of emendations made without record in the apparatus.

Mr. Berry notes that "obvious errors are not recorded" (p. 53) in the historical collation, but the footnotes include the deathless emendations i.86
"earthlye] *Shepherd;* eathlye" and iii.22 "ceaslesse] *Shepherd;* cealesse," both
of which are listed in the historical collation. Similar but inconsistent attention
to accidental and, in the main, insignificant readings characterizes the general
editor's text of *MDO* (but not his *HDM*) and Mr. Ornstein's text of *WT* (but
not his *GU*). At *MDO* II.ii.61 "spurnd] *Parrott;* spnrnd" at first glance seems
a reading which should have been silently corrected. The historical collation,
however, shows various readings of the turned letter in earlier editions: this
illustrates why it is useful to have a record of the readings of other editions
listed near the note of the editor's own readings. But II.ii.256 "the] *Dilke;* the
the" leads in the historical collation to the entry "the] *D, L, S, P;* the the *Q*,"
that is, all editions have corrected *Q*'s dittographic "the." (In *MD*, dittography
at IV.vi.37 is not listed in the historical collation). Mr. Ornstein notices *WT*
II.iv.7 "letters] *Dodsley;* letrer" (not included in the historical collation) and
III.ii.21 "may] *Dodsley;* my" and III.ii.69 "out] *Dodsley;* ont." The phrase in
which "my" was printed is "*Hymen* may cure her."; the historical collation
records "21 may] *Do, R. C. S. P;* my *Q*"; the entry for "out" is similar. It may
be that editors who make and record such emendations are merely following
the general editor's instructions to regard as "substantive or semi-substantive
any emendation which changes copy-text diction, alters copy-text meaning
through punctuation, or removes copy-text ambiguity" (p. 2), but why should
editors be instructed to bring to bear on the text *less* discrimination and common sense than they show in their everyday scholarly dealings? What is important here is not whether a reading is substantive but whether it is significant.

There are other trivialities in the footnotes to *BB*. At i.315 "We] we" could
have been corrected silently; at line 317 a footnote records "Exeunt." as the
quarto reading where *Q* in fact reads "*exeunt.*" If a silent correction was made
here, it is difficult to understand why similar corrections were not made to stage
directions in *GU* (for example, "*he studies*" [IV.ii.73]). Proper nouns are
usually supplied with capitals (for example, ii.5–6 "Hero, Leander"), but at
v.73, "cupid" is not. Editorial convention is difficult to discover when in *BB*

"greekish" (x.173) is capitalized, but in *HDM* "latine" (I.ii.49) and "christian" (I.v.6, I.iv.88) are not. Mr. Berry retains anomalous capitals at iv.27 "Then
make as If" and iv.107 "We Thanke" but normalizes the capitalization of the
only "ile" observed in *BB*, at v.145. At iii.45 "pur sued" is corrected silently to
"pursued" (and word division elsewhere, for example, *WT* I.iii.124, IV.iii.42),
but at i.174 "a while," for which the Malone Society reprint reads "awhile,"
should not have been emended or should have been footnoted at the least.
Why at vi.81 "In voking," which is certainly a misprint, was not corrected
is hard to see. Other peculiarities which involve spacing or word division are:
in *HDM*, "thousand fold" for Q "thousandfold" (I.i.34), "whereas" for "where
as" (V.ii.143), "ouerioyes" for "ouer ioyes" (V.ii.290); in *AF*, "Gentlewomen"
for "Gentle women" (I.ii.52) but not "In deed" at II.i.265; in *MDO*, "T'n
flame" at II.i.178.

   At iii.104 the editor of *BB* inserts an apostrophe in "thentent" but not at
x.53 "Thalexandrian." Apostrophes are supplied in "you'r" (vi.38, 63) and
"for't" (vi.51) but not in "hees, thats," and so forth. A peculiarity of this text
is the conflation of digraphs (for example, "cœlestiall" as "coelestiall" at x.130);
this practice is especially graceless in the speech-prefixes for "Aegiale," which
are printed "AEgi." That the printer possessed the correct sorts is shown by
"SCÆNA" (*GU* V.i) and "*Scæna*" (*MD* I.i) and elsewhere. Digraphs should
have been treated consistently throughout the edition. A few final points about
BB: the substitution of the speech-prefix "*Mem.*" throughout for "*Meni.*" (in
the Greg reprint) should have been recorded somewhere in the apparatus. At
ii.36 "suppled" looks like a misprint for "supplied" (of which it is not a
variant spelling), but it could possibly be the participial adjective "made supple;
softened"; either the correction or a textual note was necessary. The general
editor writes that "editors record even bracketed interpolations [to SD] in both
the footnotes and the historical collations" (p. 4); at v.164 the editor reads "*Exit
with* Druso." for Q "Exit."; this is not recorded in the footnotes. Lastly, the
historical collation, unlike that of the general editor's *HDM*, omits to include a
note of substantive press-variants.

   Mr. Berry's footnotes and those of the other editors to some extent are inflated with the record of the introduction of necessary and unnecessary marks
of punctuation. The kind and amount of punctuation falls far short of what a
modern reader expects to find, and it is not likely that one reader will agree
with another how much repunctuation is desirable. Nevertheless, the editors
often appear to have had different conceptions of the abilities of readers to cope
with the seventeenth-century punctuation. There is no advantage to be expected from multiplying examples of the punctuation here: two instances will
suffice. In *BB* lines ii.42–43 read:

Count. Giue me thy hand we ar louers both, shall we haue her both.
Brag.   No, good sweete *Count*, pardon me.

The pointing of line 42 is inadequate even by seventeenth-century standards; the apparatus discloses only that the terminating full stop has been added after "both." In the next line however, two commas were introduced to mark off the vocative phrase. It is hard to conceive of a reader who, while experiencing no difficulty with the first line, would require the pointing of the second. In the same text at iii.154–55 occurs what seems to be transposed punctuation:

> Now was there euer man so fortunate.
> To haue his loue so sorted to his wish,

In a "definitive" edition, this should have been corrected. Parrott reads "fortunate] $\sim_\wedge$" and "wish] $\sim?$"; but his readings are not included in the historical collation of substantive and semisubstantive variants.

The texts which follow *BB* reveal many of the same anomalies and errors, and there is not much point in enumerating them all. Occasionally, however, an editor does something exceptionally interesting. Mr. Holaday, the general editor, for instance, in *HDM* includes the notation *stet* after an apparently unexceptional lemma and does not direct the reader to consult the textual notes according to the general practice in this edition. The first two lines of *HDM* read:

> Yet hath the morning sprinckled throwt the clowdes,
> But halfe her tincture and the soyle of night[;]

and line 2 has the footnote "But] *stet.*" What this means is impossible to determine. Emendation does not seem to be called for; there is nothing in the list of press-variants or in the historical collation to show what reading the editor has rejected in favor of Q, and there is no discussion of his refusal to emend in the textual notes. At II.ii.149 there is the lemma "O what] *stet*," again without support elsewhere in the apparatus; the editor could hardly have felt obliged to record his rejection of Parrott's comma after the vocative because he did not consider that important enough to be included in the historical collation. The mystery is compounded at IV.i.43, 45 where two O's are marked in the footnotes with *stet* but are otherwise unremarked. O's at III.ii.13, IV.i.14, 16, 24, 29, and so forth, are not drawn to the reader's attention in that manner. Another text which employs *stet* in this fashion is Mr. Welsh's *MD*; at I.i.22, 203, and

I.ii.146 there is information in the historical collation which bears on the reading at point, but at II.iii.64 there is none.[5]

Another peculiarity of *HDM* is that here, but not in other texts (for example, *MD* I.ii.152), elisions of "is" like "that's" are supplied with apostrophes, and this is recorded in the footnotes (much to their inflation). However, other elisions like "nere" (I.v.147) and "lets" (I.v.177) are not modernized. More remarkable, in light of the general practice to supply apostrophes in "lou'd," difficult and unfamiliar elided words like "throwt" in the lines quoted above, remain without the benefit of editorial intervention. The footnote to I.iv.24 ("there's] thers *Q(u)*; theres *Q(c)*") besides being wrong—it is the reading of the corrected form into which the editor has inserted the apostrophe, not the uncorrected form—shows a practice of which far too many instances occur in *HDM* and in other texts. I refer to the inclusion in the footnotes of press-variant readings which, had they not occurred in variant forms, would have been corrected silently by the editor.[6] There is no reason why, when a compositor or press-corrector has removed an obvious error from the printed page, as at II.ii.39 ". . . but] *Q(c)*; bur *Q(u)*" and IV.iii.SD "*Queene*] *Q(c)*; *Q eene Q(u)*," or corrected relatively insignificant spellings like "thers" to "theres," these corrections should be recorded in the footnotes, when similar corrections by the modern editor are not (or in this case, should not be) so recorded. This practice is inconsistent, too, with the general editor's description of the function of the footnote collation to list the differences between the edited text and the copy-text. Since the editor's copy-text is generally the corrected variant form, the readings of uncorrected formes should be of no interest to him once he has decided on the authority and correctness of the readings of the corrected forme.

A check of the first scene of Mr. Holaday's text with Greg's Malone Society reprint shows these differences: I.i.34 "thousand fold,] thousandfold," I.i.40 "will] wil." At I.iv.77 "what is you busines?" contains an error which, like the others, must be attributed to the editor since there is no mention of these readings in the apparatus. I also wonder whether the reading "enough" which is credited to Parrott is correct in an old-spelling edition as the correction for "in nought" (Q, I.i.28). Although the spelling "enough" occurs at I.v.78, "inowe" (II.i.113) and many other similar spellings suggest that the manuscript read "innoughe." To this or a spelling closer to it than "enough" the text should probably have been emended.

In *MD*, one of Mr. Welsh's *stets* leads eventually to the historical collation where Dyce is shown to have emended Q "Is" to "Is't" in the phrase "Is true, Lieftenant?" (I.ii.146). This looks very much like a common kind of compositorial misprint, the *t* being liable to omission when the following word starts with *t* (cf. *Taming of the Shrew*, l. 2422, "brough to"). When an editor refuses to make an ostensibly necessary correction, he should explain the grounds for his decision in a textual note.[7] One wonders also why it was necessary to adopt Parrott's spelling "perlous" for Q "perl's" at IV.iv.3 and to revert to the ugly "AE" in the speech-prefixes when the "Æ" digraph had been used in *GU* before. On page 396, "retoration" is presumably a misprint.

In Mr. Holaday's *MDO*, besides the general features already mentioned, there are anomalies like *"Mounsieur D'oliue"* (I.ii.70); in *HDM* at I.iv.102–3 he reads "monsier *du Barto*] *monsier du Barte*," and the editor's refusal to emend the incorrect (by seventeenth-century standards) and disfiguring orthography of "mvst" (II.i.49), "withovt" (II.i.94) and "Shovld" (II.i.122). Editors retain much of the orthography of the early compositors because, for want of the author's manuscripts, they must, but they should not consider themselves obliged to treat compositorial error and inconsistencies with pious respect.[8] At V.i.230 the editor gives the lemma "th'Herculean] *Dilke*; t'Herculean," but Dilke's modernization does not represent the pronunciation as clearly to a modern reader as the original spelling and is unnecessary. (In any case, the lemma should be "th' Herculean"). Mr. Ornstein on the other hand retains "by 'thead" (*WT* I.ii.120) when "by'th head" occurs at I.iii.22: some correction or normalization was desirable. Another Dilke reading imported into the text can be seen at I.ii.177 where "it" is modernized to "its" in the phrase "in it kinde." This is a difficult case, for the "it" may be the old possessive pronoun found in Shakespeare and not a misprint as the editor takes it to be. However, most of the citations in *OED* show that "it" was followed by a vowel or semi-vowel (the phrase "it owne" is a common example) and euphony calls for the emendation. Nevertheless, *OED* cites the precise instance in Wither's *Works*, 1633 ("Each part as faire doth show In it kinde . . ."); this makes emendation much less acceptable. This is a point which surely deserved brief discussion in the textual notes.

Mr. Holaday's textual note to IV.ii.136 is interesting enough to be quoted in full:

> 136 hane] Parrott emends to "have" (i.e., "haue"). But the colloquial tone of the speech strongly supports the copy-text reading. Mugeron uses a common expression that often occurs as "I durst han swore" or "I durst han vowed" or, as here, "I durst han layed my life."

Turned "u" is so common as not to require a gloss, and my instinct here was to take "hane" as an instance of that simple misprint. However, the textual note was ostensibly instructive and further thought was necessary. There were, nevertheless, two difficulties: the editor referred to "a common expression" but gave no instances of its occurrence (which is unknown to the reader in works of this date), and the emendation he proposed in the textual note was "han," not "hane" as his text reads. Onions, Abbott, Halliwell, and Wright yielded no evidence of the commonness of this expression, although Halliwell did record that "han" was "Still in use in the North for the pres. *plur.*" The *OED* cites "han" as a spelling of the simple infinitive in the fourteenth and fifteenth centuries, too early to be relevant, and has nothing under "dare" to show the commonness of the expression "durst han" at any time. More significantly, "hane" as a spelling of "han" is unknown to *OED* and, I should think, intrinsically improbable. Unless the editor has other information which he has not brought out in his note, it is difficult to resist the conclusion that his note is devoted to the defense of a compositor's error.

All in all, one cannot conclude that this edition demonstrates the confident control of editorial and linguistic methods that could have been expected from scholars of such reputation and accomplishment. The plan of the edition was not a good one and does not seem, from the evidence I have discussed, to have been completely understood—or endorsed—by the contributing editors. A great deal of hard work has gone into the edition, and future editors will be grateful for it. The common reader, however, with any degree of scholarly competence whatever, will be bemused and dissatisfied if he dares to open its pages at all. Inconsistencies of editorial procedure, trivial as they may be in particular instances, and the absence of any commentary which might assist a *reader*, cannot but confuse him, and even the more sophisticated user of this volume should attend closely to what has been carried out in the edition, rather than what the editor has said has been done.[9]

Notes:

1. The editors pay frequent tribute to the scholarship of Professor Akihiro Yamada of Shinshu University, whose bibliographical studies of Chapman's works, largely because many of them were published in journals not widely available in English-speaking countries, are not as well known as otherwise they might be.
2. The printer of this first volume is not identified.
3. This implies that there are other categories not given in the general introduction. Other emendations to the copy-text made without record in the apparatus affect word division at the ends of lines of prose; turnovers and incorrect punctuation (e.g., *BB* i.352 "*Exeunt.*] *Exeunt*").
4. The distinction attempted here is demonstrated by the definition of textual criticism in *Webster's Third New International Dictionary:* "1. the study of a literary work that aims to establish the original text. 2. a critical study of literature emphasizing a close reading and analysis of the text."—I do not object to silent

emendation as such; indeed, part of my complaint is that there is not enough silence about accidentals in modern editions.

5. Also, *WT* I.ii.32 SD gives the lemma *"another Vsher] stet"* but the historical collation shows only that the punctuation of the appositional *"Lycus"* was in question.

6. As, for example, the turned letter in *BB* ix.39 ". . . must Q *(c)*; mnst Q *(u)*."

7. The only similar citation was supplied by Abbott who gives "Is then unjust to each his due to give" *(Faerie Queene*, I.ix.38). The modern editions I have seen do not comment on the line. Phonetically, "Is then" is not the same as *MD*'s "Is true" which is, also, part of a prose passage. The First Folio reading "ouer Test" for "overt test" in the quartos of *Othello* at I.iii.107 also illuminates this point.

8. A comment by Greg is, as is often true, refreshing: "Having no respect for the copy-text as such, I have thought myself at liberty to remove what I take to be occasional eccentricities of the scribe or compositor." *(Jonson's Masque of Gipsies* [London, 1952], p. 110).

9. The historical collation to *BB* omits to record substantive press-variants, the one to *HDM* includes them, and Mr. Ornstein in *WT* gives a selection, omitting substantive variants at I.ii.77, 84, I.iii.11, and so forth.

Hermogenes and the Renaissance: Seven Ideas of Style by Annabel M. Patterson. Princeton University Press, 1970. Pp. 240. $10.00.

Reviewer: Peter Saccio.

Hermogenes of Tarsus, the second-century child prodigy who wrote a series of texts on rhetoric in his youth and then apparently sank into a premature and wretched senility, does not loom very large in the modern scholarship that has revived the rhetorical tradition. His *Progymnasmata* is known as a Renaissance schoolbook, but his major work, *The Art of Rhetoric*, has not been generally thought an important influence outside Byzantium. *The Art* is, for example, only passingly alluded to in Bernard Weinberg's massive account of Italian criticism and not even mentioned in W. S. Howell's *Logic and Rhetoric in England, 1500–1700*, Rosemond Tuve's *Elizabethan and Metaphysical Imagery*, or Brian Vickers's recent concise handbook.

It is Professor Annabel Patterson's original and modestly argued contention that the third section of Hermogenes' *Art*, the περὶ ἰδεῶν, is a fruitful treatment of literary decorum illuminating—and perhaps accounting for—the style of much English Renaissance poetry. We have neglected Hermogenes possibly because he has never been translated into English, but he was available in the sixteenth century in a number of Greek editions, Latin translations, and Italian paraphrases, many accompanied by commentary. Sturm's Greek text of 1570–71, with Latin translation, probably achieved the widest circulation; it was accompanied by so lengthy a commentary as to earn its editor a reproach for pedantry from Bacon. Furthermore, the "Ideas" of περὶ ἰδεῶν were directly expounded in the poetics of Lullius, Minturno, and Scaliger, and used in discussion of particular critical problems by various Italians including Tasso. Unfortunately, there is difficulty (usual in matters of this sort) in demonstrating knowledge of the Ideas in England. No direct English treatment of them exists. Elyot, Harvey, Herbert, and Milton betray familiarity with them; Professor Patterson industriously collects other English references to Hermogenes, but some of these are not very sympathetic and others are regrettably vague.

The Ideas are seven aims or categories of style, one or more of which is to be striven for depending upon the sort of composition undertaken: Clarity, Grandeur, Beauty, Speed, Ethos, Verity, and Gravity. They are variously subdivided, each subdivision having a characteristic range of subject matter, method of organization, diction, group of figures, texture of vowels and consonants, rhythm, and so on. This sort of elaboration makes Hermogenes a ripe target for Baconian reproach; indeed, as Professor Patterson points out, that is what he got from J. W. H. Atkins in the *Oxford Classical Dictionary*. As in all such systems, moreover, there is backwash between categories. Clarity may be an independent style (Orazio Ariosto argued that it was the ruling Idea of the *Orlando Furioso*), but it is also a requirement for most good writing; and the distinction between Gravity and Grandeur is easily obliterated (Minturno uses the term *Gravitas* for both Gravity and a subdivision of Grandeur). Drawing on the Renaissance commentary without ignoring these difficulties, Professor Patterson expounds the Ideas lucidly in her opening chapters. Indeed, she makes the system appear remarkably attractive, substantiating her claim that the Ideas could have served as useful instruction for poets and constituted an organization of stylistic possibilities more fruitful than the frequently ambiguous and generically problematic Three-Style scheme of Cicero.

The rest of the book discusses five of the Ideas in the context of Renaissance poetry (mostly English and entirely nondramatic). The subdivisions of Grandeur fall naturally into two groups to be used for praise and reproof respectively. The former group contributes techniques to the ode and the canzone (Minturno's illustrations of Grandeur from Petrarch are carefully and perceptively pressed into service), while the latter provides a more thorough explanation of the rough qualities of late Elizabethan satire than we have previously had (although they do not explain, as seems to be suggested in a footnote, why satire should have gone "hairy" at the precise date that it did). The Ideas of Beauty and Verity are opposed in both concept and technique: these Professor Patterson sees as providing not only compositional method but also thematic centers for the sonnets of Sidney and Shakespeare. She thus suggests a firm context and function within the sequences for their anti-Petrarchanism and their highly rhetorical disparagements of rhetoric. The chapter treating the Idea of Speed illuminates the technique of *carpe diem* poetry, although I cannot see how this can be called a "new, minor genre" (p. xii). Finally, the last Idea, Gravity, which is both Grandeur under a different name and the fitting combination of all the Ideas (Eloquence, or Decorum itself), is investigated in the epics of Camoens, Tasso, Daniel, Drayton, and Spenser.

Writing this book required an impressive mastery of a bulky chunk of Renaissance learning and of a wide range of poetry. To this mastery Professor Patterson adds a deft hand at organization (it would not have done to treat the seven Ideas seriatim in the second half of the book), a clear style, a sense of humor, and an ability to select apt illustrations from modern poetry that demonstrate the occasional analytic usefulness of the Hermogenic system even when the poet cannot by any stretch be supposed to have known it. Despite the fact that the repute, importance, and pervasiveness of the rhetorical tradition have been well established—to the point where three handbooks of rhetoric for undergraduate students of sixteenth-century poetry have been published in the last three years—the work of reviving a particularly obscure rhetorician and using his system sensitively is genuinely pioneering. Aware of the hypothetical character of influence-study, Professor Patterson remains suitably tentative, even when, for example, Hermogenes nicely accounts for the combination of syntax, vocabulary, word order, and vowel sounds of Nature's judgment in the *Mutabilitie Cantos* (pp. 90–92). Unfortunately, there are some curious lapses. Sixteenth-century criticism, like twentieth-century criticism, has its share of nonsense, and it is surprising to see Professor Patterson use without qualification Vicenzo Toralto's sweeping pronouncement that end-stopped lines represent corruption from which the reader recoils (pp. 170–71). Her debts to other scholars are occasionally left too implicit: a summary of the narrative premises of *The Faerie Queene* (pp. 204–5) appears to derive from Professor Roche, but we are merely told that "all this is obvious." Perhaps it is, now that Roche's *Kindly Flame* has so carefully explained it. Above all, the book ends unsatisfactorily. Granted that discussing the decorum of five epics is a massive job, it is a double error of strategy to be so sketchy with the final, crowning Idea and to omit all direct treatment of Milton, the English epic poet most outspokenly devoted to decorum and most likely to have known Hermogenes well.

We know that the rhetorical tradition was vital to Renaissance poetry; we must attempt to distinguish the fruitfulness of the various plots in that far-flung nursery of art. We know that decorum was the grand masterpiece to observe; it behooves us to observe how the poets observed it. This book, expounding a particular system of decorum and reading the poetry in its terms, deserves attention.

Shakespeare's Lives by Samuel Schoenbaum. Oxford University Press, 1970. Pp. xxiv + 838. $12.50.

Reviewer: John Freehafer.

In 1964, at Shakespeare's grave, Professor Schoenbaum decided to write "a little book narrating the quest for knowledge of Shakespeare the man; a book describing the different, sometimes opposing ideas of him that people over the centuries had entertained. It would be called Shakespeare's Lives." The large book that Schoenbaum has published coincides with that original concept by retaining a title which no longer describes its scope. *Shakespeare's Lives* not only deals more fully with the biographers than with the lives they wrote, but devotes much space to matters that are off the highroad of Shakespearean biography. Schoenbaum's book has grown so much that his own statement that "my most ample coverage is reserved for the twentieth century" is now wrong, because he devotes twice as many pages to the nineteenth century as to the twentieth. Nonetheless, the reader who allows Schoenbaum his concept of his topic will be rewarded, because his book combines wit, liveliness, human interest, originality, and scholarship.

Presumably, Schoenbaum reverts to his plan for his "little book" when he tells us that he has dealt successively with life records of Shakespeare, the legends and traditions about him, and the formal biographies. In the book before us, however, a hundred pages are devoted to the anti-Stratfordians, and other digressions deal with such peripheral matters as plays and novels in which Shakespeare is a character, and spurious documents, portraits, and souvenirs. These excursions carry Schoenbaum into areas touched upon in books about William Henry Ireland, the anti-Stratfordians, the Shakespeare industry, and Shakespeare's reputation; but here, as elsewhere, Schoenbaum's original research is manifest. Furthermore, the extravagances of novelists, forgers, and Baconians often provide striking proofs of Schoenbaum's thesis that Shakespearean biography is unusually narcissistic and "tends towards oblique self-portraiture." As Schoenbaum demonstrates, the greatness of

Shakespeare combines with the paucity and dullness of the factual record about him to induce nearly all Shakespearean biographers to portray themselves under the guise of Shakespeare; and this tendency of each "biographer" and each generation to recreate Shakespeare in a preferred image is strikingly embodied in the naive and sentimental fabrications of Ireland and in the eagerness with which they were accepted. According to Schoenbaum, Desmond McCarthy said "that trying to work out Shakespeare's personality was like looking at a very dark glazed picture in the National Portrait Gallery: at first you see nothing, then you begin to recognize features, and then you realize that they are your own." That final realization seems, however, to have eluded most of Shakespeare's biographers.

Schoenbaum demonstrates that fundamental and pervasive errors of fact and judgment are to be found in most biographies of Shakespeare. Although he omits much that seems trivial (such as the *Annotator* controversy), he occasionally unearths errors from deservedly forgotten books; in such cases the reader can thank him for having examined and categorized "such reading as was never read." But Schoenbaum's diligent search for errors has not saved him from repeating some old ones or adding a few new ones. The first encyclopedia article on Shakespeare did not appear in 1763; Thomas Birch contributed a lengthy and important article on Shakespeare to Volume IX of the expanded English edition of Bayle's *General Dictionary* in 1739/40. Milton's well-known sixteen-line epitaph on Shakespeare is not a "sonnet," and Schoenbaum's discussion of Rowe as an editor of Shakespeare, besides being irrelevant, repeats several hoary errors of judgment. For example, Rowe was not "the first critical editor of Shakespeare"; in *Shakespeare's Seventeenth Century Editors* (1937), Black and Shaaber demonstrated that the Second Folio qualifies as a critical edition. Schoenbaum's discussion of Davenant also includes much that is doubtful or wrong; for example, Davenant did not introduce "actresses on the professional London stage." Schoenbaum's attempts to catch E. K. Chambers in error are unsuccessful, for most of the points that he cites are not errors or else have been corrected in later printings of Chambers's *William Shakespeare*. For example, Schoenbaum says that Chambers's index is "not impeccably accurate: the single citation under *Rape of Lucrece* refers the reader to II, 342, which contains no mention of the poem." But Chambers's citation appears under "PLAYS" and correctly refers the reader to a listing of Heywood's tragedy *The Rape of Lucrece*; and elsewhere in his index (II, 440) Chambers lists twelve citations of *Lucrece* (as Shakespeare's poem is called on the title pages of the four earliest editions). Schoenbaum says that Shakespeare enjoyed no great early reputation; as "proof" that in the seventeenth century Shakespeare was seldom praised, except by the wrong people, Schoenbaum notes that the First Folio contains fewer commendatory verses than later folios of Jonson and Fletcher. Surely, however, the fact that Shakespeare's plays were published much more often than Jonson's or Fletcher's counts for more than the printing of single sets of commendatory verses. Indeed, if the reputation of a seventeenth-century dramatist can be gauged by the number of commendatory verses in one collected edition, then the most esteemed dramatist of the time must have been Cartwright. Schoenbaum reveals other decided views of his own by brushing aside the plausible suggestion that Jonson had a hand in the dedicatory epistle of the First Folio and calling Alexander's theory about the transmission of the texts of 2 and 3 *Henry VI* "irrefutable." Indeed, Schoenbaum is so fond of Alexander's theory that he singles out for praise a forgotten book of 1864 in which Kenny advanced a similar view and supposedly toppled "the traditional view that Shakespeare began his stage connection as a playadaptor." According to Schoenbaum, whatever Shakespeare may have done during the "lost years" and immediately thereafter, the view that he cobbled plays at that time is a "legend." Schoenbaum seems to incline towards the view that Shakespeare spent the "lost years" as a schoolmaster.

In view of the size and scope of his book, however, Schoenbaum's errors are not especially numerous or damaging, and they are offset by his original findings from unpublished sources. Schoenbaum has found new information on Malone, Ireland, Collier, Knight, Halliwell-Phillipps, the Wallaces, and others. Along with some familiar illustrations Schoenbaum includes others that he has unearthed. He establishes the parentage and date of birth of Ireland and prints a confession which the "nearly blind" Collier wrote at the age of ninety-three. Another valuable feature of Schoenbaum's book is his effort to trace to their sources the legends, hypotheses, and critical clichés which have become part of common knowledge (or, more often, common ignorance) about Shakespeare. Who first suggested that Shakespeare held horses outside the theater; that Prospero's epilogue is Shakespeare's farewell to his art; that "Mr. W. H." is Southampton, or Pembroke, or someone else; that Bacon wrote Shakespeare's plays, or Montaigne's *Essays;* that Shakespeare's *Sonnets* are a thinly disguised autobiography in verse? Schoenbaum answers a host of such questions and sometimes traces these suggestions to obscure or unnoted sources.

Schoenbaum's "passionate interest in the lives and achievements of men" is much in evidence; he presents the study of Shakespeare's biography as an eminently human and humanistic endeavor, for all its errors and eccentricities. But the relatively few writers who appear mainly in a favorable light in Schoenbaum's pages include the no-nonsense scholars such as the lawyer Malone, the hoarder Halliwell-Phillipps, the antiquarian Fripp, and the civil servant Chambers. To be sure, Schoenbaum is correct in finding that such dedicated, but meticulous and self-effacing, scholars tend to write about Shakespeare's life in a "bleak" or "gray" style. Nevertheless, Schoenbaum's book suggests to me that a cautious and circumspect revision of Chambers's magisterial *William Shakespeare* would be a particularly welcome addition to the shelf of Shakespearean biography. The great Shakespearean scholars of the eighteenth century established a worthy tradition of crediting, preserving, and building upon the best work of their predecessors, and a new edition of Chambers would constitute a notable application of that tradition to the field of Shakespearean biography.

The least entertaining part of Schoenbaum's book is that in which he must deal with the "life records," rather than the many and colorful idiosyncrasies of Shakespeare's biographers and pseudo-biographers. Once past the "life records," Schoenbaum maintains the reader's interest at a high pitch despite the length of his book and the need to discuss such matters as the deer-poaching story again and again. He usually succeeds in the difficult task of combining and keeping in balance a lively writing style, a striving for human interest, massive original research, and tough-minded criticism. Sometimes, however, a stress upon human interest may have dictated his allotment of pages; Collier and Ireland, for example, receive far more space than Chambers. At other times, a striving for human interest may have led to questionable or erroneous conclusions. For example, Schoenbaum suggests that the "strange thoughts" of Joseph C. Hart, who was the first to argue seriously in print that Shakespeare did not write his plays, arose from "the isolation of Santa Cruz, surrounded by the Sulu Sea." Like many an older Shakespeare legend, this attractive notion will not stand factual scrutiny, because Hart was American consul at Santa Cruz in the Canary Islands, not the Philippines; and he did not become a consul until after he had published his "strange thoughts." Usually, however, Schoenbaum's views of those who wrote about Shakespeare seem to be just and correct, and they are firmly stated. For example, Malone receives at least his due in terms of space and by virtue of the judgment that he was "the greatest of Elizabethan scholars." In sum, Schoenbaum's book is a major contribution which should be read and studied by everyone with an interest in Shakespearean biography. *Shakespeare's Lives* will certainly find a place on the standard lists of scholarly books about Shakespeare.

The Hamlet of Edwin Booth by Charles H. Shattuck. University of Illinois Press, 1969. Pp. xxvii + 321. $10.95.

Reviewer: Carol J. Carlisle

One of the treasures of the Folger Shakespeare Library is a sixty-thousand-word description of Edwin Booth's performance of *Hamlet*, penned in the summer of 1870 by Charles Clarke, a twenty-one-year-old admirer of Booth. This extraordinarily detailed account, written after Clarke had memorized the entire play, studied criticisms of it and of Booth's performance, and seen Booth's Hamlet eight times, is the most complete written record that we have of any Shakespearean performance. Although Professor Shattuck has used a number of additional sources for his study of *The Hamlet of Edwin Booth*, Clarke's "massive" description is the heart and center of his book.

As Shattuck remarks, the manuscript "is not holiday reading. Every line or phrase—at times every word—that Booth uttered upon the stage carries its burdens of commentary, and the effects of any one passage can be got at only by painstaking and repeated mulling" (p. vi). His statement is a temperate one, as anyone who has tried to work with the document can attest. Readers in the Folger Library who "discover" Clarke's manuscript feel, in their first jubilation, like Balboa sighting the Pacific; but, once they have tried to make some real use of it, their excitement is likely to turn to frustration—just such frustration as Balboa would have experienced in attempting, single-handedly, to hew his way to that ocean through a nearly impenetrable jungle. To explore the dense jungle of Clarke's words, to find one's way through it and, with expert woodmanship, to clear a path for others—this is a labor not to be undertaken lightly. Professor Shattuck has dared to undertake it, however; and indeed it is difficult to imagine anyone more thoroughly equipped for the task. His intimate knowledge of the theater in all periods, and particularly the nineteenth century, his work with the Shakespeare promptbooks, and—not least—his ability to translate the mysteries of the stage into "plain English" have made him an ideal mediator between Clarke and the reader. In spite of the stringent restrictions which he placed upon himself in dealing with the manuscript, he has been remarkably successful. (Successful, that is, with the reader who is willing to become deeply involved in the analysis of Booth's performance but who needs help in doing so. Even in Shattuck's rendition, Clarke will make little appeal to the casual reader.) If Professor Shattuck had done nothing beyond making

Clarke's valuable manuscript accessible and, through his superb editing, usable, his book would have been a very substantial achievement. Actually he has done considerably more than this.

The Hamlet of Edwin Booth is a "biography," not of the actor, but of a single role played by him over a period of thirty-eight years. It is divided into three sections. Part I traces the development of Booth's Hamlet from 1853 to 1870, with chapters devoted to early efforts in the role, to the influences exerted by Adam Badeau and Mollie Devlin in shaping the role, to "the emergence of Hamlet as Booth's acknowledged masterwork," as in the 1864 production at the Winter Garden which ran for one hundred nights, and, finally, to a discussion of Booth's "definitive production of the play at his own theatre in 1870." The history of Booth's acting of Hamlet is interrupted by Part II, the longest and most fascinating part of the book, which is devoted to a detailed reconstruction of Booth's 1870 *Hamlet*. This production, though less emphasized by theater historians than the record-breaking Winter Garden production, was intrinsically the more important, as Professor Shattuck convincingly shows. Luckily, it is also the one for which we have the fullest documentation. Part III resumes the interrupted history and completes it, tracing Booth's appearances in *Hamlet* from 1870 to the final performance in 1891. The author suggests that readers who are content with an "overview" may read only Parts I and III. "Only those who wish to realize Booth's Hamlet in the utmost possible immediacy should grapple with Part II." Parts I and III will be a welcome addition to stage history both for specialists and for interested amateur readers. But the real meat of the book is in Part II.

The bulk of the reconstruction is Charles Clarke's account, already referred to. Clarke's method, as Shattuck explains it, is to mention settings briefly, to describe Hamlet's appearance "exhaustively," to report the words of other characters only as necessary to the sense, but "to record every word of Hamlet's speeches and to explicate them with succinct notations of sound and accompanying action." At the end of each scene or major passage he pauses "to generalize upon Booth's acting, to interpret the larger meanings of the scene, to express its effect upon himself. . . ." In annotating Hamlet's speeches Clarke records a word, phrase, or line, marks it for Booth's stresses and phrasings; then he inserts in parentheses vocal effects (tone, tempo, rising or falling inflection, emotional coloration) or physical effects (facial expression, gesture, movement) or both (see p. 105). The multiplicity of details makes it almost impossible at times for the reader to get a clear impression of the overall effect of Booth's acting, even in the portion of the scene that is being described. Yet it is the completeness of the description that gives it much of its value.

Professor Shattuck has rejected the idea of simply making the Clarke account the basis for an "original" and far more readable description of Booth's Hamlet. This expedient, he maintains, would have been "dishonest." At times the reader may wish that he had been less uncompromising; for, even with the considerable smoothing that Shattuck has given the original, the account is still rather hard going. Its awkwardness for all except dedicated readers may be illustrated by a passage chosen for its easy intelligibility and relative smoothness. Beginning in the middle of Hamlet's advice to the players, we read:

> ". . . for *anything* so *overdone* (upward accent of *-done*) is from the PURpose of *playing*, whose *end*, both *at the first and now* (broad sound of *and* and *now*, spoken slowly and warningly), *was*, and *is*, to *hold* as-'twere the *mirror up* (upward accent) to *nature*; to show (he speaks more freely and a little faster now, abandoning the admonitory tone) virtue-her-own-*feature* (upward accent), *scorn*-her-own-*image* (pronounced *im-aj*), and the very *age*, and *body* of the time, his *form* and *pressure*."
>
> (*p. 199*)

Yet it is hard to argue with Professor Shattuck's reasoning: "Clarke saw and heard Booth's Hamlet, and the evidence he set down is more important than would be a filtering of it through me or any single evaluator" (p. vii). What Shattuck has done is edit Clarke's account in order to make it more systematic and intelligible, but he has been scrupulously careful to omit no detail. The wording, too, is largely Clarke's own, though grammatical forms have been regularized when necessary, and the passages of general commentary have been pruned of verbiage. Professor Shattuck considers that his "greatest liberty" has been the lifting of whole statements out of parentheses, especially those reporting physical effects, and presenting them in the form of running narrative. We must be grateful for his decision to take this liberty, for it has enabled him to present a much more coherent account than would have been possible otherwise and thus to make a picture of the action more easily accessible to the imagination of the reader. As for the pruning of Clarke's prose in the passages of general commentary, I have compared several such passages with my copy of the original, and invariably I have found that, although repetitions and circumlocutions have been eliminated, all the ideas are represented, key words and phrases faithfully preserved.

In addition to Clarke's manuscript, Professor Shattuck has used a number of other documents for his reconstruction of Booth's *Hamlet*. One of the most important is a souvenir promptbook made up for Booth during or after the 1870 run of the play; it contains "the text cut as the play was then performed,

with the stage manager's notes of scenic arrangement and basic stage business," and watercolors, by Charles Witham, of ten of the eleven sets used in
the production. Shattuck has used it to resolve major contradictions in the
evidence presented by other sources; he has also drawn upon it heavily in
describing the stage settings of the 1870 *Hamlet*, and he has reproduced, in
black-and-white, all ten of Witham's watercolors. (These illustrations, clear
and excellent in quality, are very helpful to the reader as he attempts to
visualize the performance. The additional inclusion of six sets of the Winter
Garden *Hamlet*, reproduced from the Booth-Hinton edition of the play, 1866,
makes comparisons possible.) Supplementary information has been gleaned
from a number of other promptbooks and similar records of Booth's production, for example a record of all of Booth's most notable stage business from
1862 to 1891 as observed by E. T. Mason, literary critic and frequent playgoer.
Booth's own annotations in his *Hamlet* Notebooks have furnished fresh insights into his interpretation. Newspaper and magazine reviews have been used
in an interesting and discriminating way.

The method of Shattuck's reconstruction is as follows. Each scene in Booth's
1870 version of *Hamlet* is treated as a separate unit. Its heading consists of the
act and scene number in Booth's version and the designation of the setting.
A headnote gives the equivalent scene or scenes in the Globe edition and the
number of lines in Booth's text as compared with the number in the Globe
text. Then follows a description of the set, giving such mechanical details as
exact measurements and stage positions, but also evoking in graphic language
the look of the scene from the audience's point of view. An excerpt from the
description of the graveyard scene will illustrate Shattuck's successful combination of practical detail and imaginative appeal:

It is a night scene, draped in shade, with moonlight flooding the church
and falling in streaks through the branches of the trees. A faint mist, a
damp, dewy look, seems to hang about it. All the standard scenic elements
—wings, borders, cut pieces, built pieces, and backdrop—combine to
produce the most ideally romantic and yet convincingly real illusion
of a country churchyard.

The scene is framed at the sides by "Moonlight Wood Wings" showing gaunt trees through the leafage. These, according to Bensen Sher-
wood's "Stage Plans," fill five grooves at stage right and four grooves
at stage left. Overhead the scene is framed by heavily leafed branches
("Cut Wood Borders") which cross the entire stage above the downstage
entrances. The moonlight falls from stage right, so that the trees at the

left are strongly lighted. Well upstage and just to the right of center a
large bushy tree rises on two trunks; toward the left, just below the third
grooves, is a blackish pyramidal yew, also double-trunked.

                                                                    (p. 250)

The stage having been set, Shattuck begins the description of the performance
of the scene, subdividing it, for the reader's greater ease in following it, and
providing, as a heading for each new block of material, the line numbers of
the Globe edition and the quotation of a key line. For example, Act I, scene i
is broken up into two units; 1–38, "Who's there?" and 38–175, "Peace, break
thee off; look, where it comes again!" This method sounds a bit awkward in the
telling, but actually it works very well. Even the most attentive reader, when
attempting to visualize the action on the basis of a minutely detailed description, probably finds it helpful to be given only a small slice of that action to
work on at a time. The description of the action is Clarke's, edited in the
manner that has already been described. Occasional comments from other
sources (such as newspaper critiques) have been added, but they are always
clearly labeled as such. Generally such comments, along with supplementary
information about the staging of the 1870 *Hamlet* and the changes made by
Booth in later productions, are found in the notes. (Happily, these are placed
at the foot of the page, so that comparisons can conveniently be made at
specific points in the action between Booth's 1870 performance and those at
other periods of his career.) At the end of the section on each scene Shattuck
lists the specific cuts and alterations made by Booth, notes whether or not
the cuts were traditional, and lists any restorations made to the traditional text
of that time.

The study of Shattuck's reconstruction is very demanding. At times the
reader, puzzled by the gestures or the tones attributed to Booth, finds himself
trying them out before an unseen audience in an effort to imagine their effect
or to understand why Booth should have considered them appropriate. The
practice is salutary, particularly for readers who have had no stage experience,
for it helps them to separate the significant actions from the motions which
are mechanically necessary as transitions between one meaningful gesture
and another. (The "outward swing" of the hand recorded at several points
in Hamlet's scene with Horatio, pp. 200–201, so distracting and so mystifying
at first reading, seems to be something of the latter sort.)

On the other hand, there are many passages of description, for example
in the closet scene, in which the excitement of the performance itself seems
to come directly through the words. Some of these vividly realized passages
help to throw a new light—or cast a new shadow—on our usual conception of

Booth's gentle, almost "feminine" Hamlet. One such description gives us a sudden glimpse of Booth's face in the soliloquy "Now might I do it pat" which reminds us that this actor was also an excellent Iago:

> At the line "Then trip him that his heels may kick at heaven," his face gradually loses its sadness and thoughtfulness; he smiles savagely with shut teeth; a mocking, triumphant expression starts from a dozen places in his face, and his look is "terrible, almost ferocious, and *humanly* malignant."
>
> *(p. 221)*

(The soliloquy, traditionally omitted in that period, was one of Booth's restorations; he himself sometimes omitted it, however, in later years.) Even some of the passages which describe outwardly gentle or courteous behavior show us a Hamlet whose grim irony is all the more effective for being subtly toned down. Booth's Hamlet used an "ironical, yet coldly decorous" tone in the scene in which the king questions him about the body of Polonius, and he said "In Heaven" in a "solemn and earnest but bizarre" manner (p. 241). Although other actors said "Farewell dear Mother" as if "to the absent parent without reference to the King," Booth addressed the king directly, as he should, but veiled Hamlet's fantastic impudence by his serious and tender air.

> An affectionate and sorrowful look crosses his face, and he comes swiftly down to the King, falls on one knee before him, and takes both his hands in his own: "*Farewell* (sorrowful tone; prolonged and tremulous), DEAR (tender; prolonged) *Mother* (upward accent). He draws the King's hands near to his lips and respectfully and lovingly bows his head over them.
>
> *(pp. 242–43)*

Such illuminating examples could be multiplied many times. The point is that, although Clarke's description of Hamlet as a "man of first-class intellect and second-class will" (p. 96) sounds like the typical romantic conception that we have long associated with Booth's Hamlet and although his list of general characteristics—gentlemanliness, princeliness, a "controllingly phlegmatic" temperament, "more excitable in words than in deeds" (p. 180)—also sounds very familiar, the details of Booth's action, as Clarke describes them, reveal a much more complex character than we are accustomed to associate with Booth's idealized portrayal.

Professor Shattuck's own concise descriptions of Booth's 1870 Hamlet (in his introduction and at the end of Part I) are unusually successful in combining generalization and detail; insofar as the complex Hamlet of Clarke's analysis can be given a broad outline without becoming distorted in any part, the thing has been done here. Readers who lack the stamina to persevere through Part II will be grateful for these portraits in little. All readers will be interested, as well, in the Hamlet of Booth's later years as the young Hamlin Garland saw him (see the introduction and Part III)—a somewhat different character from that of 1870, more meditative and stoical, "the good man enduring."

There is one point in Shattuck's interpretation of Booth's Hamlet which I must challenge. This relates to Booth's understanding of Hamlet's mental state at some points in the play. No one can quarrel with the statement that Booth believed Hamlet to be sane, for he made this fact known repeatedly and unambiguously. Yet it seems to me too much to deny that Booth's Hamlet ever approached an abnormal state of mind. According to Professor Shattuck:

> He could break out wildly now and then, as in his convulsion at the departure of the Ghost, or in the rattle of names he hurls down to the cellarage, or in his doggerel rhymes that cap the success of the *Mousetrap*, or in his ranting at Laertes over Ophelia's grave; but these were not hysteria—they were "the very intensity of mental excitement."
>
> (p. xxii)

Perhaps my problem is merely one of semantics, but I cannot believe that the "intensity of mental excitement," as Booth understood it, was very far removed from hysteria. As I have commented elsewhere,[1] Booth considered Hamlet a type of "uneven or unbalanced Genius" and his unseasonably frivolous speeches ("old mole," and so forth) as safety valves to preserve his reason. He associated Hamlet's eccentricities with the vagaries of his own father, Junius Brutus Booth, of whom he said: "Only those who have known the torture of severe mental tension can appreciate the value of that one little step from the sublime to the ridiculous."[2] Several days after Booth had been fired at and narrowly missed by a madman at McVicker's Theatre in Chicago (April 23, 1879), he wrote to E. C. Stedman:

> My temporary self-control gave way after a day or two to a highly nervous excitement—a condition similar to that which I believe Shakespeare illustrates by Hamlet's frivolity after the ghost is gone, and the terrible tension of his brain is relaxed. I have a ghostly disposition to joke about the affair which is hardly controllable.[3]

Because of such comments as these, I find it difficult to accept as convincing the charge, made in a review by O. B. Bunce, that when Booth spoke the "wild and whirling words" they "did not spring from intense feeling rising into hysterical mirth: they were only a practical device to confound and confuse his listeners." Professor Shattuck does accept this, however, and all else that Bunce says about Booth's insistence upon logical explanations at every point where Hamlet "ought to behave hysterically."

Bunce was only one witness to Booth's Hamlet. According to another witness, William Winter:

> Booth was definite . . . as to the "madness" of Hamlet. He was not absolutely mad, but substantially sane,—guarding himself, his secrets, and his purposes by assumed wildness; yet the awful loneliness of existence to which Hamlet has been sequestered by his vast, profound, all-embracing, contemplative intellect, and by the mental shock and wrench that he has sustained, was allowed to colour his temperament.[4]

We cannot necessarily trust Winter to keep Booth's ideas separate from his own—certainly he seems to go too far when he speaks, in another passage, of Hamlet's "fatal grief . . . which sometimes drives him into delirium and must inevitably cause his death"[5]—but the passage which I quoted first, with its emphasis on Hamlet's "awful loneliness," is consonant with Booth's own comment, in a letter to Winter, that genius is a "disease" that isolates the possessor and denies him "sympathetic communion with ordinary men."[6]

The fact that two witnesses may disagree upon the details of the same performance—even upon mechanical matters like tempo and stressed words (Shattuck notes several such cases, p. 288)—serves as a caveat against too trusting an acceptance of any report of a stage interpretation. Yet, since reports are all we have of the great performances of the past, we cherish them. To work one's way through the mass of detail accumulated about Edwin Booth's performance by the dedicated and meticulous observer Charles Clarke, skillfully set in order and annotated by Professor Shattuck, and, in the case of scenery, expanded from other sources, is to come as close as is humanly possible to experiencing the whole of such a performance.

Notes:

1. *Shakespeare from the Greenroom* (Chapel Hill, 1969), p. 109.
2. Booth's comments on Hamlet as a genius and on his similarities to Junius Brutus Booth are found in a letter to William Winter, dated April 23, 1883 (MS in the Folger Library), and in his essay on his father in *Actors and Actresses of Great*

Britain and the United States, ed. Brander Matthews and Lawrence Hutton (New York, 1886), III, 95–96.

3. Quoted in Charles Copeland, *Edwin Booth* (Boston, 1901), p. 114. There is a similar passage in a letter to William Winter, written the same day, April 27, 1879 (MS in the Folger Library).

4. William Winter, *The Life and Art of Edwin Booth* (1893; New York, 1968), pp. 164–65.

5. Ibid., p. 175.

6. Letter cited in note 2.

Shakespeare's Plays Today: Customs and Conventions of the Stage by Arthur Colby Sprague and J. C. Trewin. University of South Carolina Press, 1971. Pp. 147. $4.95.

Reviewer: Robert F. Willson.

Now that Shakespearean criticism has generally recognized the value of examining the plays as dramatic scores rather than solely as texts for the study and has even given a certain weight and place to pioneering essays like John Styan's *Shakespeare's Stagecraft*, it seems appropriate that two giants of the theatrical school should publish the distillate of years of play-watching. J. C. Trewin and Arthur Colby Sprague have spent their careers exploring the realm of performance in search of the grail-like essence of Shakespeare's magic; those of us who believe in this approach and who delight in its growing acceptance owe these men a great debt. Mr. Trewin's books establish his credentials as a prominent stage historian, in particular such works as *Shakespeare on the English Stage, 1900–1964* and *Benson and the Bensonians;* his edition of Macready's Journals affords valuable insight into a nineteenth-century actor's view of tragedy. Arthur Colby Sprague's production, including such influential studies as *Shakespeare and the Audience, Shakespeare and the Actors: The Stage Business in his Plays, 1660–1905,* and *Shakespearian Players and Performances,* must certainly be recognized as the foremost achievement of American scholarship in the field. A collaborative effort by these critics, then, promises much, especially a discussion of customs and conventions of the stage.

But this little book delivers more reminiscence than researched fact and falls short in its acknowledged aim of searching out the sources of long-observed conventions. The authors' essay consists mainly of notes jotted down after performances in the 1920s and '30s by traveling companies, under the direction of legendary figures like Frank Benson, Charles Doran, and Henry Baynton. The assumption is made that these performances were crucial because they set the outlines on which today's revivals are based. This assumption is never proved in the book; the authors seem not to care to do the kind of consistent analysis required to achieve that end (indulging in statistics was "to be firmly resisted"). In fact, this hyperbolic claim of preeminence for Benson and the others is directly contradicted in the first chapter, where we learn that such stage business as survives in today's productions originated in the nineteenth century! Unfortunately the collaboration often finds the authors working at cross-purposes because of differing interests and tastes: Sprague had the major hand in chapters on stage business, additions to the text, and sights and sounds, while Trewin worked with problems of cutting the text, speaking the lines, the people of the plays, and stages and staging. And a good deal of the unevenness in style can be attributed to this plan of writing. Clearly, Trewin has done more work in digging out reviews and introducing critiques of recent productions at Stratford-upon-Avon, Edinburgh, and Stratford, Ontario; Sprague, on the other hand, relies more heavily on a sometimes faulty memory and delivers himself in an offhand manner, which, though seductive, is sometimes exasperating. When he discusses the addition of lines to Falstaff's speech after his escape from Hal and Poins ("D'ye think I did not know ye?"), Sprague haltingly concludes: "It is my impression—an impression only (alas!)—that I have heard them at least once, not a great while ago."

Yet the real dilemma in *Shakespeare's Plays Today* is that the authors have not worked together in determining the guiding purpose of the book: are we to learn about nineteenth-century origins of stage custom? are we intended to revaluate the contribution of English traveling companies of the twenties and thirties? are we supposed to appreciate how radically modern producers have swerved from tradition in presenting certain plays? The succession of chapters appears to follow no rational organization, and the book is embarrassingly devoid of generalization. A rather feeble attempt is made at synthesis in the final chapter, where modern directors are urged to refrain "from discovering new significances that Shakespeare never dreamed about, struggling to make their productions unlike any other, and playing over and over the game of 'relevance to modern life' which can be both irrelevant and tedious." Not only is the reader hard-pressed to see the relationship of this conclusion to the essay's curiosity about the practice of stage interpretation, he is also a bit dismayed when Mr. Trewin, in supporting his observation, cites the rarity of such unforgettable recent interpretations as Sir Lawrence Olivier's Othello.

How could any critic ignore the obvious and dubiously successful attempt at relevance in Olivier's West Indian accent! Instead of reasoned argument we get in *Shakespeare's Plays Today* indulgence in nostalgia; Benson and Doran look suspiciously like spirits from the past called up to purge the stage of its ambitious usurpers.

Yet if one can overcome this nagging feeling that his sensibilities are being lectured to about the good old days, when directors gave us something to look at and actors gave us something to hear, he has much to discover about the tradition of Shakespearean performance. It must be admitted that with modern attempts at uncluttering the stage, performing the entire "original" text, and generally stripping the plays of their theatrical excrescences, directors have deprived new generations of theatergoers of the knowledge that Quince was always played as a bespectacled old man, a kindly stammerer with sole knowledge among the mechanicals about the meaning of "Pyramus and Thisbe," or that Audrey of *As You Like It* always appeared barefooted. In other words, the book gives us a pretty full sense of those traditions rebels have consciously rejected—or adopted—thinking they have unearthed something new. In particular, we learn that post-World War II producers have eschewed the notion of a set repertoire. The Bensonites of the twenties and thirties kept to a familiar run of plays: *Macbeth, Hamlet, Romeo and Juliet,* and *Julius Caesar; The Merchant of Venice, The Taming of the Shrew, As You Like It, Twelfth Night,* and *The Merry Wives of Windsor.* Our modern festivals, with their attendant purist impulses, have of course cured us of such parochialism, as they also have of the disturbing habit of cutting whole swatches from the plays in order to establish scene breaks. Typically missing from the traveling companies' versions were the murder of Cinna the poet in *Julius Caesar,* the English doctor in *Macbeth,* the Latin lesson in *Merry Wives,* and the Induction to *Taming of the Shrew.* Fortinbras rarely if ever made an appearance on the circuit. Acting was highly stylized, scene breaks tended to be numerous (averaging three long intervals), and in matters of costuming, casting, and business tradition was everywhere followed; to quote Trewin, "These productions were Shakespeare of the theatre theatrical." Now, both authors conclude, no one expects to see real bridges in *Merchant of Venice,* or a complete chapel for the wedding of Romeo and Juliet (except in the movies, of course). Indeed, a most striking break with tradition has resulted from the placing of a single property. Hamlet's visit to his mother's room following the play scene has been played traditionally as taking place in a private room. But, since the critical interest in the Freudian aspects of the play has risen sharply, recent performances have turned the closet into a bedroom. One of the few genuine discoveries of the book is the citation of John Dover Wilson's

What Happens in Hamlet (1935) as the source for the phrase, "the Bedroom Scene," on which Gielgud's New York production of the next year was based. The conclusion the reader must draw for himself is that such striking modifications indicate that directors of modern versions have been found guilty of reading *literary* criticism!

Of abiding interest in the book, however, is not what happens in *Hamlet*, but what happens to it—in production. While the authors do concern themselves with a number of plays in the canon, they return regularly to this longest of the plays in order to praise or decry innovative staging. From the close of the nineteenth century we have Hamlet lying on his back and looking up at the stars as he responds to the ghost's admonitions:

> O all you host of heaven! O earth! What else
> And shall I couple hell? Hold, hold, my heart!
> And you, my sinews, grow not instant old,
> But bear me stiffly up.

Professor Sprague recalls John Barrymore carrying on like this in a twenties production, and thinking at the time how right it was; he is not so sure of its rightness now. A more recent piece of business, first introduced by Gielgud in 1934, intrigues and perplexes him even more: "The Theft of the King's Sword." This occurs as Hamlet comes upon Claudius in the prayer scene ("Up, sword, and know thou a more horrid hent"); besides qualifying as a tour de force, it also, as Sprague sensibly points out, relieves the actor from having to carry a sword in the play scene, where he does not require one, and provides him with one for the closet scene, where he needs it in order to dispatch Polonius. Succeeding actors have readily embraced this piece of business: Scofield used it at Stratford in 1948, Redgrave at the Old Vic in 1949, and Burton in New York in 1964. But Sprague's main objection wins back the scene for champions of the study. Engrossed in the game of seizing the weapon, "we no longer concentrate on the momentous inner drama which is played out in the course of the scene." The point is well taken and worth further discussion (what, precisely, is the nature of that inner drama?), but Sprague's informality does not allow for such critical evaluation.

The excision of Fortinbras has had a long tradition, with most altered versions ending on Horatio's "Flights of angels sing thee to thy rest." (In Beerbohm Tree's production of 1892, the audience could faintly hear extraterrestrial echoings of "Good night, sweet Prince.") Modern performances have restored Fortinbras, though not completely, but Voltimand and Cornelius, ambassadors to Norway, and Reynoldo are seldom met. As for scenes and speeches, they were tampered with as well by touring companies of the twenties, a point which certainly offers supporting evidence for theories about the generation of bad quartos for such plays as *Hamlet* and *Romeo and Juliet*. Hamlet's "This heavy-headed revel east and west" (I.iv), the central lines of the ghost's speech in I.v ("whose effect . . . all my smooth body"), the dumb show, and practically all of the duologue for Hamlet and Horatio at the opening of V.ii are "still the passages first endangered" by modern directors, despite their claims of truthfulness to text. In shortened versions, Hamlet keeps all his soliloquies while Claudius's and Laertes' parts suffer sharply from the director's scissors. The inescapable conclusion is that, despite the fact that *Hamlet* is a lengthy and melodramatic piece, it has suffered cutting not so much in order to fit time requirements, but to conform to directorial notions about the true interpretation of the hero. No other Shakespearean character, after all, has undergone so many psychoanalytic excavations.

Less thorough explorations have been undertaken to discover the essential beings of the other "people of the plays," as we learn from the most rewarding chapter in the book (it is Trewin's). Custom has given to Olivia the character of either a stately matron or a lively young coquette, with the former being most often favored by actresses of the nineteenth and early twentieth century. Her youthfulness, if not her coquetry, has now become established. While Feste had been stereotyped as "a tiresome fidget in cap-and-bells who would move to wistfulness with an effort," contemporary treatments have tended to make him a mature, somewhat Jaques-like fellow. Such pendulum swinging in interpretation is most evident in the case of the lovers from *A Midsummer Night's Dream*, who are now almost always played for laughs, while tradition had called for them to be straight romantics. Trewin seems disappointed that the mood has changed, and he puts his question about the dilemma facing today's directors of the comedy rather simplemindedly: "Should the lovers of *A Midsummer Night's Dream* be comic?" With such lines as "O Helen, goddess, nymph, perfect divine! To what, my love, shall I compare thine eyne?" it is difficult to conceive of them being played otherwise. Still, one senses the rightness of Trewin's disapproval of attempts to exaggerate, to play for slapstick in this and other romantic roles.

The custom of playing the duke of York in *Richard II* as a comic character deserves stronger censure; weakness and vacillation are not necessarily comic, especially in a history. However, Shakespeare has given actors and directors thorny problems of character and style to deal with in this case. York's "Come, cousin, I'll dispose of you" in the passage with the queen (II.ii), or his repeated "Get me my boots, I say," shouted while scurrying to indict his son, present real challenges to control of tone and mood. Still other customs have been secured on the basis of misreading Shakespeare's language as well as intent. For example, Hotspur had been played as a stammerer in traditional productions, on the authority of Lady Percy's line in *Part II*: "Speaking thick, which nature made his blemish." "Thick" in this context obviously connotes not clumsiness or defective speech but rapidity of delivery, as in "thick and fast"; the faulty convention was taken to its logical extreme by Olivier in his 1945 Old Vic performance, in which he elected "to halt throughout on the letter 'w'." Here interpretation of character has been shaped by mistakes of a most fundamental kind.

Today's directors still commit such errors (Andrew Aguecheek and Sir Eglamour are consistently caricatured); but on the whole they have moved away from realistic setting—a bare, flat stage is generally the rule at Stratford-upon-Avon—toward a more "Elizabethan" platform and continuous performances. Entrances from the audience, favored at the Edinburgh and Stratford, Ontario festivals, have been elected as at least one means, if sometimes awkward, of achieving greater intimacy between actor and audience. But audiences and actors must be on their guards: Eric Keown of *Punch*, a tall man in need of legroom, once nearly overturned Ophelia's funeral procession; he concluded that others in his situation should "never put an unwary foot in the sceptred aisle." Ingenious juxtaposition of scenes has become another method of keeping audience interest and excitement high. Trewin praises Frank Hauser's 1965 Oxford Playhouse *Antony and Cleopatra* for the clever opposition of Ventidius's often-cut Syrian scene (III.i) and the reveling scene on Pompey's yacht (II.vii). (One wonders how much praise this particular touch would have received had Trewin checked the text, where he would have discovered that the Ventidius scene does follow the galley revel. The juxtaposition is Shakespeare's, not Hauser's.) Modern staging has also seen more experiments with costuming, or no costumes at all, and lighting, symbolic scenic suggestions, and the collapsing of history tetralogies to make one play. It is Trewin's conclusion, and presumably Sprague's as well, however, that today's audiences still demand something to look at, and that recent productions have been deficient in "range and size."

Lamentably, the same conclusion must be reached about their little essay. Missing is any scholarly attempt to trace the history of convention and custom to uncover, as I have said, the probable origin of theatrical device. Nowhere is the question asked whether Shakespeare himself was following certain accepted practices. Not a jot appears from the pages of Pepys, or Garrick, and very little from the work of Granville-Barker, or even the directors and producers most frequently mentioned—Benson and Doran. Moreover, the survey of recent performances is random and incomplete, ignoring or overlooking radical departures by such controversial figures as Joseph Papp and Richard Schechner, whose 1969 garage-theater production of *Macbeth* certainly should have sparked some comment. Most distressing is the absence of almost any reference to contemporary film treatments of Shakespeare; even though such discussion might be considered tangential, it could introduce matters related to the influence of stage direction, or the lack of it, in another medium. For instance, the Induction was missing from the Burton-Taylor *Taming of the Shrew*, even though the film's multidimensional visual effects might have allowed for some imaginative handling of it. One might also rightly expect a comment or two about television versions, where the techniques of videotaping could and do allow for spectacular kinds of juxtaposition. Finally, the choppy, jotting style ("Forward to the tragedies: to *Hamlet* and to a sinister Osric") frustrates the reader who is interested in more than the cuttings from the authors' notebooks. It is perhaps a telling if unfortunate remark when Sprague calls for an anthology of directors' program notes, since that is essentially what we get in *Shakespeare's Plays Today*. From Arthur Colby Sprague and J. C. Trewin we might defensibly ask for more.

The Latin Passion Play: Its Origins and Development by Sandro Sticca. State University of New York Press, 1970. Pp. xix + 220. $10.00.

Reviewer: Jeffrey Helterman.

Sandro Sticca's *The Latin Passion Play: Its Origins and Development* is a rather Procrustean study of medieval Latin drama. Of its two primary purposes, the first—the evaluation of the research in the area delimited by the title—is ultimately too dependent upon the second—the placement of the little known, but very important, Montecassino Passion Play in the history of liturgical drama. For this reason, Professor Sticca's extensive analysis of the backgrounds of medieval Latin drama seems manipulated to provide a neat context for the appearance of the Montecassino play as the first full-scale passion play. Although many of the hypotheses about the origins of medieval drama in general and the passion play in particular are plausible, they are never quite convincing.

Exemplary of Professor Sticca's approach is his handling of the problem of why no passion play developed until two centuries after the earliest plays whose subject was the resurrection. His argument that the mass itself was high drama of the passion is well documented, but the conclusion that the mass, therefore, needed no amplification into conventional drama is hardly necessary. In fact, the converse argument, that the drama of the mass would inspire the medieval playwright, is equally plausible. It will be shown in a moment that Professor Sticca reaches just such a conclusion to resolve a similar problem in a different part of his study.

In addition to this kind of faulty logic, Professor Sticca's theories often lack the precision necessary to transform them into convincing arguments. When he turns from the negative to the positive side of the preceding problem (that is, why the passion finally *was* dramatized in the middle of the twelfth century), he again presents a theory which cannot be refuted, but can be seriously doubted. He contends that the Christological humanism of the twelfth century led to the portrayal of the passion in all of the arts. The dating of this movement, however, is a moot point among medieval scholars, as is the concept of the contemporaneity of style in all the arts. The existence of the humanistic trend is undeniable, but Theodore Spencer, for one, dates it later than does Professor Sticca and, in fact, uses it to differentiate the styles of Dante and Chaucer.[1] Furthermore, Millard Meiss has shown that an argument based upon the appropriateness of the *Zeitgeist* must be accurate with respect to both time and place because intellectual milieux changed rapidly in the Middle Ages.[2] Professor Sticca does not pinpoint the cultural backgrounds of the passion play with anything like the precision that Professor Meiss uses to explain the changing styles of painting in quattrocento Florence and Siena. Without such exactitude, Professor Sticca's hypotheses must remain precisely that.

Furthermore, the intellectual currents that Professor Sticca cites as evidence of the new humanism are primarily those of mystical contemplation, but nowhere does he explain the transition from meditation to drama. His mere assertion of his theory—"there can be no doubt that the mystical contemplation on the doctrine of the Incarnation must have contributed to the desire to represent the passion dramatically" (p. 43)—lacks the kind of highly articulated analysis which Louis Martz uses to show why and how Ignatian contemplation might have led to the highly dramatic poetry of the seventeenth century.[3] In addition, Professor Sticca's assertion contradicts his earlier assertion about the sufficiency of the mass as drama: ". . . originally the people appear to have been satisfied with contemplative liturgy, which possessed in itself some elements of dramaturgy" (p. 41). If contemplation is sufficient in one case, why not in both?

The book is more convincing when dealing specifically with the Montecassino play and its relation to the fourteenth-century Sulmona passion fragment. Using paleographic, metrical and stylistic evidence, Professor Sticca confirms the, until now, somewhat questionable dating of the play in the middle of the twelfth century. His proof that this play predates the two Benediktbeuern plays in the *Carmina Burana* puts to rest the theory that medieval passion drama does not begin until the thirteenth century. This evidence allows Professor Sticca to prove that the passion play was an independent development and neither a prelude to the Easter resurrection play nor an outgrowth of the *Planctus Mariae*. Also, by showing the direct ancestry of the Sulmona passion fragment in the Montecassino play, he further undermines the appendage theory of origin, since much of that theory was based on the belief that the Sulmona fragment, which was written later than plays containing the *Planctus*, was an original passion play.

The book includes the Latin text of the play. Professor Sticca provides a close analysis of the literary qualities of the play as well as an examination of its sources. The explication shows the playwright to be a man of some imagination but no great literary skill, and the research into the tradition of characterization adds interesting sidelights on such details as the appearance of the devil to Pilate's wife. The attempt to attribute sources beyond the gospels for the play, however, is unconvincing. For example, Professor Sticca claims that the playwright relied upon the earliest illustrated manuscript of the gospels, the sixth-century *Codex Pupureus Rossanensis*, for his rendering of the trial before Pilate. He uses the provenance of the manuscript to show that the playwright might have had access to the Benedictine Abbey, where the Codex was located, and does show that the scenic organization is similar to the Codex, but his clinching argument turns out to be rather flimsy. Sticca notes that the playwright substitutes *proiciat* ("throws") for the *retulit* ("brought back") of Matthew in his description of Judas's return of the pieces of silver and claims that this substitution "could only have been suggested to the dramatist by this miniature [in the codex], where indeed Judas is seen throwing the pieces of money before Caiaphas" (p. 94). In fact, the text of Matthew xxvii.5, *which Professor Sticca quotes*, suggests *proiciat*: "Et *projectis* argenteis in templo, recessit: et abiens laqueo se suspendit" (italics mine).

Since a good part of this bock is a refutation of earlier criticism about the origins and development of the Latin passion play, it might be well to interject a cavil about Professor Sticca's handling of secondary materials. The critical citations, whether in French, German, Italian, or Spanish, are at first untranslated (which is a slight annoyance to the reader without Professor Sticca's fluency in Western languages), but then, for no apparent reason, some passages are translated and others are not. Furthermore, citations are taken at random from different editions of the same book. In one chapter, for example, he cites Emile Mâle from a French edition on one page and an English edition on another.

This carelessness would scarcely need to be noted except that it is symptomatic of a more central inconsistency in the book's logic—its reliance upon scholarly opinion at critical junctures in its argument. In a study whose primary purpose is to dispose of old hypotheses all previous theories must be held suspect. The author, therefore, cannot use the opinions of scholars to buttress part of his argument, when he is questioning the views of those very scholars elsewhere. In one example, he includes O. B. Hardison among those who support his belief that modern European drama evolved from ecclesiastical rather than secular sources, but he later dismisses the major premise of Hardison's book, which should disqualify him as an authority.[4] Although Professor Sticca does not ignore primary sources in developing his theories, too often he depends upon the sheer weight of critical opinion to decide a questionable point. For example, although I agree with his contention that Hrotswitha's plays had little influence upon medieval drama, the argument from "prevalent opinion" in his conclusion has no place in a book which is questioning the whole body of criticism about medieval drama: "Whatever the literary worth of Hrotswitha's tales, and whether or not they were ever acted out, the prevalent opinion today is that her writings had no influence on the subsequent development of drama and cannot serve as ties between the classical theater and that of the Middle Ages" (p. 7).

The book, then, is useful in dating and pointing out the significance of the Montecassino play as the first Latin passion play, and the evidence marshaled in this area does the job properly. As a study of the origins of the passion play, however, Professor Sticca's work is a fabric of speculations, which, although interesting, lacks the authority of primary material which would make it definitive. Too often the book relies upon the opinion of the critics whose scholarship it elsewhere questions. Speculation is necessary to open up a field about which too little is known, but this cannot be carried out fairly when conflicting evidence is ignored or overwhelmed by assertion.

Notes:

1. Theodore Spencer, "The Story of Ugolino in Dante and Chaucer," *Speculum*, 9 (1934), 295–301.
2. Millard Meiss, *Painting in Florence and Siena After the Black Death* (Princeton, 1951).
3. Louis Martz, *The Poetry of Meditation* (New Haven, 1954).

4. Pp. 1 and 27. The first chapter of Professor Hardison's book (*Christian Rite and Christian Drama in the Middle Ages* [Baltimore, 1965]) is a model of the proper evaluation of one's scholarly predecessors and one that Professor Sticca should look at more closely.

The Fool and His Scepter: A Study in Clowns and Jesters and Their Audience by William Willeford. Northwestern University Press and Edward Arnold (Publishers) Ltd., 1969. Pp. xxii + 265. $8.50 and 63s.

Reviewer: George L. Geckle.

William Willeford is an unusual literary critic for the simple reason that he not only teaches in the Department of English at the University of Washington but is also a psychotherapist in private practice. From his many favorable references to Carl Jung's works and his generally critical attitude toward Freud, one assumes that he is a devotee of the Jungian circle. *The Fool and His Scepter*, at any rate, approaches fools and clowns primarily from the perspective of psychology and with some emphasis on anthropology and sociology, but with little stress on literary history. This is both the strength and major weakness of the book.

When dealing with real-life fools, such as court jesters, vaudeville and circus clowns, comic actors, and film comedians, and the ways in which they interact with us as audience, Willeford is able to present valid and perceptive insights about the nature of folly. As he points out in his introduction, certain attributes of folly are "an abiding possibility of human experience" (p. xvi). Willeford further argues that we worship folly because it is symbolic—that is, it has an archetypal foundation—and we can understand it only through a combination of abstraction and *Einfühlung* (or "empathic imagination"). In Part One of his book Willeford studies both the materials of folly and the audience's relationship to them. In Part Two he discusses the pattern of folly in terms of the supposed magical powers of fools and the relation of fools to order and chaos. Finally, in Part Three he analyzes what he calls "The Fool and the Kingdom," or the fool, the king, and the realm in its symbolic dimension. It is in the third part that he discusses *Hamlet* and *King Lear* in detail, and it is on Willeford's examination of those plays that I will primarily concentrate this review.

Part One of *The Fool and His Scepter* contains interesting discussions of the etymology of the terms "fool" (having medical, biblical, moral, and sexual

derivations), "clown," "idiot," and "jester"; it also traces the real-life antecedents of clowns and jesters from the Egyptians to the present and gives details
concerning their dress, psychic aberrations, and magical healing powers. Within
the same section there is detailed examination of the fool's part in mimetic representations and of the audience's relationship to these imitations; two mottoes
—*stultorum plena sunt omnia* and *stultorum infinitus est numerus*—help to
summarize the complex relationship. Willeford illustrates from such works as
Erasmus's *Praise of Folly*, Shakespeare's plays, and the Marx Brothers' films,
but one looks in vain for any examples from Samuel Beckett, surely an author
who deserved some discussion in a book on clowns and jesters.

Willeford's second part contains consideration of the fool's relative inde-
pendence of time, space, and normal concepts of order and also a good discussion of recent research on magical processes of thought, with emphasis on the
work of Claude Lévi-Strauss, Julian H. Steward, and other anthropologists.
Here Willeford also examines the ways in which the fool "breaks down the
boundary between chaos and order" and "violates our assumption that that
boundary was where we thought it was and that it had the character we thought
it had" (p. 108). After discussing the moral issues of the fool's relation to in-
fantility, social responsibility, the Devil in Christian tradition, death, and sexuality, Willeford concludes Part Two with a chapter entitled "The Fool, the
Boundary, and the Center" (the boundaries being such things as death and
ignorance, the unknown, and the center being "marked by an object full of
mana or by a sign of supernatural disposition" and also "the source of established order and uniform power" [p. 143]).

Part Three begins by providing more relevant background for Willeford's
discussions of *Hamlet* and *King Lear*. He analyzes the relationships between
kings and heroes, "representatives of the center" (p. 165), and fools, showing
the symbolic connections between the hero's sword and spear, the king's scepter ("like a sword or spear that has been crowned and sheathed and fixed at the
center, as the hero-king has in a sense come to rest in becoming king" [p. 168]),
and the fool's bauble ("like the king's scepter, phallic" and also "having
hermaphroditic overtones, since the bauble often combines a rod and a lump of
a kind that is traditionally regarded as feminine and maternal" [p. 170]). The
sexual aspects of folly, touched on in Part Two, are more explicitly explored in
Part Three in chapter 10, "The Fool and the Woman." The fool's roles here are
those of "the mother-bound son, the hermaphrodite, the bawd and lecher, the
partner of a fool double almost identical with him, and the yearning lover of
the angelically pure woman" (p. 175). The chapter, heavily weighted with
psychological commentary, contains eight of the book's thirty-six illustrations,
including woodcuts, drawings, and photographs. On the whole, the plates add

immeasurably to the book's value, often succinctly summarizing visually the points Willeford laboriously pursues in his text. I might here add that the typography of the text itself is extremely annoying since the compositors, for whatever reasons, did not justify the lines, the net effect being that of a badly typed dissertation.

For those of us especially interested in Shakespeare, the two most intriguing chapters in *The Fool and His Scepter* are numbers 11 and 13, entitled respectively "The Tragic Dimension of Folly: *Hamlet*" and "The Sovereign Fool: *The Tragedy of King Lear*." The *Hamlet* chapter is perhaps one of the more wrongheaded readings of the play in recent years. It obviously disturbed Miss Enid Welsford also, because in her two-page preface to Willeford's book, she says: "I am not wholly convinced by his study of the 'tragic dimension of Folly' in *Hamlet*." I suppose a preface writer must be tactful. But let us quote from Willeford and then see if tact is in order. The chapter begins:

> According to an anecdote, the cross-eyed Ben Turpin fell into his métier as a slapstick comedian in the silent films from the tragic heights of Hamlet, as he tried on the stage to play the role straight. Whether or not the story is true, the image of Turpin as Hamlet is horrible, funny, and somehow legitimate. Hamlet's "To be or not to be" soliloquy has been burlesqued by many comedians; if Turpin were to have done it as a gag, we might have seen Hamlet's consciousness, which Henry James called the widest in all of literature, reduced to the mindlessness of a frightened chicken and his traipsing about the stage sped up to become part of a frenzied chase.
>
> (p. 192)

The fact that most of us who have ever read *Hamlet* or seen it performed would probably not think of it as an exercise in humor does not deter Willeford from his comparison. As a literary critic, he seems to think that any demonstration of folly has some sort of relevance to any other manifestation of it regardless of context. Hence, in his chapter 12 Willeford tries to relate *Hamlet* to Buster Keaton's film *The General* (1926), mainly because "the film is concerned, as *Hamlet* is, with the division of the realm, and the main figure of the film, like that of the play, is a fool-hero" (p. 201). Hence, "Turpin as Hamlet is horrible, funny, and somehow legitimate." But it is not "legitimate" in serious literary criticism at all, because then *Hamlet* is no longer *The Tragicall Historie of Hamlet, Prince of Denmarke* but is instead some sort of joke. The point is that genre and dramatic conventions count in the world of literature, even if they do not matter in psychiatric circles.

Willeford continues his argument by stressing the similarity between Hamlet and the fool and then gets to his main thesis:

Hamlet must search for a metaphysical and moral basis for his action, because that basis, as it is provided naturally in the primitive kingship, has failed and become the lie of the person of the king, Claudius, against his office. Hamlet must find his way from his own position, with its personal motivations, to one from which he can act for the general weal. Thus the purification of purpose he must undergo in a sense leads in an opposite direction from that of Lear—from the personal to the collective, rather than the reverse; and it is in this necessity that he adopts the ambiguous, helpful, and disruptive role of the fool.

(*p. 193*)

Actually, the main emphasis for action is provided by the ghost's injunction that Hamlet avenge his father's murder at the hands of Claudius (I.v.81–112). The metaphysical and moral problems Hamlet faces derive from whether it is, indeed, "an honest ghost" (I.v.138) he has talked with. Aside from Hamlet's comment, "The time is out of joint. O cursed spite / That ever I was born to set it right!" (I.v.189–90), which *can* be interpreted to refer to a concern for "the general weal," practically all of Hamlet's interests are personal. As for the reason Hamlet decides to "put an antic disposition on" (I.v.172), Harry Levin cogently and sensibly argues as follows: "Hamlet stands in need of a new *persona*, once the Ghost has excited his suspicions, not so much in order to feel his way as to speak his mind with impunity. 'Give thy thoughts no tongue' is the first commandment in the world of Polonius (I.iii.59). From the outset Hamlet feels constrained to hold his tongue, to keep his counsel in soliloquy (I.ii.159); with his fellow courtiers, as with the players, gradually he learns to 'show fairly outwards' (II.ii.391–2)."[1] I quote Levin both because he, unlike Willeford, sticks closely to the text of the play and because Willeford refers to Levin's study in a footnote to his chapter on *Hamlet*. Willeford, however, seems unable to assimilate good criticism into his own reading of Shakespeare's play.

The *Hamlet* essay that most influenced Willeford, and from which he quotes several times, is Francis Fergusson's fine study "Hamlet, Prince of Denmark: The Analogy of Action."[2] It is Fergusson who argues that "the welfare of Denmark—the traditional order of society, with its father-king upon whom depend 'the lives of many'—is the matter of the play as a whole, rather than Hamlet's individual plight" (p. 113). (It is also, for that matter, Fergusson who tells us that Henry James called Hamlet "the widest consciousness in literature" [p. 133], but Fergusson does not compare Hamlet with Ben Turpin.) Fergusson, however, inveighs against reducing *Hamlet* to a single motive or action. He objects, for instance, to Ernest Jones's psychoanalytic reading of the play in *Hamlet and Oedipus* because "it reduces the motivation of the play to the emotional drives of the Oedipus complex. This overworks that complex, and takes us too far from the play itself" (p. 122). Lionel Trilling has had the same objection to the Freudian approach: "It is not here a question of the validity of the evidence, though that is of course important. We must rather object to the conclusions of Freud and Dr. Jones on the ground that their proponents do not have an adequate conception of what an artistic meaning is. There is no single meaning to any work of art; this is true not merely because it is better that it should be true, that is, because it makes art a richer thing, but because historical and personal experience show it to be true."[3]

The reduction of *Hamlet* to one meaning is my main objection to Willeford's study. Although he does not stress the Oedipus complex theory, he does allow its influence to penetrate his reading of Hamlet's relationship with Gertrude to the extent that he misreads the fifth soliloquy (III.ii.406–17) and says it reveals that "Hamlet's allegiance is divided between his dead father and his living mother" and that Hamlet must "admonish himself" not to harm Gertrude "in the same moment in which he is fighting to overcome what he feels to be hypocrisy" (p. 195). However, the rather painfully obvious purpose of the soliloquy is a dramatic one—Hamlet is informing the *audience* in a passage of exposition what to expect in Act III, scene iv so that we will not misinterpret his behavior with Gertrude. Willeford's version is all part of his real thesis, however, which is to reduce the play to Hamlet's "dispossession" of the throne and his "fluctuation between the possibilities of heroism and those of folly" (p. 194).

> The action of the play, the killing of the false king, requires a hero; but the problem on which the action is based, the hidden malady of the state, is one with which the hero alone, without the blessing of his folly, cannot deal; a vicious circle ensues that draws Hamlet again and again into the "imposthume" that he should stand outside and lance as though it were a monster or human enemy outside the kingdom. The vicious circle comes from the fact that the integrity of the center needs to be restored, but the abscess at the center destroys the basis for the action needed.
>
> (*pp. 194–95*)

The role of the clown seems to Hamlet to provide him with the sought-for position of a *punctum indifferens* in the midst of the action, but the role is a trap from which he must fight to get out, though he fights in vain. The fool becomes the *punctum indifferens* through the renunciation of action; and to renounce action in face of the threat of raging chaos is to become a fool either in the sense of the failed hero or in that of Lear's jester. Lear can become interchangeable with his fool, because the fool in his incapacity for action and his humble and shrewd acceptance of that incapacity leads Lear toward the moral condition in which he may find whatever salvation is open to him, a state in which he must leave off posturing as the personal agent of a might he does not have. But for Hamlet the necessity is to become the personal agent of a power that he does not have but should have. It is the power of the hero only partly differentiated from the fool, a state in which the hero is open to the dispositions of unseen powers and to the unexpected possibilities in the present moment for action, in which he is free from the inertia of his personal feelings and deaf to the play of reason when it is not immediately relevant to the task at hand. As Hamlet assumes the role of the fool actor, he becomes dissociated from the kind of folly that would have furthered heroism.

(p. 196)

Moreover, when the mousetrap springs, Hamlet, who has been the failed hero, emerges not as a hero but as a failed fool. And even if he is, as a result, moved to action, part of his energies must continue to leak into the role of the unsuccessful fool-as-mock-hero, to which he has unwittingly committed himself.

(p. 197)

In fact, in reading or seeing *Hamlet* one does not feel that a sort of heroic folly is what is needed in Denmark. What Hamlet needs is some empirical evidence that the ghost is not a devil, and to this end he devises the mousetrap: "The play's the thing / Wherein I'll catch the conscience of the king" (II.ii.632–33). The mousetrap is successful (III.ii.297–301), and Hamlet is hardly "a failed fool."

But to conclude that the final meaning of Hamlet resides in Act V, scene i is, indeed, foolish; nonetheless Willeford argues that "the hero-prince's familiarity with the cynical Gravedigger as they contemplate the skull of the jester is a final epiphany" (p. 199). We might wonder what happened to Act V, scene ii, especially Hamlet's lines of philosophical reflection about the "divinity that shapes our ends" (V.ii.10) or the "special providence in the fall of a sparrow" (V.ii.230–33) and the tragic, but at the same time, religious, recognition that "the readiness is all" (V.ii.234); these passages constitute the play's moral catharsis, as J. V. Cunningham has shown.[4] For his final explanation of Hamlet as prince and fool, however, Willeford neglects the play for some psychiatric jargon:

> The character of this amalgamation of roles, and its self-destructive motivation, may be seen in Hamlet's famous question, "To be, or not to be . . . ?" (III.i.56). The ego has no right to ask such a question; asking it is a form of psychic self-mutilation—in psychoanalytic terms, of self-castration—the deliberate abandonment of any possible basis for action. If we draw ourselves up enough to reject Hamlet's pathos, we may see this question as an intellectual equivalent of a clown's attempt to take a step with one foot while standing on it with the other. Or we may treat Hamlet's pathos more respectfully by regarding the question as an intellectual equivalent of Ophelia's suicide.
>
> (pp. 199–200)

The "ego" may have no right to ask "To be, or not to be," but dramatic characters certainly do, and philosophers certainly have exercised the right, as Harry Levin has pointed out: "That is the question, *esse aut non esse,* which metaphysicians from Plato to Sartre have pondered. Hamlet seeks the essence of things in a world of phenomena, where being must be disentangled from seeming; and since the entanglement is a personal one, perhaps a sword is the only means of escape" (*The Question of Hamlet,* p. 69). But, of course, Hamlet does not commit suicide and does not remain long in contemplation of Yorick's skull, although Willeford concludes otherwise.

> In Yorick's skull, joy is dead and laughter silenced. In Yorick's skull, too, the force is at last objectified that has blocked Hamlet from assuming his father's throne and marrying his destined bride. (This objectification takes place somewhat in the way that a feeling-toned unconscious complex of archetypal character is sometimes revealed in the course of psychotherapy.) Hamlet's encounter with the skull might thus have signaled a new and more adequate differentiation of his motives and purposes, if it were not too late. But death has already won—and death's accomplices and foes, the grave-digging clowns.
>
> (p. 200)

To which we might conclude with Horatio: " 'Twere to consider too curiously, to consider so" (V.i.227).

The chapter on *King Lear* is more reasonable, probably because the play has a bona fide fool for Willeford to discuss. But even here Willeford reduces the play to a single major issue: "The crux of the play is the question of whether or not Lear achieves enlightenment and, if so, what kind of enlightenment it is. I will here consider the ways in which the form of the kingship is dissolved in the fool show" (p. 208). To this end Willeford discusses four of the play's incidents, the first being the mock trial in the opening scene. The key to I.i. is an Empsonian-type analysis of the term "nothing," which Willeford relates to the theological doctrine of *ex nihilo nihil fit,* a probable allusion, as William R. Elton has recently demonstrated.[5] But to overinterpret Lear's "Nothing can come of nothing" (I.i.92) and conclude that "when Lear says this to Cordelia, he means, in effect, that there *is* nothing but what he allows to exist" (p. 212) seems plain silly. Lear's Fool is related to "nothing" because fools are often "not fully human and even not real in the way that nonfools are" (p. 212). Finally the concept of "the *Sovereign Fool*" (the title of the chapter) indicates "a state of mind and soul and body that is dramatized by the king and the Fool together," or "the total assimilation of kingship by folly," in psychological terms the breakdown of "the play between the king and his jester as symbolizing (in part) consciousness and unconsciousness in an interaction that accords with the complex structure of the psyche" (p. 213). So, as Lear's kingdom disintegrates, the state of "the *Sovereign Fool*" emerges.

Willeford next moves to Lear's degeneration into madness and his eventual appearance on the heath in weeds. But again in an attempt to say something new and startling, Willeford goes too far: "By the time the storm breaks on the heath, the *Sovereign Fool* rules the kingdom. The storm is Lear's madness; it is also the dissolution of cosmos in chaos and of reality in illusion" (p. 214). In fact, the storm is *analogous* to Lear's madness, since macrocosm relates to microcosm (III.i.1–11), at least according to the text of the play. Willeford concludes that as Lear goes mad "the kingdom is sustained by the fool show. If no other redemption proves possible, there is always this, that 'The worst returns to laughter' (IV.i.6). And laughter is seldom so stiff or so maniacal that it does not express a kind of foolish sanity" (p. 214). But, of course, that is not what IV.i.6 means at all; in context the line means that a change from the worst condition is a movement toward a happier condition. The iconological allusion (in IV.i.3) is to the Wheel of Fortune, not to folly. A similar type of misreading occurs when Willeford explicates the Fool's speech about knaves, fools, and "a great wheel":

Rosencrantz calls majesty
                          a massy wheel,
     Fix'd on the summit of the highest mount,

To whose huge spokes ten thousand lesser things
Are mortis'd and adjoin'd. . . .

(Hamlet, III. iii. 17–20)

The image suggests (and contrasts with) the Fool's counsel:

. . . Let go thy hold when a great wheel runs down a hill, lest it break thy
neck with following; but the great one that goes upward, let him draw
thee after. When a wise man gives thee better counsel, give me mine again.
I would have none but knaves follow it, since a fool gives it.

(King Lear, II. iv. 71–75)

The Fool would not believe the claim that the wheel of majesty is fixed,
and not on a mere hill but on "the summit of the highest mount," since
the claim denies what he knows to be the relativity of all degree, whether
social or metaphysical, and since he has the already dispossessed Lear
beside him. The Fool knows that the wheel will roll down to a plain on
which all men share the equality of homeless idiots, madmen, and jesters.
He admits that his advice is superfluous to a "wise" view of politics and
that he is knave as well as fool and thus has the self-sufficiency and natural
cunning to survive where conscious values have been broken down or have
not been organized into a structure. For nonfools, to reach this level is to
renounce the world or to be debased; for the Fool, it is to affirm both the
"nothing" of the "destructive element," linked with winter, disease, death,
and nonbeing, and his capacity for making a bridge between this "nothing"
and the fullness of natural life.

(pp. 215–16)

Willeford has trouble, it seems, identifying Dame Fortuna's Wheel, but let us
compare his reading of the lines with the following one by Enid Welsford:

Folly is the opposite of wisdom, how unwise it is to pursue a policy
which in this world of ours must lead you to the stocks. I am only a Fool,
but I can teach you better than that. But after all, do I want you to follow
my advice? No, let it be followed only by knaves, for it is the advice of a
fool—a contemptible vicious being, as all men acknowledge. But who is
this Fool who not only desires none but knaves to follow his advice, but
also defiantly proclaims that he will himself disregard it:

'I will tarry, the fool will stay
And let the wise man fly.'

After all which is which? The knave who runs away, comes out into the open, and is at once seen as the abject contemptible ludicrous creature that he has always really been. The fool is at least true to himself. He has never professed to be wise, he will not now act as though he were worldly wise.[6]

Aside from the lucidity of Miss Welsford's prose, her reading is also substantially correct. One might take similar objection to some other of Willeford's interpretations of Lear's madness. To say, for instance, that Lear "goes on ranting about his daughters, giving vent to his injured vanity, enjoying his madness" and that "his enjoyment of his madness is also self-indulgent" (p. 218) seems to me to be patently absurd; neither Lear (I.v.49–50, IV.vi.194–97) nor Edgar (III.vi.63–64, 108–16) seems to think that madness is much fun.

Analogous to Lear's madness is Gloucester's blindness, which leads him in despair to the cliff at Dover. Here Willeford eagerly accepts Jan Kott's (*Shakespeare Our Contemporary*) comparison of Gloucester's leap with clown tricks or moments in the drama of Beckett and Ionesco. "The form of Edgar's trick on Gloucester is 'absurd' and clownish, and its content is fundamental to the fool show: it is the fact that life goes on and that its doing so, even in the moments leading to death, is a miracle. That miracle is 'seeming,' but it is also grace" (p. 221). The final moment of "grace in 'seeming'" (p. 221) is Lear's belief that Cordelia is alive. Willeford compares Lear's behavior with the Clown Bébé's salted herring skit (clown enters arena sobbing, dragging salted herring by string; clown explains he had taken herring for walk, and it fell into puddle and drowned) performed at the Cirque Medrano in Paris, because "Bébé's gag touches upon ambiguities of seeming and upon the impulse to charity that are fundamental to *King Lear*" (p. 224). Finally, Willeford concludes his chapter with the following:

> Bébé's herring is an instance of the ever recurring point at which the meaningful world threatens to fall asunder and life to be swallowed up in death. But the herring is also an instance of the power that gives the world to us, that maintains its structure even when we have lost our grasp of it. And when Lear appears with the dead Cordelia in his arms and announces that she lives, we are brought by a king who is also a tragic clown to the same point of folly, an imagined breath that is a sign of connection with the hidden center that sustains us.
>
> (*p. 225*)

For *Hamlet*, Ben Turpin, for *Lear*, Bébé and his herring—such is the literary world of *The Fool and His Scepter*.

Notes:

1. *The Question of Hamlet* (1959; rpt. New York, 1961), p. 112.
2. In *The Idea of a Theater* (1949; rpt. Garden City, N. Y., 1953).
3. "Freud and Literature," in *The Liberal Imagination* (New York, 1950), pp. 48–49.
4. "The Donatan Tradition," *Woe or Wonder: The Emotional Effect of Shakespearean Tragedy* (1951; rpt. Denver, 1964), pp. 40–41.
5. *"King Lear" and the Gods* (San Marino, Calif., 1966), pp. 179–90. Willeford seems to be unaware of Elton's very valuable and thoroughly documented study of *Lear*.
6. *The Fool: His Social and Literary History* (1935; rpt. Gloucester, Mass., 1966), p. 258.

Books Received

(Inclusion of a book in this list does not preclude its being reviewed in this or a subsequent volume.)

Alexander, Nigel. *Poison, Play, and Duel: A Study in Hamlet.* Lincoln: Univ. of Nebraska Press, 1971. Pp. ix + 212.

Allen, Don C. *Mysteriously Meant: The Rediscovery of Pagan Symbolism and Allegorical Interpretation in the Renaissance.* Baltimore: Johns Hopkins Univ. Press, 1971. Pp. vii + 354.

Allen, Judson Boyce. *Friar As Critic: Literary Attitudes in the Later Middle Ages.* Nashville: Vanderbilt Univ. Press, 1971. Pp. vii + 176.

Anderson, Warren. *Theophrastus: The Character Sketches.* Kent: Kent State Univ. Press, 1970. Pp. vii + 153.

Baker, Herschel, ed. *Four Essays on Romance.* Cambridge, Mass.: Harvard Univ. Press, 1971. Pp. 87.

Beaty, Nancy Lee. *The Craft of Dying: A Study in the Literary of the* Ars Moriendi *in England.* New Haven: Yale Univ. Press, 1970. Pp. ix + 299.

Bentley, Gerald Eades. *The Profession of Dramatist in Shakespeare's Time, 1590–1642.* Princeton: Princeton Univ. Press, 1971. Pp. vii + 329.

Bolgar, R. R., ed. *Classical Influence on European Culture,* A.D. *500–1500.* Cambridge: Cambridge Univ. Press, 1971. Pp. v + 320.

Bromley, John C. *The Shakespearean Kings.* Boulder: Colorado Associated Univ. Press, 1970. Pp. ix + 138.

Brower, Reuben A. *Hero and Saint: Shakespeare and the Greco-Roman Heroic Tradition.* Oxford: Oxford Univ. Press, 1971. Pp. ix + 425.

Brown, John Russell. *Shakespeare's Dramatic Style.* New York: Barnes and Noble, 1971. Pp. ix + 191.

Calderwood, James L. *Shakespearean Metadrama: The Argument of the Play in* Titus Andronicus, Love's Labour's Lost, Romeo and Juliet, A Midsummer Night's Dream *and* Richard II. Minneapolis: Univ. of Minnesota Press, 1971. Pp. 192.

Coleridge, S. T. *Coleridge on Shakespeare: The Text of the Lectures of 1811–12.* Ed. R. A. Foakes. Folger Shakespeare Library Monographs on Tudor and Stuart Civilization, No. 3. Charlottesville: Univ. Press of Virginia, 1971. Pp. 171.

Crane, R. S. *Critical and Historical Principles of Literary History.* Chicago: Univ. of Chicago Press, 1971. Pp. v + 112.

Cubeta, Paul M., ed. *Twentieth Century Interpretations of Richard II.* Englewood Cliffs: Prentice-Hall, 1971. Pp. 121.

Cullen, Patrick. *Spenser, Marvell, and Renaissance Pastoral.* Cambridge, Mass.: Harvard Univ. Press, 1970. Pp. 212.

Curtis, Jared R. *Wordsworth's Experiment with Tradition: The Lyric Poems of 1802.* Ithaca: Cornell Univ. Press, 1971. Pp. vii + 227.

Davidson, Clifford. *The Primrose Way: A Study of Shakespeare's Macbeth.* Conesville, Iowa: John Westburg and Associates, 1970. Pp. 105.

Davies, Horton. *Worship and Theology in England: (Vol. I) From Cranmer to Hooker, Fifteen Thirty Four–Sixteen Hundred Three.* Princeton: Princeton Univ. Press, 1970. Pp. v + 482.

Davis, Norman, ed. *Paston Letters and Papers of the Fifteenth Century.* Oxford: Oxford Univ. Press, 1971. Pp. xx + 670.

DeMezieres, Philippe. *Figurative Representation of the Presentation of the Virgin Mary in the Temple.* Ed. Robert S. Haller. Lincoln: Univ. of Nebraska Press, 1971. Pp. vii + 97.

Dessen, Alan C. *Jonson's Moral Comedy.* Evanston, Ill.: Northwestern Univ. Press, 1971. Pp. 264.

Donohue, Joseph W., Jr. *Dramatic Character in the English Romantic Age.* Princeton: Princeton Univ. Press, 1970. Pp. vii + 402.

Doucette, Leonard E. *Emery Bigot, 1626–89: Another Aspect of Seventeenth Century Humanism.* Univ. of Toronto Romance Series. Toronto: Univ. of Toronto Press, 1970. Pp. 204.

Doughtie, Edward, ed. *Lyrics from English Airs, 1596–1622.* Cambridge, Mass.: Harvard Univ. Press, 1971. Pp. vii + 657.

Enright, D. J. *Shakespeare and the Students.* New York: Schocken Books, 1970. Pp. 203.

Farnham, Willard. *The Shakespearean Grotesque: Its Genesis and Transformations.* Oxford: Clarendon Press, 1971. Pp. 175.

Fletcher, Angus. *The Prophetic Moment: An Essay on Spenser.* Chicago: Univ. of Chicago Press, 1971. Pp. vii + 326.

————. *The Trancendental Masque: An Essay on Milton's* Comus. Ithaca: Cornell Univ. Press, 1971. Pp. 254.

Foakes, R. A. *Shakespeare, the Dark Comedies to the Last Plays: From Satire to Celebration.* Charlottesville: Univ. of Virginia Press, 1971. Pp. 186.

Forbes, Thomas Rogers. *Chronicle from Aldgate: Life and Death in Shakespeare's London.* New Haven: Yale Univ. Press, 1971. Pp. xvii + 251.

Fowler, Alastair. *Triumphal Forms: Structural Patterns in Elizabethan Poetry.* Cambridge: Cambridge Univ. Press, 1970. Pp. vii + 234.

Fraser, Russell. *The War Against Poetry.* Princeton: Princeton Univ. Press, 1971. Pp. 215.

Freeman, Sylvia D. *The Morality Patterned Comedy of the Renaissance.* The Hague: Mouton and Company, 1970. Pp. 165.

Galloway, David, ed. *The Elizabethan Theatre, I & II*. Hamden, Conn.: The Shoe String Press, 1970. Pp. ix + 130; pp. ix + 148.

Gellert, Bridget L. *Voices of Melancholy: Studies in Literary Treatments of Melancholy in Renaissance England*. New York: Barnes and Noble, 1971. Pp. 189.

Gibson, H. N. *The Shakespearean Claimants*. 1962; rpt. New York: Barnes and Noble, 1971. Pp. 320.

Gurr, Andrew. *The Shakespearean Stage, 1574–1642*. Cambridge: Cambridge Univ. Press, 1970. Pp. vi + 192.

Heinsius, Daniel. *On Plot in Tragedy*. Trans. Paul R. Sellin and John J. McManmon. The San Fernando Valley State College Renaissance Editions, No. 5. Northridge, Calif.: San Fernando Valley State College, 1971. Pp. iii + 176.

Heywood, Thomas. *A Woman Killed with Kindness*. Ed. R. W. VanFossen. New York: Barnes and Noble, 1970. Pp. vii + 122.

Himelick, Raymond, ed. *Erasmus and the Seamless Coat of Jesus*. Purdue University Studies. Lafayette, Ind.: Purdue Univ. Press, 1971. Pp. vii + 223.

Hobson, Alan. *Full Circle: Shakespeare and Moral Development*. New York: Barnes and Noble, 1972. Pp. 232.

Holmes, David M. *The Art of Thomas Middleton*. Oxford: The Clarendon Press, 1970. Pp. xii + 235.

Howard-Hill, T. H., ed. *Oxford Shakespeare Concordances:* Antony and Cleopatra. Oxford: Oxford Univ. Press, 1972. Pp. v + 351.

——. *Oxford Shakespeare Concordances:* Coriolanus. Oxford: Oxford Univ. Press, 1972. Pp. v + 375.

——. *Oxford Shakespeare Concordances:* 1 Henry IV. Oxford: Oxford Univ. Press, 1971. Pp. v + 388.

——. *Oxford Shakespeare Concordances:* 2 Henry IV. Oxford: Oxford Univ. Press, 1971. Pp. v + 366.

——. *Oxford Shakespeare Concordances:* Henry V. Oxford: Oxford Univ. Press, 1971. Pp. v + 357.

——. *Oxford Shakespeare Concordances:* 3 Henry VI. Oxford: Oxford Univ. Press, 1971. Pp. v + 314.

——. *Oxford Shakespeare Concordances:* Henry VIII. Oxford: Oxford Univ. Press, 1971. Pp. v + 336.

——. *Oxford Shakespeare Concordances:* Julius Caesar. Oxford: Oxford Univ. Press, 1971. Pp. xii + 249.

——. *Oxford Shakespeare Concordances:* Macbeth. Oxford: Oxford Univ. Press, 1971. Pp. v + 250.

——. *Oxford Shakespeare Concordances:* Pericles. Oxford: Oxford Univ. Press, 1972. Pp. xiii + 259.

——. *Oxford Shakespeare Concordances:* Richard II. Oxford: Oxford Univ. Press, 1971. Pp. v + 284.

————. *Oxford Shakespeare Concordances:* Richard III. Oxford: Oxford Univ. Press, 1971. Pp. v + 365.

————. *Oxford Shakespeare Concordances:* Romeo and Juliet. Oxford: Oxford Univ. Press, 1972. Pp. v + 320.

————. *Oxford Shakespeare Concordances:* Timon of Athens. Oxford: Oxford Univ. Press, 1971. Pp. 263.

————. *Oxford Shakespeare Concordances:* Titus Andronicus. Oxford: Oxford Univ. Press, 1972. Pp. 261.

————. *Oxford Shakespeare Concordances:* Troilus and Cressida. Oxford: Oxford Univ. Press, 1972. Pp. v + 346.

————. *Shakespearean Bibliography and Textual Criticism.* Oxford: Oxford Univ. Press, 1970. Pp. 322.

Hughey, Ruth. *John Harington of Stephney, Tudor Gentleman: His Life and Works.* Columbus: Ohio State Univ. Press, 1971. Pp. ix + 343.

Jones, Eldred D. *The Elizabethan Image of Africa.* Folger Booklets on Tudor and Stuart Civilization Series. Charlottesville: Univ. of Virginia Press, 1971. Pp. 52.

Jones, Emrys. *Scenic Form in Shakespeare.* Oxford: The Clarendon Press, 1971. Pp. 269.

Jonson, Ben. *Every Man in His Humor.* Ed. Gabriele Bernhard Jackson. New Haven: Yale Univ. Press, 1969. Pp. 250.

————. *Every Man in His Humor: A Parallel-Text Edition of the 1601 Quarto and the 1616 Folio.* Ed. J. W. Lever. Regent's Renaissance Drama Series. Lincoln: Univ. of Nebraska Press, 1971. Pp. v + 296.

Jorgensen, Paul A. *Our Naked Frailties: Sensational Art and Meaning in Macbeth.* Berkeley: Univ. of California Press, 1971. Pp. 242.

Joseph, B. L. *Shakespeare's Eden.* History and Literature Series. New York: Barnes and Noble, 1971. Pp. 368.

King, T. J. *Shakespearean Staging, 1599–1642.* Cambridge, Mass.: Harvard Univ. Press. 1971. Pp. 163.

Leech, Clifford. *The Dramatist's Experience: With Other Essays in Literary Theory.* New York: Barnes and Noble, 1970. Pp. 248.

Lever, J. W. *The Tragedy of State.* New York: Barnes and Noble, 1971. Pp. vii + 100.

Levi, A. H. T., ed. *Humanism in France at the End of the Middle Ages and the Early Renaissance.* New York: Barnes and Noble, 1970. Pp. 334.

Levin, Richard. *The Multiple Plot in English Renaissance Drama.* Chicago: Univ. of Chicago Press, 1971. Pp. ix + 277.

Long, John H. *Shakespeare's Use of Music:* (Vol. 3) *Histories and Tragedies.* Gainesville: Univ. of Florida Press, 1971. Pp. ix + 306.

Lowbury, Edward, Timothy Salter, and Alison Young. *Thomas Campion: Poet, Composer, and Physician.* New York: Barnes and Noble, 1970. Pp. vi + 195.

Mason, H. A. *Shakespeare's Tragedies of Love.* New York: Barnes and Noble, 1970. Pp. vi + 290.

Masters, G. Mallary. *Rabelaisian Dialectic and the Platonic Hermetic Tradition.* Albany: State Univ. of New York Press, 1969. Pp. vi + 152.

Michael, Lawrence. *The Thing Contained: Theory of the Tragic.* Bloomington: Indiana Univ. Press, 1970. Pp. vii + 177.

Muir, Kenneth, and S. Schoenbaum. *A New Companion to Shakespearean Studies.* Cambridge: Cambridge Univ. Press, 1971. Pp. ii + 298.

Muir, Kenneth, and Sean O'Loughlin. *The Voyage to Illyria: A New Study of Shakespeare.* 1937; rpt. New York: Barnes and Noble, 1970. Pp. 242.

A Nest of Ninnies and Other English Jestbooks of the Seventeenth Century. Ed. P. M. Zall. Lincoln: Univ. of Nebraska Press, 1970. Pp. ix + 260.

Notestein, Wallace. *The House of Commons, 1604–1610.* New Haven: Yale Univ. Press, 1971. Pp. ix + 598.

Partridge, A. C. *The Language of Renaissance Poetry: Spenser, Shakespeare, Donne, Milton.* London: Andre Deutsch, 1971. Pp. 348.

Patterson, Annabel M. *Hermogenes and the Renaissance.* Princeton: Princeton Univ. Press, 1970. Pp. vii + 240.

Pierce, Robert B. *Shakespeare's History Plays: The Family and the State.* Columbus: Ohio State Univ. Press, 1971. Pp. 261.

Pochoda, Elizabeth T. *Arthurian Propaganda: Le Mort D'Arthur as an Historical Ideal of Life.* Chapel Hill: Univ. of North Carolina Press, 1971. Pp. ix + 185.

Praz, Mario. *Mnemosyne: The Parallel Between Literature and the Visual Arts.* A. W. Mellon Lectures in the Fine Arts, Vol. 16; Bollingen Series, No. 35. Princeton: Princeton Univ. Press, 1969. Pp. viii + 261.

Ramsey, Peter H., ed. *The Price Revolution in Sixteenth Century England.* Debates in Economic History Series. New York: Barnes and Noble, 1971. Pp. vii + 182.

Rees, Joan. *Fulke Greville, Lord Brooke, 1554–1628: A Critical Biography.* Berkeley: Univ. of California Press, 1971. Pp. 255.

Richards, Kenneth and Peter Thomson, eds. *Nineteenth Century British Theatre.* New York: Barnes and Noble, 1971. Pp. 195.

Richmond, Hugh M. *Shakespeare's Sexual Comedy: A Mirror for Lovers.* New York: Bobbs-Merrill Company, 1971. Pp. 210.

Riggs, David. *Shakespeare's Heroical Histories:* Henry VI *and Its Literary Tradition.* Cambridge, Mass.: Harvard Univ. Press, 1971. Pp. 194.

Shakespeare, William. *Measure for Measure.* Ed. R. E. Houghton. New Clarendon Shakespeare Series. Oxford: Oxford Univ. Press, 1970. Pp. 238.

————. *The Merry Wives of Windsor.* Ed. H. J. Oliver. The Arden Shakespeare. New York: Barnes and Noble, 1971. Pp. 149.

————. *Much Ado About Nothing.* Ed. Sir Walter Greg and Charlton Hinman. Shakespeare Quarto Facsimiles, No. 15. Oxford: The Clarendon Press, 1971.

Sisson, C. J. *Lost Plays of Shakespeare's Age.* 1936; rpt. New York: Humanities Press, 1971. Pp. 221.

Smidt, Kristian. *Memorial Transmission and Quarto Copy in* Richard III. New York: Humanities Press, 1971. Pp. 93.

Soens, Lewis, ed. *Sir Philip Sidney's* Defense of Poesy. Regents Critics Series. Lincoln: Univ. of Nebraska Press, 1970. Pp. ix + 95.

Southern, R. W. *Western Society and the Church in the Middle Ages.* History of the Church Series, Vol. 2. Gretna, La.: Pelican Book Company, 1970. Pp. 376.

Sprague, Arthur Colby, and J. C. Trewin. *Shakespeare's Plays Today: Customs and Conventions of the Stage.* Columbia: Univ. of South Carolina Press, 1971. Pp. 93.

Thompson, Karl F. *Modesty and Cunning: Shakespeare's Use of Literary Tradition.* Ann Arbor: Univ. of Michigan Press, 1971. Pp. 176.

Turner, Frederich. *Shakespeare and the Nature of Time: Moral and Philosophical Themes in Some Plays and Poems of William Shakespeare.* Oxford: Oxford Univ. Press, 1971. Pp. 193.

Tuvill, Daniel. *Essays Politic and Moral and Essays Moral and Theological.* Ed. John L. Lievsay. Folger Documents on Tudor and Stuart Civilization Series. Charlottesville: Univ. Press of Virginia, 1971. Pp. 231.

Walton, J. K. *The Quarto Copy for the First Folio of Shakespeare.* New York: Humanities Press, 1972. Pp. 306.

Watermeier, Daniel J., ed. *Between Actor and Critic: Selected Letters of Edwin Booth and William Winter.* Princeton: Princeton Univ. Press, 1971. Pp. 329.

White, Harvard B. *Copp'd Hills Towards Heaven: Shakespeare and the Classical Polity.* International Archives of the History of Ideas, Vol. 32. New York: Humanities Press, 1971. Pp. 155.

Wimsatt, James I. *Allegory and Mirror.* Backgrounds in English Series. Indianapolis: Pegasus, 1970. Pp. vii + 224.

Winchcombe, George and Bernard. *Shakespeare's Ghost-Writer(s).* London: Thaab Publishers, 1970. Pp. vii + 285.

The Year's Work in English Studies, Vol. 49, 1968. Ed. Geoffrey Harlow. New York: Humanities Press, 1970. Pp. 456.

Composite Index to Volumes I–VI of Shakespeare Studies

EDITOR'S NOTE: *The Composite Index is subdivided into two parts. PART A is a name index of authors before 1640, with the exception of Shakespeare. Book titles are listed under authors' names. PART B includes authors after 1640, all anonymous works (listed under* Anonymous works*), and references to Shakespeare. Shakespeare's works are grouped together by titles in Part B under separate entries for* Shakespeare, William, PLAYS *and* Shakespeare, William, POEMS; *for topoi, concepts, and mythology, see Part B under* Concepts and motifs. *Part B is also a subject index for Volumes I–VI. Illustrations are listed in order of appearance under the heading* Illustrations. *The number of the volume referred to is given in parentheses, followed by the page reference(s).*

Part A

Abbot, Archbishop George, *A briefe Description*, (IV) 182

Aeschylus, (I) 275; *Agamemnon*, (III) 77; *Choephori*, (III) 77; *Eumenides*, (III) 77; *Oresteia*, (III) 77; *Seven Against Thebes*, (III) 77

Aesop, (I) 35

Alabaster, William, *Roxana*, (III) 281

Alberti, Leone Battista, (VI) 318

Alciati, Andrea, *Emblemata*, (I) 291 n, 292, (II) 225

Alexander, Sir William, (V) 142, 144; *Alexandrean Tragedy*, (II) 74

Alexander the Great, (IV) 285

Allen, Cardinal, (VI) 185

Alleyn, Edward, (VI) 323

Amman, Jost, *Bibliorum*, (IV) 254; *Neuwe Biblische Figuren*, (IV) 254

Andrews, Lancelot, (IV) 113–14

Aneau, Bartélemy, *Picta Poesis*, (II) 362

Anne of Denmark, (IV) 184–86, 190

Anselm, Saint, (IV) 246, (V) 341

Aphthonius, (III) 295

Appian, *An Auncient Historie*, (V) 230, (VI) 287

Apuleius, Lucius, *The Golden Ass*, (II) 215–16; *Metamorphoses*, (VI) 348

Aquinas, Saint Thomas, (II) 334, (III) 330, (V) 358, 359; *Summa Theologica*, (II) 100, (III) 88

Ariosto, Lodovico, (I) 86; *Orlando Furioso*, (I) 283, 284, 291 n, 292, (II) 217, 225

Aristophanes, *Birds*, (III) 77; *Clouds*, (III) 77; *Frogs*, (III) 77; *Wasps*, (III) 77; *Lysistrata*, (III) 77

Aristotle, (I) 142–67, 305, 326, (II) 370, (III) 63, 102, 125, 133, 264, 292, (IV) 120, 122, 146, 239, 263, 268, 269, 338, (V) 299–304, (VI) 239, 294, 312; *Nichomachean Ethics*, (I) 163, (II) 23, 110, (VI) 348; *Poetics*, (III) 349; *Politics*, (IV) 239, 268

Armin, Robert, (I) 340, 341, (VI) 340

Arrianus, Flavius, (VI) 28

Ascham, Roger, *The Scholemaster*, (II) 311; *Toxophilus*, (I) 341, (V) 157

Ashley, Robert, *Of Honor*, (I) 150, (II) 111, (V) 222, (VI) 284

Attawel, Hugh (actor), (V) 285, 295–96

Augustine, Saint, (II) 357, (IV) 148, 442, (V) 358, (VI) 28, 197–98, 209, 346; *City of God*, (II) 229, 231–56; (VI) 198; *De Doctrina Christiana*, (III) 86

Ayton, Sir Robert, (VI) 381–83

Bacon, Sir Francis, (I) 119, (II) 43, 165, (III) 119, 144, 173, (V) 142, (VI) 204, 208; *Physical and Metaphysical Works*, (V) 96 n; *Essays*, (V) 227 n

Baldwin, William, (IV) 267, (V) 345; *A Treatice of Morall Philosophy*, (II) 180; *The Mirror for Magistrates*, (VI) 199

Bale, John, *A Brefe Chronycle*, (II) 178; *King Johan*, (I) 66

Bandello, Matteo, (V) 22

Part B

(See EDITOR'S NOTE on page 473.)

Index to Volume VII

SHAKESPEARE STUDIES
*An Annual Gathering of Research,
Criticism, and Reviews*

Composed in Linotype Palatino by Typoservice Cor-
poration, of Indianapolis, Indiana. Offset printing and
binding by Kingsport Press, Inc., of Kingsport, Ten-
nessee. The book paper is Warren's University Text,
which has been specially watermarked with the University of South Carolina Press emblem. Designed by
Robert L. Nance.